Rory Gallagher

The Later Years

Lauren Alex O'Hagan
&
Rayne Morales

Rory Gallagher

The Later Years

Lauren Alex O'Hagan
&
Rayne Morales

WYMER PUBLISHING
Bedford, England

First published in 2024 by Wymer Publishing
Bedford, England www.wymerpublishing.co.uk Tel: 01234 326691
Wymer Publishing is a trading name of Wymer (UK) Ltd

Copyright © 2024 Lauren Alex O'Hagan, Rayne Morales / Wymer Publishing.

Print edition (fully illustrated): **ISBN: 978-1-915246-60-8**

Edited by Jerry Bloom.

The Author hereby asserts his rights to be identified
as the author of this work in accordance with sections
77 to 78 of the Copyright, Designs & Patents Act 1988.

All rights reserved. No part of this publication may be
reproduced or transmitted in any form or by any means,
electronic or mechanical, including photocopying, or any
information storage and retrieval system, without written
permission from the publisher.

This publication is sold subject to the condition that it shall not,
by way of trade or otherwise, be lent, re-sold, hired out or
otherwise circulated without the publishers' prior consent in any
form of binding or cover other than that in which it is published
and without a similar condition including this condition
being imposed on the subsequent purchaser.

A catalogue record for this book is available from the British Library.

Typeset/Design by Andy Bishop / Tusseheia Creative
Cover design by Tusseheia Creative
Front cover photo © Colm Henry

For Rory
"Hope you like it"

Contents

Introduction: The Celtic King Without His Crown?   9

Part 1: In the Studio

1.1 Flying in the Face of Fashion: *Jinx* (1982)   27

1.2 Blood on the Tracks: *Defender* (1987)   43

1.3 No End in Sight: *Fresh Evidence* (1990)   63

1.4 "A Great Holiday for Me": Guest Appearances and Collaborations, 1984-1991   81

1.5 "A Great Holiday for Me": Guest Appearances and Collaborations, 1992-1995   99

Part 2: On the Stage 1985-1991

2.1 Teenage Renegade Fever: The 1985 Tour of Yugoslavia and Hungary   115

2.2 "See Rory and Die?": Storming the Montreux Jazz Festival 1985   131

2.3 Hot Nights and Wailing Decibels: The 1986 Tour of Spain   141

2.4 Let's Go to Work! Rocklife 1990   159

2.5 The Vasco Da Gama of Rock: The Final World Tour (1991)   173

Interlude: Introducing the New Rory Gallagher Band   203

Part 3: On the Stage 1992-1995

3.1 Boxer Spirit: On the Road with the G-Man, 1992-1993 223

3.2 A Year of Musical Renewal: The 1994 Festival Circuit 241

3.3 Just Remember the Good Things: The Final Tour (1995) 261

Part 4: Ireland

4.1 He Came, He Saw and He Certainly Conquered: Cork Opera House 1987 281

4.2 Just A Man with a Mission (and a Guitar): The 1988 Irish Tour 297

4.3 In Sunshine or In Shadow: Irish Festivals and Cultural Celebrations, 1983-1989 315

4.4 Like a Phoenix from the Ashes: The Temple Bar Blues Festival 1992 333

4.5 Going to My Hometown: The Rebel Returns to Cork, 1992-1993 345

4.6 Carrying the Celtic Blues Torch: Television Interviews and Recordings, 1992-1994 363

Conclusion: The Rise and Rise of Rory Gallagher 383

Acknowledgements 405

Introduction:
The Celtic King Without His Crown?

*"I can't go away and vanish like some people want [...]
They'll have to find a slot for me somewhere."*
Rory Gallagher, 1991[1]

"What became of Rory Gallagher?" asked Françoise Rossi in her article on Gallagher's return to Brittany in 1994.[2] A decade had passed since Gallagher toured any of Brittany's major cities, and his appearance at the annual *Festival Interceltique de Lorient* would be his first and final visit. Rossi summarises Gallagher's ten-year absence with these noteworthy observations: "he has put on a lot of weight," "he doesn't seem to be particularly well," "he hasn't recorded for a long time," "his bassist Gerry McAvoy is no longer at his side" and "[he] has remained loyal to his Canadian lumberjack shirts."

Reading over Rossi's comments, we indeed repeat the question: what became of the man who was once described as the "fastest rising young star in Europe" following the debut of his band Taste (1966-1970)?[3] An answer soon emerges when we acknowledge that Rory Gallagher's career is typically framed within the hackneyed 'rise and fall' narrative, from a young man in the 1970s "with the world at his feet" to "fading [at] the margins" by the end of the 1980s.[4]

The 'rise' in Gallagher's narrative is shaped by a number of familiar accolades and performances that are, without question, astounding achievements in the initial stages of a professional musician's life. Taste's explosive presentation at the 1970 Isle of Wight Festival left audiences anticipating the next step for this "best new group,"[5] while two years later, Gallagher—now a solo artist—"made Irish guitarists matter" when he topped 1972's 'Best Guitarist' poll in the British magazine *Melody Maker*.[6]

As the Troubles hindered travel of international rock groups to Northern Ireland throughout the 1970s, Gallagher continued to tour the major cities, as demonstrated in the double album *Irish Tour '74*, with an accompanying film directed by Tony Palmer. This release in Gallagher's catalogue is regarded as both a musical triumph ("Gallagher reaching a new height in his expression of blues"[7]) and an important cultural moment in the Troubles by breaking "Belfast's musical drought."[8]

Outside of touring, Gallagher occasionally participated in session work, his best known—and most highly regarded—contributions being *The London Muddy Waters Sessions* (1972) and Jerry Lee Lewis's *The Session: Recorded in London* (1973). Another feat that is frequently featured in magazine articles (both then and now) is Gallagher's jam with the Rolling Stones in January 1975, the chance at being a Stone sometimes earning more recognition than Gallagher's own achievements. In 1976, Gallagher reached a "new peak" in his career, receiving critical acclaim for his album *Calling Card*. He would go on to further his "secure" reputation as "one of the most accomplished guitarists in rock" by headlining the Macroom 'Mountain Dew' Festival, both in 1977 and 1978.[9]

Although 1977 was a "triumphant" year for Gallagher, biographer Julian Vignoles has suggested that it also marked "trouble" for the guitarist, acting as the precursor to the supposed 'fall' in his career narrative.[10] Vignoles highlights "a fork in the road" regarding Gallagher's recording output, the release of *Photo-Finish* (1978) attained only after an abandoned album and change of band line-up.[11] Gallagher's "complex" and "satisfyingly interesting" blues style was now viewed in the music press as a "highly predictable" approach with "plenty of flash but very little genuine fire."[12] His media profile would further diminish over the course of the 1980s.

In Colin Harper's 1995 obituary for *Mojo* magazine, Gallagher's life was described as coming "full circle," with 21st century accounts reflecting this interpretation, as demonstrated by Vignoles and his question: "did Rory Gallagher really want to live on?"[13] Documentaries such as Ian Thuillier's *Ghost Blues: The Story of Rory Gallagher* (2010) impede any chance of settling Gallagher's 'rise and fall' narrative, particularly when many of the musical works and accomplishments from the latter half of his life are absent. After all, this is the *story* of Rory Gallagher, and yet *Defender* (1987) is breezed over in less than a minute and 1990's *Fresh Evidence* receives no airtime at all. The documentary also does not delve into Gallagher's live work in this era, aside from the portion of 'I Could've Had Religion' at the 1994 *Festival Interceltique de Lorient,* which is juxtaposed with anecdotes of how poorly Gallagher was, thereby inferring to viewers that his music was poorly at this time too.[14]

"It's so hard to tell someone's career in ninety minutes," Gallagher's nephew Daniel said at a Q&A for the first Panhellenic screening of *Ghost Blues* at the 2022 Gimme Shelter Film Festival in Athens, "But I think we did a very good job [in *Ghost Blues*] of giving an introduction to Rory."[15] We would tend to agree with this assessment if written biographies on Gallagher provided a comprehensive equivalent on the final decade of his career.[16] Instead, they tend to lean on the familiar 'rise and fall' narrative, interpreting Gallagher's withdrawal from the spotlight as a desire to withdraw from life altogether.

While Gallagher is indeed the "undisputed guitar hero" nourishing the rock-

Introduction - *The Celtic King Without His Crown?*

starved crowd in 1970s Northern Ireland, he must also be recognised as the same guitar hero at 1986's Self Aid—a benefit concert that raised awareness of the unemployment crisis in Ireland. When Gallagher played his final show with bassist Gerry McAvoy and drummer Brendan O'Neill at New York's Marquee Club in 1991, the "incredible magic"[17] produced onstage during a tense time within the group bears a strong resemblance to Taste's 1970 Isle of Wight performance, where the "cocktail of venom and exasperation," as Henry Yates of *Louder Sound* put it, "brought out the best" in the band.[18] Gallagher "made Irish guitarists matter" by topping 1972's *Melody Maker* 'Best Guitarist' poll, but we forget that he was the recipient of the Fender/Arbiter 'Hall of Fame' award in 1992. Behind James Burton of Elvis Presley's TCB band, Gallagher is the second guitarist ever to be honoured with this award. Literature regards the sessions with Muddy Waters and Jerry Lee Lewis as career high points, but where is the acknowledgement of Gallagher's work with fellow Irishman Davy Spillane on 1988's *Out of the Air*? Similarly, Gallagher's "electrifying" union with Roberto Manes and Peter Lockett for the jazz-rock fusion album *Phoenician Dream* (1999) falls in between the cracks of this unstable narrative.[19]

Despite these momentous post-1970s successes, a large majority of them appear as a footnote in scholarship or, worse, forgotten altogether. As a result, both the general public and many members of the fan community—old and new—lack the knowledge regarding this late, yet important, stage in Gallagher's life. One such example is Marc 'Jake Lee' Martin, who discovered Gallagher's music in 1976 when he was 15 years old. Martin was browsing his local record shop in Chicago and came across the album *Calling Card*, buying it "based on the cover." When Gallagher's next LP, *Photo-Finish*, hit the shelves in 1978, "it quickly became [his] favourite album of all time" and, over the next few decades, Martin would see Gallagher every time he came to the US, including eight times on his final tour in 1991.

Martin met and spoke with Gallagher on a number of occasions and even worked with former Rory Gallagher Band drummer Ted McKenna in the early 2000s. When we talked to Martin in April 2022, he confirmed that "my affection for Rory Gallagher [...] at 60 years old is the same. I've never lost interest or affection for him." Although Martin was and still is a huge fan of Gallagher, what stuck out in our conversation was his uncertainty about Gallagher's final years ("I don't know much after the '91 tour. Not much at all. I know he recorded [on *Rattlesnake Guitar: The Music of Peter Green*], [but] other than that I don't know much"). If Martin, a fan who "never lost interest" in Gallagher, knew "not much" post-1991, then how can we account for those who are less acquainted with Gallagher's career? Evidently, an updated review of Rory Gallagher's life is required.

Rory Gallagher: The Later Years is the first book to document Gallagher's musical trajectory over the final decade of his life, challenging the typical 'rise and fall' narrative with a steadied and optimistic perspective that does not discredit Gallagher's earlier achievements, yet reveals the story of a maturing bluesman broadening his horizons, rather than bidding farewell to them. Against all odds (from popularity decline to worsening health), Gallagher was embarking on a new phase in his career through exciting songwriting collaborations and the reforming of his live band. In his final years, we uncover an artist laying the foundations of a career rebirth, which was tragically cut short by his untimely passing in 1995. With *Rory Gallagher: The Later Years*, we crave a different story to that which has been told countless times before. A story that does not follow the easy and familiar pathway of a man victim to the 1980s zeitgeist, victim to 'addiction' and victim to himself and, instead, portrays him as the hero of all he was still able to accomplish. Our objective is to provide the long-awaited (and accurate) answer for those who perhaps once asked the question: "what became of Rory Gallagher?"

Dredging the Murky Waters:
What Lies Beneath the Depths of the 'Fall' Narrative

Before delving into the origins of *Rory Gallagher: The Later Years* and outlining the book format in more detail, it is important to consider what lies beneath this 'rise and fall' narrative that continues to be unfairly perpetuated in accounts of Gallagher's life. Where did it come from? And what can we do about it? We have identified various factors at work.

First is the changing music industry of the 1980s, which did considerable damage to Gallagher's reputation, as well as his own self-confidence. In an age of MTV, synthesisers and big hair, blues was seen as uncool and passé, therefore making Gallagher an easy target for the music press who derided him for staying true to his beliefs. Countless articles from this period describe Gallagher's music as old-fashioned and make cheap jibes about his "trademark" check shirts—something which played into his decision to switch to all-black clothing later in the decade, describing his shirts as having become a "stigmata" to him.[20] As Gallagher increasingly strived for perfection in the studio, his outputs also became less prolific than in the 1970s. The five-year break between *Jinx* (1982) and *Defender* (1987) led the press to describe him incorrectly as being on 'hiatus', even though he was still touring extensively across Europe during this time.

When the blues revival took place at the beginning of the 1990s, Gallagher expressed hurt at the way that his music had been overlooked throughout the 1980s and the fact that so many other acts were now capitalising upon this renaissance. In 1993, he told French magazine *Guitar World* that he felt "used up" and had ended up "caring about nothing" because he had continued to tour and play, doing "the dirty work for years without the least bit of support" or "least bit of publicity or coverage in the press." "Success, failure, honour or oblivion, none of them means anything to me anymore," he poignantly concluded.[21] Speaking to the German newspaper *Die Zeit* in 1994, Gallagher also mused that he played

Introduction - *The Celtic King Without His Crown?*

"better today than twenty years ago," but that "people probably don't think that, although I know it."[22]

Due to Gallagher's increasing disillusionment with the music industry, there is a pattern of homesickness expressed in his later interviews. "I never entirely mentally left Ireland [...] I'm constantly checking out what's going on at home," he told Kenneth Kelleher of *London-Irish News* in 1990.[23] Two years later in a conversation with Liam Fay for *Hot Press*, Gallagher stated, "The business side, you know, really bugs me," pondering the chance to leave and "live in Dublin, and let all the business side just tick over in London."[24] Although Gallagher seems to be in a transitionary period of his career, the *Hot Press* article concludes on a high note ("Rory Gallagher's profile as an artist is set to step up a gear or two over the coming months"), with Gallagher disclosing his "idea on recruiting some new musicians to give himself a fresher sound," as well as "fervently hoping" to record a new album soon.[25]

While disillusioned with the music industry, Gallagher's musical ambitions persevered and often extended into other genres. From as far back as 1975, he had raised the possibility of releasing an acoustic album and, by the 1990s, his determination to complete this "special project" seemed even greater, especially after his session with Irish folk group The Dubliners for their album *30 Years A-Greying*.[26] In a 1992 interview with Uli Twelker (published in March 1993), Gallagher approved of the recent MTV 'Unplugged' sessions and voiced his plans on how his acoustic album would sound, with one side of blues and one side of "semi-Celtic Irish Folk experimental music."[27] Folk had crept into Gallagher's playing throughout his career, but this side of his music taste began to reveal itself even more in his final years. Following his 1993 acoustic gig at the Cork Regional Technical College Arts Festival (see 4.5), Gallagher discussed with his brother and manager Dónal the possibility of "[getting] back very much to the folky root of things [without] a large PA, trucking, catering, transport, and all that stuff."[28] In later interviews, Gallagher would also frequently list folk artists with whom he would like to collaborate, such as Martin Carthy, Davey Graham, Bob Dylan, The Chieftains, Bert Jansch, Anne Briggs and Maggie Boyle. From the 1980s onwards, Gallagher also expressed an interest in completing a film soundtrack and, even as late as 1991, he was being approached with scripts, as stated in his conversation with Shiv Cariappa ("There is one vague offer, and it is the story of a blues band").[29]

Another factor contributing to Gallagher's disillusionment with the music industry was his negative experiences on US tours in particular. Gallagher was frustrated at having to "compete on a circus level"[30] with other acts and play arenas, as well as at his poor treatment by other bands when part of package tours, which, on the rare occasion, resulted in him leaving midway through a tour (as was the case in 1979 when opening for Jefferson Starship). In 1982, Gallagher supported the Canadian trio Rush on their *Signals* US tour, playing large venues such as Madison Square Garden and Nassau Coliseum. According to Dónal Gallagher, the concert dates were scheduled "months in advance," and while the tour "would be a good package" on paper, Gallagher was privately unfavourable ("Rory really didn't want to do it," Dónal was quoted in his interview with Dan Muise).[31] Gallagher later described the situation as "soul destroying," identifying the issue as venue choice (following the Rush tour, Gallagher only played the club circuit or small theatres on his return to the US in both 1985 and 1991).[32] In addition, the Rush tour revealed the generation gap of a 1980s audience. Press articles noted the "strong contrast" musically between the "Irish rock guitar master" and "Canadian progressive rock power-trio," as well as how each act was received: Rush "entertained" their fans, while the crowd received an "education" from "veteran" Gallagher.[33]

The chance to bridge this generation gap suffered from the severe lack of exposure of Gallagher's albums, particularly in the US. Although Gallagher toured the US three to four times a year in the 1970s, he obtained minimal support from the record company regarding the distribution of his albums. This issue worsened when Gallagher's contract with Chrysalis finished with the release of *Jinx* (1982), leaving him in "limbo" on the business end.[34] While there were potential offers with New York's Mercury International, these eventually fell through and, soon after, Gallagher became subjected to a music industry that favoured corporate over independent labels. Fan Marc Martin recalls that, when *Fresh Evidence* came out, "there wasn't any publicity about it [in the US]"; he only managed to track down a copy in Los Angeles one year later. The album has since become one of his "go-to" Gallagher records ("his songwriting is just as strong on those albums as it was on earlier albums").

Added to the decreased visibility of Gallagher abroad was his fear of flying, which developed in the late 1970s and prevented him from touring as frequently as he had done before. This was treated with tranquillisers, but with the accumulated stress and pressure of his relentless work schedule, Gallagher began to rely on them in his everyday life to help him deal with his anxiety. Throughout the 1980s, Gallagher also developed a series of physical health problems, leading him to undergo steroid treatment, which caused fluid retention. This did not go unnoticed by the fickle music press who frequently commented on his weight gain and changed appearance, thereby taking away from the continued high quality of his music and sowing the seeds of doubt on his ability to perform still.[35]

Press articles from the period also skirt around the issue of Gallagher's mental health, describing him as being "unhappy" or "vulnerable"[36] or reducing his very apparent struggles to mere eccentricities or quirks. This is particularly evident in the July 1990 article for *Q* magazine by David Sinclair, which calls attention to the way that Gallagher looks ("poor shape," "rheumy eyes," "grey roots [pushed] up along the crease of a ragged centre parting"), his "neurotic" attention to detail and his superstitions, asking the question: "what can do this to a man?"[37] As we

Introduction - *The Celtic King Without His Crown?*

now know in hindsight from interviews with Dónal Gallagher and bandmate and close friend Mark Feltham, Gallagher was going through a challenging battle with depression and had also suffered a series of nervous breakdowns.[38] These problems may be spoken about more openly today and with greater sensitivity, but they were poorly understood at the time in the music press. Even Dónal himself confesses that he "never really knew how ill [Gallagher] was"[39] because he "really didn't understand the body as much as [he does] now,"[40] coupled with the fact that his brother was such an introverted person and did not open up to him.

As Gallagher began to depend increasingly on prescription medication, his health failed further. Nonetheless, he continued to deliver top notch performances, from Rocklife (1990) and Bonn (1992) to Tegelen (1993) and Montreux (1994). It was only on very scant occasions that his illness affected them, but, unfortunately, it is these scant occasions that have coloured many people's views about his musicianship during this period of his life. Two of the most notorious concerts in this respect occurred in 1992 at the Scottish Fleadh and the Town & Country Club.

In May 1992, Gallagher shared the bill with such acts as Van Morrison and Christy Moore for the Scottish Fleadh, a music festival established by the Irish promotion company Mean Fiddler, which celebrated Irish music, dance and culture. The Fleadh was originally held in 1990 at London's Finsbury Park, but soon spread to New York, Boston and Glasgow. Gallagher played the festival after a 14-month break off the road. As his new live band was not quite ready for the show, he reached out to previous members McAvoy and O'Neill to fill in for the event. "Rory didn't play well at all,"[41] McAvoy wrote in his 2005 autobiography *Riding Shotgun: 35 Years on the Road with Rory Gallagher and "Nine Below Zero"*, going on to describe the experience as "a fiasco."[42] In his book, McAvoy questioned Gallagher's choice to invite Milanese violinist Roberto Manes onto the stage, judging the decision to be "a sign of how muddled Rory's thinking had become" due to a "mismatch of drink and pills."[43] Despite Manes' training at the Conservatorio di Musica in Milan, McAvoy claims that the violinist's musical skills were not "even very good."

While McAvoy couldn't "understand" why Manes was at the Scottish Fleadh, we discovered in our interview with Manes in May 2022 that he and Gallagher had struck up a friendship in the early 1990s after the guitarist saw him and his band perform at the Polo Club in London. Although Manes' work leaned more towards jazz-rock fusion, he and Gallagher "alchemised entirely from the very beginning," forming a musical connection that was "beyond words."[44] Manes highlighted their shared love of improvisation and extended soloing, which eventually led to multiple collaborations between the pair, including concert dates in Swanage, London and Leeds. In his musings, McAvoy also forgets that Gallagher's collaboration with Manes was not the first time that the guitarist had stretched his musical wings into the world of violin. In 1977, Gallagher had guest-starred on *Gaodhal's Vision* by Irish violinist Joe O'Donnell, who was a long-time fan and friend. As O'Donnell told *CVFolk* in 2020: "when Rory played at The Marquee in London [in the 70s], he'd invite me to get up and jam with him at the end of the night – a reasonably regular occurrence."[45] In the same year, O'Donnell also contributed violin to some tracks on Gallagher's scrapped San Francisco album.

In addition to McAvoy's claims, Gallagher's performance at the Scottish Fleadh has attracted negative attention in the online fan community. Memories of the event were shared in a 2012 November post on *The Rock and Roll Knife* blog, with the user detailing what a "shambolic" and "dispiriting experience" it was to watch Gallagher on the day.[46] "Moon-faced, and having piled on the beef, [Gallagher] was almost unrecognisable from the chap I had seen rock the Apollo some fifteen years earlier," the user harshly writes. Fan John Carnie also concurs that Gallagher's performance was "not good at all," although looking back on the event today, he acknowledges that Gallagher "had found a real musical and spiritual soulmate" in Manes.[47]

The media were also unfavourable to Gallagher's resurgence at the Fleadh. While Van Morrison and Christy Moore were warmly welcomed to the festival in press releases, praised as "Ireland's finest ever singer-songwriters in action," Gallagher was presented near the bottom of the bill, grouped with the "tired formula" acts like Andrew Strong and Kevin McDermott.[48] Often, the reviewers reserve a one-sentence remark for Gallagher's spot—or in the case of *The Courier and Advertiser*, just three words: "overindulgent guitar work."[49] Although anticipation was high for the Scottish Fleadh, the *Daily Record* deemed the entire day a "flop."[50] Cold weather shunned away many visitors, with reports that even Van Morrison (the festival's "big attraction"[51]) failed to draw the expected audience. Nevertheless, for many in attendance, Gallagher's brief set was not entirely the "fiasco" we have been led to believe.

Fan Mike O'Connor discovered Gallagher at a young age through listening to Taste records with his older brother, and 1992's Scottish Fleadh was his first and only time seeing Gallagher live. Overall, O'Connor's memories of the gig are positive, and although Gallagher "looked a little bloated" and initially "a bit lost" onstage, once he began to play, "[he] seemed to be right in the zone."[52] The band entertained the crowd with three or four long jams and, despite Gallagher being unable to reach "the peak of his legendary powers" that day, O'Connor reassured that "there were still real flashes of magic." Bobby Gillespie from Primal Scream was also at the Fleadh and, speaking in a radio interview several days later, he described Gallagher's performance as "great."[53] Out of the four times Roberto Manes shared the stage with Gallagher and his band, it was the Fleadh that he remembers as "the best one," recounting to us one show highlight with particularly evocative imagery: "we were completely absorbed with what

Introduction - *The Celtic King Without His Crown?*

we were doing, and during one of his solos I saw him lunging literally the notes out of his guitar to the audience, as if he was throwing flowers."

As demonstrated with the case of the Scottish Fleadh, it is important to balance accounts of Gallagher's later-day performances to take into consideration the range of factors that may have shaped negative opinions, such as his ongoing health issues, uncomplimentary treatment of him in the press and overall poor festival conditions. Three months later, Gallagher and his new band appeared at the Temple Bar Blues Festival in Dublin, where the critics applauded his performance ("Rory still so sharp,"[54] headlined the *Evening Herald*). Given the contrast in views between May and August, we can conclude that Gallagher's "terrible"[55] show at the Scottish Fleadh was part of a group of outlier shows greatly affected by his ill health at the time, coupled with a long break off the road and the anxiety of having to perform again with his old band members. As an alternative to McAvoy's assessment (a "fiasco" influenced by a "mismatch of drink and pills"), we highlight Gallagher's involvement with the Fleadh as a sign of his Irish patriotism (rather than "muddled" thinking), contributing to the growth of international appreciation of Celtic musical traditions. The addition of Manes for the show could be interpreted as Gallagher continuing to experiment with the blues format, inspired by his new musical friendship, as opposed to McAvoy's unsympathetic viewpoint ("Rory had definitely lost the plot at [this] stage"[56]).

Five months after the Fleadh, on 29 October, Gallagher performed at the Town & Country Club in London. It was the second of three dates in England before embarking on a long European tour in December. Prior to the show, Gallagher had taken his regular medication prescribed by his doctor but had mistakenly drunk one glass of brandy on an empty stomach, which caused him to appear intoxicated on stage. As Dónal recounts in the 2024 documentary *Rory Gallagher: Calling Card*, "the first four numbers [were] great, then suddenly his hands turned to jelly and then he didn't know what was happening to himself. The side effects were all kicking in." As Gallagher progressively struggled to play, the show was brought to a premature end by Dónal. The Town & Country Club was the last time he ever played in London, leaving a somewhat murky impression for those in attendance.[57] In *Rory Gallagher: The Man Behind the Guitar*, Vignoles incorrectly labels this concert as the debut of bassist David Levy and drummer Richard Newman, which has contributed to the negative way that Gallagher's final band is often understood.[58]

When Gallagher passed away on 14 June 1995 after contracting a staphylococcal infection following a successful liver transplant, several obituaries made reference to the Town & Country Club concert and wrongly claimed that he had been drunk.[59] To his credit, journalist Colin Harper called out this falsity in a 1998 article for *Mojo*, underscoring the fact that Gallagher was "seriously ill" at the time.[60] However, in the internet age, the story of the gig resurfaced and spread, often elaborated or mistold like a game of Chinese Whispers, which has continued to bolster an unfair image of Gallagher that is not in keeping with the hundreds of other concerts that he gave between 1985 and 1995.

Looking at press articles on Gallagher across his entire career—and indeed other Irish artists—there is, in fact, an uneasy pattern in journalists often falling back on long-rooted Irish stereotypes to describe him, whether in terms of his "funny" way of speaking, "leprechaun" appearance or, most relevant here, fondness for alcohol.[61] These references often wrapped Irish prejudice in a cloak of fun and frivolity, which made it seem harmless and trivial. However, such disparagement humour could foster discrimination by moulding (negative) public opinion of what it meant to be Irish, particularly at a time when Anglo-Irish tensions were already high. From as early as the late 1960s, articles about Gallagher make throwaway remarks about Guinness and whiskey, framing their consumption as innate aspects of being Irish. Therefore, when he succumbed to a liver transplant in 1995, it was (and still is) wrongly assumed to be the result of alcohol abuse, with little or no mention of the fact that his long-term reliance on prescription medication played a major role, as Dónal has often explained in interviews. Dónal notes the cruel irony that his brother spent his life "loathing drugs and drug takers," yet it was drugs prescribed to help him that ended up contributing to his premature death.[62] Much of the medication that Gallagher was prescribed has, in fact, since been banned due to its dangerous side effects on the body.[63]

Even today, the music press favour narrow perspectives when examining Gallagher's career and frequently cite the Town & Country Club gig as epitomising his 'downfall', as shown in the 2011 article by Gavin Martin for *Record Collector*.[64] Martin describes the gig as Gallagher's "King Lear on the heath moment" and goes into great detail about how "lost" and "out of it" he was. Martin expresses sadness at having once seen Gallagher "in his prime" when his power was a "thing to behold" and his "worn and battered paint-stripped Strat had lit up the world," implying that this era is long over.

This is in stark contrast to the view of long-term fan Patrick Kennedy who saw Gallagher live throughout the 1970s, 1980s and early 1990s and assures that he was "always at his prime"[65]—a belief echoed by other older fans who maintain firmly that "Gallagher never lost it."[66] Added to the unfair picture that Martin paints of Gallagher is his discussion of Mike Batt's 1979 *Tarot Suite* album, where he claims Gallagher had "pints of Guinness lined up in the studio" while he recorded his contributions. The original quote from Batt, in fact, offers a different perspective: Batt had just received a call that 'Bright Eyes' had hit number one in the charts, so both he and Gallagher enjoyed a few pints of Guinness together to celebrate as they worked.[67] Martin's selective citation biases readers' views towards Gallagher and his alcohol 'problem' so that their minds are already made up about him before the Town & Country Club bombshell is dropped several paragraphs later.

Introduction - *The Celtic King Without His Crown?*

Martin similarly paints a dismal picture of Gallagher's presence in the studio during work on Energy Orchard's 1994 album *Pain Killer*, suggesting that he simply turned up, did not talk to anybody, plugged in his guitar and—to quote frontman Bap Kennedy—"went mad," which he describes as "bizarre." This account is a far cry from what keyboardist Kevin Breslin told us in May 2022 (see 1.5), describing Gallagher as active, collaborative and even unguarded in the studio as he chatted and made suggestions about the song they were working on. Martin inserts this Energy Orchard quote between the story of Gallagher forgetting the riff to 'Shin Kicker' during a rehearsal (first recounted in McAvoy's *Riding Shotgun*) and an unkind description of him "looking like Jake 'Raging Bull' La Motta" on his final 1994 Montreux performance, further contributing to the image of Gallagher as somebody who was 'past it' and even 'unstable' by the late 1980s.

Overall, when we look back over what has been written to date about Gallagher, we see that there are several components at the root of this 'rise and fall' narrative: the (in)visibility of his final decade in most publications to date and, consequently, a lack of information about his achievements; an overwhelming focus on his physical appearance, leading to misconceptions about his ability to perform; 'fuzzy' knowledge about his illness and death; and damage caused by shoddy journalism—both within Gallagher's lifetime and posthumously—that often relies on selective citations, calculated framing or Irish stereotyping to perpetuate certain discourses, which have subsequently been spread by social media. All these reasons compelled us to start our *Rewriting Rory* project, where we have been dedicated since day one to dredging the waters of Gallagher's written past and sifting out the mud to offer a more balanced and objective account of his later years.

The Origins of *Rory Gallagher: The Later Years*

The roots of this book began somewhat unexpectedly in November 2021 with the *Rewriting Rory* project. For some time, we had been feeling frustrated at the lack of attention given to Gallagher's final decade and how it is often portrayed as less significant than the two decades of his career that came before. We were tired of the constant focus on the 1970s in publications, of repeatedly hearing the same 'rise and fall' narrative, of press articles and biographies splitting Gallagher's career into *before* and *after* periods, with *Defender*—or even *Jinx*—frequently marked as the start of a downward spiral simply based on the fact that Gallagher's health worsened during the recording of the albums. And we were saddened to find similar claims made by many fans on social media that Gallagher's 'best years' were behind him by the mid-1980s.

One day, I (Lauren) decided to channel those frustrations into a long piece of writing about how Gallagher's later years needed reappraising, needed to be understood with greater sensitivity, needed recognition that he might have faced many struggles, but that he tackled them head on in the way that he knew best: by continuing to perform with his heart and soul night after night. I sent it to Rayne—a close friend I had met through the Rory Gallagher Instagram community—with no real intention of publication. But she was very supportive and asked whether I had ever thought about setting up a blog. I had not. "Would anyone even want to listen to my rants?" I joked.

But the more we spoke, the more we realised that we might be onto something. It was not just a matter of two 'angry, young women' getting aggravated about people's preference for one period of Gallagher's music over another. Of course, everyone is entitled to their opinion. Rather, it was the injustice of Gallagher's alleged fall from grace stemming not from any critical assessment of his music or performances, but rather from the way he looked in photos or videos, as well as hearsay about his poor health. As we delved deeper, we realised that many fans were unaware of what Gallagher was doing musically from 1985 to 1995 and only knew this period as one when he 'put on weight' or 'became ill'. We were surprised just how many thought that Gallagher's career ended after *Fresh Evidence* or following the departure of McAvoy and O'Neill, or that many could not name one single member of Gallagher's final band. Reflecting critically rather than emotionally, we realised that much of this narrative boiled down to visibility, or rather the *lack* of visibility and dearth of knowledge when it comes to this later stage in Gallagher's career, and we wanted to do something about it.

So, on 13 November 2021, we launched the *Rewriting Rory* blog with a bold opening post that aimed to foster a greater appreciation of the later years of Gallagher's career and encourage people to think differently about them. We wanted to set the record straight by showcasing everything that he continued to achieve during this time, despite great personal challenges. We were blown away by the positive response that we received from day one, not just from fellow Gallagher fans, but also from those close to Gallagher.

As many of the topics that we wanted to cover had not previously been written about—or at least not written about in any detail—we began to dig deep into newspaper archives and library collections, gather first-hand accounts from fans and interview musicians and photographers who had worked with Gallagher over the years, as well as family members and friends. As a result of the kindness and generosity of these people, we were able to start producing monthly articles full of new research and content. We also added exclusive interviews to our website, as well as previously unpublished photographs, a large body of translated press articles from the 1985-1995 period and links to our academic work on Gallagher.

Speaking to those who knew Gallagher or saw him perform during the last decade of his life, we found that our assumptions were indeed correct and that the 'rise and fall' narrative that is so often peddled in relation to his life just did not stick. Everybody told the same tale: yes, Gallagher was clearly unwell and even fragile, but his musicianship never faltered and he still performed with fire and intensity.

Introduction - *The Celtic King Without His Crown?*

Rayne and I were excited that the stories we uncovered so clearly challenged standard accounts of Gallagher's life.

Over long Zoom calls, we planned our future posts and it soon became apparent that we had enough material for at least three years. So, as the blog continued to gain momentum and take on a life of its own, our thoughts shifted towards the idea of writing a book. And the result of this shift is the volume you hold in your hands today.

The Format
Rory Gallagher: The Later Years seeks to reappraise the last ten years of Gallagher's career by using previously unexplored archival materials and fresh interviews with those who knew him to challenge the 'rise and fall' narrative of his life. It aims to fill in the many blanks about his musical achievements during this period and correct the assumption that his decline in health somehow translated into a decline in musicianship.

The book is not a chronological account of Gallagher's life, but rather a series of essays dedicated to particular aspects of his musical career during the 1985-1995 period—a period that is too often forgotten or misunderstood when telling his story. It consists of four core sections, in which 19 chapters are grouped together in a cohesive and sequential manner; however, each chapter can be read independently of the others. Although the book's focus is squarely on 1985 to 1995, occasionally we stray to encompass important earlier achievements in the 1980s that have been neglected in previous works on Gallagher.

The first part of the book—'In the Studio'—looks at Gallagher's three final studio albums: *Jinx* (1982), *Defender* (1987) and *Fresh Evidence* (1990). It also covers the wide range of session work and collaborations that Gallagher carried out between 1985 to 1995, with particular attention to the original musical directions in which he was heading towards the end of his life.

Given how much Gallagher toured, it is perhaps unsurprising that a large chunk of our book is dedicated to this topic. 'On the Stage 1985-1991' covers the period when Gerry McAvoy and Brendan O'Neill were members of the Rory Gallagher Band. We recount such major events as Gallagher's tours of Yugoslavia and Hungary (1985), Spain (1986) and the United States, Australia and Japan (1991), as well as headlining performances at major European festivals. 'On the Stage 1992-1995', on the other hand, is concerned with the years that David Levy and Richard Newman joined the Rory Gallagher Band. The Bonn Blues Festival (1992), the Montreux Jazz Festival (1994) and Gallagher's final tour of the Netherlands (1995) are just some of the live shows that we discuss. The two 'On the Stage' sections are partitioned by 'Introducing the New Rory Gallagher Band', which provides the first full account of the members of Gallagher's final band (including Mark Feltham), as well as occasional guests, such as John Cooke, Jim Leverton and Geraint Watkins.

Considering the importance of Ireland to Gallagher, it is fitting that the last section of the book is dedicated to his many musical achievements on the island. We shine a spotlight on his 'comeback' show at the Cork Opera House in 1987, his 1988 Irish Tour and his involvement with major Irish events and festivals, such as Lisdoonvarna (1983), Self Aid (1986) and Rock on the Lough (1989). We also look at the Temple Bar Blues Festival (1992)—one of Gallagher's crowning achievements—and a number of important 1992-1993 shows in Cork, including Lark by the Lee and the Regional Technical College Arts Festival.

We end the book with a reflection on Gallagher's legacy in the 21st century, considering posthumous accomplishments and releases, his growing young fanbase and influence on young musicians, as well as increased recognition of his significance within the academic field of Irish musicology.

Ultimately, with *Rory Gallagher: The Later Years*, we aim to change the way that Gallagher's final decade is understood. Through our book, we encourage fans—old and new—to rethink the 1985-1995 period and stop viewing it as a sad coda in Gallagher's life. Gallagher's talent did not wane at this stage of his career; it, in fact, became finetuned and seasoned as he developed into a true bluesmaster. In the 2011 Gavin Martin article we mentioned earlier, Gallagher is described as a "Celtic King without his crown" towards the end of his life. We strongly object to this. As we will demonstrate, Gallagher's crown may have been a little worn around the edges and perhaps even glued back together in places, but it still fit like a charm and was firmly on top of his head like the glorious leader he always had been and still remains today.

****

If you'd like to find out more about our *Rewriting Rory* project, then please visit our website (www.rewritingrory.co.uk) or find us on Instagram, Facebook, X and YouTube @rewritingrory. Alternatively, you can contact us at rewritingrory@gmail.com.

LAO and RM

Introduction - *The Celtic King Without His Crown?*

Footnotes

1 Stephen Roche, 'King of the Blooze', *Seconds*, no. 15 (1991), http://www.roryon.com/blooze412.html
2 Françoise Rossi, 'Rory Gallagher marche au blues', *Ouest-France* (10 July 1994), n.p.
3 'Sound Sandwich', *Hit Parader* (March 1970), http://www.roryon.com/sound.html
4 Colin Harper, 'Ballad of a Thin Man', *Mojo* (October 1998), http://www.roryon.com/mojo.html
5 'Sound Sandwich'.
6 Kenneth J. McKay, 'Tar liom', *Strum and Bang* (March 2020) https://medium.com/strum-and-bang/tar-liom-2423328b8c8d
7 Mark J. Prendergast, 'Rory Gallagher, Taste, and the Blues Guitar', *Isle of Noises: Rock n Roll's Roots in Ireland* (1987), http://www.roryon.com/isle.html
8 Steve Carr, 'The Night Rory Gallagher Broke Belfast's Musical Drought', *Every Record Tells a Story* (27 January 2017), https://everyrecordtellsastory.com/2017/01/27/the-night-rory-gallagher-broke-belfasts-musical-drought/
9 Both quotes from 'Live Lines: Rory Gallagher for Macroom Festival', *Hot Press* (9 June 1977), http://www.roryon.com/liveline374.html
10 Julian Vignoles, *Rory Gallagher: The Man Behind the Guitar* (London: Collins, 2018), 153.
11 Ibid., 156.
12 'Rory Gallagher, 'Irish Tour '74', *The Scene* (August 1974), http://www.roryon.com/it304.html; Mike Boone, 'Gallagher Has But No Fire', *The Gazette* (16 November 1979), 73.
13 Colin Harper, 'Rory Gallagher (1948-1995)', *Mojo* (August 1995), http://www.roryon.com/colin.html; Vignoles, *Rory Gallagher*, 258.
14 The recently released *Rory Gallagher: Calling Card* documentary (*The Rory Gallagher Story* in the UK) fares much better in this regard. However, it is disappointing that the 52-minute version broadcast on Irish television — cut by six minutes to account for RTÉ's advertisements — chose to remove segments on *Defender* and Gallagher's songwriting abilities, which led to a gap in the narrative on his continued musical excellence in the 1980s.
15 'Gimme Shelter Film Festival Q&A' (14 March 2022), https://vimeo.com/698242549
16 See, for example, Jean-Noël Coghe, *Rory Gallagher: A Biography* (Cork: Mercier Press, 2001); Dan Muise, *Gallagher, Marriott, Derringer & Trower* (Milwaukee: Hal Leonard Corporation, 2002); Marcus Connaughton, *Rory Gallagher: His Life and Times* (London: Collins, 2012); Marcelo Gobello Chapurri, *Rory Gallagher: El Último Héroe* (New York: Lenoir, 2016); Fabio Rossi, Il bluesman bianco con la camicia a quadri (Genoa: Chinaski Edizioni, 2017), Vignoles, *Rory Gallagher* (2018).
17 This is how US fan Marc Martin described the concert when we interviewed him on 10 April 2022. All subsequent quotes from Martin come from this interview.
18 Henry Yates, 'Taste - What's Going On: Live at the Isle of Wight', *Louder Sound* (1 December 2015), https://www.loudersound.com/reviews/taste-what-s-going-on-live-at-the-isle-of-wight
19 Richard Whitehouse, 'Roberto Manes - Fihavanana', *Classical Source* (July 2003), https://www.classicalsource.com/cd/roberto-manes-fihavanana/.
20 Liam Fay, 'Tangled Up in Blues', *Hot Press* (July 1992), http://www.roryon.com/Tangled.html. For more on how Gallagher was depicted in the music press, see: Lauren Alex O'Hagan, 'Fashioning the "People's Guitarist": The Mythologization of Rory Gallagher in the International Music Press', vol. 9, no. 2 (2022), *Rock Music Studies*, 174-198.
21 J.P. Sabour and X. Bonnet, '...et vogue la galère', *Guitar World* (February 1993), https://rewritingrory.co.uk/2022/06/03/guitar-world-february-1993/
22 Christopher Dieckmann, 'Rory Gallagher, Legende des Bluesrock, besucht seine ostdeutschen Fans', *Die Zeit* (December 1994), https://rewritingrory.co.uk/2022/06/13/die-zeit-december-1994/
23 Kenneth Kelleher, 'Interview from the London-Irish News', *London-Irish News* (December 1990), http://www.roryon.com/kenneth164.html
24 Fay, 'Tangled Up in Blues'.
25 Ibid.
26 Uli Twelker, 'Rory Gallagher: Good Times', *Good Times* (March 1993), http://www.roryon.com/uli209.html.
27 Ibid.
28 Connaughton, *Rory Gallagher*, 151.
29 Shiv Cariappa, 'Conversation with Rory Gallagher', *Christian Science Monitor* (29 July 1991), http://www.roryon.com/conversation1.html
30 'Rory Gallagher - Dublin TV appearance, Interview & Ride On Red, Ride On. 1983', https://www.youtube.com/watch?v=b8IYzOAsdAo&t=336s
31 Muise, *Gallagher, Marriott, Derringer & Trower*, 57.
32 Cariappa, 'Conversation with Rory Gallagher'.
33 Michael St. John, 'Gallagher Teaches, Rush Entertains', *Wisconsin State Journal* (11 October 1982), 35; John Taylor, 'Rush Blasts Sellout Crowd at Auditorium', *The Nashville* (21 October 1982), n.p.
34 Muise, *Gallagher, Marriott, Derringer & Trower*, 57.
35 See, for example, David Sinclair, 'The Show Must Go On', *Q* (July 1990), http://www.roryon.com/q8.html
36 Michael Ross, 'Praying at the Temple of the Blues', *Sunday Tribune* (16 August 1992), http://www.roryon.com/praying.html
37 Sinclair, 'The Show Must Go On'.
38 Michael Ross, 'While My Guitar Gently Weeps', *Sunday Times* (17 May 1998), http://www.roryon.com/rorytimes.html
39 'Remembering Rory Gallagher 2024', https://www.youtube.com/watch?v=xE8LArN63VA
40 Gerry McAvoy and Pete Chrisp, *Riding Shotgun: 35 Years on the Road with Rory Gallagher and "Nine Below Zero"* (Chicago: SPG Triumph, 2005), 274-275.
42 Muise, *Gallagher, Marriott, Derringer & Trower*, 86-87.
43 McAvoy and Chrisp, *Riding Shotgun*, 274-275.
44 Interview with Roberto Manes, 27 April 2022. All subsequent quotes from Manes come from this interview.

45 'Total remix and relaunch for Joe O'Donnell's celtic-rock masterpiece', *CVFolk* (3 November 2020), http://www.cvfolk.com/cvfolk-news-archive-2020/
46 'Van Morrison - Scottish Fleadh - 1992', *The Rock and Roll Knife* (19 November 2012), http://therockandrollknife.blogspot.com/2012/11/van-morrison-scottish-fleadh-1992.html
47 Interview with John Carnie, 28 April 2022.
48 'All Set for Scottish Fleadh', *The Courier and Advertiser* (21 May 1992), 7.
49 'The Fleadh was No Flop', *The Courier and Advertiser* (26 May 1992), 7.
50 'Fleadh Flop', *Daily Record* (25 May 1992), 5.
51 'All Set for Scottish Fleadh'.
52 Interview with Mike O'Connor, 22 April 2022.
53 As recounted by John Carnie in our interview.
54 Eugene Maloney, 'Rory Still So Sharp', *Evening Herald* (17 August 1992), 12.
55 McAvoy and Chrisp, *Riding Shotgun*, 274-275.
56 Muise, *Gallagher, Marriott, Derringer & Trower*, 86-87.
57 Gallagher was able to perform the next night at the opening of the Town and Country Club in Leeds. However, the set was shorter than usual and, according to fan Pete Wood (1 November 2022), Gallagher appeared "flat" and "strained." Show promoter Alan Robertson booked the band Dr. Feelgood as a stand-in should Gallagher be unfit to perform.
58 Vignoles, *Rory Gallagher*, 190.
59 See, for example, Michael Ellison, 'Roaring Rory in Denim', *The Guardian* (16 June 1995), http://www.roryon.com/roaring238.html and Jonathan Buckley, *The Rough Guide to Rock* (New York: Penguin, 1996).
60 Harper, 'Ballad of a Thin Man'.
61 See: Lauren Alex O'Hagan, '"Rory Gallagher's Leprechaun Boogie": Irish Stereotyping in the International Music Press', vol. 4, no. 2 (2023), *Review of Irish Studies in Europe*, 38-72.
62 Maeve Quigley, 'Booze didn't kill my brother Rory, it was the drugs to help his fear of flying', *Sunday Mirror* (14 April 2002), https://www.thefreelibrary.com/Booze+didn%27t+kill+my+brother+Rory%2C+it+was+the+drugs+to+help+his+fear...-a084782459
63 As Dónal told Dan Muise, *Gallagher, Marriott, Derringer & Trower*, 68.
64 Gavin Martin, 'The Man Who Sweated Rock 'N' Roll', *Record Collector* (9 June 2011), https://recordcollectormag.com/articles/the-man-who-sweated-rocknroll
65 Patrick Kennedy, 'Rory Gallagher: He Lived, Loved, and Died with the Blues' (May 2004), http://www.roryon.com/lived255.html
66 'In Love with the Blues', *Irish Times* (13 June 1998), http://www.roryon.com/news11.html
67 'Mike Batt Talks to Phacemag', *Phacemag* (8 May 2020), https://www.phacemag.com/mike-batt-talks-to-phacemag-618347.html

Part 1: In The Studio

1.1 Flying in the Face of Fashion: *Jinx* (1982)

As Rory Gallagher entered the 1980s, he was feeling optimistic about the future of music. Speaking to broadcaster Mal Reding, he described the 1970s as a "cynical" time where rock bands became "aristocratic" and expressed hope in the resurgence of creativity, spontaneity and "grittiness"[1] in this new decade. He repeated similar thoughts to Gary Weimer of the *Illinois Entertainer* in December 1982, stating that he anticipated the 1980s would see more "meat and potatoes" music and less sensationalism in terms of "innovations or craziness." "We might come out the other side of the decade in better shape," Gallagher concluded.[2]

Despite Gallagher's optimism, the decade ahead was not particularly kind to him, and he became somewhat of a "lone figure holding out against the march of pop glamour, the ever-present synthesizer and the decline of guitar rock."[3] Throughout the 1980s, Gallagher would see himself increasingly worn down by an ever-fickle, image-conscious music industry who largely ignored some of the best outputs that he had ever created. This is something which journalist Michael Ross believes fuelled the guitarist's anxiety and depression, leading him to push himself ever harder and, ultimately, "exposed an already vulnerable man" to the "quick-fix quackery" that contributed to his untimely death.[4] In a 1991 interview with *Seconds*, Gallagher reflected sombrely on the 1980s, admitting: "I felt adrift […] I was developing my music, but I didn't fit in the music press or in a social way […] I felt that within the music industry I was getting nowhere."[5]

According to music journalist Harry Shapiro, the 1980s were a challenging time for many musicians, with the blues rock scene "pretty much disappearing in Britain."[6] So, when Gallagher decided to release his "rootsiest album in years"[7] with *Jinx* on 1 May 1982, it perhaps was never destined to be a huge commercial success or have wide appeal to the music press. *Jinx* was a return to a more blues-oriented sound, Gallagher having strayed into hard rock territory with his previous studio albums *Photo-Finish* (1978) and *Top Priority* (1979). For Gallagher, *Jinx* was "an attempt to get the sound that you used to hear in records before it was all computerised."[8] A brave move indeed in 1982. But then Gallagher was never one to follow trends or care what the public thought; as he later told Derek Oliver of *Kerrang!*: "I've never consciously worked in a way where I've been swayed by fashion. I just record for me. It's a personal statement of what I want to achieve."[9]

Notwithstanding some positive reviews in the music press, *Jinx* was generally met with a lukewarm response, particularly in the US, where the album was seen as archaic and redolent of another age. Even today, *Jinx* is still the target of negative descriptors, described frequently as "the weaker album"[10] and seen as "lacking the spark"[11] of earlier records or an example of Gallagher "treading water musically rather than striking out in any new direction."[12] Some frame the album as the beginning of the 'fall' in Gallagher's story or a sign that he needed a break. Furthermore, *Jinx* is constantly left off lists of Top Ten Rory Gallagher albums compiled by music magazines, considered an irregularity in Gallagher's long recording career or even a disappointment for some fans, particularly those who prefer his harder edge.

This essay offers a critical reappraisal of *Jinx*, exploring the making and recording of the album and diving deeper into the factors that led to its muted reception, both then and now. In doing so, we demonstrate that it was not 'weaker' than Gallagher's other albums, but rather overlooked and underrated because it was 'in the right place at the wrong time'. *Jinx* provides evidence of Gallagher's dedication to his blues roots, his integrity and honesty as an artist and his ability to "fly in the face of fashion."[13] Yet, it also shows his progression and maturity, particularly as a songwriter, his quasi-autobiographical lyrics about ill fate and misfortune offering a rare and privileged insight into his psyche. *Jinx* also marks revitalisation for Gallagher, with a return to a more bluesier sound with drummer Brendan O'Neill, who replaced Ted McKenna the year before. Ultimately, with its mixture of "fiery hard rock and smouldering blues,"[14] strong lyricism and raw sound, *Jinx* had all the components to be a smash hit, but it was simply a victim of circumstance.

Marching to the Beat of a Different Drum

In February 1981, after almost three years with the Rory Gallagher Band, drummer Ted McKenna made the decision to leave. As McKenna told Dan Muise in 2002, although the job was "secure and ongoing,"[15] he had reached a stage where he wanted to try something new and explore a different style of music. McKenna decided to visit Gallagher to break the news. Gallagher was at home with his mother Monica who, according to McKenna, "made [him] very welcome." The three of them went out to get a takeaway and, on the way back, McKenna told Gallagher that he wanted to leave the band. Gallagher accepted his decision amicably and wished him all the best.

Meanwhile, Belfast-born drummer Brendan O'Neill had heard through the grapevine about Ted McKenna's departure and phoned his long-term friend Gerry McAvoy (bassist with the Rory Gallagher Band since 1971) to ask if he could put in a good word for him with Gallagher. O'Neill was already relatively well acquainted with Gallagher, having first met him in 1973 at the Ashling Hotel in Dublin and again in early 1976 at a house party thrown by Rod De'Ath (drummer with the Rory Gallagher Band from 1972 to 1978). When Gallagher reverted his band to a three-piece format in 1978, O'Neill had, in fact, auditioned as drummer on McAvoy's request. However, O'Neill admits that he was satisfied playing with his own band Swift at the time and that it was "obvious" that his jazzy style of playing did not suit the direction in which Gallagher was then heading.[16]

The situation was very different in 1981. O'Neill's band Swift had broken up, he was running out of money, found himself in an unhappy marriage and was looking for a new musical adventure to take him out of "the doldrums."[17] He was, therefore, delighted to receive a phone call from Gallagher several evenings after speaking to McAvoy, inviting him to the Nomis rehearsal rooms behind the Olympia in London for an audition. O'Neill recalls answering the phone with the rather formal, "Hello, Rory, what can I do for you?" which he says immediately broke the ice because Gallagher found it hilarious.

In McAvoy's view, Gallagher was not entirely sure where he wanted to take his band at the time. There had been some talk of adding a rhythm guitar player and he had even auditioned one potential candidate, Tommy Willis, who had once been a roadie for the band. He had also discussed the possibility of auditioning Derek St. Holmes, best known for his work with Ted Nugent. However, neither option amounted to anything. According to McAvoy, Gallagher had also tried out a number of other drummers before calling O'Neill, including "a guy from Birmingham" who had played with Stan Webb's Chicken Shack ("a good drummer but he never stopped talking") and Fran Byrne from Ace ("a bit too square for Rory's liking").[18] Gallagher had heard O'Neill's drumming on McAvoy's first solo album and was impressed that it had "hardened up" since 1978; O'Neill had now moved away from his early jazz influences, but maintained a blues shuffle that Gallagher particularly admired and saw as potentially fitting well into the new edition of the Rory Gallagher Band.

Writing in his 2020 autobiography *Meet Mr Sticks*, O'Neill describes the first audition as "torture."[19] He remembers being "uptight" and unable to relax as Gallagher gave him "no direction at all" and "just wanted to play, to see what [his] instincts were." When the audition ended, O'Neill felt pessimistic about his chances. Despite his negative opinion of his own performance, he was, however, blown away by Gallagher: "Just with his guitar, Rory was the piano player, the sax player and the guitar player all rolled into one. He filled the sound completely and nothing compared with Rory in terms of energy and intensity. Nothing."

O'Neill was surprised to get a call back from Gallagher, inviting him for a second rehearsal. This time, the playing was "harder, more intense and much longer [...] extremely physical," but O'Neill felt more confident. Nonetheless, he was unable to read Gallagher's reaction, describing it as "like having a go at Braille for the first time," so he was, once again, surprised to receive another call back. For O'Neill, the third rehearsal was "much more fluid," lasting well over four hours in length. When they had finished, Gallagher invited O'Neill and McAvoy for a pint and then on for a meal at an Italian restaurant. As they walked to the restaurant, Gallagher turned to McAvoy, pointed at O'Neill and said, "Meet Mr Sticks." And with that, O'Neill became the new drummer, staying with the Rory Gallagher Band until 1991.

O'Neill's entrance into the band was, to some extent, a baptism of fire: they would be setting off for Dieter Dierks Studios in Germany to record *Jinx* almost immediately. The idea of a baptism of fire was nothing new for drummers in Gallagher's band, Rod De'Ath having made his debut at the Limerick Savoy Theatre (the first show aired in colour on Irish television) and Ted McKenna before 20,000 spectators at the Macroom 'Mountain Dew' Festival (Ireland's first major open-air event). Added to O'Neill's difficulties, however, was the bombshell news that his wife Brenda wanted a divorce, delivered to him just days before rehearsals for *Jinx* started. O'Neill was understandably devastated and turned up at rehearsals in poor shape emotionally. He describes the session as "a struggle from the start" and worried whether Gallagher would regret having hired him.[20] When they were packing up, McAvoy convinced O'Neill to tell Gallagher why he was off form. According to O'Neill, Gallagher "just listened and let [him] talk." Typical of Gallagher's graciousness, he was sympathetic to O'Neill's problems and even agreed to give him an advance on the album fee. "That says everything about the man," O'Neill summarises in his autobiography.

The Making of *Jinx*
When Gallagher arrived at Dieter Dierks Studios in the small village of Stommeln in north-west Cologne to record *Jinx*, there was a sense of positivity in the air. He felt invigorated by the new band formation and was keen to capture this fresh energy on record. Moreover, having previously recorded at Dierks, Gallagher was well acquainted with his surroundings and felt at ease in its peaceful countryside location rather than the usual claustrophobia from which he often suffered in the studio.

Established in 1968, Dierks Studios swiftly became the home of the first generation of German rock bands, from Tangerine Dream and Wallenstein to Guru Guru and Cosmic Jokers. Throughout the 1970s, as the Studios expanded and were promoted in the music press, it gained international renown, coming to the attention of Gallagher's brother and manager Dónal at just the right time.

In 1977, Gallagher and his band had flown to San Francisco to begin work with producer Elliot Mazer on what would later become *Photo-Finish*. The sessions were plagued with difficulties due to a conflict in working style between Gallagher and Mazer, leading the recording to "drag on" for "what seemed like an eternity," according to Gerry McAvoy.[21] Unsatisfied with the record's final mix, Gallagher made the bold decision to scrap the album on the day it was due to be presented to Chrysalis by Dónal. Leaving Dónal with the arduous task of breaking the bad news to the record company, Gallagher went to the cinema to watch Bob Dylan's film *Renaldo and Clara*. However, distracted and upset, on the way back to the hotel he shut his thumb in the taxi door and broke it, putting him out of action for six weeks.

Speaking to Dan Muise in 2002, Dónal describes this period as Gallagher's "first major depression"[22]—a heightened version of the depression that he had first noticed in his brother following the demise of Taste seven years earlier. McAvoy remembers bumping into roadie Tom O'Driscoll in London at the time and asking after Gallagher. "He wasn't well, in fact, he was quite ill," McAvoy was shocked to hear.[23] The whole San Francisco experience had "affected [Rory] quite badly" from a psychological perspective and, feeling despondent, he sought solace back home in Cork with his mother Monica. Dónal recalls Gallagher chatting "until the dawn"[24] with him and their mother about the next direction he should take. As we now know, this involved parting ways with Lou Martin and Rod De'Ath, recruiting Ted McKenna and moving towards a hard rock sound, inspired by the energy of the punk movement. Under obligation to deliver a new album to Chrysalis within a couple of months, it was paramount to find a new studio to start recording as soon as possible. Remembering "the nice setup" and "vibe"[25] that he had sensed on a brief visit to Stommeln the year before, Dónal convinced his brother to pay a visit to Dierks Studios with him.

Unlike many other studios, Dierks had residential facilities so that all musicians could live on site, with home-cooked meals provided by Dierks' mother Ursula. This "homey"[26] atmosphere instantly appealed to Gallagher, offering an ideal recording environment that was in sharp contrast to His Master's Wheels in San Francisco. Gallagher was also impressed by the studio's equipment and hit it off immediately with both Dierks and his mother who found him to be "a most warm-hearted and friendly person."[27] Sealing the deal was Gallagher's familiarity with Germany (having toured the country since as early as 1965 with the Impact Showband), his good command of the German language and the friends that he and Dónal had in nearby Cologne who they had met through their connections with the WDR television network.

Satisfied that Dierks Studios was the right place for him, Gallagher returned to Stommeln with his band and recorded *Photo-Finish*, delivering it to Chrysalis at the "eleventh hour of the eleventh minute of the eleventh day" (hence its title).[28] The whole experience was so seamless that Gallagher chose Dierks Studios once again for the follow-up album *Top Priority*, the title being a cheeky reminder to Chrysalis who promised to make this album their "top priority." Parts of Gallagher's 1980 live album *Stage Struck* were also mixed at Dierks. Therefore, when it came to recording the next studio album, *Jinx*, two years later, Gallagher had no hesitation in going back to Dierks Studios once again. This time, Gallagher and his band were also joined by Bob Andrews on keyboards and Ray Beavis and Dick Parry on saxophone. The return of keyboards and the addition of saxophone clearly marked the end of Gallagher's heavier rock era, signalling the new ideas that he had for his music in the 1980s.

Having co-produced *Photo-Finish* and *Top Priority* with Alan O'Duffy, Gallagher decided to return to his role as sole producer for *Jinx*, working alongside Jürgen Krämer as engineer. Gallagher wanted more of a live feel for *Jinx*, with everybody performing in the same space rather than the drums in a separate booth. Therefore, a considerable amount of time was spent for the first few days trying to find the right set-up to produce the best sounds from the instruments. Speaking to journalist Wolfgang Bongeriz in 1982, Gallagher explained that he was aiming for "the natural sound of a Howlin' Wolf record," where the percussion sounded "as natural as [...] in a practice room." To this end, he also used vintage tube microphones to obtain "the old Presley-sound."[29]

Reflecting on the early days of recording *Jinx*, Brendan O'Neill admits that that they did not go well because of his lack of experience in a studio. He could sense Gallagher's frustration and vowed to himself not to take it personally and up his game. Slowly, as O'Neill relaxed into the sessions, the situation improved, and they started to lay down several tracks. A particular high point came for O'Neill when he overheard Gallagher tell McAvoy, "I think he's getting into it now."[30] Nevertheless, it was not all plain sailing and the whole recording process took much longer than anticipated, reflective of Gallagher's growing search for an unattainable perfection in the studio.

Since the days of Taste, Dónal had worried about the emotional effect that making an album had on Gallagher, noting how he would start with great gusto, but could not discipline himself and ended up overworking to the point of "verging on a nervous breakdown" by the end.[31] Any attempts by Dónal to get Gallagher to "impose discipline"[32] on himself fell on deaf ears, while whenever he suggested that his brother finish early and take a rest, he was "cast from the studio" and told "never to come back."[33] Gallagher himself recognised that he was getting into a "dangerous syndrome"[34] of expecting too much from himself in the studio and, consequently, finding it more difficult to make albums. He told *International Musician and Recording World* in February 1982 that he was driving "harder to get more out of [himself]" with *Jinx*, but that this came with the risk of going "over the top" and losing his "vision."

Despite his gruelling work schedule, Gallagher did find some time to relax. Dierks Studios was next to a small pub called Anno 1900, where Gallagher and the band often went for a "change of scene" and to play darts.[35] Soon, they began to compete against the locals and a "healthy rivalry" developed, leading Gallagher to establish a darts team made up of him, O'Neill, McAvoy, Tom O'Driscoll, Jürgen Krämer and Peter, the pub landlord. They called themselves the Kamikaze Darts Team and even had black sweatshirts made with the team's name printed on the front. According to Brendan O'Neill, the Kamikaze Darts Team were challenged to play against a pub team in the neighbouring village of Pohlheim, but were "soundly beaten," so they retreated back to Dierks Studios where they played table tennis until the early hours.

Jinx was originally set to be released in late autumn of 1981, but it was delayed because Gallagher was keen to get back out on the road and halted mixing to do a British tour throughout November and December. He then returned to the studio to revise certain tunes and begin mixing, ready for a mid-December release. However, this date got pushed back because the mixes were not satisfactory and Gallagher did not want to rush the album out before Christmas and it "get lost in the shuffle."[36] The album release was rescheduled for February 1982, but was postponed again, finally coming out on 1 May.

Jinx: A Low-Down on the Tracks

In the liner notes for the 2018 re-edition of *Jinx*, Dónal Gallagher writes that his brother "had become quite frustrated with the way life was unfolding for him" at the time and that many of the songs were autobiographical. "From a spiritual standpoint, Rory [ ] probably knew of his own destiny," Dónal told Shiv Cariappa in 2003, "[In his songs], he refers to it often about fading away, about being taken away by depression."[37]

The inner turmoil that Gallagher felt around the time of *Jinx* seemed to be channelled creatively into his lyrics, which show a mature and developed songwriter, someone who is able not just to convey emotions, but to tell stories and paint a whole imagined world around them in which listeners can immerse themselves. While Gallagher was always highly adept at doing this ('Philby', 'Daughter of the Everglades', 'Moonchild', to name but a few examples), his lyrics were often overshadowed by his virtuosic guitar-playing and many journalists unfairly discounted them as throwaway lines before getting to the 'big' guitar solo—something to which he strongly objected. According to fan Robert Gannon, Gallagher was refreshing in that he did not "sing about girls, sex and drugs" like most other bands.[38] Television and radio broadcaster Dave Fanning seconded this in his interview with us in April 2022,[39] agreeing that Gallagher's lyrics have been overlooked because of his ability on the guitar ("he was more than what a lot of people sometimes think he is [...] he was a great songwriter as opposed to just a guy who brought the blues into some more decades from the old blues guys"). Photographer Jean-Pierre Sabouret equally believes that Gallagher's lyricism needs to be reappraised as "on the same level as Bob Dylan or John Lennon." *Jinx* sets out a very strong case for this.[40]

The album has two standout songs from a lyrical point of view—the title track 'Jinxed' and the ballad 'Easy Come Easy Go'—both expressing Gallagher's melancholy yet tinged with "optimistic self-encouragement."[41] Gallagher described 'Easy Come Easy Go' as "kind of a mirror"[42] to 1973's 'A Million Miles Away', which is often considered to be his theme song, offering a "description of his terrible depression."[43] In 'Easy Come Easy Go', Gallagher reflects on how he is "lost inside" himself, "just hears sad notes lately" and has to "break out soon," before reassuring himself not to "paint it all so sadly" and "burn out completely." Similar themes emerge in 'Jinxed' as Gallagher states that he "feel[s] like a lost child searching in the dark" and is "sinking down into the endless sea," as well as rhetorically asking if the "heavy weather" that he is going through will ever end. Gallagher was particularly proud of 'Jinxed', which he described as a "bluesy type of thing with a Latin American beat"[44] that was "quite interesting" and had a "spooky atmosphere."[45] Nonetheless, in his typically modest style, he added that it "sounds bad on paper but it sounds all right on disc!" and stated that he was not the first to try this type of thing, citing Junior Wells' 'Cha Cha Blues'. 'Lonely Mile'—a track that was included on the 2018 re-release of *Jinx*—is another fine example of Gallagher's progression as a songwriter. Its poignant lyrics recount the nights when, suffering from insomnia, he would walk up and down Fulham Road alone.

However, even the album's more up tempo and less introspective songs show Gallagher's lyrical prowess. The hard-hitting 'Big Guns', for example, is heavily inspired by Gallagher's love of crime fiction and gangster movies, telling the tale of a hapless character who is desperately trying to flee from the mob—a theme that would be revisited on *Defender* (1987). The character's sense of urgency is reflected in Gallagher's fast-paced slide-playing, which is truly electrifying in live extended versions, such as the recorded concerts at *Rockpalast* 1982 and Ulster Hall 1984. "The same sense of nemesis [is] internalised"[46] in 'Bourbon', which covers themes of transit, restlessness and the sad illusion of freedom that they convey. Dónal believes that Gallagher had outlaw musicians, such as Waylon Jennings and Johnny Paycheck, in mind when he wrote the song, although it could arguably also be semi-autobiographical in its idea of a man whose "mind feels like crazy pavement," music being the only thing that "befriends" him. The slick album closer 'Loose Talk' also touches on personal themes, particularly manipulative people in the music industry, with Gallagher tenaciously affirming that he will not let it "faze" him or "play their games" and will "keep on pushing." The album opener 'Signals', on the other hand, draws on the "telepathy" between Gallagher and his brother Dónal, its lyrics speaking to Gallagher's strong sense of perception. "We all used to have in depth family conversations and he could sum up a situation in one word,"[47] Dónal told Mark McClelland in 2000.

Other tracks showcase Gallagher's expertise in drawing upon the roots of rock and blues, yet firmly putting his own stamp on them, such as the energetic 'The Devil Made Me Do It', which he described as a "very fast Eddie Cochran sort of thing"[48] or the raunchy 'Double Vision', which offers some of the best slide licks on the album. Gallagher also demonstrates his fine ability to take a classic blues number and very much turn it into his own, in this case with a fiery rendition of Louisiana Red's 'Ride On Red, Ride On'. While the album version is recorded electrically, Gallagher often played this acoustically in live shows and television performances, showcasing his versatility as a musician and what made him stand out from other rock guitarists. Although not on the original *Jinx* release, the 2018 re-edition featured a cover of Lightning Slim's 'Nothin' But the Devil', played in finger-picking style on Gallagher's 1932 National Triolian Resonator, further displaying his proficiency and depth as a guitarist.

Jinx: The Reception Then and Now

Never one to rest on his laurels, Gallagher was already thinking about how to make his next album better, even before *Jinx* had hit the shelves. Speaking to *International Musician and Recording World* in February 1982, he stated that he wanted to "try and simplify" the process of making future albums by giving himself the "challenge" of using an eight- or 16-track studio and setting a fixed time limit.[49] He cited Neil Young's *Tonight's The Night* and *On the Beach* as benchmarks, liking the fact that they were "rough" and "spontaneous" and "mixed as you hear it back rather than mixed later."

Despite feeling that there was some room for improvement with *Jinx*, Gallagher was generally pleased with the end product, telling Thierry Chatain of *Rock and Folk* that he had "returned to the feeling of *Tattoo* and *Against the Grain*," which was "less hard and more powerful." [It's] me at my most natural,"[50] he summarised succinctly. Gallagher elaborated on this in an interview with Mal Reding, explaining how *Jinx* was "quite gritty" and "more R&B" with a "mixture of ideas, tempos, sounds and styles."[51] In a nod to the heaviness of his two previous studio albums, he also added how he hated "to be stuck in one mould" and that *Jinx* was "impossible to fit into any real category." Overall, for Gallagher, while the album had taken much longer than he had originally planned, it was ultimately "worthwhile"[52] in achieving his desired sound.

Although Gallagher had undoubtedly produced an album of which to be proud, it failed to make much headway following its release on 1 May 1982, receiving a generally muted critical reception. "It has to be said that [*Jinx*] is not one of Rory's most successful albums on any level," wrote Gerry McAvoy in his autobiography *Riding Shotgun*.[53] When thinking about *Jinx*, it is important to remember that *success* has nothing to do with quality and everything to do with circumstances, which, in this case, were very unfavourable to Gallagher. The music scene of the 1980s was not conducive to an album like *Jinx*, which bucked the New Romantic, New Wave and electronic dance trends and bravely went back to the roots of the blues. Competing with it on the market were such records as *Rio* by Duran Duran, *The Hunter* by Blondie, *Avalon* by Roxy Music and *Hot Space* by Queen—all a far cry indeed from the stripped-back sounds of songs like 'Ride On Red, Ride On' or 'Jinxed'. Mainland Europe had a more open attitude towards *Jinx*, being far less influenced by mainstream fashions or fads, but both Britain and the US posed challenging markets.

Another major factor that hindered the commercial success of *Jinx* was issues with

Gallagher's record company. Chrysalis had certainly not fulfilled their promise to make Gallagher their "top priority" and there was little or no promotion or radio spots around the release. Gallagher was unhappy that Chrysalis was increasingly catering to their new pop sign-ups (e.g. Gen X, Ultravox, Spandau Ballet) and not investing in publicity for him because they took it for granted that he would self-promote the album through his constant touring. This problem reached a head in the US where, according to Dónal, Chrysalis was rapidly "going down the tubes."[54] None of Gallagher's albums were visible in US record stores, making it difficult for fans to source his music.

Always looking out for his brother's best interests, Dónal negotiated a deal to get a "free release" of *Jinx* in the US with Mercury International, which was now run by Dan Young, who had previously been responsible for Chrysalis in Germany. Although *Jinx* was released, there was no contractual deal signed, so Dónal arranged a tour supporting Rush to promote the album. In hindsight, he recognises that this was a "wrong move" because Young was quickly removed from his post at Mercury, leaving Gallagher in a state of uncertainty. The Rush tour, therefore, became a "tour of convenience." According to Gerry McAvoy, "everything about the tour just felt wrong" and Gallagher found it "difficult to get any sort of reaction" from the Rush fans,[55] which greatly upset him. McAvoy also notes that Gallagher's fear of flying had become so bad at this stage that they had to travel around the US by bus, which was an added stress that contributed to the generally negative atmosphere of the tour. While Vignoles writes in *Rory Gallagher: The Man Behind the Guitar* that Chrysalis "dropped"[56] Gallagher at this point, this was not the case; *Jinx* fulfilled his contractual obligation with the record company and he decided to seek a better deal elsewhere, given his poor treatment from them.

In the music press, *Jinx* received little attention and, even when it was reviewed favourably, these reviews were often tinged with jokes about Gallagher's age, appearance, supposed 'hiatus' or dogged loyalty to the blues. This attitude was also carried over into television interviews of the period, with Eamonn Holmes of *Good Evening Ulster*, asking Gallagher if seeing young fans at his concerts made him "feel old" and questioning why he "shunned all the trappings" of a rockstar.[57] Gallagher was no stranger to what he often referred to as "backhanded compliments," having been used since the early 1970s when the press framed his check shirt as a sign that he was the "People's Guitarist" or gave him the nickname the "Hardest Working Man in Rock" because of his constant touring schedule.[58]

In the context of *Jinx*, Paul Strange of *Melody Maker*, for example, starts his review with the rhetorical question "Whaddya mean, you thought he was dead?" making reference to the three years since Gallagher's last studio album *Top Priority* and, in doing so, overlooking the live album *Stage Struck* (1980) and the 300+ concerts that Gallagher had done since 1979. Although Strange goes on to describe the album as "one of the finest examples of a man rising from the grave," this narrative again feeds into the idea that Gallagher had been doing nothing for the past three years. The suggestion that Gallagher had lost his way musically is also emphasised by Strange's claim that he is "back on form with a vengeance" with *Jinx*, despite both *Photo-Finish* and *Top Priority* having been critically acclaimed at the time of release. Although Strange concludes that *Jinx* is "one of the best blues rock albums of the year," he adds that the "dinosaur theory was made to be broken," conceiving Gallagher as a veteran or old-timer, despite only being 34 years old at the time.[59]

Equally, Chas de Walley of *Kerrang!* begins his review of *Jinx* by referring to Gallagher as "Ol' Rory Gallagher," this value-laden language setting up readers' opinions of the bluesman as a member of the old guard before they have even started reading. His next lines are more positive, describing *Jinx* as a "real gutbucket job" that is "oozing with blues" and praises Gallagher for "taking a step backwards in time" and "flying in the face of fashion." However, his concluding statement that *Jinx* sounds like "Phil Lynott and Van Morrison [...] teamed up with Rory Gallagher on guitar" is confusing and seems to namecheck other major Irish musicians in a somewhat incoherent manner that takes away from the album itself and Gallagher's own talent.[60]

Similar assertions are made in Wolfgang Bongeriz's article about *Jinx* and its supporting tour, which takes off from the incorrect statement that Gallagher has had "three years' abstinence of touring." It then states that, after so many years in the business, it is unsurprising that "this or that guitar run has been heard before," implying that *Jinx* is made up of recycled material. Gallagher assures Bongeriz that he does not "fall back on old riffs" and "keeps developing." Despite this critique, Bongeriz concedes that *Jinx* is full of "untamed energy" and offers proof that Gallagher "in no way is ready to be discarded." Towards the end of the article, Bongeriz makes an unnecessary reference to Gallagher's weight gain, to which Gallagher feels obliged to state that it "will be gone by the end of the tour." Following up Gallagher's response, Bongeriz wonders if he has "clothes in different sizes in his luggage?" this flippant remark shifting the focus from Gallagher's music towards his physical appearance—something that can be noted in the music press from as early as 1979.[61]

In a 1988 interview with Irish music magazine *Hot Press*, Gallagher reflected on the unfair way that he felt *Jinx* had been largely received by the music press, his hurt still apparent six years on:

> I had taken it on the shoulder for a couple of years. They were really ostracising me. There's no two ways about it. I'm not a cry baby, but it's a bit hard to take sometimes when you've worked very, very hard [...] [*Jinx*] had a lot of plusses that were overlooked at the time. I do take it to heart a wee bit [...] I'm still trying to hold my own with what's happening now."[62]

Bucking the trend of most other publications, *Illinois Entertainer* wrote a highly favourable, non-caustic review of *Jinx*. Journalist Gary Weimer praises Gallagher for maintaining respect for his roots and "a solid blues foundation" in his work, calling *Jinx* "a statement to that very end." He commends Gallagher's decision to move away from the "metallic overtones" of *Stage Struck* in favour of a "60s R&B album," which he sees as a strong "reaction against a sterile, computerized sound." Weimer also expresses disappointment in American radio for missing Gallagher's "intention" and not catching onto the "warmth and vibrance" of *Jinx*. However, he points out that this has nothing to do with Gallagher's talent, citing the fact that he remains well received in concert and that his recent show at Park West was sold out on a night when The Who were also in town.[63]

Perhaps the best reviews of *Jinx* come from *Hot Press*, which Gallagher and his brother Dónal played a pivotal role in establishing in 1977. Editor Niall Stokes describes *Jinx* as Gallagher both "reinvestigating a more down-home slant on his original R&B base" and further exploring "his penchant for short sharp dramatic and [...] melodically endowed songs." For Stokes, "there isn't a weak track on *Jinx*"; Gallagher's guitaring is "leaner" and "cleaner" and his songs "tighter" and "more focused" than earlier albums. Stokes also lauds Gallagher's authenticity, integrity and willpower to "play the game the way his heart says," even if that is to the "detriment of his career potential." These are the terms of which Gallagher's contribution "should be evaluated and criticised in the future."[64]

John Waters of *Hot Press* also shows great sensitivity to Gallagher's artistic vision, moving beyond the Gallagher 'as Guitar God' status to recognises his development as a songwriter on *Jinx*. Waters applauds Gallagher's "remarkable sense of melody and of song structures," as well as his "unerring feel for putting the right words in the right places," concluding that *Jinx* "has put the final seal" on Gallagher's recognition as a lyricist, which has been "underestimated" for so long. He also notes that *Jinx* marks a return to the "groove [Gallagher] is happiest with" and "what he does best"[65] "a statement that echoes Dónal's own thoughts. Speaking to Robert Haagsma in 2000, Dónal explained that, in the late 1970s, Chrysalis tried to push Gallagher in the direction of the New Wave of British Heavy Metal. Although his brother "tried the best he could," his heart was not in it.[66] For Dónal, *Jinx* is stronger than *Photo-Finish* and *Top Priority* because it was "well arranged and thought out" and Gallagher "finally had the space to create a record that was more than an ennobled live recording."

But how does the album stack up now over forty years later in an age where music is more accessible and people have greater access to information online? Unfortunately, it would seem that the answer is rather mixed.

A 2002 review by Marc Giguere of the Manitoba Blues Society claimed that *Jinx* was one of Gallagher's "weaker albums" and was "more pedestrian and lackadaisical" in style. He also added that the album "lived up to its prophetic title" by marking the start of Gallagher's "peripety."[67] Too often, posthumous reviews of *Jinx* latch onto its sombre title and link this to Gallagher's personal challenges over the last decade or so of his life. By applying hindsight to this 1982 album, they run into the timeworn trap of associating his personal 'jinx' with his musical 'jinx', implying that his decline in physical and mental wellbeing also marked a decline in musical quality—a claim that does not stand up when listening to Gallagher's last three studio albums or watching his later live performances.

One of the most scathing contemporary reviews of *Jinx* comes from George Starostin's *Only Solitaire* blog, where he describes the album as "mediocre," "inconsistent," "faceless" and a "pale shadow" of what Gallagher did before, which clearly indicated that he "needed a break." In stark contrast to John Waters of *Hot Press*, Starostin argues that *Jinx* does "very little to eliminate the rumour of Rory not being a good songwriter"[68]—a point that seems to suggest his unfamiliarity with the material, given the lyrical dexterity of songs like 'Easy Come Easy Go' and 'Big Guns'.

Both Hal Harowitz of *All Music* and Pete Pardo of *Sea of Tranquility* also fall into the trap of looking at *Jinx* from the perspective of what we now know about Gallagher's final decade. Harowitz frames the album as a sign that Gallagher's "personal fortunes were on a downslide from which they would never recover," while Pardo claims that it signals the "decline" in Gallagher's recording career and is "not as strong" as earlier albums. These initial disparaging remarks diverge from their later claims that Gallagher still "sounds inspired" and on "full fiery form" throughout *Jinx*, producing a "tough and confident" "spirited set of blues rock" where his "vocals take on a new emotional depth not previously heard."[69] Again, this leads us to ask the question to what extent are contemporary opinions on *Jinx* influenced by hindsight on Gallagher's poor health rather than actual album quality?

On rare occasions, contemporary reviews are overtly positive. *Gold Mine Magazine*, for example, calls *Jinx* a "solid, overlooked album" that is "more laidback" than the "flashier and more expensive-sounding" *Photo-Finish* and *Top Priority*, yet "still infusing various blues rock ideas with lots of electricity and energy."[70] *uDiscover* also compliments the album's broader scope than Gallagher's previous two studio albums and his ability to mix "muscular rockers" with "subtler material,"[71] while *Louder Sound* see his "no nonsense blues rock" as sounding "revitalised" in *Jinx*.[72] These two latter reviews come from 2022, expressing a tinge of optimism that *Jinx* is finally starting to get the recognition that it deserves, although much work is still needed to reappraise it as an album on the same calibre as *Tattoo* or *Blueprint*—as Chas O'Whalley of *Kerrang!* predicted that it would become over time.

Swim or Sink? Reappraising *Jinx*

After a three-year period where his music took on a hard rock edge, Gallagher went back to his blues roots with *Jinx*. Reinvigorated by new drummer Brendan O'Neill, he returned to the familiar Dieter Dierks Studios in Germany and worked hard to achieve a gritty sound in the style of an old Howlin' Wolf record. Gallagher pushed himself ever harder in a bid to make the 'perfect' album, leading the initial release date of *Jinx* to be postponed by almost a year. When the album finally hit shelves in May 1982, it was beset with all sorts of challenges—from lack of promotion and record company issues to the changing music scene and unfavourable journalism—which resulted in a general apathy towards the record and poor sales. These challenges had a negative impact on Gallagher's already fragile state of mind. Dónal Gallagher notes that his brother's depression worsened in this period, while Gerry McAvoy states that Gallagher became "very reclusive" from this point on and stopped spending time with him socially.[73] McAvoy also claims that the muted reception of *Jinx* drove Gallagher to take "a step back" from the music industry and, instead of competing, he "waited and bided his time."[74]

While Gallagher's touring schedule noticeably slowed down at this point, he was, by no means, sitting back and relaxing. Throughout the supposed five-year 'hiatus' period ahead, he participated in a wide range of session work (see 1.4 and 1.5), created a whole new album *Torch*, which was scrapped and eventually morphed into *Defender* (see 1.2), and branched out into new territories, delivering concerts in both Yugoslavia and Hungary (see 2.1). According to biographer Julian Vignoles, Gallagher "was not prepared to accept that his more creative days had passed."[75] And that is because they affirmatively *had not*, as we demonstrate throughout this book. Although Vignoles adds that Gallagher was prepared to "keep striving," his comment casts doubt over Gallagher's musical ability from the early 1980s onwards.

Too often, when *Jinx* is spoken about, conversations overfocus on Gallagher's personal unhappiness at this stage in his life, leading both fans and critics to see the album as the start of his 'fall'. Persisting negative attitudes towards *Jinx* also seem largely to be reflective of persisting negative attitudes towards the latter part of Gallagher's career more generally and the continued (in)visibility of his post-1970s work. *Jinx* is often absent from lists of Top Ten "essential" Rory Gallagher albums, but then again, so are *Defender* and *Fresh Evidence*, showing a heavy bias in journalism towards the early part of Gallagher's career.[76] Furthermore, when Gallagher's albums were rereleased in 2018, it was *Jinx*, *Defender* and *Fresh Evidence* that sold the least copies (along with *Notes from San Francisco*). Had any of these three albums been associated with the earlier period of Gallagher's life when he was younger, slimmer and healthier, they may well have made the Top Ten list or achieved greater record sales. We see a persisting negative stigma attached to all three of these albums that *must* be changed in order to reappraise them and truly appreciate their musical quality. We must separate what was going on for Gallagher personally from what was going on for him musically. When we focus solely on the music and the lyrics, we recognise that *Jinx* stands up as a strong album, definitely in the same vein as *Tattoo* or *Blueprint*, and that it represented not the beginning of Gallagher's 'decline', but his evolution into a mature storyteller of the blues—a position that he would consolidate further with *Defender* and *Fresh Evidence*.

LAO

Footnotes

1 'Rory Gallagher talks Jinx' (May 1982), http://malreding.com/interview/rory-gallagher/
2 Gary Weimer, 'Despite Radio's Hex, Rory Gallagher's Back to What He Does Best', *Illinois Entertainer* (December 1982), http://www.roryon.com/hex259.html
3 Julian Vignoles, *Rory Gallagher: The Man Behind the Guitar* (London: Collins, 2018), 137.
4 Michael Ross, 'While My Guitar Gently Weeps', *Sunday Times* (17 May 1998), http://www.roryon.com/rorytimes.html
5 Stephen Roche, 'King of the Blooze', *Seconds*, no. 15 (1991), http://www.roryon.com/blooze412.html.
6 Cited in Marcus Connaughton, *Rory Gallagher: His Life and Times* (London: Collins, 2012), 128.
7 Chas de Walley, 'Rory Gallagher Jinx', *Kerrang!* (May 1982), http://www.roryon.com/gutbucket342.html
8 Weimer, 'Despite Radio's Hex…'
9 Derek Oliver, 'Defender of the Faith', *Kerrang!* (14 November 1987), http://www.roryon.com/faith322.html
10 Marc Giguere, 'Rory Gallagher - Irish Tour (1974)', *Manitoba Blues Society* (summer 2002), http://www.roryon.com/manitoba175.html
11 George Starostin, 'Rory Gallagher', *Only Solitaire* (2020), https://starling.rinet.ru/music/rory.htm
12 Vignoles, *Rory Gallagher*, 138.
13 De Walley, 'Rory Gallagher Jinx'.
14 Pete Pardo, 'Gallagher, Rory: Jinx' (reissue), *Sea of Tranquillity* (16 August 2011), https://www.seaoftranquility.org/reviews.php?op=showcontent&id=11297
15 Dan Muise, *Gallagher, Marriott, Derringer & Trower* (Milwaukee: Hal Leonard Corporation, 2002), 54.
16 Brendan O'Neill, *Meet Mr Sticks* (New York: Glimmer Twin Publishing, 2020), 323.
17 Ibid., 355.
18 Gerry McAvoy and Pete Chrisp, *Riding Shotgun: 35 Years on the Road with Rory Gallagher and "Nine Below Zero"*, (Chicago: SPG Triumph, 2005), 234.
19 O'Neill, *Meet Mr Sticks*, 356-358.
20 Ibid., 363-364.
21 Muise, *Gallagher, Marriott, Derringer & Trower*, 38.
22 Ibid., 39.
23 McAvoy and Chrisp, *Riding Shotgun*, 204.
24 Liner notes to *Notes from San Francisco* (2011).
25 Muise, *Gallagher, Marriott, Derringer & Trower*, 45.
26 Ibid.
27 Vignoles, *Rory Gallagher*, 119.
28 Muise, *Gallagher, Marriott, Derringer & Trower*, 45.
29 Wolfgang Bongeriz, 'Playing as Magically as ever – Rory Gallagher', *Deuce Quarterly* (1982 interview, reproduced in March 1986), http://www.roryon.com/magic176.html
30 O'Neill, *Meet Mr Sticks*, 329.
31 Pete Makowski, 'Rory Gallagher: The Remarkable Story of a Blues Brother's Hot Streak' (2 March 2020), *Louder Sound*, https://www.loudersound.com/features/rory-gallagher-the-remarkable-story-of-a-blues-brothers-hottest-streak
32 Ross, 'While My Guitar Gently Weeps'.
33 Muise, *Gallagher, Marriott, Derringer & Trower*, 46.
34 'International Musician of the Month - Rory Gallagher', *International Musician and Recording World* (February 1982), http://www.roryon.com/month145.html
35 O'Neill, *Meet Mr Sticks*, 366.
36 John Waters, 'Rory Gallagher - A Rap on the Road', *Hot Press* (18 December 1981), https://www.roryon.com/rap262.html
37 Shiv Cariappa, 'Wheeling and Dealing' (March 2003), http://www.roryon.com/donalshiv352.html
38 Interview with Robert Gannon, 31 March 2022.
39 Interview with Dave Fanning, 24 April 2022.
40 Interview with Jean-Pierre Sabouret, 13 October 2022.
41 Liner notes to *Jinx* re-edition (2018).
42 John Waters, 'The Rory Gallagher Interview', *Hot Press* (1981), https://www.hotpress.com/music/the-rory-gallagher-interview-14356357
43 Interview with Dónal Gallagher in *Songs & Stories: New York Remembers Rory Gallagher* (2005) documentary.
44 'International Musician of the Month…'

45 Waters, 'The Rory Gallagher Interview'.
46 Niall Stokes, 'On This Day in 1982: Rory Gallagher releases *Jinx*', *Hot Press* (2 May 2019), https://www.hotpress.com/music/day-1982-rory-gallagher-releases-jinx-22772465
47 Mark McClelland, 'Why We Won't Let Rory Be Forgotten', *Evening Echo* (13 July 2000), http://www.roryon.com/forgotten.html
48 Waters, 'The Rory Gallagher Interview'.
49 'International Musician of the Month...'
50 Thierry Chatain, 'The Blue Line', *Rock and Folk* (April 1982), http://www.roryon.com/rgfr482.html
51 'Rory Gallagher talks Jinx'.
52 Chatain, 'The Blue Line'.
53 McAvoy and Chrisp, *Riding Shotgun*, 235.
54 Muise, *Gallagher, Marriott, Derringer & Trower*, 57.
55 McAvoy and Chrisp, *Riding Shotgun*, 241.
56 Vignoles, *Rory Gallagher*, 139.
57 'Rory Gallagher - It's good to be back in Belfast HD', https://www.youtube.com/watch?v=RAf9gCxCi70&t=92s
58 See: Lauren Alex O'Hagan, 'Fashioning the "People's Guitarist": The Mythologization of Rory Gallagher in the International Music Press', vol. 9, no. 2 (2022), *Rock Music Studies*, 174-198.
59 Paul Strange, 'Rory Gallagher - Jinx', *Melody Maker* (22 May 1982), http://www.roryon.com/jinx321.html
60 Chas de Whalley, 'Rory Gallagher - Jinx', *Kerrang!* (May 1982), http://www.roryon.com/gutbucket342.html
61 Bongeriz, 'Playing as Magically as ever...'
62 'Talkin' Blues', *Hot Press* (1988 quote, reprinted 12 July 1995), https://www.roryon.com/talkin.html
63 Weimer, 'Despite Radio's Hex…'
64 Stokes, 'On This Day in 1982'.
65 John Waters, 'Rolling with Rory', *Hot Press* (May 1982), http://www.roryon.com/rolling163.html
66 Robert Haagsma, 'Rory Gallagher: An Irishman Not to be Forgotten!', *Aardschok* (July 2000), http://www.roryon.com/Aardschock.html
67 Giguere, 'Rory Gallagher - Irish Tour (1974)'.
68 Starostin, 'Rory Gallagher'.
69 Hal Harowitz, 'Jinx', *All Music* (2000), https://www.allmusic.com/album/jinx-mw0000196559/credits; Pete Pardo, 'Gallagher, Rory: Jinx (reissue)', *Sea of Tranquility* (2010), https://www.seaoftranquility.org/reviews.php?op=showcontent&id=11297
70 'Rory Gallagher - Jinx', *Gold Mine Magazine* (2 March 2013), https://www.goldminemag.com/reviews/album-review-of-rory-gallaghers-jinx-reissue
71 Tim Peacock, 'Fresh Evidence: Revisiting Rory Gallagher's Sublime 80s Albums', *U Discover* (2 March 2022), https://www.udiscovermusic.com/stories/rory-gallagher-80s-albums/
72 Paul Elliott, 'The Rory Gallagher Albums You Should Definitely Own', *Louder Sound* (14 June 2022), https://www.loudersound.com/features/rory-gallagher-best-albums
73 Muise, *Gallagher, Marriott, Derringer & Trower*, 58.
74 Vignoles, *Rory Gallagher*, 140.
75 Ibid.
76 See, most recently, 'Top 10 Rory Gallagher Albums', *Blues Rock Review* (29 August 2022), https://bluesrockreview.com/2022/08/top-10-rory-gallagher-albums

1.2 Blood on the Tracks: *Defender* (1987)

"I've got to admit that life without Rory Gallagher has been a bit like having to suffer fish 'n' chips without salt 'n' vinegar," writes Derek Oliver for the November issue of *Kerrang!* in 1987.[1] "I mean, one minute he was busy thrashing out solid slabs of blues-boogie to all and sundry at every available opportunity and then, in the wink of an eye, he was gone. But where?" While Oliver compliments Gallagher on his recent release of *Defender* (particularly after 1982's "lacklustre" *Jinx*), he also does not shy away from keeping the reader aware that "Rory is a member of the *old* school of guitar giants." Compared with the "speedy whiz kid axe maniacs like Yngwie J. Malmsteen," Gallagher's blues sounds "rather passé" to the young ears of 1987 and, as we read on, even his "old and battered 1961 Stratocaster" is under attack from Oliver: "Surely he could afford to buy a new one by now?"

As mentioned in 1.1, in 1977, Gallagher abandoned finished recordings in San Francisco in order to make *Photo-Finish* (1978). A similar decision occurred during the mid-80s when he scrapped a completed album called *Torch* for the release of *Defender* on 1 July 1987. Although much has been said about Gallagher's time in San Francisco (to the point of his Estate even releasing the original tapes in 2011 as the album *Notes From San Francisco*), his 'lost years' between 1982-1986 are either overlooked altogether or the truth is embellished. In a recent conversation thread on the Rory Gallagher Official Forum,[2] fans expressed confusion about exactly what the *Torch* project was and when it occurred, as well as its connection with the San Francisco album, signifying such gaps in Gallagher's history.

In his biography *Rory Gallagher: The Man Behind the Guitar*, Julian Vignoles lists off speculations about Gallagher's movements during the five years, suggesting the possibility of a creative block, despite Gallagher's own confirmation to Dave Fanning that, "I wrote so many songs [in the mid-80s] it was ridiculous."[3] Gerry McAvoy reflects in his memoir that the *Defender* period was the catalyst for Gallagher's "deterioration" and that extended lapses off the road "left Rory with too much time on his own where he would sit and mope and inevitably drown his sorrows with increasing amounts of alcohol."[4] Despite such assertions, Gallagher frequently describes the making of *Defender* as a high point in his creativity. As stated in a conversation with Uli Twelker in 1992, "[*Defender*] was a turning point in my career and in my life. It was a very special album to me personally."[5]

In this essay, we separate fact from fiction by providing a comprehensive overview of Gallagher's five year 'hiatus', from his business ventures—such as the establishment of Capo Records—to a complete timeline of the *Torch* album. We also discuss the media's spotlight on Gallagher's health problems, and how this could, on more than one occasion, obstruct critics view of *Defender*, particularly in a contemporary setting. On a final note, we track the reception of *Defender*, from then to now, and how the album showcased maturation in Gallagher's songwriting and production style.

"I'm breaking out": Gallagher's Struggle for Independence
"Mr. Blues is back!"

While only a headline, we had to wonder, was it truly fair to say that Rory Gallagher was... 'back'? Fair or not, it was the narrative printed in the March 1988 edition of *Hot Press*. In the article, Gallagher reminisces with Bill Graham about his showband days in the early 1960s, as well as his updated philosophies on touring and musical ambitions, while accounting for his temporary "exile from Irish stages and record shops."[6] He quips, "Maybe people thought I was sheep farming." Gallagher, in fact, dedicated much of his time in the mid-80s to the studio, from session work (see 1.4) to mixing tracks for the *Self Aid* album, as well as regularly touring the European festival circuit. While, in the past, the new wave of music magazines such as *Metal Hammer* expressed derision towards Gallagher, on this occasion, Al Simpson (partially)[7] supports the guitarist, claiming that "Rory Gallagher doesn't play the rockstar" by "sunning himself on some exotic island."[8] Instead, he continues to work on his music, even if out of the spotlight.

Up until his death, Gallagher would often discuss this cycle—or "funny head things,"[9] as he wryly described to Fanning—of abandoning albums. In *Ghost Blues: The Story of Rory Gallagher* (2010), Dónal Gallagher recounted his frustration of watching his brother toss away the San Francisco recordings before a meeting with record executives in 1978. The transition between *Torch* to *Defender* unfolded in a similar manner, as demonstrated in Gallagher's conversation with Grahame Bent in late 1988. "One day I just woke up and thought, 'That's it. It's over, and that's the end of that. To hell with it.' And I started laying plans for what became *Defender*."[10] Gallagher displayed confidence in his decision, despite the fact that it "cost a fortune"[11] to remake an entirely new record. "Sometimes it's good to get really disgusted with the stuff you're doing and give yourself a real ticking off and start again," he said on RTÉ's *Borderline* in 1988.

Years on, Gallagher continued to reflect on the 82-86 period with an optimistic outlook, recognising the downside of too much time on the road. "You can't get a third eye of yourself," he stated in 1991's *Cleveland Scene*, "[...] when you're doing constant touring, you don't get a chance to assess what you're doing or what you could be doing."[12] Gallagher used this time to re-evaluate his relationship with the blues, both as an admirer and interpreter. "At home I just played more blues records [and] I became more of a blues fan than I had for a while."[13] He also realised the risk of "getting too rocky" onstage and forgetting to "have fun at just playing the groove," concluding that "things worked out for the better" during the five years.[14] Paul Charles, his agent at the time, considered *Defender* "[Rory's] best collection of songs"[15] and observed a rejuvenated Gallagher as a result of the break. As he told us in our October 2023 interview:

> I really love the *Defender* record. I felt it was new [and] it was fresh. It benefited, to my ears, greatly from the five-year layoff [...] They were all songs that wouldn't have felt out of place on the Taste setlist from the Marquee Club days. The album brought back memories to me about what it used to be like to be involved (as an agent) with a new exciting gigging band.

While Gallagher indeed had time to spare to reassess his musical direction, there was also the danger of *too* much time and the effects of this on his lingering depression, which always intensified when off the road. Music had always been an outlet, with the guitar a source of "therapy"[16] for Gallagher, and while he was "more inclined to take more time out"[17] following *Top Priority* (1979), the unpredictable nature and pressure of the music business must have also taken a toll. In fact, many *Defender* songs allude to this restless and stagnant state of mind, from the narrator being "close to the edge" ('Road to Hell') to the verge of "breaking out" of "my cell" ('Doing Time'). Even "Heaven has to *wait*" for Gallagher in 'I Ain't No Saint'.

Daniel Gallagher highlights 'Kickback City' as encapsulating "Rory's despondency with having to exist in the business side of music,"[18] particularly the lyric, "You try to learn all your lines, and you try to play the part." With London viewed as the 'mecca' of the music industry during the 1960s-1970s, Gallagher's Irishness could often marginalise him, as demonstrated in his confession of feeling like an "exile"[19] while living in England, therefore adding to this search for liberation. And even when trying to fit in, Gallagher could not recognise the business he once knew in the 70s, telling Bill Graham in 1987: "Now it's the project, the stew, the movie. Everything has to be Cecil B. De Mille."[20] Gallagher mentions instances when record companies showed interest in him during his 'hiatus', admitting that these deals "usually fell down" because he was "being too obstinate" and "not commercial [enough]," which "caused a lot of tension for me, [in myself]."[21]

Overtime, Gallagher's health problems have stirred up many misconceptions, particularly those around the *Torch* era. Gallagher's depression has often been associated with the mid-80s period, as if his symptoms *suddenly* appeared. In reality, key moments throughout Gallagher's life triggered depressive episodes, going back to the break-up of Taste in 1970 which, according to Dónal, "caused a huge depression in [Rory]."[22] Similarly, Gallagher's health anxiety has attracted fictitious holes in his narrative, like the claim that he "became a hypochondriac in the 80s,"[23] when "even as a kid, Rory had a tendency to be a little bit of a hypochondriac," says Dónal.[24] "Rory had an anxiety problem and always had," agrees Mark Feltham.[25] As the public struggled to piece the puzzle together, so too did the band. "The problem had sort of crept up on all of us," wrote McAvoy, "[...] we all hoped that having the new album to focus on would get Rory back on track health-wise."[26]

Unfortunately, Gallagher's many health battles during the *Defender* period have undermined the focus on the album itself in both the past and contemporary press. For Dan Muise, Gallagher is "driven" to complete the *Photo-Finish* sessions, documenting the studio atmosphere with lengthy passages from co-producer Alan O'Duffy. With *Defender*, however (which O'Duffy also co-produced), the only noteworthy point is to ask him whether there was a noticeable "change in Rory's character or outlook," as opposed to his direction for production and instrumentation.[27] Muise is instead distracted by the contentious side, and we lose the opportunity to understand an album that Gallagher dedicated most of his studio time to: "I was probably working harder [on *Torch* and *Defender*] than I had been at certain points in the 70s."[28] Gallagher's musical vision had significantly shifted from 1979 to 1987, and through misdiagnosing his strive for perfection as a superstitious symptom, Muise fails to document a flourishing artistry.

From the late 1980s until his passing, Gallagher rid his check shirts in favour of wearing plain black clothing. While the black attire was a "disappointment"[29] to some, for Gallagher, black signified "a new start."[30] Comparatively, Gallagher fondly referred to his first solo album as 'the black album', again associating the colour black with fresh beginnings in his career. In any case, Gallagher quickly decided to wear black when, over "the course of several nights in the studio, [he felt] something unpleasant and even threatening came over him."[31] The press clung onto Gallagher's new wardrobe,[32] with both past and present articles projecting black as symbolic of "his health [deteriorating]."[33] The *Irish Press* attributed the change to Gallagher's "notoriously superstitious nature" mixed with "boredom."[34] Above all, however, Gallagher felt the check shirts were "distracting people from the enduring quality of his work."[35] He would discuss this dilemma in *Hot Press* with Liam Fay.

> I know it's peculiar but it's just a psychological thing. That denim jacket and check shirt have become like a stigma to me. I never treated it as a uniform but that's what it has become over the years, a uniform that I just don't want to wear anymore. Lately, I wear an ordinary black shirt and a black jacket when I'm onstage. Right now, I feel a lot happier in black.[36]

As stated in 1.1, Gallagher's contract with Chrysalis was fulfilled with the completion of *Jinx*. His decision to move away from the major record companies and instead start an independent label was, according to Dónal, "a calculated move."[37] He further explains: "After *Jinx*, it did take a long time. [Rory] took a sabbatical then. 'What's the point in rushing? Who's the new company?' That was when the Chrysalises, the Islands, the A&Ms, who were tall Rory-type companies if you like, started being bought up by the big majors who Rory had steered clear from."[38] From there, the next—and most logical—step was to establish his own label, doing so in 1986 under Capo Records. The name shows inspiration from two areas of Gallagher's life: as the accessory used for a guitar, as well as his appreciation for crime fiction (*capo dei capi* being the Boss of the crime family). Speaking with the *Tuam Herald*, Gallagher outlined the process of forming Capo. "Legally I had some difficulty in setting up the record label. It might not be very viable in a commercial sense, but it has a fantastic feeling of independence [...] I feel that the pop merchants have had enough sway and they will have to contend with me for a while."[39] Gallagher also mentioned in an interview with the *Evening Herald* about the possibility of signing new artists to Capo if the situation ever arose. However, this plan was never executed.

Over two decades of experience in the music world had left Gallagher alert to the "suspicious"[40] attitudes of executives, particularly if their artists were uncooperative. "If you don't please everyone (press officer, label representative, producer etc.) you end up like me: in a situation where one day you speak to the record company and the next day it's all over. There's a cold war for years."[41] Although Gallagher would admit that he was "not that organised" regarding the music business, he did have expectations for matters "to be under control" and, most importantly, "I want the final say on things."[42] Around the same time, Gallagher signed with the distribution company Demon Records in the UK, per the recommendation of his new agent Paul Charles. The two first met backstage during one of Taste's many performances at the Marquee Club in London, maintaining contact throughout the 1970s. Charles continued to attend many Gallagher shows and even phoned him after the break-up of Taste to enquire about the progress of his solo career. He also organised and promoted Guitarists' Night in 1984—a set of shows featuring Gallagher, along with David Lindley, Richard Thompson and Juan Martín (see 1.4).

Two years later, Charles was approached by Dónal to be Gallagher's agent. "I felt very privileged. I was a major fan," he told us, "[Rory] was the perfect artist for an agent to represent. Absolutely every promoter I knew wanted to book [him]." Charles understood what kind of artist Gallagher was, made clear by his encouragement to choose Demon Records. Prior to this, Gallagher was "on the verge" of accepting an offer from "one or two major companies," though soon declined as "the way they saw my future [wasn't] quite right."[43] Demon, on the other hand, expressed immediate "artistic trust"[44] in Gallagher, understanding his desire to simply "make some music, record it and put it out" rather than "sell a million [records]" or participate in "miming sessions for TV."[45] In addition, with Demon "not competing with big pop names or anything else," Gallagher found himself "more in [his] neck of the words."[46]

And so, after a spell of legal trouble, Gallagher had perhaps achieved momentary peace. Charles recalls the atmosphere backstage at Sheffield City Hall, three months after the release of *Defender*: "Rory was in great form. He was feeling good and very happy with the way things were going with the album and the touring. He was positive, but never big headed, about the path he was on."

From *Torch* to *Defender*: The Similarities and Differences

In 1983, Gallagher returned to Ireland for his annual Christmas tour. Although our timeline is a rough estimate, we can conclude from Gallagher's interviews at this time that the making of *Torch* began around the middle of the year and was scheduled for release in March 1984. Gallagher explained in an interview with Philip Nolan that, beginning in October, sessions for the new album alternated between The Point and West Three Studios in Central and West London, respectively. Three months until release and time seemed to disappear like quicksand, with Gallagher admitting that the long days and nights were "getting a bit out of hand."[47] He continues, "You go into the studio to mix at seven, and suddenly it's a dozen coffees later and five or six in the morning, and it's silly really."[48] At that stage, the album was untitled, "but it will probably be after 'Failsafe Day' or 'Early Warning'," Gallagher stated.[49]

'Failsafe Day', as we know, would make its formal debut on *Defender*, but was already in the rotation of new material Gallagher was previewing at his concerts. As Cathal Dervan reported in his review of Gallagher's shows in Ireland around January 1984, the audience were treated to the "mellow" 'Lonely Mile', 'Fallback [sic] Time' (the song "began in a slow mood, but had the masses rocking with delight"), as well as 'Kickback City', "which highlights yet again Gallagher's penchant for writing classic rock n roll tunes."[50] During Gallagher's travels around Scandinavia in June 1984, he discussed his (still nameless) album with journalists Trond Hansen and Per Wollen, feeling optimistic about an early August completion: "we're in the mixing stage now, [with] a few overdubs left."[51] Though an explanation for the delay is undisclosed, we can hypothesise a combination of factors, as highlighted in Gallagher's conversation with Dave Fanning in 1988.

> We had some contractual problems and tying up the rights deals and getting artistic freedom from various companies [...] and then if you throw in a couple of tours and festivals and so on, I just don't know where the five years went.[52]

Compared with previous years, Gallagher's touring schedule had dropped significantly by the mid-80s, his flying phobia being a major contributor. Regardless, Gallagher's appearance at many European festivals, such as the Calpe Rock Festival (Spain, 1984) and Out in the Green (1986, 1987), were listed in *Guitarist* magazine as the primary reason for his new album stalling. Gallagher reassures readers that the trouble is not a lack of material:

> We have about fifteen songs that we're working on. We've got keyboards on one track and sax on another, and there will be one or two other people involved [...] the fifteen songs will be narrowed down to about ten with proper mixes. It's looking good–I'm confident about it.[53]

Dónal attended an afterparty of the 1986 Self Aid Festival in Dublin, updating the press about his brother's (now completed) album, which was expected to be released sometime in September. Unfortunately, an unfulfilled prophecy. In the June 1987 issue of *Guitarist*, Gallagher revealed the name that fans would read once his LP hit the shelves next month. "The album will either be *Torch* or *Loan Shark Blues*, which is one of the tracks on the album."[54] It is interesting to note that, even at this late stage, the name *Torch* was still resonating with him.

Gallagher's 'sudden' resurgence with the release of *Defender* prompted much media attention on where the Irish guitarist had vanished. When the abandoned *Torch* was mentioned, journalists were undoubtedly intrigued. However, when the subject was raised, Gallagher seemed distant from the project, as demonstrated by his insistence to Dave Fanning that "*Defender* was like a brand new thing from start to finish."[55] Therefore, *Torch* and *Defender* were separate identities that we could categorise as a 'pre-*Defender*' and 'post-*Defender*' Rory Gallagher:

> In and around the *Defender* thing, I just got a whole new lease of life [and] I don't feel at all weary. Not just a new mind, I got a whole new strength. When people read all these rock histories they expect you to be some decrepit icon in a wheelchair. Right now I still feel like I'm fifteen years old and that's the way I want to keep it.[56]

It goes without saying that if this was indeed a different album—even a different Rory Gallagher—then a different title was essential. In an article for *Guitar*, Dónal speculated on the meaning behind 'torch' and the link with Gallagher's album vision. "Rory would have thought of it as handing over the torch [...] of [him] being the torch carrier for blues music."[57] Of course, this interpretation is weighted by his brother's untimely passing. Nevertheless, Gallagher referred to himself as "a crusader of the blues,"[58] and so regarded his music as a continuation of the tradition,[59] even if sometimes unintentionally, such as 'Last of the Independents'. Additionally, Gallagher being a devout Catholic, we cannot overlook the biblical symbolism of 'torch' as a beacon of knowledge and truth.

Nor the use of a 'torch' as an instrument used by a police officer to bear light on the evidence, to find the right clue.

As part of a Rory Gallagher exhibition some years ago, the proposed album cover for *Torch*, as drawn by Gallagher, was put on display. Gallagher has depicted a figure in black, perhaps camouflaging himself in the similar way a criminal would in the night, reflecting themes of illegal activity and the law that would later appear on *Defender* ('Doing Time', 'Loanshark Blues'). When fans held a copy of *Defender* in their hands for the first time, they were met with a photograph of Gallagher leant against the hood of a red Chrysler Saratoga, stare fixed straight ahead. As opposed to the illustrated *Torch* version, Gallagher himself has now transformed into the figure in black, shrouded in darkness, illuminated only by the glowing dashboard. The cover bears slight reminiscence to the boldly colourful French New Wave film posters, with Gallagher cloaked in mysterious and brooding undertones. Gallagher opted for the title *Defender* as a reference to the Chicago newspaper of the same name, highlighting the "direct linking up with the blues roots"[60] on the album. Although the argument has been made that—like carrying the 'torch'—Gallagher was also a *defender* for the blues, many overlook the obvious connection to legal jargon: public defender. We could even interpret Gallagher's stance behind the car as behind the witness box of a courtroom.

While *Defender* is characterised by a rural blues atmosphere and clean production, without the original sessions, we can only provide assumptions about *Torch*'s aural mood. Speaking with *Overdrive* in 2020, Daniel Gallagher briefly mentioned his discovery of tapes from the *Torch* period, circa 1983 in Dublin. "[The tapes] sounded much different to the version that was made public [i.e., *Defender*], as [Rory] had saxophone players involved during those sessions."[61] Daniel's mention of saxophones alludes to Gallagher's prior work on *Jinx*, presuming he was carrying over ideas from the early 80s to his next record. Gallagher described *Torch* as "innovative" in terms of sound, and that his experimentation with "rhythms and melodies" would "break new ground."[62] Gallagher kept a handful of *Torch* tracks for *Defender*, such as 'No Peace for the Wicked' (originally released as a 7" single), adjusting them to "different keys [and] different tempos,"[63] with the addition of new songs.

Hardboiled Blues: Songcraft and Storytelling on *Defender*

Gallagher always revered a song that told a story. He took inspiration from the "little gems and masterpieces" of rock & rollers such as Chuck Berry and Bo Diddley, meanwhile idolised his peers, like "the greatest songwriter in the world" Bob Dylan.[64] Gallagher even revealed to a magazine Q&A in 1985 that a dream of his was to pen his own screenplay. Therefore, finding the right words for the right story was a significant part of Gallagher's songcraft, and *Defender* exhibits experimentation in his storytelling, attracting much critical acclaim. In the past, critics were not as complimentary, with *Rolling Stone* describing Gallagher's lyrics and vocal delivery on *Calling Card* (1976) as not being "particularly arresting."[65] Gallagher adapted his lyrics to "fit in with the music"[66] as opposed to "throwaway material for guitar breaks,"[67] despite some critics not always agreeing. By *Defender*, however, the press proudly acknowledged Gallagher's songwriting progression, as shown in a review from the *Harrow Leader*: "Amid the extraordinary guitar playing [...] it is almost impossible to overlook the lyrics, which are crammed with atmosphere and imagery."[68] Three months after the release of *Defender*, Gallagher sat down with Spencer Leigh to discuss his songwriting. "I have worked very hard and seriously on [my] lyrics," judging those on *Defender* to be "pretty good" and "important to [him]."[69] One such track was 'Loanshark Blues', inspired by the plotline of *On the Waterfront* (1954). "When I was recording 'Loanshark Blues', I thought, 'if I die tomorrow, I'll be proud of that one'."[70]

Defender showed a unity within the track list, and thematically it was considered Gallagher's "most consistent and composed record" to date by "fusing his musical pre-occupation with the blues [and] his fascination with film noir and thriller authors."[71] Gallagher's interest in the crime fiction genre, both in film and literature, was sparked during early adolescence. Dónal recalls watching *Purple Noon* (1960), a loose adaptation of Patricia Highsmith's *The Talented Mr. Ripley* (1955), as having a "significant impact on [Rory]" during his teenage years.[72] Throughout his life, Gallagher read the likes of Highsmith, Raymond Chandler, Roger Borniche, Ian Fleming and John le Carré. From Dónal's observations, the plots and characters his brother encountered in such hardboiled novels and films reflected in his attitude. Gallagher "identified" with "the rebel" of these stories, admiring "anybody who stood their ground," regardless of moral conviction.[73] Prior to *Defender*, Gallagher's appreciation for crime fiction was peppered into the title and lyrics of his discography, such as 'In Your Town' (*Deuce*, 1971), 'Secret Agent' (*Calling Card*, 1976) and 'Public Enemy No. 1' (*Top Priority*, 1979). 'Philby', also off *Top Priority*, would become widely known to fans and the press as representing Gallagher's fascination with espionage, influenced by British double-agent Kim Philby.[74]

Defender, by Gallagher's account, revolved "around the whole idea of the cops and robbers story,"[75] and this is most evident on the second track 'Continental Op', a tribute to the character developed by novelist Dashiell Hammett. Gallagher related to the world penned by Hammett, often comparing the life of a musician to that of a detective as "neither have a nine to five job and both come under certain mental pressure."[76] In conversation with Fanning, Gallagher referred to the Op as an "ideal" subject for a song as "he's very pushy and vain and he's a bit high-minded as a detective."[77] Gallagher also admired Hammett's "short, snappy and straight to the point" writing style.[78] This is demonstrated not only in Gallagher's lyrics, but also the sharply vigorous guitar strokes throughout the track. Gallagher's use of the pause before such lines as "there's a menace on the streets" effectively enhances the suspenseful nature of the song. In a retrospective review from *Hot Press*, Pat Carty argues that "if a Dylan or Springsteen had written ['Continental Op'], the critics would have been falling over themselves."[79]

The world sculpted by Gallagher in *Defender* is founded on "double dealings" ('Kickback City') and fuelled by rumour, warning us to not "believe the papers" ('Smear Campaign'). If the turmoil is not in the streets, then it is found in the mind, tormenting the narrator. "In the night I hear that rumbling, keep on hoping that it's just a dream," pleads Gallagher in 'Failsafe Day'. Or from the perspective of a prisoner facing the electric chair in 'Seven Days', "the feeling in my head is like all-out war." Gallagher even eliminates divine salvation from his narrative; corruption has run so deep that he "won't make it through the pearly gates" ('I Ain't No Saint') as "the devil's got a jump on me" ('Road to Hell'). Gallagher's lyrical output had evidently (and very successfully) gone beyond the "12 o'clock/ got the blues" tropes and "moon-in-June" sentimentalities.[80] While Gallagher references the blues structure in his compositions, he also did not want to limit himself so that "[he] couldn't put a middle-eight with nothing to do with the blues in a song."[81]

In a 1991 interview with Shiv Cariappa, Gallagher opened up about the "isolated [and] unusual city" he wrote of in 'Failsafe Day', forming the idea after "a holocaust [or Armageddon] type of situation"—a theme that would later appear in 'Middle Name' (*Fresh Evidence*, 1990).[82] In the track, Gallagher recalls the stranger motif established on 'Philby' ("there's a stranger in my soul"), which has now transported outside of himself: "there's this stranger in the air I breathe." Gallagher's intentions with the song were to remind the narrator to "keep your control [and] keep your grip" against "the people running the world" who do not "[play] by the rules."[83] As he sings: "the voice inside just tells me one thing, keep on hoping that it's just a dream." Moreover, Gallagher's passion for crime novels was, in Brendan O'Neill's mind, "part of [Rory's] make-up" and reflected his tendency to "be undercover" and "never [show] his hand too readily."[84] On occasion, biographies have overemphasised such personality quirks, like Julian Vignoles claiming Gallagher's preoccupation with "fictional crime [and] political corruption" as "both a unifying and a worrying feature" on *Defender*.[85] Further misinterpretation is exacerbated by McAvoy's comments to Dan Muise that Gallagher's fascination with spies "took a different shade in his life," causing him to "get very paranoid about silly things."[86] However, for *Defender* to be solely a metaphor for Gallagher's depressive and melancholic headspace is almost too narrowminded. As such, could *Defender* be more than simply art imitating life?

While *Defender* could be Gallagher, it could also be the general population living in the 1980s under the Thatcher era ("dirty tricks department"), or those suffering from the AIDS crisis and widespread famine ("feel six feet under" in 'Seems to Me' or the death date looming in 'Seven Days'). The rise of the corporate world and "greed is good"[87] philosophies under the Reagan-Thatcher regimes is subtly referenced in 'Kickback City' ("this town ain't got no soul") or compared to "a pantomime" in 'No Peace for the Wicked'. By the same token, this could also refer to Gallagher's conflict with the changing climate of the 80s music industry, as addressed in a 2013 interview with his nephew Daniel. "Rory's later songs" often use the "villain/mob type" as a metaphor for the music business in that "he has to duck and weave in and out to survive."[88] In our interview, Paul Charles measured the ramifications of Gallagher's attitudes to the music business throughout his career:

> I fear that in order to protect the purity of his art and his music, Rory made a lot of commercial sacrifices. In other words, it could be said that Rory could have been a lot more successful commercially if only he'd played the record company's game: prioritised singles; allowing himself to be 'produced'; be agreeing to special edits and mixes; duets; chat shows, game shows and developed a celebrity status.

Above all, *Defender* demonstrates a Rory Gallagher willing to broaden his songwriting capabilities, crafting a story with different meanings—and on different levels—to represent something more than solely an obsession with fiction and create his own unique style of 'hardboiled blues'.

"The real meat": Balancing the Old with the New on *Defender*

In an interview with *Guitarist* to commemorate the release of the *Rory Gallagher 50th Anniversary Edition* (2021), McAvoy discussed Gallagher's natural approach to recording and production. "Rory wanted it to be as live as possible," he said, which Gallagher believed created "a great performance" and, therefore, "a great song."[89] Over time, Gallagher familiarised himself with the studio and became comfortable utilising certain techniques. As he told Adam Sweeting in 1979:

> On [past] albums I sang live, played live lead guitar and then overdubbed a bit of rhythm. I suppose in retrospect it was a bad idea, but at the same time I wanted to get something as truth as possible, mistakes and all. But with the last three albums I've been a bit more intelligent about it. I'm not averse to overdubbing vocals and lead parts if need be, or a rhythm part.[90]

Although Gallagher had increased his time in the studio, this did not mean that he had turned against his organic style of recording. "Mentally, I still like to start as though it's just a tape recorder taping music, more or less live," said Gallagher to *Making Music*'s Jon Lewin in late 1987.[91] In the past, Gallagher was known to schedule studio time around touring, preferring to flesh out songs in a live setting for an audience. During the recording of *Defender*, however, Gallagher abandoned this method, preferring to finetune the details of each track through lengthy rehearsal sessions. "I laid down every song at least twice, sometimes more, and ultimately ended up with around twenty songs to choose from."[92]

Mark Feltham stated in our October 2023 interview that he was not involved with the *Torch* project, and instead attended the *Defender* rehearsals at Nomis Studios in West London. These "extremely intense" rehearsal sessions, as Feltham described, unfolded without formal structure and often ended with Gallagher "dripping in sweat."[93] "He would never say, 'Stop there. I want to do it this way. He just kind of knew without him having to say anything. Absolutely [like an instinct]." When time came for recording, Feltham was usually the final addition to the track. "Rory and the guys would put a loose backing track together in the afternoon and then I would go up in the evening and we'd all try and cut the record live [...] He never directed me. I was given complete artistic freedom."

Gallagher would then fall into a procrastination stage of determining the best take to put on the album. "There'd be four or five takes that were on tape and he'd often reference back to them [...] I think he suffered a great deal from his procrastination. He was tormented by his inability to know [what was the better take]." With *Defender* suffering multiple delays—partly a result of business complications—Gallagher eventually felt the "pressure" to make his new album "better" and "prove that [he] could still cut it" in the industry.[94] It could be said that Gallagher was perhaps *too* involved with his albums, taking on the roles of writer, producer and performer, which he admitted increased the risk of "[losing] all perspective."[95] As a result, Gallagher often became "run-down"[96] during the mixing process. Speaking with Kenneth Kelleher in 1990: "No matter how long you have been doing it, you never feel absolutely secure or satisfied. You are always a bit conscious that you might be able to change this or improve that."[97] Feltham has identified similar behaviour with many musicians and that Gallagher "was certainly no more precious than anybody else [he] worked with." As an artist, Feltham distinguishes Gallagher's key strength as a "performer" rather than a "producer" or "engineer."

Once released, Gallagher expressed satisfaction at *Defender*'s overall mood and sound, telling *Guitarist* magazine, "I wasn't very happy with the sound on *Jinx* compared to this one."[98] Although Gallagher applied a similar mentality when recording his next album, the distinction lay in his "mellow" approach to *Fresh Evidence*, whereas *Defender* had "a lot more of a rock production."[99] Gallagher was looking to capture a "roots sound"[100] reminiscent of the records by Leonard and Phil Chess or Sun's Sam Phillips. But "at the same time, [I want] a 1987 feel. It's hell trying to get the two together because I hate pop rock or pop blues."[101] One method Gallagher used to try and capture the "old magic"[102] was to start breaking up the recording cycle with touring. "I think sometimes that's the best way to do it–do it in bits instead of starting on January 1 and being at it for the next X weeks," which, in Gallagher's view, can "dull your sense of decision."[103] According to Brendan O'Neill,

> A lot of [*Defender*], believe it or not, was very impromptu. [Rory] would come along with a riff and we would work on that. And then

he would go off on a tangent or an offshoot from it [...] And he didn't block-book time then. We would just get a call and say, 'I've got an idea. Are you free tonight?' And we'd go and record. Maybe that's why it took so long. He wouldn't pressure himself by block-booking a studio for a month and go into a think-tank.[104]

Compared with Gallagher's "painfully anaemic"[105] recordings of the past, *Defender* has layered guitar tones and instrumentation, including saxophone on 'I Ain't No Saint', Coral sitar on 'Kickback City' and guest pianist Lou Martin on 'Seven Days'. Though synonymous with the Fender Stratocaster, Gallagher was an avid guitar collector, occasionally utilising his finds for the studio, such as playing his Silvertone 1323 on 'A Million Miles Away' and 'Cradle Rock' for *Tattoo* (1973). Maintaining this experimental streak, *Defender* substitutes the Strat in favour of a Telecaster[106] sound, as heard in 'Continental Op', 'Failsafe Day' and 'Don't Start Me Talkin''. Gallagher favoured the Tele for rhythm playing due to its accuracy, "you have to work harder—no free gifts."[107] In addition, Gallagher increased his use of his 1963 Gretsch Corvette, exhibited mainly on 'Road to Hell', 'Doing Time' and 'Loanshark Blues' as either rhythm or slide. Outtakes for the *Defender* photoshoot show Gallagher posed with his 1965 National Airline and another Gibson, again distancing himself from the Strat (and, therefore, his past), in a similar way to how his wardrobe changed at this time. Onstage, Gallagher could be seen swapping guitars for different songs, such as the Airline for 'I Wonder Who' at 1985's Montreux Jazz Festival or his 1960 Gibson Melody Maker for 'Bad Penny' at 1987's Wiener Stadfest (Vienna City Festival). Around the same time, Gallagher was reassessing the set-up of his rigs, which we discuss further in 2.2.

Gallagher's tendency to be "fairly meticulous"[108] with production has divided critics. Dónal has identified his brother's "perfection" in the studio as having less to do with "preciseness" and more to do with a rejection of sounding "diluted [or] sweetened."[109] Gallagher's mixes, therefore, tended to be "introverted" and "subtle."[110] While, on the one hand, *Defender* could be heard as "sparse,"[111] to the contemporary ear, Gallagher has achieved a timeless quality on his latter recordings. *Defender* encapsulates "the usual Gallagher with his Chicago sounds and country blues," but, at the same time, exhibits "not a trace of eighties sounds," writes *The Outlaw* blog.[112] As such, Gallagher's strive to achieve "that old magic with modern material"[113] will still relate for generations to come, encapsulating "the real meat"[114] of authentic blues playing while transcending the epoch in which it was created. As critiqued himself in the *Belfast Telegraph*: "At no point does [*Defender*] reek of being neutered by the engineer or the desk or the equipment."[115]

"The one worth waiting for": *Defender*'s **Reception in the Press, Then and Now**
Gallagher frequently expressed contentment with the material on *Defender*. On more than one occasion, he ranked the record among his favourites from his

catalogue and, as late as January 1995, stated that *Defender* (along with 1973's *Tattoo*) was his "best album" and "pretty complete" in terms of mixing and mood.[116] "Of all my albums, *Defender*'s my absolute favourite purely because it was blood on the tracks," Gallagher told Grahame Bent for *Sounds* magazine in 1988, "It's the usual Barry Manilow quote: 'I really put a lot of myself into the album'. It's not going to change the world, [but] it says what it means and it means what it says."[117] Although Gallagher was often noted for his integrity, for playing "natural"[118] and representing "the real thing,"[119] the exercise of distancing himself from the mainstream music world and maintaining blues purity appears more prevalent in 1987 than ten years before, as shown by his descriptions of *Defender* in interviews: "convincing," "gritty," "honest" and "to the point."

Although hesitant to admit he was "entirely satisfied"[120] with the finished result, Gallagher was, nevertheless, adamant about *Defender*'s value—both to his existing output, as well as the blues market. "I was fighting against what was the current theme and attitudes in a lot of production and a lot of music," Gallagher stated to Fanning, "I made the album for my own headstone, not for great success or anything. That's genuine."[121] Although fans are accustomed to humble remarks such as this, the words hold greater significance when acknowledging the loosened shackles around Gallagher as a result of forming Capo. *Defender* was shaped truly to Gallagher's vision and, "without any help or assistance,"[122] he was finally untied from company obligation, the direction of label executives and even allowed to remove his flannel 'uniform'. Gallagher had become "hell-bent on making [*Defender*] the best" of his career and "not connected with [his] past albums," but rather indicating "a fresh beginning."[123]

Gallagher's 'fresh beginning' was regarded by critics as a return to form. *Defender* was immediately positioned with "the classics like *Tattoo* and *Blueprint*,"[124] and proved to be the best indication that he had not "lost [his] touch"[125] musically. Tony Kentwright of the *Daily Post* hailed *Defender* as "the one worth waiting for," complimenting Gallagher's pairing of "excellent bluesy-rock [with] his best lyrics to date" to create "angry and vengeful tales."[126] Kentwright concludes that Gallagher recent efforts represent "real music played by a true musician." Upon release, *Defender* reached over 60,000 sales, making it one of Demon's all-time Top Ten bestsellers.[127] The album generated further success for Gallagher when it topped the UK Independent Albums Chart, as well as re-establishing him in the public sphere, as highlighted by his (well-deserved) inclusion on a Reader's Poll Best Musician list for *Sounds* magazine in 1988. Gallagher later commented on the "morale boost" such an achievement brought to him, considering the challenging process to complete the record: "[*Defender*] was really the Van Gogh album. You know, the cutting of the ear job."[128]

Retrospectively, *Defender* has divided critics. When the catalogue was rereleased in 2011, Wesley Britton regarded *Defender* and *Fresh Evidence* as epitomising "what Gallagher [was] best known for."[129] *Defender* featured two bonus tracks,

'Seems to Me' and 'No Peace for the Wicked', which were regarded as "actually better [if not] certainly as good" as the original tracks.[130] *Defender* was released to a generation that felt frustrated with "the 80s creative void," triggering a "realisation that maybe the 'old stuff'"—i.e., artists from the late 60s and 70s—"had something going for it."[131] Although many young Gallagher fans still yearn for the 'old stuff' (see Conclusion), not all critics of the 21st century do, exemplified in the sour reception of *Defender* recently. To Paul Elliott's ears, *Defender* is not at all a 'fresh beginning', but simply the "one to avoid" from Gallagher's albums.[132] Ryan Sagadore from *Spill Magazine* recognises a "slight improvement" from *Jinx*, but disapproves of the production style, equating *Defender* to "lounge music [as opposed to] the top tier blues rock Gallagher was capable of [making]."[133] Decades on, perhaps Gallagher's 'fresh beginning' does not sound so fresh anymore when listened against his other albums, and instead *Defender* is now "watered down basic rock," as assessed on the *rateyourmusic* database.[134] On the upside, Gallagher's songwriting on *Defender* continues to be praised. "Some of Gallagher's best lyrics really make themselves apparent on this album," as written by Bruce Forrest for *Vintage Rock*.[135]

"Gallagher survives": *Defender*'s Place in the 21st Century

Since 1987, *Defender* has been honoured in a variety of ways, with particular attention on Gallagher's composing. In 2011, his Estate assembled *Kickback City*—a boxset of Gallagher's crime fiction themed songs. Novelist Ian Rankin contributed a 40-page novella based on the selected 14 tracks, five of which are from *Defender*. 'The Lie Factory'—narrated by American actor Aidan Quinn—closes the album and was conceived as "a homage to the golden age of the American detective story," while upholding "the [Dashiell Hammett and Raymond Chandler] style Rory would have appreciated."[136] Although a longtime fan of Gallagher's music, Rankin seized the opportunity to re-familiarise himself with the Irishman's catalogue as inspiration for the novella. "I tended to focus on the guitar and the very raw, passionate vocals, not really the lyrics," said Rankin to *Classic Rock*. On these recent listens, Rankin was impressed by Gallagher's "strong [and] one-liner" lyrics, appreciating "bloodstains on the dress of the millionairess" from 'Continental Op' in particular as "it forms a picture." In addition, Rankin admired Gallagher's merging of the blues with crime fiction, suggesting that the link between the two lies in the "basic human emotions." *Kickback City* was not "just a boxset," but rather "a murky underworld you can reach out and touch," therefore breaking the mould of what the compilation could be: based on concept instead of an artist's hits. Henry Yates from *Classic Rock* was pleased to discover that, as advertised, *Kickback City* was indeed "a unique immersive album," while Bernard O'Rouke complimented Gallagher's ability to combine "incredibly atmospheric and moody lyrics around masterful guitar work."[137]

Around the same time *Kickback City* was in development, author and educator Wesley Callihan spoke at Idaho's New Saint Andrews College on the portrayal of

Hammett's Continental Op character in various media over the years. Based on Hammett's brief period in the Pinkerton Detective Agency, the Continental Op—as connected by Callihan—has evolved from print to film, (as seen in the Man with No Name from Sergio Leone's *Dollars Trilogy*) to finally music (as heard in Gallagher's track). Callihan sampled Gallagher's many crime fiction themed songs throughout the lecture, such as 'Secret Agent', 'Public Enemy No. 1' and 'Philby'. Coincidentally, Callihan's lecture occurred at roughly the same time as the *Continental Op* 10" release for Record Store Day in April 2013, which—along with the title track—features three other songs: 'I Ain't No Saint', 'The Loop' and 'Loanshark Blues'.

If we look to the future, there are many ways that we can continue to celebrate *Defender*. In a similar manner to how Gallagher's self-titled debut and *Deuce* were commemorated with an anniversary boxset in 2021 and 2022, respectively, *Defender* would be a suitable candidate for such treatment. A boxset could allow fans to follow the arc from 1983's *Torch* production to what would then become an album of "subtlety and sophistication"[138] in 1987. In recent years, Eoin Gallagher has digitised his uncle's notebooks and journals from across his career. "It was fascinating to learn about [Rory] as a writer," said Eoin, "[and] to see the creativity of an artist, and how they come about to write songs was really an eye-opener."[139] An accompanying booklet with Gallagher's lyric sheets could enhance the listener's experience of *Defender*'s themes while gaining insight into his songwriting technique.

As touched upon throughout the chapter, the composing, recording and eventual release of *Defender* was a very precious and arduous process for Gallagher. It was a clear labour of love, perhaps hate at some times, and ultimately symbolised (in Gallagher's mind) one of his most important contributions to the blues tradition. As he told *Sounds*, "If I retired from the stage tomorrow, I think *Defender* would stand up as, at least, a semi-important album in years to come."[140] The years have indeed come and gone since Gallagher's statement, so how has *Defender* shifted from the 'semi-important' to Paul Elliot's 'one to avoid' category? Suppose Gallagher had discarded *Defender* (in addition to *Torch*), waiting until 1990 to release *Fresh Evidence*—would we examine his latter discography in a different light? Such questions can unveil the value of Defender.

As a standalone album, *Defender* exhibits more shade than light, consisting of both high and low points. Gallagher attempts lyrical vulnerability without falling trap to cliché, using literary influences to express himself. His gutsy riff-making, on most occasions, is fresh and never stuffy, though does have the tendency to sound rigid at times ('Doing Time', 'Failsafe Day'). Nevertheless, on the whole, Gallagher succeeds at his modernised blues-making, such as 'Loanshark Blues' (easily his best composition), 'Continental Op', 'Seems to Me', 'No Peace for the Wicked' and 'Seven Days'. While *Defender* is not the Sgt. Pepper of Gallagher's career, I would refrain from the 'one to avoid' distinction all the same, instead

Part 1 - *Blood on the Tracks*

viewing the album as a stepping stone to his next idea. As Gallagher himself proclaimed in the *Sunday Press*: "Your career shouldn't rest on one album or one stretch or three months or six months—you should learn from your mistakes."[141] *Defender* was the product of immense transition in Gallagher's life, navigating his personal and professional identity—perhaps he's not defending the blues as much as himself on the record? Unlike the photograph on his debut album (1971), Gallagher does not shyly bow his head; rather, he stares (and connects) with his audience.

As Bill Graham defiantly wrote: "Gallagher survives."

And he certainly proves it with *Defender*.

RM

Footnotes

1 Derek Oliver, 'Defender of the Faith', *Kerrang* (14 November 1987), http://www.roryon.com/faith322.html
2 See: https://rorygallagher.boards.net/thread/74/torch-lost-interview-states-defender (2 October 2021).
3 'Rory Gallagher - Dublin 1988 + Interview', https://www.youtube.com/watch?v=JZVjd8JaI-A
4 Gerry McAvoy and Pete Chrisp, *Riding Shotgun: 35 Years on the Road with Rory Gallagher and "Nine Below Zero"* (Chicago: SPG Triumph, 2005), 247-251.
5 Uli Twelker, 'Rory Gallagher: Good Times', *Good Times* (March 1993), http://www.roryon.com/uli209.html
6 Bill Graham, 'On this day in 1987: Rory Gallagher released *Defender*', *Hot Press* (1 July 2023), https://www.hotpress.com/music/on-this-day-in-1987-rory-gallagher-released-defender-22977026
7 On the whole, Simpson frames Gallagher in a positive light. However, he does slightly backhand compliment him, commenting how "time off the road has taken its toll on his waistline."
8 Al Simpson, 'Defender of the Faith', *Metal Hammer* (July 1987), http://www.roryon.com/mhammer155.html
9 'Rory Gallagher - Dublin 1988 + Interview'.
10 Grahame Bent, 'Have Guitar Will Travel', *Sounds* (10 December 1988), http://www.roryon.com/have147.html
11 'Rory Gallagher on Borderline – 1988', https://www.youtube.com/watch?v=drQW3EJiz2s&t=51s
12 Judy Black, 'Rory Gallagher: Back to the Basic Blues Roots', *Cleveland Scene* (March 1991), http://www.roryon.com/black403.html
13 Graham, 'On this day in 1987'.
14 Ibid.
15 Interview with Paul Charles, 24 October 2023. All subsequent quotes from Charles come from the same interview.
16 Vivian Campbell, 'The Wearing of the Blues', *Guitar for the Practicing Musician* (August 1991), https://www.roryon.com/guitar91.html
17 Dan Muise, *Gallagher, Marriott, Derringer & Trower* (Milwaukee: Hal Leonard Corporation, 2002), 54.
18 'Kicking Back with Daniel Gallagher', *Shadowplays* (23 September 2013), https://shadowplays.com/blog/?p=2874
19 Kenneth Kelleher, 'Interview from the London-Irish News', *London-Irish News* (December 1990), http://www.roryon.com/kenneth164.html
20 Graham, 'On this day in 1987'.
21 Ibid.
22 David Cavanagh, 'Taste—I'll Remember', *Uncut* (27 August 2015), https://www.uncut.co.uk/reviews/taste-ill-remember-70479/
23 See: https://www.thegearpage.net/board/index.php?threads/opinion-no-way-rory-gallaghers.2106324/page-3 (22 December 2019).
24 Peter Makowski, 'Rory Gallagher: the remarkable story of a blues brother's hot streak', *Louder Sound* (3 May 2022), https://www.loudersound.com/features/rory-gallagher-the-remarkable-story-of-a-blues-brothers-hottest-streak
25 Colin Harper, 'Ballad of a Thin Man', *Mojo* (October 1998), http://www.roryon.com/mojo.html
26 McAvoy and Chrisp, *Riding Shotgun*, 247-251.
27 Muise, *Gallagher, Marriott, Derringer & Trower*, 61.
28 Bent, 'Have Guitar Will Travel'.
29 Oliver, 'Defender of the Faith'.
30 'Radio Clyde Interview' (4 October 1987), http://www.roryon.com/clyde349.html
31 Michael Ross, 'While My Guitar Gently Weeps', *The Sunday Times* (17 May 1988), http://www.roryon.com/rorytimes.html
32 For further commentary on Gallagher's wardrobe and physical appearance in the press, see: Lauren Alex O'Hagan, 'Fashioning the "People's Guitarist": The Mythologization of Rory Gallagher in the International Music Press', vol. 9, no. 2 (2022), *Rock Music Studies*, 174-198.
33 Ross, 'While My Guitar Gently Weeps'.
34 Dermott Hayes, 'Rory Is Still Rocking All Over the World', *Irish Press* (12 August 1992), 19.
35 Ibid.
36 Liam Fay, 'Tangled Up in Blues', *Hot Press* (July 1992), https://www.roryon.com/Tangled.html
37 Muise, *Gallagher, Marriott, Derringer & Trower*, 61.

38 Ibid.
39 N.E. 'Rory Gallagher: Defender of Rock and Blues Traditions', *Tuam Herald* (12 March 1988), 9.
40 G. Zimmerman, 'On the Road Again', *Guitare et Claviers* (February 1989), https://rewritingrory.co.uk/2022/05/30/guitare-et-claviers-february-1989/
41 Ibid.
42 Marcus Connaughton, *Rory Gallagher: His Life and Times* (London: Collins, 2012), 138.
43 Oliver, 'Defender of the Faith'.
44 Ibid.
45 Peter Clark, 'Road Test: Catching Up with Rory', *Metal Hammer* (1987), https://www.roryon.com/Catching.html
46 'Radio Clyde Interview'.
47 Philip Nolan, 'The Man with the Golden Fingers', *Evening Herald* (30 December 1983), http://www.roryon.com/fingers193.html
48 Ibid.
49 Ibid.
50 Cathal Dervan, 'Rory Gallagher A Class Apart', *Meath Chronicle* (7 January 1984), n.p.
51 'An interview with Rory Gallagher 04.06.1984', https://www.youtube.com/watch?v=SGpXZbqjT2s&t=61s
52 'Rory Gallagher - Dublin 1988 + Interview'.
53 Bob Hewitt, 'Rory Gallagher', *Guitarist* (February 1985), http://www.roryon.com/guit231.htm
54 Neville Marten, 'Rory!' *Guitarist* (June 1987), https://www.roryon.com/guitarist.html
55 'Rory Gallagher - Dublin 1988 + Interview'.
56 Bent, 'Have Guitar Will Travel'.
57 Bob Hewitt, 'Rory Gallagher Remembered (1948-1995)', *Guitar* (16 June 2015), https://guitar.com/news/rory-gallagher-remembered-1948-1995/
58 Graham, 'On this day in 1987'.
59 As stated in a 1975 interview prior to his performance at the Ruisrock festival, Gallagher described his method: "We try to progress our music, but we still keep our roots in the music."
60 'Radio Clyde Interview'.
61 Oran, 'Feature Interview: Rory Gallagher was one of the biggest rock acts of the 70s', *Overdrive* (22 October 2020), https://www.overdrive.ie/interview-rory-gallagher-was-one-of-the-biggest-rock-acts-of-the-70s-daniel-gallagher
62 Nolan, 'The Man with the Golden Fingers'.
63 Twelker, 'Rory Gallagher: Good Times'.
64 Hewitt, 'Rory Gallagher'.
65 'On this day in 1976: Rory Gallagher released *Calling Card*', *Hot Press* (24 October 2022), https://www.hotpress.com/music/on-this-day-in-1976-rory-gallagher-released-calling-card-22934769
66 Bert van de Kamp, 'Rory Gallagher: Hooked on Guitar', *OOR* (March 1976), http://www.roryon.com/oor220.htm
67 'A 1987 interview with Rory Gallagher by BBC broadcaster Spencer Leigh', *Shadowplays* (4 January 2012), https://shadowplays.com/blog/?p=2147
68 Mark Kearns, 'Rory's Return', *Harrow Leader* (2 October 1987), 11.
69 'A 1987 interview…'.
70 Bent, 'Have Guitar Will Travel'.
71 Graham, 'On this day in 1987'.
72 Muise, *Gallagher, Marriott, Derringer & Trower*, 50.
73 Ibid., 50-51.
74 Gallagher's love for crime fiction aligns with his other fascination with the life of a cowboy, as evident in his early interest of Roy Rogers and Gene Autry, as well as his cover of Leadbelly's 'Out on the Western Plain'.
75 N.E. 'Rory Gallagher…'
76 Ibid.
77 'Rory Gallagher - Dublin 1988 + Interview'.
78 N.E. 'Rory Gallagher…'
79 Pat Carty, 'Brute Force: Rory Gallagher and *Photo-Finish*', *Hot Press* (15 July 2020), https://www.hotpress.com/opinion/brute-force-rory-gallagher-and-photo-finish-22822497
80 Graham, 'On this day in 1987'.
81 Ibid.
82 Shiv Cariappa, 'Conversation with Rory Gallagher', *Christian Science Monitor* (June 1991), https://www.rorygallagher.com/conversation-with-rory-gallagher/
83 Ibid.
84 Ross, 'While My Guitar Gently Weeps'.
85 Julian Vignoles, *Rory Gallagher: The Man Behind the Guitar* (London: Collins, 2018), 177.
86 Muise, *Gallagher, Marriott, Derringer & Trower*, 51.
87 Pushan Dutt, 'The rise, fall and rise again of businesses serving more than just their shareholders', *The Conversation* (10 October 2019), https://theconversation.com/the-rise-fall-and-rise-again-of-businesses-serving-more-than-just-their-shareholders-124618
88 'Kicking Back with Daniel Gallagher'.
89 Grant Moon, 'Rory Gallagher bassist Gerry McAvoy remembers making the great bluesman's debut album', *Guitar World* (27 October 2021), https://www.guitarworld.com/features/rory-gallagher-gerry-mcavoy
90 Adam Sweeting, 'Gallagher: The Rory Details', *BEAT Instrumental* (March 1979), https://www.roryon.com/beat.html
91 Jon Lewin, 'Rory's Story', *Making Music* (October 1987), https://www.roryon.com/Rorystory.html
92 Oliver, 'Defender of the Faith'.
93 Interview with Mark Feltham, 19 October 2023. All subsequent quotes from Feltham come from the same interview.
94 Oliver, 'Defender of the Faith'.

Part 1 - *Blood on the Tracks*

95 Michael Leonard, 'The Spotlight Kid', *The Guitar* (December 1998), https://www.roryon.com/spotlight.html
96 Kelleher, 'Interview from the London-Irish News'.
97 Ibid.
98 Marten, 'Rory!'.
99 Chris Heim, 'Rory Gallagher Roars Back with a Roots-Blues Album', *Chicago Tribune* (22 March 1991), https://www.chicagotribune.com/news/ct-xpm-1991-03-22-9101260191-story.html.
100 Clark, 'Road Test'.
101 Ibid.
102 Lewin, 'Rory's Story'.
103 Marten, Rory!'.
104 Muise, *Gallagher, Marriott, Derringer & Trower*, 62.
105 Vignoles, *Rory Gallagher*, 108.
106 The main Telecaster used on the album was Gallagher's early 1980s Eccleshall Tele, gifted to him by fan Gordon Morris.
107 Lewin, 'Rory's Story'.
108 David Randall, 'Album review: Rory Gallagher—Blues', *Get Ready to Rock* (23 April 2019), https://getreadytorock.me.uk/blog/2019/04/album-review-rory-gallagher-blues/
109 Muise, *Gallagher, Marriott, Derringer & Trower*, 45.
110 Ibid.
111 Oliver, 'Defender of the Faith'.
112 'Rory Gallagher "Defender" (1987)', *The Outlaw* (30 July 2019), https://theoutlaw76.blogspot.com/2017/01/rory-gallagher-defender-1987.html#more
113 Lewin, 'Rory's Story'.
114 Gwyneth Jones, 'Rory Gallagher – "real meat…no messin"", *Belfast Telegraph* (13 February 1988),11.
115 Ibid.
116 Rory Gallagher interview with Jip Golsteijn, *De Telegraaf* (December 1994), http://www.roryon.com/famous221.html
117 Bent, 'Have Guitar Will Travel'.
118 Raj Babadur, 'Gallagher uses 'natural approach', *Scene Spotlight* (26 Nov-3 Dec 1975), http://www.roryon.com/natural386.html.
119 Niall Stokes, 'Rory Gallagher—Pressing Ever Onwards', *Hot Press* (9 June 1978), http://www.roryon.com/pressing149.html
120 'Rory Gallagher - Dublin 1988 + Interview'.
121 Ibid.
122 Bent, 'Have Guitar Will Travel'.
123 'Radio Clyde interview'.
124 Al Simpson, 'Defender of the Faith'.
125 Jean-Pierre Sabouret, 'Rory Gallagher—Defender of the Faith', *Hard Rock* (December 1987), https://rewritingrory.co.uk/2022/06/05/hard-rock-december-1987-1-article/
126 Tony Kentwright, 'Rock', *Daily Post* (10 September 1987), 18.
127 Bent, 'Have Guitar Will Travel'.
128 'Interview with Rory' (12 April 1989), http://www.roryon.com/casey169.html.
129 Wesley Britton, 'Music Review: Rory Gallagher—*Defender, Fresh Evidence, BBC Sessions* and *Wheels Within Wheels*', *Blogcritics* (13 August 2011), https://blogcritics.org/music-review-rory-gallagher-defender-fresh/
130 Hal Horowitz, 'Defender (Remastered)', *All Music Guide*, https://www.highresaudio.com/en/album/view/qvhb53/rory-gallagher-defender-remastered
131 Dan Collins, 'Rock of Ages', *Cork Examiner* (11 July 1990), n.p.
132 Paul Elliott, 'The Rory Gallagher albums you should definitely own', *Classic Rock* (14 June 2022) https://www.loudersound.com/features/rory-gallagher-best-albums
133 Ryan Sagadore, 'REMEMBERING RORY GALLAGHER 25 YEARS LATER A RETROSPECTIVE RANKING', *Spill Magazine* (2020), https://spillmagazine.com/spill-retrospective-remembering-rory-gallagher-25-years-later-a-retrospective-ranking
134 See: https://rateyourmusic.com/release/album/rory-gallagher/defender/
135 Bruce Forrest, 'Rory Gallagher I 2011 Reissues – CD Review', *Vintage Rock* (2011), https://vintagerock.com/rory-gallagher-summer-2011-reissues/
136 Henry Yates, 'How Rory Gallagher inspired author Ian Rankin', *Classic Rock* (November 2013), https://www.ludersound.com/features/how-rory-gallagher-inspired-author-ian-rankin
137 Bernard O'Rouke, 'Dónal Gallagher Interview', *Goldenplec* (6 December 2013), https://www.goldenplec.com/featured/donal-gallagher-interview/.
138 Dave Fanning, 'Rory Gallagher: The Blues Alone', *Irish Times* (13 February 1988), n.p.
139 'Barry O Neill interviewing Rory Gallagher's nephews Ballyshannon 2022', https://www.youtube.com/watch?v=L-KZiQP47Z0
140 Bent, 'Have Guitar Will Travel'.
141 Peter Marriott, 'Commercialism Frightens Rory', *Sunday Press* (24 May 1987), 2.

1.3 No End in Sight: Fresh Evidence (1990)

> *"The compass has come round again all right.
> It's not that nice when you're out there in the cold."*[1]

Rory Gallagher uttered the above words to music journalist David Sinclair in 1990 when asked what he thought about the sudden resurgence of interest in the blues. While the blues—and indeed Gallagher—had always maintained a core audience, for much of the 1980s, popular opinion was unfavourable towards the genre, considering it outmoded and irrelevant. Stevie Ray Vaughan's commercial breakthrough in 1983 marked a ripple of hope for the blues that slowly turned into a full wave later in the decade with the growing success of Robert Cray, Bonnie Raitt and Jeff Healey. The wave grew stronger under the renewed enthusiasm for old masters like Muddy Waters, following the use of 'Mannish Boy' in a 1988 commercial for Levi's 501 jeans, and John Lee Hooker, as a result of his Grammy award-winning 1989 album *The Healer*. By the end of the 1980s, increasing numbers of blues societies, festivals and nightclubs had emerged in major cities across the world. This blues 'revival' continued into 1990 as long out-of-print material was reissued in compact disc format, including the complete collection of 1930's bluesman Robert Johnson, and new albums were released, such as Gary Moore's *Still Got the Blues*.

Throughout the ebbs and flows of public appreciation for the blues, Gallagher had represented that "one fixed point,"[2] always remaining true to the musical style, even if this frequently made him the target of criticism from the music press. With two long periods off the road in the late 1980s due to ill health, Gallagher found himself with rare free time to reflect on the future of his career. Looking for new ideas, he delved back into his large record collection and reacquainted himself with the music of the early blues pioneers, which had long been a source of inspiration for him. Re-energised, he decided to make an album where he "defined the blues roots"[3] more than he had ever done so before. The result was *Fresh Evidence*.

Released in May 1990, *Fresh Evidence* was a powerful statement to the blues, encapsulating all of Gallagher's musical loves from Son House and John Lee Hooker to Slim Harpo and Scrapper Blackwell. The album was recorded using vintage equipment, which encouraged a raw, earthy and even haunting sound. However, with *Fresh Evidence*, Gallagher also made it clear that he was not simply "pandering to the past," but rather renewing the blues and updating it by "hitting it on the head and coming up with new chord changes and tunes."[4] *Fresh Evidence* also saw Gallagher wearing his heart on his sleeve, many of the songs being autobiographical in nature. As he told Emmanuel Potts of *Hard Force*, the album was "truly personal" and contained "all the sounds and emotions that I am currently experiencing in my life."[5]

When *Fresh Evidence* is talked about today—either in the music press or fan community—it is this autobiographical element of the album that is latched onto. The heavy themes of illness and death are seen as harbingers of what was to come, reflective of Gallagher's fragile mental and physical health at the time. But to look back at initial reviews of *Fresh Evidence* tells a different story, which is all too easy to forget when looking in hindsight. After being on the receiving end of much unfair treatment during the 1980s, Gallagher was highly praised by critics for his new album who saw it as representing a period of renewal for him. So, how has this positive narrative turned sour over time?

We address this question in this essay by reassessing the importance of *Fresh Evidence* and moving beyond typical discussions of the album's portending themes. Instead, we consider the album as a fine example of Gallagher's development in the studio and his continued evolution as a songwriter. We also explore the making of the album, the general context around its release and how it stands up today, particularly in relation to another major blues album of 1990: Gary Moore's *Still Got the Blues*. Overall, we show how, with *Fresh Evidence*, Gallagher was looking to the future, not the past, and was enthused with refreshing, mature ideas for his music. The album was supposed to mark the beginning of a new chapter in his life, not the end.

Keeping Technology at Arm's Length:
The Making of *Fresh Evidence*

Throughout his career, Gallagher's relationship with the studio was fairly ambivalent. In interviews, he often described being in the studio as a "grind," admitting that he was "not the greatest person in an enclosed space" and much preferred giving live performances.[6] A constant challenge for Gallagher was trying to capture on tape what he had envisaged in his head. He preferred records to be "rough and echoey" and disliked overproduced, clean mixes, which "[took] the rough edges off some very good pieces of music."[7] Even when recording at home on cassette, Gallagher was "never happy that the best [went] on tape."[8] He was also disheartened by the irresolvable issue that a song always improved after several weeks of playing and, therefore, it was never in its best form when recorded for an album. Gallagher also felt weighed down by the music press who constantly argued that his albums took "second place"[9] to his live shows and failed to reflect their raw energy.

However, as much as Gallagher expressed his dislike for the studio, it was never far from his mind. From as early as 1975, he outlined his goal to "make a definitive studio album."[10] This was something that he repeated over the next two decades, even stating in his last filmed interview for Ulster Television's *Rock 'n the North* (1994) that he wanted "two great albums in the charts" for the "people that have supported [him] over the years."[11] On his first albums, Gallagher had strived for an "honest approach"[12] by recording live in the studio with all band members in the same room. However, by 1976, he recognised the pitfalls of "leaving it to chance"[13] and agreed that it was better to treat albums as a studio project rather than try and obtain on-stage excitement. By *Top Priority* (1979), Gallagher felt that he had become "more intelligent"[14] in the studio and was no longer averse to overdubbing if necessary. However, with this increased intelligence came "terrible doubts"[15] and Gallagher began to deliberate endlessly over the value of his music.

While these doubts had crept in with the scrapped San Francisco album, they worsened throughout the 1980s and Gallagher spent more and more time in the studio in his quest to make the 'perfect' record (see 1.2). Speaking to *The Fuze* in 2003, Dónal Gallagher likened the process of Gallagher delivering an album to the record company to "post-natal depression,"[16] noting how he would constantly return to the studio to remix or resequence tracks. Gallagher's punishing work rate also concerned bandmates Brendan O'Neill and Gerry McAvoy who believe that his dedication to music "took over his life" and "became an obsession" that "drained every last bit of energy" from him.[17]

In Dónal's view, Gallagher never learned how to delegate and, even on the rare occasions when he did delegate the role of producer (e.g. Elliot Mazer, Roger Glover), he was never fully content with not being in the driving seat. Any time that he worked with producers, there was a "clash" because they attempted to "sweeten the music up too much" for his liking.[18]

Engineers could also pose a problem; speaking to Christopher Dieckmann of *Die Zeit* in 1994, Gallagher recalled with horror the time when he asked an engineer to record the bass drum "with the reverb of Howlin' Wolf" and was met with the response: "Who's Howlin' Wolf?"[19] So, when it came to *Fresh Evidence*, Gallagher was adamant that he would leave nothing to chance, taking on the duties of singer, songwriter, guitarist, producer and creative director all himself, which put a considerable strain on his already delicate health.

Work on *Fresh Evidence* began in May 1989, with Gallagher intending to do "something very raw"[20] within three months. However, it took almost one year later for the album to be completed, despite its deliberately simple and primitive sound. Writing in his autobiography *Riding Shotgun*, Gerry McAvoy describes *Fresh Evidence* as a particularly "strenuous" album to make,[21] with Gallagher experiencing various health challenges along the way. Over the course of the sessions, he suffered a serious bout of flu and severe exhaustion, even falling asleep in the studio at times, while upon the album's release, he stated that he felt "broken" as if he had "given birth to [his] own child."[22] Reflective of the toll that the album took on him, Gallagher subsequently ended up in a clinic (on Dónal's request "to save himself from himself"[23]) and later caught a viral infection, which put him out of touring action over the summer of 1990 (see 2.4). Speaking to David Sinclair of *Q* about the recording of *Fresh Evidence*, Gallagher recognised that the studio was "dangerous"[24] for his health because he stopped eating and sleeping and got no fresh air or exercise. He also explained the problem of leaving the studio satisfied only to go home, listen to his favourite artist and become "very depressed" about the quality of his own music.

Initially, *Fresh Evidence* began by Gallagher casually running through some tracks in the rehearsal rooms for several weeks before booking any studio time. He had hoped that this would enable him to then "get straight into recording [...] without anticipating the long tour ahead."[25] However, reflecting a pattern throughout his career, he was unable to find a studio with which he was satisfied once he was ready to record, which set the album off to a rocky start. Early recording sessions took place in Maison Rouge in South London, but were cut short when Gallagher found the studios "too clinical."[26] Sessions then moved briefly to Music Station in Chelsea, before Gallagher finally settled on Redan Recorders in Bayswater. Once at Redan, Gallagher soon established an intense work schedule, with the band meeting in the pub every evening at 7PM for drinks and then working solidly in the studio from 9PM until 5AM or 6AM, according to McAvoy.

Gallagher immediately felt far more at home in Redan because of its old-school feel and vintage equipment, and it was here where *Fresh Evidence* really took shape. Gallagher had always preferred the ambience of old studios, which he believed carried a certain energy. Dónal Gallagher jokes that his brother "practically specialised in playing in studios that were on the point of falling down," with at least six or seven closing shortly after he recorded there, including Redan.[27] Although *Fresh Evidence* was recorded with 24-track, Redan's vintage equipment and the sounds it produced enabled Gallagher to achieve his aim of creating a record that was mellow, rootsy, ethnic, natural and "a little bit demo-ish."[28]

For this purpose, he relied predominantly on Neve desks, tape echoes, spring reverbs, valve compressors and, in his own words, "microphones not favoured by disco people," using "just enough modern tricks to help out" (i.e., noise gates to improve sharpness).[29] Speaking to Steve Morse of *Boston Globe* in 1991, Gallagher explained that new sound decks made things too "synthetic and tinny."[30] As he preferred a "nice rumble on bass, openness on guitar and drums that breathe,"[31] using vintage equipment left things "fairly woolly and casual"[32] and ensured that the music remained "rough around the edges."[33] For Gallagher, the "deficiencies"[34] of older recording equipment and echo machines were integral to achieving the sound that he wanted, while most effects "should come from the hands."[35] In short, *Fresh Evidence* would keep technology "at arm's length."[36]

While Gallagher had also made heavy use of vintage equipment for *Jinx* with the same intention of going back to his roots and creating an authentic blues record (see 1.1), what he had visualised for the 1982 release properly came into its own with *Fresh Evidence*. Aided by his experience and maturity as an artist, Gallagher seemed much more at ease with the recording process and "finding the essence" of the tracks.[37]

Taking the reins as producer also allowed him to bring in his widest range of instruments and guest musicians to date, which added considerably to the album's tone. Gallagher played electric and acoustic guitar, as well as the dulcimer, electric sitar and mandola, while, in addition to regular band members Gerry McAvoy and Brendan O'Neill, he was joined by Mark Feltham (harmonica), Lou Martin (keyboards), Geraint Watkins (accordion) and John Earle, Ray Beavis and Dick Hanson (brass).

For Gallagher, "instinct" also played a major role in *Fresh Evidence*, a feeling that was "stronger than [him] and part of [his] personality."[38] Guided by this instinct, he recorded as many songs as possible in the first take in order to prioritise the performance rather than the production. However, unlike earlier albums, he was also more willing to do repair work if necessary. According to Gallagher, the "feel" was already there on the first takes for *Fresh Evidence*, but it was during the mixing and overdubbing when he became a "perfectionist."[39] Indeed, it would take four cuts of the master before Gallagher was satisfied. He admitted to Anil Prasad that, in an ideal world, he would love to play the album once and "have it all perfect," but he felt "at the mercy" of too many things out of his control.[40] Despite his concerns, Gallagher's painstaking perfectionism ultimately paid off and the end result was a natural and intimate album, which, according to Uli Twelker of *Good Times*, sounds "as if Rory is sitting next to you."[41]

"Salvation, inspiration and just a hint of sadness": Rethinking the Songs of *Fresh Evidence*

In addition to the use of vintage equipment and Gallagher's enhanced knowledge of production, the quality of his songwriting was another factor that contributed to the power of *Fresh Evidence*. While Gallagher's songwriting had blossomed with *Jinx* and flourished with *Defender*, it hit new heights with *Fresh Evidence* in terms of lyrics, arrangement and instrumentation. Posthumous reviews of the album consistently point to its themes of illness and death, describing Gallagher's "art and life" as becoming "entangled."[42] However, in doing so, they miss many of its finer points. Looking closer at Gallagher's lyrics, most, in fact, speak of redemption, purification, inner strength and resilience—characteristics that he always possessed and that kept him going whenever times got tough. *Fresh Evidence* reads not as the tale of a man who is tired of life and ready to surrender, but rather, of a man who is struggling, yet ready to face his challenges head on and keep persevering. Beyond its personal motifs, it is also a benediction to the blues, a love letter to the music and masters that set Gallagher on the path of his vocation as a young boy. But it is also about resurgence, stretching the boundaries of the blues further than they have gone before. Ultimately, it marked the "starting point of the new Rory that would have emerged."[43]

On the topic of illness and death, most critics and biographers have referenced songs like 'Heaven's Gate', 'Walkin' Wounded' and 'Ghost Blues', but such songs need reappraising both lyrically and musically to fully appreciate their depth and complexity. For Gerry McAvoy, the lyrics of 'Heaven's Gate' are "quite frightening" and indicate "where Rory's head was at the time"[44] ("the darkness 'round your neck is like a metal claw"). While Gallagher himself saw the song as the story of "a man being haunted in a room in a terrible condition" or "somebody going through a very bad patch and facing up to mortality,"[45] he was also keen to state that it was a "semi-redemption" song, inspired by Robert Johnson's 'Hellhound on My Trail', and "slightly preaching" in its lyrics about being unable to "bribe St Peter" to enter heaven. For Gallagher, faith was an important part of his life on many levels, whether faith in God, in himself or in music itself. This is something that journalist Michael Ross picks up on in a 1992 interview, arguing how it is "faith" that keeps Gallagher going "through the bad spells" and that "keeps him focused on getting something new from the blues."[46] 'Heaven's Gate' is a song that both encapsulates this faith and injects the blues with something new, Gallagher's emotive solo marking a particular strong point.

Equally, most posthumous reviews see 'Walkin' Wounded' as a song about a man who has given up on life. However, Gallagher himself did not view it in this way. Again, in candid conversation with Shiv Cariappa, he acknowledged that he wrote the song at a time when his health was poor, but wanted to convey that the character still had "fighting spirit," despite being "at a very low ebb."[47] Like 'Heaven's Gate', the song carries a heavy redemption element, the protagonist's hesitancy at the beginning about moving back to the "southern coast" if they "had some sense" turning to conviction by the end of the five minutes. The song is a turbulent journey leading up to that decision, with the figure torn between despair and hopelessness ("I'm truly wounded like a fox in a snare"; I feel suspended, got no lust for life") and tenacity and courage ("don't cross me no more, had enough of you"; "I'm breakin' out, got no time to lose"). The supporting brass section and brash slide solo expertly drive these emotions forward as he presses on, unwilling to give up.

Much has also been written about 'Ghost Blues', seen as a haunting epitaph of Gallagher's life, which was further emphasised by its choice as a title for Ian Thuillier's 2010 documentary on Gallagher. Although Gallagher explained in a 1992 interview with *Guitar Magazine* that the song was inspired by the loneliness that he felt at the time of its composition (it was New Year and he was away from family in Ireland), for him, its main themes were, in fact, "salvation, inspiration and just a hint of sadness."[48] "Good blues always comes from situations of strong emotion [...] a little pain," he added in the same interview, explaining that he was able to channel his melancholy into something positive.

For Gallagher, 'Ghost Blues' was an important track and his favourite on *Fresh Evidence*, inspired by the blues of Reverend Robert Wilkins and Robert 'Pete' Williams, which he had been absorbing frequently at the time. In Gallagher's artistic vision, 'Ghost Blues' was a "Gospel" song that spoke of "redemption" and felt like "church on a Sunday morning" or "Maxwell Street on a Saturday afternoon." Despite this optimism that lay at the root of 'Ghost Blues', it is the song's 'sadness' factor that posthumous reviews have overwhelmingly tended to hone in on, feeding into the 'Gallagher had concluded his life' narrative first posited by Colin Harper in a 1995 obituary and revived by Julian Vignoles in his 2018 biography.

This overemphasis on the link between 'Ghost Blues' and Gallagher's poor mental state has unfairly drawn attention away from the magic of the song itself and how it came together in the studio. On the day of recording, Gallagher had the flu and was feeling "very weak," but this created a "huge haze" that made him "more open to strong emotion."[49] 'Ghost Blues', thus, became an act of "purification" for him—a thought that he would reiterate in an interview with Jas Obrecht, telling the journalist that "music can heal [...] cool down the savage breast [...] [be] good for your mental health."[50] The unique sound of 'Ghost Blues' was also influenced by a curious engineering error: Gallagher and his band were playing in the same room and the engineer did not mic up the drums properly, which led them to feed back into the acoustic guitar microphone. Gallagher liked the immediate and "eerie" sound that it produced because it reflected the style of old blues records or Bob Dylan's *Highway 61 Revisited*, so he decided to keep playing, not wanting to lose the mood of the session.

'Ghost Blues' also stands as a clear demonstration of Gallagher's refined studio knowledge, its multitracked dulcimer, synths, bass and harmonica at the beginning of the song creating an "overture." Added to this magical tone is the strong rhythm running throughout the song, "akin to a Big Joe Williams track, that sorta chugs it along like a train," as Gallagher told *Guitar Magazine*.[51] To obtain this "deep sound," Gallagher "doubled up the six string," using a Sigma, then a 12-string Danelectro and, finally, his Stratocaster, showing his technical advancement from early rawer albums like *Rory Gallagher* and *Deuce*.

The constant aggrandizement of the illness and death themes of *Fresh Evidence* has also led to an underappreciation of the two sonically adventurous instrumentals on the album—'Alexis' and 'The Loop'—which signal Gallagher's ability to keep progressing the blues while staying true to its roots. 'Alexis' was written as a tribute to Alexis Korner, the Father of British Blues, who had died in 1984. Gallagher was an admirer of Korner and had previously played a tribute concert in his honour at the Pistoia Blues Festival. Speaking to Emmanuel Potts of *Hard Force,* Gallagher explained that he did not want to seem "pretentious," but that he liked to do a "little homage" whenever one of his heroes passed away.[52]

According to Gallagher's friend Shu Tomioka, 'Alexis' represented "a new challenge," being Gallagher's first foray into electric instrumentals and drawing heavily on the jazz tradition, which he had not employed on record since 1973's 'They Don't Make Them Like You Anymore'.[53] For Dónal Gallagher, the song indicated a different side to his brother's playing, with echoes of both Stevie

Ray Vaughan and Freddie King. Equally, 'The Loop'—dedicated to Chicago's overhead railway system, but perhaps a tribute to Chicago Blues more generally—was another number that pushed the boundaries of the blues and became a staple of Gallagher's later live set. The upbeat song displays the strong interplay between Gallagher and harmonicist Mark Feltham, while its horn section adds a touch of swinging urban jazz. Both 'Alexis' and 'The Loop' indicate the way in which Gallagher's musical interests were developing and serve as powerful precursors of his later jazz fusion instrumentals with Roberto Manes and Peter Lockett in 1994 (see 1.5).

Continuing his series of homages to his musical heroes, Gallagher also penned 'The King of Zydeco' for *Fresh Evidence* in honour of American Creole musician Clifton Chenier who he greatly admired and who had died in 1987. Gallagher had once been on the same bill as Chenier at the Montreux Jazz Festival, but was admittedly "too shy" to say hello to him.[54] For Gallagher, Chenier's music had a "casual air" that dreamily evoked "a simpler time,"[55] which is what he hoped to capture with his tribute: "an escape from the stress and pressure of modern life in the big city to go to this mythical juke joint in the south." In true zydeco style, Gallagher employed maracas and accordion on the song, the latter played expertly by Geraint Watkins, and had even tried to incorporate a washboard.

Like 'Ghost Blues', Gallagher saw the song as evoking a "quasi-depressing" ambience, yet being a key example of the "melancholy leading to something positive."[56] In a break with tradition, he had even envisaged an accompanying music video for the song of a "depressed man driving into the night, unsure if life is worth living, but he keeps going," although this never came into fruition. Autobiographical? Perhaps. Yet, once again, it demonstrates Gallagher's undying resilience and willingness to persevere in the face of challenges, not a sign that "the shadows were now closing in on [his] life."[57]

Side 1 of *Fresh Evidence* closes with another tribute to an old bluesmaster: a stunning cover of Son House's 'Empire State Express'. Deemed by many as the centrepoint of the entire album, Gallagher recorded the song on his 1932 National Triolian in just one take late in the evening of St Patrick's Day. The song's rawness and immediacy stems from the fact that Gallagher had misplaced his copy of the Son House record, forcing him to make up his own arrangement and rely on lyrics that he had luckily jotted down in a notepad several months before. The decision to record the track in a drum booth with drum mics to make it "as responsive as possible"[58] also led the song to have a "starker, more desolate tone than the original,"[59] once again showcasing Gallagher's ability to draw inspiration from his heroes yet interpret the blues in his own unique way. Although Gallagher admitted that he found the song difficult to record because the rhythm of the vocal line broke up with the guitar, he mused that he "didn't do too badly on it."[60] Critics (both contemporary and posthumous) were certainly in agreement, with Hal Horowitz of *Blues Review* declaring the track as "all one needs to grasp the essence of Gallagher's talent."[61]

In the remaining songs on the album, it is Gallagher's magnificent capacity for storytelling that is most apparent. 'Middle Name' tells the evocative tale of a man in the Bible Belt who is stuck in a hopeless situation and desperately searching for someone before a big storm comes. Gallagher conceived the setting as one inspired by Tennessee Williams, with the "big storm" itself being open to interpretation and perhaps more to do with "Armageddon or the Holocaust" than a physical weather event.[62] Continuing *Fresh Evidence*'s musical memorial tradition, the swampy feel of 'Middle Name' pays an indirect tribute to Slim Harpo, one of the leading exponents of swamp blues. Here, Mark Feltham's harmonica alternates hypnotically with Gallagher's rhythm guitar, the occasional pinch harmonics adding a touch of drama that accentuates the overwrought atmosphere conjured up by the lyrics.

If 'Middle Name' evokes a swampy Mississippi atmosphere, then 'Slummin' Angel' instead transports the listener to a gritty urban context. The narrative recounts the misfortune of a young girl who has fallen in with the wrong crowd and finds herself in a bad situation. Tapping into the album's overall messages of salvation, redemption and perseverance, Gallagher adopts the role of Good Samaritan, recognising the good in the girl, sending her a warning ("take off these rose-coloured glasses, this place is no wonderland") and, ultimately, offering her some friendly advice ("go home to your daddy where you ought to go"). Accompanying the powerful lyrics is a hammering rhythm section, intersected by a roaring guitar solo that is tinged with Celtic overtones that offers a throwback to 'Overnight Bag'. With its "eyebrow-singeing blast of attitude"[63] (as journalist Nick Deriso nicely put it), 'Slummin' Angel' is the ideal album closer.

In a similar vein, the rousing 'Kid Gloves' is the ideal album opener, its combination of rock & roll guitar, rolling piano and brass setting the benchmark for the 45 minutes ahead, both musically and lyrically. Inspired by the John Garfield film *Body and Soul* and Gallagher's love for hardboiled detective novels, the song chronicles the life of a boxer who refuses to take a dive and now has the mob on his case. Below the surface level, however, 'Kid Gloves' works as a metaphor for the music business and serves as a statement of defiance for Gallagher against the status quo. In an interview with John Sakamoto of the *Toronto Sun*, Gallagher admitted that the song's themes of "taking on life's struggles with a pugilistic tenacity" and not "putting a good man down"[64] could be interpreted as autobiographical—much in the same way as 'Last of the Independents'. However, he jokingly added that it was deliberately "tongue-in-cheek" and if he was as "bitter" as the character, he would "be in trouble."

The two bonus tracks to appear on the 2018 rerelease of *Fresh Evidence* also exhibit Gallagher's unique storytelling ability. Like 'Kid Gloves', 'Bowed Not Broken' takes inspiration from the world of noir, recounting the story of a gambling addict who cannot pay back the money that he has borrowed from a loanshark. As with many of the characters that Gallagher depicts in songs, the man is determined not to give up without a fight, despite his difficulties. The other song, 'Never Asked You for Nothing', returns to the Cajun blues sound, thanks to Geraint Watkins' exhilarating accordion-playing and Brendan O'Neill's brush drums, as well as the exchange between Mark Feltham and Gallagher. Again, tapping into the world of crime, Gallagher's lyrics speak of a man who has ended up in prison unfairly and is feeling hard done by.

"The guy on the sidelines":
In the Face of *Still Got the Blues*

When *Fresh Evidence* finally hit shelves on 14 May 1990, it was met with immediate warmth by the press. For Phil Alexander of *RAW*, *Fresh Evidence* showcased Gallagher's "genuine love of the [blues] rather than any misguided attempt to jump on the tailboard of the blues boom bandwagon."[65] Carol Clerk of *Melody Maker* equally praised the way that Gallagher "explored old fields of influence with the authority of someone who has all of the experience to be confident in his craft," but also recognised that the album "bristled with a contemporary sense of adventure and wit."[66] The most important achievement of *Fresh Evidence* for Clerk, however, was that it re-established Gallagher as "something more than an electric guitar virtuoso," serving as proof that he was a "master" with a "supreme feel for the instrument and the song, whatever its mood."

As a result of new worldwide licensing deals, initial sales of *Fresh Evidence* were strong and the album would, in fact, go on to become one of the bestselling of Gallagher's career. The album was released on his own independent label Capo in the UK, while it came out in the US under I.R.S. Records. The material from *Fresh Evidence* was also extremely well received by fans when Gallagher toured Europe later in the year (after a four-month delay due to illness) and Japan, Australia and the US in 1991. Gallagher expressed satisfaction that the album seemed to be attracting a "new audience" and that he was no longer being "judged on his past material."[67]

Despite these major accolades, *Fresh Evidence* did not quite reach the heights of critical acclaim that it deserved. Rather unfairly, it became overshadowed by another album that had been released two months earlier and was swiftly being held up as a gamechanger for the blues: *Still Got the Blues* by Gary Moore. *Still Got the Blues* marked a dramatic change of direction for Moore who had worked predominantly in the field of hard rock to date. Fed up with the shred guitar sound that was now dominating rock music and encouraged by new blues talent like Jeff Healey, Moore wanted to create an album that took a step back and paid homage to the great British blues guitarists who had first inspired him. Initially, Moore conceived the album as a side project; in fact, his management had such little faith in its success that they decided that it would be a non-contractual album. However, once Moore played his early demos to Virgin, they recognised its commercial potential and began to invest large sums of money in its development. The bigger budget enabled Moore to bring in Albert King, Albert Collins and George Harrison as guest stars, as well as a larger band and horn section.

Upon its release, *Still Got the Blues* received major press attention, with journalists eager to interview Moore about his return to the genre that had first shaped his music taste. The critical response to the album was astounding, with high praise from the press and *Q* listing it in its top 50 best albums of 1990 (*Fresh Evidence* was not in this list). *Still Got the Blues* went on to sell over three million copies, obtaining platinum, gold and silver across the globe and breaking the top 100 on the US Billboard chart.

In promotional interviews for *Fresh Evidence*, Gallagher was frequently asked about Moore's album. While the press was, no doubt, genuinely interested in his views as someone who had played the blues for almost three decades, there also appeared to be an underlying antagonism in their question, almost a hope to pit the two old friends against one another.[68] Characteristic of his gentle nature, Gallagher never rose to the bait and was always diplomatic. In an appearance on the Channel 4 programme *Rocksteady*, he praised Moore's album, telling presenter Dave Fanning that "there's room for us both" in the world of blues.[69] He was also keen to point out the differences between the two albums, *Fresh Evidence* being a "southern album" motivated by country blues and country electric blues and *Still Got the Blues* being more influenced by "modern" blues.

Although Gallagher and Moore had a deep mutual respect for one another, it is hard to believe that Gallagher's sensitive nature was not wounded by the constant references to *Still Got the Blues* in interviews, as well as its runaway chart success and critical reception. In an interview to promote his album, Moore outlined that it had enabled him to relearn and strip down his sound, go "right back to the essence" and rediscover "all the things you'd forgotten over the years, all the reasons you started playing in the first place."[70] But Gallagher had always done this and, what is more, had been criticised throughout the 1980s for remaining true to exactly that. "I've always been a blues artist. I'm not a heavy metal guitarist or pop artist who suddenly starts playing the blues," Gallagher stated frustratedly in a 1992 interview with Henry Knegt, perhaps alluding to Moore, as the editor suggests.[71] Gallagher's hurt was still apparent one year later when speaking to *Guitar World*. Although his comments were not overtly directed at Moore, they are telling of just how much the music industry had damaged his confidence and self-belief:

> When no one has paid you the least attention for many years and then to see some people in this business come back because [blues] becomes the new trend, I just can't put up with that. It's a fairly perverse attitude. You end up caring about nothing and you can only look at this circus with a distant and discouraged glance [...] I've given so much of myself to this business that I really have difficulty getting enthused about anything nowadays. Often, I think that I'd be better off dropping everything and going fishing or back to my paintings. I don't have a desire anymore to inspire sympathy in others or any other sentiment for that matter.[72]

While Gallagher's words can be seen as partially reflective of his depression, they are understandable, especially if we consider how the two albums have stood up over the past three decades since their release.

Of all Gallagher's albums, *Fresh Evidence* is the one that has received the least contemporary reviews, often cast aside as the "final" album and, therefore, not as important as those that came before.[73] Furthermore, on the scant occasions that the album is reviewed, most articles focus on its illness and death narratives, rather than the high quality of the music and lyrics themselves. Even the 2024 *Rory Gallagher: Calling Card* documentary disappointingly chose this angle when speaking about the album. One of the most recent reviews of *Fresh Evidence* by *Live About* describes the album as "for collectors only" and claims that it "doesn't meet the lofty standard established by Gallagher during his incredible string of solid 1970s era albums."[74] As if to add insult to injury, it also incorrectly labels the album's release date as 1988. *Fresh Evidence* is also frequently absent from lists of the 'Top 10 Rory Gallagher Albums You Should Own'; recent countdowns by *Louder Sound* and *Blues Rock Review* both bemusingly overlooked it.

This is something that Barry Barnes—lead singer and guitarist of the legendary Gallagher tribute band Sinnerboy—laments. While many Gallagher fans and reviewers continue to cite *Irish Tour '74* or *Tattoo* as his best albums, Barnes sees every new Gallagher album as "better than the last one," with *Fresh Evidence* being the greatest of all. "He'd got [his guitar sound] down to a fine art... very bluesy, very dark... it was just beautiful and it would have carried on being better [but], unfortunately, he died."[75]

This is in sharp contrast to *Still Got the Blues*, which still continues to top lists of the best Gary Moore albums and is widely praised for singlehandedly "reigniting the blues scene"[76] and being *the* moment that "redefined who Gary was."[77] While *Fresh Evidence* is viewed as not in the same league as Gallagher's 1970s albums, there is general agreement across the contemporary music press that "Moore plays better than ever" on *Still Got the Blues*, "spitting out an endless stream of fiery licks that are both technically impressive and soulful."[78]

In a recent 200-page Blues Special by *Classic Rock* magazine, ten pages were dedicated to Moore's album and its transformative effect on public perceptions of the blues. The very same issue gave no attention whatsoever to *Fresh Evidence*. In fact, it gave no attention to Gallagher at all, bafflingly erasing him from their history of the blues. This erasure was helped on its way—perhaps unintentionally—some years earlier by Moore himself who claimed in a 2007 interview with *Classic Rock* that "nobody was doing [the blues] at the time" and that, rather than jumping on the bandwagon, he was "the fucking bandwagon."[79]

So, what is it that makes *Fresh Evidence* unjustly pale in comparison to *Still Got the Blues*, both then and now? Biographer Julian Vignoles blames Gallagher himself, suggesting that he was "perhaps past caring enough" and simply did not have the "will or energy left to capitalise in this apparent resurgence of blues."[80]

Vignoles' statement is unfair, not only in its reduction of Gallagher's physical and mental health struggles at the time to him simply "past caring," but also in its belief that Gallagher would somehow want to "capitalise" upon anything. It is well documented that Gallagher was not interested in commercial success or passing trends and saw music as a "compulsive hobby" and "lifetime affair," not some get-rich-quick scheme.[81]

Furthermore, Gallagher was not remotely bothered about whether the blues was popular or unpopular. As he told Richard Skelly of *Central New Jersey Home News* in 1991, he was "delighted" that people like John Lee Hooker and Albert Collins were doing well, but he "didn't need that to keep [his] interest in blues."[82] Equally, in an interview with Susan Whitall of *Detroit News*, he expressed concern that the blues was now becoming a "yuppie hit" and that he wished that people dug deeper than the "obvious influences" of Albert King and BB King and listened also to old acoustic blues or electric Chicago blues.[83] Gallagher quite simply played for the love of playing; while he may have been glad that the climate was more favourable to him again, he was not thinking about this favourability in terms of album sales or stadium tours.

Indeed, following the resounding success of *Still Got the Blues*, it was the album sales and stadium tours that ended up becoming a heavy cross to bear for Gary Moore. As Moore's biographer Harry Shapiro notes, with *Still Got the Blues*, success had "crept up behind Gary and tapped him on the shoulder when he wasn't looking."[84] The album swiftly became the greatest success of his career in terms of sales. However, this came with a price and, just one year later, Moore was under pressure from his record company to follow up *Still Got the Blues* with another equally successful album. Through great emotional strain, Moore managed to produce *After Hours* in 1992. Although not as critically acclaimed as its predecessor, the album hit the charts at number 4, making it Moore's highest-charting album in the UK.

Throughout his career, Gallagher had always shied away from releasing singles, one of the reasons being his fear of having to follow up one hit with another, which would create pressure and make him lose sight of the bigger picture. Had *Fresh Evidence* sold in the numbers that *Still Got the Blues* did, one could argue that Gallagher would have felt similar stresses. The making of *Fresh Evidence* had already been damaging to his health; having to follow it up immediately with another album would have had further detrimental effects on his wellbeing. Much like Gallagher himself, *Fresh Evidence* was successful in its own modest way, journalist Colin Harper making the very good point that chart statistics "fail to reflect the sheer scale of [Gallagher's] consistent popularity."[85]

Demand for *Still Got the Blues* grew so much that Moore soon found himself undertaking the biggest tour of his life, which dragged him back into the rock circus from which he had sought to get away. For six months, he travelled across Europe, playing stadiums and festivals. The requirement to perform in large venues with flashy stage shows, pyrotechnics and a full entourage would have been anathema to Gallagher, particularly as it was these very things that had contributed to him staying away from the US throughout much of the 1980s. At this time in his career, Gallagher was travelling in quite the opposite direction, wanting to move more towards folk music and increasingly intimate settings with a smaller band. Had the success of *Fresh Evidence* come at this price, then it would not have had a happy outcome for Gallagher. Again, starting a quiet revolution with *Fresh Evidence* was far more suited to Gallagher's lowkey, self-effacing nature.

There have been suggestions that the guest stars on Moore's album were a major factor in the success of *Still Got the Blues*. Certainly, the chance to hear the guitarist trade licks with Albert Collins, Albert King and George Harrison was a draw for some. There have also been questions raised about why Gallagher never thought to do the same. To answer this, we must again go back to the fundamentals of who Rory Gallagher was: a humble, unassuming man who did what he did because he believed in it, not because he sought glory, fortune or fame. Although Gallagher enjoyed guesting on albums (see 1.4 and 1.5), he did not actively seek to promote himself through these collaborations and, if anything, played down his own contributions.

Dónal Gallagher himself has explained that his brother was also far "too shy and petrified"[86] to approach his idols, once shunning the chance to talk to John Lennon when they were both on the same plane. In an interview with Uli Twelker, Gallagher described himself as a "schoolboy" who still "hero worshipped,"[87] recognising that it was a "terrible thing" for a man of his age. Therefore, it would have been most out of keeping with his character and beliefs to give too much importance to the inclusion of guest stars and how they may affect the reception of his album. Given its personal themes, *Fresh Evidence* was very much Gallagher's album and no one else's; a "true baby that I have to look after day or night," as he told Emmanuel Potts of *Hard Force*.[88] In the same interview, he explained that the album had demanded a "lot of effort and attention," but he took "enormous" comfort in the fact that "everything" belonged to him.

Gallagher's own health limitations also played a part in the initial reception of *Fresh Evidence*. He had pushed himself so much during the making of the album that, once released, he fell ill and had to cancel a string of dates and promotional events throughout the summer as he recovered. In his scant press appearances, Gallagher looked exhausted, telling Felix Parbs of *Ohne Filter* that it had "been very hard" to finish up the album.[89] Ill health meant that it was not until later in the year when Gallagher began to tour the album, kicking off with a performance at Rocklife on 17 October (see 2.4).

Although Gallagher continued to write new songs and make demoes over the next five years until his untimely death, he never recorded another album, therefore confining *Fresh Evidence* to the annals of music history as the *final* album, rather than the album that marked his rebirth. *Still Got the Blues*, on the other hand, has acquired the rebirth tag, with Moore portrayed as the powerful phoenix rising from the ashes of the fickle 1980s music scene. Talking to Anil Prasad about his place in the blues scene, Gallagher mused that he was "probably the guy on the sidelines."[90] Evidently, a move to centre stage for both him and *Fresh Evidence* is long overdue.

(Re)freshing the Evidence

Throughout his career, Rory Gallagher had a difficult relationship with the studio, always striving to capture the electricity of his live shows on record and often being disappointed with the result. For Gallagher, his enthusiasm and love for playing went "down the swanny"[91] when he entered the studio, often leading the recording process to become protracted and even painful. Despite Gallagher's mixed feelings, he remained committed to the ambition of recording *the* perfect album, investing hours of time in finetuning his knowledge of production techniques, equipment and resources. This investment paid off with his final album *Fresh Evidence*, which perhaps represents the pinnacle of his studio wizardry.

Gallagher had always been known as a live performer; his studio albums often (unfairly) considered to fall short of capturing that magic. But *Fresh Evidence* flipped this narrative. Upon its release, music journalists were astounded by the high quality of Gallagher's studio work and widely approved of the album's production and composition. Furthermore, they praised Gallagher as an accomplished recording musician and highly skilled lyricist, rather than just a guitar virtuoso. Some even went as far as to say that they now drew more pleasure from his later albums than his concerts.

Ultimately, *Fresh Evidence* was seen as representing a period of rebirth for Gallagher, not death. However, somewhere along the way since Gallagher's passing in 1995, this positive narrative shifted. Focus instead began to be placed on the heavy themes of Gallagher's lyrics and the fact that this was his studio swansong. Viewing *Fresh Evidence* as Gallagher's farewell to the world is a sign of lazy journalism, much in the same way as *Jinx* became later reframed as Gallagher's own jinx. It ignores the frequent glimmers of hope that shine through the sorrow, of the tenacity that Gallagher always maintained, even in the depths of his depression. This, in turn, has played down the enormous contribution that the album made to the world of blues and marred its legacy.

Across the music press, *Fresh Evidence* has disappeared from view, omitted from lists of the best Rory Gallagher albums or overshadowed by Gary Moore's *Still Got the Blues*. While *Still Got the Blues* is undoubtedly an excellent album, one must ask the extent to which its album sales, guest stars and press attention feed into contemporary perceptions around its quality and the continued belief that it singlehandedly reignited the blues. How much of its material can truly be viewed as groundbreaking or authentic? Or does its acclaim lie mainly in its huge commercial success and its popularisation of the blues? Was it really a case of getting back to one's first musical love or was it jumping on the bandwagon? Perhaps there are no clear answers, but it would do good for music critics to reflect more on these questions.

Fresh Evidence is the sounds of a man who is feeling increasingly confident in his own abilities. A man who has finally mastered the studio and understands how to get the best from the equipment. A man who is keen to keep the blues alive and recognises its source point, but is not afraid to bring it a step forward with new arrangements, unconventional chord positions and jazz and Celtic-inspired licks that break its traditional tempo. A man who creates characters, tells stories and brings visions to life through his words. In short, the album is an artistic triumph, proving not only that Gallagher's creativity was still "intact" (as biographer Julian Vignoles questions), but that it was more flourishing than ever before.

Fresh Evidence promised an exciting future for Gallagher and laid the groundwork for what was to come. Although he did not record any more studio albums, he put his knowledge to fine use on a range of session work and collaborations with Energy Orchard, Roberto Manes and Samuel Eddy, to name but a few examples (see 1.5). As Gallagher moved into middle age, the studio seemed the natural pathway to cut down on his gruelling touring schedule. Songwriting for others may have also been a possible option, as Dónal acknowledged in the sleeve notes for the recent *Deuce 50th Anniversary* boxset release.

Fresh Evidence lit a creative fuse and, on his 1991 US tour, Gallagher found himself writing every night in his hotel room—something that he continued when back home in Ireland. By the end of 1992, he had compiled enough material for a complete electric album and was also working on songs for his long overdue acoustic album. Gallagher told *Guitar World* that he wanted to learn from past mistakes where he had "abused his physical and mental health" by recording both albums fairly quickly and in different studios. This would allow him to be "like a gypsy going from town to town," which would keep things fresh and energetic and help him better express himself.[92] Sadly, neither album came to pass.

When promoting *Fresh Evidence*, Gallagher had stated his desire for someone to come along soon with an "outrageous" and "raw" blues album that would "change the way things are."[93] *Fresh Evidence* did just that. But it is high time that the rest of the world woke up to the fact.

As Carol Clerk of *Uncut* wrote in 1998, "there was no end in sight."[94]

LAO

Footnotes

1 David Sinclair, 'The Show Must Go On', *Q* (July 1990), http://www.roryon.com/q8.html
2 Ibid.
3 Judy Black, 'Back to the Basic Blues Roots', *Cleveland Scene* (March 1991), http://shadowplays.com/blog/?p=193
4 Chris Welch, 'Flying Back to the Blues with Rory Gallagher', *Metal Hammer* (1990), http://www.roryon.com/flying.html
5 Emmanuel Potts, 'Gallagher comme a la guerre', *Hard Force* (June 1990), https://rewritingrory.co.uk/2022/06/04/hard-force-june-1990/
6 Neville Marten, 'Rory!' *Guitarist* (June 1987), http://www.roryon.com/guitarist.html
7 Shiv Cariappa, 'Conversation with Rory Gallagher', *Christian Science Monitor* (June 1991), https://www.rorygallagher.com/conversation-with-rory-gallagher/
8 Ray Hammond, 'Strat Stories', *International Musician and Recording World* (April 1975), http://www.roryon.com/hammond265.html

Part 1 - *No End in Sight: Fresh Evidence*

9 Harry Doherty, *Rory Gallagher Songbook* (1977), http://www.roryon.com/songbook.html
10 Hammond, 'Strat Stories'.
11 'THE BIRTH OF BELFAST BLUES - Rock 'n' The North', https://www.youtube.com/watch?v=O7b29vYQg70
12 Harry Doherty, 'Rory of the Crowd', *Melody Maker* (16 October 1976), http://www.roryon.com/crowd.html
13 Ibid.
14 Adam Sweeting, 'Gallagher: The Rory Details', *BEAT Instrumental* (March 1979), https://www.roryon.com/beat.html
15 Sinclair, 'The Show Must Go On!'
16 'Interview with Donal Gallagher', *The Fuze* (November 2003), http://www.roryon.com/fuze229.html
17 Michael Ross, 'While My Guitar Gently Weeps', *Sunday Times* (17 May 1998), http://www.roryon.com/rorytimes.html; Gerry McAvoy and Pete Chrisp, *Riding Shotgun: 35 Years on the Road with Rory Gallagher and "Nine Below Zero"* (Chicago: SPG Triumph, 2005), 252.
18 Michael Leonard, 'The Spotlight Kid', *Guitar Magazine* (December 1998), http://www.roryon.com/spotlight.html
19 Christopher Dieckmann, 'Rory Gallagher, Legende des Bluesrock, besucht seine ostdeutschen Fans', *Die Zeit* (December 1994), https://rewritingrory.co.uk/2022/06/13/die-zeit-december-1994/
20 Phil Alexander, 'Rory Gallagher', *RAW Yearbook* (1990), http://www.roryon.com/raw260.html
21 McAvoy and Chrisp, *Riding Shotgun*, 255.
22 Potts, 'Gallagher comme a la guerre'.
23 'Remembering Rory Gallagher 2024', https://www.youtube.com/watch?v=xE8LArN63VA
24 Sinclair, 'The Show Must Go On!'
25 Alexander, 'Rory Gallagher'.
26 McAvoy and Chrisp, *Riding Shotgun*, 255.
27 Ezequiel, 'Magia para los oídos', *This Is Rock* (October 2022), https://rewritingrory.co.uk/2022/10/08/this-is-rock-october-2022/
28Y GALLAGHER INTERVIEW WITH KRUSHER 1990 (EXCERTS ONLY)', https://www.youtube.com/watch?v=IPC31-CFiyw&ab_channel=DAVESTICKLEY-AQUATARKUS
30 Steve Morse, 'Rory Gallagher - Hard to Forget', *Boston Globe* (29 March 1991), http://shadowplays.com/blog/?p=165
31 Ibid.
32 'Rory Gallagher - The Complete 1991 "Guitar Player" Interview', https://www.youtube.com/watch?v=9gA9vGWieAs&t=2434s
33 Jeff Gilbert, 'Lost and Found', *Guitar School* (March 1992), http://www.roryon.com/school219.html
34 Cariappa, 'Conversation with Rory Gallagher'.
35 Dan Hedges, 'Rory Gallagher', *Excerpt from British Rock Guitar* (1977), http://www.roryon.com/british.html
36 Phil Alexander, 'Power Tools Sound Advice Pure Genius', *RAW* (November 1988), http://www.roryon.com/power.html
37 Marcus Connaughton, *Rory Gallagher: His Life and Times* (London: Collins, 2012), 142
38 Potts, 'Gallagher comme a la guerre'.
39 Anil Prasad, 'Rory Gallagher Outside the Establishment', *Inner Views* (1991), https://www.innerviews.org/inner/rory-1
40 Ibid.
41 Uli Twelker, 'Rory Gallagher: Good Times', *Good Times* (March 1993), http://www.roryon.com/uli209.html
42 Julian Vignoles, *Rory Gallagher: The Man Behind the Guitar* (London: Collins, 2018), 171.
43 Dave McHugh, cited in ibid., 150.
44 *Rory Gallagher: Calling Card* (RTÉ and BBC NI, 2024).
45 Cariappa, 'Conversation with Rory Gallagher'.
46 Michael Ross, 'Praying at the Temple of the Blues', *Sunday Tribune* (16 August 1992), http://www.roryon.com/praying.html
47 Cariappa, 'Conversation with Rory Gallagher'.
48 'Rory Gallagher', *Guitar Magazine* (April 1992), http://www.roryon.com/interviewextra.html
49 Ibid.
50 'Rory Gallagher - The Complete 1991 "Guitar Player" Interview'.
51 Ibid.
52 Potts, 'Gallagher comme a la guerre'.
53 Liner notes for 2018 rerelease of *Fresh Evidence*.
54 Cariappa, 'Conversation with Rory Gallagher'.
55 Susan Whitall, 'In the Midst of a Blues Boom, Rory Roars Back', *Detroit News* (March 1991), http://www.roryon.com/midst393.html
56 Potts, 'Gallagher comme a la guerre'.
57 Vignoles, *Rory Gallagher*, 151.
58 Twelker, 'Rory Gallagher…'
59 Vignoles, *Rory Gallagher*, 150.
60 Twelker, 'Rory Gallagher…'
61 Hal Horowitz, 'Ireland's Prodigal Blues Son', *Blues Revue* (July/August 1999), http://www.roryon.com/br.html
62 Cariappa, 'Conversation with Rory Gallagher'.
63 Nick Deriso, 'Rory Gallagher – Fresh Evidence (1990, 2011 reissue)', *Something Else* (16 August 2011), https://somethingelsereviews.com/2011/08/16/rory-gallagher-fresh-evidence-1990-reissue/
64 John Sakamoto, 'White Knuckle Guitarist', *Toronto Sun* (21 March 1991), http://www.roryon.com/knuckle159.html
65 Alexander, 'Rory Gallagher'.
66 Carol Clerk, 'Rory Gallagher - Fresh Evidence', *Melody Maker* (May 1990), http://www.roryon.com/freshevidence325.html
67 Skelly, 'The Irish Guitar Wonder'.
68 Gallagher and Moore knew each other well, having first met in the 1960s at Club Rado in Belfast, where they would leave a spare guitar on stage to share because they could not afford extra strings (as Moore recounts in the song 'Business as Usual'). They would later jam together in Hamburg when Thin Lizzy were on their 1979 *Black Rose* tour and crossed paths again in Dublin at the 1986 unemployment benefit concert *Self Aid*. At the end of Gallagher's life when he lived at the Conrad Hotel, Moore also visited him.

69 'Rory Gallagher - interview Rocksteady 1990 HD', https://www.youtube.com/watch?v=h2lg3B5ATSs
70 Harry Shapiro, *Gary Moore: The Official Biography* (London: Outline Press, 2022), 203.
71 Henry Knegt, 'Rory Gallagher Interview', *NOIZE Rockmagazine #2* (1993), https://harrypater.nl/2024/06/rory-gallagher-interview/
72 J.P. Sabour and X. Bonnet, '...et vogue la galère', Guitar World (February 1993), https://rewritingrory.co.uk/2022/06/03/guitar-world-february-1993/
73 The one notable exception is Colin Harper ('Ballad of a Thin Man', *Mojo* (October 1998), http://www.roryon.com/mojo.html) who recommends *Fresh Evidence* as one of the three albums that newcomers should check out to get a sense of who Gallagher is.
74 Reverend Keith A. Gordon, 'Rory Gallagher Album Buying Guide', *Live About* (31 March 2019), https://www.liveabout.com/rory-gallagher-album-buying-guide-404302
75 Interview with Barry Barnes, 11 September 2023.
76 Harry Shapiro, 'How Gary Moore Reignited the British Blues Scene with the Help of a Famous Guitarist', *Louder Sound* (6 February 2022), https://www.loudersound.com/features/gary-moore-the-story-of-still-got-the-blues
77 Shapiro, *Gary Moore*, 204.
78 Daevid Jehnzen, 'Still Got the Blues', *All Music* (12 September 2015), https://www.allmusic.com/album/still-got-the-blues-mw0000208220
79 Sian Llewellyn, 'Gary Moore: "I Jumped On the Blues Bandwagon? I Was the Bandwagon!"' *Louder Sound* (23 March 2007), https://www.loudersound.com/features/gary-moore-i-jumped-on-the-blues-bandwagon-i-was-the-bandwagon
80 Vignoles, *Rory Gallagher*, 150.
81 Colin McGinty, '"Music Is Not a Job, More of a Hobby," Says Rory', *Evening Herald* (1983), http://www.roryon.com/job156.html
82 Skelly, 'The Irish Guitar Wonder'.
83 Whitall, 'In the Midst of a Blues Boom, Rory Roars Back'.
84 Shapiro, *Gary Moore*, 211.
85 Harper, 'Ballad of a Thin Man'.
86 Liam Davenport, 'Rory Gallagher', *Record Collector* (11 May 2018), https://recordcollectormag.com/articles/rory-gallagher
87 Twelker, 'Rory Gallagher…'
88 Potts, 'Gallagher comme a la guerre'.
89 'Rory Gallagher - Interview Germany 1990', https://www.youtube.com/watch?v=im4YdY-Ed2k
90 Prasad, 'Outside the Establishment'.
91 "RORY GALLAGHER INTERVIEW WITH KRUSHER 1990'.
92 Sabour and Bonnet. '...et vogue la galère'.
93 Alexander, 'Rory Gallagher'.
94 Carol Clerk, 'Rory Gallagher Reissues', *Uncut* (October 1998), https://www.rocksbackpages.com/Library/Article/rory-gallagher-reissues

1.4 "A Great Holiday for Me" Guest Appearances and Collaborations, 1984-1991

In a 1980 interview for *The Rock Show* on RTÉ's Radio 2, presenter Dave Fanning asked Rory Gallagher what it was like to "do stuff" outside the Rory Gallagher Band. "It's a great holiday for me!" Gallagher exclaimed, "The responsibility is off your shoulders, and you can just become a guitar player."[1] For Gallagher, session work was "straightforward" because he played whatever was suitable for the artist. However, he equally saw it as an opportunity to learn and develop as a musician. When Gallagher was off the road, he had a tendency to "languish" and became "very insular" and "very depressed."[2] Although his brother Dónal encouraged him to go on holiday, Gallagher was never interested and described time off as "agony"[3] for him. Session work was, therefore, an ideal busman's holiday, enabling him to continue pursuing his vocation, yet without the pressure of being both bandleader and producer.

For Gallagher, the "high point of his life"[4] came early when he worked on *The London Muddy Waters Sessions* (1972). He never forgot Waters' kindness and patience, which he believes turned him into a much better guitarist, and even kept the car that Dónal drove Waters around in as a "shrine," leaving it permanently parked outside his mother Monica's house.[5] Throughout his career, Gallagher also spoke positively about the Jerry Lee Lewis sessions in 1973. Despite there being a "strange sense of violence and madness" in the studio, Gallagher found this "borderline of danger" integral to creating real rock & roll and bonded with Lewis over their shared love of country music.[6] When Lewis flew into a fit of rage during the recording of 'Satisfaction' by the Rolling Stones and kicked the other musicians out of the room, it was Gallagher who he asked to stay and teach him the song, stating four words of affirmation: "I trust you, boy."[7]

Receiving a seal of approval from both Waters and Lewis meant a great deal to Gallagher, but also to critics who frequently cited—and continue to cite— him being chosen for these sessions as a mark of his talent. However, these sessions represent just a very small cross-section of the many guest appearances and collaborations that he undertook. From 1971 to 1995, Gallagher, in fact, contributed to 19 different albums—some with well-known artists and others with up-and-coming bands who he was keen to support.[8] Furthermore, over half of these contributions came in the last ten years of his career, challenging the myth of his 'slow output' during this time. While Gallagher may have only released two albums (*Defender* and *Fresh Evidence*) in the final decade of his life, he was frequently in the studio working with others. Even a week before his final show in Rotterdam in January 1995, he was recording new material with young Irish blues player Samuel Eddy (aka Eamonn McCormack).

Over the next two essays, we will delve—for the first time—into Gallagher's many guest appearances and collaborations throughout the 1980s and early 1990s, telling the stories behind them and shining a spotlight on the tracks that he recorded. These albums on which Gallagher guested demonstrate his flexibility as an artist and the way that he drew upon his Celtic roots yet blended them and experimented with different genres. They also suggest new, creative avenues for him, moving towards acoustic music and working more with jazz fusion, folk and flamenco artists. Too often, the final ten years of Gallagher's life are depicted as ones of creative barrenness, with the fact that he only released two studio albums during this time held up as 'evidence' to support this. We argue that the number of sessions in which Gallagher took part in show otherwise and indicate that his enthusiasm for music was still there, despite growing personal challenges. Furthermore, his confidence in the studio was increasingly building as he fully embraced the opportunity to experiment, share ideas and develop new approaches to recording. He had truly come into his own as a recording musician, not just a live performer.

'Flight to Paradise' (1984)
(recorded with Juan Martín, released posthumously on *Wheels Within Wheels*, 2003)

In March 1984, Gallagher took part in a short acoustic tour with David Lindley, Richard Thompson and Juan Martín. Billed as 'Guitarists' Night', the tour was the brainchild of Northern Irish concert promoter Paul Charles who wanted to bring the four world-renowned guitarists together under one roof (Charles would go on to become Gallagher's agent). Writing in his autobiography *Adventures in Wonderland*, Charles stated that his decision to bring these four guitarists together was because they were "masters in their own field" and "had a hunger to explore other styles."[9] According to Charles, they all "bought into the idea immediately" and after finally managing to sync their schedules, three shows were organised in Guildford, Cambridge and London. All three shows followed the same format: the four guitarists introduced themselves to the audience and played several numbers together, then each played an individual set, before all reassembling at the end for a jam.

For critics, the series of concerts was a curate's egg. David Lindley, who performed first in his unique lap-steel style, was extremely crowd-pleasing. However, the sets by Juan Martín and Richard Thompson that followed were less well received. Martín's long compositions and introductions were said to make the audience "restless," while Thompson was "off-form" due to a bad case of flu.[10] Gallagher, who appeared last, was widely described as having "put a show together that was head and shoulders above anything else." Although the concert was pitched as acoustic, Gallagher alternated between his National Triolian Resonator, Martin D35 and Fender Stratocaster, the loud cheers and applause from the audience making it clear that most people had turned up to see him. Simon Rouse of *Blue Suede News* was so in awe of Gallagher's performance that he pondered why the Irishman had never recorded a live acoustic album.[11] The concert ended on a high with a jam between the four guitarists, the interplay between Gallagher and Lindley singled out by critics as a "treat to the ears."

Despite mixed reviews about the choice of musicians and the extent to which they worked well together, Gallagher enjoyed the experience, thriving on the opportunity to jam in a range of styles on his acoustic guitar. As an enthusiast of flamenco music, Gallagher formed an "immediate connection" with Juan Martín and particularly enjoyed the part of the show where they played together. The two musicians had first met several days earlier at the Aer Lingus Hotel in London, where they ran through some songs together in preparation for the short tour. Speaking to us in March 2023, Martín recalled Gallagher's instant respect for his playing, as well as an appreciation for the technical difficulty of flamenco music: when the Spaniard played a fast scale high up on the fretboard, a stunned Gallagher uttered, "We can't do that. It looks too difficult!"[12]

On stage, Gallagher encouraged Martín to sing *rumba* (something that the Spaniard had never done previously in public) as he responded on his Stratocaster playing improvised flamenco scales—a memory that Martín treasures. They also experimented with Martín's song 'Flight to Paradise' (originally recorded as 'Vuelo a Paraíso')—a beautiful flamenco-inspired instrumental which enthralled Gallagher when he first heard it. 'Flight to Paradise' went down well with audiences on the tour, so when Gallagher and Martín were invited to perform on BBC Radio 1, they had no doubt that they would choose this song. They recorded it in just one take, with Gallagher on his National and Martín on his 1972 Sobrinos de Esteso flamenco pegboard guitar.

After its original broadcast in March 1984, the performance was filed away and did not see the light of day until 2003 on *Wheels Within Wheels*—an attempt by Dónal to fulfil his brother's lifelong desire to release an acoustic album. It was worth the wait, the instrumental amply displaying the virtuosity of both Gallagher and Martín. The song title 'Flight to Paradise' is fitting because the song does just that, taking the listener on a transcendent voyage that grows in magic and mysticism as the tempo increases. There is a certain sense of joy and freedom in the song as the two guitars splendidly combine and interact in a compelling call and response, sometimes giving the impression that a whole room of guitarists are playing. The result is a melting pot of sounds as Spanish and Celtic, flamenco and blues, come together to form a bold, unique and emotional piece of music, showcasing yet another string in Gallagher's extremely versatile musical bow.

'The Edge' and 'Into the Dark' (1984)
(recorded for *Box of Frogs* by Box of Frogs)

Gallagher made no secret of the fact that he was a big fan of the Yardbirds. He frequently described them as his favourite group of the mid-1960s and spoke fondly about seeing them at the Marquee Club when he first went to London with the Fontana Showband in 1965. Things seemed to go full circle when in June 1983, Gallagher was invited back to the Marquee Club to perform as part of a series of shows to mark the venue's 25th anniversary. Also on the bill with him were three of the original Yardbirds: Paul Samwell-Smith, Chris Dreja and Jim McCarty.

The success of the live shows encouraged the ex-Yardbirds to get together and record new music. Adding Medicine Head's John Fiddler on vocals, they formed a band and were joined in their Christmas Eve recording session by Jeff Beck. Gradually, more and more musician friends became involved in the sessions, leading the group to call themselves Box of Frogs. One of these musicians was Rory Gallagher.[13] Speaking to journalist Dmitry M. Epstein in 2014, Jim McCarty said that Gallagher was an obvious first choice for them because he was "always good" and they "always liked what he did."[14] They were also aware that he liked the Yardbirds and, therefore, had a good understanding of their musical style.

Gallagher performed on two tracks with the band: 'The Edge' and 'Into the Dark', the former showing off his formidable slide playing and the latter his proficiency on the sitar. 'The Edge' opens with a catchy riff in the style of ZZ Top, before Gallagher enters with his distinctly identifiable slide guitar. The same riff runs throughout the song, peppered with the occasional squeal of Gallagher's slide, which calls to mind some of his finest work on *Jinx* like 'Double Vision' and 'Big Guns'. The song also incorporates two short solos by Gallagher, bringing this dynamic rocker up-to-date and making it clear that Box of Frogs was not just a pining for the past.

With its independent bassline and reggae rock feel, 'Into the Dark' is much more like a lost Sting song. The way that Gallagher's 1968 Coral sitar slips into the introduction gives it an eery quality and creates an ominous atmosphere, which melds well with the lyric's themes of darkness, shadows and mysteries of the night. Gallagher's use of sitar is subdued, yet every note that comes from it is evocative.

Box of Frogs was released in September 1984 to a mixed reception. While critics generally relished in the idea of bringing the Yardbirds' sound to a modern audience, music fans were less convinced about its place in the 1980s and saw it as "boring."[15] Fiddler was quick to strike back, arguing that the album was not a nostalgia trip and that the "music and ideas [were] fresh and [had] an eighties feel to them."[16] Over time, the album has come to be seen as a "curiosity" that lacked the spark, sound or style" of the Yardbirds.[17] Gallagher's contributions, however, are still seen by critics as the strongest parts of the record.

'Trick of the Night' (1985)
(recorded for *Echoes in the Night* by Gary Brooker)

Part 1 - *Guest Appearances and Collaborations 1984-1991*

Throughout the days of Taste and his early solo career, Gallagher often passed Procol Harum frontman Gary Brooker like a ship in the night: they played within days of each other at Mothers in Birmingham in 1969 and at the Felt Forum in New York in 1973, they appeared on the German programme *Beat Club* one week apart in 1971 and they were both signed to Chrysalis Records. Their first proper meeting came in 1978 at Lonnie Donegan's *Puttin' on the Style* sessions, where Brooker played piano on 'I Wanna Go Home' and Gallagher played guitar on 'Rock Island Line', 'Drop Down Baby' and 'Lost John'. Flash forward to 1985 and Brooker was looking for guest guitarists to feature on his forthcoming solo album *Echoes in the Night*. On the suggestion of his manager Nick Blackburn, Brooker phoned Gallagher who agreed right away.

Echoes in the Night is often described as the album for fans who had been waiting for a Procol Harum reunion, the band having broken up in 1977. Although a solo record by Brooker, it featured the band's organist Matthew Fisher, lyricist Keith Reid and drummer B.J. Wilson, leading many to call it the 'lost' Procol Harum album. At the time of its release, Brooker was eager to stress that it was not so much a "recapture" as "a meeting of new ideas that are just as meaningful yet much less complicated."[18]

The album brought together the AOR soft rock sound of the 1980s with traditional orchestral arrangements and gospel music, meaning that guest performers such as Eric Clapton and Ray Cooper were just as at home on the album as the National Philharmonic Orchestra and the London Gospel Community Choir. While this eclectic blend of music may seem far removed from Gallagher's bread and butter, he was always open to different musical genres and welcomed the opportunity to participate, guesting on the closing track 'Trick of the Night'.

'Trick of the Night' is a quintessential power ballad with strong Mike and the Mechanics vibes. Brooker's stirring vocal performance gels throughout with the sax-playing of Jamie Talbot, a former member of the National Jazz Youth Orchestra. Gallagher's influence on the song is very subtle here, with Brooker not making the most of the guitarist's musical prowess: there are no grand guitar solos and the emphasis is very much on the saxophone. Gallagher plays slide guitar, but this is somewhat buried for most of the track—a peculiar decision given that the album's eponymous track benefits from an emotional Clapton guitar solo. Nonetheless, even in the rare moments when Gallagher is allowed to shine, he shows his proficiency, his guitar's wails always taking place at the right moments to accentuate the song's heartfelt lyrics about an old friend. According to Matthew Fisher, it was Gallagher's own suggestion to play slide rather than just fretting chords. He remembers Gallagher playing well in the studio, but was surprised at just how "battered" his Fender Stratocaster was up close.[19]

Van Morrison's Blues Album:
The Session That Never Was (1985)

Around the same time as *Echoes in the Night*, Gallagher was approached by Van Morrison to form a grouping to make a blues album. Morrison had heard about

Gallagher's recent performance at an Ethiopian benefit concert in Edinburgh with Charlie Watts, Jack Bruce, Ian Stewart and Dick Heckstall-Smith, and hoped to collaborate with all five musicians, bringing in Brian Auger on keyboards. Concurrently, RTÉ was developing a television series called *The Sessions* and planned to include Gallagher and Morrison. Known for his notoriously temperamental behaviour, Morrison suddenly changed his mind at a lead-up meeting and, in Dónal's words, "he left and the whole session fell apart."[20] RTÉ wanted to continue without Morrison, but the whole experience "depressed" Gallagher and he scrapped the idea, despite his initial enthusiasm.

This was not the first time that Morrison had messed Gallagher around; in 1978, Gallagher was invited to play on *Wavelength*,[21] but Morrison arrived several hours late and then disappeared altogether, leading Gallagher to abandon the session.[22] Known for his professionalism, Gallagher was frustrated by the incident and later told *Hot Press* that he and Van were like "the meeting of the waters" and that he hoped to "get together soon," but not "just on Van's terms."[23] Sadly, the two never did record together, although they remained good friends and had a mutual respect for each other; when Gallagher passed away, Morrison attended his memorial service at the Brompton Oratory.

'You Mix Me Up', 'Heart Full of Soul', 'House on Fire' and 'Hanging from the Wreckage' (1986)
(recorded for *Strange Land* by Box of Frogs)

Box of Frogs enjoyed working with Gallagher so much on their first album that they invited him back for their follow-up *Strange Land* in 1986. *Strange Land* featured an even bigger rollcall of guest musicians than *Box of Frogs*, including Steve Hackett, Jimmy Page and Graham Gouldman. This time, however, vocalist John Fiddler only appeared on half of the tracks, the others sung by Graham Parker, Ian Dury and Roger Chapman. This was due to a ruckus between Fiddler and the other band members, which had led him to walk out halfway through the recording sessions. Although the precise details have been lost to history, the story goes that Box of Frogs were asked to do a US tour because their first album had been particularly popular on college campuses. However, much to Fiddler's dismay, Samwell-Smith, Dreja and McCarty hated the idea and refused. Jeff Beck, who had been considered for the US tour, was reportedly also disappointed by this decision and took no part in their second album as a result.

Gallagher contributed to four songs on *Strange Land*: 'You Mix Me Up', 'Heart Full of Soul', 'House on Fire' and 'Hanging from the Wreckage'. As with everything he did, Gallagher fired on all cylinders for the sessions, even to the detriment of his own health. Writing in the liner notes to the 2006 rerelease, Chris Dreja described Gallagher as a "complete perfectionist," standing in the middle of the studio floor at 2AM "simply refusing to listen to his body which was telling him 'I can't go on and we need to stop'." Dreja also praised Gallagher's fine ear for music, noting how he dispatched a roadie to pick up his sitar to give an extra edge to 'Hanging from the Wreckage'.

Part 1 - *Guest Appearances and Collaborations 1984-1991*

It is fair to say that *Strange Land* has not aged particularly well. The majority of the songs have a strong 1980s pop-rock feel and can be described as catchy, radio-friendly tunes with fairly repetitive, somewhat superficial lyrics and heavy use of synthesisers. This was a view also shared by critics who expressed surprise that an album with such a high calibre of guest musicians was not as good as one would expect. Even contemporary reviews of the album are unkind and consider it to lean too heavily on "boom-bash drumming and pedestrian pop arrangements."[24] Nonetheless, Gallagher is one of the record's saving graces, able to bring his own unique edge to the songs on which he appears, which keeps them fresh and stops them from falling too deep into the clichéd 1980s sound trap.

'You Mix Me Up', for example, is a track that begins with Huey Lewis style harmonies and a foot-tapping synthesiser. It is certainly not something that one would associate with Rory Gallagher who regularly described synthesisers as "soulless stuff."[25] Much of the song is rather forgettable, with Gallagher's short guitar solo midway through—complete with his classic string-pulling technique—being one of its redeeming features.

Although a Yardbirds cover, 'Heart Full of Soul' also suffers from an overuse of synthesisers and gated reverb, but is saved somewhat by Roger Chapman's powerful vocal performance and Gallagher's musicianship. Gallagher shines, playing the song's iconic riff on his sitar, before switching to his Stratocaster to deliver a breathtaking guitar solo and then deftly back to the sitar again. Chapman's wailing vocals magnificently intertwine with the notes that Gallagher plays, but not enough is made of this melding, and the final minute of the song gives way once more to a classic 80s Phil Collinesque sound.

'House on Fire' fares much better from the get-go with its slick opening guitar riff by Gallagher and the boogie woogie piano of Geraint Watkins (who went on to play with Gallagher on *Fresh Evidence* and his 1990 tour). John Fiddler's vocals are also en pointe. Here, Gallagher revels in the more bluesy feel of the song, playing a much longer guitar solo—perhaps one of the best in the history of his session work—as well as interweaving short bursts of slide into the playing of rhythm guitarist Dzal Martin. It is by far the standout track of the album.

Finally, 'Hanging from the Wreckage' is an unusual song that begins with quasi-mystical chanting from John Fiddler and the other band members, before the supernatural sounds of Gallagher's sitar kick in. After the opening verse, the chanting resumes as Gallagher takes up a beautiful sitar solo that is arguably stronger than that of the better known 'Philby', even managing to incorporate more of his adept string-pulling. It stands as a fine example of his ability as a multi-instrumentalist and begs the question of why he did not make greater use of the sitar in his solo work and live performances.

'Tara Hill' and 'If You Should Go' (1988)
(recorded for *The Scattering*
by the Fureys and Davey Arthur)

Although it was the blues that captivated Gallagher as a child, in interviews, he often acknowledged his great appreciation for Irish folk music. His father Danny was an Ulster champion accordion player who had his own céilí dance orchestra, while his mother Monica and uncle Jimmy were good singers, meaning that no family gathering was complete without a traditional singsong around the piano. Growing up above his grandmother's Modern Bar in MacCurtain St in Cork, Gallagher also came face-to-face with Irish folk music every day in the bar and even once met composer Seán Ó Riada who drank there.[26]

In later years, Gallagher's appreciation for traditional Irish music grew further, with him frequently expressing a desire to play more acoustic material and collaborate with other Irish folk artists. This desire seemed to stem from his increasing homesickness and yearning to return to Ireland. In a 1992 interview with Liam Fay, he stated that he was "constantly thinking mentally about Ireland"[27] and listened to RTÉ radio every night, read the Irish papers every Sunday and kept up with all the latest Irish album releases. Despite Gallagher's desire to move back home, Dónal believes that his brother was "too much of a rolling stone" to settle: "It was almost as if he liked Ireland so much, he was afraid he would end up liking it too much and not move on and travel. That he'd end up almost in retirement."[28]

Gallagher's longing for Ireland is apparent in the way that he tended to weave 'She Moved Thro' the Fair' into later live performances of 'Out on the Western Plain' or burst into impromptu versions of traditional songs like 'Dan O'Hara'. Shortly before his passing, Gallagher was also planning to record with The Chieftains, while the posthumous release *Wheels Within Wheels* features many traditional-inspired tracks.

Given Gallagher's affinity for the music of his homeland, it may come as no surprise then that when the Fureys and Davey Arthur—well-established Irish folk musicians—approached him about guesting on their 1988 album *The Scattering*, he was eager to oblige. This marked the first of a series of guest appearances that Gallagher did around this time that put him in touch with Irish traditional music. *The Scattering* is generally seen as the Fureys' best album, bringing together a collection of melancholy folk songs that romanticise Ireland and reflect the experiences of the Irish immigrant who yearns for home. Given these themes, it is understandable that Gallagher was so taken by the idea of contributing to the album, appearing on two songs: 'Tara Hill' and 'If You Should Go.' The album also featured guest performances from Ralph McTell, Dave Stewart and Siobhan Fahey-Stewart.

'Tara Hill' is an emotional ballad that personifies the famous hill in County Wexford as a beautiful female. Its chorus goes on to describe the hill as "a treasure," praising its splendour and how if the hill "were a dream," the narrator would "stay asleep." Accompanying these words is an exquisite, understated piece of slide guitar by Gallagher that heightens the emotional intensity of the song. He then leads into a short country style solo that harks back to 1973's

'Tucson Arizona', yet given a Celtic makeover by the accompanying uillean pipes and whistle, bringing this song of homesickness and love to a wonderful conclusion.

'If You Should Go', on the other hand, is a sweet little ditty in the popular Country and Irish style. It is essentially a tale of love, the narrator pleading anxiously with his darling never to leave him. In this song, Gallagher takes more of a backseat role, supporting the Fureys' vocals with his solid rhythm guitar-playing and occasional sweeps of slide that echo earlier songs like 'If I Had a Reason'. Although seemingly simple, the song has many layers: the female backing vocals, the beautiful uilleann pipes and whistle solo, the octave change towards the end. It showcases how perfectly Gallagher could fit in with any musical ensemble, yet firmly putting his own stamp on the music.

'Litton Lane', 'The Road to Ballyalla' and 'One for Phil' (1988)
(recorded for *Out of the Air* by the Davy Spillane Band)

In the same year that Gallagher guested with the Fureys and Davey Arthur, he had another opportunity to become more involved in traditional Irish music, this time with Davy Spillane—the renowned Irish uilleann pipes and low whistle player—who was working on his latest album *Out of the Air*.

Out of the Air was the follow-up to Spillane's debut solo album *Atlantic Bridge* and, in the same style, it blended Irish traditional music with bluegrass and country rock. The album was partially compiled from live recordings for BBC Radio 1 with Spillane's touring band (Anto Drennan on guitar, James Delaney on keyboards, Tony Molloy on bass and Paul Moran on drums), as well as additional studio sessions at Windmill Lane Studios in Dublin.

The sessions with Gallagher came about thanks to a chance meeting with radio presenter and record producer P.J. Curtis who was co-producing Spillane's album (he had also produced *Atlantic Bridge* and went on to produce Spillane's third album *Shadow Hunter*). As Curtis told us in March 2023, he was working as a sound engineer on the road with The Chieftains at the time.[29] The band was touring the UK in 1987 and found themselves with a rare night off in Glasgow. By chance, Curtis learnt that Gallagher was also in the city playing at the Pavilion and decided to attend the concert with several band members, managing to get backstage to meet him. Curtis was "thrilled" to learn that Gallagher was familiar with his work and listened regularly to his RTÉ blues show (*The House of R&B*) when back home in Ireland. Such was Gallagher's love for Curtis's radio show that he even asked Dónal to record and send him cassette copies when he was out of the country. Curtis told Gallagher that he was about to start working on Davy Spillane's new album and the guitarist expressed his admiration for Spillane's work. Right there and then, Curtis asked him if he would like to play on the album and he immediately said yes. They decided to plan a session with Spillane and his band for the next time that Gallagher was in Dublin.

As promised, several months later, Gallagher arrived at the Windmill Lane Studios in Dublin along with his trusty Stratocaster. It was the first time that he and Spillane had ever met, and the two men hit it off instantly. Curtis describes watching them work out their common musical ground as "something to behold." In the course of just one morning, they recorded three tracks: two Spillane compositions—'Litton Lane' and 'The Road to Ballyalla'—and a joint penned new track— 'One for Phil'—written in memory of Thin Lizzy frontman Phil Lynott who had passed away two years before. On Curtis's request, they had also tried out an old Robert Johnson song (Gallagher on acoustic and Spillane on low whistle), but "it didn't really work out."

For the first track—'Litton Lane' (dedicated to a small cobbled street in central Dublin) —Spillane provided Gallagher with a guitar, which he described as a "thirty-year-old lady-size harmony guitar."[30] However, in true Gallagher style, he played it effortlessly. The song begins with the unmistakable sounds of Gallagher's acoustic slide—highly reminiscent of his later work with Roberto Manes (see 1.5)—before breaking into some bluesy rhythm-playing. As the song progresses, the piano kicks in, followed by the uillean pipes, the result being an unusual yet beautiful blend of Ireland meets the Mississippi. This is further accentuated by Brian Palm on harmonica who plays in unison with the pipes (his own suggestion). As recounted by Palm in an April 2023 interview with us, Spillane was struggling with the arrangements for his solo as he was not used to playing the blues scale.[31] To keep him on track, Palm came up with the idea of "trading lines like a musical dialogue" instead. Palm notes that he "skied completely off piste" during his own solo, but managed to make it out "intact." Following a solo by Gallagher—now on his electric guitar—all the instrumentalists come together for a big crescendo. Keen ears will pick up Palm's laugh at the end of the song, followed by his comment, "We nailed it!"

Palm recalls the session as "exceptionally exciting." He is particularly pleased that the unique sound of his amp and "crazy old microphone" (originally from a 1960s Irish police car) is immortalised on the record because it was later stolen and he never saw it again. Much to Palm's regret, this was the only time that he recorded with Gallagher (there were plans for Gallagher to record with Palm's partner Mary Stokes, but they never materialised). Nonetheless, he has fond memories of a later jam session together at The Waterfront in Dublin. Gallagher had come as a spectator and quietly sat down in the audience. Spotting the guitarist from the stage, Palm invited him forward to jam and they went on to perform Little Walter's 'Can't Hold Out Much Longer', with Gallagher using Dermot Stokes' Telecaster.

The second song involving Gallagher on *Out of the Air*—'The Road to Ballyalla'—is a nine-minute dazzling and thought-provoking instrumental whose shifts in rhythm and tempo take the listener through an auditory journey to the village of Ballyalla in County Clare. Here, Gallagher swops his guitar for a sitar, bringing a touch of India that flawlessly complements this otherwise traditional Irish song (Gallagher, in fact, frequently spoke in interviews about the surprising links between Indian and Irish folk music). Spillane's accompaniment is hypnotic, starting slowly before picking up pace midway through and turning into a quasi-jig. The song takes another unique twist towards the end, the piano, bass and sitar interplay giving it a late-night jazz feel, before Spillane's pipes take over once again, bringing the song to a potent end.

Finally, 'One for Phil' is a funky short number that begins with a guitar riff from Gallagher with echoes of the live version of 'In Your Town'. Soon, Gallagher is joined by Spillane, resulting in a striking combination of the raw and the refined. Although an instrumental, the song features stretches of humming by Gallagher that integrate with the guitar and pipes, adding a layer of depth. The song came about when Gallagher and Spillane were taking a break during rehearsals and started discussing Phil Lynott and how sad his death was. Within a few minutes, they had come up with 'One for Phil'. Although not close friends, Gallagher had performed with Lynott on several occasions, including at Punchestown Racecourse (1982), and was deeply "shocked" by his death.[32]

For P.J. Curtis, the session is one that he "will never forget." He remembers Gallagher as somebody "so gentle, without ego, respectful and reserved, shy even... just a dream to work with." The other members of the band were also "totally captivated" by Gallagher's humility and talent. In the 1995 *Hot Press* tribute to Gallagher, Spillane described the guitarist as "very generous with his time, friendly and accessible," noting how he "showed an interest" in traditional Irish music at a time when few people were focused on it.[33]

In an interview with Colin Harper in the same year, Spillane added that, although he did not know Gallagher well, he "greatly enjoyed his company" and found him to be a "very generous, personable man."[34] Gallagher, in turn, had described Spillane several years earlier as "very pleasant" and felt their project had turned out "quite well,"[35] especially because he had never recorded with uilleann pipes before and was anxious about how it would work.[36]

Will Ye Go Lassie Go'   (1989)
(recorded for *Words and Music* by Phil Coulter)

One year after his sessions with the Fureys/Davey Arthur and Davy Spillane, Gallagher was approached by Phil Coulter—the celebrated Irish musician, songwriter and record producer—about featuring on his new album *Words and Music*. *Words and Music* was a collection of 15 traditional Irish classics and popular melodies, arranged by Phil Coulter and featuring 'the best' of the folk world, including Ralph McTell, the Dubliners and Liam Clancy.

Gallagher's response to Coulter was resoundingly positive for two reasons. First, because he wished to continue his liaison with Irish traditional music, but also because Coulter hailed from Derry (the birthplace of the Gallagher brother's father Danny, and where Gallagher himself had lived from ages 1-8), which made Gallagher feel an immediate warmth towards him. However, typical of Gallagher's lack of self-confidence, he worried that he would not be able to pull it off and asked Coulter whether he was sure about his choice. In his 2019 autobiography *Bruised, Never Broken*, Coulter revealed that the record company was also hesitant about Gallagher; in fact, "horrified" because they thought that his playing would not suit the style of the album. However, as a long-term Gallagher fan, Coulter was adamant that the guitarist was perfect for the record and that he "would prove it."[37]

On the allotted day, Gallagher arrived at Livingston Studios (London), and he and Coulter decided together which track he would play on. After some deliberation, they selected an instrumental version of 'Will Ye Go Lassie Go'. Also known as 'Wild Mountain Thyme', the lyrics and melody of the song are a variant of the 18th century Scottish poem 'The Braes of Balquhither', which was adapted by the Belfast musician Francis McPeake in the 1950s. As Coulter played Gallagher the orchestral track, "a big smile" spread over the guitarist's face as he concentrated on where to fit in his playing. Gallagher asked politely to listen again. Then, he nodded and said, "Mmm, the red lad, I think," selecting his chosen guitar from the rack of instruments that roadie Tom O'Driscoll had brought in. Already in the first run-through, Coulter was bowled over by Gallagher's licks and melody lines and told him that there was no need for another take. Gallagher seemed "confused" and "a little reluctant," asking Coulter whether he was sure that he did not want him to try again. "Rory, it's fucking brilliant!" Coulter replied, encouraging him into the control room to listen back. As Gallagher did, "a look of childish delight" spread across his face, which Coulter describes as "priceless […] a rare and precious" moment.[38]

In the liner notes to *Words and Music*, Coulter added further details about 'Will Ye Go Lassie Go', stating that it was the first song that he had ever learnt to play and that he never thought that he would record a version with Gallagher. He also wrote that he was "lost in admiration" for the sensitivity of Gallagher's playing on the track. And it is easy to see why when listening to the hauntingly beautiful rendition. Coulter's lasting impressions of Gallagher are of somebody "quiet, self-effacing and even shy […] the humblest of men"[39] and, here, the guitarist's emotive playing truly encapsulates these characteristics. Coulter's piano assimilates the soft tones of Gallagher's guitar, strongly evoking the lush, green fields and rugged coastline of Ireland. Towards the halfway point, the piano and drums momentarily stop, leading into a stunning piece of weeping guitar by Gallagher, before the instruments resume and the song rises an octave and then gradually fades out.

'I Can't Be Satisfied' and 'Comin' Home Baby' (1989)
(recorded with Chris Barber, released posthumously on *Memories of My Trip*, 2011 and *Blues*, 2019)

When legendary jazz musician Chris Barber passed away, aged 90, in 2021, Dónal Gallagher described him as a "god-father figure" to him and his brother.[40]

Part 1 - *Guest Appearances and Collaborations 1984-1991*

It was Barber's show on BBC radio in the 1950s that introduced both brothers to blues and jazz and fostered an early childhood hero for Gallagher in the form of Lonnie Donegan who was then banjo player in Barber's band. Barber was also co-owner of London's Marquee Club, where Gallagher and his band Taste got their first big break in the late 1960s. Barber had been informed of Taste's talent by his wife Ottilie Patterson, a blues singer from Belfast, and quickly took a keen interest in Gallagher, describing him as "the person to carry the blues torch for the next generation."[41]

A friendship blossomed between the two men, leading Barber to invite Gallagher to play two songs on his 1972 album *Drat That Fraddled Rat*. The album's fusion of jazz rock with prog swiftly turned it into a cult classic, with Gallagher singled out for his skilful bottleneck guitar on 'Sleepy Louie' and "earthy guitar sounds" and "emotional solo" on the album's eponymous track.[42] The two men's paths crossed again in 1980 when Gallagher played the Reading Festival for a record-breaking fourth time. As Barber was a founding member of the Festival (then the National Jazz and Blues Festival), he came up on stage to present a surprised Gallagher with an award.

Barber and Gallagher remained in touch and, in 1989, Barber asked the guitarist if he would like to do several UK tour dates with him and his band. Gallagher willingly accepted and the somewhat unusual combination took the road together. Fans who attended their opening concert at the University of Warwick recall the curious scene: half the audience with long hair and motorcycle jackets, the other half in suits and formal dresses. The first part of the concert saw Barber and his band perform jazz and blues standards, before Gallagher took to the stage for his typically rollicking show. He and Barber also performed several numbers together, some of which were recorded.

To date, two of these recordings—'I Can't Be Satisfied' and 'Comin' Home Baby'—have emerged. The first track appeared on Chris Barber's 2011 double album *Memories of My Trip*, released to mark his 80th birthday and featuring rare recordings and collaborations from across his career with such A-grade musicians as Muddy Waters, Van Morrison, Mark Knopfler, Alexis Korner and Keith Emerson. 'I Can't Be Satisfied'—an old Muddy Waters song—was recorded at the Wyvern Theatre in Swindon and, in the liner notes, Barber sings Gallagher's praises, complimenting his singing and playing, particularly his ability to obtain a "slightly distorted" guitar effect simply by adjusting his instrument's volume levels. Barber also applauds Gallagher's unique Irish twist on the blues, singling out 'Out on the Western Plain' as a key example.

Gallagher performed 'I Can't Be Satisfied' many times over the years, no one version ever being the same. Television footage shows him variably playing the song alone on his National, accompanied by Mark Feltham on harmonica or even joined by German presenter Götz Alsmann on banjo. This 1989 version is no exception, with Chris Barber adding a singular touch on the double bass. This is improvisation at its finest, Gallagher playing a riff and Barber closely following, both men going where the feeling takes them, as all good blues and jazz does. Gallagher's vocals are strong and immediate here, making the listener feel as if they are intruding on a private performance by the two men. His slide solo is also impeccable, accentuated by Barber's slick accompanying groove. Towards the end of the song, Gallagher hands over to Barber for his own solo, which demonstrates the jazz musician's aptitude on the double bass. In the album liner notes, Barber expressed his delight at having "the chance to play the bass for once," being most typically associated with the trombone.

'Comin' Home Baby', also recorded at the Wyvern Theatre in Swindon, was released by the Gallagher Estate in 2019 on the *Blues* album—a collection of rare and unreleased recordings of Gallagher playing his favourite blues material. The song was popularised by Mel Tormé in 1962 and was suggested to Barber by Gallagher during an afternoon rehearsal for their concert. Their fine rendition of the song later that evening demonstrates Gallagher's profound knowledge of music and perception of what would work well for the two performers together. Fully instrumental, Gallagher takes the role of bandleader here, starting with a slow, opening lick on his guitar and then guiding each instrument's entrance. His superb jazz-playing fuses perfectly with the accompanying brass, indicating yet another possible musical pathway that he could have taken, had he wanted. His confidence and freedom are evident as he continually builds off the recurring riff, letting himself be guided by his instincts rather than any set rules. As Barber himself noted, Gallagher also brings his own Irish touch to what he plays, straying far from the Tormé version and into new creative territory.

'Human Shield' (1991)
(recorded for *Flags and Emblems* by Stiff Little Fingers)

It may seem an unlikely combination, but, in 1991, Gallagher teamed up with Northern Irish punk band Stiff Little Fingers, guesting on the track 'Human Shield' for their *Flags and Emblems* album. Although from seemingly different musical traditions, Gallagher often spoke about how he admired the energy of punk and praised Stiff Little Fingers for their "Irish approach" to music, which had a "special style of songwriting" that gave their songs a "truly different feel."[43] For their part, Stiff Little Fingers were, in fact, long-term admirers of Gallagher. In a 2021 interview with *Spin*, frontman Jake Burns described Gallagher as his "initial inspiration" and discussed the life-changing experience of seeing Taste's Ulster Hall farewell concert on television in 1970:

> Seeing, and more importantly 'hearing' Taste changed my world. That guitar tone literally stopped me in my tracks. I really mean that. I was walking out of the room when they started playing 'Morning Sun' and I froze. "What WAS that? And how is he doing it?" I sat back down and within ten minutes or so had decided that I wanted to 'be' Rory Gallagher![44]

Immediately, 12-year-old Burns went out, bought a guitar and began to teach himself a repertoire of Gallagher songs, including 'Messin' with the Kid' and 'Walk on Hot Coals', which he described as "a bit above [his] pay grade at the time." Then, in 1977, Burns and his schoolmates formed Highway Star and regularly performed Gallagher covers, before discovering punk and changing their name to Stiff Little Fingers. In 1979, Stiff Little Fingers released their first album *Inflammable Material* on the independent label Rigid Digits. However, its swift success led them to sign their label to Chrysalis Records who also happened to be Gallagher's record company at the time. Through Chrysalis, the band were introduced to Gallagher who Burns describes as "charm and friendliness personified," recalling that the guitarist became "embarrassed" and said "oh, don't be like that" when Burns mentioned that he was a huge fan.[45]

Although Gallagher and Stiff Little Fingers did not move in the same circles, Burns kept in touch with Gallagher's brother Dónal. So, when guitarist Henry Cluney ran into trouble doing the guitar solo for 'Human Shield' on their 1991 comeback album *Flags and Emblems*, they decided the solution would be to get a "legend" in to complete it. In 2003's *Stiff Little Fingers Song by Song*, Burns said the following:

> I phoned Dónal Gallagher and said, 'Look, we're in the studio doing an album, we've got this track and I think it would sound fucking great with slide guitar on. For my money, the best slide guitar player on the planet is your brother - is there any chance he'd be interested?'[46]

Dónal relayed the message back to his brother and Gallagher, always keen to support Irish artists, agreed immediately.

Burns recalls Gallagher arriving with a whole van full of equipment, plugging in his guitar and doing his solo in just one take, which he describes as "astonishing." By all accounts, all Burns could do was stand and stare, thinking to himself, "Fuck me! That's Rory Gallagher!" He at least managed to pull himself together for long enough to ask Gallagher if he could buy him a drink afterwards.

In many ways, *Flags and Emblems* is a typical Stiff Little Fingers album with its blend of personal and political lyrics mixed with punk energy and catchy riffs. And 'Human Shield' is characteristic of this. It opens with a punchy guitar hook by Cluney, in a similar vein to Living Colour's 'Cult of Personality' released three years earlier, before bursting into touching lyrics that reflect the need to come together to overcome fear and hate.

Although the situation in Northern Ireland had much improved since Stiff Little Finger's 1978 release of 'Alternative Ulster' at the height of the Troubles, political unrest was still rife, with an attempted assassination of British prime minister John Major and his war cabinet by the IRA shortly before the release of *Flags and Emblems*. The topic of overcoming fear and hate was, therefore, still extremely relevant on a personal, Irish level and a view that Gallagher shared and was keen to advocate, even though he made it clear throughout his career that he never wrote political lyrics himself.

As Burns predicted, Gallagher's slide solo indeed improved the song and offered the missing component that they were looking for. The way that he builds the solo to a crescendo, before dropping back as Cluney retakes the opening riff is a stroke of genius. Burns still recalls the entire recording experience with Gallagher as "the thrill of a lifetime" for him. He speaks on behalf of many of those who collaborated with Gallagher in the studio, as we will continue in the next chapter.

LAO

Footnotes

1 'The Rory Gallagher Dave Fanning Interview 1980', https://www.youtube.com/watch?v=WNsbNT51MlQ
2 Shiv Cariappa, 'Wheeling and Dealing' (2003), http://www.roryon.com/donalshiv352.html
3 Bill Graham, 'Rory Gallagher: Revisiting his classic 1987 interview with Hot Press legend Bill Graham', *Hot Press* (17 July 2020), https://www.hotpress.com/music/rory-gallagher-revisiting-his-classic-1987-interview-with-hot-press-legend-bill-graham-22822714
4 Michael Leonard, 'The Spotlight Kid', *Guitar* (December 1998), https://www.roryon.com/spotlight.html
5 Colin Harper, 'Ballad of a Thin Man', *Mojo* (October 1998), http://www.roryon.com/mojo.html
6 Ibid.
7 Daniel Seah, 'The Best of Rory Gallagher to Feature a Rare Stones Cover with Jerry Lee Lewis', *Guitar* (20 August 2020), https://guitar.com/news/music-news/the-best-of-rory-gallagher-jerry-lee-lewis-satisfaction/
8 This does not include Gallagher's live contributions, such as Albert King *Live* (1977), Albert Collins & The Icebreakers *Jammin' with Albert* (1986) and *Live for Ireland* (1987).
9 Paul Charles, *Adventures in Wonderland* (Dublin: Hot Press, 2023), 117.
10 Newspaper clipping from https://www.facebook.com/RoryGallagher/photos/a.322997981806/10157427923706807
11 Ibid.
12 Interview with Juan Martín, 16 March 2023. All subsequent quotes from Martín come from the same interview.
13 Interestingly, harmonicist Mark Feltham was also on the sessions. He would go on to become a member of the Rory Gallagher Band later that year.
14 'Interview with JIM McCARTY (THE YARDBIRDS) – Part 1', *DME* (June 2014), https://dmme.net/interviews/interview-with-jim-mccarty-yardbirds-pt1.html
15 'Jump… to the Frogs' New LP', *Sandwell Evening Mail* (15 September 1984), 24.
16 'On the Comeback Trail…' *Nottingham Evening Post* (3 August 1984), 8.
17 Stephen Thomas Erlewine, 'Box of Frogs/Strange Land', https://www.allmusic.com/album/box-of-frogs-strange-land-mw0000089159
18 'Echoes in the Night Mercury/Polygram Press Release' (September 1985), https://www.procolharum.com/gb_echoes_press.htm
19 Interview with Matthew Fisher, 9 March 2023.
20 Todd Whitesel, 'Rory Gallagher: His Enduring Legacy', *Rock Cellar* (14 June 2014), https://www.rorygallagherfestival.com/latest-festival-news/rory-gallagher-his-enduring-legacy-rock-cellar-magazine
21 In the above cited interview, Dónal Gallagher states that the album was *Period of Transition* (1977). However, Rory Gallagher told Liam Fay of *Hot Press* ('Tangled Up in Blues', July 1992, http://www.roryon.com/Tangled.html) that it was *Wavelength*.
22 Later, during the recording of *Fresh Evidence*, Gallagher invited Morrison to play harmonica on 'Walkin' Wounded. Not forgetting the events of 1978, when Morrison entered the control room, Gallagher disappeared without saying where he was going. According to bassist Gerry McAvoy, Gallagher returned several hours later with a "wry smile" on his face. Morrison had left by then and never did play on the track.
23 Fay, 'Tangled Up in Blues'.
24 Paul Hightower, 'Box of Frogs – Box of Frogs/Strange Land' (1 March 2007), *Exposé Online*, http://expose.org/index.php/articles/display/box-of-frogs-box-of-frogs-strange-land-13.html
25 Carol Clerk, 'Life with Last Year's Model', *Melody Maker* (12 September 1981), http://www.roryon.com/model278.html
26 Ó Riada played a major role in reviving traditional Irish music, created an iconic film score for *Mise Éire* and composed the first Irish language mass. His mass setting was, in fact, Gallagher's favourite and his song 'Ag Críost an Síol' was performed by a choir at Gallagher's memorial service at Brompton Oratory, where the guitarist regularly attended mass (this was the first time that an Irish language song was performed there).
27 Fay, 'Tangled Up in Blues'.
28 Treacy Hogan, 'The Legend's Going Strong', *Irish Independent* (26 June 2004), 21.
29 Interview with PJ Curtis, 10 March 2023. All subsequent quotes from Curtis come from the same interview.
30 'Rory Gallagher: Tributes from Famous Friends', *Hot Press* (June 1995), https://www.hotpress.com/music/rory-gallagher-tributes-from-famous-friends-14356545
31 Interview with Brian Palm, 24 April 2023. All subsequent quotes from Palm come from the same interview.
32 Bill Graham, 'Rory Gallagher: Revisiting His Classic 1987 Interview with Hot Press Legend Bill Graham', *Hot Press* (17

Part 1 - *Guest Appearances and Collaborations 1984-1991*

July 2020), https://www.hotpress.com/music/rory-gallagher-revisiting-his-classic-1987-interview-with-hot-press-legend-bill-graham-22822714
33 'Rory Gallagher…'
34 'Rory Gallagher', *Record Collector* (August 1995), http://www.roryon.com/harper.html
35 Kenneth Kelleher, 'Interview from the London-Irish News', *London-Irish News* (December 1990), http://www.roryon.com/kenneth164.html
36 In 2001, Spillane teamed up with Barry McCabe, whose band Albatross had once toured with Gallagher, to compose an instrumental dedicated to his memory: 'The Emigrant'. According to McCabe, they recorded the track looking out at the Atlantic Ocean from Spillane's studio window. The sound of Spillane's whistle reminded McCabe of waves and made him think of all the Irish people who had to leave home and start a new life abroad, including Gallagher.
37 Phil Coulter, *Bruised, Not Broken* (Dublin: Gill Books, 2019), 204-206.
38 Ibid.
39 Ibid.
40 Dónal Gallagher, 'RIP Chris Barber', https://www.rorygallagher.com/rip-chris-barber/
41 Hal Horowitz, 'Ireland's Prodigal Blues Son', *Blues Review* (July/August 1999), http://www.roryon.com/br.html
42 Jan Foerster, 'Chris Barber & Band – The Outstanding Album', https://gallaghersblues.net/discography/chris_barber.outstanding.html
43 Hérve Picart, 'Eire de fête', *Best* (March 1982), http://www.roryon.com/Best233.html
44 Liza Lentini, 'What the World Needs Now', *Spin* (1 January 2021), https://www.spin.com/2021/01/jake-burns-stiff-little-fingers-interview/
45 Ali McMordie, '[INTERVIEW] STIFF LITTLE FINGERS Interview', *Subculture Entertainment* (31 January 2020), 'https://subcultureentertainment.com/2020/01/interview-stiff-little-fingers-interview/
46 Jake Burns and Alan Parker, *Stiff Little Fingers Song by Song* (London: Sanctuary Publishing Ltd, 2003), 133-134.

Part 1 - *Guest Appearances and Collaborations 1992-1995*

1.5 "A Great Holiday for Me": Guest Appearances and Collaborations, 1992-1995

'Barley and Grape Rag', **'Will the Circle Be Unbroken'**
(recorded for *30 Years A-Greying* by the Dubliners, 1992)

From the beginning of Gallagher's career, The Dubliners have closely followed. In a 1992 interview with *Hot Press*, Gallagher recalls his initial meeting with the group during his early adolescence.

> We were playing a show with Dickie Rock and The Miami Showband in the Savoy in Cork. And because we were way down the bill, we weren't even allowed to change in the dressing room. So we were out in the hall changing when Ronnie opened the door—The Dubliners were second on the bill so they had a room to themselves—and he said come on in and use our room with us. Luke was there and Ciaran Burke and all the rest and they were very nice. It was a small gesture but I'll never forget it.[1]

Over the years, a friendship grew between Gallagher and The Dubliners, leading to their London session in 1992. The Dubliners' *30 Years A-Greying* celebrated their 30th anniversary as musicians, and similar to their *25 Years Celebration* (1987), featured many special guests such as the Pogues, Billy Connolly, Hothouse Flowers and, of course, their good friend Rory Gallagher. The first track Gallagher played on was a reworking of his song 'Barley and Grape Rag', which originally appeared on his 1976 release *Calling Card*. Gallagher contributes harmonica, tambourine and acoustic guitar to the track, as well as sharing lead vocals with Ronnie Drew.

'Barley and Grape Rag' is sloppily arranged: solos weave throughout, laughter creeps in-between phrases and voices linger beneath the instrumentation. Instead of polished wood, the song is splintering bark, capturing the atmosphere of comrades rather than entertainers. As a result, us as listeners feel personally welcomed into this wonderfully improvised moment of musical gaiety. In contrast, Gallagher's harmonica playing on the country adaptation of an old Christian hymn, 'Will the Circle Be Unbroken', showcases his great emotional flexibility, this time a sorrowful echo of the song's lyrics: the funeral procession of the narrator's mother. Gallagher's use of the 'wah' technique imitates mournful cries, intensifying the duet between Drew and Eleanor Shanley.

In the 1995 documentary *Gallagher's Blues*, Ronnie Drew remarked upon the effect Gallagher had on him, claiming that he "didn't have the overconfidence that the mediocre have, [rather] he had the quiet unassuming way that the great have–and he was one of the greats."[2] Gallagher expressed a similar appreciation towards Drew. As stated in his December 1992 conversation with Uli Twelker, Gallagher's recurring desire to record an acoustic album was greatly spurred on by his session with The Dubliners. "I get on with [The Dubliners] so well. Those people are so kind," Gallagher said, contrasting the attitudes of the folk and rock world.[3] "The folkies are a lot more caring about people. The rock guys have so much ego and so many bloody trips going on… Folkies are not into the big bucks."[4] Overall, Gallagher's collaboration with The Dubliners is a strong beginning to a new musical pathway which, while prematurely concluded due to his untimely passing, showcased exciting potential.

'She Moved Thro' the Fair/Ann Cran Ull'
(recorded with Bert Jansch in 1993,
released posthumously on *Wheels Within Wheels*, 2003)

Throughout his career, Gallagher often cited Bert Jansch as an influence, as heard on compositions such as 'Just the Smile' on his self-titled debut. Additionally, Gallagher once listed Jansch's *Birthday Blues* (1969) as one of his favourite records. The chance to collaborate with the guitarist took place late in Gallagher's life and had even flown under the radar for his brother and manager Dónal. Catching up with Jansch in 2003, Dónal was made aware of an unfinished recording from 1993. Jansch offered to finish the track, and it was included on the *Wheels Within Wheels* compilation later that year. The Irish traditional 'She Moved Through the Fair/Ann Cran Ull" has been covered by a range of artists and, therefore, transformed through frequent interpretation, from lyrical appropriation (Paddy Tunney, for example) to the basis for instrumentals ('White Summer' by The Yardbirds). Here, Gallagher and Jansch trade lilting guitar lines, with simple yet effective embellishments.

Gallagher had hoped to bring in folk singer Anne Briggs for the final recording. He had even sent her a tape but, according to Jansch, she assumed that Gallagher was a "pop star" and "rejected it out of hand."[5] Jansch instead suggested Maggie Boyle, who agreed and came down to London especially to meet Gallagher, but he did not show up, having seemingly "[drawn] a blank" and forgotten that it was arranged. Unfortunately, by this point, Jansch grew "disheartened" and gave up on the project, describing it as a "palaver" to have to constantly go through Dónal to speak to Gallagher.

'Bratacha Dubha'
(recorded with Martin Carthy in 1994,
released posthumously on *Wheels Within Wheels*, 2003)

Part 1 - *Guest Appearances and Collaborations 1992-1995*

Another unexpected discovery for Dónal was the incomplete version of 'Bratacha Dubha' on a discarded tape machine, featuring Gallagher playing with Martin Carthy. For the release of *Wheels Within Wheels*, Carthy cleaned up his guitar parts, while Dónal brought in harp/guitar duo Máire Ní Chathasaigh and Chris Newman to complete the track. Dónal insisted Chathasaigh and Newman feature, as the pairs' show at the Troubadour was the final gig that his brother attended. Chathasaigh's rendition 'Carolan's Farewell to Music', a favourite of Gallagher's, was played at his funeral. Gallagher's elegant arrangement of the traditional tune shows a departure from blues to what Dónal characterises in the album's liner notes as "almost like Irish-Elizabethan music," indicating the guitarist's persistent (as well as unexplored) musical curiosities.[6] To read more about Gallagher's friendship with Carthy, see 3.2.

'Remember My Name'
(recorded for *Pain Killer* by Energy Orchard, 1995)

"Rory Gallagher was a big influence in music in Belfast," Kevin Breslin, keyboardist for Belfast group Energy Orchard, recalled in our interview with him in April 2022, "People had a great affinity with Rory."[7] From his brief residence in the early Taste days to playing the Ulster Hall regularly throughout the Troubles, Belfast was a place always close to Gallagher's heart—and this connection only strengthens when we delve into his 1994 recording session with the band Energy Orchard. The group formed in the late 1980s and, following a few years developing their sound through live performances around London, they released their first single titled 'Belfast', written by bass player Joby Fox.

In the early half of 2022, we reached out to Fox and asked about Gallagher's influence on the band. He shared with us his "electrifying [and] religious experience" of watching Gallagher perform live at the Ulster Hall.[8] When forming Energy Orchard with Bap Kennedy, Fox remembers "Rory [being] around." However, "I was star struck, [and] I wasn't really able to talk to him... which is unusual for me to say the least [laughs]." Unfortunately, following the release of 'Belfast' (1990), Fox parted ways with Energy Orchard and, therefore, was absent on the session for 'Remember My Name' with Gallagher.

Kevin Breslin's career in music began when he moved to London and became involved in the group 10 Past 7, along with Spade McQuade and Bap Kennedy. Together with percussionist David Toner and guitarist Paul Toner, 10 Past 7 would eventually reform into Energy Orchard. Musician Steve Earle discovered the group during one of their many gigs in London. "His wife was a Vice President of MCA," Breslin explained, "so we ultimately sang to MCA through that connection." Energy Orchard would sign to MCA Records in 1990, achieving critical laud for their debut album and embarking on an extensive touring schedule. By 1994, the group had released two other albums (1992's *Stop the Machine* and *Shinola* in 1993) and, as Breslin described, "we were becoming a musician's musician band [due to the fact that] quite a few people [wanted] to play on some of our songs."

One of these people included Rory Gallagher, who, according to Breslin, "got a message through [to us] saying he would like to come in and play on one of the tracks. So, of course, we jumped up and down and went 'yeah, great, brilliant!'" The sessions for 'Remember My Name' occurred towards the final stages of what would be known as the album *Pain Killer* (released in 1995), with the entire evening dedicated to Gallagher to suggest and record whatever he felt suitable for the track:

> [Rory] was just a lovely guy. I call him the gentle man of rock & roll because he was. He was just such a gentleman. [During the 1994 session] he had this thing where you had to take your shoes off and the shoes had to go together a certain way, and then [he would say] 'it's good luck'. So I think I took my shoes off and put them the same way for him [laughs].

For most of the session, Gallagher stayed in the studio and made minimal visits to the control room, preferring to get as many different ideas down on tape for the band to select from. Gallagher contributes guitar, harmonica and Dobro to the song, each layer complementing the initial rhythm track provided by the group. To Breslin's recollection, the addition of the Dobro was Gallagher's idea, which all members agreed lifted the song.

As highlighted in the book introduction, Gavin Martin negatively framed Gallagher's session with Energy Orchard in his 2011 article 'The Man Who Sweated Rock N Roll' for *Record Collector*. Martin drew upon Bap Kennedy's descriptions of Gallagher as "mad [and] bizarre" during the session, enhancing this misguided portrayal of the guitarist as passive, inward and even distant during his later career. Contrastingly, our discussion with Breslin uncovers a different and—most notably—*positive* perspective:

> [Rory] took a break and came [into the control room and] started talking to me about keyboards he liked. He loved the Rhodes piano sound, and Hammond sound. He was really into that, chatting away. And then he'd go back [into the studio] and say 'alright, let's move onto another section'.

Although playing on another artist's song, Breslin noticed that Gallagher "took a great interest in 'Remember My Name', and he wanted to make sure that what he was playing was not for the sake of playing, but that it worked out best for the song." Following a fruitful session, Energy Orchard crossed paths with Gallagher again in 1995 when they supported him on his final tour. We pick up their story in 3.3.

'Leaving Town Blues', 'Show-biz Blues'
(recorded for *Rattlesnake Guitar:
The Music of Peter Green*, 1995)

In his official statement following Peter Green's passing in 2020, Dónal Gallagher brought to light the bond between his brother and Green, beginning in the Taste days: "[Rory] was very fond and an admirer of Peter, and they enjoyed each other's company."[9] When attending a Doors gig at the Camden Roundhouse, Dónal recalled Gallagher and Green engaging in conversation for most of the night, and so when news reached Gallagher in 1994 that Peter Green's health was declining, he readily accepted the opportunity to pay tribute to an old friend.

Rattlesnake Guitar: The Music of Peter Green was released in 1995 and featured an array of musical legends, including Jethro Tull's Ian Anderson, Arthur Brown, Billy Sheehan and the Yardbirds' Jim McCarty. A portion of the profits generated from album sales was donated to the Willie Dixon Blues Heaven Foundation, which was established in 1981 by the blues artist himself to help preserve the blues tradition and publications. In a retrospective review following the 2003 album rerelease under the title *Peter Green Songbook (A Tribute to His Work in Two Volumes)*, critic Michael Fremer praised the musicianship and production, claiming "this record is not to be missed both because of the stinging performances and the superb sound."[10]

Gallagher's session for the Peter Green tribute album has always been of great interest to us, but we were initially disheartened by the scarce information about these wonderful recordings. Part of the mystery was lifted when we ordered the highly recommended book *Rory Gallagher: 25th Memorial Edition* published by Shinko Music Entertainment, which highlights Gallagher's tours in Japan (1974, 1975, 1977, 1991). The final chapter of the book ('In Rory's Later Years') showcases the photographs taken of Gallagher by his close friend Shu Tomioka, some of which—to our delight—were previously unseen images of the Peter Green tribute session. In late April 2022, we reached out to Shu Tomioka, and he graciously agreed to help us on our mission to gain further insight into these two tracks.

Tomioka was born in Tokyo, Japan, and began his career as a freelance photographer in 1985. When moving to London in 1990, Tomioka would take pictures of many of the live acts he saw regularly, before getting in contact with the organisers of a benefit gig at the 100 Club for the saxophonist Dick Heckstall-Smith and asking to photograph the event. On the night, Tomioka photographed a number of British musicians, leading to an article for Japan's *Record Collectors* magazine about the show. Eventually, his own column called 'Portraits in British Rock' was created for the magazine, which Tomioka has run since 1993 to the present day. Tomioka's aims for the articles are to "highlight some of the musicians who don't usually take centre stage, yet make an enormous contribution to British rock."[11]

Through the benefit concert for Dick Heckstall-Smith, Tomioka made friendships with many names in the music world, including Cream's Jack Bruce and lyricist Pete Brown. When Brown was producing the Peter Green tribute album, Tomioka was appointed as the official photographer of the sessions. According to Tomioka, Gallagher came in on the second session for the album, which occurred at the Roundhouse venue in London:

> On 30th May, 1994, I met Rory face to face for the first time. Because he loved Japan we clicked immediately and had a nice chat. He was friendly and even invited me to visit him in [the] Conrad Hotel in Chelsea Harbour to make an article [for the 'Portraits of British Rock' series]... In the dark area of the studio there was his beloved Stratocaster, white Telecaster, Dobro, 12 string Stellar acoustic, old Japanese TEISCO guitar, and a flat mandolin. Rory kindly let me play his Stratocaster. That was like my dream came true... Later I became a good friend of [Rory's long-time roadie] Tom [O'Driscoll], [and] he told me that he was watching me playing the Strat closely in case I made a scratch on it!

On the initial session, drummer Richard Newman joined Gallagher in the studio and, as Tomioka remembers, they were musically a "strong [and] powerful unit." The second (and final) session was a month later on 18 June and was primarily devoted to completing overdubs. On this occasion, keyboardist John Cooke was brought in, as well as two female vocalists. Tomioka recalled the name of one, Deborah Welch, who was on the chorus. On the official release, Gallagher did not include the female voices, though it is interesting to note his experimentation with vocal textures here, absent in his earlier studio work.

> This session was harder and took a long time. Pete Brown and the co-producer John Mackenzie took Rory to a nearby pub for a break. Rory asked me to come along and I took the pictures of them chatting together at the bar. Rory also chatted to other customers at the bar who were keen to talk to him about his music. He was always happy to talk about his music with his fans whenever they approached him.

Also present in the studio was cameraman and close friend of Gallagher, Rudi Gerlach, who filmed parts of the session. On his website (now run by Volker Grupe), Gerlach has mentioned that the session lasted well after he retired to his hotel room, with Gallagher slipping a note underneath his door that read he had just returned from the studio at 5:45AM.

As Gallagher always did when covering an artist, he made the songs his own. 'Leaving Town Blues' originally appeared on the 1971 compilation album *The Original Fleetwood Mac*, which featured outtakes of the first line-up of the group from 1967-1968. The arrangement is minimal, with Peter Green's soft vocals drifting in-between the fiddle melody and clear guitar line. Gallagher updates 'Leaving Town Blues' with multiple layers of instrumentation, from mandolin to the Dobro and electric guitar (Gallagher's technique here on slide is powerfully screeching in some places of the track). Richard Newman's use of the drum brush and prominent beat on the kick drum offers a hypnotic backdrop to Gallagher's interweaving guitar lines, generating a bluegrass feel. Despite the maturing of his voice, Gallagher's singing still showcases impressive emotional range, from a whimper ("Got the blues so bad, baby") to a growl ("Operator, operator, operator").

'Show-biz Blues' featured on the 1969 album *Then Play On*, which was the last Fleetwood Mac album with founder Peter Green. The original is poignantly arranged, with sweeping rhythm guitar, tambourine and bass. Alternatively, in the 1994 version Gallagher, again, colours his version with layers of sound, including keyboards, electric guitar, tambourine and shakers, hard-hitting drums and overdubbed vocals.

'Raga for G.M. Volonté', 'Voices from the Bazaar'
(recorded in 1994 for *Phoenician Dream* by Roberto Manes, released posthumously in 1999).

On his 1999 album *Phoenician Dream*, Roberto Manes fuses violin with tabla percussions to create a harmonious blend of jazz, blues and Eastern influences. On 22 December 1994, Gallagher guested on two tracks for the album. Manes shared his high praise for Gallagher in the album's liner notes, describing him as "one of those rare people in whom art and life combine as one... [with] tremendous inner strength and belief." Manes added brief comments about the collaboration, reflecting on the contrast between how anxious Gallagher was in the studio compared to the "absolute calmness" he felt afterwards. Sadly, Gallagher passed away before the titles of either track were finalised, but he had told Manes that he wanted to dedicate one of them ('Raga for G.M. Volonté') to his favourite actor Gian Maria Volonte, who had died earlier that month, and the other to the spirit of a street market in Africa ('Voices from the Bazaar').

Since our first listen to these recordings, they have undoubtedly stayed with us, even haunted us, if you will. We did not know where to begin with our analysis, our minds carried off on this rich musical voyage, and yet whenever we tried to pen these thoughts, our fingertips froze over the laptop keyboard. The music we heard was grandiose, yet organic, somehow foreign, yet addictively inviting. The chemistry between Gallagher, Roberto Manes and percussionist Pete Lockett is explosive, very passionate and respectful, one talent does not dominate the other; together, all three elegantly fuse. We were entranced by how they crescendo as effortlessly as they simmer in 'Raga for G.M. Volonté' or how we could taste every flavour from spice to grain then dirt in 'Voices from the Bazaar'. Every influence seemed to creep into Gallagher's playing, from Celtic to Delta blues to flamenco, and when combined with Manes' graceful lines on the violin and Lockett's fluctuating and expressive rhythms, the music created sharply contrasts to anything Gallagher had previously recorded. As we continued to listen and digest the sounds, our curiosity grew to the point of contacting both Roberto Manes and Pete Lockett in April 2022, eager to learn more about this collaboration.

To our excitement (and surprise), Manes and Lockett expressed great interest in participating in our project. During our conversation, we found Manes to be extremely warm, both of us in awe of his wisdom and enthusiasm to tell his story. We rarely had to prompt him with questions, one memory sparking a series of others, as we quietly listened. In 1990, Manes relocated from his birthplace in Milan to London after he was offered a publishing deal with Warner Chappell

Music. This presented many musical opportunities for him, including forming his own band. "My style was jazz-rock fusion, so it was a band but it was instrumental, it wasn't pop or rock with a singer," Manes told us and, instead of a person, "the violin would be the singing part."[12] In addition to his group, Manes worked on various projects at this time, including regular session work for television and movies, collaborating with artists in the studio, as well as joining a separate band to his own, which covered American songs and featured a singer from Texas. It was around this time in the early 1990s that Manes and Gallagher crossed paths:

> So, [the band which covered American songs] played in a club, a nightclub I would call it, on Fulham Road, and that's where Rory Gallagher used to live. He had a little–on the corner there–he had a little apartment [...] But how we met was one night we had this gig in this club called The Polo, as in the Polo sweets, like that one. In fact, they had those little sweets on the bar as well.

> [...] So that club I think it just opened late, like it would open when the pubs would close... We would start and play at night, around midnight [or] one o'clock in the morning at that place [...] So what happened is that at that gig Rory was there [...] he was there for his enjoyment [...] [and] it was handy for him to come down from his apartment and just go there and have a couple of hours there. I believe he enjoyed the gig, and particularly enjoyed my playing because after the gig we ended up having a chat. Of course I knew him from before because I knew Rory Gallagher–I even had [a couple of Rory's albums] in my vinyl collection in Milan.

Manes was unsure as to whether he was playing with his own band or the American covers band when he met Gallagher for the first time at The Polo. However, he recalls that he continued to see Gallagher at that particular club on different occasions, and he was complimentary of both bands:

> We clicked from the start [...] most of us when [we] meet someone new somehow you do connect or you don't, most of us are like that, and in the case of Rory and I we alchemised entirely from the very beginning. I could feel he was entirely connected to me, despite the fact my English wasn't very good [...] so it was beyond words, it was a connection on a musical level definitely; we had a similar way of doing music, especially the soloing.

One of the features from Gallagher's musicianship, which Manes strongly related to, was his natural sense of improvisation. "My violin playing has always been based on improvisations," Manes explained, which attracted him to the form of jazz, "and [on the *Phoenician Dream* collaboration with Rory and Pete] it was entirely improvised. We didn't decide anything, which is like the jazz mentality, and it was one take." Soon after meeting Gallagher, an acquaintance developed into a special friendship, which we could sense from Manes' words, was a friendship still very dear to his heart:

> I asked [Rory] at some point if he wanted to come and join me [on some of the *Phoenician Dreams* recordings]. I mentioned I had a friend playing the percussion [Pete Lockett] and I thought it could work altogether... I don't remember whether I played him something before, [such as] previous recordings and then he heard the percussionist, or he just trusted my word and then he popped in with his guitar. I don't remember exactly how I presented [the idea]... but he did come. It wasn't very early [in the day], but he did come [laughs].

Manes shared many details about this "smooth" collaboration, from the close privacy of the studio ("It was just Rory, Peter Lockett, the sound engineer [Andy Fryer] and me") to the talk outside the studio, "in the corridor [and] office doors, [because] they were aware that we had Rory Gallagher... because he was quite a legend, I would call it." Manes continues:

> We didn't rehearse or anything... I allowed Rory–of course, he was the guest, and I want to be the host–and I said, 'you go, you start', and we follow you, I follow you, Pete follow you... So we just follow, and create the sound together. And I think Rory was the only one who did a couple of overdubs afterwards, but not because of mistakes, just because he wanted to add some slide guitar and then he wanted to have some harmonica, [which] you will hear at some point [slide is on both tracks, and harmonica on 'Voices from the Bazaar'].

> [Rory] was very kind. I would even use the words tender and sweet. But a couple of times I did see him upset. I remember once he even called me in the middle of the night, [and] he wasn't too impressed with Warner postponing the release of what we did. He wanted to have it happen. Actually, he wanted to get them to help me more. I remember he found me possibly [a] very soft type of person, but I perceived him as a soft person, but then he told me in the middle of the night... 'Roberto, sometimes we have to get tough'. So I suppose ... if he was disappointed, he could tell you.

Manes remembers Gallagher as "also very clever, intelligent, curious [and] a cultural person." When listening to the *Phoenician Dream* recordings, Manes recalled Gallagher referring to a specific passage of his violin playing as "'very Prokofiev', and [Sergio] Prokofiev is a famous Russian composer. So that means he knew not just *his* work."[13]

As our conversation with Manes drew to a close, we felt we could have listened to him for another hour or so. When we reflect on our meeting with Manes years later, one passage distinguishes itself from the others, prompting re-evaluation of our relationship with Gallagher's music. When putting on that first Rory Gallagher album, we never predicted that we would come into contact with each other, form a friendship and create a blog site that would eventually transform into the book you read today. Each of these events has had a major impact on our personal and professional lives. We never forced the fate of Gallagher into our lives; he naturally fell into it.

> Somehow I felt that we were on the same wavelength [...] because I believe that somehow things happen magically in your life, you know? And [Rory] believed in the same way. You don't force things to happen. If you are ready, things open and the connections are there also, it's not you forcing them. And this philosophy of mine, it's just been with me all my life. And I find it [...] was also Rory's mentality; he had exactly the same thing. He believed it was magic, really [...] And when I see how my career went, somehow I can tell it's all happening, I never forced anything, [like] meeting Rory. Some people would queue [to meet Rory], but for me it was just natural [...] I think he was a free spirit, so [we were] very similar.

When we contacted Pete Lockett in early 2022, he preferred to write a collection of memories for us to include and so, with his permission, we conclude our review of *Phoenician Dream* with these insightful reflections:

> I recall this recording very clearly. It was early in my career and to be in the situation to not only record with the great legend of Rory Gallagher but to also collaborate, improvise and compose with him as well. It was a massive honour. One always approaches such a situation with an air of caution. There is no way of knowing the personality type of the person you will be working with. There are some massive egos out there and getting caught in that steam is wholly unpleasant. Thankfully, Rory was the complete opposite. An absolute gentleman. Down to Earth, polite and to my amazement, not standing behind any ego whatsoever. Being so incredibly sensitive, one might even say he was a little vulnerable. In my humble opinion, artists who allow this degree of 'feeling' can really get into the emotionally creative side of music making in a much more intense and meaningful way.

> The studio was one of those old Warner Chappell studios upstairs off the back of Oxford Street in London. A pretty unassuming small studio for such a personal collaboration. It was the perfect fit. We spent the day exploring a few different set ups and improvisational approaches and went with the flow. Rory was great at 'allowing' it to happen and let the music grow organically from the situation. Seeing how he thought and felt about the energy and music was incredibly inspiring and truly pulled out the best from Roberto and

myself. Once his 'sound' kicked it was like being pulled into an infinite musical vortex. I honestly had never experienced anything like that before. Words are poor messengers in conveying exactly how that manifested. It was not long after this that Rory sadly passed away. It was devastating to realise that he was gone and that his a priori energy was only going to remain with us as recordings and audio.

I have been lucky to have worked with a lot of great performers over the years. Two really stand out for me are Rory and Steve Gadd. They both had that incredible degree of 'purity'. In creating with them you become intensely aware of the 'gravity' they generated. They pulled you into their orbit in such an inspiring way that tuned in all your receptors and allowed your creative integrity to remain perfectly intact. It's a rare thing indeed.[14]

'Falsely Accused'
(recorded for *Strangers on the Run* by Samuel Eddy,
aka Eamonn McCormack, 1995).

As we began our research for this particular session, we discovered Rory Gallagher's impact on Eamonn McCormack to be undeniably clear, with the majority of his interviews mentioning Gallagher at least three or four times. McCormack became an immediate fan at eleven years of age when he came across a Gallagher concert playing on television. He first met his musical idol backstage at the 1982 Punchestown Festival in Ireland, with the two establishing a proper relationship a few years later when McCormack was touring around America and bumped into Gallagher in Los Angeles. Reflecting in December 1995, McCormack admitted that "[Rory and I] became closest throughout the last six months of his life"[15] and, between long phone conversations, Gallagher participated in one of his final recordings, which would be released in September of that year on McCormack's album *Strangers on the Run* (later rereleased on 2012's *Kindred Spirits* under his given name).

Strangers On the Run was McCormack's second release under his stage name Samuel Eddy and helped to establish him as an artist in Ireland after touring across the Continent and America for many years. The first mention of collaboration between McCormack and Gallagher surfaced publicly in Eamon Carr's column for Dublin's *Evening Herald,* where McCormack recalls a rare day off from his band's busy touring schedule in December 1992. "We crossed paths with Rory Gallagher in Bremen. We went to his gig and he was great," McCormack said.[16] The two friends hung out following the concert, where Gallagher brought up McCormack's recent work with guitarist Jan Akkerman (both as a support act and in the studio) and teasingly asked "what about me?" The idea was left up in the air. "We might get together in Ireland, [but] we've got to sort things out," McCormack confirmed to Carr at the conclusion of his 1993 article, until a session was scheduled for January 1995 shortly after New Year's Day.

In 'Falsely Accused', McCormack coolly talks us through the injustice of Billy Ray, a man at the wrong place and wrong time during a holdup in a gas station and, as a result, becomes "suspect number one" to the police. The lyrics and mood allude to the many plotlines from some of Gallagher's favourite detective stories and, therefore, it is not too surprising that he agreed to collaborate on this particular track. In an interview with Gallagher from December 1994, journalist Jip Golsteijn conjures up a sensitive portrait of a man in physical decline ("a bit uncertain on his legs," "difficulty composing a swollen face into a smile," and "his eyes don't join").[17] However, on 'Falsely Accused', for someone clearly fighting a physical (and mental) battle, there is not a trace of evidence to suggest that Gallagher is in a musical decline. From trading fiery solos with McCormack following the second chorus and towards the conclusion of the song, to providing electrifying suspense with slide interludes in the fourth verse ("silence in the courthouse, feel the atmosphere, jury passed the verdict…"), Gallagher proves that not only can he keep up with young talent, but that he is *still* young talent himself.

In another interview with *Evening Herald* reporter Eamon Carr, McCormack talks about the "tremendous experience" of watching Gallagher transform from a "shy, somewhat nervous" demeanour when arriving at the studio, to then putting on his guitar and "[becoming] larger than life."[18] McCormack adds, "The whole studio shook with the sound. [Rory] was ten years younger. He was jumping around and you could feel the experience he had." We as the listener can gain a sense of Gallagher's enjoyment from not only his guitar playing, but his animated shouts in the background which echo some of McCormack's verses. McCormack confirms in Carr's article that Gallagher participated in every aspect of the session and showcased his wisdom in the studio, from "telling the sound engineer what graphics to change for sound," to "pushing me on the vocals… he even changed a few of the words for me before I sang it." As a final point in Carr's article, McCormack highlights the far-reaching influence of Gallagher:

> It's only when you travel that you realise how big Rory was, and how respected he was. He moved and influenced a lot of people to take up guitar. I don't think he himself realised the impact he had on musicians, not just Irish ones, but throughout the world.

Although many decades have now passed, Gallagher's impression on McCormack's life has not diminished. In a 2018 interview for a Dutch music blog, McCormack was asked to name his favourite collaboration throughout his career:

> Well, as always top of the list is my old friend and hero Rory Gallagher. Rory is always the most special one. I do what I do because of Rory. He owns a part of every note I play.[19]

To commemorate the 25th anniversary of Gallagher's death in 2020, McCormack was invited to play at the International Online Tribute Concert, along with acts such as Dom Martin and Paul Rose. McCormack told *Blues* magazine that he was honoured to be involved in the event.

Musical Cubism: Striving for Success in the Studio
This two-part essay originally appeared as a post in April 2022 on our blog *Rewriting Rory*. When preparing the article, we were, quite frankly, alarmed by the lack of information and analysis in literature regarding Rory Gallagher's session work from 1985-1995. If mentioned, then these sessions take on the format of a footnote, and we might be lucky if there is a whisper of acknowledgement in documentaries. We are reminded of the quote mentioned in the introduction of this book from Colin Harper in the *Mojo* obituary for Gallagher, "[Rory's] life was coming full circle."[20] As we have argued, unfortunate commentary such as Harper's has led to a 'rise and fall' pattern in Gallagher's story, and his creative accomplishments during the latter half of his life have been swept up in it.

Assumptions have been made that, due to a steep reduction of studio output, releasing only three albums (excluding the shelved *Torch*) in the final 15 years of his life, Gallagher had officially retreated—he had, in Brendan O'Neill's words, "concluded his life [and] maybe felt it was time."[21] However, if anything, 'Part One: In The Studio' reveals Gallagher broadening his musical horizons and ambitions, in spite of his struggle to overcome physical and mental health battles. We hear in his final recordings Gallagher participating in a diverse range of music: new wave rock (Energy Orchard), country blues (tribute to Peter Green), eastern and jazz (Roberto Manes and Pete Lockett) and raunchy blues (Eamonn McCormack). Furthermore, this section highlights Gallagher stepping into the role of mentor, particularly to Manes and McCormack, as they navigated the unsteady waters of the music industry.

In a 1985 interview for *Guitarist* magazine, Gallagher was asked what he would be doing ten years from now. He reflected that he wanted to do "the same thing really – perhaps in a more accomplished way," singling out "more success in the studio" as a particular aim.[22] Although often thought of as a live performer, throughout his career, Gallagher strived to 'succeed' in the studio and leave a legacy on record. In his final decade, this ambition intensified, and he dedicated growing amounts of time to recording, whether with his band or as a guest musician. "Something happens to you when you go into recording studios quite often," he told Vivian Campbell in 1991, "A lot of song writing ideas hit you, because the equipment's set up, the tapes are hot, the lights are on, you're in the mood, and it's like you're in a factory."[23]

In other words, Gallagher's attitude to the studio was shifting; he felt increasingly inspired, excited and even reinvigorated by the musical possibilities of the setting and had really come into his own as an experienced and knowledgeable recording musician. As Roberto Manes told us, Gallagher was taking constant inspiration from the "new sounds" and "fresh energy" around him. Who knows what he would have gone on to achieve and with whom he would have worked?

So, we have to shake our heads as we read Colin Harper's words 'full circle' because Gallagher's life was not even *mid* circle. Instead, we read of a musician progressing from his, if you will, blues to Cubist period, and in any other universe the stars would have lined up, but sadly Rory Gallagher's body gave out before another destiny could take its course.

RM

Footnotes

1 Liam Fay, 'Tangled up in Blues', *Hot Press* (July 1992), http://www.roryon.com/Tangled.html
2 'Gallagher's Blues documentary(Full documentary)', https://www.youtube.com/watch?v=VZ1E3LFN3XM
3 Uli Twelker, 'Rory Gallagher: Good Times', *Good Times* (March 1993), http://www.roryon.com/uli209.html
4 Ibid.
5 Colin Harper, 'Rory Gallagher: Requiem for a Guitar Hero', *Irish Folk, Trad & Blues: A Secret History* (London: Cherry Red Books, 2004), 240.
6 Gallagher included the song as an extended introduction to 'Tattoo'd Lady' at his concert in Bremen, Germany on 10 December 1992.
7 Interview with Kevin Breslin, 10 April 2022. All subsequent quotes from Breslin come from this interview.
8 Interview with Joby Fox, 3 April 2022.
9 Dónal Gallagher, 'RIP Peter Green' (25 July 2020), https://www.rorygallagher.com/rip-peter-green/
10 Michael Fremer, 'Legendary Guitar Great Peter Green Feted By All-Star Cast', *Analog Planet* (1 November 2005), https://www.analogplanet.com/content/legendary-guitar-great-peter-green-feted-all-star-cast-0
11 Interview with Shu Tomioka, 24 April 2022. All subsequent quotes from Tomioka come from this interview.
12 Interview with Roberto Manes, 27 April 2022. All subsequent quotes from Manes come from this interview.
13 Manes' comment is unsurprising to us as Gallagher's curiosity for classical music has been documented, e.g. during the band's jam session in Cork for the *Irish Tour '74* documentary film, Gallagher is shown trying to learn the chords with Lou Martin from Mozart's Piano Sonata No. 11: III Alla Turca.
14 Email exchange with Pete Lockett, 22 April 2022.
15 'Albums, Guest Appearances. Samuel Eddy: Strangers on the Run', *Gallagher's Blues*, https://gallaghersblues.net/discography/samuel_eddy.strangers.html
16 Eamon Carr, 'Sam's D.I.Y. Triumph', *Evening Herald* (29 January 1993), 22.
17 Jip Golsteijn, 'Popscore', *De Telegraaf* (7 January 1995), https://www.roryon.com/tele214.htm
18 Eamon Carr, 'Who's Eddy?', *Evening Herald* (5 September 1995), 21.
19 Anneke Schrijft, 'Interview with Blues-Rock Guitarist Eamonn McCormack', *Anneke Schrijf* (24 August 2018), https://annekeschrijft.com/2018/08/24/interview-with-blues-rock-guitarist-eamonn-mccormack/
20 Colin Harper, 'Rory Gallagher (1948-1995)', *Mojo* (August 1995), http://www.roryon.com/colin.html
21 'Gallagher's Blues…'
22 Bob Hewitt, 'Rory Gallagher', *Guitarist* (February 1985), https://www.roryon.com/guit231.htm
23 Viv Campbell, 'The Wearing of the Blues', *Guitar for the Practicing Musician* (August 1991), http://www.roryon.com/guitar91.html

Part 2: On the Stage 1985-1991

2.1 Teenage Renegade Fever: The 1985 Tour of Yugoslavia and Hungary

In early January 1985, simple black and white posters began to spring up across some of the major cities in Yugoslavia and Hungary. From Maribor to Miskolc, Belgrade to Budapest, advertisements bombastically announced a spectacular concert from "THE GREATEST GUITARIST OF BLUES ROCK." Just a few years before, Alvin Lee had been promoted as the "Hero of Woodstock" and Chuck Berry as the "Prince of Rock & Roll," leading local newspapers to joke that the forthcoming concerts of Jethro Tull and Deep Purple would be marketed as the "Champion One-Legged Flautist" and "The Deepest Purple Orchestra of the Universe."[1] But in the case of Rory Gallagher, journalists were largely in agreement: this bold epithet was not an exaggeration. Those who immediately queued to buy tickets also believed that this grandiose statement was not far from the truth. Many of these fans had watched Gallagher from afar since the days of Taste and, in the case of Yugoslavia, had followed him on Radio Luxembourg and the popular *Rockpalast* broadcasts. Now, their time had finally come to see this "living rock legend"[2] in the flesh.

Yugoslavia was not exactly a rock-starved country (it had always maintained a strong relationship with the West and consistently welcomed foreign acts from the 1970s onwards), but since the death of President Tito in 1980, constitutional tensions and political dissidence had been on the rise, threatening its vibrant musical ecosystem. Hungary, on the other hand, had been governed by the Hungarian Socialist Workers' Party since 1949, which was under the influence of the Soviet Union, meaning that rock music had been historically condemned by the authorities and local groups were subject to censorship by a Song Committee. While the 1980s saw a steady relaxation in rules, with increasingly accepted visits from international groups (e.g. Dire Straits, Queen), such visits remained few and far between.

For Gallagher, no political, religious or ethnic divides were going to prevent him from bringing his music to the masses. His ambitious 1985 tour would see him play six dates in modern-day Slovenia, Croatia, Serbia and Bosnia (Maribor, Ljubljana, Zagreb, Belgrade, Novi Sad and Sarajevo), as well as four dates in Hungary (Pécs, Budapest, Miskolc and Debrecen). According to Gallagher's brother Dónal, the guitarist took it in his stride and was not concerned with the potential significance of his act. "That was just Rory's way [...] he just liked doing that for the kids,"[3] he later told the *Dallas Observer*. Gallagher was, in fact, thinking more about the opportunity to soak up the Cold War atmosphere first-hand, given his fascination with detective novels and undercover agents.[4]

The tour was an overwhelming success, with concert halls full of a "teenage-renegade excitement" that Gallagher fed off to "whip the audience into a complete frenzy."[5] At a time when other European countries had forgotten about Gallagher or poked fun at his 'tired' blues, Yugoslavia and Hungary—thrilled at the opportunity to see a music icon on home soil—welcomed him with open arms. When Gallagher hit town, "all barriers crumbled like a house of cards"[6] and his "instinctive musicianship"[7] made it clear that—regardless of music trends, age or physical appearance—he still represented *the* ultimate live experience.

Tussles and Tensions

As far back as 1974, Gallagher had stated that he would love to play "behind the Iron Curtain"[8] one day because nobody else was willing to perform there. He achieved that goal very early on when, in 1976, he was invited by the Polish Jazz Society to perform three dates in Warsaw, Katowice and Gdansk. Although Poland was under Communist rule at the time, the country had a more liberal attitude to youth culture than its neighbours. Furthermore, its censorship policy was openly contested by intellectuals and undermined by foreign radio and television broadcasts and *samizdat* (the clandestine distribution of government-suppressed literature), which led to a burgeoning rock scene in the 1960s. Gallagher's concerts were, therefore, sanctioned by the Polish government, his Irish nationality also making them more sympathetic towards him. Nonetheless, they were not without difficulties; the *politburo* ordered Gallagher not to play any encores and, when Dónal argued in support of his brother, his passport was confiscated and he was detained for one week.

Despite this drama with the authorities, Gallagher's performance and down-to-earth nature quickly won over the Polish public, with fans delighting at the fact that he dressed in a pair of Polish-bought jeans and check shirt, drank Polish beer and asked them about historical places to visit in the country. Speaking about the concerts in *Rock* magazine in 1977, Gallagher noted that the audience was "awfully quiet [...] very attentive and extremely polite."[9] Always one to play down the importance of his actions, he also stated that he did not view performing in Poland as "that much different" from performing anywhere else in the world. Decades later, drummer Rod De'Ath reflected on the Polish concert for the *Stagestruck* fanzine and how the crowd had "not seen and heard anything like us before."[10] He describes the last concert as a "very emotional event" because coachloads of East Germans had travelled to Poland to see them and came backstage after the show with "tears in their eyes." The event was so significant at the time that it received international press attention.

It was not until 1985 that Gallagher returned to Eastern Europe again, this time on a far larger scale. He had spent much of the last decade touring the US, as well as travelling further afield to Japan, Australia and New Zealand. Now, he wanted to "catch up" in Europe and "forge inroads" into new territories.[11] He had started this venture into new territories in 1981 when he performed a now-legendary concert at the Nea Filadelfeia stadium in Athens. 15,000 tickets had been sold, but news of the concert spread by word of mouth and 40,000 people ended up in the stadium. Anticipating violence, the police turned heavy on the crowd. This tension spread quickly through the stadium and, soon, a full-scale riot had erupted, resulting in 300 people getting injured, while outside the stadium, local shops and restaurants were burnt down.

In a 1982 interview with *Hot Press*, Gallagher described it as "the most frightening gig" of his life, where he genuinely feared that he was going to die.[12] He recalled flames at the back of the stadium, CS gas that made his eyes water uncontrollably, mass confusion backstage as semi-militia patrolled and being unable to stop trembling, even when he was safely back at the hotel. Turbulence aside, Gallagher was satisfied with the concert ("it was a great gig really if I say so myself"[13]) and stated that the events had not put him off returning to Greece again.

Although the 1985 tour of Yugoslavia and Hungary went smoothly compared to the turmoil in Greece, it was still fraught with hostility along the way. The very first date in Maribor (13 January 1985) saw the police getting rough with the crowd, which led two angry fans to submit a letter to the editor of the Slovenian newspaper *Delo*. Entitled 'Permitted Forms of Violence', Mario Manzidovšek and Drago Guntner—on behalf of the young people of Bistrica—wrote how "completely innocent listeners" who simply wanted to "express their excitement" were "immediately physically disabled" by the guards. They described this act as a "cold shower," which spoilt their enjoyment of the concert. Manzidovšek and Guntner were particularly concerned that many of these guards were just "young boys," leading them to question whether the youth should "fear the future of elitism in their own ranks."[14] The outrage felt by these fans is reflective of the broader resentment that the Slovenian student movement of the time was starting to have of the repressive Yugoslav authorities. This would reach a head over the next few years, with increasing resistance against military conscription, for example.[15]

Similar events were noted in Zagreb two days later when "three hours of honest blues rock" was ruined by "three minutes of tear gas."[16] According to journalist Aleksandar Kostadinov, the audience of 3,500 was "happy and exhilarated" to see Gallagher perform, but the mood was changed to one of sorrow when a guard decided to let off tear gas. This happened during the encore, prompting Kostadinov to conclude that it was "one of the saddest ends" to an evening on Zagreb rock stages. This was a particular shame for Kostadinov as he deemed Gallagher to be "at the very top" of all the guitarists who had ever visited Yugoslavia. Such incidents provide evidence of the Yugoslav authorities' increased suspicion towards youth subcultures in the mid-1980s. Later in the decade, more and more non-Serbs started to view these types of incidents as evidence that the Yugoslav system (in the form of police and military) was biased against them in ethnic terms.[17]

In conversation with Dan Muise in 2002, bassist Gerry McAvoy noted the strong military presence at concerts, particularly in Hungary. "We were being watched all the time," he stated, with 70% of the audience at one concert close to the Soviet border consisting of soldiers in uniform.[18] Throughout the tour, there was also a Communist representative that travelled with the band alongside the promoter to make sure that they were on their best behaviour. These Hungarian concerts were organised by the Youth Director's Office (Ifjúsági Rendező Iroda), an independent department of the Express Youth and Student Travel Office (Express Ifjúsági és Diák Utazási Iroda)—a tourism company that belonged to the Hungarian Communist Youth Association. Prior to its founding in the early 1980s, domestic concerts were arranged by the National Director's Office (Országos Rendező Iroda)—a state-monopoly organisation—and only foreign musicians considered not to 'rock the boat' were permitted to perform. While the Youth Director's Office had a little more freedom, as McAvoy's testimony makes clear, Gallagher and his band were still closely monitored at all times.

In addition to unnecessary force, military presence and constant surveillance, Gallagher and the band were also witness to the ethnic tensions in Yugoslavia between Croats, Slovenes and Serbs. According to Dónal, they were all somewhat naïve to this before the tour and ended up directly "in the middle of it," yet coming from Ireland had "taught [them] well" and they were, therefore, not fazed to play in a place with similar issues.[19] The overt discrimination could still be disturbing at times, however. Dónal remembers an incident in Belgrade when the Yugoslav promoter, Toni Sabol, was refused entry to the radio station because he was Croatian, despite the fact that he was a figure of major importance on the Yugoslavian rock scene. Sabol had started out in the late 1960s as a concert organiser and manager to a number of bands, before achieving international success in the 1970s when he introduced Tina Turner to Europe. Throughout the 1980s, he brought many major artists to Yugoslavia, including Dire Straits and Uriah Heep. For Sabol to be subjected to such discrimination at home was an unsettling forewarning of the issues that would come to head in the later Yugoslav Wars.

Another challenge to Gallagher's 1985 tour was the lack of promotion. As he told *Borderline* in 1988, everything was "lowkey" with no "big, glossy colour posters" to advertise the concerts.[20] Nonetheless, he felt that the lowkey approach suited him. Speaking to *Déli Hírlap*, Gallagher explained how the Hungarian leg of the tour was a last-minute decision; they were in Yugoslavia and the promoter mentioned a small detour. According to Gallagher, he "didn't know what we were getting into," but was not disappointed, even though the stands were emptier than in Yugoslavia.[21] The January weather—which Dónal remembers as "atrocious" and "very bleak" at times[22]—also posed difficulties throughout the tour. Some concerts required Gallagher and the band to travel long distances by train across barren wintery landscapes, which Dónal likens to "being an extra in Dr Zhivago." As harmonicist Mark Feltham recounted to us in October 2023, the national football team coach was even co-opted as a tour bus to drive them around in Hungary.[23] "It's amazing that at the time of the 'Iron Curtain', events fell into place at all," added Dónal in an email exchange.[24]

Come Taste the Band

Given that Gallagher's reputation around the world was built on his live performances, it is interesting—although perhaps unsurprising in the political climate—that his reputation in Yugoslavia and Hungary came primarily from his studio albums. Promotional articles leading up to the tour noted how he was "known and loved"[25] in Eastern Europe for his LPs and that he had sold 60 million records in the last 15 years, which stood as a testimony to his talent. Perhaps even more interestingly, however, is that this reputation stemmed predominantly from his work with Taste, not as a solo artist, with advertisements for Gallagher's concerts repeatedly describing him as "ex-Taste," "the founder of the band Taste" or "former guitarist in Taste." The association between the public's knowledge of Gallagher and Taste was frequently emphasised by journalists, who wrote that most people buying tickets for his concerts hoped to hear some of his "biggest hits," including 'Same Old Story', 'What's Going On?' and 'Born on the Wrong Side of Time'.[26]

Why Yugoslavian and Hungarian audiences were particularly familiar with Taste is worth exploring further, especially given the countries' different political contexts. From 1948 onwards, Yugoslavia adopted a non-aligned internationalism approach which, according to music journalist Aleksandar Žikić, made it more relaxed to Western musical influences and even steadily encouraged them as long as they did not provoke the political system.[27] Hungary, in contrast, was historically more restrictive of international rock music, despite having a healthy national rock scene with such bands as Omega, Locomotiv GT, Illés, Metró and Karthago. The so-called "Three Ts" (*Tiltott, Tűrt, Támogatott*: Forbid, Tolerate, Support) guided Hungarian cultural policy at the time and many of these bands fell into the *Tűrt* (Tolerate) category.[28] International jazz and blues were more widely accepted. In 1965, Louis Armstrong had delivered a concert at Budapest's National Stadium in front of 70,000 people, while, in 1968, Traffic performed at the capital's Kisstadion. The city of Debrecen also held regular international jazz meetings from the late 1950s. In both countries then—based on their nationality and musical style—Taste fit into the category of 'acceptable' music.

Despite their diverse political situations, Yugoslavia and Hungary had one thing in common: there was no reliable way to find information about recent releases in Western markets. News tended to be received in dribs and drabs through both imported magazines and international radio stations with special programmes dedicated to rock music, such as Radio Luxembourg, Radio Free Europe and Voice of America. Doru Pop, a Professor in Film and Media Studies, describes these stations as "one of the most important factors of dissemination and influence" for rock music in Eastern Europe.[29] It was through them that many Yugoslavians and Hungarians first discovered Rory Gallagher or, rather, Taste. Speaking to us in December 2022, photographer Ferenc Kálmándy recounted how he heard Gallagher for the first time on the radio in 1968.[30] Then unable to buy records in Hungary, this introduction to a new form of music was revelatory for him. Later, Kálmándy's friend smuggled back some of Gallagher's albums from Germany for him; in 1985, Gallagher signed two of them (*On the Boards* and *Live at the Isle of Wight*) at his Pécs concert.[31]

Throughout the 1960s, a growing number of nationally produced music and youth magazines were published in Yugoslavia and Hungary, which served as an entry point to Taste for many. *Džuboks*—the first rock magazine in a communist country—was established in 1966 in Belgrade. Drawing inspiration from *New Musical Express* and *Melody Maker*, its first issue featured the Rolling Stones on the cover and its ambitious circulation of 100,000 copies sold out in days, demonstrating the clear demand and desire for such music news in Yugoslavia. Taste featured in the magazine on multiple occasions. Similarly, in Hungary, *Ifjúsági Magazin* was set up in 1965 and aimed at young people, offering a colourful picture of both national and international music. Again, Taste appeared regularly—as well as in other local publications—although often their musical uniqueness was downplayed in unfair claims that they "filled the void created by the breakup of Cream and Traffic."[32] Both magazines were closely monitored (the former by the City Committee and the latter by the Hungarian Communist Youth Association), yet they still offered a platform for Yugoslavians and Hungarians to access and learn about Western music.

It was these early engagements with Gallagher's music—whether through international radio or imported and locally produced magazines—that stuck with Yugoslavian and Hungarian fans. While they continued to access his solo records (when possible) throughout the 1970s and 1980s and watched him on *Rockpalast* (in the case of Yugoslavia), it was Taste to which many were drawn back, perhaps for what the band's music had represented for the young people of the 1960s: the spirit of creative freedom and expression. Understood in this broader landscape, it is clear then why so many people were excited about Gallagher's 1985 tour. For many who had loyally followed him since the days of Taste, they would finally have the opportunity to experience his music live and unrestrained rather than relying on sporadic radio broadcasts and imported records or just looking at photographs in magazines. And for those not so familiar with Gallagher's music, their curiosity was piqued by the mysterious advertisements about the "ex-Taste guitarist," so they also snapped up tickets. An international musician coming to Yugoslavia and especially Hungary—which had such tight entry and exit restrictions at the time—was a big deal, a rare event not to be missed.

The wide range of people that Gallagher attracted to his concerts is nicely captured in a review of the Budapest show. Journalist Gábor Kapuvári notes that of the 6,000 people in attendance, many were "music fanatics" and "Rory Gallagher devotees" who had dashed straight from work and had been waiting 20 years for this occasion. But equally, there were young couples, pregnant women and even children, as well as members of some of Hungary's national blues bands and curious spectators who had "heard something about Taste" from their peers.[33] With his words, Kapuvári paints a picture of the Gallagher concert as a communal experience, one that does not require a pre-existing knowledge of his music—or even a love of blues or rock—to enjoy. The concert represents so much more than the musical act itself; it is a chance to be transported to another world for a while and return renewed and restored.

The Blues Don't Lie
Although many people had come to Gallagher's concerts with the hope of hearing a Taste song, they certainly did not go away disappointed at the absence. In fact, they were amazed at just how much Gallagher had developed as an artist and performer since then. Of course, some had heard him on imported copies of *Live! in Europe*, *Irish Tour '74* and even *Stage Struck*, but this was nothing compared to experiencing a Gallagher concert first-hand. Reviews of his shows—from both fans and critics—were overwhelmingly positive. Not even Alvin Lee or Peter Green could gather the number of visitors that Gallagher did in Yugoslavia, wrote *Večernji List*...[34] If we compare Gallagher's concerts to those of Lee, Green and even Clapton, he has no equal, added *Oslobođenje*...[35] No other foreign artist to Hungary has ever been so successful as Gallagher, reported *Rock Révkalauz*...[36] No other foreign artist to Hungary has ever played such long sets, reminded *Képes Ifjúság*...[37] And so, the praise for Gallagher just kept coming in the weeks following his concerts.

While many had been expecting a hard rock sound from Gallagher and his band, they were pleasantly surprised at the bluesiness of his concerts. In fact, it was the slow blues and acoustic elements that truly captured both Yugoslavian and Hungarian audiences who felt that these parts of the show revealed Gallagher as being in a league of his own. In a review of Gallagher's Budapest show for *Rock Révkalauz*, János Sebők noted how there were many skilled Hungarian blues bands, but with Gallagher, for the first time, Hungarian audiences could discover "what it means when someone plays not only with technique, but with feeling."[38] For Sebők, Gallagher "lived the blues in every song, movement and sweep of the string" and, while he paid respect to the old bluesmasters, he very clearly had his own unique identity. Showing a good understanding of the subtleties of Gallagher's music, Sebők also described the performance as "one long song"; by listening carefully, the "individual beauty" of each element could be picked out, yet these elements worked best when they came together to create "one experience" for the listener—like all the best folk artists do.

Equally, journalist Peter Vanicsek, who was also at the Budapest concert, felt that the slow blues and acoustic numbers enabled Gallagher to show "not just his technical but also his mood-creating ability."[39] Vanicsek reserved particular praise for Gallagher's improvisation skills, where his own "musical commentaries" were inserted into "melodic circles," thereby showcasing the real "charm" of his music. The journalist was also extremely impressed by Mark Feltham's harmonica-playing—echoing comments of others who described him as a "first-class partner" to Gallagher.[40] The Budapest bootleg is a fine example of Feltham's contribution to the band, his subtle touches on 'I Wonder Who', 'Banker's Blues' and 'Nadine' enhancing the songs. Gallagher's cover of Bo Diddley's 'Hey Mama,

Keep Your Big Mouth Shut' — also expertly supported by Feltham and with backing vocals by Gerry McAvoy — is another highlight of the bootleg. The midpoint when the entire Budapest crowd sings along to the chorus anticipates the iconic Queen 'Love of My Life' moment one year later, captured in the *Hungarian Rhapsody* recording. But for Vanicsek, the real value of Gallagher was just how effortless he made playing the blues: "his fingers gallop so naturally on the strings during a solo that his technical virtuosity is barely noticeable [...] he is a wonderfully skilled musician who knows practically everything about the guitar."[41]

Reviewing the Sarajevo concert, Ognjen Tvrtković remarked that Yugoslavian audiences might know Gallagher as "an excellent boogie heavy rock guitarist," but his performance sealed his status as "a blues connoisseur."[42] Reporting about Belgrade and Budapest, Attila Beder also agreed, noting that Gallagher played "with heart and soul," [feeling] each note individually and passing this experience onto the audience."[43]

This is something that Aleksandar Kostadinov — who was at the Zagreb show — also recognised. For Kostadinov, Gallagher had a refreshing approach to old blues numbers, knowing how to bring them alive and keep them exciting. The "mesmerising" and "magically played" 'Out on the Western Plain' was a clear example of this.[44] Kostadinov's highlight of the night, however, came with a cover of Sam Cooke's 'Bring It on Home to Me' — a song that Gallagher also played in Budapest, delivering a spectacular 8-minute rendition full of such feeling (Mark Feltham again showing his worth in spades).

"Beef Stew" Rock
When describing Gallagher's performance at the Budapest Sportcsarnok, journalist János Sebők likened it to "beef stew," noting how it is a staple dish that he never gets tired of, despite trying many delicacies, treats and specialties. He explains how he might consume "cotton candy-soul, teenybopper chewing gum, new wave whipped cream or (hotel) menthol rock & roll sweets," but he will always return to beef stew as no other dish quite compares. For Sebők, this beef stew personifies Gallagher, always able to serve up a "musical menu" that he enjoys and proving to be "a master chef worthy of his reputation."[45] In comparing Gallagher to the traditional Hungarian dish, Sebők taps into the authenticity of his music — something that would have been recognised by Hungarian readers. Indeed, Gallagher himself often referred to him and his band as playing meat and potatoes music — a basic, straightforward formula, yet full of substance and grit.

While Gallagher's blues was what caught the attention of most spectators at his Yugoslavian and Hungarian gigs, his meat and potatoes — or "beef stew" — approach to music was also frequently lauded. A review of Gallagher's Belgrade concert, for example, noted how he brought the audience to their feet with the first number and, from then on, almost every number was met with "thunderous applause."[46]

An evocative description of Gallagher's Stratocaster is provided as "an object that had undergone all the horrors of the Allied landings in Normandy," but is still capable of firing out all the right notes when in the hands of its owner. This is a sentiment with which fan Csaba Mester, who caught Gallagher in Miskolc, also agrees, describing the concert as a "life-changing event [...] a revolution [...] pure magic."[47]

For Mester, Gallagher had a "Chuck Berry thing" going on, pouring with sweat and totally focused as he delivered "pure rock and roll" and "lots of great moves" across the stage. Today, Mester runs *Master-Lab Comics*, a company that makes rock-related short stories, and has plans to develop a comic about Gallagher because, in his words, "we owe him a lot; he was a superhero." Mester's friend László Lukács travelled to Debrecen the next day to see Gallagher, describing it as "an inspirational start" for him to play music. He is now bassist in the Hungarian rock band Tankcsapda.

Writing for *Oslobođenje* about Gallagher's Sarajevo concert, Ognjen Tvrtković noted that Gallagher played with "a surprising intensity worthy of the best heavy metal bands."[48] Integral to this was the "granite sound mass" of Gerry McAvoy and Brendan O'Neill who, together with Gallagher, "gave the last atom of power on stage." Mark Feltham also provided a "delicious" complement to the "fiery barrage of guitar riffs" and the "frantic pumping" of the rhythm section. Tvrtković makes the important point that trios can sometimes sound cliché and expected, but Gallagher knows how to avoid monotony by "never allowing the tension of the performance to drop." Gallagher was a master in playing off the crowd, always astutely calculating whether to bring up the pace or drop the tempo—an approach that Dónal has described as "making love to the audience."[49]

Throughout the tour, journalists also frequently commented on Gallagher's incredible stamina, consistently performing three-hour sets. In reference to the Budapest concert, *Képes Ifjúság* noted how when Gallagher finished, the audience "went into complete ecstasy" and called him back "with such a thump that it was almost like the ceiling was going to fall down on us."[50] Keen to oblige, Gallagher came back twice more, performing with such power that the spectators "could barely stand up" by the end, and he left the stage "in the knowledge of complete success." This was after a shaky start to the concert when the guitarist's amplifier broke down and had to be repaired, leading to a one-hour delay. According to János Sebők, Gallagher certainly made up for this, rocking the crowd of 6,000 for over three hours and "taking hold of the whole arena" by the fourth number.[51]

Gallagher's Zagreb concert was recorded and broadcast live on Radio Zagreb, while Magyar Rádió recorded his show in Budapest. There were plans to use this material for a forthcoming live album, which never came to light, but would certainly be a welcome future release from the Gallagher Estate. *Check Shirt Wizard – Live in '77* (2020) filled the 1975-1979 gap in Gallagher's live albums, while *All Around Man – Live in London* (2023) provided a long overdue testimony of Gallagher's *Fresh Evidence* era material. However, Gallagher's mid-1980s period still remains overlooked. An official release from Zagreb or Budapest would cover a previously undocumented period in Gallagher's career, displaying his continued development—rather than supposed decline—as a live performer.

Ageless and Indestructible
Throughout the 1980s, Gallagher was the target of much negative press in the UK, US and even Ireland, where his everyday clothes and cherished guitar were often turned into gimmicks and used to ridicule him, framing both his loyalty to the blues and his appearance as obsolete. This was in strong contrast to Yugoslavia and Hungary where Gallagher's age was seen as a sign of his knowledge, wisdom and experience—all of which contributed to making him one of the greatest guitarists of all time. As Dónal Gallagher told Dan Muise in 2002, "When you play to an audience that's starved for music or they've never seen a western/ rock player [...] there's a fever, a sense of excitement. People in New York or London... we're so blasé about it."[52] In other words, by the 1980s, audiences used to seeing Gallagher regularly had become a little complacent and took him and his music for granted. Being exposed to him more frequently, they had come to see him as "good old reliable RG"[53] and failed to appreciate the continual development of his music.

Yugoslavian and Hungarian audiences, on the other hand, had an entirely different attitude. Less accustomed to international musicians performing on their home ground—and certainly not international musicians of Gallagher's calibre—they appreciated him for what he was: 36 years of age with over two decades of professional experience that made him an exceptional performer. Despite all the references to Taste beforehand in the press, nobody dared compare Gallagher to his former band after or claim that he came up short. Instead, they wanted him now as he was in 1985, not as a time capsule from 1970. To them, Gallagher represented "a real rock experience," showing that rock was truly "ageless and indestructible" if it was played the way that he played it.[54]

A review in *Esti Hírlap* of Gallagher's Budapest concert noted that his guitar-playing was "better than ever,"[55] while in reference to Zagreb, *Vecernji List* wrote that Gallagher was "still in very good shape" and that the finer parts of guitar work were, in fact, "even better" than his peers.[56] Writing about Sarajevo in *Oslobođenje*, Ognjen Tvrtković also made it clear that Gallagher's time had "not yet passed" and that he was, in fact, now "at the height" of the reputation he had gained in the last 20 years.[57] Likewise, speaking of Zagreb, Aleksandar Kostadinov stated that, when someone succeeds to attract so many people to their concerts after so many years, that is something that commands due attention and respect.[58]

Honesty is also another descriptor that comes up frequently in articles about Gallagher in both the Yugoslavian and Hungarian press, with journalists remarking how he comes across as genuine in both his music and as a person. For Ognjen Tvrtković, Gallagher's "basic qualities" have remained "unchanged" and he has not lost any of his "primary charm, immediacy and communicativeness."[59] Others linked this honesty to the way that Gallagher continually thanked his audience or recalled past anecdotes, such as a memorable concert in Zurich in 1973, when, despite being on the verge of collapse, he sat on the edge of the stage and talked to fans until after midnight. A comment on YouTube from a fan who was at Gallagher's Novi Sad show also indicates the power that the unassuming Irishman held over his audience: when some teenagers threw cans and coins at Gallagher as a sign of respect, he stopped playing and politely asked them to refrain from doing so because he was not a punk musician; they immediately stopped.

Breaking the Ice
While Gallagher's schedule was too tight to engage in many press events, he did take the time out to give some interviews when possible. Following his concert at the Zagreb Sports Hall, he spoke backstage to Maja Razović of *Vjesnik* newspaper. The interview captures many of the defining aspects of Gallagher's attitude to music, as well as his own self-effacing personality. Gallagher tells Razović that he has "never been completely satisfied" with the songs he has written, the albums he has recorded or the concerts he has played and that he is "still trying to get better."[60] He worries particularly about getting lazy, becoming too relaxed or "surrendering to success," outlining that all he wants to do is "just play."

When pressed on his unwillingness to release singles or engage in publicity, Gallagher explains that he is happy to "sacrifice" success if it means that he can "live in peace" and maintain a private life. He also emphasises how he sees himself as belonging more to "the group of traditional musicians" and tries to be "a normal human being" instead of pushing himself like some "personality." Gallagher also talks about the difference between Irish folk and blues, the former being "in [his] blood" and affecting the way that he writes and thinks, and the latter automatically "in [his] soul" with a sound "so incomparably deeper than rock & roll." Gallagher's ethos of valuing personal authenticity above conformity to what mainstream society and ideology expected of him resonated strongly with both Yugoslav rock journalists and the Yugoslav 'new wave' scene in general. It stood in stark contrast to the way that others got ahead in a career in late socialist Yugoslavia (i.e., through patronage and knowing how to say the *right* things to the *right* people).[61]

On the topic of the Yugoslavian tour, Gallagher tells Razović how he has been "extremely surprised" by the response to date. He adds that he was unsure what type of songs to perform or what the audience would accept better, but so far both the rock and blues songs have gone down well. "Now that we've broken the ice, I would be glad if we came back again, maybe after the new album in nicer weather," he concludes on a positive note.

Gallagher also gave a backstage interview after his concert in Budapest, which was later broadcasted on the Hungarian music programme *Rock News*. Here, Gallagher reflects on the evening, speaking of the "personal" atmosphere that he tried to create with the acoustic part of his set and the "good feeling" of seeing older fans in the crowd because they have remained loyal to him through the years.[62] Given Taste's popularity in Hungary, naturally, the conversation then turns to this topic and the possibility of a reunion. For Gallagher, this is "not a very good idea" because "the old stuff belongs to the past [...] this time is over." When asked whether he would ever join a "super band," he modestly replies that he has been approached various times, but does not like the idea. "There are too many 'super problems' among the 'super musicians' who are in 'super groups'," he explains somewhat tongue-in-cheek. Instead, he prefers to have his own band and do occasional session work.

On the same evening, Gallagher also spoke briefly to László Gurály and Zsolt Tuza of *Polifon* magazine. Challenged about his reputation of "fighting against showbusiness," Gallagher gives yet another fascinating insight into his attitude to music:

> Perhaps I wouldn't put it quite so self-consciously because you have to make a living from something... But I'm against the pop phenomenon that puts too much emphasis on image and is excessively 'shiny'. Me, I'm more interested in music and natural development, not constant 'big publicity' and big stories. Sometimes, of course, record sales also depend on publicity, but for me, this is not the main thing. I want to care about music.[63]

Gallagher is also requested to reflect on his "experiments" with the blues, to which he explains that he is "changing as a songwriter" and has noticed a progression in his songwriting in recent years as he comes up with new ideas and themes for songs. He also outlines that he is "still learning" and enjoys experimenting by blending blues with jazz and folk. These personal reflections by Gallagher are significant because they counter many claims made in the press at the time that he was stagnating and his music offered nothing new. They show how Gallagher was constantly looking to develop his music and inject something new into the blues, whether breaking genre boundaries and fusing different styles of music together or incorporating new lyrical motifs by drawing on his love for noir — both of which he clearly achieved on record with *Defender* (1987) and *Fresh Evidence* (1990).

Amongst the many other topics, Gallagher also speaks about why he returned to a trio ("much more rhythmic, more powerful and somehow much freer in terms of form"), his favourite part of his career ("people always love the present best"), his future plans ("finish the new LP [...] and record an acoustic album in the autumn"), comparisons to Clapton ("Not appropriate. We make the same kind of music but in a different way") and, inevitably, the break-up of Taste ("I just 'grew up'. I wanted to play a different kind of music"). Finally, he shares his delight with how well the Pécs and Budapest concerts have gone, how "very surprised" he is that so many people know him and his desire to return next year. He also apologises for not having had time to catch any local bands live, which he had hoped to do.

It is unsurprising that Gallagher did not have any free time on this tour, especially when he kept continually adding to his already busy schedule. Originally, there was to be a day off between the Belgrade and Sarajevo dates, but he decided to make a small detour to Novi Sad, playing the Sajmište Hall. At just two hours, Novi Sad was the 'shortest' performance on Gallagher's tour (still a respectably long set, yet 'short' by his standards) because he had to undertake a gruelling eight-hour car journey to Sarajevo after. Nonetheless, he still put on a performance that photographer Zoran Veselinović remembers as a "great joy" and "beautiful experience."[64] Veselinović was permitted to shoot the entire concert, not just the first three songs, and Gallagher even allowed him to get up close with the camera, resulting in dozens of authentic photographs of the guitarist captured in full flight. Equally, fan Žikica Ivković—just 17 at the time—recalls being "instantly won over" by Gallagher's performance, describing the concert as "special" and the "best" he has ever attended.[65]

Following the concert, Ivković hung back to meet Gallagher, along with three Hungarian fans. After a short wait (during which Ivković met the other band members), Ivković spotted Gallagher and excitedly approached him, leading the guitarist to stop abruptly and exclaim, "Oops!" Soon, Gallagher was surrounded by the small group of fans. Not wanting to bother Gallagher with their complicated names, the Hungarians asked him simply to sign their tickets to "Joe" and "John." However, unable to speak English, Ivković presented his ticket to Gallagher and pronounced his name—Žikica—in the normal Serbian way, indicating that he wanted an autograph. Seeing that Gallagher did not understand, Ivković air-spelt the "Z" and repeated each syllable of his name slowly. Gallagher tried to copy his actions and sounds with a felt tip on the ticket, but the ticket ended up signed "Zeketsr" (to which Žikica added the caron ˇ on top of the "Z" with his pen). When Gallagher asked if he had spelt his name correctly, Ivković simply smiled and told him that it was great. Gallagher then patted him on the shoulder and said goodbye.

Gallagher reached Sarajevo in the early hours of the morning, but immediately had an important press engagement to fulfil. The city was hosting its annual winter sports competition and, as the visiting international celebrity, the authorities had asked him to open their official ceremony for television. Despite his exhaustion after a long journey and busy week of touring, Gallagher good-naturedly agreed to the request. Speaking to us in February 2022, Dónal shared more about this intriguing event:

> Despite travel that saw us arrive at the Holiday Inn hotel at 4 a.m., my brother got up early to do this. We were driven in a tiny car to the top of a mountain, which had the toboggan run and didn't have suitable shoes or clothes. Rory did his bit. We then sat in a toboggan type structure with their sports guys for a photo and then got pushed down the 'run', which was both exhilarating and scary, but quicker and safer than the car that brought us up![66]

Unfortunately, no surviving photographs have yet been found from the event.

Same Old Story?

When Rory Gallagher went to Yugoslavia and Hungary in 1985, he was known by many as the fresh-faced guitar virtuoso from Taste. Less familiar with his solo work, fans expected a throwback to the late 1960s, with performances of Taste classics like 'What's Going On' and 'Same Old Story'. Advertisements leading up to the tour were replete with interchangeable descriptions of him as "ex-Taste," "the founder of the band Taste" or "former guitarist in Taste." However, as Gallagher so often emphasised, "memories should remain memories."[67] Fifteen years had now passed since the band's break-up and he wanted to be appreciated for what he was doing today instead.

Gallagher had no need to worry. As soon as he stepped out on stage—whether in Ljubljana, Novi Sad, Pécs or Debrecen—all thoughts of Taste were swiftly forgotten. Standing before the crowd was a mature bluesman, an accomplished musician who had taken the fire and passion from Taste and honed it to perfection over the intervening years, developing his own unique style. Alvin Lee, Eric Clapton and Peter Green had all visited the countries in recent years, but both fans and critics were in agreement that they did not hold a candle to Gallagher. For them, Gallagher played with a rare authenticity and honesty, remaining true to the core values with which he had started out, yet unwilling to live in the past and always seeking to revitalise the blues. It was these values of holding onto personal truth, even at the expense of mainstream success and recognition, that resonated so strongly with the attitudes of rock fans in both Yugoslavia and Hungary. Many saw parallels between their own subjectivities in a corrupt, authoritarian system and the choices that Gallagher made about the type of musician that he wanted to be within a corporate music industry dominated by image. In other words, Gallagher's willingness to stay true to himself was seen by fans through the prism of choices that they themselves were making to maintain integrity rather than concentrate on climbing up the Party ladder. By the time Gallagher left, both Yugoslavian and Hungarian audiences largely agreed that Taste should be a happy distant memory and that Gallagher should be appreciated in the here and now.

Gallagher's concerts attracted a diverse range of spectators, including many youths who were simply curious to know more about this 'mystery' guitar man that they had heard so much about from their elders. It was not unusual for international musicians to come to Yugoslavia, but their visits were, nonetheless, always heralded with great fanfare—and Rory Gallagher's visit was no exception. Hungary, contrastingly, was still a fledgling in this respect. Gallagher's tour was, therefore, of major significance, representing a rare window into an alternative view of the world—an alternative view that Slovenian reporter Srečko Niedorfer believes would eventually help bring down "the symbolic and symbolist" Berlin Wall.[68]

Queen's 1986 concert in Budapest is frequently held up as an event that broke new ground, but we must remember that Gallagher had blazed the trail one year earlier, setting the precedent for those who followed. At the time, Gallagher's concerts were the most successful ever in Hungary, while his Yugoslavian dates attracted far larger numbers of spectators than earlier concerts by Alvin Lee and Peter Green. He also held the record for playing the longest sets in both countries. However, as is so often the case in Gallagher's career, these firsts are often forgotten as he was never one to blow his own trumpet about them. Gallagher also made his mark in both countries because of his kindness towards fans, always taking time to meet them no matter how tired or hungry he was. The fans made a huge mark on Gallagher too; when the devastating Yugoslav Wars later broke out, Gallagher immediately organised a Red Cross benefit concert in Cork for the refugees (see 4.5). A keen believer that music should transcend political boundaries, he had also planned to perform in Tallinn (Estonia) in 1989, but due to logistical challenges, this concert never went ahead.

Gallagher's performances in Yugoslavia and Hungary inspired a whole generation of young people and are still remembered fondly today by those who attended. Ferenc Kálmándy is instantly transported back to that wintery night in Pécs when he looks through the photographs that he took of Gallagher. There is one shot that he holds particularly dear: Gallagher with his head back and eyes closed, a full smile on his face, totally lost in the moment as he reaches for a note on his beloved Stratocaster. "When I look at the photo, I can just hear the music," Kálmándy reminisces. Above all, he remembers Gallagher's joy as he performed, an infectious joy that he spread to all those around him and which endeared him to so many people. According to Kálmándy, for this reason and so many more, "we should never forget Rory."

Amen, brother. Amen.

LAO

Footnotes

1 Gábor Kapuvári, 'A gitáros, aki 1966-ban felejtette magát', *Magyar Ifjúság* (15 February 1985), 30.
2 Advertisement for Rory Gallagher's Budapest Concert, *Pesti Műsor* (6 February 1985), 69.
3 Rick Koster, 'Rory in the Sky', *Dallas Observer* (27 November 1997), http://www.roryon.com/sky.html
4 As recounted by Dónal Gallagher in Dan Muise, *Gallagher, Marriott, Derringer & Trower* (Milwaukee: Hal Leonard Corporation, 2002), 59.
5 Ibid., 60.
6 Ognjen Tvrtković, 'Legenda koja živi', *Oslobođenje* (22 January 1985), 10.
7 Kapuvári, 'A gitáros, aki 1966-ban felejtette magát', 33.
8 Linda Solomon, 'Rory: Rockin' Irish Rover', *The Gig* (15 September 1974), http://www.roryon.com/gig408.html
9 Darcy Diamond, 'Rory Gallagher – Just Straight Ahead Rock', *Rock* (May 1977), https://www.roryon.com/diamond.html
10 Jakob Mulder, 'Interview with Rod De'ath', *Signals* (autumn 1996), http://www.roryon.com/rod211.
11 Muise, *Gallagher, Marriott, Derringer & Trower*, 80.
12 Liam Fay, 'Tangled Up in Blues', *Hot Press* (July 1992), http://www.roryon.com/Tangled.html
13 John Waters, 'Rory Gallagher: A Rap on the Road', *Hot Press* (18 December 1981), http://www.roryon.com/rap262.html
14 Mario Manzidovšek and Drago Guntner, 'Dovoljene oblike nasilja', *Delo* (13 February 1985), 7.
15 Ljubica Spaskovska, *The Last Yugoslav Generation: The Rethinking of Youth Politics and Cultures in Late Socialism* (Manchester: Manchester University Press, 2017), 140.
16 Aleksandar Kostadinov, 'Rory Gallagher u Zagrebu', *Oko* (14 February 1985), 29.
17 My thanks to Dr Catherine Baker, a specialist in post-Cold War history, for her insights on this topic.
18 Muise, *Gallagher, Marriott, Derringer & Trower*, 80.
19 'Donal Gallagher Interviewed For Live at Cork City Libraries', https://www.youtube.com/watch?v=_9D42OSXUeM

20 'Rory Gallagher on Borderline – 1988', https://www.youtube.com/watch?v=drQW3EJiz2s
21 'Rory és csapata', *Déli Hírlap* (26 January 1985), 22.
22 Muise, *Gallagher, Marriott, Derringer & Trower*, 59.
23 Interview with Mark Feltham, 19 October 2023.
24 Email exchange with Dónal Gallagher, 16 October 2023.
25 'Rory Gallagher Miskolcon', *Déli Hírlap* (14 January 1985), 11.
26 Aleksander Kostadinov, 'Rory Gallagher', *Vecernji List* (9 January 1985), 10.
27 Aleksandar Žikić, 'Belgrade Rock Experience: From Sixties Innocence to Eighties Relevance' in *Made in Yugoslavia: Studies in Popular Music*, edited by Danijela Beard and Ljerka Rasmussen (New York: Routledge, 2020), 56-70.
28 My thanks to Éva Mihalovics, a PhD student at Durham University, for sharing her knowledge of this with me.
29 Doru Pop, 'Pop-Rock and Propaganda During the Ceausescu Regime in Communist Romania' in *Popular Music in Eastern Europe: Breaking the Cold War Paradigm*, edited by Ewa Mazierska (London: Palgrave Macmillan, 2016), 51-69.
30 Interview with Ferenc Kálmándy, 11 December 2022.
31 Unlike Hungary where many records had to be smuggled in from abroad, Yugoslavia had several of its own record labels which released foreign titles for the Yugoslav market. The only drawback was that they only released select albums according to commerciality and world sales charts. For this reason, only the following Gallagher/Taste albums were released in Yugoslavia: *On the Boards*, *Against the Grain*, *Calling Card*, *Photo-Finish* and *Top Priority*, as well as the compilations *The Best Years* and *The Story So Far* (all by PGP-RTB or Jugoton).
32 'Taste', *Csongrád Megyei Hírlap* (1 March 1970), 51.
33 Kapuvári, 'A gitáros, aki 1966-ban felejtette magát'.
34 M. Ambruš-Kiš, 'Trpki Blues', *Vecernji List* (23 January 1985), 10.
35 Tvrtković, 'Legenda koja živi', 10.
36 János Sebők, 'Vendégünk volt: Rory Gallagher', *Rock Révkalauz* (January 1985), 3-4.
37 Attila Beder, 'Rory Gallagher', *Képes Ifjúság* (6 February 1985), 40.
38 Sebők, 'Vendégünk volt: Rory Gallagher', 3-4.
39 Péter Vanicsek, 'Rory Gallagher Magyarországon', *Magyar Hírlap* (4 Febraury 1985), 28.
40 'Gallagher gitározott', *Esti Hírlap* (23 January 1985), 2.
41 Vanicsek, 'Rory Gallagher Magyarországon', 28.
42 Tvrtković, 'Legenda koja živi', 10.
43 Beder, 'Rory Gallagher', 40.
44 Kostadinov, 'Rory Gallagher u Zagrebu', 29.
45 Sebők, 'Vendégünk volt: Rory Gallagher', 3-4.
46 Beder, 'Rory Gallagher', 40.
47 Interview with Csaba Mester, 13 March 2023.
48 Tvrtković, 'Legenda koja živi', 10.
49 Shiv Cariappa, 'Wheeling and Dealing' (2003), http://www.roryon.com/donalshiv352.html
50 Beder, 'Rory Gallagher', 40.
51 Sebők, 'Vendégünk volt: Rory Gallagher', 3-4.
52 Muise, *Gallagher, Marriott, Derringer & Trower*, 59.
53 'Rory Gallagher - Dublin 1988 + Interview', https://www.youtube.com/watch?v=JZVjd8JaI-A
54 Sebők, 'Vendégünk volt: Rory Gallagher', 3-4.
55 'Gallagher gitározott', *Esti Hírlap*, 2.
56 Ambruš-Kiš, 'Trpki Blues', 10.
57 Tvrtković, 'Legenda koja živi', 10.
58 Kostadinov, 'Rory Gallagher u Zagrebu', 29.
59 Tvrtković, 'Legenda koja živi', 10.
60 Maja Razović, 'Bard bjelačkog bluesa', *Vjesnik* (19 January 1985), 11.
61 My thanks again to Dr Catherine Baker for her insights on this.
62 'Interview 1/85', *Deuce Quarterly*, no. 38 (January 1986), http://www.roryon.com/hungary171.html
63 László Gurály and Zsolt Tuza, 'Rory Gallagher', *Polifon* (1 March 1985), 3.
64 Interview with Zoran Veselinović, 30 May 2023.
65 Our thanks to Žikica Ivković's friend and neighbour, Milan Živančević, for translating this story and sharing it with us.
66 Email exchange with Dónal Gallagher, 26 February 2022.
67 'Interview 1/85'.
68 Srečko Niedorfer, 'Yugoslavian Liverpool in 60's – Maribor', *KMCS Media* (20 January 2018), https://homocumolat.com/2018/01/20/yugoslavian-liverpool-in-60s-maribor/

2.2 "See Rory and Die?" Storming the Montreux Jazz Festival 1985

In a review of Rory Gallagher's 1985 performance at the Montreux Jazz Festival, Beat Odermatt posed the rhetorical question, "See Rory and die?"[1] The question alluded to the Irishman's incredible ability as a live performer, suggesting that he set the bar so high that spectators need not watch anybody else after seeing him. Indeed, for many, a Gallagher concert was akin to a religious experience, enabling them to be taken momentarily to another realm. Music promoter Paul Charles, who became Gallagher's agent in the 1980s, recalls seeing Taste at the Marquee Club back in 1969, poetically noting how Gallagher seemed to "levitate" above the heads of the audience, such was his magic and sorcery as a performer.[2] And when it came particularly to the festival scene, Gallagher could always be relied upon to deliver strong and memorable performances, making him a musician with major drawing power.

Taste's now-legendary performance at the Isle of Wight Festival in 1970 set a precedent for Gallagher's festival reputation, which was only consolidated in the decade ahead through frequent appearances across the European festival circuit, leading *Melody Maker* to joke that the guitarist had played more festivals "than most people have had cold hamburgers."[3] Gallagher set all sorts of records, from headlining the first Irish rock festival in Macroom in 1977 to being presented with an award in 1980 for playing the Reading Festival more than any other act. While Gallagher preferred the intimate setting of a club, he saw great value in festivals, considering them "a good challenge" to win over new audiences.[4] Colm O'Hare of *Hot Press* notes that it was rare for a musician to be a "master" of both settings, yet Gallagher was, which he proved time and time again throughout his career.[5]

While the mid-1980s are often framed incorrectly as a period of 'hiatus' for Gallagher, the guitarist continued to tour all over Europe and keep up his track record of festival appearances, where he remained regularly called upon to headline. Furthermore, far from the claim that he was "comfortable" doing the "same stuff"[6] that he always had, Gallagher was constantly seeking to get something new from his music, to "keep hold of [his] roots while still progressing as a musician."[7]

This is exemplified by the increasing sophistication of his rigs during this time as he experimented with different amps, pedals and even effects in both the studio and live setting. The Montreux Jazz Festival in 1985 offers an important window into both the power of Gallagher's live performances during this period of his career and the sound that he was trying to achieve. Through an overview of Gallagher's long relationship with Montreux and his changing rigs, coupled with an analysis of his 1985 performance, we demonstrate that he still had plenty to offer and that his music was still capable of hitting the hearts of spectators from across generations, genres and genders.

"Gallagher and Montreux again and again"
Founded in 1967 by Claude Nobs, Géo Voumard and René Langel, the Montreux Jazz Festival is a world-famous music event held every July in Switzerland, which has featured a diverse range of performers over its 57-year history. The first Festival lasted for three days and was headlined by the jazz artists Charles Lloyd, Jack DeJohnette and Keith Jarrett. Throughout the 1970s, the Festival opened up to broader musical styles, including blues, soul and rock, attracting a list of names that reads like a roll call of musical legends: Led Zeppelin, Pink Floyd, Canned Heat, Deep Purple, Van Morrison, BB King, Stevie Ray Vaughan, Eric Clapton... In the 1980s, the Festival developed into a true world music festival (although it continued to specialise in jazz), while the 1990s saw the growth of an off-festival site with workshops, competitions and themed shows around the town's lakeshore promenades and cafes. This expansion led the festival to move in 1993 from its usual location of Montreux Casino (rebuilt in 1975 following a fire during Frank Zappa's 1971 set that was immortalised in Deep Purple's 'Smoke on the Water') to the Montreux Convention Centre, which has two concert halls: Auditorium Stravinski (3,500 capacity) and Miles Davis Hall (1,800 capacity). Today, the Festival is the second largest annual jazz festival in the world (after Montreal), lasting two weeks and drawing some 200,000 visitors. It has welcomed over 1,300 artists to date, one of whom was, of course, Rory Gallagher—a guaranteed crowd-pleaser.

Gallagher first came to Montreux with Taste in 1970. In August of that year, Claude Nobs had attended the Isle of Wight Festival, hoping to convince The Doors and Jimi Hendrix to play at his new jazz festival. Blown away by Taste, he decided to hire them too. The band agreed and, just three days later, they performed at Montreux Casino, a performance that was unofficially released as *Live Taste* in 1971. "My friendship with Rory was immediate as we both love the blues," recalled Nobs in 2006, "[He] was one of the nicest people I ever met, as quiet backstage as he was wild on stage."[8] Throughout his solo career, Gallagher returned to Montreux five times: 1975, 1977, 1979, 1985 and 1994.

The liner notes by Chris Welch in the 2006 *Rory Gallagher: Live at Montreux* DVD describe Gallagher's appearances at the festival as a "homecoming." Welch states how Gallagher always greeted the cheering audience with "self-effacing charm," before strapping on his Fender Stratocaster and transforming into an "aggression-fuelled performer." Gallagher made an immediate impact at Montreux 1975 when he took part in Guitar Night along with John Martyn, Philip Catherine, Larry Coryell and Steve Khan. He later described the jam session as a "music shop gone mad"[9] as there were no rehearsals and Coryell's rhythm machine broke down at the very beginning of the performance. Gallagher instinctively took the lead, calling up each soloist one by one, before delivering his own solo acoustic set. "It was a test for me. I was alone, but I knew I could do it," he said in a rare display of confidence.[10] Spectators and journalists were in agreement that Gallagher stole the show, "setting light to the audience" and "inspiring the other players" to give the best of themselves.[11]

The next day, the guitarist performed with his own band. "You can't get rid of me," he joked as he walked out on the stage, before delivering a dynamic set which, according to Welch, "brought happiness" to the audience with the "seductive power of [his] unstoppable enthusiasm and energy." It was at this 1975 edition that Gallagher also had the opportunity to jam with Albert King, who was being recorded for a live album (released in 1977). Although he was "chuffed to bits" to perform with the blues legend, the experience was rather daunting. As Dónal told *Music Radar*:

> When eventually [Rory] was called on stage, the band didn't make it very pleasant for him; there were no keys written down and it was a case of being thrown in the deep end. If you could swim, fine - if you couldn't, tough! Rory tried looking at Albert's fretboard to see what key he was in, but that didn't help. Albert King had such a unique system of playing - the guitar was upside down and he was left-handed. Rory asked one of the brass players, who just said, 'B natural, boy - B natural.' And that was it![12]

Despite being "really up against the wall," Gallagher performed strongly, defying King's brazen statement at the beginning of the Festival: "I'm gonna hang these young boys by their toes up here tonight."

Two years later, Gallagher returned to Montreux with another impressive performance, which responded to the arrival of punk with its harder, faster and more aggressive edge. Away from the stage, archive footage from Swiss television captures a happy Gallagher piloting a speedboat on Lake Geneva and entertaining a crowd of young fans with a rendition of 'Mystery Train' on a borrowed banjo. In 1979, Gallagher was back again for an explosive performance, which is perhaps best remembered for the epic ten-minute version of 'Shadow Play', where he places his guitar on the ground, drags it across the stage and then skips towards it, pointing animatedly before fanning it with a white towel. Despite some critics expressing disappointment at Gallagher's preference for hard rock over blues in his set, others enjoyed this "evolution" of his music, noting that he attracted the most applause from the audience and "provoked hysteria" with his solos "worthy of the greatest hard rock guitarists."[13] After this concert, the guitarist was awarded with a prize from Nobs to mark his many appearances at Montreux to date.[14]

It was not until 1985—the focus of this chapter—that Gallagher performed at the Festival again. His final appearance was nine years later in 1994 (see 3.2).

"How do you get your sound, Mr Gallagher?"
The iconic Rory Gallagher sound is frequently attributed to a simple Vox AC30 amp and Dallas Rangemaster Treble Booster. However, Gallagher's rigs, in fact, changed throughout his career and, by the time of the Montreux Jazz Festival in 1985, they were perhaps the most ambitious to date.

Gallagher had started to use a Vox AC30 when he joined the Fontana Showband in 1963. He saw it as "the most reliable amp... really, very loud and solid,"[15] but acknowledged that the addition of a Treble Booster provided a "nice rough edge without getting into a very fuzzy sound."[16] It was this simple set-up that he used the first time that he played the Montreux Jazz Festival with Taste in 1970 and which impressed Brian May of Queen who regularly saw Taste play at the Marquee Club in London. One night, the young May stayed behind to speak to the guitarist after the show and asked, "How do you get your sound, Mr Gallagher?"[17] Gallagher told him and, the next day, May went out and bought the very same equipment. He has used this set-up, albeit with a few tweaks, ever since.

Gallagher was, of course, synonymous with his 1961 Fender Stratocaster. He summarised the "beauty" of the Stratocaster to be its "ability to mix the distorted sound of the amp with the clear guitar sound of, say, Buddy Holly or Hank Marvin."[18] However, much difficulty presented itself in finding "the perfect amp" to capture this ideal "dirtiness,"[19] leading Gallagher to fiddle with his amplification over the years. When his band changed to a four-piece in 1973, for example, he moved away from the Vox AC30 in favour of Fender amps, which blended better with the sounds of Lou Martin's keyboards. He started by using a 1956 Fender Twin, which, in his view, offered a cleaner sound, made him "work a little harder" and sounded nicer when playing slide guitar.[20] He also experimented with a 1954 Fender Bassman (as seen in footage from his 1975 Montreux Jazz Festival appearance), often combining it with the Twin when playing large outdoor venues in the US to create a more powerful sound. By 1977, Gallagher was linking the Bassman with a 1960 Fender Concert (a set-up employed in his 1977 Montreux performance), sometimes adding a Hawk II Expander/Booster (first used in 1974) "to roughen it up a bit."[21] In the studio, he would prefer his 1950s Fender Champ tweed amp, which accompanied him most notably to the 1975 jam with the Rolling Stones in Rotterdam.

In 1978, Gallagher reverted to a three-piece with Ted McKenna on drums and he began playing around with Ampeg VTs, eventually linking a VT-40 to a VT-22 which gave him a "good mid-range" and "natural distortion."[22] The VTs were often combined with the Hawk II Expander/Booster, later replaced with a Furman PQ-3 Parametric EQ. In line with the band's harder sound during this period, Gallagher sought a louder and more reliable set-up, which led him to experiment with two Marshall 50-watt JMP combos. He hooked them together with a Boss DB-5 pedal acting as a graphic equaliser to produce a "meaty" sound.[23] The set-up for his 1979 Montreux concert consisted of the Ampeg VT-22 combined with the 50-watt Marshall. While Gallagher was never too keen on effects, he did have an MXR Phase 90 for "fooling around with"[24] in the studio at this time. However, he frequently emphasised that effects "should come from the hands"[25] rather than from equipment.

Moving into the *Jinx* era, Gallagher revived his Vox AC30 (the "best all-around European amp I have ever come across"[26]), but used it with the Marshall 50-watt combo to augment his sound. At the 1985 Montreux Jazz Festival, two Marshall heads with two speaker cabinets can be spotted, combined with the Vox AC30. In a 1988 interview with *RAW*, Gallagher stated his growing tendency to "go through different phases" and "vary" his amps in particular "about every six months."[27] Hence, by the time of his final Montreux performance in 1994, a Marshall 100-watt Super Bass amp had now been added to the AC30/Marshall 50-watt combo, which he converted to sound more like a Super Lead. According to Gallagher, the amp, which was borrowed from Gerry McAvoy, gave his sound more "body."[28] He placed the Super Bass atop a 4X12 cabinet (often covered by a cloth) and used a Boss DB-5 pedal for equaliser along with a DOD 680 delay to achieve slap echo, which he felt "can really change the character of your guitar."[29]

Although remaining "very wary" of guitar effects and pedals[30] and still wishing to get "as much from the guitar and amp as possible,"[31] Gallagher did display gradual experimentation with effects throughout the 1980s. He employed an Ibanez TS808 Tube Screamer and a script-logo MXR Dyna Comp to "drive the songs from the leads [...] as a form of compression" rather than for effect.[32] By 1988, this was "on almost all the time" and mostly used "as a signal booster."[33] He also added a Boss BF-2 flanger on certain songs such as 'Shadow Play', 'Moonchild' and 'Bad Penny' for some "variety and mystique,"[34] while his OC-2 Octaver—which he described as his "favourite effect"[35]—reflected his growing interest in subtle modulation and pitch manipulation. Gallagher also sometimes used the Boss OD-1 Overdrive in his live performances. Speaking to Viv Campbell in 1991, the guitarist admitted that he had been against Overdrive for many years, but recognised the benefit in some solos.[36] The only rack-mounted effect that Gallagher used periodically was a Boss ROD-20, which he praised for its "midrange possibilities."[37] In the studio, he expanded his knowledge on programmable effects boards, such as the Boss ME-5. For the majority of the time, however, he never "bothered" to program the ME-5, preferring to "leave all that up to an engineer."[38]

Throughout his career, Gallagher preferred Fender Rock 'n' Roll 150 strings for his electric guitars and Martin medium gauge strings for his acoustic guitars. He also varied his picks accordingly: Herco Flex 75s for electric guitar and Fender tortoiseshell picks for acoustic guitar. When playing slide guitar, early in his career, Gallagher tended to use a brass slide, which he believed added bite and aggression to his tone and produced a sharp sounding slide. He later switched to a glass Coricidin medicine bottle to produce a softer and less harsh tone, although he would continue to use the brass for acoustic playing, particularly on his National. By the early 1980s, Gallagher had gone back to a brass slide for electric (as can be seen in 'I Wonder Who' from Montreux 1985), but also had a fondness for steel socket wrenches, describing them as "fantastic," despite tending to "wear your small finger down"[39] and tire the hand by the end of a concert. When using a capo, he tended to rely on the Bill Russel model (see 4.6 for details of Gallagher's guitar techniques).

"Still makes the walls vibrate"
Amid Gallagher's experimentation with different amps, equipment and effects, he was always keen to emphasise that the "perfect compliment" would be if his music sounded "as if [he was] plugging straight into the amp," indicating—to his ears—that he was "using the effects correctly."[40] The guitarist undoubtedly achieved this aim, with reviews from the 1985 Montreux Jazz Festival emphasising his "natural" and "straightforward" sound that is "as credible [now] as it was at the beginning of his solo career.[41] According to *Der Bund*, Gallagher "devoted himself body and soul to the music, savouring every note of his guitar as if it were a drop of his heart's blood."[42] Through his guitar tone, he produced a "subtle dialogue"[43] with the audience, showcasing his sensitivity and nuanced understanding as a musician.

Given this rave review of his performance, it is rather surprising that Gallagher was, in fact, not the first choice for the Festival's 19th edition. Keen to attract a younger audience, the organisers had signed up English pop singer Kim Wilde and synth-pop group Talk Talk. After both acts pulled out at the last minute, Gallagher was then drafted in as headliner, travelling out to Switzerland directly from an intense two-month US tour. Joining him on the bill were Big Sound Authority and the Blues Band, reformed especially for the occasion thanks to the persuasive abilities of Claude Nobs.

At this stage in Gallagher's career, the press often poked fun of the guitarist and his dogged allegiance to the blues. Leading up to his appearance at Montreux, one Swiss newspaper claimed (incorrectly) that he would "undoubtedly be very happy to earn a few Swiss francs," given that he has been unable to find a new record deal since his departure from Chrysalis in 1982.[44] Others joked that he had "come back to life" in reference to his supposed 'hiatus' and that he could not be more different than Nina Hagen—the "Godmother of German Punk"—who was also performing at the Festival that weekend.[45] Despite the fact that Gallagher was only 37 years old at the time, some journalists drew attention to his 'old' age, describing him as a "well-oiled old Harley"[46] and his "prehistoric"[47] blues like "a cardigan of the same nostalgic fabric."[48]

However, as was often the case with such comments, Gallagher's performance immediately laid to rest any rumours that he was no longer the live performer that he once was. Most journalists were in agreement that he "saved the evening" not just with his "generosity" by stepping in at the last minute, but also with his "legendary punch."[49] As Rolan Tillmanns of *Le Matin* noted, Gallagher required no "fireworks or sophisticated orchestration"; his "naturalness" and "energy" was enough to "hit the mark" and provide "two long hours of blues and rock at its best."[50] "Gallagher's music had lost none of its shine and freshness," admitted *Der Bund*, "It couldn't have been more authentic, more honest and more vital."[51]

According to press reports, Gallagher had rehearsed for over an hour in the afternoon before the concert, treating a small crowd of spectators that had gathered to a repertoire of old blues numbers, but he showed no signs of tiredness when he hit the stage that evening. "The one and only Rory Gallagher!" introduced Claude Nobs, before the guitarist broke into a storming rendition of 'Double Vision', followed by 'Shin Kicker' and 'Brute Force and Ignorance', clearly meaning business and proving why he should never just be a fallback option.

Throughout the concert, Gallagher "pulled out all the stops of his abilities,"[52] offering extended versions of many of his songs. There is the sultry 13-minute version of 'Off the Handle, for example, which features some smouldering slide-playing and fabulous interplay with the newest addition of the Rory Gallagher Band: harmonica player Mark Feltham. And the ten-minute rendition of 'Bad Penny', which gives bassist Gerry McAvoy a chance to shine, with his extended solo, accompanied by some playful dancing from Gallagher. Not to mention a 16-minute show-stopping 'I Wonder Who', played on Gallagher's unique 1965 National Airline (JB Hutto model). While the Res-O-Glas-bodied guitar is today associated with Jack White, Gallagher was ahead of the curve, inspired to purchase the guitar because of its unusual appearance and its JB Hutto connection.

"Who's gonna kiss and hug you when all your so-called friends have packed up, sold your home, sold your car, stole your soul, but *they can't get this guitar*!" he growls. In his improvised lyrics, Gallagher also acknowledges tennis player John McEnroe's shock departure from Wimbledon the day before ("when John McEnroe packs up his kit bag and goes on home. Sorry, John!"). Perhaps an unexpected namecheck for the audience, yet Dónal notes that his brother identified strongly with the tennis player, admiring his willingness to stand his ground and defend his convictions.[53] Gallagher's flawless slide solo offers a perfect counterpoint to his gutsy vocals. His tone here is clear, sharp and confident—a real high point in the set and perhaps one of the greatest renditions of this song that he ever did.

Concert reviews constantly make reference to Gallagher's stamina and express surprise at his "unbridled energy on stage."[54] It was "full steam ahead for two and a half hours without the slightest sign of tiredness," notes François Cuvit of *Berner Zeitung* with surprise, "And that's after twenty years of performing almost every evening!"[55] "The Irishman has lost none of his legendary energy," Jeans-Blaise Besençon of *24 Heures* concurs.[56] This is perhaps most apparent in the fiery 'Moonchild' and the cover of Sonny Boy Williamson's swing blues 'When My Baby She Left Me', which again demonstrates the splendid musical chemistry between Gallagher and Feltham as they engage in a jaunty call and response with one another. 'Big Guns' also sees Gallagher play ferocious slide, ending the song with a sprint from one end of the stage to the other as he kicks his right leg up and down.

Unlike many other artists, Gallagher has the remarkable ability to create such connections with his audience in both fast- and slow-paced numbers. In 'Tattoo'd Lady', for example, he teases the crowd with his exciting staccato playing, continually stopping and starting to elicit cheers and claps and raising his Stratocaster like a machine gun towards them. In contrast, in 'Out on the Western Plain', all he needs is his voice and Martin D35 acoustic guitar to silence them as they watch in awe at his fingers moving along the fretboard and picking strings to evoke the sound of multiple guitars.

It is no surprise then that Gallagher's versatility is also frequently emphasised in reviews, as is the fact that he is "still full of ideas,"[57] particularly in the way that he adds "idiosyncratic Celtic-coloured harmonies"[58] to the blues and clearly takes great pleasure in playing with no concern about financial reward. While the lack of new songs is frequently commented upon (it had been three years since *Jinx*), most journalists agree that the addition of Mark Feltham added a freshness to the old material, his contributions particularly noteworthy in the acoustic set on numbers like 'Walkin' Blues' and 'Banker's Blues'. Both songs offer an early insight into the union that would develop further between Gallagher and the harmonica player who was such a fundamental part of the guitarist's final decade. According to Robert Magnenat of *Gazette de Lausanne,* by the end of his set, Gallagher had a "good part of the room standing up and shouting his name."[59] This offered a sign of hope that the "the era of technicalisation of rock music is over and that good old rock & roll is coming back into fashion instead."[60]

In fact, Gallagher's performance went down so well that he returned for an encore of 'Philby', which took him over his pre-allotted timeslot. This led one of the technicians for the Blues Band—who were up after him—to threaten to cut the power. Trying to mitigate the tension, Claude Nobs asked Gallagher to wrap up his set after 'Philby'. The guitarist obliged, but immediately locked himself in his dressing room in frustration. Gallagher had been expected to return to the stage to jam with the Blues Band, but—in a classic example of his passive stubbornness—he instead waited in his dressing room and "snuck away surreptitiously" when he was called up.[61]

"A rocker with heart and soul"

In the liner notes to *All Around Man – Live in London* (2023), Nigel Summerley remarks that Duke Ellington's advice to "never start with a finisher" was not something that Gallagher ever came across, judging by the fact that he "played every number as if it were his last of the evening – sometimes the last he would play." Watching or listening to any of Gallagher's performances, you would be hard pressed not to agree with Summerley. But specifically watching or listening to any of Gallagher's performances at the Montreux Jazz Festival, this statement is even more meaningful. Whether 1970, 1975, 1977, 1979, 1985 or 1994, Gallagher's appearances are abundant with all sorts of musical snapshots that offer a reference point into the multifaceted performer that he always was, as well as his continuous development as an artist, whether in terms of style, tone, rigs, voice and mood.

Part 2 - *Storming the Montreux Jazz Festival 1985*

To look at 1985 alone, we see the humble working musician in his Western shirt and denim cutoff; the pioneering bluesman with his acoustic guitar, peppering his songs with unique Celtic embellishments; the red-hot rocker unleashing all sorts of implausible sounds from his Stratocaster; the skilful leader directing his bandmates with subtle head cues and hand gestures; the consummate showman (although Gallagher would, no doubt, hate the term) teasing the crowd with his duckwalks and machine gunning; the musical shaman, capable of putting listeners into a trance and taking them along on a spiritual journey with him... And then there are occasional glimpses of the offstage Gallagher, his polite and frequent "thank yous" and self-effacing "hope you like it," his shy smile in response to the audience's applause, his silly dancing.

But with all these many sides to the musician, *warmth* is the overwhelming characteristic that shines through. As Stephen Hunter of the Cork Folklore Project notes, Gallagher might "unleash an explosive flurry of growling, bent notes" on his guitar, but there was always a "sensitivity" and "aesthetic precision" behind them.[62] He always played with space—whether between guitar phrases, for the different instruments in the band or for the audience to interact—and instinctively understood when and where to make use of speed and volume. In short, he had a deep knowledge, honed through years of experience, of what made a solid live performance. And his performance at the Montreux Jazz Festival in 1985 epitomises this. Gallagher's music was never meant to be "fashionable" or "disposable"; it is "something that is there forever."[63]

LAO

Footnotes

1 'Ein Monument', reproduced in *Deuce Quarterly*, no. 37 (1985), 7.
2 Paul Charles, *Adventures in Wonderland* (Dublin: Hot Press Books, 2023), 79
3 'Festivals', *Melody Maker* (9 September 1975, https://www.roryon.com/festivals239.html
4 Ibid.
5 Colm O'Hare, 'Rory Gallagher: The Rebirth of a Legend', *Hot Press* (September 1998), https://www.roryon.com/FRESH135.html
6 'Rory Gallagher - I Can't Be Satisfied - Germany 1987', https://www.youtube.com/watch?v=QTG5UnXcCPQ
7 Thierry Chatain, 'The Blue Line', *Rock & Folk* (April 1982), https://www.roryon.com/rgfr482.html
8 Liner notes to *Rory Gallagher: Live at Montreux* CD (2006).
9 Chris Welch, 'Rory gets the acoustic bug', *Melody Maker* (19 July 1975), https://www.roryon.com/acoustic.html
10 Ibid.
11 Liner notes to *Rory Gallagher: Live at Montreux* DVD (2006).
12 Julian Piper, 'Rory Gallagher: the magic, the modesty and Muddy Waters', *Music Rader* (14 October 2015), https://www.musicradar.com/news/guitars/rory-gallagher-the-magic-the-modesty-and-muddy-waters-628127
13 Thierry Dénervaud, 'Un autre point de vue', *Le nouvelliste* (31 July 1979), 3.
14 'Quand il y a blues et... blues', *Le nouvelliste* (20 July 1979), 37
15 Nick Robertshaw, 'From Showband Kid to Electric Blues Ace', *New Musical Express* (9 November 1974), http://www.roryon.com/gadget250.html
16 Stefan Grossman, 'Rory Gallagher: An Irish Guitarist Traces His Roots In Acoustic And Electric Blues, And Tells How He Plays Them', *Guitar Player* (March 1978), http://www.roryon.com/GP78.html
17 'Brian May Interview On Taste & Rory Gallagher', https://www.youtube.com/watch?v=2xG4mnm0bBQ
18 'International Musician of the Month: Rory Gallagher', *International Musician and Recording World* (February 1982), https://www.roryon.com/month145.html.
19 Bob Hewitt, 'Rory Gallagher', *Guitarist* (February 1985), https://www.roryon.com/guit231.htm
20 Jeffrey Pike, 'Jeffrey Pike interview with Rory Gallagher', *Guitar Magazine* (May 1973), http://www.roryon.com/guitarpike306.html
21 Grossman, 'Rory Gallagher'.
22 'Rory Gallagher', *Music Maker* (June 1978), http://www.roryon.com/mm678-315.html
23 'International Musician of the Month'.

24 Dan Hedges, 'Rory Gallagher', *Excerpt from British Rock Guitar* (1977), http://www.roryon.com/british.html
25 Ibid.
26 Grossman, 'Rory Gallagher'.
27 Phil Alexander, 'Power Tools: Sound Advise Pure Genius', *RAW* (November 1988), https://www.roryon.com/power.html
28 Ibid.
29 'Rory Gallagher: A Question of Taste', *Sounds* (29 July 1989), https://www.roryon.com/Question.html
30 Ibid.
31 Hewitt, 'Rory Gallagher'.
32 Vivian Campbell, 'The Wearing of the Blues', *Guitar for the Practicing Musician* (August 1991), http://www.roryon.com/guitar91.html
33 Alexander, 'Power Tools'.
34 Henry Yates, 'Messin' with the Rig', *Guitarist* (August 2023).
35 'Rory Gallagher: A Question of Taste'.
36 Campbell, 'The Wearing of the Blues'.
37 'Rory Gallagher: A Question of Taste'.
38 Ibid.
39 Jas Obrecht, 'Rory Gallagher: The Irish Blues-Rocker Slides Again', *Guitar Player* (June 1991), https://www.roryon.com/slides.html
40 'Rory Gallagher: A Question of Taste'.
41 'Rocker mit Leib und Seele', *Der Bund* (8 July 1985), 23.
42 Ibid.
43 Ibid
44 Robert Magnenat, 'Festival: plus fort que le rock fort', *Gazette de Lausanne* (8 July 1985), reproduced in *Deuce Quarterly*, no. 37 (1985), 9.
45 'Rockbotschaften aus tiefsten Seelen', *Der Bund* (8 July 1985), reproduced in *Deuce Quarterly*, no. 37 (1985), 3.
46 Magnenat, 'Festival...'
47 JAL, 'Blues-rock prehistorique avec Rory Gallagher', *Vevey-Riviera* (8 July 1985), reproduced in *Deuce Quarterly*, no. 37 (1985), 12
48 Jeans-Blaise Besençon, 'Montreux: seul Rory...' *24 Heures* (8 July 1985), reproduced in *Deuce Quarterly*, no. 37 (1985), 11
49 Rolan Tillmanns, 'Montreux: seul Rory...' *Le Matin* (7 July 1985), reproduced in *Deuce Quarterly*, no. 37 (1985), 11.
50 Ibid.
51 'Rockbotschaften aus tiefsten Seelen'.
52 François Cuvit, 'Kontrastreiches Programm am 19. Jazzfestival Montreux', *Berner Zeitung* (9 July 1985), reproduced in *Deuce Quarterly*, no. 37 (1985), 4.
53 Dan Muise, *Gallagher, Marriott, Derringer & Trower* (Milwaukee: Hal Leonard Corporation, 2002), 51.
54 Cuvit, 'Kontrastreiches Programm...'
55 Ibid.
56 Besençon, 'Montreux: seul Rory...'
57 Cuvit, 'Kontrastreiches Programm...'
58 'Rockbotschaften aus tiefsten Seelen'.
59 Magnenat, 'Festival...'
60 'Rocker mit Leib und Seele'.
61 LM, 'Untitled', *Le Matin* (8 July 1985), reproduced in *Deuce Quarterly*, no. 37 (1985), 10.
62 Stephen Hunter, "Won't See His Like Again", *The Archive* (January 2000), https://www.roryon.com/archive.html
63 Ibid.

2.3 Hot Nights and Wailing Decibels: The 1986 Tour of Spain

When Rory Gallagher returned to Spain in 1986 for what would be his last tour of the country, it was a far cry from his first visit more than 20 years earlier in 1965. Spain was a changed nation, having recently gone through a lengthy process of democratisation following 36 years of dictatorship. Now, the Spanish Socialist Workers' Party (PSOE) was in charge and, eager to move on from its troubling past, they embraced narratives of modernity, progress and cultural transformation.

These attitudes extended out into popular culture and were adopted by the countercultural movements—*las Movidas*—which started in Madrid in the late 1970s and gradually spread to other cities, such as Barcelona, Bilbao and Vigo. *Las Movidas* looked towards the future as a period of liberation and progressiveness and were characterised by greater sexual expression and drug use, as well as an aesthetic influenced by dadaism, futurism, punk rock and synth pop music. This aesthetic was reflected in street fashion, with both women and men sporting unconventional clothing, bright colours, heavy make-up and voluminous hair.

The popular press was quick to endorse similar narratives and create a dichotomy that split public figures into *past* and *future*. In the world of music, previously well-loved stars were now out of favour, replaced instead by image-conscious icons like Madonna, Prince and Michael Jackson who represented a new generation of frivolity and adventure. With his undeterred devotion to the blues and his preference for check shirts, it is no surprise then that Gallagher was unfairly cast into the former group and framed by much of the Spanish media as a relic of a bygone age.

While Gallagher still had a dedicated fanbase in Spain who were eagerly anticipating his return in 1986, the press was more unfavourable. Leading up to his visit, articles described him as a musician in decline and claimed that his tour was an attempt to fruitlessly "exploit his glorious past"[1]—a calculated lexical choice reflective of the country's general desire to turn its back on former times. In other words, Gallagher was representative of the old guard and, therefore, to like him and his music was deemed not in keeping with the image of a modern Spain.

Across four nights in Barcelona, Madrid, Gijón and Leikeitio, Gallagher proved that he still had plenty to offer and that his years of experience were beneficial—not detrimental—to his popularity and relevance. In their concert reviews, the

Spanish press was torn; although they reluctantly admitted that Gallagher's performances remained high quality and he still had an overwhelming connection with his audience, they were also quick to claim that most people in attendance were simply "blurred by the fog of nostalgia."[2]

But to what extent did the "fog of nostalgia" really play a role? Were press reports in line with actual evidence from audio recordings and first-hand testimonies? Or were they simply reflective of Spain's social situation and a desire to break with the past? And what was the long-term significance of Gallagher's 1986 tour for the people of Spain? These are questions that we seek to answer in this chapter.

The Spanish Connection

Although Gallagher's first trip to Spain took place in 1965 when he was 17 years old, his relationship with the country, in fact, goes back much further than this. According to his brother Dónal, Gallagher's love for all things Spanish began when he was a young child and first stared into the sound hole of an acoustic guitar, sold in Ireland at the time as a "Spanish" acoustic guitar—a then-mysterious instrument, uncommon in Irish folk music.[3]

Gallagher's interest in Spain continued throughout his teenage years as he discovered the music of Andrés Segovia and Manitas de Plata, fuelling his lifelong love of flamenco music. He also developed a passion for Spanish art when attending night classes at the Crawford College of Art and Design in central Cork. When Gallagher joined the Fontana Showband at 15 years of age, he added 'Spanish Gypsy Dance' to their setlist, giving him an opportunity to experiment with flamenco guitar, although he would always humbly claim throughout his life that he could never play the style of music well and that he just "faked it for [his] own ears."[4]

The young Gallagher expressed a keen desire to visit Spain, so he was delighted when the opportunity arose to play a four-week residency with his showband at a US Air Force Base in Alcalá de Henares, 31km outside of Madrid. Gallagher flew out to Spain just one day after completing his Leaving Certificate examination. Dónal notes that his brother's excitement about his first trip abroad was stymied by one stipulation of the contract: he had to cut his hair. Gallagher begrudgingly agreed to the decision, although he was not happy to find the *Cork Examiner* waiting at the airport to snap a photograph of him—with his newly cropped hair—boarding the plane (he would wait six weeks for it to grow back before playing for fans in Ireland again!).

In many ways, Spain was a rite of passage for Gallagher. In addition to performing every night for an audience who was well-versed in rhythm and blues, he learnt to swim, attended his first bullfight (which he did not enjoy) and made friends with many US soldiers at the base, who let him borrow their records and introduced him to a range of blues artists that he had not encountered before. There was only one downside: he missed the chance to see the Beatles play in Madrid because his military pass to leave the base did not arrive in time. Dónal remembers

Gallagher's sense of depression at not attending the concert still looming large weeks later when he returned to Cork. However, it was not enough to kill his joy for Spain and he read extensively about the country, soaking up its history and culture, and looking forward to returning one day.

It was May 1974 when Gallagher—now an accomplished solo artist—set foot in Spain again, performing three concerts in San Sebastián, Madrid and Barcelona, respectively. Although Gallagher was more or less unknown when he arrived, his performances quickly turned him into "one of the most significant music acts" to ever happen in Spain.[5] With the country still in the grips of Franco's dictatorship, the Spanish people were hungry for rock music. Just as he did in Northern Ireland, Poland, Hungary and countless other places, Gallagher brought his music to them at a pivotal moment, representing hope, freedom and a new future.

Gallagher returned to Spain one year later, this time with greater press attention and anticipation around his tour now that he was better known. Once more, he performed in San Sebastián, Madrid and Barcelona, stunning audiences with his authentic rock and blues. 1979 saw him back again for three dates in Irún, Badalona and Madrid. He also made history when he crossed the border into Portugal, playing one of the first rock concerts in the country since the Carnation Revolution.

Although it would be July 1984 before Gallagher revisited Spain, with an appearance at the Calpe Rock Music Festival in Alicante, he maintained close ties with the country, most notably through his friendship with flamenco guitarist Juan Martín who recalls Gallagher as a "friendly, respectful, warm, talented guy"[6] (see 1.4). Inspired by the passion, style and rhythm of Spanish music, Gallagher would also introduce elements of the genre into his later live performances, from extended openings to 'Tattoo'd Lady and 'Out on the Western Plain' to a revived version of 'I'm Not Awake Yet' at Vienna Rockhaus in 1992 (see 3.1). According to Dónal, Gallagher's troubadour and Gypsy spirit fit with the Spanish way of life, and he is sure that his brother would have one day bought a house in Spain.

The Wanderer Returns (to a 'New' Spain)
Despite being absent from Spain between 1979 and 1984, Gallagher sustained a small but loyal fanbase in the country. For those growing up during Franco's dictatorship, Gallagher's music had been a "fundamental influence" and he was considered "one of the most important musical interpreters."[7] Therefore, there were waves of excitement about his long overdue return to Spain for the Calpe Rock Music Festival. Unfortunately, these waves of excitement did not sweep the music press who, once highly favourable towards Gallagher's music, now tended to view it as archaic and tired in this 'new' Spain.

A case in point is an article from the November 1984 edition of *Disco Exprés*, published several months after Gallagher's appearance in Calpe. Despite the performance being warmly received by Bob Hewitt of the British magazine *Guitarist* ("the performance was outstanding. It was like watching a magician with that Stratocaster on stage [...] sheer mesmerising power and skill turned into musical perfection"[8]), *Disco Exprés* instead opted for the strapline "He's not what he used to be,"[9] before making a series of claims about Gallagher that feeds into this idea. According to journalist Kike Alvareda, watching Gallagher perform live is like "witnessing the fall of an idol." Moreover, he has been "going downhill" over time and is now "a shadow of his former self." The article concludes by stating that Gallagher is "clearly old and has little left to say." Not only was Gallagher just 36 years old at the time—hardly old by anyone's standards—but Alvareda's claims stand in strong contrast to eyewitness accounts of Calpe, as well as other extremely well-received performances from the same period, such as the Pistoia Blues Festival and Tegelen Bluesrock Festival.

In the interview part of the article, Alvareda also shows disrespect for Gallagher, asking him rather caustically, "How long do you plan to keep going?" With his usual politeness, Gallagher responds that he feels "okay" at the moment and still has a following, so he will keep going "as long as [he has] the strength." Alvareda also enquires how Gallagher thinks new generations see him, to which he responds, "hopefully as a hard-working guitarist who never gives up and keeps going." Put differently, Gallagher was tenacious and happy to continue playing, regardless of fluctuating levels of popularity or critical opinions reflective of the zeitgeist rather than his talent.

If Gallagher was deemed irrelevant in 1984, this condition only worsened by the time of his return to Spain two years later. 1986 saw Spain build its platform on the world stage, with entry to the European Economic Community and a referendum that ratified its continued membership in NATO. It was also the year that the PSOE gained an absolute majority for the second time in a snap election. Embracing the future was in full swing and, according to much of the press, this was a future of which Gallagher had no part. An article for *La Hoja de Lunes* by Joaquín del Río, for example, introduces Gallagher with an extremely disparaging description:

> He is halfway between being a down-and-out hippy big shot and a classic heavy drinker of Irish beer. He voted a firm no in the recent referendum on divorce in his country. He carries behind him twenty years of experience that becomes an insurmountable handicap when trying to communicate with an audience much younger than him. In the absence of another alternative, the image of a corpse in an incipient state of artistic decomposition parades around the world's stages. His few unconditional fans, however, remain convinced that he is one of the best guitarists in the world. He is Rory Gallagher.[10]

The article's opening line shows a flagrant lack of understanding about Gallagher's character, wrongly associating him with the hippy movement, as well as claiming that he is pretentious and associates with the wrong kind of people. Moreover, it taps into long-held stereotypes about the Irish as heavy drinkers, which was a common feature of the music press at this time.[11] The reference to Gallagher's position on the legalisation of divorce in Ireland is also an unnecessary remark, used to call attention to his Catholic faith. The Catholic Church had been complicit in Spain's dictatorship, being one of the closest allies of Franco. There was, therefore, much animosity towards Catholicism in Spanish society and many Spaniards rejected the faith following the rise of democracy. Consequently, framing Gallagher as a devout Catholic further serves to portray him as out of place in a modern Spain. Likewise, twisting his many years of experience into something negative that prevents him from connecting with younger audiences is unfounded, as eyewitness accounts from the 1986 tour demonstrate.

The subsequent interview with Gallagher is also full of attempts to depict him as passé, with questions focused on his love for old musicians and his dislike for music videos, aesthetics and pyrotechnics. Del Río is almost gleeful when Gallagher feeds into the narrative by remaining true to his firm beliefs and critiquing the strong attention to image and the lack of improvisation and feeling in many new bands. Gallagher astutely remarks that musicians "should not be asked to become an instrument of the videomaker" and that cinema and video should be "at the service" of groups only. However, Del Río sees this as a sign of "bitterness" on Gallagher's part because the medium has turned against him for not adopting it.

Like in the 1984 interview, Gallagher is asked again where he fits on the contemporary music scene. He replies that he is only interested in creating music "as a means of expression" so that he can "look at himself in the mirror of [his] songs" and "check that [he is] still the same." Unable to rile Gallagher, Del Río ends by provocatively asking him if he wishes he had been born Black. Gallagher tactfully states that the question is "too complex" to deal with, especially after having played a two-hour concert.

Reading these journalistic accounts transmits a very negative image of Gallagher, an image unrecognisable from the man who set Spain alive in the 1970s with his "great blues" that "shook everyone's veins" and "intoxicated" them.[12] "Fashions pass but the blues never dies," *Extra!* had claimed in its review of Gallagher's Madrid show in 1975.[13] Yet clearly, those words had been forgotten just a decade later. Nonetheless, among fans, Gallagher's performances on his 1986 tour left no room for doubt that he might still play the blues, but his music was just as relevant as it always was—even in a 'new' Spain—and was attracting new generations of supporters.

Palau Blaugrana 2, Barcelona (9 July 1986)
Gallagher kicked off his 1986 tour of Spain with a return to Barcelona—a city that had played host to him on three previous occasions. Of these former visits, his first concert in 1974 at the Palau d'Esports was particularly memorable due to the fact that there was a power failure mid-set. Unfazed by the challenge, Gallagher kept the atmosphere going by pulling out his acoustic guitar and singing without a microphone, which *La Vanguardia* reported as the highlight of the evening.[14] Gallagher's 1979 show at the Pabellón Polideportivo del Club

Juventud in Badalona is also remembered positively by fans for his "vigorous and energetic" long set; he returned for three encores, followed by an additional thirty minutes of playing when the cheers from the crowd would not stop. "He gave it his all until the point of visible exhaustion," reported journalist Alberto Mallofré[15]—words that could equally hold true for any of Gallagher's live performances throughout his career.

Given Gallagher's earlier triumphs in the city, expectations were running high for his return in 1986. Momentum built on the day of the concert, with local newspapers reporting on his return and using positive adjectives like "mythical," "legendary" and "virtuoso" to describe him. However, they also could not resist pondering whether this "veteran" who was no longer a "rising star" and was "going through a decline in popularity" would still be capable of exciting audiences.[16] As if to support this, articles frequently referenced *Live! in Europe* and *Irish Tour '74*—albums from over a decade past—as the "best expression" of Gallagher's talent and claimed that he had "evolved little in the eighties" and "failed to connect with new generations."[17] Although Gallagher's supposed lack of evolution was praised for maintaining a sense of "purity" compared to the growing commercialism of Eric Clapton, it, nevertheless, tapped into the idea that he had nothing new to offer in the 1980s and was going through the motions.

On the evening of 9 July, fans poured into the Palau Blaugrana 2, excited to see Gallagher back on their home soil. It was a particularly sticky summer evening, with a "suffocating heat" inside the arena by the time the concert started at 10PM with support act Dinkremea—a local rockabilly group from Sant Gervasi. According to *La Vanguardia*, the crowd "listened respectfully" and gave them "polite applause," but they were all impatiently awaiting the main act of the night.[18]

Just after 11PM, Gallagher fireballed onto the stage with 'Moonchild', followed closely by 'Double Vision', before taking the audience on a whistlestop tour of his career. Songs from *Photo-Finish* and *Top Priority* featured heavily in the set, but he also made sure to throw in old favourites from *Tattoo* and classic covers like 'I Wonder Who' and 'Nadine'. Playing up to the Spanish crowd, Gallagher played a beautiful flamenco opening to 'Tattoo'd Lady', which was met enthusiastically with prolonged claps and cheers, as was the extended version of 'Bad Penny' full of stunning improvisation and interplay with bassist Gerry McAvoy. 'Off the Handle' and 'Messin' with the Kid' also scaled new heights with the addition of Mark Feltham on harmonica.

For Toni Mantis—a fan since 15 years of age—it was "very exciting" to finally have the opportunity to see Gallagher live. According to Mantis, Gallagher "gave himself to the fullest" for the whole time that he was on stage, adding that he "knew no other way" to perform.[19] This echoes Dónal Gallagher's own view of his brother: "every gig was an absolute cup final that had to be won... every show was performed as if it were the last."[20] However, Mantis admits that he was slightly disappointed at the fact that Gallagher—known for his legendary three-hour concerts—only played for around one hour that evening. Mantis also remembers that the guitarist had to be helped to and from the stage—perhaps an early indication that all was not well with his health. Nonetheless, he affirms the high quality of Gallagher's performance and is grateful for having had the opportunity to witness the "strength and technique" live.

Despite the evidence left by bootleg recordings and eyewitness accounts by fans, Gallagher's concert was received unfavourably by the Spanish press. However, rather peculiarly, none of the reviews fault the quality of his actual performance. In fact, they all unwillingly admit that the concert was electrifying. Instead, the only way to signal that he is no longer relevant is by targeting his changed appearance, age and dedication to the blues. Alberto Mallofré of *La Vanguardia*, for example, entitles his review 'An Already Watched Film' and opens with the line that Gallagher is back in Barcelona "a few kilos heavier."[21] Notwithstanding the unnecessary remark about Gallagher's weight gain, the review then begins seemingly positive with the claim that his "energetic rock blues [...], voice, loose hair, movements and presence were 100% the same as ever" and everything was in place "like the great nights of the 70s." However, Mallofré follows this up with the assertion that he felt a "strange sensation" overcome him as he watched Gallagher, as if he was "going to see an old film that we used to enjoy but now when we watch it again, we enjoy the nostalgia more than real pleasure." Continuing his use of cinema as a metaphor for Gallagher, Mallofré claims that "the film is the same but we have all changed." In other words, times are different now and Spain has moved on, transforming into an exciting, modern country in which there is no longer a place for a musician like Gallagher. Even the one difference about Gallagher's performance that Mallofré points out—the addition of Mark Feltham on harmonica—is cast aside as being "of little relevance."

It is somewhat curious that, just the year before, blues legends Buddy Guy and Junior Wells performed in Barcelona and were hailed by the press for their mastery of the blues and for keeping the genre alive into the 1980s. We have to ask ourselves why was Gallagher criticised for doing exactly the same thing? For Guy and Wells, age and experience were an asset, whereas for Gallagher, they were seen as impediments that made him out of place. For them, playing old blues numbers was a sign of their authenticity, while for Gallagher, it was associated with stagnancy, despite the fact that he never played a song the same way twice. This critique is something that Gallagher himself reflected on in a 1987 interview for German television programme *Aktuelle Stunde*. When asked why he has played the same music for 22 years, Gallagher states that he has a "strong style of [his] own," which is "a gift from God" and while 1% of what people say may be true, "99% is work, new ideas, new materials with respect for the roots of the music."[22]

Sala Canciller, Madrid (10 July 1986)

"For me, Rory Gallagher is a grandmaster and an inspiration. I still listen to him every day," legendary Spanish rocker Rosendo told *MariskoRockTV* back in 2018.[23] A Gallagher fan since the late 1960s, the young Rosendo jumped at the opportunity to see his idol at the Teatro Monumental in Madrid on his first Spanish tour back in 1974. So much so, in fact, that Rosendo has the distinction of being the first person in Spain to obtain a ticket for the concert, "queuing like a bastard from early in the morning"[24] to secure his place. The night turned out to be extremely memorable for Rosendo, and like so many others both before and since (e.g. Brian May, Johnny Marr), it inspired him to pursue a career in music.

It was, in fact, Gallagher's 1974 concert in Madrid that helped him make his name in Spain, so that by the time he returned to the same theatre just over a year later, tickets were long sold out and the venue was jampacked. A memory shared on the *Rockliquias* music blog by an attendee of the 1975 Madrid show evocatively describes the atmosphere: "the air full of smoke, flashing lights behind the stage, people on their feet, knowing glances between us all, incredible applause, a sea of sweat."[25] These scenes can be viewed on the video footage of the concert, recorded for Spanish television and capturing the full dynamism of Gallagher and his band at this time. "Pure adrenaline for a youth that ate and dined on fascism, censorship and repression," writes one fan on YouTube.

On his return to Madrid in 1979, Gallagher's popularity had soared to such an extent that he upgraded from a theatre to an indoor arena—Pabellón del Real Madrid—which held over 5,000 spectators. Again, tickets sold out quickly. While the concert went down just as well as previous ones with fans ("Gallagher's performances in Madrid are always a great success,"[26] noted *El País*), it was hampered by poor sound due to the venue's acoustics. "Although his Madrid recital was not completely convincing, it is good to know that he is still alive and well," *El País* concluded sympathetically.

Seven years had passed when Gallagher set foot in the Spanish capital again in 1986, this time supported by the Pedro Calvo Group and opting for a return to a smaller venue—the Sala Canciller, which had swiftly made a name for itself as a temple to rock and metal. Gallagher was the second foreign artist to perform at the venue, pipped only by fellow Irishman Bernie Tormé who played there in March 1985. Just as in Barcelona, articles leading up to the concert generally expressed excitement about Gallagher's "comeback," yet these emotions were tempered by the usual cliches around his "old" age and choice of attire, as well as his stubborn resistance to trends. Despite the mixed views of the press, as usual, Gallagher's performance spoke for itself, silencing any suggestions that pushing 40 meant a dip in the quality of his live shows.

To hear the bootleg is to hear two and a half hours of pure lightning in a bottle. From the moment that Gallagher hits the stage with 'Moonchild', he is full of vigour and intensity, and does not let up until the end note of the fourth encore—'All Around Man'. He surpasses the already high standards set the night before in Barcelona, with powerhouse versions of 'Double Vision', 'Shadow Play' and 'Messin' with the Kid', contrasted with the dulcet acoustic tones of 'Out on the Western Plain' and 'Walkin' Blues'. Gallagher always works best when feeding off an audience and the Madrid audience is particularly wild, inspiring him to push boundaries. Covers of The Beatles' 'Come Together' and Chuck Berry's 'Nadine' are extremely well received, while there is a point in 'Follow Me' where the crowd is so loud that Gallagher hands over vocals to them—a truly moving thing to witness.

Juan Lloret, a long-term Gallagher fan, was at the Sala Canciller back in 1986, and describes the concert as "the best thing [he's] ever seen."[27] Echoing what the bootleg evidences, Lloret remembers Gallagher opening with an impassioned version of 'Moonchild', which set the pace for the several hours of music that followed. Apart from the music, what Lloret—along with other fans—most remembers about the evening is just how stifling the venue was, with Gallagher taking several attempts to remove his denim jacket as he was so heavily soaked with sweat. He and the band even required oxygen in their dressing rooms after the show to recover from the suffocating heat.[28]

Despite these challenges, Gallagher put "so much feeling into every song," bringing "sheer joy" to fans and filling them with "positive energy and a lot of optimism." More than 45 years later and Lloret still has the ticket, treasured "as if it were a piece of gold." Equally, José Martos Arellano, drummer in iconic Spanish rock band Barón Rojo, recalls that "the venue was beyond full capacity" and that Gallagher's hands were "soaked in sweat due to the suffocating heat." Nonetheless, he "gave it his all as usual."[29]

Unlike Barcelona, Gallagher's Madrid concert received generally positive reviews from the press. However, it is interesting to note that, even these positive reviews, are tinged with sarcasm. "And the award for loyalty goes to... Rory Gallagher,"[30] opens a review in *El País*, the type of statement that Gallagher often bemoaned. "It's an easy cop out," he told *Melody Maker* back in 1975, "I'd prefer them to say that they don't like my music."[31] The article continues by lauding Gallagher's former visits to Spain when he "calmed the General's former subjects who craved live music" and contrasting this with his current "chubby face," "usual cowboy uniform" and "marginalised" status on the music scene.

Despite the lukewarm introduction, Gallagher's blues are then described as a "formula that is still working" and which attracts old and new fans to his shows, both generations bonded as they "jump, punch their fists in the air and play invisible guitar." Even the "marine boiler temperatures" of the Sala Canciller are not enough to put off fans, so long as "good old Rory" keeps playing. Although the article acknowledges that fans were highly entertained, it concludes with a derisive description of Gallagher's talent, claiming that he "resurrects venerable phrases from the rusty blues rock repertoire," "barks cliches about bad women sentencing the desperate singer to death" and "squeezes angry sentiments" from his covers of 'Come Together' and 'Nadine'.

Equally, Luigi Almarza of *La Nueva España* claims that Gallagher "put on a splendid display of his talents," producing "powerful high-quality hard rock, yet did not "invent anything new."[32] As if to indicate Gallagher's 'decline', Almarza points out that the concert took place in "one of the shabbiest places" in the city. Pedro Calvo of *Diario 16* gives the concert three out of five stars. The ambiguous review states how Gallagher is "no longer fashionable," but this is "a point in favour of his music" because it makes it "beyond judgements of good or bad."[33] He praises Gallagher for "vibrating and roaring as if participating in a battle where his own life is at stake." However, like Almarza, he still uses the venue as an indication of Gallagher's 'decline', describing it as a "dirty heater that leaves you dehydrated." Somewhat contradicting their claims of a 'decline', both articles note that the venue was "packed with young rockers" who were "15 years younger than Rory."

Plaza de Toros, Gijón (12 July 1986)

The day after his Madrid performance, Gallagher travelled up to Gijón in the north-west province of Asturias in preparation for his concert the next evening at the Plaza de Toros. Gijón had never played host to Gallagher before, so the date was marked firmly in the calendar of rock and blues lovers across the city. There was a general feeling of elation in the air, especially when news circulated that Gallagher and his brother Dónal had arrived early and had just checked into the Hotel León. Once settled, the brothers decided to take a look around the city centre, stopping off at El Busgosu rock bar on the Avenida de la Costa for a quick pint. Their accents immediately aroused curiosity from the patrons and, through whispers, the identities of the two strangers were slowly revealed. Soon, Gallagher was approached by a group of fans with whom he politely conversed, before inviting the entire bar to his concert—on the house, of course.[34]

Despite making a good first impression with the local *gijoneses*, just as in Barcelona and Madrid, the press was more mixed about Gallagher's forthcoming concert. Once again, articles emphasised his age and rigid attitude towards music, pointing out that he is "an old rock figure" who "had his heyday in the past decade," that his "popularity is starting to decline" and he has "little knowledge of current music."[35] Some, less familiar with his background, even mistakenly called him English or British, while others moaned that his concert was the most expensive of the summer, costing 1,200 pesetas (approximately £6)—hardly expensive for an artist of Gallagher's renown. However, this was also allayed by more supportive comments about him being one of the "more conscientious musicians," citing his recent Self Aid appearance, and praising him for maintaining a relationship with the traditional music of Ireland.

It was Gallagher's affinity with his country's traditions that particularly seemed to resonate with the *gijonés* press. This marked sense of regional identity was something that Gallagher himself also appreciated about the people of Gijón, telling journalist Joaquín del Río that he was "very interested" in the "strong regional feeling" because, as an Irishman, he felt the same way.[36]

Gallagher also spoke in interviews about his fondness for the sound of the *gaita* (a type of Asturian bagpipe), comparing it to the uilleann pipes and stating how he wished that he had somebody in his band tonight who could play them. Both Gallagher's knowledge of Spanish music and cultural issues also endeared him to the *gijonés* press; in interviews, he expressed praise for the music of Los Brincos and Los Bravos, as well as his concern about playing in a bullring, given his negative feelings about bullfighting.

With the absence of bootlegs for Gallagher's Gijón concert, we must rely on press and fan reviews to build a picture of the evening. According to *El Comercio*, 3,000 people were in attendance, despite the bullring's 9,000-person capacity. The concert opened with a short set from local rock band Stukas, who pulled out all the stops to get the crowd going before Gallagher's arrival. Just as in Madrid, Gallagher played for over two and a half hours, showing an "extraordinary mastery of the guitar,"[37] particularly during the blues numbers. However, press opinions were generally divided between those who considered the show to be a nostalgia trip and others who thought it was novel and exciting. Articles describe Gallagher as a "mythical figure" who put on "an exhibition of old school rock," delivering all that was expected of him with no surprises. However, they acknowledge that, in doing so, he "never disappointed" and formed a strong connection with the audience who were on his side from the very start.[38] Indeed, the crowd was so animated that Gallagher had to dodge a bottle of gin thrown up on stage halfway through the show. Furthermore, while some journalists thought that it was real value for money to attend such a long concert, others found it "boring" and wished that it had ended sooner.[39]

One person who did not want the concert to end was Nacho Fernández Campuzano who shared his memories on Reiko's Rory Gallagher website.[40] Fernández Campuzano had attended a Kinks concert at the Plaza de Toros several months earlier and, while there, had seen a poster on the wall advertising Gallagher's forthcoming concert. Having been a huge Gallagher fan for many years, he immediately bought a ticket and eagerly anticipated the big day in July. He was not disappointed. The Spaniard can still picture Gallagher running out onto the stage holding his Fender Stratocaster, before treating the audience to a blend of "energetic songs, high octane rock, blues and much more delicate songs." For Fernández Campuzano, seeing Gallagher was a "religious experience" and he could not keep his eyes off the guitarist, who was smiling from ear to ear for the whole time that he played. Fernández Campuzano believes that there has been no artist before or since who had such a bond with the audience. "Intense, natural, passionate [...] it seemed as if the guitar was part of his own body [...] Right after his guitar solo, you couldn't even blink." He remembers leaving the bullring "flying on a cloud"—an experience that he will never forget.

Frontón Santi Brouard, Lekeitio (13 July 1986)

Gallagher was no stranger to performing in places that others might deem too risky and shy away from. As is well documented, he was one of the few artists to give concerts in Belfast during the Troubles, returning annually throughout the 1970s as part of his Irish tour. "It's the same as playing anywhere else, except for the odd explosion," he told *happytimes* in 1976, glossing over the significance of his act.[41] When visiting Spain, he viewed the Basque Country with exactly the same attitude.

Located in the western Pyrenees straddling the border between Spain and France, the Basque Country has a long history of political turbulence. Between 1959 and 2011, an armed and political conflict took place between Spain and the Basque National Liberation Movement, which sought independence from Spain and France. The movement was built around the separatist organisation ETA, which evolved from a group promoting traditional Basque culture into a paramilitary group who carried out bombings, assassinations and kidnappings throughout Spanish territory.

While this volatile political situation prevented many international musicians from visiting the region, Gallagher was not one of them. Between 1974 and 1986, he performed in the Basque Country four times, setting a record in the process. Gallagher also stands as one of the first international musicians to have played a concert in the Basque Country; he was beaten to the title by Dutch band Golden Earring who performed in Bilbao several months before him.[42]

Gallagher's first and second performances both took place at the Anoeta Sports Centre in San Sebastián in 1974 and 1975, respectively. At this time, still under Franco's dictatorship, many rock & roll records were banned from Spain, meaning that dedicated *vascos* would travel across the border to France and pick them up from Hendaye or Bayonne. Those who had purchased a ticket to see Gallagher in San Sebastián, therefore, had little idea what to expect from a live rock concert and were blown away by what they witnessed. "My hair stands on end and I'm almost in tears [when I think about it]," commented one fan on the Rory Gallagher Fans Spain Facebook group, "It left me stunned. It made me love blues and rock. I adore Rory and will always look up to him."

Gallagher returned to the Basque Country in 1979, this time playing at the Frontón Uranzu in Irún. Franco was now dead, and the region was shortly to take part in a referendum on the Statute of Autonomy. However, just a few months before Gallagher's visit, there had been two terrorist attacks by ETA in San Sebastián and Getxo, killing five civil guards. As usual, Gallagher was undaunted and proceeded to perform to a sold-out audience. During the concert, he was presented with a *txapela* (a Basque beret) embroidered with the words "Welcome, world champion of musicians," which he wore for several songs.

Speaking to *Naiz* in 2018, Josema Martínez—one of the men behind JF Promociones Musicales who organised Gallagher's 1970s concerts in the Basque Country—shared a funny anecdote from after the concert in Irún. He and Gallagher had one too many drinks in the bar and tried to head back to their room at the Alcázar hotel. They made it to the lift, but once it reached their floor, they both tried to exit at the same time and got stuck in the doorway. They promptly fell onto the floor laughing and could not stand up. Martínez still does not remember how they got out in the end.[43]

By the time Gallagher came back to the Basque Country in 1986, Santi Ugarte of Tiburón Concerts was now the major promoter, having taken over from JF Promociones Musicales. Again, Gallagher was returning at a complex political time when negotiations were taking place between ETA and the Spanish government in Algiers and when regional elections were set to take place in the Basque Country. However, as usual, he saw no reason why this should affect his decision to perform, this time at Frontón Santi Brouard in the small town of Lekeitio.

Once again, press reports leading up to the concert were unkind. An article in *El Correo* starts promisingly by describing Gallagher as "one of the most legendary blues rock guitarists of all time," but then proceeds to criticise his "eternal jeans and check shirts and old-fashioned hairstyle."[44] It goes on to refer to him as a "musician in decline," supporting this unfair point by the simple fact that he has never strayed far from the blues. The article also compares him to Eric Clapton, claiming that he falls short of Slowhand because he "does not know how to do anything else" but play the blues. It concludes by bluntly stating that Gallagher is "out of the loop" and his way of "thinking, composing and playing is no longer of this time."

Despite the negative press, Gallagher's performance said otherwise. Fan Carlos Olabarria remembers the concert as "the best [he has] ever seen." Olabarria was just 19 years old at the time and had bagged front row tickets with his friends. He was so "impressed" by Gallagher's energy and humility, noting that the guitarist "seemed genuinely surprised by the affection and fervour of the audience." For Olabarria, Gallagher transmitted something "impossible to explain," but which made him "feel like a friend forever." He recalls a particular funny anecdote during the acoustic section when his "enthusiastic" friend removed his t-shirt and threw it onto the stage; he went home topless after the concert!

Olabarria later saw a photograph of Gallagher wearing that very same t-shirt. Speaking of the press reports, Olabarria says that they are simply not true, that Gallagher "wasn't boring at any time" and that he has "rarely seen an audience leave so happy." He also adds that Basque fans felt an affinity with Gallagher because of his Irish nationality. "Rory played for pure enjoyment, not for money," Olabarria concludes, "He gave himself to the audience without thinking about how long he would play for."[45] That evening, Gallagher played for almost three hours, in fact, to the point where the venue had to cut off the lights to make him finish.

Sadly, ill health and a worsening fear of flying prevented Gallagher from ever returning to Spain again. Nonetheless, his 1986 tour secured his reputation among fans as a musician who "mastered the guitar like few others, with great wisdom and tremendous intensity, letting himself be carried away by wherever the audience took him."[46]

Blurred by the Fog of Nostalgia?
The transformation of Spain from Gallagher's first visit in 1965 to his last in 1986 was dramatic. The 'new' and democratised Spain was unrecognisable, no

longer under the grips of Franco's dictatorship and warmly welcoming a future of modernity, progress and cultural change. These attitudes were reflected in the popular press, who were generally unsympathetic to or sceptical of public figures no longer considered to be in keeping with this fresh country. Gallagher's style of music, clothing and age unfairly found him classified into this category. Both prior to and after his concerts—whether in Barcelona, Madrid, Gijón or Lekeitio—many reviews claimed that, despite his undoubtable prowess, his blues were not something for the modern age and that fans were simply "blurred by the fog of nostalgia."[47]

This view does not quite fit with reality. To hear a Gallagher show from his 1979 Spanish tour and compare it with 1986 is to witness major progression. Gallagher had shed his hard rock sound, moving towards a more consolidated blues style. However, this blues style was not just a tired and cliched formula, but rather peppered with his own unique touches, drawing on his extensive knowledge of jazz, Irish folk, flamenco and rock & roll. By this time, Gallagher had solidified his position as a true bluesmaster, developing greater command of the stage and his instrument. The addition of Mark Feltham on harmonica and the inimitable musical chemistry between them had further sharpened his act. However, his continued preference to wear check shirts and sport sideburns—at a time of power dressing and big hair—made it easy for the press to use them as shortcuts to claim that he was not progressing. Claims of nostalgia are also somewhat contradictory when the very same articles report on the number of young people in the audience, coming together with old Spanish fans and delighting in Gallagher's music.

And if we are to agree that a certain element of enjoyment in Gallagher's live shows came from nostalgia, then that is not necessarily a bad thing. We must remember that those who first discovered Gallagher's music were living under a brutal dictatorship full of murders, censorship and repression. For them, Gallagher represented freedom, escapism and youth. Therefore, it is only normal that Spanish fans might relive his 1986 concerts with a certain sense of nostalgia, recalling what his music meant to them at a particularly awful time in the country's history and counting their lucky stars that they got through it.

Like in Belfast, Gallagher's concerts in Spain throughout the 1970s temporarily united communities, tore down barriers, suspended politics, gave people hope, encouraged a common goal and promoted music as a healing force. At the time, the Spanish press had praised him for the very same reasons. But how soon they were to forget. How capricious their motives became once democracy was established and the 1980s arrived in full force with its cultural revolution.

But Gallagher's small yet dedicated Spanish fanbase never did forget. In 1986, they still turned out in their thousands for the return of a man who had done so much musically for them. It was clear that Gallagher was an element of the past with which they did not want to break, despite the best efforts of the press. And for Gallagher, it was only ever the fans that mattered, not the critics. "It'd be a sad day if I let [comments in the press] get to me and I started thinking, 'They must be right—they don't think I'm valid, therefore I can't be any good'," the guitarist later told *Sounds*.⁴⁸

Once Gallagher had passed away in 1995, the Spanish press was suddenly filled with praise for him and his attitude towards music. Ironically, all the things that he had been criticised for on his 1986 tour were now being commended by the very same press: his unwavering commitment to the blues, his resistance to the whims of the music industry, his originality as a guitarist and lyricist, his integrity, even his down-to-earth clothing. The obituaries were also filled with recognition of Gallagher's strong relationship with his audience:

> Seeing Rory perform was like becoming friends with him. He gave the impression that the energy transmitted by his music had no limits, that his batteries were fed by the vibrations that the public sent him [...] When Rory picked up his guitar and began to sing with his sweet but raspy voice, you knew unequivocally that he was addressing you. His main virtue was to communicate, to easily get inside of those who listened to him.⁴⁹

Now there was no mention of Gallagher's age, weight or 'sleepy' blues; rather, he was applauded for "opening the path" in 1974 for all the international acts who came later and performed in Spain.⁵⁰ The acknowledgement that Gallagher blazed a trail for all those who came after is a pattern that can, in fact, be found across the international music press following his death. Liam Mackey of *Irish Express* reflected on this sorry state of affairs, writing that it was a shame that it took death for Gallagher's immense contribution to music to be acknowledged.⁵¹ This was echoed by Dónal Gallagher who, speaking in 2000, expressed anger at the fact that nobody had told his brother how much they appreciated his music when he was alive and that he had spent the last decade or so of his life thinking that nobody cared about him anymore.⁵²

In October 2023, Carlos Marcos wrote a reflection piece for *El País* on Gallagher and why "the guitarist who should have reigned did not reign." He puts this down to Gallagher's "incorruptible ethics" and "100% pure" devotion to the blues. Marcos also briefly reflects on Gallagher's Spanish tours, noting that his interaction with the audience was "a spectacle in itself" where his "vibe could almost be seen, not just felt."⁵³ It is recent articles such as these that offer hope that attitudes in Spain (and indeed across the world) are changing towards Gallagher and that his significant place in the history of rock/blues is finally being recognised. However, coming almost 30 years after his death, such recognition is bittersweet.

LAO

Footnotes

1 Joaquín Del Río, 'El rock es un medio de comunicación hiperpoderoso', *La Hoja del Lunes* (14 July 1986), https://rorygallagher.es/prensa/entrevistas/entrevista-realizada-el-12-de-julio-de-1986-y-publicada-por-la-hoja-del-lunes-el-14-de-julio-de-1986-por-el-baboso-joaquin-del-rio/
2 Alberto Mallofré, 'Una película ya vista', *La Vanguardia* (11 July 1986), 32.
3 Dónal Gallagher, 'Prólogo' in Marcello Gobello, *Rory Gallagher: El Último Héroe* (Lenoir Ediciones: Girona), 7.
4 'Rory Gallagher - The Complete 1991 "Guitar Player" Interview', https://www.youtube.com/watch?v=9gA9vGWieAs&t=2436s
5 'Una reliquia', *Extra!* (14 March 1975), 22.
6 Interview with Juan Martín, 16 March 2023.
7 Juan Casas Rigall, 'Rory Gallagher visto desde España' in *As Others Saw Us: Cork Through European Eyes*, edited by Joachim Fisher and Grace Neville (London: Collins Press, 2005), 403-404.
8 Interview with Bob Hewitt, 27 May 2023.
9 Kike Alvareda, 'El viejo corázon irlandés', *Disco Exprés* (November 1984), https://rewritingrory.co.uk/2022/09/15/the-old-irish-heart-rory-gallagher-disco-expres-november-1984/
10 Del Río, 'El rock es un medio de comunicación hiperpoderoso'.
11 See Lauren Alex O'Hagan, '"Rory Gallagher's Leprechaun Boogie": Irish Stereotyping in the International Music Press', vol. 4, no. 2 (2023), *Review of Irish Studies in Europe*, 38-72.
12 J. Moya Angeler. 'Rory – Gran Reserva', *Extra!* (14 March 1975), 22.
13 Ibid.
14 Alberto Mallofré, 'Concierto de Rory Gallagher', *La Vanguardia* (31 May 1974), 65.
15 Alberto Mallofré, 'Concierto triunfal de Rory Gallagher', *La Vanguardia* (1 March 1979), 47.
16 Alberto Mallofré, 'Rory Gallagher, un veterano del rockblues, - en el Blaugrana 2', *La Vanguardia* (9 July 1986), 25; 'Rory Gallagher reaparece con su trepidante rock de siempre', *El Periódico* (9 July 1986), 47.
17 Ibid.
18 Mallofré, 'Una película ya vista', 32.
19 Interview with Toni Mantis, 10 July 2023.
20 Treacy Hogan, 'The Legend's Going Strong', *Irish Independent* (26 June 2004), 21.
21 Ibid.
22 'Rory Gallagher - I Can't Be Satisfied - Germany 1987', https://www.youtube.com/watch?v=QTG5UnXcCPQ&ab_channel=ScottishTeeVee
23 'Rosendo rinde homenaje a Rory Gallagher, una de sus mayores influencias', https://www.youtube.com/watch?v=VtK3qxiZnmw
24 Jorge Aldea, 'Rosendo: "Yo compré la primera entrada para ver a Rory Gallagher en el Monumental"', *Cadena Ser* (13 May 2012), https://cadenaser.com/ser/2012/05/13/cultura/1336864629_850215.html
25 'RORY GALLAGHER - Live Madrid 1.975', *Rockliquias* (20 December 2014), https://www.rockliquias.com/2014/12/rory-gallagher-live-madrid-1975.html
26 José Manuel Costa, 'Recital madrileño de Rory Gallagher', *El País* (2 March 1979), https://elpais.com/diario/1979/03/03/cultura/289263605_850215.html
27 Interview with Juan Lloret, 8 January 2023.
28 'Rory Gallagher en la sala Canciller', *Los Mejores Rock* (30 January 2024), https://losmejoresrock.com/rory-gallagher-en-la-sala-canciller-el-otro-rock-de-una-noche-de-verano-pero-en-1986/
29 Our thanks to Jesús Ruipérez for sharing this memory with us (4 March 2023) on behalf of José Martos Arellano.
30 Diego A. Manrique, 'Top-less', *El País* (13 July 1986), https://elpais.com/diario/1986/07/14/cultura/521676009_850215.html
31 Harry Doherty, 'Rory: play for today, tomorrow you die', *Melody Maker* (29 November 1975), http://www.roryon.com/play142.html
32 Luigi Almarza, 'Un mito del rock duro', *La Nueva España* (11 July 1986), 27.
33 Pedro Calvo, 'Rory Gallagher, una guitarra heroica', *Diario 16* (12 July 1986), 39.
34 Monchi Álvarez, 'Oscarín', *Mi Gijón* (26 November 2021), https://migijon.com/oscarin-aprendiz-playu/
35 'Tres mil personas presenciaron en Gijón a Rory Gallagher', *La Nueva España* (15 July 1986), 33; 'Rory Gallagher y Stukas, hoy, en la plaza de toros', *La Nueva España* (12 July 1986), 7.
36 Del Río, 'El rock es un medio de comunicación hiperpoderoso'.
37 Ibid.
38 'Review', *El Comercio* (13 July 1986), https://rewritingrory.co.uk/2022/07/10/el-comercio-13-july-1986/
39 Del Río, 'El rock es un medio de comunicación hiperpoderoso'.
40 See: https://sites.google.com/view/rory-gallagher/home/memories-of-rory
41 Don Waller, 'Ireland's Powerhouse Blues Man', *happytimes* (1 December 1976), https://www.roryon.com/powerhouse394.html
42 Pablo Cabeza, 'Rory Gallagher, un irlandés conectado con Euskal Herria', *Naiz* (15 August 2018), https://www.naiz.eus/en/info/noticia/20180815/rory-gallagher-un-irlandes-conectado-con-euskal-herria
43 Ibid.
44 J. Fuentenebro, 'El guitarrista Rory Gallagher y su 'blues rock', mañana en Lekeitio', *El Correo* (12 July 1986).
45 Interview with Carlos Olabarria, 11 June 2023.
46 Beatriz Torreadrado, 'Obituary', *Heavy Rock* (1 July 1995), https://rewritingrory.co.uk/2022/07/09/heavy-rock-june-1995/
47 Mallofré, 'Una película ya vista'.
48 Graham Bent, 'Have Guitar Will Travel', *Sounds* (10 December 1988), https://www.roryon.com/have147.html
49 Oscar Bastante, 'Obituary', *Guitar Player* (July 1995), https://rewritingrory.co.uk/2022/07/10/guitar-player-july-1995
50 Don Sincero, 'Primer concierto en España (Donostia, 1974)', in Gobello, *Rory Gallagher*, 61.

Part 2 - *Hot Nights and Wailing Decibels*

51 Liam Mackey, 'Rory Gallagher: Remember Him This Way', *Irish X-Press* (16 June 1995), http://www.roryon.com/remember.html
52 Mark McClelland, 'Why We Won't Let Rory Be Forgotten', *Evening Echo* (13 June 2000), https://www.roryon.com/forgotten.html
53 Carlos Marcos, 'Rory Gallagher: por qué no reinó el guitarrista que debió reinar', *El País* (1 October 2023), https://elpais.com/cultura/2023-10-01/rory-gallagher-por-que-no-reino-el-guitarrista-que-debio-reinar.html?rel=buscador_noticias

2.4 Let's Go to Work! *Rocklife* 1990

Gallagher's appearances on the German music television programme *Rockpalast* are considered landmark occasions in his touring history, capturing the greatest features of his performance skills from the mid-1970s to the early 1990s. As stated on the *Rockpalast Archive* website, fans could be "guaranteed" to "work up a sweat [and] have a great time" at Gallagher's *Rockpalast* gigs, with the guitarist himself even remarking on his particular fondness for the programme.[1]

His five recorded shows—first released in full under *Rory Gallagher: The Complete Rockpalast Collection* in 2005[2]—represent the guitarist "at his very best,"[3] according to Dónal, whether in 1976 or 1990. The DVD includes numerous memorable scenes that continue to be cherished within a growing fanbase, such as Gallagher's offstage interview with Albrecht Metzger in 1976 or his onstage jam with Scottish singer-songwriter Frankie Miller three years later. In his essay for the DVD liner notes, music critic Chris Welch argues Gallagher's "greatest accolades" to be "from the audiences who loved him and the many musicians who admired him," concluding that his "glorious" *Rockpalast* shows in particular "were his true Rock & Roll Halls of Fame."

In this chapter, we summarise Gallagher's record-breaking four appearances at *Rockpalast* throughout the years: Cologne 1976, Essen 1977, Wiesbaden 1979 (as part of the *Mai Festspiele*) and Loreley 1982. We then focus on Gallagher's concert for the *Rocklife* programme (deviated from the original *Rockpalast*) on 17 October 1990. Through press articles and our interview with *Rockpalast* co-founder Christian Wagner, we examine Gallagher's strengths as a performer, as well as his role in the German music scene, specifically in regard to rock and television. In addition, we track the many projects lined up for Gallagher in 1990, coinciding mostly with the release of *Fresh Evidence* in May, that were either sidelined due to ill health or revisited posthumously, such as the Town & Country Club recordings from December 1990.

A History of Rory Gallagher at *Rockpalast*

Peter Rüchel and Christian Wagner developed the concept of *Rockpalast* in 1974. Together, they proposed a series of live concerts, especially for German television and radio, featuring performances by internationally known bands and musicians. Viewers were encouraged to watch the concerts on television, yet tune into the radio to listen to the music in stereo. For many viewers, *Rockpalast* was more than just a music show; it became "the philosophy of a generation."[4] By

Dónal Gallagher's account, *Rockpalast* revolutionised the relationship between artist and television by eliminating regulations, such as PA volume or a "three-minute" time slot for performances.[5] *Rockpalast* provided musicians with "the finest" equipment and a "relatively" flexible schedule, creating a "relaxed rock & roll" environment in order to produce "the best performances" for audiences to enjoy.

The first *Rockpalast* concerts took place in late 1974, with performances by Electric Light Orchestra (4 October, Studio Hamburg) and Lynyrd Skynyrd (5 December Musikhalle Hamburg). By the next year, the programme—mostly now based in Studio-A, Cologne—was attracting such names as Alexis Korner, Steeleye Span and the David Bromberg Band. Momentum having grown, 1976 saw concerts broadcast on a monthly (sometimes bimonthly) basis. An ever-growing list of international musicians took to the stage, from Procol Harum and Frankie Miller to Wishbone Ash and Eric Burdon. It was in this year on 6 October that Gallagher first appeared on *Rockpalast*, performing in front of a small audience in Cologne's WDR studios.

Enveloped in deep midnight blue and soft crimson lighting, Gallagher opened his set with a 45-minute solo acoustic spot, inviting the band onstage for 'Goin' to My Hometown', before launching into the electric portion of the show. Gallagher plays a wide selection of tracks from his soon-to-be released album *Calling Card*, interspersed with cuts from his previous LP *Against the Grain* (1975), such as 'I Take What I Want' and 'Bought and Sold'. Though clearly fatigued, Gallagher participates in a 20-minute interview with Albrecht Metzger once the concert has concluded and seats have emptied. Reminiscent of his guitar demonstration at the soundcheck in Cork in the *Irish Tour '74* documentary film, Gallagher highlights the trademarks of bottleneck playing and his 1932 National Triolian Resonator. Metzger also enquires about Gallagher's influences, what the blues means to him as self-expression and his thoughts on being a guitar idol to many. "It's a nice boost to say that people like you and what you do. It also gives you a duty to be as good as they want you to be."[6]

Rockpalast co-founder and cameraman Christian Wagner described his impressions of Gallagher as "a bit shy, very polite [and] very sympathetic" during their first meet in 1976.[7] Wagner was already aware of Gallagher's music since the days of Taste in the late 1960s, as he recalled in May 2024: "Taste seemed to be a bit different [than Cream or the Jimi Hendrix Experience]. [They were] more raw, more bluesy and more direct." Wagner was "pretty impressed" by the energy captured on 'Blister on the Moon', as well as 'What's Going On' off the trio's second album *On The Boards* (1970). Wagner continued to be a fan as Gallagher shifted to a solo artist post-1970, deeming the Irishman's "performing abilities" as a perfect pairing with his and Rüchel's concept for "live music in its best form." Overall, Wagner was "pretty happy" to feature Gallagher on multiple broadcasts of *Rockpalast*, sharing fond memories of the 1976 programme in particular. Gallagher was "inspired" to complete "a real acoustic set" in front of the studio audience and, as a result, Wagner revealed that it was, in fact, the guitarist's idea to split the show into an acoustic and electric section. Wagner viewed this suggestion to be a great success as it "warmed up the audience quite nicely," in addition to demonstrating Gallagher's exquisite skills on the acoustic. Years later, Wagner regards this to be "one of [his] nicest memories of [Gallagher]," which indicated the beginning of a friendly rapport between the *Rockpalast* team and the guitarist.

As the popularity of *Rockpalast* grew, Rüchel and Wagner moved away from the small clubs and venues across Germany, seeking a larger stage. 23 July 1977 marked the launch of this new 'Rock Night' format, with an all-night concert scheduled at the Grugahalle in Essen and, for the first time, broadcast live all across Europe. In late 1976, Dónal was working at the Stramp factory when a call came through from Rüchel about building a 40,000-watt PA system. The request seemed outrageous, but coincidentally appropriate for Dónal, who was in the midst of designing a 10,000-watt PA ("one of the biggest in Europe at that time") for the Rory Gallagher band.[8] On behalf of Stramp founder Peter Streuven, Dónal travelled to Cologne to meet with Rüchel and discuss plans for the first international broadcast of *Rockpalast*. According to Dónal, a Muhammad Ali match on American soil was to reach European television audiences many hours later and, therefore, an empty slot needed to be filled prior to the fight.

At first, Dónal suggested Bob Dylan fly over to perform a European 'Rolling Thunder' tour, inviting many musicians across Europe to join him onstage. When this idea fell through, the Beach Boys were next considered due to their abundance of hit songs, which was convenient at the chance of overtime. Although the group was already set to appear at an open-air concert, they also detested the format: "television will kill your box office."

Dónal had flown back to Ireland and begun preparations for the first Macroom 'Mountain Dew' Festival when Rüchel phoned and suggested that Gallagher, along with Little Feat and the Byrds' Roger McGuinn, join the bill for *Rockpalast* on 23 July 1977. Dónal agreed that it sounded like a great idea; the only trouble was that Gallagher was playing the Montreux Jazz Festival the night before. He consulted with Gallagher, who did not want to pass up the opportunity ("have guitar will travel" was his motto, jokes Dónal[9]). So, on little sleep, they flew straight from Geneva to Frankfurt, then took a car to Düsseldorf and onwards to Essen. "We had a nice evening [in Montreux], had two hours' sleep and got up here to Essen, so the energy wasn't too lost," Gallagher said in a post-concert interview.[10]

The Rory Gallagher Band were greeted with "a lovely reception"[11] upon arrival, socialising with Roger McGuinn and the members of Little Feat, and (as per Dónal's recommendation) awarded with a pendant from Rüchel. The gift was modelled off the tradition of teams trading football pendants at European cup games. Due to time restrictions, a pendant could only be made per band (as opposed to per member). However, "[by] the next Rockpalast all the musicians managed to get one [since] it [had] become such a popular item."

Gerry McAvoy details in his memoir the rising tension between management over what band should open the concert. As the situation began "to get a bit heated," McAvoy recalls Gallagher interjecting with, "You lot argue amongst yourselves. I'm going on first," before "[walking] off in disgust."[12] Dónal recalls the situation unfolding differently, with Gallagher apparently agreeing on the condition that his friend and musician Roland Van Campenhout be the opening act. Ironically, Gallagher's instinct to "avoid confrontation"[13] resulted in his set attracting a higher viewing rate at 9:30PM (28 million), compared to Roger McGuinn's closing performance at 2:30AM (1 million) when most of "the audience had gone to bed."[14] As a result of the "incredible publicity," Gallagher's reputation as an outstanding live performer escalated across Europe and beyond, such as those viewers witnessing "the first 'rock' act they'd even seen"[15] behind the Iron Curtain.

During sessions for *Top Priority* (1979) at Dieter Dierks studio in Stommeln, Gallagher was asked by the *Rockpalast* team to appear in Wiesbaden, which "felt like having the weekend off"[16] following a few busy weeks of recording time. Gallagher's performance on 6 May has since been remembered as legendary— and not only for what occurred onstage. For the encore, Gallagher and his band jammed with Frankie Miller, covering old tunes such as 'Sea Cruise', 'Roll Over Beethoven' and 'Walkin' the Dog'. This encore continued well after the venue lights shut off and the band had returned to the hotel. "They very kindly let us set up a few amplifiers in the hotel and we played there till the dawn. And then we got the acoustics out and we had breakfast and we were still singing," explained Gallagher in a 1982 interview.[17] While his recollections were (understandably) "fairly blurred," it was overall "a great night [and] atmosphere," according to Gallagher.

Gallagher reunited with Miller for the next *Rockpalast* in 1982 at the open-air theatre atop Loreley Rock, overlooking the river Rhine. Gallagher postponed the beginning of his US tour to join the likes of David Lindley, Eric Burdon and Bap at what would be the first stereo simulcast of a European rock concert. Gallagher celebrated with an over two-hour spectacular, delighting crowds with classics from his catalogue, as well as showcasing tunes off the recent *Jinx*. In the DVD liner notes, Welch commends Gallagher for his "hard-edged 1980s flavour" on 'Bourbon' and 'The Devil Made Me Do It', while also recognising the "unusually adventurous arrangement" on 'Philby'. Gallagher was again experimenting with instrumentation, layering his sound with saxophonists Ray Beavis and Howie Casey, as well as John Cooke on keyboards. Gallagher and his band participated in the all-star encore, delivering such songs as Dylan's 'Knockin' On Heaven's Door' and Larry Williams' 'Slow Down'. Gallagher acknowledged his pre-show jitters in an interview with Alan Bangs: "a little bit of nerves is healthy, but if it's too much then it's destructive. I'm feeling reasonable."

After 12 successful years, it was decided that 1986 would be the last of the all-night, "Rock Night" *Rockpalast* shows. To mark its end, Rüchel hosted a *Best of Rockpalast* programme on WDR in July 1986, featuring clips from its 12-year run and interviewing guest stars. Naturally, given Gallagher's strong association with the show, Rüchel invited him to take part. As Gallagher was already in Germany at this time to play at the Out in the Green Festival in Dinkelsbühl and St. Goarshausen, he willingly accepted. Accompanying Gallagher was Miller, who took time out of his German tour to appear on the show. Gallagher voiced his opinion on whether the 1980s is "still a time for live music," as well as the reception of blues artists by a younger audience. He also briefly mentions the various delays surrounding his new album, but remains hopeful it will be ready by August (eventually released in July 1987 as *Defender*).

"Dynamic as ever": Gallagher at *Rocklife* (17 October 1990)
1990 proved to be a particularly challenging year for Gallagher. While prosperous in some respects (such as his critically acclaimed new album *Fresh Evidence*), his increasing physical and mental health problems continued to interfere with fulfilling many career endeavours. Quite notably, Gallagher's health failed following the release of *Fresh Evidence* in May. As disclosed by Dónal in his recent interview with Dave Fanning, he subsequently "engineered Rory into a clinic" for a period of several weeks ("it wasn't a voluntary situation") in the hope that he would recover.[18]

Upon examination, doctors were "quite alarmed" about the medication that Gallagher had been prescribed, and Dónal was made aware of his brother's naivety regarding not just what he was taking and why, but also about the effects of mixing his medication with alcohol, even in small quantities. In the mid-1980s, Gallagher had begun steroid treatment, which "[was] absolutely the wrong thing for him," Dónal subsequently acknowledged, recognising both the physical and mental effects on his brother: "[the steroids] would swell his body [...] not least what it was doing [by] messing his head up."[19]

Gallagher's friend and fellow musician Martin Carthy recalls seeing the Irishman's photograph in a magazine around this time and immediately asking himself, "Why on earth is he taking steroids?"[20] Dónal has recently stated that Eric Clapton even reached out to Gallagher at this time, offering to "sponsor Rory" as his health worsened with prescription medication overuse.[21] Such anecdotes highlight the advice and support that the guitarist was receiving from his musical peers, in addition to family and band members.

As a result of his medical treatment and worsening health, Gallagher had to cancel prearranged concerts throughout the summer. He was set to headline the Blues Festival in Bolsward on 29 June, for instance, accompanying the Skid Row Bluesband and Magic Frankie. As reported in the *Leeuwarder Courant*, the guitarist had supposedly "collapsed,"[22] prompting a quick replacement from concert organisers. In late July, Gallagher was forced to pull out of the Cambridge Folk Festival after being hospitalised for "suspected glandular fever."[23] His "critically ill" condition continued to make the press when his scheduled appearance at the Waterpop Festival in the Netherlands on 18 August was also cancelled. According to *Het Vrije Volk*: "At the end of last month, it was reported from Ireland that the intended top act, guitarist Rory Gallagher, had been admitted to hospital with serious health problems and therefore cannot perform. The reports about the Irishman's health are now becoming increasingly gloomy."[24] Two June dates in Amsterdam were also postponed, first until August and then later pushed back to December.

Despite his continued health struggles, Gallagher—always keen to support the new generation of musicians[25]—put time aside in June to judge a Fender Young Guitarist competition. Around 1,000 guitarists from across the UK were invited to play without any pedals in their local music shops. Their performances were filmed, and Gallagher was presented with the edited videos to watch and select his favourite. The lucky winner was Paul Rose who has since gone on to play with Band of Friends. At a promotional event in Tower Records, Gallagher watched Rose perform, describing him as a "hot player with a hot future."[26] As a prize, Rose received a 1962 reissue Fender Stratocaster and a Vox AC30 amplifier. He went on to win a Rory Gallagher custom Stratocaster in 1994 in Fender's custom guitar competition.

Gallagher's next few months were dedicated to rest and recovery in a bid to get back into shape to promote *Fresh Evidence* properly later in the autumn. His return to the stage finally occurred on 17 October at the Live Music Hall in Cologne for the first recording of *Rocklife*—a successor to the popular *Rockpalast*—which ran from 1990 to 1995. Rüchel and Gerd F. Schultze took responsibility for booking the music acts at this time, which, according to Christian Wagner, created some "difficulties" to organise "good musicians for the recording dates." Despite "very short notice," however, Rüchel and Schultze were able to "talk Dónal [and Rory] into joining the *Rocklife* concert."

Wagner was "delighted" to work with Gallagher again, though did observe that he had "changed a bit" since the Loreley show in 1982. "He seemed to be a bit more remote than I remembered him to be," while appearing "to be not older, but fuller." Nevertheless, while only a "short meeting [offstage]," Wagner claimed that Gallagher was still the "very polite and rather quiet" man he had come to know, who was "fully concentrated on his upcoming performance." Once onstage, Gallagher was "as energetic and dynamic as ever," with the audience "[responding] well to what he had to offer." Wagner could not "see or hear any difference" in Gallagher's playing at this time and unable to detect "any features or signs of [him] deteriorating."

The atmosphere captured at the Live Music Hall is equivalent to a small club venue, which lends itself well to Gallagher's performance style. Gallagher highlighted in his 1991 interview with *Young Guitar Magazine* the importance of "[creating] different moods [in one night],"[27] which he demonstrates to a great extent at his *Rocklife* performance. He guides the audience through various emotions, from the Slim Harpo-esque 'Middle Name' to the very punchy and feverish 'Don't Start Me Talking', and even playful in 'Garbage Man'. Many tracks from *Fresh Evidence* are also showcased, from 'Kid Gloves' to 'The King of Zydeco', with special guest Geraint Watkins joining the band on accordion and piano for a few numbers. Gallagher settles the mood with a short acoustic interval, delivering a soulful cover of Son House's 'Empire State Express'. He balances a tender and subdued vocal line over fervent bottleneck strokes, enhancing the folky-blues elements of the track. *Rocklife* photographer Philipp J. Bösel reflected on the evening for our blog site in September 2022: "When Rory played his acoustic guitar, [it] was a very special moment for me. He played with and from his soul."[28] Though Bösel was not too familiar with Gallagher's work, he nevertheless enjoyed the lively atmosphere and Gallagher's bond with the crowd. "The concert hall freaked out. It was a really great performance."

When *Rory Gallagher: At Rockpalast* hit the shelves in 2004, it rapidly climbed the German Music DVD charts to number 1. "I think it indicates that there is an overwhelming interest in the real thing—classic blues and rock played by the master," said Peter Rüchel at the time.[29] In a 2008 review for the DVD's reissue in full, Brian Elliot complimented the "stunning quality" of Gallagher's musicianship at *Rocklife*, "unlike the output of any artist [in the early 2000s]," boldly suggesting that guitarists such as "America's Joe Bonamassa" are "nowhere near the astonishing catalogue of the Ballyshannon legend."[30] In a more recent article, Gallagher's *Rocklife* performance is "still a sensation," with critic Elly Roberts arguing the "call and response" between harmonica and guitar on 'Mean Disposition' to be "the best bit" of the DVD.[31] In his liner notes essay, Chris Welch values the *Rocklife* concert in terms of seeing Gallagher as "a more mature performer," noting the warm response the Irishman continues to evoke from his loyal fans.

Gallagher's Encore with Jack Bruce at *Rocklife*

For many, like photographer Phillip J. Bösel, "the best" part of Gallagher's *Rocklife* performance was his unexpected jam with Jack Bruce—a musician with whom he shared a lengthy history.

Gallagher first crossed paths with Bruce in Hamburg's Star Club in 1966. Dónal even recalls receiving a postcard from Gallagher about his "pleasant conversation"[32] with Bruce following Cream's set. This initial contact sparked a friendship between the two, with Taste often spotted on the same bill as Cream in the subsequent years. In 1968, Cream played their farewell concert at the Royal Albert Hall—which Taste supported—where, supposedly, management approached Gallagher to collaborate with Bruce and Ginger Baker for Cream Mark II. Although Gallagher declined, soon embarking on his own solo career, this did emphasise an obvious admiration for the Irishman's musicianship. Bruce was highly favourable of Gallagher's "Celtic approach" to the blues and his balance for "an incredibly melodic lyrical style" while still maintaining an "edge" and "tremendous energy."[33] Bruce and Gallagher reunited on 9 December 1984 when Scotland's Usher Hall hosted the Ethiopia Benefit Concert, which was in aid of the Save the Children Fund for famine relief. Joining them on the all-star line-up were Charlie Watts, Ian Stewart, Bert Jansch, Rick Wakeman and John Martyn.

As stated by Wagner, it was Rüchel's suggestion that Gallagher jam with Bruce for the encore at *Rocklife*. Bruce had completed a solo performance (mainly on the piano) for the programme, but had also brought his bass along with him to the venue. For three numbers ('Born Under a Bad Sign', 'I'm Ready' and 'Politician'), Gallagher and Bruce sounded "like a jollier version of Cream,"[34] seeming to be "more than delighted to play alongside each other." On 'Politician', in particular, Jean-Noël Coghe noted, between the "sweat and laughter," Gallagher and Bruce played "as if in a dual," generating the "magical voice" of the 1960s rock trios.[35] The *Rocklife* rendition of 'Born Under a Bad Sign' has since been included in the *Blues* (2019) release, while 'Politician' is a particular fan favourite because backstage footage captures Bruce quickly reminding Gallagher how the song goes, before the guitarist steps out on stage, gets into the groove and puts his own mark on the song. In 1996, Bruce was among the many musicians honouring Gallagher at the Fender 50th Anniversary Concert.

In a 2023 interview for *Stef's Podcast*, Dónal revealed that there was an opportunity for Gallagher and Bruce to record together in 1991. A journalist friend of his was looking for ways to raise money to support the Lebanon hostage crisis at the time. Dónal suggested an all-star recording of Cream's 'White Room', given its lyrics about entrapment and hopelessness. He managed to get his brother on board, as well as Van Morrison, and was also planning to approach Charlie Watts. He suggested the idea to Bruce in the hotel bar after *Rocklife*, but was disappointed that the Scot did not quite seem to understand the rationale for using 'White Room'. However, in the middle of the night, it "suddenly dawned" on Bruce and he slipped a note under Dónal's hotel room door the next morning to say that it was an "excellent idea." Sadly, the project never moved further forward.

Gallagher's Lost Projects (1990-1991)
The unfulfilled session with Jack Bruce was one of many missed opportunities for Gallagher in the early 1990s as a result of ill health. During Gallagher's appearance on *Ohne Filter* (30 March 1990), presenter Felix Parbs reveals the recent news that Willie Dixon had telephoned the guitarist earlier that day to propose a studio session with his band, as well as with Eric Clapton and Keith Richards. "We'll see what happens," Gallagher states, "It looks good."[36] Due to unknown circumstances, this session never occurred.

In the months leading up to Gallagher's notorious July interview with David Sinclair for *Q* magazine (see Introduction), a warm-up show in Hamburg, a concert in Cologne, two London meetings and a television appearance in Baden Baden were abandoned (although Gallagher did reschedule Baden Baden's *Ohne Filter* show for March). The discarded plans were likely a mixture of conflicting schedules and poor health on Gallagher's part. "I'm not the most organised guy in the world," he modestly confessed to Sinclair.[37] In the case of Gallagher's originally scheduled *Ohne Filter* appearance, McAvoy recalls the cancellation being based on the fact that the band "were allocated a small stage" due to Feltham's absence. "In the old days, [Rory] would have gone ahead and done the show, but his mind and judgement had begun to be affected by alcohol [and medication]."[38] There had also been plans for Gallagher to appear at a benefit concert on 28 October at the Point Depot in Dublin for Brian Keenen, the Northern Irish writer who spent four years as a hostage in Beirut. While the concert took place with Paul Brady, Donovan, Roger Cook, Clannad and Midge Ure, Gallagher was absent from the final bill.

Another unfulfilled project took place in June 1990 when Gallagher was invited to audition for the role of Joey 'The Lips' Fagan in the screen adaptation of the 1987 Roddy Doyle book *The Commitments*. According to Dónal, his brother was "the model" for Doyle's character, "the kid who wanted to change music in Ireland."[39] But Gallagher was not keen on taking part:

> They were pleading with Rory to do a screentest, but he was saying, 'No, no' and when Rory read the book, there were so many swear words in it, he felt it was just a sad commentary. I managed to get Rory as far as Alan Parker's [the director] office, but Rory just refused. Rory did eventually meet with Alan and he wouldn't allow me into the room to meet with him [...] Rory stopped during the reading and said, 'Look, I'm not the one. To be quite honest, the musician in the book is a totally different character to me. Why don't you get Van Morrison?' He had almost a completely self-destruct aspect about it [...] When he came out, I asked him how it went and Rory said he should stick to the trombone. I was shocked really and annoyed with him.[40]

In a bid to find more balance in his brother's life, Dónal was constantly encouraging Gallagher to explore other "business ideas" outside of music. While Gallagher was generally reluctant and wanted to just "stick to the music," he was entertained by the idea of starting "a weekly magazine on crime" because he felt that "there [was] no magazine for crime writing" at the time.[41]

In his August 1991 conversation with Vivian Campbell for *Guitar*, Gallagher discussed his involvement with three projects, one of which was a live album. As his last live output was *Stage Struck* in 1980, he admits that "it would be nice [...] [because] when we do a live album it's not just fulfilling the contract," but rather to showcase "unrecorded songs."[42] Campbell immediately encourages the idea, telling the bluesman that he is a great live performer with an "exceptional band" and that the "outrageous" talent of Mark Feltham needs to be captured on record.

While Gallagher's wish was never fulfilled in his lifetime, it was achieved posthumously in 2023 when the Estate released *All Around Man: Live in London*.

The album brings together the best of Gallagher's two nights at the Town & Country Club, which ended his six-date English tour on 28 and 29 December 1990. A year before the album hit stores, Daniel Gallagher had told *Hot Press* about his recent discovery of a tape of the two concerts. The intentions for such recordings remain unknown, with even the sound engineer unidentified. Nonetheless, Daniel expressed a keen interest in releasing them, recognising a gap in official Gallagher live material: "With the *Check Shirt Wizard: Live in '77* (2020) live album, that recording period hadn't been documented, so that went down really well. I'd like to do the same with the *Defender* and *Fresh Evidence* periods."[43]

Journalist Nigel Summerley attended the first of Gallagher's two shows at the Town & Country Club and wrote a rave review at the time for the *Evening Standard* that sums up the cosmic, quasi-spiritual journey of seeing Gallagher live.[44] Summerley references the "blue flashy thing" in the new Star Trek series that "sends the Enterprise" from here to beyond eternity" and claims that it must be in Gallagher's possession because of his ability to send the audience into "rhythmic hyperspace" with his "fierce grooves." He lauds the way that Gallagher works his guitar, turning the blues into his "own special monster" as he constantly drives forward. Summerley reserves special praise for Mark Feltham who he sees as a "faultless foil" to Gallagher and singles out the material from *Fresh Evidence* for its "keener edge" which promises that "the best of Gallagher is perhaps yet to come."

Fan Tom Mitchell was at the same show and agrees that Gallagher was "on great form, lively, moving well, leaping well high on occasion, in great voice, great screams in true old bluesman style."[45] He managed to meet the guitarist after the show and rather poignantly "implored him not to work too hard" because "we all care about his health and wellbeing and look forward to the vintage years (musically) being long and enjoyable for all." Gallagher politely thanked him and mentioned that he would be heading overseas in the new year for another tour. Other eyewitness accounts published in the *Fresh Evidence* fanzine note that the venue was at full capacity with a good cross-section of fans in attendance, while there were no shouts for old material from fans—a clear sign of the robustness and validity of Gallagher's new songs. They also comment on the fact that, while Gallagher's shows have always been full of improvisation, this element now seems to be even more at the forefront, with a "loose" format that allows him to be guided purely by his emotions and instincts.

Almost 35 years on and the concerts—captured on *All Around Man: Live in London* have re-defined the media's perception of Gallagher's musicianship at the latter stage of his career and, according to Howard King, serve as "a perfect introduction"[46] to the Irishman's catalogue. Daniel Gallagher acknowledges the "tightrope balance" of not "over-saturating" the fans.[47] While he strives not to "dilute the importance of the *Irish Tour* album," he does identify the "pockets" of his uncle's career, particularly the last decade, that deserve "another light put on them." *All Around Man* demonstrates a step in the right direction towards, as Gallagher would put it, "[covering] the rainbow [of sounds]" in his career.[48] Critics raved about Gallagher's quality as a bluesman ("he effortlessly varies his tone, touch and attack, without ever resorting to crowd-pleasing shtick"),[49] leading Andy Thorley from *Maximum Volume* to deem the record "the finest live album released in a very, very long time."[50] Howard Kind of *At the Barrier* even claimed that it "matches" the quality of Gallagher's classic albums *Live! In Europe* and *Irish Tour '74*.[51] The album reached number 1 in the Official Jazz & Blues Albums Chart, staying in the Top 20 for 15 weeks.

Bridging the Two Different Worlds:
Gallagher's Legacy in Germany

Ani from Karlsruhe in southwestern Germany only discovered Gallagher's music recently, yet was instantly captivated by the Irishman's warmth and connection with his audience, particularly on his *Rockpalast* appearances. She identifies an important moment during Gallagher's 'Too Much Alcohol' rendition at the 1976 *Rockpalast* show when he "encourages the thrilled audience to clap along" and immediately responds with "That's dufte, ja!"—a phrase that roughly translates to the "German 70s teenage slang equivalent of 'smashing'." Ani argues that such instances demonstrate Gallagher's ability to make "an audience feel special and appreciated." She continues:

> It comes as no surprise that Rory's wild and exciting playing style found a lot of young fans in a country that's famous for being a bit grey and uptight. Naturally the youth thirsted after some excitement and that still hasn't changed. With YouTube the next generation of German Rory fans rediscovered his stellar performances and it's still a touching little moment when the shy man they adore so much throws some crumbs of their own language in their direction.[52]

According to Christian Wagner, Gallagher was "a vital part" of *Rockpalast*'s success, simply because he "brought out the energy that we always wanted to put [across] to the audience via television." In this sense, Gallagher helped bridge the "two different worlds" that were television and rock music in 1970s Germany, with Wagner—like Ani—identifying the guitarist's strong relationship with his audience as a "significant" element of his *Rockpalast* concerts:

> He didn't care if it was five people or five hundred. He just gave his best and was very successful, and the people were very excited. They felt instantly that he didn't care who or how the situation was; he always gave his best and served the audience as good as possible. That's the thing that people feel, and they honour that. That's what impressed me and my partners as well, and that's one of the reasons why eventually Rory ended up playing five shows for us.

Gallagher was honoured in a tribute concert at *Rockpalast* in 1996, organised by his brother and Rüchel. Nine Below Zero & Band of Friends performed together, with a line-up of guitarists Bobbie McIntosh, Brian 'Robbo' Robertson and Paul Rose, as well as Lou Martin, Mark Feltham and De Dannan. While Slash and Jack Bruce had been invited to join them, both—to Dónal's great disappointment—cancelled a few days prior.

Through the DVD releases of Gallagher's *Rockpalast* concerts, the guitarist has since become a key figure in the "rich archive of German TV material." In addition, critics and fans alike are provided with a "video diary" of various points in Gallagher's musical journey, "showcasing the bands, the albums and changing mood of the time." Dónal has emphasised the significance *Rockpalast* concerts played in "[helping] bring the [Berlin] Wall down," with specific reference to the 1977 Essen show transmitted to viewers in the Eastern Bloc. Gallagher's collaborations on the programme, therefore, contribute to the progression of the European rock music scene in the late 20th century, as well as ensure that his live catalogue can be viewed by his growing legion of fans. His music continues to resonate with a younger generation, evident by the many tribute groups in Germany, such as Etched in Blue, Brute, Force & Ignorance and Double Vision.

As young German fan Amelie notes, it's "nearly impossible" to attend a blues rock concert in Germany "without finding at least one person wearing a Gallagher shirt."[53] Furthermore, it was through speaking to such people at concerts that she first learnt about *Rockpalast*'s legendary Rock Nights and Gallagher's important relationship with the programme. "*Rockpalast* was the introduction to Rory's music for many Germans. It was the start of a love that has lasted long after his death," she concludes.[54]

RM

Footnotes

1 '1. Open Air Festival Loreley 28.8.1982', *Rockpalast Archive*, https://www.rockpalastarchiv.de/l1_e.html#rory
2 *Rory Gallagher: At Rockpalast* was released by the Gallagher Estate in 2004, but only contained Gallagher's *Rockpalast* concerts from 1976 and 1977, as well as the Frankie Miller jam in 1979.
3 Dónal Gallagher, quoted in the *Rory Gallagher: Live at Rockpalast* (2007) DVD liner notes.
4 'Rockpalast – A Magical Journey Through the World of Rock Music', *Mig Music*, http://www.mig-music.de/en/rockpalast-3/
5 Dónal Gallagher | 40 Jahre Rockpalast', *WDR* (22 July 2017), https://www1.wdr.de/mediathek/video/sendungen/rockpalast/video-donal-gallagher---jahre-rockpalast-102.html
6 'Rory Gallagher | Interview | 1976', https://www.youtube.com/watch?v=Yuv_mYB29-0
7 Interview with Christian Wagner, 15 May 2024. All subsequent quotes from Wagner come from this interview.
8 'Dónal Gallagher'.
9 Dónal Gallagher, *Rockpalast* liner notes
10 'Rory Gallagher – Gruga Halle Essen – 1977', https://ok.ru/video/1402742114823.
11 'Dónal Gallagher'.
12 Gerry McAvoy and Pete Chrisp, *Riding Shotgun: 35 Years on the Road with Rory Gallagher and "Nine Below Zero"* (Chicago: SPG Triumph, 2005), 193.
13 Ibid.
14 Figures cited in Niall Stokes, 'Rory Gallagher - Pressing Ever Onwards', *Hot Press* (9 June 1978), https://www.roryon.com/pressing149.html
15 Chris Welch, *Rockpalast* liner notes.

Part 2 - *Let's Go to Work!*

16 Dónal Gallagher, *Rockpalast* liner notes.
17 'Rory Gallagher Rockpalast 1982 (video interview)', https://www.youtube.com/watch?v=-0mcx5hECd8
18 'Remembering Rory Gallagher 2024', https://www.youtube.com/watch?v=xE8LArN63VA
19 *Ghost Blues: The Story of Rory Gallagher* (2010).
20 Colin Harper, 'Ballad of a Thin Man', *Mojo* (October 1998), https://www.roryon.com/mojo.html
21 'Remembering Rory Gallagher 2024'.
22 'Gallagher niet op festival Bolsward', *Leeuwarder Courant* (28 June 1990), 9.
23 Chris Elliot, 'Rock star out of city folk festival', *Cambridge Evening News* (27 July 1990) 7.
24 'Waterpop mist doodzieke topact Rory Gallagher', *Het Vrije Volk* (14 August 1990), 16.
25 In July 1991, Gallagher would also write a letter of support to the Musicians Collective and Gweedore Bar in Derry for arranging a 'Battle of the Bands' competition to encourage young musicians.
26 See: https://bluguitar.com/en/artists/paul-rose
27 'Rory Gallagher Interview 1991', https://www.youtube.com/watch?v=fNpaun5s1CE&t=536s
28 Interview with Philipp J. Bösel, 19 September 2022.
29 'Rory Gallagher live DVD number 1 in Germany', *Hot Press* (27 April 2004), https://www.hotpress.com/music/rory-gallagher-live-dvd-number-1-in-germany-2724604
30 Brian Elliott, 'Rory Gallagher: Shadow Play (3 Discs)', *My Reviewer* (3 September 2008), https://www.myreviewer.com/DVD/106829/Rory-Gallagher-Shadow-Play-3-Discs/107321/Review-by-Brian-Elliott
31 Elly Roberts, 'Rory Gallagher: The Complete Rockpalast Recordings', *DVD Fever* (4 May 2017), https://dvd-fever.co.uk/errory/
32 Jamie Dickson, 'Dónal Gallagher: 'Playing with Muddy Waters was Rory's badge of honour'', *Music Radar* (11 June 2019), https://www.musicradar.com/news/donal-gallagher-playing-with-muddy-waters-was-rorys-badge-of-honour.
33 'Rory: The blues genius who did his own thing', *Irish Independent* (4 June 2005), https://www.independent.ie/news/rory-the-blues-genius-who-did-his-own-thing/25978756.html.
34 Welch, *Rockpalast* liner notes.
35 Jean-Noël Coghe, *Rory Gallagher: A Biography* (Cork: Mercier Press, 2001), 153.
36 'Rory Gallagher - Interview Germany 1990', https://www.youtube.com/watch?v=im4YdY-Ed2k&t=1s
37 David Sinclair, 'The show must go on!', *Q* (July 1990), https://www.roryon.com/q8.html
38 McAvoy and Chrisp, *Riding Shotgun*, 250-251.
39 Karen Howard, 'Donal Gallagher', *Music News* (23 March 2019), https://www.music-news.com/review/UK/13694/Interview/Donal-Gallagher
40 Ibid.
41 'Remembering Rory Gallagher 2024'.
42 Vivian Campbell, 'The Wearing of the Blues', *Guitar for the Practicing Musician* (August 1991), https://www.roryon.com/guitar91.html.
43 'On this day in 1971: Rory Gallagher released *Deuce*', *Hot Press* (28 November 2022), https://www.hotpress.com/music/on-this-day-in-1971-rory-gallagher-released-deuce-22940588
44 Nigel Summerley,'Warp-Mongering Blues', *Evening Standard* (31 December 1990), 25.
45 Tom Mitchell, 'Town and Country Club, Kentish Town, London 28-12-90', *Fresh Evidence* vol. 1 (1990), 20-21.
46 Howard King, 'Rory Gallagher—All Around Man, Live in London: Album Review', *At The Barrier* (14 July 2023), https://atthebarrier.com/2023/07/14/rory-gallagher-all-around-man-live-in-london-album-review/
47 Ed Power, 'Rory Gallagher: New live album created from 1990 concert in London', *Irish Examiner* (11 July 2023), https://www.irishexaminer.com/lifestyle/artsandculture/arid-41180998.html
48 'Rory Gallagher – Interview Germany 1990'.
49 Doug Collette, 'Rory Gallagher: All Around Man: Live in London', *All About Jazz* (13 August 2023), https://www.allaboutjazz.com/all-around-man-live-in-london-rory-gallagher-ume-cadet-records
50 Andy Thorley, 'Review', *Maximum Volume* (30 July 2023), https://maximumvolumemusic.com/review-rory-gallagher-all-around-man-live-in-london-2023/#google_vignette.
51 Howard King, 'Rory Gallagher – All Around Man, Live in London: Album Review', *At the Barrier* (14 July 2023), https://atthebarrier.com/2023/07/14/rory-gallagher-all-around-man-live-in-london-album-review/
52 Interview with Ani, 17 June 2024.
53 Interview with Amelie, 17 June 2024.
54 Gallagher is also commemorated in Hamburg's public landscape: his name is on both the city's Große Freiheit 36 building and a plaque on the site of the former Star Club.

2.5 The Vasco Da Gama of Rock: The Final World Tour (1991)

"Other kids were driving down the street in their Holden station wagon with their stereos blaring Led Zeppelin, [but] mine was 'Follow Me'. That was my jam in my car."[1]

Australian musician, Gwyn Ashton

In the mid-1970s, British music magazine *NME* half-jokingly created the 'Vasco da Gama touring award' to recognise Gallagher's gruelling tour schedule.[2] The name was inspired by the Portuguese explorer who united Europe and India by sea. In a similar way, Gallagher united folk with blues while roaming every possible musical landscape. Fans can learn about Gallagher's travels and his impact on audiences around the world through an extensive amount of visual material.[3] Having said this, minimal effort has been made to document Gallagher's final world tour[4] in the early months of 1991 — a tour we strongly consider to be one of his most impressive.

A few dates around England in December 1990 kickstarted Gallagher's return on the road following a lengthy period of absence due to illness (see 2.4). After the Christmas break, he began his final tour of Northeast Asia, Australia and America in mid-February, concluding in New York on 31 March. However, the weeks leading up to the tour were not quite as pleasant as the shows themselves. "Rory knew [Gerry McAvoy and I] were leaving the band six months prior to [the final tour]," Brendan O'Neill stated in an interview with Dan Muise, "We wanted to form Nine Below Zero again and we wanted to get involved with writing more. Basically just have a bit more control ourselves."[5] Despite resigning in late 1990, O'Neill and McAvoy would accept Gallagher's offer to return to the road for what would be their farewell tour.

Adding to the unease was Gallagher's lingering fear of flying, which had previously limited his travel abroad. Before his concert in Toronto on 26 March, he visited the deejays at radio station Q107-FM, discussing the missed opportunities for touring as a result of his "Buddy Holly complex":

> We cancelled or postponed some dates in America and North America, Japan, and Australia last year and the year before. All of a sudden after all these years I had a couple of bad flights and that affected me [...] I could only fly one hour or something. That

would be maximum [...] I certainly couldn't consider flying—like we've just done from London to Tokyo—this time last year. But I can do it now [...] It's like any phobia, you eventually roll over it and feel great again and then you start enjoying the speed of flight and so on.[6]

Unfortunately, additional delays impacted Gallagher's positive state of mind, with flight restrictions put in place as a result of the Persian Gulf War (1990-91). The US and British airlines were initially affected as "the home countries were seen as the most high-profile protagonists in the war" and were subject to frequent re-routings, raised fares and cancellations.[7] McAvoy reveals in *Riding Shotgun* that the band received confirmation of the tour only three weeks prior, with the Liberation of Kuwait occurring on the day Gallagher landed in Melbourne for the start of the Australian leg of the tour.

As you, the reader, will hopefully discover, the Rory Gallagher we present here is a man at one of the many high points in his career (despite the many obstacles, both professional and personal), embarking on a world tour at the tail end of a critically acclaimed new album, *Fresh Evidence*. We divide this chapter into three sections to correspond with each destination, modelled off our original article of this tour from our September-November 2022 posts on *Rewriting Rory*. Part 1 explores Gallagher's relationship with Japan and how his music is remembered today through the Rory Gallagher Tribute Festival. Part 2 tracks the link between Gallagher and the Australian blues landscape while providing a personal perspective from the author. Finally, Part 3 offers a definitive guide to Gallagher's final trip across America, culminating in the farewell concert in New York.

PART 1: Japan

"It's wonderful whenever I come over to Japan. Japanese audiences have a really good vibe [...] they can bring my technique out more than my ability"[8]

Gallagher delivered these comments to Japanese music magazine *Ongaku Senaka* in 1977 while on his third tour of Japan in four years. Although Gallagher would never single out a favourite country, Japan always held a special place in his heart and he would talk warmly about his memories of Japanese concerts and fans in interviews throughout his career. His love affair with the Land of the Rising Sun goes back long before he had even visited the country for the first time, however. The erudite that he was, Gallagher had a great interest in Japanese culture. He was particularly fascinated by the country's rich cinematic history and was a huge fan of the old black and white movies of Akira Kurosawa, Yasujiro Ozu and Nigisa Oshima, while Ken Takakura was one of his favourite actors.[9]

The feeling was mutual and, from the days of Taste, Japan had always embraced Gallagher, the music press showering him with praise and framing him as "the hope of young guitarists." When Gallagher first toured the country in 1974, he was given an extremely warm welcome, met by hordes of fans at Haneda Airport who offered him flowers and boxes of chocolates—much to his embarrassment. The 1974 tour was so successful that Gallagher returned to Japan just one year later, this time playing to sell-out venues across the country as word had spread about his breathtaking live performances. Then, two years later, he was back again for a slightly longer tour, this time taking in Nagoya, Hiroshima, Osaka and Tokyo, often performing twice a day in each city.

After this flurry of activity, it would be 14 years until Gallagher returned to Japan again, his acute fear of flying leading him to cancel scheduled visits in 1980 and 1988. Ex-president of the Japanese Rory Gallagher fan club, Mutsumi Mae, believes that this undoubtedly affected Gallagher's popularity in Japan: "When he didn't visit, he was forgotten about a little. And on the flipside, more and more bands had started coming to Japan, so everyone forgot about Rory."[10]

According to Mae, Gallagher kept reassuring his Japanese fans, through announcements in the fan club newsletter, that he would return to the country, but he could not follow through on this promise. When Mae visited London in the mid-1980s, she stopped by Dónal's office to find out when Gallagher would return to Japan, but he told her that his brother could not handle the thought of a long-haul flight. In 1988, finding herself in London again, Mae tried to convince Gallagher directly, popping into a rehearsal session to meet him. She now worked for Virgin Records and told him about the recently established Virgin Atlantic airlines. "I told Rory, 'I'm with Virgin now. You could come to Japan first class with Virgin Atlantic,'" said Mae. "I'm sorry, I can't,'" was Gallagher's reply.

Despite the importance of Japan in Gallagher's career and his large Japanese fanbase, his tours of the country have been overlooked in all biographies to date.[11] One significant exception is the *Rory Gallagher 25th Memorial Edition* book, published by Shinko Music Entertainment Co. Ltd. in 2020, which offers a comprehensive guide (in Japanese) to Gallagher's four tours of Japan and is a valuable resource for understanding more about his legacy in the country.

Gallagher's Final Visit to Japan

Gallagher's 1991 tour consisted of five dates, starting with two nights at Club Città in Kawasaki (19 and 20 February), one night at Osaka IMP Hall (22 February), one night at Nagoya Club Quattro (23 February) and one night at Shiba Mielparque Hall in Tokyo (24 February). Although just one full bootleg exists from Gallagher's Tokyo concert, it showcases a mature, confident musician with full command of his audience. Although Gallagher was nervous about returning to Japan after so many years and was unsure how fans would take his new material, as well as his changed appearance, you would not know it to listen to his performance. His vocals are dazzling—stronger than they have been in years—and his musicianship exemplary, while his band offers solid support.

The setlist over the last years of Gallagher's life did not change too much, made up largely of material from *Defender* and *Fresh Evidence*, as well as fan favourites from *Tattoo* and *Calling Card*. Most nights in Japan saw some or all of the following songs: 'Continental Op', 'Moonchild', 'Mean Disposition', 'The Loop', 'Tattoo'd Lady', 'Bad Penny', 'Don't Start Me Talkin'', 'I Wonder Who', 'Out on the Western Plain', 'Walking Blues', 'Pistol Slapper Blues', 'Loanshark Blues', 'A Million Miles Away', 'Kid Gloves', 'Middle Name', 'Shadow Play', 'Messin' with the Kid' and 'Bullfrog Blues'. However, Gallagher also threw in some delightful surprises like 'I'm Leaving', 'Keep Your Hands Off Her', 'I Ain't No Saint', 'Nadine' and 'Roberta'. Personal highlights include a gritty version of Robert Nighthawk's 'Going Down to Eli's', a dynamic encore of Little Richard's 'Keep A Knockin'', a fiery 'Laundromat', back in the set again after many years (all from the Tokyo show) and a sample of Elvis Presley's 'Heartbreak Hotel' (from Club Città, Kawasaki), enhanced by Feltham's sultry accompaniment.

On his first day in Japan, Gallagher went guitar shopping in Kawasaki, returning with a Takamine Dreadnought Style acoustic guitar, which he used as a back-up/live alternative for his Martin D35 from this point forward. In a later interview with *Guitar for the Practicing Musician*, Gallagher said that he was "impressed" with the Takamine and described it as being "as close to the Martin" as he had heard.[12] Gallagher must have felt in guitar heaven as later that day he was presented with a red prototype Guyatone Marroly before his first show at Club Città. The guitar company had heard that he was a big fan of their guitars and offered one to him as a gift. "I jumped into the swimming pool straight away and tried it. That's the only way to try a guitar," he told Steve Harris of *Young Guitarist Magazine* a few days later.[13] Gallagher played it for the opening numbers of 'Continental Op' and 'Moonchild', delivering his verdict that "it sounded good, it was nice."

At the Club Città performances was Mr Utam. Sharing his memories on Reiko's Rory Gallagher Japanese website,[14] he said that, although Gallagher seemed "tired and unwell," as soon as he started playing, it was clear that his ability had not changed at all. Press reviews of the Club Città performances were likewise extremely favourable, with journalists expressing delight that Gallagher threw in a few Japanese words between songs: "konbanwa" (good evening), "arigato" (thank you) and "sayonara" (bye bye). Japanese guitarist Kouki 'Dannie' Taniguchi agrees, remembering the concert as a "great experience [...] really incredible." Taniguchi brought along his own battered Stratocaster to the concert after encouragement from his friend to get it autographed by Gallagher. After the gig, he waited at the back door and, sometime later, Gallagher emerged. Despite looking "very tired," he came immediately over to Taniguchi and his friend and treated them "very kindly." When Taniguchi showed him his guitar, the Irishman "frowned," his eyes seeming to tell the young man to take better care of his guitar. He then asked Taniguchi whether he was really sure that he wanted his autograph on the guitar, before agreeing to sign it. For Taniguchi, that guitar remains his "gem" and, thanks to Gallagher's words, he has taken much better care of his guitars since![15]

Mutsumi Mae also attended the Club Città concerts. She was thrilled that Gallagher had finally made it back to Japan and met him and Dónal backstage to express her happiness. By that time, she knew Dónal particularly well through her fan club work, so he told her to hop on the tour bus and head back to the hotel with them to have dinner. Mae remembers talking to Gallagher about his love for Akira Kurosawa films, as well as his general interest in Japanese culture and history. Although she felt that she never knew Gallagher that well, she did get on "tremendously well" with Dónal, who she describes as a "good person." Concerned about Gallagher's appearance, she asked Dónal (out of Gallagher's earshot) about his brother's health.

> When I met Rory in the 80s, he didn't seem very well. So, whenever I met his brother, I remember I always asked, 'How is Rory?' [When he came to Japan in 1991], he obviously wasn't in great physical condition [...] I heard that his immune system was so strong, and because of his genetic makeup, it somehow damaged his liver. Therefore, he started taking medication and, as a side effect of those drugs, his face became swollen, and he experienced weight gain. That's why he looked that way. Hence, his body had been in a poor condition for a long period of time.[16]

Their meeting in Kawasaki was the last time that Mae saw Gallagher. Her lasting impressions of him are of somebody "sincere" who was "married to his music" and was "happy that way." Given his dedication to his craft, she really hoped that his time "would come again" with the blues revival of the 1990s, but, as we know, things sadly did not turn out this way.

The day after Gallagher's first show at Club Città in Kawasaki, he gave a 30-minute interview for *Young Guitar Magazine* in his room at the Takanawa Hotel. He sounds unusually relaxed and open here, speaking at length about the blues scene of the 1990s, creating depth and soul in a live atmosphere and comparing up-and-coming guitarists to his generation. His advice to those recently picking up the guitar is to:

> Open your ears to other kinds of guitar players. Don't think that unless they are speed merchants that they're not worth listening to. It's worth checking out some of the old acoustic players. Even if you're an electric player, if you can afford it, you should have an acoustic at home because it keeps the hands tough and you hear different things.[17]

After one day of rest, Gallagher travelled to Osaka, where he performed at the

IMP Hall. In attendance was K.G. Takeda. Takeda told us how he felt "nervous" before the concert about seeing Gallagher live for the first time and wondered if he would live up to expectations. However, he was not disappointed and found Gallagher's guitar sound to be even "harder than earlier."[18] Other views from fans at the Osaka concert have been published on Shinolez's Japanese Rory Gallagher blog.[19] "I was a little surprised by his appearance," admits one anonymous fan, "But even if he was heavy, he was still Rory." Gallagher "played with passion," the live version of 'Continental Op' somehow being "even more beautiful" than the studio version. Similar remarks come from another anonymous user who explains how he rushed to the concert from work and "was surprised for a moment" at how Gallagher looked when he appeared on stage. However, "that didn't matter once the performance started." "Even though he had put on weight and become older, Rory is still Rory!" he concluded. In the same vein, 'Kumi' says that he was "relieved to hear Rory's sound" and that, although he had "become older," he clearly hadn't "changed at all." To be in such a small venue "where you can see the whites of Rory's eyes" was a "precious experience" for him.

The following day saw Gallagher in Nagoya at the Club Quattro. A review by fan Mr Tsutsumi on Reiko's Rory Gallagher Japanese website really captures the mood of the concert:

> When I rushed [to the concert hall] after work, I saw a line of people on the stairs from the 8th floor to the 1st floor even before the show started. I think most of the songs were from *Fresh Evidence*, which had been released that year. [...] There was a great sense of unity on stage with the performance and the audience singing along. A performance with flavours of blues, zydeco and Ireland, a raw and intense performance with glimpses of a naïve side, mysterious harmony and emotional performance. [Rory's] guitar playing was great, but the songs were [also] good too. I saw Keziah Jones at Rainbow Hall and Clapton at the Prefectural Gymnasium and I thought they were wonderful, but Rory Gallagher's songs are equally wonderful. It was a moving live performance.[20]

The final concert on this tour took place at the Mielparque Hall in Tokyo. This concert has been nicknamed "Rory's First Live & Last Live in Japan" by Japanese fans due to a curious bit of trivia: the first concert that Rory ever played in Japan (23 January 1974) was at the same venue (formerly called Shiba Yubin Hokin Hall). Originally, Gallagher was scheduled to play at 5PM at a venue called MZA Ariake. However, the management company went bankrupt, so the venue was changed and the concert was pushed back to a later start time of 7PM. Although a small newspaper advertisement announced this change, many fans unknowingly went to MZA Ariake and then had to rush to Mielparque Hall after the concert had already begun.

Press reports from the Tokyo concert note that many long-term Gallagher fans–now in their 40s–had gathered in the hall still wearing their business suits because they had dashed straight from work to see him. According to *Ongaku Senaka*, when Gallagher first walked out on stage, whispers went around the auditorium of "Who is he?" because he looked so different from 1977. However, as soon as he started to play, they were "silenced" and realised that he was the "same person." Echoing the words of so many other Japanese fans, the magazine wrote, "Rory was Rory. His exciting playing never changed."[21]

New Possibilities to Come:
Honouring Gallagher in Present-Day Japan
On 19 September 2010, Megumi Manzaki (along with four long-time Gallagher fans) organised the first Rory Gallagher Tribute Festival in Japan. The event had been in development for a number of years, cultivated by the hard work and dedication of a small group. Much like John Ganjamie of the *RoryON!!* website (see Conclusion), Manzaki found herself welcomed by the Gallagher online fan community, mainly through Japanese social media in the late 2000s, and this group would occasionally meet up. Towards the end of 2009, a note was sent to Dónal Gallagher expressing a desire to "hold the first Rory Gallagher festival in Japan,"[22] which was positively received, spurring motivation to schedule a gathering the subsequent year.

The initial festival was held at a small venue (with a capacity of only 80) in Tokyo, as a "very satisfied" audience enjoyed five hours of celebrating Gallagher's music. Although the Great East Japan earthquake prevented tribute plans in 2011, encouragement from fans and Japanese musicians ensured the festival would resume in 2012. That year, crowds were treated to a "special message" from Dónal, as well as "official approval from the Irish Embassy in Japan." Due to the reduced size of guests, the festival switched to the Crawdaddy Club in 2014. In the festival posters, images of Gallagher are often incorporated with Japanese artwork, as shown in 2014 and 2023, which feature the woodblock painting *The Great Wave off Kanagawa* by Hokusai. Japanese musician Kouki 'Dannie' Taniguchi, who met Gallagher on his 1991 tour, has appeared at the Crawdaddy Club on many occasions, overlooking an audience "full of love for [Rory]."[23] Taniguchi cites his jam with Innes Sibun Torio from the UK as a "very exciting experience" and "best memory" from the festival.

Another frequent performer at the Rory Gallagher Tribute Festival in Japan is O.E. Gallagher. Guitarist for the group, Takayuki Oi, attributes Gallagher's improvisation and dedication as a major influence on his musicianship. "Each performance [was] different and the songs are in various styles," Oi told us in May 2024. He favours Gallagher's 1980 release *Stage Struck* and Taste's concert at the 1970 Isle of Wight in particular, which taught him to become "conscious of playing with my soul in every note." The decision to start a Gallagher tribute act arose from a missed opportunity to see the Irishman on his 1991 Japan tour.

"I regret that very much," Oi reflected. Despite the 2024 festival being cancelled, Oi continued to commemorate the 29th anniversary of Gallagher's passing by appearing at the Crawdaddy Club on 15 June.[24]

According to Taniguchi, Gallagher's popularity has waned in Japan since his passing in 1995:

> I rarely hear about him from young musicians, but his music is living among musicians who love his music deeply. Each time we hold the festival, there are always multiple fans in the audience who saw Rory's performances in Japan [...] Nevertheless, audience numbers have not increased since peaking at the first festival in 2010. So I can't think that our festivals are contributing to Rory's popularity in Japan after his passing."

When contributing to the *Rory Gallagher 25th Memorial Edition* (2020), Manzaki realised the "pessimistic reality" that Gallagher's long-time Japanese fans are "getting older and older," raising the possibility that the Irishman's memory might fade with them. Nevertheless, Manzaki has noticed the "happy phenomena" as a result of the festival, such as the ongoing friendships between Gallagher's fans at the Crawdaddy Club. In addition, many new bands (members of both young and older age) have applied to appear at the festival, indicating a steady interest in keeping Gallagher's memory alive. Manzaki remains optimistic: "With Rory, new possibilities may still be waiting for us in the years ahead." As 2024 marks the 50th anniversary of Gallagher's first trip to Japan, his rendition of 'In Your Town' from Nagoya on 27 January 1974 was uploaded to the festival YouTube site, preserving "[Rory's] legacy in Japan [for many years to come]."

PART 2: Australia

2025 will mark 50 years since Gallagher's first visit to Australia. Many highlights come to mind when thinking of the Irishman's three Australian tours, such as the photograph of him feeding a kangaroo in 1975 to the inside sleeve of *Stage Struck* (1980) featuring a backstage look at the Gold Coast's Playroom or even Gallagher's interview with Steve Vizard on the eve of his 43rd birthday following his final appearance at Sydney's Enmore Theatre in 1991. For myself, however, the terms 'Rory Gallagher' and 'Australia' are associated with exactly 27 seconds of music. And that is Gallagher's solo on Mike Batt's track '(Introduction) The Journey of a Fool' from the 1979 album *Tarot Suite*. While an obscure and often forgotten Gallagher contribution, to many Generation X Australians, this solo is nostalgia. It is the jingle to their favourite radio station. It is Triple, Triple, Triple Your Music.

Triple M was launched in August 1980, and along with 2Day FM, was the first commercial FM radio station in Sydney. The station predominantly played hard rock and set out to appeal to a blue-collar audience, contrasting with other stations around the country. Throughout the decades, the 'Dr. Dan' theme song for Triple M has been rerecorded by many guitarists. The first rendition in 1980 by New Zealand-Australian guitarist Kevin Borich closely resembles the fiery, sharp and wailing 1979 original, albeit without Gallagher's string-pulling/tremolo technique. As we headed for the 90s, Australian guitarist Dieter Kleemann chose to reflect the end of a decade by incorporating heavy synthesisers into his version, which was also released as a single on Mushroom Records in 1990. More recently, in celebration of Triple M's 30th anniversary in 2010, Guns N' Roses guitarist Slash was invited to put a 21st century West Coast LA feel to the theme. And so, what was once a long-lost Rory Gallagher solo hidden between the grooves has transformed into a tradition of musical reinterpretation in Australian radio history. Although this iconic riff has accompanied the Australian population for years, the question remains: do Australians even know who Rory Gallagher is?!

According to Australian blues musician Gwyn Ashton, the answer is quite simple: NO.

I spoke with Ashton over the phone one afternoon in September 2022 as he drove around South Australia to his next show. Late into our conversation, he shared with me this performance ritual:

> Every gig I [play in Australia], I go, 'here's a Rory Gallagher song', and the place goes quiet. I say, 'are there any Rory Gallagher fans here?' and not one person will put his hand up. And I'll say something like 'you people need an education'. These people need to hear his music.

From 2000-2005, Ashton played lead guitar with Band of Friends, a group formed by Gallagher's ex-bandmates that is dedicated to honouring his music and the blues. During his time with Band of Friends, Ashton headlined the first two Rory Gallagher Festivals in Ballyshannon, Ireland. Ashton spoke of another anecdote that involved the possibility of a Band of Friends in Australia featuring "Kevin Borich, myself and Rory Gallagher's rhythm section [bassist Gerry McAvoy and drummer Ted McKenna]." Unfortunately, when Ashton contacted music agents across Australia about this fantastic line-up, "nobody was interested" and the idea was never revisited. To hear about the lack of support from the Australian music business in Ashton's story was unsurprising when we consider the poor appreciation of Gallagher's relationship to Australia, beginning with his first tour here.

Despite Gallagher visiting Australia in 1975, 1980 and 1991, neither the international nor Australian press in the decades since his passing have attempted (or cared) to acknowledge and document his ties with Oceania. According to local newspapers, there was a cancelled tour in 1976, and a visit to America was scheduled instead. There has been suggestion that Gallagher visited Australia in

1977; however, archival research does not confirm this. This section contributes to the long-overdue exploration of Rory Gallagher's connection to the Australian people, memory and popular culture.

"Takes away the aches and pains":
Gallagher and His Australian Fans

In 1975, following a night out with his mates, John Spreckley was "immediately excited"[25] when flicking through the newspaper and discovering an advertisement about a Rory Gallagher concert in Adelaide on 6 February. Spreckley was already a "huge fan" of Gallagher and, to his recollection, "[I] hadn't heard anything about [Gallagher] touring [in Australia] before seeing that ad." On the day of the concert, Spreckley and a few mates endured the train ride in the sweltering summer heat to the Festival Theatre, hanging out at the pub before the show. Gallagher was "wonderful and intoxicating," mesmerising the crowd with "lots of slashing slide guitar" that "filled the Theatre." Gallagher indeed lived up to his reputation for outstanding performances ("Rory and his band blew the roof off, and had everybody going crazy!"), but as Spreckley reminisces, he soon mentions that, "I didn't really notice at the time [but] the Theatre was probably only half full." To Spreckley's knowledge, there is an interview where Gallagher addressed the moderate ticket sales. "[Gallagher] wasn't [disappointed] because people didn't know his music, but once people know his music, more people will come to the concerts." Gallagher's 1975 show at the Hordern Pavilion in Sydney on 8 February saw a repeat of Adelaide, although in a disclosed interview with Australian journalist Paul Dufficy, when asked about the low attendance at the Sydney gig, Gallagher brushed it off as an issue with advertising.

As such, Australia in 1975 seemed to be a time when people did not know Rory Gallagher's music. However, this is not to say that there was not an effort to make Australians aware of who he was. Paul Dufficy became a Gallagher fan during his final years at boarding school, remembering his first exposure to the Taste debut as "unbelievable."[26] As he recalls, "I hated being [at the boarding school] [...] [and] Rory Gallagher's music took me out of that place and made me think of things beyond that situation, so therefore I loved it." When reaching out to Dufficy in May 2022, he generously passed down some of his Gallagher memorabilia, such as newspaper clippings, to Lauren and myself. A few pieces in his collection are of his own work published in the 70s for Australian music publications. One such article (c.1975) opens with the current problem ("Rory Gallagher has had limited exposure in Australia") and offers a solution to "fill this gap" by summarising Gallagher's career from his first group Taste to solo work ("His latest *Irish Tour '74* gives us Rory Gallagher in his most expressive environment, before a wildly enthusiastic crowd").

Critics for the *Sydney Morning Herald* expressed high hopes for Gallagher's visit in 1975 ("it should be a good tour"), and Grant Thompson was an immediate fan after a "few days" with *Irish Tour '74*, hailing it as the "best tradition of rock and blues."[27] Gallagher's character as portrayed in the Australian press mirrors the usual adjectives synonymous with the guitarist, contrasting his "quiet, soft-spoken" manner offstage to his "dominating" and "driving blues."[28] In *Rolling Stone Australia*, Paul Comrie-Thomson praised Gallagher's show at the Hordern Pavilion as "one of the finest showings of white blues guitar we have seen in Australia."[29] Comrie-Thomson greatly detailed the physicality of Gallagher's performances ("he crouches coaxing the audience [...] in three seconds the slide has shot up ten frets [...] he has crashed an open chord resolution and spun around"), as well as documenting the crowd diversity ("most of the people dancing were guys. Eastern suburb surfs, North Shore denim overalls, Mediterranean's [sic], a couple of Chinese"). Above all, Comrie-Thomson determined Gallagher's "total lack of pretension" and his "no flash clothes" or "no flash talk" to be the catalyst that "won" over the Australian audience. "Australians love a 'battler'," wrote Donald Horne in his 1964 book *The Lucky Country*, "an underdog who is fighting the top dog,"[30] and, as suggested by Comrie-Thomson, it was Gallagher's 'underdog' quality that left the greatest impression on the Australian public and "made us all feel better."

While in Australia, Gallagher stopped by Sydney's radio station Double J. Created under the Gough Whitlam government as a 'National Youth Radio Network', Double J began a month prior to Gallagher's February 1975 tour. As former presenter Mark Colvin stated, Double J was "a voice of youth [when] there had been no real voice of youth heard before. There was a sense of rebellion, radicalism [and] trying not to do what everybody else was doing."[31] Double J was responsible for turning many young Australian listeners onto Gallagher's music. Australian fan Bob Hall recalled in our 2023 phone call that English presenter Mac Cocker played the Gallagher tracks 'Sinner Boy' and 'Crest of a Wave' on Double J, which began Hall's great love and appreciation of the Irishman's music. Hall became friendly with another Double J presenter, Mike Parker, and remembers that "a mate and I sometimes visited him in the studio and I tended to bring in a Rory album and he was always happy to put some of the alternate tracks on the turntable."[32]

The station took influence from overseas broadcasts by inviting rock groups and artists to come into the studio and perform live. Supposedly, Gallagher took part in a performance and interview at Double J, but only the interview can be found in the Library of NSW archives. Gallagher sounded very upbeat at Double J studios, stating that there had been "a very good reaction" from crowds in Perth and Adelaide, and that the band were enjoying some relaxation between gigs, "The weather is suiting us. We're getting a bit of a tan [...] It's been enjoyable."[33] Paul Dufficy remembers sitting in the car with a few friends at Central Station when the Double J broadcast came on, listening to Gallagher playing acoustic while "stoned and enjoying ourselves thoroughly," before driving to the gig at the Hordern Pavilion. Afterwards, Dufficy and his friends drove up to Brisbane for the concert on 11 February, this time scoring front row seats and even shaking hands with Gallagher.

Gallagher's 1980 *Top Priority* tour marked an important moment for his recording history, with tracks recorded in Melbourne at the Palais Theatre for his release *Stage Struck* (1980). Photographs of Gallagher posed in front of the Playroom on the Gold Coast were taken by Patrick Jones and used for the inner sleeve. Without question, Gallagher's visit in 1980 was to be his most successful in Australia. As advertised in the *Sydney Morning Herald*, management were forced to add a show in Sydney at the Capitol Theatre for 29 June, contrasting to the 'half full' attendance five years earlier. Kim Trengove described Melbourne's Palais Theatre as "numb" and "reeling" following Gallagher's "high-power" and "fiery" performance on 24 June.[34] According to Trengove, Melbournians were so captivated by Gallagher that they "demanded three encores from him, and Gallagher's playing seemed to improve each time." As a matter of fact, the entire continent appeared to be struck with a case of 'Rory-fever' in June 1980, with the tour deemed a "success beyond expectation," which led Gallagher to "pledge a return in 1981"—a promise he sadly was unable to fulfil.[35] Newspapers reported on the rise of Gallagher's single 'Philby' from the album *Top Priority* (1979), despite being "completely ignored on original release"[36] in early 1980. Apart from a passage of time, what had changed for an Australian audience to suddenly become Rory Gallagher fans?

For a start, by this stage in history, Australia's popular music landscape had significantly developed into its own brand of hard rock with the influx of bands like Midnight Oil, Dragon, Cold Chisel and Australian Crawl. Gallagher's output during this time, such as 'Bad Penny', 'Shadow Play' and 'Shin Kicker', fit into this gritty, hard rock edge that Australians were craving. Furthermore, if Gallagher's first tour was tainted by advertising difficulties, then this issue appeared to be resolved by the second tour. New Zealand artist Chris Grotz, known for his tour posters of blues acts such as Taj Mahal and Ry Cooder, designed the 1980 *Top Priority* posters for Oceania. Grotz discovered Gallagher's music through Taste, and particularly enjoyed the "passion and unstoppable action-packed-attack" of Gallagher's sound and soloing.[37] At the time, Grotz was working for Australian Concert Entertainment when he was approached to design the posters, tour programme and backstage passes. Grotz paired the colours orange and green "to suggest some form of coming together during The Troubles [as well as to convey Gallagher's] slash and burn style of Fender Strat playing.

By the time Gallagher returned in 1991 for the third and final time, playing dates in Adelaide, Melbourne and Sydney, the Australian critics had slightly recovered from 1980's 'Rory-fever'. Though deeming Gallagher to be a "very talented [and] perfectly competent performer," Bruce Elder nevertheless criticises the Irishman's set at Sydney's Enmore Theatre to be "nothing more than vehicles for guitar solos," even arguing that Gallagher "lacks the ability to make the [blues] his own."[38] For the most part, Elder uses Gallagher's music as a pawn to explore the question, "whether white boys can play the blues," expressing outrage to audiences who "pay twice as much" for "a [white] imitator" as opposed to "half the price" for "the real thing [i.e., African American blues artists]" such as "Louisiana Red or Lonnie Brooks." By comparison, Bruce Gutherie of *The Age* argues *Fresh Evidence* to be indicative of Gallagher's "open mind"[39] within the blues idiom, citing 'The King of Zydeco' as a primary example. Gutherie praises Gallagher's "enduring ability to come up with irresistible guitar hooks," and that, if anything, his new album provides "several [reasons]" for readers to purchase a ticket for his upcoming Melbourne concert. As stated by author Clinton Walker, young Australian listeners of the early 1990s "wanted something of [their] own,"[40] as attention shifted to the indie-rock scene (evolved from the punk movement in the late 1970s). It is a plausible suggestion that Gallagher's unpretentious attitude and roots-orientated style would have appealed to this new faction of Australian music listeners.

Gallagher's Connection with the Irish-Australian Community

In the 2011 Census, approximately one in three Australians claimed to have Irish heritage. Since the transportation of Irish convicts in 1788, Australian and the Irish diaspora have shared a long history—a history that has, unfortunately, faced class discrimination, racism and religious segregation. As outlined in Mick Armstrong's 2017 article, "anti-Irish racism" in Australia "was a direct product of British imperialism," with many Irish communities perceived as "lazy welfare cheats, drunken, dirty, uneducated, violent criminal, stupid [and] with hordes of kids."[41] Gallagher was no stranger to such discrimination, with the subhead to Kim Trengove's 1980 review comparing the veracity of his Melbourne concert to that of "an IRA raid," reinforcing the stereotype of the Irish as violent, particularly within the context of The Troubles. On the same tour, Gallagher was unfairly targeted when he was "abused" by an employee from the Wrest Point Casino in Hobart who called him an "obnoxious little bastard" when he refused to leave the venue.[42] Gallagher was deeply disturbed— later referring to the event as "the most disgusting incident of my fifteen years on the road"—and proceeded to catch the next plane to Queensland ahead of schedule. This conflict could have been the result of the 'anti-Irish racism' Armstrong alluded to in the Australian character.

While, on the one hand, some factions of Australian society reflected prejudice, others discovered connection and solidarity with their Irish roots through Gallagher's many visits, such as fan Paul Patrick Martin. Though Martin's first recollection of Gallagher was watching him on Irish television with his band Taste, it was during Martin's stay in Adelaide in 1975 when the opportunity arose to see his musical idol in concert. "[Rory] was so humble and polite to the audience, and tore the roof off the place! His energy onstage could light up a city."[43] Through mutual acquaintances, Martin was able to meet Gallagher after the show, with their Irish background fuelling the conversation:

> A mate of mine worked for Festival Records, who distributed Rory's label Chrysalis in Australia. He picked Rory and the band up at the airport and drove them to the gig. I saw him in the foyer at the interval (his band did the support slot) and he invited me to a wine bar where he was taking Rory for a drink after the show. I didn't have to be asked twice! Rory spotted the t-shirt I was wearing, with a Celtic harp and the Irish-Gaelic greeting 'Cead Mile Failte' (a hundred thousand welcomes) on it. He walked over and said the greeting and asked me where I was from! I was blown away that he came over to talk to me—no big star bullshit! He asked for my name, how long had I been [in Australia] and [we had] a general chat.

Years later, Martin and his wife attended Gallagher's "fantastic gig" at the Old Lion Ballroom (also in Adelaide) on 27 February 1991:

> When [the band] had finished, I gave a bouncer a piece of paper with 'Cead Mile Failte a Ruari' and asked him to please give it to Rory. He came back and said, 'I don't know what you wrote, mate, but he wants to see you'. We went backstage to the dressing room. I shook hands with Rory and said that he might not remember me from our previous meeting, but he said, 'I do, yeah'. I introduced my partner, and then told him that I had named my son after him. His reaction was very gracious, [but he also] looked a bit embarrassed!

To the present day, Martin cherishes the impression of Gallagher as "a very lovely [and] humble gentleman" and credits him as an important musical influence ("he inspires me to do my best when I perform"). Hence, Gallagher's impact on the Irish-Australian community spreads across many levels, from the personal to the creative.

Coincidentally, on the final night of his 1991 Australia tour, Gallagher bumped into a few musicians from Ireland prior to boarding his flight from Sydney to the US. Fiachna Ó Braonáin, guitarist and vocalist for the Irish group Hothouse Flowers, describes the moment he had a chat with Gallagher at Sydney's Sebel Townhouse Hotel as "like meeting a hero."[44] Braonáin recounts: "Rory was nervously preparing for a long-haul flight and Hothouse Flowers had just arrived into town to kick off an Australian tour. So we sat and shot the breeze about music and touring and what a wonderful way of life it was." From a contemporary standpoint, Braonáin now recognises the privilege of sharing "company [with] a kind, gracious and generous human being."

"It was like an epiphany":
Gallagher's Influence on Australian Musicians

Part 2 - *The Vasco Da Gama of Rock*

In addition to connecting with his Irish roots, Gallagher also reached out to many up-and-coming musicians during his brief 1991 tour of Australia. Gwyn Ashton, for instance, became aware of Gallagher as a teenager in the 1970s. At this stage in his life, he was already a music fanatic, absorbing ("like a sponge") "twenty years of music in about two years" from the British blues boom and fifties rock & roll to the California sound. Ashton was introduced to Gallagher's music by a fan in his neighbourhood who had often heard Ashton and his band rehearse.

As a starting point, Ashton was given three albums: *Live! In Europe*, *Irish Tour '74*, and *Calling Card*. "That night I listened to them, and it was like an epiphany," Ashton told me over the phone, "I thought, 'Wow, why haven't I heard this before?' It was probably the best guitar playing I'd heard, and the songs were really good as well." Gallagher's impression on Ashton was so immense that he took a three-month break from his band in order to study the guitarist, spending endless hours rewinding the needle on his records to decipher the guitar work. Although other bands such as ZZ Top and Budgie were also in the rotation, it was Gallagher that was "on top of all the other ones," partly due to the blues foundation of his sound.

In 1980, Ashton had the chance to swap the records for a seat in the Festival Theatre when Gallagher played Adelaide, vividly recalling the "blinding show." Luck was certainly on his side that night as Ashton had purchased tickets at the last minute. "The only ticket to get was right at the back, and I've been to concerts before and right up the back of the room is not a fun place to be." But as Ashton explained, "Rory was on fire that night and it was so good that the energy even hit the back of the room, and that's really unusual for any gig. You've normally got to be right down the front." The concert was important to Ashton for two reasons: foremost, as a fan ("I hadn't seen him before, I hadn't seen videos, [and] I had no idea what he looked like apart from the album cover"); and secondly, as an inspiration ("I took all of what I'd seen and adapted it to how I played, and sort of added it to my textbook of guitar licks"). Seeing Gallagher live only intensified Ashton's passion for the Irishman's music, and now he was permanently hooked.

In 1991, after begging the promoter to let his band do the show, Ashton found himself moved from offstage to *on* the stage as the support act for Gallagher in Adelaide. The opportunity deeply impacted Ashton as both "a fan of Rory [and] as a musician and a peer." Before the 1991 gig even started, Ashton experienced his first taste of Gallagher history when he struck up a conversation with Gallagher's long-term roadie and friend Tom O'Driscoll at soundcheck and was offered the chance to play Gallagher's 1961 Fender Stratocaster ("I said I'd *love* to"). Ashton has fond recollections of chatting with Gallagher backstage, noting how "quiet" and "shy" he was. "Rory didn't look particularly healthy" at this late stage in his life; nevertheless, his set was "brilliant" that night at the Old Lion Hotel. Gallagher's stage gear was supplied by Adelaide's Derringers, and the next day Ashton and his band happened to rehearse with the same gear. Ashton played through the same amp Gallagher had. "I didn't touch a single knob. I just wanted his sound, [and] to tap into a little bit of his psyche."

Perhaps some of Gallagher's 'psyche' did indeed stay with Ashton as his career progressed, beginning in 1996 when he left Australia for England. During a quick stop in America, he managed to obtain Gerry McAvoy's phone number, which eventually led to him joining Band of Friends in 2000. Ashton replaced both Brian Robertson and Robbie McIntosh in the band, the reality soon hitting him: "I had to replace not only Rory in the band, but I also had to replace these two hotshot guitar players. I thought, 'I better pull my socks up here and do something right' [laughs]."

Ashton's position in the preservation of Gallagher's legacy and music continues to the present day. To celebrate what would have been Gallagher's 73rd birthday in 2021, the estate uploaded a video of Ashton's 'Pickin' on Rory', which featured Gallagher covers as well as Ashton originals. These recordings are in the current process of being remixed for a studio release in the near future. For Ashton, the timeline of Gallagher's entanglement in his life, from "discovering the music" and "doing a gig with him" to finally being "in the band" with McAvoy and McKenna during 2000-2005 has played a significant role "as far as the stepping stones in music go."

Another musician to be influenced by Gallagher is Australian singer-songwriter Jeff Lang who was the support act for Gallagher's Melbourne and Sydney shows on 28 February and 1 March 1991, respectively. In an email exchange, Lang shared a few insights on how watching Gallagher onstage contributed to his own style of roots-oriented folk and blues:

> [Gallagher's] sound was his own, a purring, buttery, touch sensitive sound that could really sting the notes. The brief acoustic portion of his set was the thing I really dug [...] He just played into a microphone in these fairly large venues, right in the middle of a raucous electric gig. Took it right down in dynamics.[45]

Lang highlighted Gallagher's practice of weaving "traditional Irish music into his blues-rock music" as an influence on his own songcraft, as well as the "intensity" of Gallagher's performances, "which was something to witness." Lang confirms that Gallagher was "complimentary" of his playing, adding that it was "kind of him, as I was pretty young and just finding my way with my music."

This friendly bond between Gallagher and young Australian musicians went beyond the blues world, also into the glam rock scene, as Candy Harlots guitarist Marc Lee De Hugar reminisced on *The Australian Rock Show* in 2021:

> I got to know [Gallagher] really well, which was great. On his Enmore Theatre show [in Sydney], I was invited for a backstage

thing, and next thing you know we just fucking hooked it [...] They let us use the studio, and he told me how to wire pick-ups [and] it was like [being with] my grandpa or my dad, you know?"[46]

Despite the session being short, De Hugar claimed that Gallagher and he "bonded."

"Are there any Rory Gallagher fans here?":
Building on Gallagher's Legacy in Australia

To use Gwyn Ashton's phrasing, Gallagher has certainly provided the 'stepping stones' for many factions of my life, both personally and professionally. Since becoming a fan in 2021, his presence has metamorphosed from a CD spinning on the machine to forming international friendships, expanding musical tastes and co-writing this book based on our blog site *Rewriting Rory*. Social media has allowed me to connect with Gallagher fans across the globe, though more times than not, the fans I connect with never live in the same country as me. I return to the question posed earlier: do Australians even know who Rory Gallagher is? And if so, where are they?

Gallagher's legacy in Australia has ridden the tidal wave, shifting from the unknown, to the known, and now back to unknown. But if the case of 'Rory-fever' in 1980s Australia has been cured, then how do we attain another outbreak? Fans hold a candle to their hero through international Rory Gallagher tribute bands and festivals (as demonstrated in Germany, Italy, Japan, Ireland, France and the UK), but when it comes to Australia, the wick has extinguished and we fail to see our appreciation for a musical figure that was the soundtrack (even the radio jingle) to many in this country. Films such as *Phil Lynott: Songs for While I'm Away* and *Crock of Gold: A Few Rounds with Shane McGowan* have played at the annual Irish Film Festival in Australia. In the near future, we Australian fans might like to see Gallagher debut at the festival, screening either *Irish Tour '74* or *Ghost Blues: The Story of Rory Gallagher* (2010) in order to reconnect with a long-lost musical figure. In the meantime, however, those Australians reading this chapter are encouraged to pick up their Gallagher albums and catch that 'Rory-fever' one last time.

PART 3: USA

Throughout his career, Gallagher racked up a whopping 23 tours of the US. He first visited the country in 1969 when Taste were asked to support Blind Faith and Delanay, Bonnie & Friends on their summer tour. The tour was somewhat of a disaster, with Taste given no time for sound checks and no PA system, and Gallagher uncomfortable with the fact that manager Eddie Kennedy decided to travel on the musicians' bus, which "created a business vibe."[47] Gallagher also disliked playing daytime gigs in large arenas and hoped to stay on in America to do a tour of smaller clubs instead, but Kennedy did not allow this. According to Dónal, Gallagher felt that Kennedy had used the trip as a holiday rather than a chance to cultivate agencies, venues and promoters, which added to the friction that led to the eventual break-up of Taste. As a result of his unhappiness, Gallagher retreated to the back of the tour bus on his own to read rather than socialise with anybody. Nonetheless, the tour had some positives—namely that it enabled Gallagher to see Muddy Waters perform for the first time in Ungano's (New York). A rollcall of stars was also in attendance that night, including Buddy Miles, Steve Marriott and Jimi Hendrix. While in Chicago, Gallagher also visited a 'no-go area' of the city to see Hound Dog Taylor.

Once established as a solo artist, Gallagher was keen to return to the US on his own terms. In October 1971, he arrived for a short tour, sharing the bill with such stars as Little Feat, Buddy Miles, Frank Zappa, Fleetwood Mac, Lee Michaels, Mylon LeFevre and Holy Smoke. Gallagher subsequently came back to the US almost every year throughout the 1970s, often twice or three times, and always for extensive three- or four-month periods. Some key highlights during this time include upstaging Aerosmith at the Schaefer Music Festival in Central Park (1974), diffusing a potentially violent incident between John Lennon and Jerry Lee Lewis backstage at West Hollywood Club (1974) and delivering a stunning WNEF.FM live broadcast from The Bottom Line (1978).

As discussed in the introduction, Gallagher's acute fear of flying as well as negative experiences supporting US 'supergroups' prevented him from visiting the US for several years. There was still clear demand for him, however, when he returned in 1985 for a two-month tour, and even after a six-year break from visiting the country, he was welcomed once again with open arms in 1991. Gallagher had hoped to tour the US again in 1993, but his ill health sadly prevented this. Nevertheless, on those 19 dates in 1991, Gallagher made sure to make a lasting impression on North America, sealing his reputation as a first-rate performer and ensuring that—although he never returned to the continent—he most certainly would never be forgotten.

"Playing for the people":
Gallagher in the US Press

Having been away from the US for so long, Gallagher's schedule between concerts was filled with press and radio interviews, the media keen to find out what the Irishman had been doing in his six-year absence from the country. Gallagher always thought carefully over his answers when being interviewed, and this time was no exception, each offering fascinating insights into his character and attitude to music. "I don't actually tour the States to make money and I don't play music for money as such,"[48] he told the *Central New Jersey Home News*, also sharing his fears of the blues becoming too popular, his scepticism about the blues revival and his hopes for his new record company. He confessed that he had experienced a "couple of cranky years" and felt "fed up" with the music business, but he still liked to "play for [the] people" to keep his music "real."[49] Speaking to the *Toronto Sun*, Gallagher expressed his belief that young people were getting tired of "video" music and looking for the "raw bones and roots of rock again,"[50] while to the *Detroit Free Press*, he elaborated on his musical philosophy:

> You see, I just believe in what I'm doing. I can see the commercial pitfalls of taking the wrong detours, but I don't want to be a pop star, number one, and I don't mind experimenting with music. For myself, I just like the honesty and rawness; you can still be progressive in your lyrics and in the way you use chords and notes. And if you match that with a rootsy sound and mood, you've achieved something.[51]

Similarly, in an interview with *The Daily Spectrum*, Gallagher stressed that he was "not trying to outsell Presley or the Stones," but that he thought there was still a "valid place" for his music.[52] With his typical dry wit, he added, "Somebody in Europe wrote recently that I'm so unfashionable that it's actually a plus for me!" and that he has deliberately tried to "stay out of the 'getting old' syndrome" and avoid joining "the rank-and-file" of his generation. Gallagher also speaks often of how he has been feeling particularly inspired to write on this tour, his songwriting having had a "boost" in recent years since he came up with "some new ideas, some new themes and new approaches" and started to "define the blues roots a lot more."[53]

One of the best interviews of Gallagher's career took place in Santa Cruz with music journalist Jas Obrecht on 15 March. The sign of a great interviewer, Obrecht knows how to immediately put Gallagher at ease, jumping straight in with a question about the blues. Gallagher responds warmly, and the two men go on to speak for an hour, exchanging tale after tale that clearly emphasises their love for and deep knowledge of the blues. The full transcript of their conversation can be read on the *Rewriting Rory* website (published with Obrecht's permission).[54]

The Conquering Irish Hero

When thinking of Gallagher's 1991 US tour, his gig at the Roxy in Los Angeles on 9 March is perhaps one of the first to come to mind, known for his jam with Guns N' Roses guitarist, Slash. Press reports and fan reviews recall the crowds of people waiting to get into the venue, causing "the strongest queue in recent memory,"[55] as well as the faces of numerous well-known musicians hidden within the crowd. Despite initial concerns over how Gallagher looked, critics were soon proved wrong, acknowledging that "his skill as a performer, guitarist, and blues-rock storyteller has not diminished at all."[56]

Slash joined Gallagher for an extended encore of 'Bullfrog Blues', which included a "terrific" rendition of Chuck Berry's 'Nadine' and "Little Queenie". According to Bill Holdship of *Bay Area Music* magazine, Gallagher ultimately came out on top and "outclassed" the young talent of Slash.[57] For fan Marc Martin, who caught eight of Gallagher's gigs on the tour, there was simply "no comparison" between the two guitarists ("Rory was so much better").[58] All spectators were in agreement that it was Gallagher's night and perhaps the Irishman himself felt it too, leaving the show with "a big grin that reached everybody in the room."[59]

Gallagher spoke about the jam in a 1993 interview with *Guitar World*, describing Slash as "a charming boy" with "respect for the music and its origins" and praising him for his ability to "let loose a riff that will freeze your blood."[60] Speaking again to *Hard Rock* on the topic, Gallagher noted that he had to adjust his style, but once they started playing together, it "worked like clockwork." Gallagher was "very touched" when Slash stated that it was "an honour" to play with him, although he was disappointed that he did not have the chance to jam with Izzy Stradlin as well.[61] Slash still frequently talks about the jam in interviews, noting that Gallagher left a "great impression" on him[62] and that he was a "genuinely affectionate and sweet" man who did not realise the effect that he had on young guitar players.[63]

But the Roxy was just one of many incredible concerts on Gallagher's tour, attested to by bootleg recordings such as *Tearing Down the Empire* (24 March, Cleveland) and *Live from the Guthrie Theater* (20 March, Minneapolis). Fan Dave Mangin was at the Minneapolis concert, describing it as the "best concert" that he has ever seen. Mangin had "no idea" that Gallagher was coming to his city until his mother called him at work and said, "That Irish blues guy you really like, Rory Whatshisname, is here tonight at the Guthrie. Can I get you a couple of tickets?" "Hell yeah!" was Mangin's reply! Although it was evident to Mangin that "the road was wearing" on Gallagher, the guitarist "never let up" for over two hours. Particular standout moments for Mangin were the few bars of 'Tumblin' Dice' that Gallagher threw in during 'Bullfrog Blues' ("you could really get why the Stones had him on the list of players to replace Taylor") and 'Off the Handle' where Gallagher changed around some of the lyrics ("when the cat's away, the mice play") and he and Mark Feltham exchanged notes that Mangin has "never heard anyone replicate" and which sent him and his friends "nuts."[64]

Gallagher's concert at Park West in Chicago on 22 March was another standout. Martin Hayes, the prolific Irish fiddler, was living in Chicago when Gallagher rolled into town and, as a long-term fan, he knew that he had to get tickets. Speaking to *Hot Press* in 2020, Martin recalled the experience:

> The concert was sold out by the time I found out about it, but since I'd never managed to see [Rory] live, I felt compelled to go and see if I could somehow get in. I did eventually, after much pleading and effort, but I had missed the first twenty minutes in the process of trying to talk my way in. By the time I got into the venue, an incredible atmosphere had built up in the room. Rory was in full command of the evening, it was an amazing display of pure

charisma, energy, and passion, with nothing held back. The great blues town of Chicago embraced Rory Gallagher and his music with wild enthusiasm and he was for me, on that night, the conquering Irish hero that my teenage imagination had always envisioned. I remember saying to myself, this is how the stage should always be approached: give everything, hold nothing back and be completely yourself. That occasion showed me the enormous power that one individual with a deep commitment could generate.[65]

However, the Chicago gig is tinged with bittersweet memories for fan Marc Martin who remembers meeting McAvoy and O'Neill the night before in a blues club on Lincoln Avenue. When he asked them where Gallagher was, they replied, "You don't wanna know. He really doesn't go out." It is somewhat painful to contrast this image of a reclusive Gallagher offstage with the "conquering Irish hero" (as Martin Hayes put it) that he was onstage, especially when being in a city so deeply rooted in the blues and brimming with live music. Martin had previously met Gallagher after his concert at San Diego's Bachanal (6 March) and recalls that he carried an inhaler and had evident "health issues," yet he "had not lost any of his personality" and "was still friendly and talkative."

Drawing Energy from the Crowd
Other concerts posed more challenging for Gallagher and his band. The Westport Playhouse in St Louis, for example, had a strange revolving stage, which was frustrating for some fans. But this evidently did not mar their enjoyment, given the standing ovations which "followed almost every number" and their amazement at the way Gallagher "succeeded in eliciting tones from his guitar" and became increasingly "adventurous" in response to the applause.[66] A review in the *St Louis Post Dispatch* notes that 'Ghost Blues' received the longest ovation of all, its "tight, powerful riff nearly mesmerising the capacity crowd."[67]

During the Sayreville show, there was potential trouble from an audience member, which Gallagher expertly handled. As one spectator recounted on Facebook:

Some guy jumped up on stage during 'A Million Miles Away' and when a stagehand tried to get him off he went into karate mode and the stagehand backed off. The guy was doing karate moves to the guitar of 'A Million Miles Away' and Rory walked the guy off the stage while still playing and nobody got hurt or in a fight. You had to see it to believe it. Wish it had been filmed [...] Pretty cool when you think how [Rory] had the power to calm a bad situation down and no one got hurt or thrown out.[68]

It was technical difficulties, on the other hand, that affected Gallagher's concert at the Paradise Theatre in Boston on 29 March. Speaking to Shiv Cariappa in 1997, Brendan O'Neill recalled the Boston gig being a "nightmare" due to the rostrum being too small for the drumkit, leading the cymbals to constantly fall off and Tom O'Driscoll having to keep running on stage to put them back.[69] Those in the audience noticed the difficulties, yet could not believe the remarkable sight they witnessed before them that evening: of Gallagher undeterredly playing, drawing energy from the crowd and progressively getting better and better. Keen to ensure that his fans did not go away disappointed, he ended up playing the longest show of the entire tour at just over three hours in length. As Marc Martin recalls:

> [Rory] was having an off night. Any musician on a tour is gonna have an off night. It happens. But what he did was… it was amazing! He played for three hours. He kept pushing. He kind of got over it, and he started playing songs that I hadn't heard on the tour. I think he played 'Souped Up Ford' and 'Walking Wounded', or 'Slumming Angel', I think it was.

Mark Morrison—another fan who was also at Paradise Theatre that evening—told a similar account:

> [Rory] looked quite ill and overweight to my eyes that evening and wore a heavy leather coat to try and disguise the fact [...] But if there was ever a performer who drew energy from an audience, it was Rory, and the crowd that night was absolutely rabid. As the evening progressed, he seemed to become stronger and more engaged. And towards the end, when he hit the first chords of 'Used to Be', the collective roar from the audience damn near blew the roof off the joint. That moment is how I love to remember him.[70]

Derry Bray even managed to meet Gallagher after the gig. Originally hailing from Ireland, Bray had first met Gallagher at the Savoy Theatre in Limerick back in 1972. Drummer Rod De'Ath was running late for his inaugural concert and, mistaking Pennywell for Jack Costello of Grannie's Intentions, Dónal asked him to sit in for De'Ath during rehearsals. By 1991, Bray was living in the US and went along to Gallagher's "typical powerful workhouse show" at Paradise Theatre:

> As the venue emptied out, I worked my way to the side stage door manned by two burly bouncers and said, 'I know you have heard every story by backstage wannabes' and I explained how I had met Rory and the circumstances and said, 'Tell Dónal Gallagher that a Jack Costello from Limerick wants to say hi'. It being Boston, of course, the two lads were 'Irish' and that seemed to make it all work out [...] In we went where I quickly explained the truth of the matter. Much to my amazement, Dónal remembered the night their drummer almost missed his first gig with Rory and gladly introduced me to 'The Gally'. I thought he looked tired and put it down to the show and the tour, but he was his quiet, polite usual self

[...] That was the last time I saw or heard of Rory until the shocking and sad news he had passed away all too young. That little boy from Donegal, with minimal outside influence and lessons, blazed his own trail through the pages of rock and roll history where he wrote his own story, a story still being read.[71]

Kindness and Connections

Other anecdotes from the tour capture Gallagher's kind heart and appreciation for his fans. Coleen Phillips had been a Gallagher fan since the early 1970s, often attending his concerts in San Francisco with her husband (and later her daughter). Gallagher's 1991 appearance at the city's Stone venue happened to coincide with Phillip's birthday, so her daughter Carolyn decided to organise a special birthday surprise for her. Days before the show, Carolyn mailed an addressed letter for Gallagher to The Stone, explaining what big fans her parents were and that it was her mother's birthday on 16 March. She told Gallagher that her mother's favourite song was 'Moonchild' and asked if he could dedicate it to her that night. To Phillips' great surprise, at the concert:

> [My husband and I] were standing about halfway back in the audience. Rory had just finished his opening song. Then he said, 'This next one is for Colleen!' and began tearing into 'Moonchild'. My jaw dropped wide open. I looked to my right and some people were holding up their drinks saying, 'Here's to Colleen!' and the house rocked with the wild sounds of 'Moonchild' with people dancing, jumping up and down having a great time! It's probably my best birthday gift ever. I was beyond surprised that something like that actually happened and was grateful nobody knew where I was in the audience. But it also shows the character of Rory Gallagher. A single letter to him from my daughter requesting a song could have simply been tossed aside or into the trash bin, or never even looked at. But it wasn't and I'll never forget that night.[72]

Equally, Marianne Murphy "cherishes the blessing" of seeing Gallagher play live and meeting him several times. Murphy's first Gallagher concert was at the Royal Oak Music Theatre in Michigan in 1976, where she presented him with a homemade Irish flag that he draped over his amp. She saw him again in 1985 at Harpos in Detroit, this time giving him a cross-stitch picture of his guitar in a frame. When Gallagher returned to Detroit in 1991—this time to the Key West Club—Murphy was sure not to miss the concert, which she described as "fantastic." After the show, she waited with her husband to meet Gallagher. Although he was "exhausted," Gallagher was "gracious" and autographed her copy of *Defender*. When they were driving home and stopped at a red traffic light, her husband noticed Gallagher in a van alongside looking across at them. Murphy said that she deliberately could not look at him because she felt that she had "taken up enough of his time already." As a working musician, Murphy sees

Gallagher as a tremendous influence:

> Rory's music makes connections between different genres. It can have some blues, jazz, folk and good old rock and roll. Rory's music brings people together in a mutual admiration for his talent of which he so generously gave us [...] Rory was hugely inspiring for me [as a musician]. I used to play lots of slide blues acoustically. I started listening to the old masters like Robert Johnson, Muddy Waters, Son House, Charley Patton...

After this final meeting with Gallagher, Murphy was inspired to write a song about him called 'Hero from the Emerald Isle'. She had hoped to give it to him one day, but instead she passed it on to Paddy Maloney of the Chieftains. The song did, however, end up on the Gallagher tribute tape *They Don't Make Them Like You*, compiled by Rick Oppegaard shortly after Rory's passing.[73]

Another example of Gallagher's connection with fans is shared by Jon B Wilder who attended his show at The Strand in Redondo Beach (8 March) with a group of friends. Wilder sat at one of the tables near the stage, soaking in the "blistering" and "larger than life" onstage persona of Gallagher. "I will never forget how quiet, almost solemn, the club became while Rory sang the poignant and haunting 'Out on the Western Plain'," he notes.[74] When the show was over, Wilder approached the stage to shake Gallagher's hand. "He looked me directly in the eyes, and gave a wan, little smile." In half shock, half inebriation, Wilder confesses that, as he "squeezed" his idol's hand, he said, "I love you, Rory." And while Gallagher did not reply, he gave Wilder "a knowing look like, 'We had a good time together, didn't we, mate?' And then he was gone…"

All Good Things Come to an End

As the saying goes, all good things come to an end. And so, on 30 March, McAvoy and O'Neill played their last official gig[75] with Gallagher at the Marquee Club in New York. The 30 minutes of surviving footage show an extremely tight band at the top of their game and there is no indication of the tensions beneath the surface or that McAvoy and O'Neill were about to go their separate ways. A beautiful moment towards the end of the video shows Gallagher hugging his Stratocaster to his chest and kissing its neck for several seconds—his faithful companion and constant source of comfort, particularly on what must have been a deeply emotional night for him.

Having a strange premonition that it was going to be the last time that he would ever see Gallagher, Marc Martin rented a car from Boston to New York for the concert without even booking a hotel room. He arrived at the venue only to find out that they had lost his ticket, but thanks to the kindness of Patrick Kennedy—a sorely missed fan and close friend of the Gallagher family—Martin was able to borrow his *Fresh Evidence* backstage pass and get into the Marquee Club. For

Martin, the New York concert was "the best" he ever saw in his life. He knew from McAvoy and O'Neill that the band was breaking up after the tour and found that this seemed to fuel them on to give an unforgettable last performance together:

> They were unbelievably tight. I'd heard all the concerts on the tour and none of them were bad, but [New York] was incredible. It was like magic. When you hear a band that is really on, when they hit a note at the same time, it was one of those nights. And Rory was lighting it up on guitar. All of a sudden, as I recall, he played 'Shadow Play' and he was holding the guitar up, it's a picture I'll always remember, and then the lights go off. There's no encore, it's over. It was only 45 minutes long, less than an hour. It was so weird. I remember hearing something about that he had to catch a flight back to London the next day, and that's why they had to cut it early. I probably could have gone backstage, but I didn't. Part of me just wanted to give him his privacy. And that was the last time I saw him live.

Although Gallagher had told the crowd that he could only play a short set because he had an early flight back to London the next day, it was, in fact, due to trouble with the New York Fire and Police Departments as a result of overcrowding in the venue. Word had spread around New York that Gallagher was going to part company with McAvoy and O'Neill after the tour, which had increased hype around the concert and led the promoter to capitalise upon this huge demand for tickets. As Dónal told the *Irish Examiner*,[76] the Marquee Club was "absolutely packed" and both the New York Fire and Police Departments got wind of it and showed up. Dónal spent the duration of the show trying to negotiate between the fire officer who wanted to shut down the venue, the police who were threatening to arrest the promoter and Gallagher who wanted to continue playing on stage:

> I said, 'Look, if you pull the plug and [Rory] has to go off stage, that's going to cause even more damage'. I asked the fire department guy if he could just do two more numbers, and he replied: 'Ok, he can do two more numbers, as long as one of them is 'Messin' With The Kid'! Rory duly obliged, and then finished out his set with 'Bullfrog Blues'!

Long-term Gallagher fan, Vince Rampino, who was also at the New York concert, painted a colourful picture of the atmosphere inside the club for us. He noted the extreme contrast in temperature within and outside the venue ("about 90 degrees, extremely hot" versus "30 degrees, very cold"), the celebrities in attendance ("Kathleen Turner was at the show!") and the intensity of Gallagher's performance ("Rory was a trouper. [He] looked a bit bloated and tired but his playing was still strong").[77] Outside the venue were hundreds of fans unable to get tickets yet hoping to catch the sounds of the concert from within.

In *Riding Shotgun*, McAvoy recalls the strange mood when Gallagher and the band walked off the stage for the final time together:

> As we climbed some stairs through a section of the crowd, we were virtually mobbed. Everyone was patting us on the back and trying to shake our hands. I was very aware that this was probably the last time in my life I would ever experience anything quite like this. We got back to the dressing room and we all just sat in silence. Everyone seemed to be feeling the same way, but nobody could find the words to express it. It was a very strange atmosphere. Eventually people started to make small talk but still nothing of any importance was said until Brendan stood up and walked over to Rory. He took Rory's hand and shook it and said, 'Good tour, Rory. Well done'. And then Rory turned to me and shook my hand and said, 'Well done, Gerry'. And that was it. No embraces. No tears. Just a huge sense of sadness that overwhelmed the room.[78]

From the Marquee Club, McAvoy and O'Neill headed to a bar that was owned by an old friend from Belfast, Sammy O'Connor. They asked Gallagher if he wanted to join them for a few drinks. He said that he probably would, but ended up sending Dónal in his place and going back to his hotel room alone.

"Rory was always Rory": Remembering the 1991 World Tour

As was often the case in his life, Rory Gallagher's 1991 world tour was an event that took place in the face of so many challenges: his crippling fear of flying, his worsening health, the Iraq war which threatened global travel restrictions and the news that McAvoy and O'Neill were leaving his band. In *Riding Shotgun*, McAvoy wrote that he would have rather "untied the knot completely" and that although Gallagher was "amicable" on the tour, there was—understandably—a lot of tension in the air.[79] Just as with Taste's performance at the 1970 Isle of Wight Festival, this growing tension spurred Gallagher on to ensure that this line-up of the band went out on a high. There was so much at stake and he needed to prove to himself, to his fellow band members and to his Japanese, Australian and American fans that he was still able to pull off world-class performances, to show that nothing had changed, even if, on a surface level, things may have.

All of Gallagher's shows across Japan, Australia and North America were sold out, demonstrating the strong demand that still existed for his music. Throughout the chapter, we have encountered so many tales that represent why Rory Gallagher the *person* is loved just as much as Rory Gallagher the *musician*: from turning shows around (Boston) to pacifying rowdy fans (Sayreville) through remembering and reuniting with old fans in Kawasaki and Adelaide. Gallagher's constant kindness shines through, whether dispensing friendly advice and words of support to young musicians or simply taking the time to speak to journalists, no matter how tired or unwell he was feeling. "Grace" is the word that folk musician Martin Carthy has often used to describe Gallagher, and he is absolutely right. As he wrote in the Order of Service for Gallagher's requiem mass, Gallagher "graced music as he graced humanity. [Grace] is the person who makes life worthwhile by example, who loves his trade and the people who play it and one who tells them so, who makes his peers feel good by his simple presence."

McAvoy's autobiography states that Gallagher's career "stalled" after he left the band and that the guitarist took the split "to heart more" because McAvoy had a "new career to look forward to."[80] He says that Gallagher needed something to "get his career back on track" and that he never capitalised on the success of the 1991 international tour. McAvoy's words are unfair as Gallagher's career was never *off track* and it was only his ill health that prevented him from 'capitalising' on anything. There is a general assumption that 1991 marked the end of Gallagher's career and that he never toured again after McAvoy and O'Neill left the band. While 1991 marked the closing of the door on this line-up's history, we nevertheless feel the cool air from a window being opened when we think about Gallagher's efforts to put together a new band in 1992 with David Levy and Richard Newman (see Interlude).

Gallagher was revitalised by his new band who gave him a boost of fresh energy and ideas and were an essential part of his later performances. Perhaps he was no longer the globetrotting 'Vasco Da Gama of Rock', but we like to see him as an Emperor Augustus or Trajan, continuously expanding across Europe and leaving towns and cities dazzled in his wake by the power of his music.

We conclude with a short quote from Marc Martin when reflecting on Gallagher's 1991 international tour:

> He didn't lose it. Health wise, he may have had some issues with that, but he was still a tremendous guitar player. He just struck an emotional chord with me that he still had in '91 that he had in '77 the first time I saw him. He just was older.

Martin's words get right to the crux of this book. Whether older, heavier or sicker, it does not matter. Rory was always Rory.

RM and LAO

Rory Gallagher - *The Later Years*

Footnotes

1 Interview with Gwyn Ashton, 16 September 2022. All subsequent quotes from Ashton come from this interview.
2 Chris Jones, 'Rory Gallagher - Sinner Boy', *Jones Is Dying* (8 May 2014), https://jonesisdying.blogspot.com/2014/05/rory-gallagher-sinner-boy.html.
3 This includes the documentary film *Irish Tour '74*, centered on Gallagher's performances in late December/early January 1973-1974 in Ireland during the height of the Troubles; the German *Rockpalast* documentary (1997), which provides an in-depth look at Gallagher's many visits to the popular rock festival in Germany; and *Cowtown Ballroom...Sweet Jesus* (2009), a documentary about the venue in Kansas City, Missouri.
4 As we know, Gallagher continued to perform in and around Europe until his passing; for the purpose of this section, we define 'world' as outside of Europe.
5 Dan Muise, *Gallagher, Marriott, Derringer & Trower* (Milwaukee: Hal Leonard Corporation, 2002), 66.
6 'Rory Gallagher Interview 1991 audio', https://www.youtube.com/watch?v=aY2SLLnC-rs&t=167s.
7 Evelyn Thomchick, 'The 1991 Persian Gulf War: Short-Term Impacts on Ocean and Air Transportation', *Transportation Journal*, vol. 33, no. 22 (1993), 48.
8 'Rory Gallagher Japan Tour 1977', *Ongaku Senaka*, (December 1977), https://www.roryon.com/japan77-392.html
9 Interview with Shu Tomioka, 24 April 2022.
10 Interview with Matsumi Mae in *Rory Gallagher 25th Memorial Edition* (Japan: Shinko Music Entertainment Co. Ltd, 2020), 124-136.
11 Our original blog post on *Rewriting Rory* (24 September 2022) provided extensive coverage of Gallagher's 1974, 1975 and 1977 Japan tours. However, we have omitted these sections here due to space and relevancy.
12 Vivian Campbell, 'The Wearing of the Blues', *Guitar for the Practicing Musician* (August 1991), https://www.roryon.com/guitar91.html
13 'Rory Gallagher Interview 1991', https://www.youtube.com/watch?v=fNpaun5s1CE
14 See: https://sites.google.com/view/rory-gallagher/home
15 Interview with Kouki 'Dannie' Taniguchi, 10 February 2024.
16 *Rory Gallagher 25th Memorial Edition*, 124-136.
17 'Rory Gallagher Interview 1991'.
18 Interview with K.G. Takeda, 20 March 2022.
19 See: http://shinolez.blog39.fc2.com/
20 See: https://sites.google.com/view/rory-gallagher/home
21 All press reports can be found at https://sites.google.com/view/rory-live-archives-by-megumi
22 Interview with Megumi Manzaki, 11 May 2024. All subsequent quotes from Manzaki come from this interview.
23 Interview with Kouki 'Dannie' Taniguchi, 4 May 2024. All subsequent quotes from Taniguchi come from this interview.
24 Interview with Takayuki Oi, 9 May 2024.
25 Interview with John Spreckley, 6 February 2023.
26 Interview with Paul Dufficy, 3 June 2022.
27 Grant Thompson, 'Glitter Scene', *Sydney Morning Herald* (2 February 1975), 81.
28 Ibid.
29 Paul Comrie-Thomson, 'Performance', *Rolling Stone Australia* (27 February 1975), n.p.
30 Donald Horne, *The Lucky Country* (Sydney: Penguin Books, 1964), 21.
31 '1975-1985: 40 Years of triple j', *ABC* (5 February 2015), https://www.abc.net.au/listen/programs/the-j-files/1975-1985-40-years-of-triple-j/10274876.
32 Interview with Bob Hall, January 2023.
33 Rory Gallagher Interview with Tony Maniaty, Double 2JJ studios (8 February 1975), Library of NSW archives.
34 Kim Trengove, 'Rory strums up a storm', *The Sun* (25 June 1980), 44.
35 'Guitarist Gallagher Ejected', *Billboard* (13 September 1980), https://www.roryon.com/ejected.html.
36 Ibid.
37 Interview with Chris Grotz, 1 June 2022.
38 Bruce Elder, 'A pale imitation of blues', *Sydney Morning Herald* (4 March 1991), 12.
39 Bruce Gutherie, 'Fresh Evidence', *The Age* (24 February 1991), 30.
40 Clinton Walker, *Stranded: Australian Independent Music, 1976-1992* (Clifton: The Visible Spectrum, 2021), 347.
41 Mick Armstrong, 'Anti-Irish racism in Australian history', *Red Flag* (27 January 2017), https://redflag.org.au/node/5651.
42 'Guitarist Gallagher Ejected'.
43 Interview with Paul Patrick Martin, 21 March 2022.
44 Interview with Fiachna Ó Braonáin, 6 August 2022.
45 Interview with Jeff Lang, 14 August 2022.
46 'Marc De Hugar Interview - Candy Harlots | Dragon (RIP 1969 - 2022)', https://www.youtube.com/watch?v=smaU9eRgLoE.
47 Muise, *Gallagher, Marriott, Derringer, Trower*, 13.
48 Richard Skelly, 'Fine Irish Guitarist to Play Club Bene', *Central New Jersey Home News* (24 March 1991), 1.
49 Ibid.
50 John Sakamoto, 'White Knuckle Guitarist', *Toronto Sun* (21 March 1991), https://www.roryon.com/knuckle159.html
51 Gary Graff, 'Rockin' Good Days', *Detroit Free Press* (25 March 1991), 2E.
52 George Varga, 'Rory Gallagher', *The Daily Spectrum* (31 March 1991), 14.
53 Judy Black, 'Back to the Basic Blues Roots', *Cleveland Scene* (March 1991), https://shadowplays.com/blog/?p=193
54 See: https://rewritingrory.co.uk/2022/06/17/previously-unpublished-1991-interview-with-rory-by-jas-obrecht/
55 John Sutherland, 'Rory Gallagher Roxy Theater Los Angeles', *Metal Hammer* (March 1991), https://www.roryon.com/roxy157.html
56 Ibid.
57 Bill Holdship, 'Newsreels', *Bay Area Music* (22 March 1991), https://www.roryon.com/newsreel257.htm

Part 2 - *The Vasco Da Gama of Rock*

58 Interview with Marc Martin, 10 April 2022. All subsequent quotes from Martin come from this interview.
59 Sutherland, 'Rory Gallagher...'
60 J.P.Sabour & X.Bonnet, '...et vogue la galère', *Guitar World* (February 1993), https://rewritingrory.co.uk/2022/06/03/guitar-world-february-1993/
61 Dominique Dujean, 'Le blues toujours', *Hard Rock* (February 1993), https://rewritingrory.co.uk/2022/06/03/hard-rock-february-1993/
62 *Ghost Blues: The Story of Rory Gallagher* (2010).
63 'Old Grey Whistle Test with Rory Gallagher (1976)', https://www.youtube.com/watch?v=vcDxYbQ9yzw&t=95s
64 Interview with Dave Mangin, 22 March 2022.
65 'Martin Hayes on Rory Gallagher: "The conquering Irish hero"', *Hot Press* (17 July 2020), https://www.hotpress.com/opinion/martin-hayes-on-rory-gallagher-the-conquering-irish-hero-22822686
66 Louise King, 'Rory Gallagher Makes Energetic Return Here', *St Louis Post Dispatch* (25 March 1991), 5A.
67 Ibid.
68 See: https://www.facebook.com/RoryGallagher/posts/pfbid0hzz2qLWj42yyE36D1NiwEiToEzCodgr1qfgUTcLCVVs1jAw-6d7RWfkURiebgW7yLl
69 Shiv Cariappa, 'Interview with Brendan O'Neill' (26 March 1997), https://gallaghersblues.net/articles/bon_int_97.html
70 Interview with Mark Morrison, 26 April 2022.
71 Interview with Derry Bray, 17 August 2022.
72 Interview with Coleen Phillips, 28 March 2022.
73 Interview with Marianne Murphy, 21 March 2022.
74 Jon B. Wilder, 'The Strand', https://www.roryon.com/wilderstory.html
75 Though McAvoy and O'Neill would come back as 'special guests' for several dates in 1992 while Gallagher got his new band together.
76 Des O'Driscoll, 'Rory Gallagher remembered 25 years on in five iconic gigs', *Irish Examiner* (9 June 2020), https://www.irishexaminer.com/lifestyle/artsandculture/arid-31004315.html
77 Interview with Vince Rampino, 30 March 2022.
78 McAvoy and Chrisp, *Riding Shotgun*, 266.
79 Ibid.
80 Ibid.

Interlude:
Introducing the New Rory Gallagher Band

Preparations to arrange a new band for Rory Gallagher were slow to begin with. The departure of McAvoy and O'Neill following the 1991 US tour seemed to aggravate old wounds within Gallagher of the Taste break-up in 1970, leaving him vulnerable, resentful and, most of all, cautious. In a 2016 interview with *Classic Rock*, director of the *Irish Tour '74* documentary film Tony Palmer commented on the impact of McAvoy's departure on Gallagher.

> [Rory and Gerry] were bonded together, no question of that. When your family fractures, it can leave you not knowing what to do. I think that left him lonely, and loneliness brings other things along [...] He did his best to keep his feet on the ground, but sometimes it gets to you, and it got to him. I think he felt quite depressed about it.[1]

While disheartened, Gallagher was, nevertheless, looking towards the horizon, regarding the split as "beneficial"[2] for both McAvoy and O'Neill as well as himself. Speaking with *Hard Rock* in February 1993, Gallagher stated: "There's no bitterness on my part [...] There is no animosity between us. Sometimes an important change is necessary."[3] During the same year, Gallagher discussed with *Guitar World* his intentions for the next set of members. "Having a 'loyal' group behind you is nice, but that can also become very restrictive [...] I've learnt to be more flexible with the musicians I choose to accompany me [...] My policy with the current line-up is to act and to live day to day without worrying if the guys will be on the next album or the next tour."[4] According to Gallagher, band flexibility created other serendipitous outcomes: "If I want to go from a three-piece band to a four-piece band or vice versa mid tour, I'll do it more freely. It's a good challenge for me because that allows me to put forth the most variety and freedom in my playing."[5] Mark Feltham offered a balanced perspective of the situation in our 2023 phone exchange:

> I think Rory felt a little bit letdown by the fact that Gerry and Brendy had strayed, but in another way, I think that they were frustrated that they weren't working enough. There was certainly no bad feeling or no animosity towards Rory about all this. No one

ever fell out with him at all. Never. He was just too nice to fall out with. But musicians have to work and I remember they were on the payroll... I think that they wanted to be creative and wanted to get out and do stuff, and I think that when they said to Rory, 'Look, we'd like to move on', I think it was quickly arranged to get some guys in to do something else.[6]

Feltham confirmed that, initially, Jim Leverton filled in on bass along with drummer Richard Newman, while "I just seamlessly drifted into the new band from the old band." Shortly after, David Levy, a session musician who had played on records by Tina Charles, Bonnie Tyler and ex-Duran Duran member Stephen Duffy, replaced Leverton on bass. The first rehearsal was scheduled in London at Nomis Studios.

"The talk of the town":
The New Rory Gallagher Band's First Show

In an article for the *North Wales Weekly News*, it was reported that Gallagher would make a "surprise date" at the Marina Hotel in Rhyl, Wales.[7] Photojournalist and friend of Gallagher, Bob Hewitt, helped organise the event, as well as providing the support act on the night with his band the Misery Brothers. According to Hewitt, apprehensive about debuting his new band at the forthcoming Temple Bar Blues Festival, Gallagher wanted to use the Rhyl gig as a "warm-up for himself and the new band."[8] As Hewitt elaborated in an August 2022 interview with us:

> Dónal contacted me to say that he and Rory were calling in to say hello on their way through to Dublin (via Holyhead). As we got talking, Don suggested arranging a low-key gig in my hometown as a warm-up with Rory's new bassist and drummer [...] I got together with my bass player [and] pal Chris White to try and find a venue, and to sort publicity/poster campaign. Eventually a guy called Hughie Shaw came to the rescue. He said we could use his Marina [Hotel] venue right on the Rhyl seafront and overlooking the Irish Sea. It was perfect–just the right intimate atmosphere and sufficient capacity (about 1,000) for a short notice gig... or so I thought!

> It was a £5 entry on the door, and on the evening of the show it was warm and sunny, [and] as I arrived, [I saw] a queue down the promenade as far as the eye could see! I soon realised we would have to turn people away to avoid exceeding the capacity licensing laws [...] As it transpired, we managed to squeeze everyone in who came along that evening–including the local fire safety officer![9]

Hewitt said that introducing Gallagher to the crowd was the "greatest thrill" of the night for him, the audience's warm reception "deafening" when Gallagher finally walked onto the stage. Despite the small venue and lowkey publicity, the gig became "the talk of the town," with Hewitt recalling Gallagher's new band as "brilliant." Unfortunately, this would be Hewitt's final meeting with Gallagher prior to his passing. "The last thing I did was write his obituary for *Guitar Magazine*," Hewitt said, "I didn't write anything else for ten years after that. I was heartbroken."

For the newest members of the group, the Rhyl show represented the electrifying atmosphere a Gallagher performance could rouse. "[It] was a good gig. [I] found out who Rory was that night... [he] blew the roof off," Richard Newman told us.[10] David Levy expressed a similar reaction:

> I remember thinking, 'Oh, this is really strange', because after the sound check I went outside to get some fresh air and there was a queue right around the corner. It was a weeknight and it hadn't been advertised, and I thought not many would be there. [But] it was madness. And that's when I thought, 'Ah, right, okay, now I understand'.[11]

During our initial phase of becoming Gallagher fans, we discovered a lengthy and scathing review on the *Loose Talk* forum concerning Gallagher's behaviour at this show. Since then, the Rhyl gig has been of great interest to us. The user writes:

> Rory eventually came out at nearly midnight looking bloody awful. In the last twelve months I was talking to a guy who was a bouncer there that night. He told me Rory was absolutely pissed and refused to go onstage. They had to pour black coffee down him and talk him into going on [...] Apart from the band being so bloody untalented, Rory himself was not really there. It was just some overblown bumbling guy who I didn't recognise.[12]

For many months, we theorised whether such a cruel anecdote could be true. Had Gallagher become "a shell of the great performer" or were we reading the tantrums of a long-time fan who was, as they stated, "in a bad state of mind" because "Rory replaced the great Gerry McAvoy with an unknown?" When we questioned Hewitt about the authenticity of the *Loose Talk* review, he contested the claims as "absolute rubbish" and "a pack of lies."[13] Hewitt elaborated, "Rory went onstage on time and played a blistering set. The crowd loved him. He wasn't in the best of health back then, *but* that didn't affect the way he played that night."[14]

Similar remarks were made during our conversation with Gallagher fan Robert Orr. Orr was "hooked" after hearing Taste's *On The Boards* in 1970, attending the trio's Liverpool show that same year, as well as watching Gallagher throughout the 1970s. Orr admitted that the Rhyl show "was very emotional [as I had] not seen Rory play for a while. Rory played his heart out, but he looked very ill [...] As for the band, they did Rory well and the night was amazing."[15] Feltham agreed with Hewitt and Orr's testaments. "[Rory] was still playing well then and, of course, the other guys [David and Richard] were in awe of being around him." According to Orr, a camera was placed on the mixing desk and the show was recorded, though no footage has surfaced online of this night.

"We're going to be right behind you":
Forging the Dynamics

Feltham confessed that memories of this time have slightly faded for him because although Levy and Newman were "great players," the group dynamic had shifted. "Sometimes there is nothing like the original band and I think that when Gerry and Brendy left, part of the soul went out of the band." Levy was "more melodic" and "less of a rock bass player" than McAvoy, and while Newman "was a fine player" and "could do everything that Brendan did," Feltham observed a lack of spontaneity during the latter years, which we presumed to be the reason why Gallagher's final line-up played more or less the same setlist every show:

> Gerry had been there a long time. Brendan had been there playing with Gerry a long time. And Gerry knew where Rory's head was gonna go as well, so Gerry was kind of the second in command there [...] Rory could quite often call a song that we hadn't played for a long, long time and Gerry and Brendy would know it. They didn't have that with the new band [...] they didn't know the songbook.

The argument could be made that the reduced touring schedule limited opportunities for musical experimentation to completely develop with the new Rory Gallagher Band. If we were to compare McAvoy's bass soloing from 'McAvoy Boogie' at the 1972 *Beat Club* show, say, with 'Tattoo'd Lady' from *Rockpalast* in 1979, we hear a clear progression in confidence brought about by familiarising himself with Gallagher's playing as well as forming strong band relationships. Amidst Gallagher's worsening health, change in artistic direction and even cancelled performances, such circumstances could never wholly unfold in the short three and a half years he played with Levy and Newman.

When joining the band, Levy was immediately mindful of the fact that Gallagher was in the middle of immense change and, therefore, in a fragile state of mind, since farewelling McAvoy and O'Neill. "I think it was a difficult time for Rory and Dónal because they'd had a band for a very, very long time and had some great success. So, it must have been very difficult and very odd for [Rory] to gain the trust of other people and vice versa." Levy recognised that the split would dishearten Gallagher's 'diehard fans' "because they've grown up with Gerry and Brendan for a long time." When we asked Levy if he ever felt pressure to fill in the void that McAvoy left, he shared these insightful words about his role in the band:

> I've been lucky that I've worked with a lot of artists before [working with Rory]. And whatever went on [with Gerry and Brendan] had nothing to do with me. It was just a privilege [to work with Rory]. I was learning so much. It was a real education, and so from that

point of view there was no pressure in as much as wanting to try and do a good job for Rory. He was brilliant and unbelievable, but you know, it wasn't easy. And there was pressure in that. But in general, I saw part of my role with Rich was to actually do the best we could musically so that [Rory] felt comfortable to do his thing without worrying about what was going on behind him.

Levy's position as a foundation to the song and, as a result, the overall mood of the music reflects his lessons as a session musician:

> Rory is the man at the front. Rory is the reason that we're there. And my job is to try and do what Rory wants me to do so that it came across looking like we are a unit [...] And looking back now, you know, it's a while ago, but if you look at those clips, we are looking at Rory to basically say, 'We've got you. You do your thing. We're going to be right behind you'.

In the time the final band were together, the playing never transferred to the studio walls. Levy recalls attending a session at Roundhouse Studios in Camden with Gallagher and Newman, though details of this memory have vanished with time as to whether tracks were recorded or not. "I think, ultimately, we would have recorded," Levy stated, "I think the more we would have done, the more diverse the audience would have become, especially if there was newer material." Levy sensed the band's progression was on the upward. "Rich and I felt like we were on a rollercoaster about to go [...] But I think, at that stage, Rory had to be in the right place and the right state of mind [...] I think he was trying to find his feet with us and to make sure that he was happy."

Recovering 'The Forgotten Musicians'[16]

Fans generally express a mixed reaction to the final Rory Gallagher Band. Negative perceptions tend to come from long-time fans and range from the subjective (the music is "rigid" and "the drummer [plays] like he's driving nails") to echoing Feltham's opinion about band chemistry ("there's a lack of flexibility").[17] One user on the *Loose Talk* forum wrote that Levy, Newman, Feltham and Cooke represented "a backing band more than a real band."[18] Meanwhile, newer fans demonstrate a more sympathetic outlook. One fan we interviewed from the Gallagher community on Instagram said she noticed a "new burst of energy" when watching performances of the final band and that they were "as strong as any [band] he'd had." During her six years of listening to Gallagher's music, she noticed the pattern of Levy and Newman being overlooked by both fans and publications. "I feel they're seen as poor replacements for Gerry and the handful of drummers Rory had worked with [...] I find this view to be a disservice."

Dónal has often spoken fondly of the final band, stating that his brother was "very happy" with the group's progression.[19] "It is a shame when Rory [passed] because the band would have matured as things got along. It was one of the better recording bands."[20] In spite of encouraging comments such as this, there has been severe underrepresentation of the band with "huge promise,"[21] such as minimal exposure in Gallagher biographies and the admission from some fans that they do not even know the members' names from the final line-up. If information were scarce on the final Rory Gallagher Band, would the same apply when accessing listening material?

In terms of Estate releases, the only choice is the 1993 gig at the Paradiso Club in Amsterdam, issued officially in 2003 under the name *Meeting with the G-Man*—an expanded edition of a bootleg available previously in the 2001 boxset *Let's Go to Work*. One fan posted online that, while the recording is "really great and displays all the extraordinary capability of Rory Gallagher as a live performer," the listening experience is diminished due to the very poor sound quality.[22] The fan concludes their review, "I hope there will be the opportunity in the future to listen to a good Gallagher recording of the period between 1990 and 1994."[23] Since 2001, only one album from the 1990-1994 period has surfaced—*All Around Man: Live in London* (2023)—but this featured McAvoy and O'Neill rather than the final line-up. Concerts such as the 1994 Montreux Jazz Festival have been released on DVD and highlight how dynamic and powerful the final Rory Gallagher Band could be. However, other brilliant gigs such as the 1994 *Festival Interceltique de Lorient*, 1994 Pistoia Blues Festival and 1992 Temple Bar Blues Festival are yet to receive the special treatment of an official remaster and release.

Due to a lack of documentation on the final Rory Gallagher Band in the past, we provide a detailed biography of each member in this Interlude chapter. We have devoted a section to each core member of the group (Mark Feltham, Richard Newman and David Levy), chronicling their timeline in the band and what they contributed to the sound, as well as reflections of their time with Gallagher. In addition, we cover members who were never permanent fixtures but rather floated in and out of the band, whether in the studio or onstage, such as John Cooke, Jim Leverton and Geraint Watkins. We hope that this essay marks the start of their recovery in the Rory Gallagher story.

The Main Men
Mark Feltham (1984-1995), harmonica
For a man with a long career as a prolific session musician, a major figure in rhythm and blues band Nine Below Zero and one of the greatest harmonica players of the last century, it is rather astounding that Mark Feltham is not better known. For those unfamiliar with Feltham's abilities, there is perhaps no greater introduction than 'When My Baby She Left Me' from Rory Gallagher's 1987 concert at the Cork Opera House. Over seven glorious minutes, viewers will learn why Feltham is in a league of his own as a musician, from his authentic blues and stunning improvisation skills to his beautiful chemistry and interplay with Gallagher, the two exchanging riffs and smiles with infectious joy in their eyes.

According to Dónal, Gallagher found a musical "kindred spirit" in Feltham and saw him as a "lovely person with a wonderful manner."[24] From the very beginning, he "felt a huge empathy" with the harmonica player and "cultivated a role for him in the band"[25] — a role that grew stronger over the years. Although Feltham admitted to us that he "never actually felt part of the band" and always saw himself as a "hired hand," he quietly shaped Gallagher's music, broadening out its sound and becoming an integral member. The live shows and recordings in Gallagher's final decade would not be quite the same without Feltham's exceptional musicianship. Offstage, Feltham was also someone on whom Gallagher came to increasingly rely. Gallagher had a complex personality and few — if anyone — ever got close to him, yet Feltham showed a true understanding of his sensitive nature and formed a connection with him in a way that arguably no other band member did away from the stage.

Born in 1955 in Bermondsey, London, Feltham had dabbled with the harmonica from the age of six, but only started to become seriously interested in the instrument in his late teens after hearing the famous opening tune of the music show *Old Grey Whistle Test*: Stone Fox Chase by Nashville country rock band Area Code 615. Immediately, he sought out other Nashville musicians, developing a particular fondness for the playing style of Charlie McCoy.

Feltham's first musical break came in 1977 when he was approached by Dennis Greaves to form Nine Below Zero. Over the next five years, the band built a core audience, particularly fans of the New Wave of British Heavy Metal who were attracted by their high-energy, fast-tempo sound. Following the band's break-up in 1982, Feltham became a highly sought-after session musician, going on throughout the decade to record with such artists as Talk Talk, Roger Daltrey, Manfred Mann's Earth Band, Godley and Creme, Deacon Blue and Paul Young, to name but a few examples.

Nine Below Zero often played at the Bridge House Club — a seminal rock venue in the East End of London. Gerry McAvoy and Brendan O'Neill were regular patrons and reported enthusiastically to Gallagher on how talented the band's harmonica player was. In 1983 — a year after the break-up of Nine Below Zero — Gallagher and Feltham met for the first time. On 26 July, the Rory Gallagher Band were playing a gig at the Marquee Club to commemorate its 25th anniversary. Feltham came along to watch and, after being introduced to each other by McAvoy, Gallagher invited him up for a jam. Feltham's initial impression of Gallagher — one that never changed over the many years that he knew the Irishman — was that he was an "absolute angel of a man" and a "very gifted musician."[26] Even though Feltham was not used to the loud sound of "aggressive blues rock," Gallagher made him feel immediately "at ease."[27]

In 1984, Gallagher was asked to support Jimmy Page and Ginger Baker at the Pistoia Blues Festival. Knowing that Feltham was looking for work, Gallagher invited him along. Feltham describes the concert as a "nervous initiation,"[28] having accidentally sat on Baker's drum cart and received a tongue-lashing from the irate drummer in return. He also recalls making the mistake of "walking too far forward" on the first solo in 'I Wonder Who' and being promptly warned by McAvoy to "keep watching Rory's shoulders" and "never cross the barrier." "From that point onwards, I never wandered within 1.5m away from my hand," Feltham recalls with a laugh. While he posits that Gallagher's need for control came from a "crisis of confidence,"[29] he believes that he learnt a great stagecraft lesson from him, which he likens to football:

> The band is always a V-shape. Always. Accept you're playing a right back in a football team or a midfielder. You're never a striker. You're never a Harry Kane. Rory is the Harry Kane and you've got to keep your eyes on the back of his shoulders.

After his first appearance at Pistoia, Feltham remained a key band member, touring regularly with Gallagher up until January 1995 and featuring on both *Defender* (1987) and *Fresh Evidence* (1990).[30] These years may have been marked by deep unhappiness for Gallagher offstage, but, onstage, him and Feltham were having a ball. The moments when they both become lost in the music, bouncing off one another and trading licks are truly magical, while the great affection that Gallagher had for Feltham is apparent from his terms of address ("maestro of the harp," "our good friend," "Mr Harmonica") to moments when he whispers in his ear or rests his head on his shoulder as they perform.

The feeling was mutual. Talking to Shiv Cariappa in 1998, Feltham stated how he loved being on the side of the stage watching Gallagher perform and that he had never seen anybody with so much dedication to his craft.[31] "46 years now I've been pro and I've not worked with a guitarist as good as him," he told us affectionately.

As Gallagher's health got progressively worse towards the end of the 1980s, Feltham took on an unofficial guardian role. Concert footage of the time often captures him looking across in concern at Gallagher and he is always at hand to give the guitarist a friendly pat on the back or a reassuring smile. When failing health affected Gallagher's final performance in Rotterdam on 10 January 1995 (see 3.3), Feltham was the first person to come to his rescue and escort him off stage. Feltham was there again when Gallagher was hospitalised in March 1995 and fell into a coma, staying at his bedside and playing country blues on his harmonica to try and wake him. In a 2018 radio interview, Feltham discussed the difficulties of playing for Gallagher under these circumstances: "they put little things over his eyes to stop [them] getting very dry because his eyes were open. And he was kind of looking at me and I was playing to him, although… the lights were on, but there was no one in."[32]

When Gallagher passed away at 10:46AM on 14 June, Feltham was present, along with Dónal and Gallagher's mother Monica. However, it was not until he saw the headline on the *Evening Standard* later that the news truly sunk in. "That was when I lost it," he reflected emotionally to us, "That's when it finally hit me." Feltham took the role of one of the pallbearers at Gallagher's funeral and also stepped up for the daunting task of playing 'A Million Miles Away' at the Church of the Descent of the Holy Cross. Through tears, he also played 'Amazing Grace' at Gallagher's final resting place in St Oliver's Cemetery, throwing his harmonica into the grave when he had finished.

"I would have done anything for [Rory], I loved him, I adored him," Feltham told Australian radio in 2018.[33] Elaborating further to us in October 2023, he stated:

> If you were a first-time fan going to see Rory, you'd think, 'Oh, he's fierce. I'd be terrified of him backstage'. But it was completely the opposite. He was an absolute angel. A lovely person [...] Although he was an amazing guitarist, he didn't have that rock image. He was always very, very quiet and subdued, calm, and he just didn't do things the way you'd think a rock & roll man would. He was such a peaceful man, although not peaceful within himself... He had time for everyone and he'd just sit there quietly. He was diplomacy to the end. Right to the end. He was a wonderful guy.

Over the years, Feltham has shared many moving anecdotes about Gallagher, from how he would often stop a conversation in mid-sentence just to cross the road and give money to a homeless person or busker to how he would reprimand band members for eyeing good-looking women or making suggestive comments about them. Reiterating the words of so many others, Feltham has also stated how Gallagher never swore, never had a bad word to say about anybody and treated women with the utmost respect, even standing when they walked into a room. He jokes that everybody always had to be careful what they said or did around Gallagher because he had such high moral standards.

Gallagher also got on well with Feltham's parents. As Feltham still lived at home in the early 1980s, his father or mother often answered the phone when Gallagher called. Without fail, Gallagher would ask Feltham's father about horseracing and if he had any tips and speak to Feltham's mother about the latest books she had been reading (she shared his passion for crime fiction). Feltham notes that his parents thought Gallagher was "a lovely, beautiful man [...] such a gentleman." Although Gallagher was shy and taciturn by nature, according to Feltham, on the rare occasions when he spoke:

> his 10 words were the equivalent and more powerful than 1,000 words from others. He made every statement a milestone in a learning curve going forward with your life, both as a musician and/or the local postman, it mattered not [...] This is the power that decent people can have over us mere mortals.

Since Gallagher's death, Feltham has continued to perform live and carry out session work for such diverse artists as Oasis, Robbie Williams, Dido, Zucchero, Johnny Cash and Gary Moore. In 2015, he rejoined Nine Below Zero and continues to tour regularly with them. 2024 saw the band release a double acoustic album *DenMark* and perform at the Rory Gallagher International Festival in Ballyshannon.

Richard Newman (1992-1995), drums

Richard Newman grew up surrounded by music. His father, Tony Newman, was the drummer in Sounds Incorporated and later worked with such artists as Jeff Beck, David Bowie and Marc Bolan, while his mother, Margot, sang with the Vernon Girls and their spin-off group, The Breakaways. As his parents were often away touring, Newman spent much of his childhood with Joe and Vicki Brown who lived nearby; Joe was part of the first generation of British rock stars, while Vicki had been in the Vernon Girls with Newman's mother. The couple, in fact, later went on to foster Newman after he was taken into care at the age of ten following his father's struggle with drug addiction and his mother's subsequent nervous breakdown. The Browns had their own recording studio, and their house was often visited by all kinds of musical figures. So, it was somewhat written in the stars that Newman would follow in both his parents' and the Browns' footsteps and become a professional musician.

From the tender age of two, Newman was already tinkering with his father's drum kit and, by age six, he had learnt to set it up and his father had taught him the basics. Newman's earliest musical influences were John Bonham, King Crimson, Pink Floyd, Yes and Billy Cobham, but he saw jazz drummer Buddy Rich as "the absolute king of rudiments and drum technique."[34] By ten years old, Newman had developed into a capable drummer. During the brief time that he lived at a children's home in North Wales, his interest in drumming was encouraged and he was bought a drum kit to play for children in the local Wrexham area. This interest developed further once he was fostered by the Browns, and it was here that he got his first break in the music industry.

Steve Marriott (Small Faces, Humble Pie) was a regular visitor to the house. One day, 14-year-old Newman was in the back room jamming with the Browns' children, Sam and Pete, when Marriott called in. Impressed by what he heard, Marriott asked Newman and Sam to play a gig with him at a pub in London. Being Newman's first professional gig, he was extremely nervous and remembers freezing partway through the set. "Get on with it!" Marriott yelled, which quickly snapped him back into reality. After leaving school, Newman moved to London and put together his first band, Yip Yip Coyote, whose cowpunk style made them a firm favourite of DJ John Peel. He also occasionally helped out in Powerplant Studios, where Pete Brown was working as an engineer. Rather serendipitously, Newman—only just 19—received a call from Marriott while he was at the studio, inviting him on tour as it was "about time [he] came to work with the big boys."[35]

Over the next year, Newman toured extensively with Marriott, finding his "road legs," yet admitting that he has never really enjoyed touring and still finds it a "grind."[36] This tour was followed by live dates and a studio album with Sam Brown, now a successful solo artist, but this came to an abrupt end when Vicki Brown became terminally ill and Sam gave up everything to care for her. Vicki passed away in June 1991; Marriott had tragically passed away two months earlier in a house fire. This marked a low point in Newman's life, where he had to take up painting and decorating to make ends meet.

Then, an unexpected phone call came from his former bandmate Jim Leverton. Leverton told Newman that Gallagher was putting together a new band and asked him if he would like to come along for a jam. Gallagher had known Newman's father and was a great admirer of his drumming. At just 26 years old, Newman was unfamiliar with Gallagher's work at the time, yet he agreed to meet him and "got on immediately," finding him to be "very fierce" and "very passionate" about his music.[37] The first rehearsal went well, and Newman was immediately blown away by Gallagher's guitar skills ("I couldn't believe his playing!" he told us in May 2022). He was offered the job shortly after.

For Newman, working with Gallagher was the "biggest eyeopener" of his life and a "real high point" of his career. He remembers Gallagher's 94-95 *Walkin' Blues* tour in particular as featuring some of the best performances that he can remember, with a great camaraderie between all band members. Newman also had the opportunity to record with Gallagher, playing drums on 'Show-biz Blues' and 'Leaving Town Blues' for the 1994 Peter Green tribute album *Rattlesnake Guitar* (see 1.5). Newman's studio work with Gallagher is often forgotten, which has contributed to unfair claims by some fans that the final Rory Gallagher Band lacked experience in the studio and, therefore, may have had difficulties recording an album with Gallagher.

According to Newman, Gallagher put himself under immense pressure and struggled to live up to the expectations that people had of him. Although aware that Gallagher was ill, his death still came as a huge shock for Newman when he received the news in a phone call from Mark Feltham. Newman was extremely upset, having considered Gallagher a "good friend" who remained the same down-to-earth "young lad from Donegal" throughout his life.[38] When reflecting in 2020 on his time in the Rory Gallagher Band, Newman noted that Gallagher was always good to him and always paid him fairly (contrary to McAvoy's claims in *Riding Shotgun*). In his view, every concert with Gallagher was a favourite simply *because* he was "going out to play with Rory Gallagher."[39] His lasting impression of the guitarist is a "lovely person [...] a great, great man," while the key lesson he took away from his time in the band is that "you'd better know how to play."

After Gallagher died, Newman did some work with Glenn Hughes (Deep Purple, Black Sabbath), but then he suffered an unexpected breakdown that led him to develop a "terror" of the drums.[40] The deaths of Vicki Brown, Steve Marriott and Gallagher in quick succession had taken a toll on him, while the constant touring had triggered unhappy flashbacks of accompanying his father on tour as a child, which he found "disorienting" and "scary."[41] Through the support of the Browns—to whom he feels that he owes everything[42]—Newman was able to resume drumming and went on to work with Alvin Lee, Jefferson Starship, Jeff

Beck, Mark Knopfler and, most recently, Deborah Bonham. Along with bassist David Levy, Newman has also played with Paul Rose on both his 2004 album *Half Alive* and at the Rory Gallagher festival in Ballyshannon, as well as Bernie Marsden on his 2009 *Bernie Plays Rory* tribute album and subsequent related live shows in 2010 and 2019. For Newman, good drumming is about "light and shade, subtlety and feeling,"[43] which takes time to perfect. Watching his performances with Gallagher, it is clear that he certainly possesses all these qualities and has a great sense of musicality.

David Levy (1992-1995), bass

David Levy, quite naturally, "fell" in to playing with Rory Gallagher, and the same could be said about his introduction to the bass guitar. During early adolescence, a friend left a Fender Precision bass at Levy's home for safekeeping. "We were lucky enough to have a garage, so when I got a few friends together to try and play music, I became the bass player by default as I had a bass in my house!" Levy was in and out of bands throughout the 1970s, including a group called Blitzkrieg, who released the LP *Survival* (1979) and toured around the UK. "My first professional tour and album was with White and Torch, an act signed to CBS/Sony in 1983." And with that, Levy, again, 'fell' into his next line of work. As a session musician, Levy played on a range of tracks, from new wave (John Foxx) to pop and soul (Five Stars, Big Big Sun, Sam Brown).

In 1992, Levy received a phone call from his friend Richard Newman asking him to join a rehearsal with Rory Gallagher at London's Nomis Studios. "Of course I knew who Rory was, but I only had one record of his in my collection," Levy confessed. The day unfolded in "Rory's style," which was more of a relaxed jam rather than a formal rehearsal. Gallagher's only request was that Levy play with a plectrum as opposed to fingers, which was not the preferred method by McAvoy's original replacement Jim Leverton. Fortunately, Levy agreed:

> I met Rory [on a Friday afternoon] and we played for a couple of hours and it was very cool. And he said, 'What are you doing tomorrow?' And I said, 'Yeah, I'm around. If you want to work'. He said, 'Yeah, I want to work'. I said, 'Okay, well, ring me up and let me know what time you want me to come down'. I got a call about 8 o'clock [the next] evening. By that time it was a bit too late for Saturday, but we then heard from Dónal, who had booked a weekend of rehearsals. That's actually how it started, and it wasn't like, 'Oh, you're in my band now'. It was just a process that we were playing. [At that time] it was only me, Rich, and Rory. Rory was happy.

Following a warm-up appearance in Wales, the final Rory Gallagher Band travelled to Dublin for the Temple Bar Blues Festival, which, along with the Montreux Jazz Festival in 1994, remain treasured experiences for Levy many years later. "The Temple Bar was fabulous for many different reasons, but it was a very early show and therefore I don't think we'd relaxed into it. So, it was fantastic on certain levels. But when Montreux came round, we kind of knew a bit more, [plus] Rory was on fire [that night]."

Offstage, Levy and Gallagher's friendship developed into a mentorship, relating to topics other than music:

> My highlights are the one-on-one, just talking to Rory, because he was a very passionate, but compassionate, man. He was quite well read, and he always had a view on things, and I loved listening to that. The man had been on the road since he was fourteen, and that's amazing from the experience you can draw on that musically and otherwise.

Levy was in disbelief when receiving the news from Dónal that Gallagher had passed away. Initially, "I was shocked Rory was actually in hospital, [although] that gave me some comfort that, you know, he was with doctors. You always think things would be alright." Levy attended a memorial service for Gallagher in London on 8 November 1995. "It was a bit of a weird time because I felt, or realised, that [Rory] was a bigger presence on my being," Levy said sombrely, "Even now, I think about Rory quite a lot." Levy has honoured Gallagher's memory on many occasions, such as joining Bernie Marsden and Mark Feltham onstage at the Buxton Opera House tribute concert in 1996, as well as collaborating with Marsden on his *Bernie Plays Rory* (2009) album.

He has maintained contact with Feltham and Dónal, and still plays with Newman on occasion. Levy could not imagine cutting ties and moving on from the other members of the Rory Gallagher Band. "Although it was a comparatively short time, a lot went on. Bonds were forged. And that was really instigated by Rory and the kind of person he was." Levy also remarked upon the "timeless" existence Gallagher's music has in the world today. "My kids have discovered Rory, which is amazing." Levy's current musical projects include touring with Chris De Burgh, Andrew Roachford and the Tex-Mex group Los Pacaminos.

Side Men

Bob Andrews (1981 and 1986-1987), keyboards and piano
In 1981, Rory Gallagher invited keyboardist Bob Andrews to participate in sessions for his forthcoming album *Jinx*. Gallagher and Andrews had known each other since the 1970s when Taste and Andrews' band Brinsley Schwarz had shared a bill at two major blues festivals (Buxton and Inverness). Andrews was also a founding member of the Rumour, having worked regularly with Ray Beavis, so it made musical sense that he would play keyboards on *Jinx* alongside the saxophonist. As Andrews told us in September 2023, he was "thrilled" by Gallagher's offer and, although he was busy producing other records at the time, willingly agreed.[44] Five years later when working on *Defender*, Gallagher invited Andrews along once again, this time to Olympic Studios in London, where he contributed piano to 'Don't Start Me Talkin''. The song had originally been

recorded for *Jinx*, but did not make the final cut (it was released posthumously on 2019's *Blues*). Both versions are excellent, although Andrews' piano playing has a more prominent place in the *Jinx* sessions. Due to his busy schedule as a producer, Andrews never performed live with Gallagher; this role was instead taken up by John Cooke, Jim Leverton and Geraint Watkins (depending on availability).

John Cooke (1982-1995), keyboards
Gallagher fondly remarked in a 1991 interview with *Young Guitar Magazine* on the "mystery" of some of the past blues artists due to scarce (or sometimes inaccurate) details in books. We encountered a similar process gathering research on keyboardist John Cooke, which certainly piqued our curiosity, though did at times prove frustrating. Information on Cooke's career barely exists online, with only the briefest mention in biographies of his association with Gallagher, despite regularly appearing at gigs and guesting on his albums since 1982. Adding to the confusion is that occasionally his surname is spelt without an *e*.[45]

Prior to meeting Gallagher, Cooke was a seasoned session musician, playing on Mungo Jerry's 1973 hit 'Alright, Alright, Alright', Alan Ross Band's 1978 album *Restless Nights*, Ozzy Osbourne's *Diary of a Madman* (1981) and *Rough Diamonds* (1982) by Bad Company. Bassist Bob Daisley was also involved in the Mungo Jerry single and remembers Cooke as "easy to work with" and "very into the current Stevie Wonder albums in particular."[46] During the recording of *Diary of a Madman*, keyboardist Don Airey was unavailable due to touring commitments with Rainbow, so Cooke was booked for the session. Daisley was delighted to see him again, but found it a "disgrace" that the keyboardist ended up not credited on the album and even had to get the Musicians' Union involved to be paid. Speaking to us in June 2024, Daisley recalled Cook as being "a good Funk player, along the lines of Stevie Wonder, for sure, and he had good groove and feel, with tasteful note choice." During the 1990s, Cooke collaborated with Tokyo-born British guitarist Saiichi Sugiyama. When we contacted Sugiyama in February 2024, he disclosed to us that Cooke's "tenure didn't last long" due to a "disagreement with [his] regular dep-bass player" and has, therefore, not heard from Cooke since.[47]

Members of the final Rory Gallagher Band could add little about Cooke's life. When asked in 2022, Richard Newman revealed that he had not seen Cooke for "about eighteen years," though did recall he was previously "in Spain." David Levy also expressed uncertainty: "No one knew him when he was in the band." Cooke, as we soon discovered, seemed to have a very elusive nature. As Mark Feltham explained, "John was a real outsider. Nobody knew much of him, [and] he's disappeared without a trace I'm afraid."[48] Despite his "enigmatic character," Feltham believes that "Rory liked [Cooke's] contributions" to his live sound. In his memoir, Gerry McAvoy touched upon Cooke's impact during the band's 1982 Rush tour. Tensions arose between the keyboardist and McAvoy, particularly at Cooke's addition of synthesisers and effects, such as on the solo of 'Moonchild'.

"It had nothing to do with Rory Gallagher, it just sounded 80s. For some reason Rory insisted, but it was very difficult for me to get used to."[49] Interestingly, Steve Morse from the *Boston Globe* commended the inclusion of Cooke's Prophet 5 synthesiser at Gallagher's Paradise Rock show on 28 September. Morse wrote: "It was convincing proof that a synth could work with ageless boogie and not just with ambient, fashionable pop."[50]

Gallagher's approval of Cooke's synthesiser sound suggests that he was not entirely against using the instrument, indicating brief experimentation with his blues playing (and simultaneously impressing the critics!). In a 1983 interview with the *Evening Herald*, Gallagher, in fact, admitted that he enjoyed the music of Kraftwerk, Brian Eno and Tangerine Dream ("I thought their score for the remake of 'Wages of Fear' was very underrated"). He acknowledged, however, that he would "swop them all for a Fats Domino record."[51] Likewise, in a 1981 *Hot Press* article, Gallagher stated that he was "not against synths," but he disliked the current New Romantics trend and preferred music "that sounds fairly human."[52]

Cooke featured on Gallagher's 1987 album *Defender*, as well as *Fresh Evidence* in 1990. In addition, he appeared alongside Gallagher on his 1994 tour, spotted in footage at the Montreux Jazz Festival, SDR3 Festival in Stuttgart and the *Festival Interceltique de Lorient*.

Geraint Watkins (1989-1990), piano and accordion
Accomplished pianist and accordionist Geraint Watkins is often described as the "embodiment of the journeyman musician."[53] Known for his multi-instrumental wizardry, good humour and professionalism, it is no wonder that Gallagher felt such an affinity with the Welshman. Watkins and Gallagher first met in 1984 when they appeared on Box of Frogs' eponymous debut album, collaborating on the fourth track 'House of Fire' (see 1.4). They continued to cross paths throughout the decade as Watkins played the local pubs of London with the Balham Alligators—a band that blended rock & roll, cajun, country and R&B. When Gallagher was looking for an accordionist to contribute to his zydeco-feel songs on *Fresh Evidence* ('King of Zydeco', 'Never Asked You for Nothing'), Watkins' name was top of his list. Watkins delivered a stellar performance on the two tracks and went on to play with Gallagher and his band on the album's supporting tour in 1990. The *Rocklife* 1990 concert and 2023's *All Around Man – Live in London* release showcase the very best of Watkins.

Jim Leverton (1992-1994), keyboards and bass
In an interview with Uli Twelker, Rory Gallagher reminisced about his first encounter with musician Jim Leverton during the late 1960s. Leverton played in Fat Mattress, a group he formed with Noel Redding, who toured with Taste throughout Europe. Gallagher reconnected with Leverton in the early 1990s through Dónal organising the rerelease of two Fat Mattress albums. "Jim is a very fine player, [and] he plays a good guitar, too […] at the moment he's doing an Al Kooper thing for me, because he's a very good keyboard player for my kind of music."[54]

Between the years that Leverton lost contact with Gallagher, he worked with Henry McCullough and Savoy Brown, as well as a lengthy stint with Humble Pie co-founder Steve Marriott, lasting from 1978 until Marriott's passing in 1991. From 1992 onwards, Leverton and John Cooke alternated playing keyboards for Gallagher, both onstage and in the studio. Leverton accompanied Gallagher on sessions, such as 'Barley and Grape Rag' for The Dubliners' 1992 record *30-Years-A-Greying*, and contributed bass for 'Leaving Town Blues' on the *Peter Green Songbook* (1995). He also played at the 1993 show at the Paradiso in Amsterdam, which featured on the fourth disc of the *Let's Go to Work* boxset in 2001.

Ray Beavis (1981-1982, 1989-1990), tenor saxophone
Dick Parry (1981-1982), tenor saxophone
Howie Casey (1982), tenor saxophone
John 'Irish' Earle (1990), tenor saxophone and baritone saxophone
Dick Hanson (1990), trumpet

In the early 1980s, Gallagher decided that he wanted to broaden out his sound by adding horns to his band on particular songs, both live and in the studio. He was, of course, no stranger to this, having taught himself alto saxophone in the days of Taste and memorably learning to play the instrument in the closet of the bedsit that he shared with his brother Dónal. He put his sax skills to good use on early songs like 'On the Boards' and 'It's Happened Before, It'll Happen Again' and continued to use it sporadically in the studio throughout the 1970s on such tracks as 'Can't Believe It's True', 'Hands Off', 'Seventh Son of a Seventh Son' and 'A Million Miles Away'.

Testing the waters with the idea of expanding his band, in early 1981, Gallagher asked Dónal to call saxophonist John 'Irish' Earle and see if he would join him for a concert at the Palais des Sports in Paris on 19 February. Earle was part of the Rumour Brass—the four-man horn section who played with Graham Parker and the Rumour. He was also the man who played the legendary sax solo on the *Live and Dangerous* version of Thin Lizzy's 'Dancing in the Moonlight'. Earle was unavailable for the Paris concert, but put Dónal in touch with Ray Beavis—the other saxophonist in the Rumour Brass—who keenly agreed to play. As Gallagher wanted two sax players, Beavis then contacted Dick Parry to join him. Parry is a name synonymous with Pink Floyd, known particularly for his iconic sax solos in 'Money' and 'Us and Them'. He had first met Gallagher when they featured on Mike Vernon's *Bring It Back Home* album in 1971.

Recalling the Paris concert, Beavis told us that he and Parry very quickly ran through the set in the dressing room with Gallagher. Gallagher had clear ideas of what he wanted from the saxes ("very sparse, but quite specific") and explained these by singing the parts to Beavis and Parry.[55] Considering that the three men had not performed together before, their sound is incredibly tight, as bootleg recordings exemplify. Gallagher performs Chuck Berry's 'Nadine' (a song from his showband days) and Howlin' Wolf's 'I'm Leavin'' with great gusto, the saxes embellishing his guitar and vocals. The horns also make an interesting addition to 'I Wonder Who', completely transforming the song from earlier versions.

Beavis and Parry went on to play many Gallagher shows together during this period, including the SWF3 festival in Offenberg whose video offers a taste of the saxophonists' prowess, particularly on the cover of Willy Dixon's 'What in the World'. On one occasion, Parry had a prior engagement with Pink Floyd, leading Howie Casey to fill in for him at Gallagher's 1982 concert at the Loreley for *Rockpalast*. Casey was an established saxophonist in his own right, having come to prominence in the early 1960s as a member of Derry and the Seniors and going on to do session work for Paul McCartney and Wings, T. Rex and the Who. Although this was the only concert that Casey played with Gallagher, he "loved every minute of it,"[56] as is apparent from the video.

The live shows with Beavis and Parry went well, so much so that when Gallagher began recording his new album *Jinx* in 1981, he asked them to join him in the studio. According to Beavis, the story was much the same: Gallagher wanted the saxes to reinforce his music, rather than to feature heavily. This is certainly apparent in 'Jinxed', the two saxes building a solid foundation for the powerful slow blues number. Some years later when Gallagher was working on his *Fresh Evidence* album, he called on Beavis again. This time, Beavis was joined by two of his friends from the Rumour Brass: John 'Irish' Earle and Dick Hanson on trumpet. Like his fellow band members, Hanson also boasted an impressive musical CV, having worked with the likes of Shakin' Stevens, Dave Edmunds and Paul Brady. The three men showcase their talents on the jazzy 'Alexis' and gritty blues 'Walkin' Wounded', bringing the semi-redemption song to a triumphant end. While Gallagher did not work further with Beavis, Earle and Hanson, he did continue to experiment with sax, jamming in 1994 with violinist Roberto Manes and Ingrid Laubrock, the sax player in Manes' band, in his room at the Conrad Hotel.

Beavis remembers Gallagher as "an extremely dedicated and virtuoso guitarist, with boundless energy throughout his epic long shows," while offstage, he was "very quietly spoken, sensitive, kind and intelligent" and enjoyed staying up late in hotels after a concert just shooting the breeze with the other musicians. "Rory is missed by millions around the world. He lived and breathed for his art," Beavis concludes.

Frank Mead (1994), harmonica and saxophone
Frank Mead's part in the Rory Gallagher story was fleeting yet impactful when he filled in for Mark Feltham at several summer festival dates in 1994, including the Pistoia Blues Festival in Italy. Mead came equipped with his harmonica, but also his saxophone, bringing a unique take to Gallagher classics like 'Shadow Play' and 'Messin' with the Kid'. Throughout the 1970s, Mead had built his reputation on London's thriving pub rock scene, which is where Gallagher first became aware of him. As Mead's reputation grew, he had the opportunity to perform with a wide range of artists, including Steve Waller, Gary Brooker and Jo Ann Kelly,

and became a member of the R&B band Juice on the Loose in 1983. Through Gary Brooker, he also participated in charity concerts with Eric Clapton, Phil Collins, David Gilmour, Mark Knopfler and Andy Fairweather Low, which subsequently led to him meeting Gary Moore and providing the horn section for *Still Got the Blues*. "Well, it certainly beats working for a living!" Mead jokes on the 'About' page of his website—a sentiment with which Gallagher himself would, no doubt, concur.[57]

RM and LAO

Footnotes

[1] Gavin Martin, 'Rory Gallagher: The Making of Irish Tour '74', *Classic Rock* (1 August 2016), https://www.loudersound.com/features/rory-gallagher-the-making-of-irish-tour-74.
[2] Dominique Dujean, 'Le blues toujours', *Hard Rock* (February 1993), https://rewritingrory.co.uk/2022/06/03/hard-rock-february-1993/
[3] Ibid.
[4] J.P. Sabour and X. Bonnet, '...et vogue la galère', *Guitar World* (February 1993), https://rewritingrory.co.uk/2022/06/03/guitar-world-february-1993/
[5] Ibid.
[6] Interview with Mark Feltham, 19 October 2023. All subsequent quotes from Feltham come from this interview, unless otherwise stated.
[7] Newspaper clipping posted on the official Rory Gallagher Facebook page: https://www.facebook.com/photo?fbid=10159001248751807&set=a.322997981806
[8] Ibid.
[9] Interview with Bob Hewitt, 15 August 2022.
[10] Interview with Richard Newman, 22 May 2022. All subsequent quotes from Newman come from the same interview, unless otherwise stated.
[11] Interview with David Levy, 22 February 2024. All subsequent quotes from Levy come from the same interview, unless otherwise stated.
[12] The *Loose Talk* forum has since been shut down and a new Rory Gallagher Official Forum established (https://rorygallagher.boards.net/)
[13] Interview with Bob Hewitt, 14 June 2023.
[14] Ibid.
[15] Interview with Robert Orr, 28 June 2022.
[16] This title is inspired by a joking comment made by Mark Feltham in our interview that he felt like the "forgotten musician in the band."
[17] Comments shared on https://rory-gallagher.forumactif.org/t69-rory-gallagher-band-mk-5-1992-1995-le-dernier-groupe.
[18] While this might be the case, we could also argue that, from 1971 onwards, Gallagher only ever had a backing band, since he was always billed as the Rory Gallagher Band following the split from Taste.
[19] Shiv Cariappa, 'Wheeling and Dealing' (March 2003), http://www.roryon.com/donalshiv352.html.
[20] Ibid.
[21] 'Album review: RORY GALLAGHER – Blues', *Get Ready to Rock!* (February 2012), https://getreadytorock.me.uk/blog/2019/04/album-review-rory-gallagher-blues/.
[22] 'Rory Gallagher: Meeting With The G-Man', *Swap-A-CD* (9 August 2005), https://www.swapacd.com/Rory-Gallagher-Meeting-G-Man/cd/888854/.
[23] Ibid.
[24] Dan Muise, *Gallagher, Marriott, Derringer, Trower* (Milwaukee: Hal Leonard Corporation, 2002), 75.
[25] Ibid, 62.
[26] 'MARK FELTHAM... THE HARP MASTER... AUSTRALIAN RADIO INTERVIEW', https://www.youtube.com/watch?v=58xR8GXvk7g&ab_channel=DAVESTICKLEY-AQUATARKUS

Dierks Studios in Cologne, Germany, where *Jinx* was recorded in 1981 *(Vincent Wolting)*

Two posters from 1982 promoting the recently released *Jinx* (*Wim Wezenberg*)

Concert ticket for the sixth, and what was to be final, Lisdoonvarna Festival on 30-31 July 1983.
(*Byrne Norry*)

At the concert and encore in Pecs, Hungary 1985
(*Ferenc Kalmandy*)

Posters announcing Gallagher's tour of Hungary and Yugoslavia in 1985 (*Wim Wezenberg*)

With the 1965 National Airline, onstage at the Montreux Jazz Festival in 1985 *(Joseph Carlucci)*

A ticket from the Self Aid festival in Dublin, Ireland in 1986 *(Byrne Norry)*

Playing his 1960 Gibson Melody Maker at the Out in the Green festival in 1986 *(Wolfgang Gürster)*

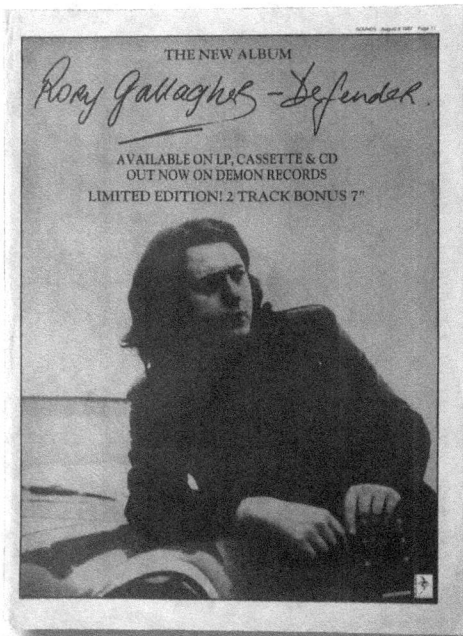

Advertisements for the 1987 release *Defender* (*Wim Wezenberg*)

On the advice of his new agent Paul Charles, Gallagher signed with Demon Records in 1986 (*Wim Wezenberg*)

Backstage at the Muziekcentrum
Vredenburg in Utrecht in 1987
(Herman Nijhof)

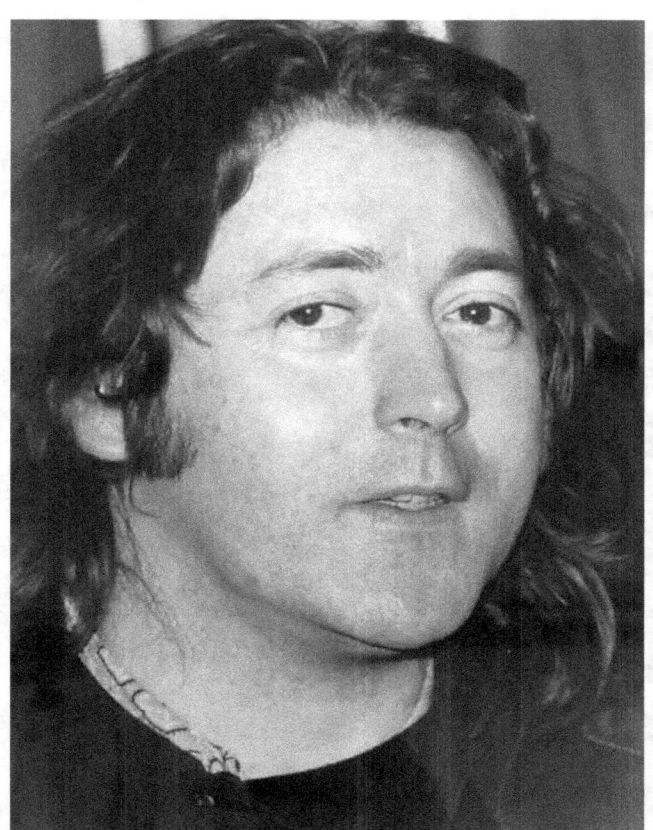

40th birthday celebration at the Moor Lane Tavern in Cashel in 1988 *(Liam M. Malone)*

Below and top two photos next page: Onstage during the UK tour in 1988
(Bob Hewitt)

With harmonica player Mark Feltham during his UK shows in 1988 *(Bob Hewitt)*

A powerful portrait with fans during the UK tour in 1988 *(Bob Hewitt)*

Commanding both the electric and acoustic during the UK tour in 1988 *(Bob Hewitt)*

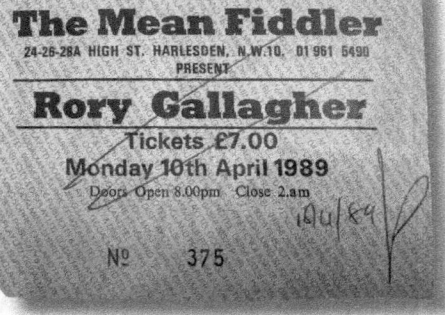

Gallagher enjoying himself onstage at Heppenheim Open Air Festival in 1988 (*Wolfgang Gürster*)

A ticket for the show at the Mean Fiddler in 1989 *(Byrne Norry)*

Above and top next page: Posters promoting the then latest recording achievement, *Fresh Evidence*, in May 1990 *(Wim Wezenberg)*

Gallagher (featuring accordionist Geraint Watkins) for the filmed *Rocklife* program in 1990 (*Philipp J. Bösel*)

Poster for the show at the Town and Country club in London 1990 *(Wim Wezenberg)*

Posters advertising the final tour of Japan in February 1991 *(Wim Wezenberg)*

1991 Guyatone LGX-II Marroly 6 guitar that was gifted to Gallagher during his final visit to Japan *(Vincent Wolting)*

With Australian blues guitarist Gwyn Ashton at the Adelaide Old Lion Hotel in 1991 *(Gwyn Ashton)*

A signed ticket from the show at the Everyman Theatre in 1992 *(Jim Roche)*

The Everyman Theatre in Cork, Ireland, in the present day (*Lauren Alex O'Hagan*)

Accompanied by his brother and mother during the civic reception at Cork City Hall in 1992 *(Tony O'Connell)*

Onstage in Aalen in 1992
(Wolfgang Gürster)

Performing at the Aladin Music Hall in Bremen, 1992
(Harry Pater)

Before the concert at the Bonn Blues Festival in 1992 *(Lothar Trampert)*

In a musical trance as he entertains fans at Amsterdam's Paradiso in 1992 *(Gerard Koot)*

Gallagher's scarf that he handed to a female fan at Amsterdam's Paradiso in 1992
(*Jan Van Bodegraven*)

Signing autographs at Bad Reichenhall in 1993
(*Wolfgang Gürster*)

One of many outstanding performances during the summer of 1994: the Pistoia Blues Festival in July
(Luca Guiotta)

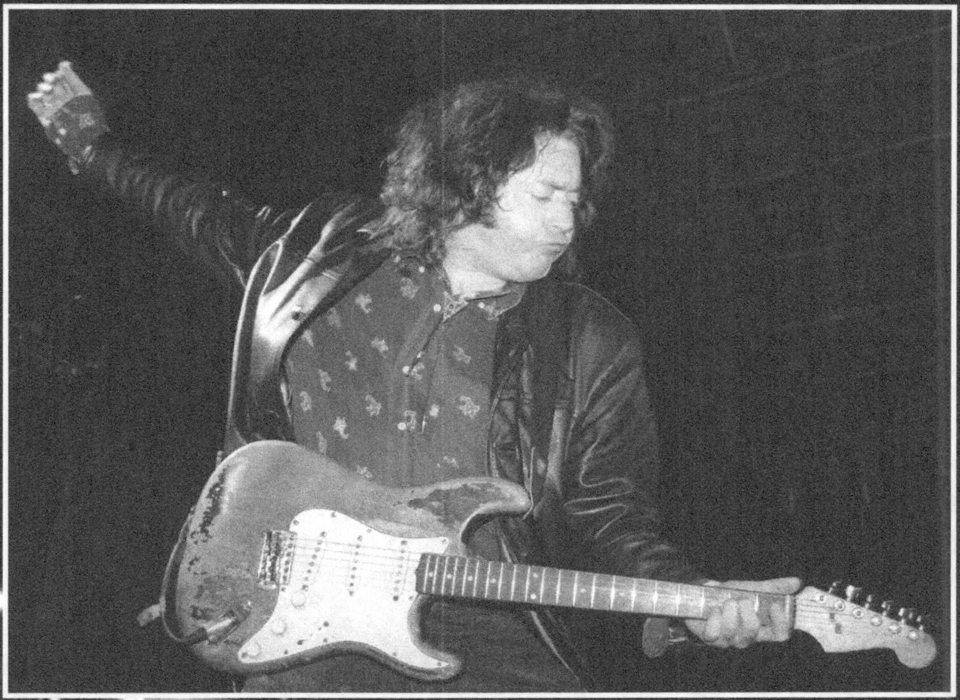

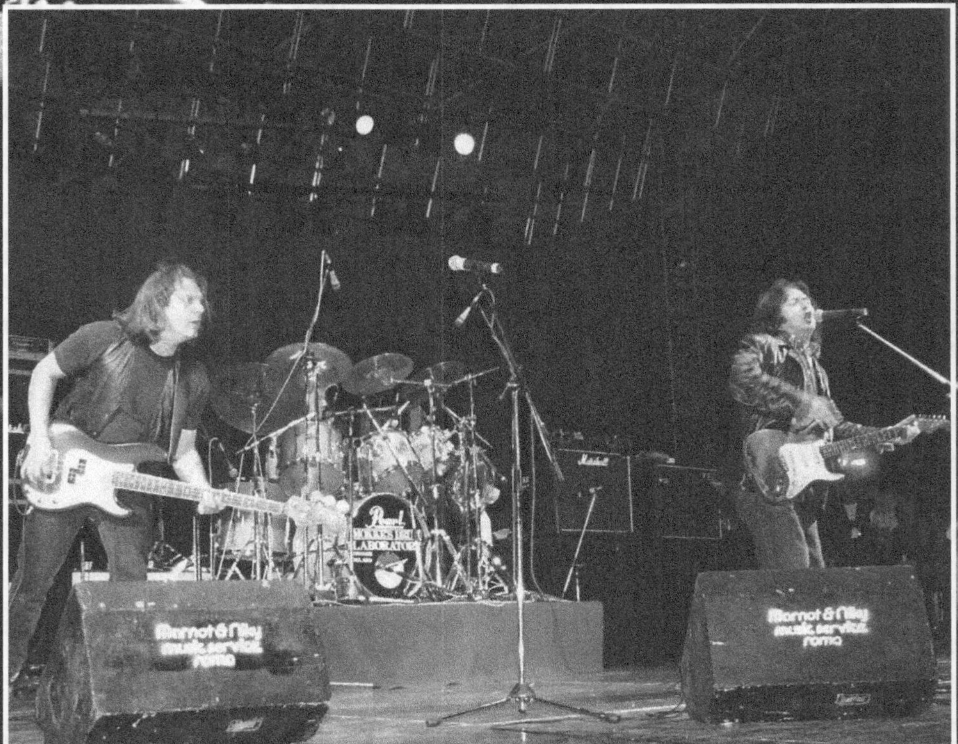

Gallagher pictured backstage before his concert at the *Festival Interceltique de Lorient* in August 1994 (*Nathalie Simon*)

Above: With Richard Newman and below with Pete Brown, relaxing after sessions for the Peter Green Songbook in 1994 (Shu Tomioka)

At the microphone during sessions for the Peter Green Songbook
(Shu Tomioka)

Testing out Shu Tomioka's camera in his room at the Conrad Hotel in 1994
(Shu Tomioka)

Above: In conversation with Pete Brown after sessions for the Peter Green Songbook in 1994
(Shu Tomioka)

Peter Green Sessions 1994
(Shu Tomioka)

A serene moment with David Levy, onstage at Langenau in 1994
(Wolfgang Gürster)

Posters advertising what would be the final tour in the Netherlands in 1995 (Wim Wezenberg)

Snapshots from the show in Enschede during the final tour in 1995
(Herman Nijhof)

Toine van Berlo's signed copy of *Tattoo* (*Toine van Berlo*)

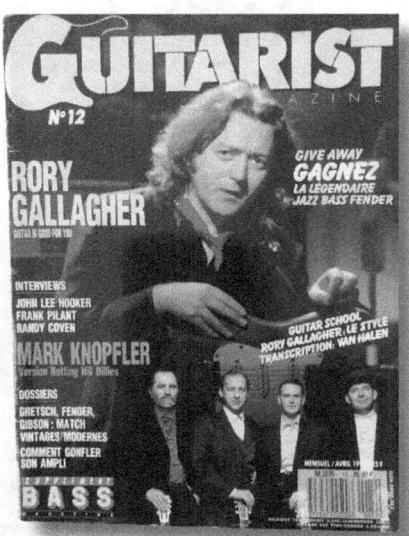

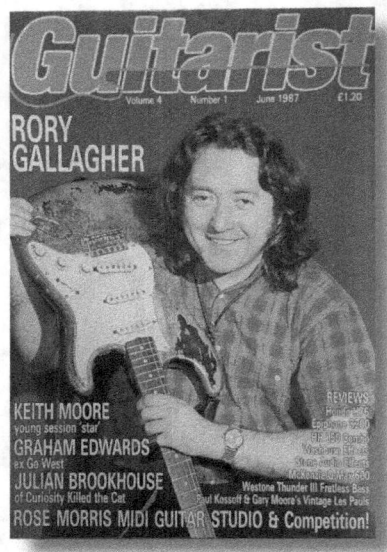

A selection of magazines with Gallagher featured on the cover, late 1980s-90s (*Lauren Alex O'Hagan* and *Wim Wezenberg*)

With his 1961 Fender Stratocaster for an IRS promotional shoot
(Wim Wezenberg)

James Roche's copy of *Macbeth* featuring inscriptions from Rory Gallagher on the inside cover
(Jim Roche)

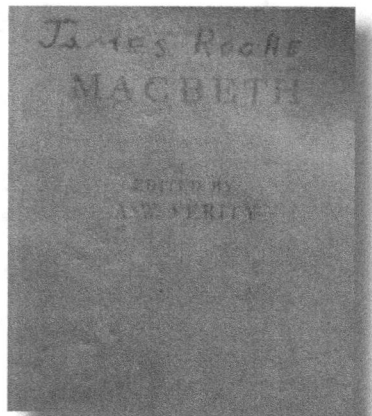

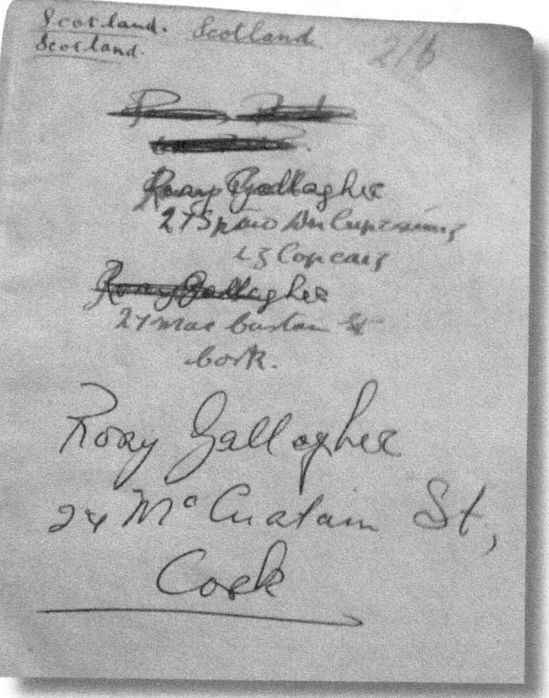

Rory Gallagher's final resting place in Cork, Ireland (*Lauren Alex O'Hagan*)

The Rory Gallagher Theatre in Cork, Ireland (the location of Gallagher's final Irish show in 1993) (*Ann Wilson*)

Rory Gallagher Place in Cork, Ireland
(*Lauren Alex O'Hagan*)

The Rory Gallagher Music Library in Cork, Ireland
(*Lauren Alex O'Hagan*)

Part 3: On the Stage 1992-1995

3.1 Boxer Spirit:
On the Road with the G-Man, 1992-1993

"Dónal, take him off, for fuck's sake." Seven little words that make my skin crawl and blood boil every time I hear them. The date is 29 October 1992. The scene: the Town & Country Club in Kentish Town, London. It is roughly 45 minutes into Rory Gallagher's set—a set that very clearly indicates that something is not quite right with him this evening. As his nimble hands fail to move in their usual magical way down the fretboard, the venue fills with boos and jeers that gradually increase in volume. Midway through a lacklustre version of 'Out on the Western Plain', Gallagher suddenly stops playing altogether and stands bewildered before the heckling crowd. Their taunts continue, but are soon mixed with encouraging claps and chants of "Rory! Rory!" from the other sympathetic half of the audience who recognise his anguish. The bootleg goes on for 25 more painful minutes in this awkward toing and froing until it abruptly cuts off. It is heartwrenching and extremely tough to listen to, especially for a diehard fan like me.

As we now know, Gallagher was seriously ill at the time and had suffered a bad reaction to his medication, which had led him to fall apart on stage in a rare display of unprofessionalism. However, as the old adage goes, a lie can travel halfway around the world while the truth is putting on its shoes, and in the ensuing years, this show has circulated in trading circles and online under the harmful and incorrect name 'The Drunk Show'. It is the spectre of this Town & Country Club concert that still today skews views on the quality of Gallagher's performances at this latter stage of his career. However, this concert truly is an exception to the rule and should be treated as such. 1992-1993 was a powerful first year on tour with new band members David Levy and Richard Newman, marking an exciting beginning and a fresh creative chapter for Gallagher.

This time in Gallagher's life was undoubtedly difficult, with increasing physical and mental health challenges and a growing dependency on medication, coupled with changes to both his living circumstances and band structure. Yet, he always maintained a strong sense of perseverance, or "boxer spirit"—as his brother Dónal calls it. No matter what life threw at him, how much pain he was in or how many obstacles in his path, Gallagher kept going through thick and thin. In one of his final interviews for the Irish press, he told Paul Dromy that music was his "reason for living" and was still the "driving force" of his life.[1] It was this deep passion for music and respect for his fans that spurred Gallagher on, come what may.

While personal conditions may have led Gallagher to tour less than usual in the 1992-1993 period, it did not stop him from putting blood, sweat and tears into every concert that he performed—as he always had done. So, join us as we spend a year on the road with Gallagher and his band, stopping off at notable concerts, such as the Bonn Blues Festival and the 40th Anniversary Celebration of the Fender Stratocaster, and recounting highlights, fan memories and personal stories along the way. Dónal notes how, in his later years, Gallagher had a growing "disbelief"[2] in himself and his talent. Here, we show that Gallagher's talent was just as vital and meaningful as it was in the 1970s and that he was still so deeply loved by fans across Europe.

Between the Devil and the Deep Blue Sea

After a warm-up gig at the Hotel Marina in Rhyl (see Interlude), the new Rory Gallagher Band made their official debut at the Temple Bar Blues Festival in Dublin in August 1992—a concert that has gone down in the annals of Gallagher history as one of the best performances in his long career (see 4.4). In sharp contrast, the Town & Country Club concert—described by Gallagher himself as a "real disaster [...] perhaps the worst concert that I've ever given"[3]—followed this two months later. Despite claims by the media that Gallagher was "lost" and "out of it,"[4] he was back on the road again just one month later for a short European tour that took in Switzerland, Austria, Germany, Holland, France and Belgium. Dónal had considered cancelling the tour, but he worried that leaving his brother alone was "probably the wrong thing to do" as he would "crawl back in a shell."[5] Speaking to Dave Fanning in 2024, Dónal disclosed that he had even started to become "afraid" that his brother would "damage himself" if left alone and that being on tour with him was the best way to "keep him safe."[6] Feeling caught "between the devil and the deep blue sea," he decided to press ahead with the planned dates.

While Dónal had been concerned about his brother's health for some years now, it was on this European tour that the full extent of Gallagher's health problems truly became apparent ("I realised that we really had a serious medical problem") and that the medication that was supposed to be helping the guitarist was, in fact, making him sicker.[7] On the opening night in Zurich, Gallagher had taken his usual medication before going on stage, but 20 minutes into the concert, his fingers suddenly went numb and he could not move them properly. Concerned for his brother's welfare, the next evening in Vienna, Dónal staged a burglary, stealing Gallagher's baggage from the dressing room and later taking the medication to a German chemist. The chemist was horrified at the "evil concoction"[8] he saw, telling Dónal that all these drugs were banned in Germany because of their harmful side effects. He replaced them with placebos, which Dónal gave back to the unsuspecting Gallagher. This worked for several days and, according to Dónal, there was an immediate change in his brother: he slept better, regained his appetite and voluntarily stopped drinking alcohol. In the 2024 documentary *Rory Gallagher: Calling Card*, Dónal revealed:

Part 3 - *Boxer Spirit*

> Just the other day, I found [Rory's] '92 diary and I was looking through the lists of what the poor man was taking and how many prescriptions he had. Where did he get all of this medication from? Some of it, you would only get if you were in a psychiatric ward and under supervision.

Despite the drama surrounding the Vienna concert, Gallagher delivered an incredibly sharp performance. As attested by the bootleg, his vocals are impeccable as he takes the audience through particularly heartfelt renditions of 'I Wonder Who', 'A Million Miles Away' and 'I Could've Had Religion' and gets them hyped with the high-energy onslaught of 'Don't Start Me Talkin'', 'Bullfrog Blues' and 'Nadine'. But the magnum opus is the surprise addition of 'I'm Not Awake Yet', reintroduced to the set for the first time in almost two decades and played electrically on his Stratocaster. While the original acoustic recording was tinged with nostalgia (written from the perspective of the young Gallagher awaiting his father's return from working away), this electric version has a more melancholic edge, Mark Feltham's harmonica offering a haunting and emotionally charged accompaniment. The song builds slowly over its nine minutes, taking on a heavier turn towards the midpoint as Richard Newman's drumming accelerates and Gallagher's rhythm-playing builds. This culminates with a dazzling harmonica solo by Feltham, which showcases his integral role in the later Rory Gallagher Band.

Like Dónal, friends were also aware of Gallagher's particularly morose air offstage on this tour. Journalist Jean-Noël Coghe attended the last date of the tour in Ghent on 19 December, along with his daughter Leslie and Flemish guitarist Roland Van Campenhout. They met Gallagher before the concert and Coghe notes that his behaviour seemed "strange";[9] at one point, Gallagher placed his hands on Leslie's shoulders, looked intensely into her eyes and said, "Look after your father's health, won't you. Health is a very precious thing." During the concert, the group met up with Catherine Mattelaer—Van Campenhout's ex-partner and an old friend of Gallagher and Dónal (the brothers had lived briefly with the couple in Ghent in 1977). "Something's up with Rory," Mattelaer whispered to Coghe as they watched Gallagher thanking them from the stage. After the concert, Gallagher and his friends went out for food and drinks, but he ate very little and talked to Mattelaer "like he'[d] never done before [...] almost as if he sensed that his days were numbered."[10] Fan Joël Winkin also followed Gallagher to the restaurant, but seeing that the guitarist was with friends, decided not to approach him. Nonetheless, when Winkin went to pay for his meal, he found that Gallagher had already taken care of it, which made him feel "embarrassed."[11]

Despite Gallagher's personal difficulties behind the scenes, accounts of his performances onstage are highly positive. The concerts seemed to mark a real return to form and, undeterred by his ongoing health issues, he consistently played three-hour sets. It was almost as if Gallagher saw the tour as an opportunity to push himself ever more and show himself—as much as his fans—that he was still capable of delivering. Indeed, he told David Sinclair of *Q* just that: "extreme touring [is] the best therapy of all. Every night you get a chance to prove yourself."[12] There are numerous high points to be found in surviving bootlegs, from 'Bratacha Dubha' at Bremen's Aladin Hall and 'Mean Old Woman' at Zurich's Volkshaus to 'I'm a Man/Hoochie Coochie Man' at Babenhausen's Stadthalle and 'I Shall Be Released' at Kehl's Stadthalle. The latter is a song that still sends shivers down Dónal's spine. Speaking to Dan Muise in 2002, he explained how, in his later tours, Gallagher would suddenly throw in 'I Shall Be Released' or 'Don't Think Twice It's Alright', which he believes was his brother "deliberately telling [him] a message."[13] In Dónal's view, Gallagher felt that "his days were numbered" and performing such songs fit with his "fatalistic" view of life.

While many fans expressed concern about both Gallagher's appearance and state of mind, they could not find fault in his concerts, delivered with his usual stamina and vitality. Photographer Harry Pater recalls meeting Gallagher backstage after a three-hour show in Bremen, having "given so much of himself that he could barely speak,"[14] while photographer Bertrand Alary, who had seen Gallagher many times in concert, still believes that his 1992 gig at the Paris Bataclan was the best ("a long concert where he was in really good shape and the sound was great"[15]). Newspapers likewise reported favourably on Gallagher's two nights at the Amsterdam Paradiso: "He rocked that place, kept coming back for encores, then looked at his watch and said, 'This man has to go to sleep' but he kept on going!"[16] Fan Jan Van Bodegraven, who was in the front row of the Paradiso with his then-girlfriend, recalls a comical anecdote from the occasion:

> My girlfriend was [wearing] a low-cut shirt, [and showing] noticeable cleavage. We were standing right at the stage, so every time Rory walked up to the edge of the stage, he [had view] of her cleavage. For a few times he smiled, shook his head, and walked away. At one point he came up to us again—I'm not sure if it was mid-solo or in between songs—and he bent down to my girlfriend, took off his scarf, and tied it around her neck to cover up the cleavage. It was hilarious, I can tell you. He smiled again, gave her a thumbs up, and he would not be distracted anymore! We took the scarf as a trophy.[17]

The scarf was framed in Bodegraven's bar, Café The Rose, until its closure in 2009. It is now in the possession of Theo Van Baar, a committee member of the Rory Gallagher Tribute Festival in Holland.

For many, Gallagher's standout performance was at the Bonn Blues Festival on 13 December. Like with many performances at this time of his life, it is shaded with bittersweet offstage memories, yet they take nothing away from the continued stage presence of the man who remained the "one unspoilt coastline left in the land of the blues."[18]

Bonn Blues Festival (13 December 1992)

Despite frequently touring Germany since the mid-1960s, Gallagher had never played in Bonn. He was, therefore, elated to headline the city's annual blues festival in December 1992. As an avid reader of crime fiction, there was something else about being in Bonn that equally delighted him: the John le Carré connection. "*A Small Town in Germany*? Did you read that?"[19] Gallagher greeted journalist Uli Twelker for their interview in his hotel room, referring to le Carré's 1968 espionage novel set in Bonn against the threat of a German-Soviet alliance. Gallagher was tired from the long car journey and had not eaten any dinner yet, but was happy to be in such a beautiful setting on the banks of the River Rhine and eagerly spoke to Twelker about music.

Although Gallagher was excited to be in a city of such political importance, he was also feeling rather nervous about the festival for one major reason: on the bill with him was Nine Below Zero, featuring his old bandmates Gerry McAvoy and Brendan O'Neill. Not only would Gallagher be crossing paths with them for the first time in months, but it would be the first time that they saw him perform with the new Rory Gallagher Band. There was also ongoing tension between harmonicist Mark Feltham and McAvoy and O'Neill. A previous member of Nine Below Zero, Feltham had suffered a mental health crisis in 1991 and left the band mid-tour, to which the members had responded unsympathetically. Later attempts to make up with Feltham had broken down, and he was still not speaking to guitarist and vocalist Dennis Greaves.

On the day of the festival, McAvoy and O'Neill visited both Gallagher and Feltham briefly in their dressing room, noting that Gallagher was "pleasant, if a little stand-offish."[20] This was the last time that they ever saw him. Blues guitarist Walter Trout—also performing at the festival—remembers seeing Gallagher backstage sitting in a chair looking bloated and ill, and wondered how he would be able to play.

Glancing at photos of Gallagher taken by journalist and photographer Lothar Trampert in his hotel room on the afternoon before the concert, it is easy to understand Trout's concerns. Gallagher is perched on top of the bedside cabinet, clinging to his red component Telecaster, and looks exhausted. His face is flushed and covered with psoriasis, his lips are pursed tightly and the grey roots of his dyed black hair are showing. Speaking to us in April 2023, Trampert recalled that Gallagher was "very calm, friendly and answered all [his] questions," but it was difficult to see him in such poor health, especially as Trampert had last seen him at Saarbrücken Open Air Festival in 1979. For the photographer, it was saddening to witness such a "hurt man, ill and lost in his life." However, his lasting impressions are of "an original, a guitar hero […] and a great singer" who he will never forget.[21]

Whenever Trampert's photos of Gallagher appear on social media, so many assumptions are made about the 'decline' in his musicianship simply based on his appearance. The photos may have captured Gallagher's vulnerabilities, yet they stand in marked contrast to the explosive figure that he became when he hit the stage in the Biskuithalle. Perhaps incentivised by the fact that his former bandmates were watching, Gallagher played for three hours—all traces of fragility washed away within the opening notes of 'Continental Op'. While Gerry McAvoy felt that Gallagher's concert "wasn't the way [he] remembered" and that the band "lacked interplay,"[22] Walter Trout was stunned by Gallagher's performance. Before an audience at Buxton Opera House in June 2022, Trout stated how amazed he was at the Irishman's transformation from front to backstage, describing him as "one of the greats."[23]

To truly get a well-rounded sense of the concert, it is helpful to frame it within the context of Twelker's interview conducted the day before, where Gallagher talks candidly about all aspects of his career. On the topic of the blues, Gallagher asserts that he has become "more independent"[24] with age and is increasingly inspired by himself as opposed to other players. This is apparent in songs like 'I Wonder Who', which evolved considerably from early performances, such as *Irish Tour '74*. By the time of Bonn, the song has been truly made into Gallagher's own, with its improvised lyrics, gritty vocals, slick guitar licks, devastating slide solos and exquisite accompaniment by Mark Feltham. While the song showcases Gallagher at his bluesy best, he introduces it with a self-deprecating statement: "I can't really do it very well, but I'll do my best."

'Off the Handle' is another example of Gallagher's blues virtuosity, the Bonn version giving David Levy and Richard Newman their moment in the spotlight with bass and drum solos. However, it is Mark Feltham who shines the most brightly, working in unison with Gallagher throughout, his vibrato and slurs on the harmonica enhancing the Stratocaster's soulful sounds. Such is Feltham's skill that Gallagher pulls him to the front of the stage at the end of the song and embraces him. His accompanying words show the high esteem in which the harmonicist is held: "Larry Adler, Tommy Reilly, Walter Horton, Little Walter, Sonny Boy Williamson, Rice Miller and, the greatest of them all, Mr Mark Feltham."

While the acoustic segment was always an important aspect of Gallagher's live concerts, his strength in this area further developed in the latter part of his career, as exemplified in Bonn. Here, he performs a beautiful rendition of the traditional Irish song 'She Moved Thro' the Fair', segueing into 'Out on the Western Plain', 'Mercy River' and 'Walkin' Blues'. The set is a fine example of Gallagher's own unique Celtic approach to acoustic blues, as well as his growing enthusiasm in incorporating Irish folk music into his performances. In his interview with Twelker, Gallagher had praised MTV Unplugged for bringing "a whole new respect back for acoustic music" and expressed plans for his long-awaited acoustic album ("if God spares me"). With his modest words, Gallagher plays down the fact that he uniquely—and successfully—incorporated acoustic music into his concerts throughout his career. Using just the sounds of his National or Martin (and, later, Takamine), he was able to create an intimate rapport with his typical rock audience, not only holding their attention but imbuing them with a new appreciation for this musical style. With Twelker, Gallagher also reflected on his recent collaboration with The Dubliners, his fondness for the folk scene and desire to record with Martin Carthy, Bert Jansch and Davey Graham.

Although Gallagher's sets and personal interests were increasingly moving towards folk, he was keen to stress to Twelker that he could "still hit it hard" when necessary. Judging from his performance at Bonn, there is no doubting this statement. The perennial 'Tattoo'd Lady' is loose and impassioned (despite his self-effacing comment that the song is "a bit of baloney"), while the surprise encore of 'Shin Kicker' is delivered with the same energy as its *Photo-Finish* heyday. 'Messin' with the Kid' and 'Shadow Play' also still have the power to stop the audience in their tracks, and the ten-minute closer 'La Bamba' is full of vigour and even a touch of humour. Integral to all these songs is the sounds of Gallagher's beloved Stratocaster, which he affectionately calls "the business" in his interview with Twelker. Elaborating further on why he still has a penchant for his 'battered' guitar, Gallagher notes its versatility ("you can beat the hell out of it and you can also caress it"), as well as the fact that as a young boy, owning a Sunburst Stratocaster was "the absolute maximum dream" and "still is" for him.

Gallagher remained loyal to his Stratocaster throughout his life, but he still enjoyed the opportunity to try out new guitars. Here at Bonn, he switches to a Fender Telecaster that was given to him by his friend Rudi Gerlach to play a blistering rendition of 'I Could've Had Religion'. Gallagher had first seen the Telecaster at Gerlach's house in 1987 and enjoyed playing it, so during the recording of *Rocklife* 1990, Gerlach presented it to him as a gift. Gallagher made some modifications to improve the sound, adding a Seymour Duncan pick-up in the lead position and changing the tuners to Schaller M6 Mini to give it a "Keith Richards type set-up." This resulted in a versatile tone, illustrated best in 'I Could've Had Religion' as Gallagher moves between warm mellow and rich cutting inflections throughout the song, creating an atmospheric mood. As David Levy recounted to us, even today his "ears are still ringing" from the powerful howls of Gallagher's Telecaster on this song.[25]

Over the course of Gallagher's career, he always spoke about his love for Bob Dylan and his dream of having the opportunity to work with him. This is something that he brings up again with Twelker, stating that he is "very inspired" by Dylan's new album *Good As I Been To You*, which is a "fantastic project." He says how his ultimate goal is to be Dylan's "Mike Bloomfield," but that he is too shy to approach him directly. Gallagher's next best thing is to pay tribute to the man himself and he does this in style at Bonn with a moving cover of 'Just Like a Woman'. Gallagher switches to his Gretsch Corvette and throws in the song off the cuff, but Feltham is quick to respond with his harmonica. The outcome is a deep, profound and simply stunning interpretation. Yes, it is sloppy in places, with Gallagher forgetting some lyrics, laughing and apologising ("sorry, Bob"), but that makes it all the more heartfelt. It comes straight from the soul, delivered with so much feeling, a true sign of Gallagher's love for one of his biggest inspirations. This love stayed with him for the rest of his life: when in hospital, he would cherish the telegram that he received from Dylan, keeping it on his bedside table right until the very end.

In the final section of the Bonn concert, Gallagher does something unexpected: he momentarily breaks into the opening riff of the Taste classic 'What's Going On'—much to the crowd's delight—before abruptly stopping and chuckling at his playful teasing. Following the band's break-up in 1970, Gallagher had vowed never to play a Taste song on stage again and kept true to his word. Legal battles with management had dragged on for decades and were only resolved shortly before the Bonn concert, which had put much strain on Gallagher. In conversation with Twelker, he reflected on the "dreadful time" following Taste's demise, his lack of money and how the press attacked him, describing it as "traumatic," "very, very cruel" and something that "battered his confidence." However, showing his Christian spirit, Gallagher also told Twelker that the manager of Taste was now "D.E.A.D, God rest him in heaven" and he had, therefore, "forgiven it all." Furthermore, now that the legal battle had been resolved, it might be fun to play a Taste song again "for old time's sake." Perhaps this conversation with Twelker was fresh in Gallagher's mind and what inspired the tantalising opening of 'What's Going On' at Bonn. Sadly, the pain did not seem healed enough for Gallagher to see it through, and he never would perform a Taste number in full again, nor would he commit to a mooted reunion concert in Belfast with former members John Wilson and Charlie McCracken.

Gallagher ended his Bonn concert by wishing the audience "a good future"—an interesting choice of words which fit with his "strange" mood on this European tour and concerns over his precarious health. While Gallagher's words were tinged with doubt about his fate, Twelker, nonetheless, was adamant that Bonn showed Gallagher as "a dedicated, no-nonsense, unpretentious musician" who was still "a considerable, tough force to be reckoned with on the country blues and rock blues front." Fan Simon Grundy—also in attendance—had similar thoughts. Despite Gallagher being "overweight and unwell," he "knocked it out the park" and "didn't seem to want to leave the stage."[26] Overall, it was "a very memorable night from the great man" that left Grundy with "a big smile." Following Gallagher's death in June 1995, Twelker reflected on his memories of the guitarist in an obituary for *Good Times*. He describes their interview as more like a "unforgettable fireside chat full of lively rock history," yet poignantly notes that Gallagher was "characterised by vulnerability and deep-seated depressive feelings."[27]

Lightning Over Water
Gallagher's European tour had been an overall success, firmly establishing his place and relevance in the 1990s. Following the tour, he immediately set to work on a compilation album *Etched in Blue* and the *G-Men Bootleg Series*—a canny attempt to "bootleg the bootleggers" by releasing a triple-CD boxset of three

unofficial live albums that had been circulating around Europe for just £15. Released through the UK indie record label Castle Communications, Gallagher hoped that it would "set a legal precedent"[28] by claiming back the rights to his own recordings. It would not only protect his own interests, but those of the different companies who licensed his music across the world. At the time, Gallagher was the most bootlegged artist in Western Europe alongside Bob Dylan and the Rolling Stones.

So, from a musical perspective, the future was looking bright for Gallagher moving into 1993, on both the touring and recording front. However, his health continued to pose an ever-growing challenge. When not on tour, Gallagher always had a tendency to isolate himself and become increasingly depressed. Although Dónal had settled Gallagher into his own flat in London in the late 1970s, the guitarist "wasn't domesticated whatsoever as regards simple things like laundry or eating or cooking."[29] Furthermore, while Dónal had hoped that having his own place would encourage his brother to invite people over, it did the opposite and he began to socialise less and less. According to Dónal, Gallagher had always lacked "the art of interacting"[30] and was "bad on one-on-one relationships,"[31] but this got increasingly worse over time, to such a point that he would not even let the gasman inside to read the meter.

Dónal was also becoming increasingly mistrustful of Gallagher's doctors and felt that the medication he was being given to treat his depression was "not the right ones."[32] "[Rory] was sick all the time, he had stomach pains […] and his mind was also starting to get disturbed,"[33] he stated in a 2011 interview with *Paris Move*. Gallagher had always been a superstitious man, but his medication progressively heightened these superstitions, causing great distress to his daily life.[34] Dónal worried that his brother had become trapped in a "terrible, vicious circle,"[35] being prescribed a series of drugs that he thought he needed to keep fit, yet which only exacerbated his health problems. Mark Feltham agrees, emphasising that Gallagher "used to worry about all sorts of ills" and probably believed that his medication was "the answer" and would give him "a little relief."[36] Dónal particularly worried about one doctor who was treating Gallagher's stomach pains (in hindsight, the onset of liver disease) with large doses of co-proxamol—an analgesic that contains paracetamol and dextropropoxyphene, which was later withdrawn from the UK market due to its dangerous reaction with alcohol and toxicity in overdose. He spoke secretly to the doctor, pleading with him to wean Gallagher off his medication, and even later contacted a lawyer out of fear that his brother was "being slowly killed,"[37] but this was to no avail.

Running out of ideas, in early 1993, Dónal recommended that Gallagher go back to Cork for several months to stay with their mother Monica and have some well-deserved rest. Gallagher had always been very close to Monica—she was his "constant confidante"[38] who he called every night no matter where he was in the world—so he agreed, anticipating that it would help improve his health. Speaking on Dutch radio later in the year, Gallagher spoke about the benefits of having been in Cork for an extended period of time: "I wrote a lot of songs. I got back to eating three meals a day and playing with animals and playing guitar and just being a human being again."[39]

On returning to London, however, Gallagher's depression set in again. Unable to keep a constant eye on his brother, Dónal arranged for him to move into the Conrad Hotel in Chelsea Harbour, hoping that it would help replicate life on the road and make him feel less lonely. At first, Gallagher settled into hotel life, enjoying the chance to converse and play with fellow musicians passing through London and staying at the hotel, such as Gary Moore, but both management and guests soon became frustrated with the late-night jams taking place in his room. The hotel manager called Dónal, complaining that Gallagher was using his room as a recording studio and warning that he would have to move out if it happened again. Several nights later, Dónal received a less friendly call. This time, Gallagher had borrowed the piano player from the hotel bar who had become so drunk that he could no longer play for the customers. As a result, Gallagher was moved into an apartment block across the street that the hotel serviced. According to Dónal, this move compounded his brother's depression to the extent that he refused to see anybody. He adopted the pseudonym Alain Delon (one of his favourite actors), which had to be said by those phoning reception in order to put the call through to him.

What was meant to be a short-term solution became long-term, with Gallagher living at the Conrad Hotel for the rest of his life. When asked by friends why he did not move back to his apartment, Gallagher would often state that he had a leaking roof that needed to be fixed. This was an "excuse," says Dónal, pointing out that the roof problem was a "minor thing," but that Gallagher did not want anyone but him or roadie Tom O'Driscoll in the apartment to try and fix it.[40] Speaking to friend Rudi Gerlach, Gallagher stated that he did not trust people and did not want anybody around him. Rather more painfully, he added that he did not want to be on his own, but "had to," describing himself as "very precarious" and praying that the Lord would allow him his "talent, [his] nerves and health."[41]

While in the Conrad Hotel, Gallagher developed a somewhat unhealthy fascination with *Lightning Over Water*—a Wim Wenders autobiographical film that documents the final days of film director Nicholas Ray. In Dónal's view, the film's understanding of one's own destiny appealed to Gallagher who saw parallels between himself and Ray, as somebody who was "being closed in upon or didn't have long to live."[42] Believing that his copy of the film had been confiscated, Gallagher asked Gerlach to send him another one. Around the same time, Gallagher also obtained audience footage from his concert at the Bonn Blues Festival and began to rewatch it over and over, chillingly describing it as his own *Lightning Over Water*. He told Gerlach that he had gone through a long period of being unable to watch himself because he disliked the way he looked, but that he thought the Bonn footage was "fantastic" and "very interesting" as it was "not unlike what Wenders was doing."

Dónal was relieved when the festival season restarted in May 1993 and Gallagher could resume his busy touring pattern. Once again, Dónal would be able to monitor what his brother ate and how much he slept and make sure that he interacted with others. Like the European tour of December 1992, Gallagher's festival appearances were extremely well received by spectators, demonstrating his remarkable ability to disconnect from his problems offstage to put on an unforgettable show for fans.

Festival Season
Gallagher's 1993 festival season kicked off with a headlining appearance at the Portsmouth International Blues Weekend on 28 May. The event was held in a large marquee on Southsea Common and also featured Snooky Pryor, the Fabulous Thunderbirds, the Nighthawks and Marcia Ball, among others. As with many of Gallagher's later concerts, cameras were prohibited and he had to be chaperoned to and from the stage. This, however, did not prevent him from delivering an inspired performance. Scott Duncan, founder of the British Blues Collection and editor of *Blueprint* magazine, was at the festival and remembers that Gallagher "pulled out more punters for his one appearance than showed up for the rest of the weekend," which served as testimony to both his "great drawing power" and the "genuine affection" in which he was held.[43] Duncan met Gallagher backstage and recalls that the guitarist was "well chuffed" when Duncan told him that he had inspired him to set up his blues society and magazine. He met Gallagher again several months later at London's Hard Rock Café and was surprised that the Irishman recognised him and even asked about the magazine.

Gallagher travelled straight from Portsmouth to Bad Reichenhall in Germany, this time for a small concert in Sternenzelt. In attendance was photographer Wolfgang Gürster who had formed a friendship with the Gallagher brothers back in 1982 and was often allowed to photograph the guitarist on stage. Speaking to us in August 2022, Gürster affirmed that Gallagher was on top form and the concert was up to his usual high standards. However, what stood out even more for him was Gallagher's post-concert selflessness and cordiality. Gürster had brought along a stack of bootleg albums for him to sign and was welcomed backstage after the concert. He was surprised to see Gallagher wrapped up in a thick coat and scarf and was informed by Dónal that his brother had a bad cold and was running a fever, so he wanted to get him back to the hotel as soon as possible. Not wanting to disturb Gallagher, Gürster decided to leave, but Gallagher insisted that he stayed, signed all his bootlegs and asked detailed questions about them. Gallagher had always been "intrigued" by his bootlegs and enjoyed being shown them by fans, even going out to buy his own copies.[44] Gürster was astonished that the Irishman was so gracious, despite being unwell, and fondly recalls him as a "true gentleman [...] quiet and shy with no rock star behaviour."[45]

After a few weeks' break, Gallagher was back in Germany again to perform at the Freiburg Zelt Musik Festival and St Wendel Bosenbachstadion, while August saw him headline the first Geel House Rock Festival in Belgium, with

Golden Earring and old friend Roland Van Campenhout accompanying him on the bill. The auspices for Geel were unfavourable when Gallagher arrived in Brussels only to find that the suitcase containing his lucky leather jacket—which had once belonged to his uncle Jimmy[46]—had missed the flight from London. Given its sentimental value, Gallagher understandably did not want to leave the airport until it had arrived on the next flight. Wanting to help his friend out, Van Campenhout organised a helicopter to catch up part of the delay, enabling Gallagher to reach the festival by midnight. Despite arriving late, Gallagher—clad in his lucky leather jacket—quickly won over the audience, delivering such a prodigious performance that organiser Dis Van Eyck immediately invited him back to headline in 1994. Fan Joël Winkin was there and agrees that Gallagher delivered a musical masterclass: "It was the best concert I ever attended. Rory had recovered all the precision and virtuosity like 10 years before." 'Messin' with the Kid' was a particular standout moment for Winkin, performed in a softer tempo that echoed the original Junior Wells version, with Mark Feltham on harmonica and Gallagher emulating the guitar tricks of Buddy Guy. According to Winkin, there was something moving about Gallagher "courageously struggling with his health issues and still giving out all his talent, passion and love for his fans."[47]

Winkin went backstage after the concert to meet Gallagher and notes that the bluesman was in a good mood, smiling and joking with fans. The atmosphere was lively, with fans constantly talking over each other and interrupting Gallagher to ask questions. However, he listened politely to everyone and even apologised for being cut off—his subtle way of highlighting their bad manners. When Winkin asked Gallagher why he did not perform certain songs that evening, he jested in response, enquiring whether Winkin was "friend or foe." The tone became a little more serious when asked about 'Fuel to the Fire', with Gallagher replying that the song was "too sad" to perform, but it lightened again when they discussed Johnny Winter and his approach to the blues ("a bit too short-sighted, excuse the cruel play on words"). For almost three hours, Gallagher gave fans his full attention, hardly eating and only drinking half a small bottle of lager.

After Geel, the rest of August 1993 was quiet, with Gallagher only playing two festival dates in France and Switzerland. At the beginning of September, he headed to Holland to perform at the Zalen Schaaf in Leeuwarden. Leeuwarden was yet another strong performance from Gallagher, but it is the radio interview for Countdown Café that he gave so affably from his hotel room after the concert that is of more significance here. It is an interview that is rather uncomfortable for the listener, with Gallagher clearly exhausted and audibly distressed when the topic turns to personal matters and his health.[48]

When asked by presenters Alfred Lagarde and Kees Baars about where he currently lives, he gives a convoluted answer, before sighing and stating, "I don't know where to live, to be honest with you," while on the topic of cancelling shows in Amsterdam three years earlier, the conversation becomes full of stunted pauses and tension as Gallagher justifies that "everyone gets ill sometimes." "What do you want me to say?" he adds with a nervous laugh, before continuing to explain his fear of flying, getting anxious before a show and, therefore, not eating. In response, the interviewer asks if he also stops drinking. Given speculation in the press at the time, Gallagher assumes that he is referring to alcohol and becomes defensive.

Sensing his upset, the presenter tries to steer the conversation onto another topic, but Gallagher insists on staying with the topic to lay current rumours to rest and talks once more about the "dangerous territory" of flying, suffering from stagefright and not eating. Although Lagarde manages to change the topic back to music, Gallagher is clearly unnerved for the rest of the interview. When told later that Belsonic Sounds—a post-punk Cork band—are also in the studio, Gallagher becomes embarrassed at them having listened into the conversation. He is asked to introduce 'Laundromat' and explain what it is about but, conscious of Belsonic Sounds' presence, he makes a disparaging remark that the track is "corny" and that they will be "listening there with red ears."

Despite its awkward moments, the interview is also full of some fantastic insights from Gallagher into his planned acoustic album. He explains how he is playing more African style rhythm guitar and that the album will feature a cover of Blind Willie McTell's 'Statesboro Blues' and the Irish traditional song 'Crann Úll', as well as many redemption blues songs in the style of Reverend Robert Wilkins. Gallagher states firmly that his turn towards acoustic is not part of a "he wants to fade away" narrative and that his acoustic playing has always been "aggressive" and "upfront." He also talks about his three "commandments" for a successful concert—"the blues", "let it rock" and "have something in between"—clarifying nicely that concerts are "not Apple computers" so they cannot be too premeditated.

Gallagher successfully followed these three commandments the next day at Tegelen Bluesrock Festival, delivering a dynamic double set when C.J. Chenier—who was second on the bill—cancelled due to problems crossing the border. Tegelen was like being back on home territory for Gallagher, having previously performed at the festival in 1984 and 1989. The 1993 performance—captured on video—shows a confident Gallagher in total command of the stage and his band, whether playing powerful rockers like 'Continental Op' and 'Moonchild' or stirring blues like 'I Wonder Who' and 'I Could've Had Religion' through to the dual attack encore of 'Messin' with the Kid' and 'Bullfrog Blues'. Here, Gallagher is in a playful mood, removing his jacket, dancing frivolously and laughing before strapping his Telecaster back on for a big finish.

**40th Anniversary Celebration
of the Fender Stratocaster (15 September 1993)**
On 15 September 1993—just eleven days after the Tegelen Bluesrock Festival—a very special concert was organised at the Manchester Free Trade Hall to celebrate the 40th anniversary of the Fender Stratocaster. Part of the Boddingtons Manchester Festival of Arts and Television and entitled "Curves, Contours and Body Horns", the concert promised a celebrated bill, with Frankie Miller,

Sherman Robertson, Sonny Curtis, Debby Davies and perhaps the most iconic user of the Stratocaster: Rory Gallagher. Leading up to the event, promotional articles in the *Manchester Metro News* also mentioned Eagles guitarist Joe Walsh and E-Street Band member Nils Lofgren, but both artists declined at the last minute due to other commitments. All proceeds from the concert were given to the charity Relate—a national charity that provides relationship counselling.

Speaking before the concert to the *Manchester Evening News*, Gallagher stated that he was "delighted" not only to be honouring the Stratocaster, but also to be performing on the same bill as his "hero" Sonny Curtis.[49] Gallagher had the privilege of closing the show, playing the longest set of the evening and—never one to follow the rules—"straying from the 100% Stratocaster policy"[50] by using both his Telecaster and Takamine Dreadnought during his performance. To date, only footage of the opening number 'Continental Op' has emerged online, but it shows a poised Gallagher "whose pleasure at being back in Manchester was evident."[51]

Fan Andrew Thompson testifies to this. Thompson had originally bought tickets for the concert when he heard that Joe Walsh would be performing. He was "devastated" when Walsh subsequently pulled out, but thrilled when he arrived at the Free Trade Hall to find that Gallagher was headlining instead. Thompson had seen Gallagher twice previously (Rock on the Tyne Festival, 1981; Newcastle City Hall, 1982) and was blown away by both live performances. Speaking of the Manchester 1993 concert, Thompson states that, despite the stiff competition, Gallagher "didn't miss a beat" and was "simply the best on the night." Thompson recalls leaving the venue and hearing people talk animatedly about Gallagher's performance, thoughts of Joe Walsh long forgotten. A report by Chris Sharratt of the *Manchester Evening News* concurs that "the most enthusiastic applause of the evening was saved for Gallagher [...], proving that it was music, not machines, that the audience had come from."[52] "I never saw Gallagher in what some say was his true prime early to mid-1970s, but he was still better than most I have seen and certainly for me the best blues guitarist I've ever seen," Thompson concludes.[53]

Around the same time as the "Curves, Contours and Body Horns" concert, a documentary of the same name was put together by Ray Minhinnett and Bob Young. The documentary sought to tell the history of the Fender Stratocaster and featured interviews with some of the most famous Stratocaster players in the world, from Eric Clapton and Buddy Guy to Keith Richards and Mark Knopfler and, of course, Rory Gallagher. However, rather scandalously, when the documentary was prepared for television release in December 1993, the editors "crudely or cruelly"—as Dónal told us—cut Gallagher out.[54] Dónal challenged the television company who responded that the edit was made to include Frank Zappa (and his son), who had just passed away. Unhappy with this decision, Dónal withdrew his brother from the video. Nevertheless, an extended version of the programme was broadcast at a later date, with Gallagher's interview included. Luckily, the year before, Gallagher had featured in the *Stratocasters* documentary, directed by Michael Bayley Hughes and Bob Hewitt and broadcast on the Welsh television channel S4C. An extended version of his interview was used in Bayley Hughes and Hewitt's 2007 documentary *Stratmasters* (see 4.6).

Two years after the *Curves, Contours and Body Horns* documentary, a book was also released: *The Story of the Fender Stratocaster: Curves, Contours and Body Horns* (1995). This time, part of Gallagher's interview—which had been recorded in his room at the Conrad Hotel—was included. The rest of the interview was published in *Modern Guitars* magazine in 2005. Gallagher talks passionately about his early influences, his love for Robert Johnson, Buddy Guy and Jimi Hendrix, and the tunings that he favours when playing guitar. The crowning moment comes, however, when Ray Minhinnett asks, "What is important to you?" and Gallagher replies by waxing lyrically about his Stratocaster:

> This is the best, it's my life, this is my best friend. It's almost like knowing its weak spots are strong spots. I don't like to get sentimental about these things, but when you spend 30 years of your life with the same instrument it's like a walking memory bank of your life there in your arms [...] I hate using your one-line clichés, but this guitar is part of my psychic make-up [...] I love playing it, I play it every day[55]

From Gallagher's words, it is clear that there is perhaps no better representative of the Stratocaster than him. Gallagher's Stratocaster was not a separate entity, but rather an integral part of himself. As Dónal reflected emotionally when speaking about Gallagher's death in the *Ghost Blues* (2010) documentary, "All I could do was look at his hands and look at his guitar and say, 'You poor orphan. Who's ever gonna play you like he did?'" At Gallagher's funeral in June 1995, the guitar was also laid next to his coffin "like an ineffably poignant still life," as Niall Stokes of Hot Press called it.[56]

Meeting with the G-Man

Following a concert in Berlin and an astounding return to Cork in November 1993 (see 4.5), Gallagher's final performance of the year took place at the Paradiso in Amsterdam on 20 December. As stated in the Interlude, this concert was released officially in 2001 as part of the *Let's Go to Work* boxset and is the only live release to date with Gallagher's final band. Coming from an original bootleg recording, the release suffers from poor sound quality, but this is not enough to spoil the scorching performance of Gallagher and his band. One could argue, in fact, that the rough mix adds to the club atmosphere and gives the listener an authentic sense of what it must have felt like to be up close and personal at a Gallagher concert. The intimacy of Gallagher's acoustic set, which includes a magnificent acoustic performance of the Irish folk song 'William of Green' (the only known performance), the blues number 'Mercy River' and the Christian hymn 'Amazing Grace', are reasons enough to purchase it. The album stands as a testimony of the new energy that David Levy and Richard Newman brought to the Rory Gallagher Band and a bittersweet reminder of all the successes that were on the horizon for this new line-up.

Bowed Not Broken

In the song 'Rory' by Black 47, lead singer Larry Kirwan talks about the volts of lightning that shot from Gallagher's fingers whenever he played guitar and then poignantly asks in the final verse, "What the hell happened, head? Where did the lightnin' go?" He reflects on whether it "burnt right through [his] fingers to the cockles of [his] soul," ultimately leaving him "stranded a million miles away from the rest of us." It is a powerful visual metaphor for a man who gave so much to everyone else and left little for himself.

Life on the road can be hard, tiring and lonely, yet life *off* the road could be much harder, more tiring and lonelier for Gallagher. As Dónal notes, on stage is where his brother came alive and filled with fire, while offstage he "would vegetate" and "couldn't function"[57]—a Jekyll-Hyde aspect of Gallagher's personality that has often been commented upon. He recalls how his brother "wasn't satisfied until he would almost physically fall down"[58] and would often stand looking longingly at the stage after a concert, almost reluctant to leave and return to his everyday life. "A lot of us were going home to a girlfriend or family [...] none of us ever realised Rory was going home just waiting for the next gig," recounted guitarist Bernie Marsden in a 2010 interview with Dave Fanning.[59] Fanning himself shared a similar poignant reflection with us about Gallagher:

> Dónal would say, 'Nobody knew Rory Gallagher as well as I did and I didn't know Rory Gallagher at all' [...] And if Dónal says that he never really knew him, I can tell you nobody really knew him. It's kind of sad, it really was. Rory didn't leave a wife or kids, guitars, a house, a car, a dog. He left nothing. He didn't really have anything. He just wanted to be on tour. He wasn't a happy person, I don't think really [but] he was such a nice, quiet guy, really introverted, very gentle and almost frail, very, very, very shy.[60]

Paul Charles, Gallagher's agent from 1986-1988, concurs:

> Off-stage, [Rory] was one of the shyest, politest gentlemen I've ever had the pleasure of meeting [...] I always had the feeling that at some deep level, Rory found things hard. Then again, you couldn't possibly play the blues the way Rory played the blues without being connected to... the blues. I have a feeling the off-stage gentleman was as keen as his adoring fans were to meet the extrovert, who appeared the moment he plugged his beloved Strat into his trusted VOX AC 30.[61]

In his biography *Rory Gallagher: The Man Behind the Guitar*, Julian Vignoles uses Kirwan's lyrics in 'Rory' to suggest that the "triumphant Gallagher years" were in the past and "the elation had gone" at seeing him live.[62] Despite

Part 3 - *Boxer Spirit*

Gallagher's many struggles offstage, we demonstrate throughout this chapter that the "volts of lightning" in his fingers were most definitely still there *onstage*. From Bonn to Manchester, Ghent to Tegelen, Vienna to Amsterdam, Gallagher routinely delivered electrifying performances, graciously meeting fans and agreeing to press interviews, even at times when he was not feeling his best. "I don't recognise myself when I'm on stage," Gallagher often said, and that is something that is certainly apparent through his 1992-1993 tour. The stage acted as anaesthesia for the bluesman, enabling him to temporarily numb his physical and mental pain and focus only on the here-and-now, putting on the very best performance for his fans. Even at this later stage in his career, Gallagher remained in great demand, with the phone "constantly ringing with offers to play huge stadiums all over the world."[63] It promised that the best was yet to come and that—as Gallagher sang on *Fresh Evidence*—he may have been bowed but he most definitely was not broken.

LAO

Footnotes

1 Paul Dromy, 'Playing for Keeps', *Irish Examiner* (23 December 1993), 15.
2 Ivan Little, 'Rory Gallagher: 20 Years Later', *Belfast Telegraph* (13 June 2015), https://www.belfasttelegraph.co.uk/entertainment/music/news/rory-gallagher-20-years-later-id-love-to-bring-rory-back-and-tell-him-to-look-at-his-talent-and-legacy/31298650.html
3 'Rory Gallagher: 'Le blues toujours', *Hard Rock* (February 1993), https://rewritingrory.co.uk/2022/06/03/hard-rock-february-1993/
4 Gavin Martin, 'The Man Who Sweated Rock 'N' Roll', *Record Collector* (9 June 2011), https://recordcollectormag.com/articles/the-man-who-sweated-rocknroll
5 Shiv Cariappa, 'Wheeling and Dealing' (March 2003), http://www.roryon.com/donalshiv352.html
6 'Remembering Rory Gallagher 2024', https://www.youtube.com/watch?v=xE8LArN63VA
7 Cariappa, 'Wheeling and Dealing'.
8 Maeve Quigley, 'Booze didn't kill my brother Rory, it was the drugs to help his fear of flying', *Sunday Mirror* (14 April 2002), https://www.thefreelibrary.com/Booze+didn%27t+kill+my+brother+Rory%2C+it+was+the+drugs+to+help+his+fear...-a084782459
9 Jean-Noël Coghe, *Rory Gallagher: A Biography* (Cork: Mercier Press, 2001), 154.
10 Ibid.
11 Interview with Joël Winkin, 9 March 2023.
12 David Sinclair, 'The Show Must Go On', *Q* (July 1990), http://www.roryon.com/q8.html.
13 Dan Muise, *Gallagher, Marriott, Derringer & Trower* (Milwaukee: Hal Leonard Corporation, 2002), 72.
14 Interview with Harry Pater, 1 May 2023.
15 Interview with Bertrand Alary, 8 August 2022.
16 Reported on Rory Gallagher official Facebook: https://www.facebook.com/RoryGallagher/photos/rory-played-paradiso-amsterdam-on-15-12-1992he-rocked-that-place-kept-coming-bac/10153958074271807
17 Interview with Jan Van Bodegraven, 21 January 2024.
18 Shane Loftus, 'Gallagher Remains True to the Blues', *Irish Examiner* (12 August 1992), 4.
19 Uli Twelker, 'Rory Gallagher: Good Times', *Good Times* (March 1993), http://www.roryon.com/uli209.html.
20 Gerry McAvoy and Pete Chrisp, *Riding Shotgun: 35 Years on the Road with Rory Gallagher and "Nine Below Zero"* (Chicago: SPG Triumph, 2005), 276.
21 Interview with Lothar Trampert, 27 April 2023.
22 Ibid.
23 Our thanks to Peter Wood who was at Walter Trout's concert and fed back this anecdote to us.
24 Twelker, 'Rory Gallagher…'
25 Interview with David Levy, 29 April 2022.
26 Interview with Simon Grundy, 8 June 2023.
27 Uli Twelker, 'Rory Gallagher – "They don't make them like you anymore"', *Good Times* (June 1995), https://rewritingrory.co.uk/2022/06/13/goodtimes-june-1995/
28 'Bootleg Blues', *Hot Press* (16 December 1992), https://www.roryon.com/bootleg425.html
29 Trevor Hodgett, 'Timeless – Trevor Hodgett Remembers Rory Gallagher', *R2* (5 August 2015), https://shadowplays.com/blog/?p=3148
30 'Songs & Stories NY Remembers Rory Gallagher', https://www.youtube.com/watch?v=j8yOANNTTuQ

31 Alan di Pern, 'Against the Grain: The Rise and Fall of Rory Gallagher', *Guitar World* (2009 holiday edition), https://shadowplays.com/blog/?p=708
32 'ITW de Donal Gallagher – Une affaire de famille', *Paris Move* (May 2011), https://www.paris-move.com/portrait/itw-de-donal-gallagher-une-affaire-de-famille/
33 Ibid.
34 Mark Feltham recalls Gallagher becoming very upset when he only saw one magpie from the tour bus window. On multiple other occasions, Gallagher would worry about having bad luck because Feltham lined his shoes up from right to left instead of left to right or Gerry McAvoy put a pair of shoes on the dressing room table (Muise, *Gallagher, Marriott, Derringer & Trower*, 75.)
35 Rick Koster, 'Rory in the Sky', *Dallas Observer* (27 November 1997), https://www.roryon.com/sky.html
36 Muise, *Gallagher, Marriott, Derringer & Trower*, 74.
37 Ibid.
38 Treacy Hogan, 'The Legend's Going Strong', *Irish Independent* (26 June 2004), 21.
39 'Interview with Rory Gallagher on Countdown Café Radio 3 Holland' (3 September 1993), https://ia902907.us.archive.org/8/items/RoryGallagher1993-09-03CountdownCafeRadio3Holland/RoryGallagher1993-09-03CountdownCafeRadio3Holland.mp3?cnt=0
40 Muise, *Gallagher, Marriott, Derringer & Trower*, 80.
41 Ibid.
42 Ibid, 63.
43 Scott Duncan, 'Rory Gallagher – No More Messin' with the Kid', *Blueprint* (August 1995), https://www.roryon.com/blueprint307.html
44 Cariappa, 'Wheeling and Dealing'.
45 Interview with Wolfgang Gürster, 20 August 2022.
46 As Jim Roche—Rory's cousin—jokes, "The story, often told is that my father went to Canada to work in a car factory to raise money for college. He brought back the leather jacket and a song, 'Moving On' by Hank Snow. Rory borrowed both. 'Moving On' ended up on the first Taste album and the jacket ended up touring the world!"
47 Interview with Joël Winkin, 7 March 2023.
48 'Interview with Rory Gallagher...'
49 Carl Johnston, 'Party Time on the 40th Birthday of Star Guitar', *Manchester Evening News* (22 September 1993), 13.
50 Chris Sharratt, 'Curves, Contours and Body Horns', *Manchester Evening News* (16 September 1993), 19.
51 Ibid.
52 Ibid.
53 Interview with Andrew Thompson, 16 October 2023.
54 Email exchange with Dónal Gallagher, 16 October 2023.
55 Ray Minhinnett, *The Story of the Fender Stratocaster: Curves, Contours and Body Horns* (1995), http://www.roryon.com/contours.html; Ray Minhinnett, 'Rory Gallagher: A Previously Unpublished Interview', *Modern Guitars Magazine* (21 July 2005), https://www.guitarinternational.com/archives/000931.html
56 Niall Stokes, 'Down All the Days', *Hot Press* (15 June 1995), http://www.roryon.com/downday.html
57 'Songs & Stories...'
58 Ibid.
59 'Dave Fanning 2010 Rory Gallagher Tribute Show', https://www.shadowplays.com/jukebox/Fanning_Donal.mp3
60 Interview with Dave Fanning, 24 April 2022.
61 Paul Charles, *Adventures in Wonderland* (Hot Press: Dublin), 117-118.
62 Julian Vignoles, *Rory Gallagher: The Man Behind the Guitar* (Cork: Collins, 2018),111.
63 Nick Dent-Robinson. 'Richard Newman - Interview', *Pennyblack Music* (23 February 2013), https://pennyblackmusic.co.uk/Home/Details?Id=20894

3.2 A Year of Musical Renewal: The 1994 Festival Circuit

1994 was a busy year in the world of music. It saw the rise of West Coast pop punk and the continued chart success of hip hop, contrasted with the fall of grunge following the death of Nirvana frontman Kurt Cobain. It was a time when the Eagles reformed and Pink Floyd split up, when alternative bands like Nine Inch Nails and Beck moved into the mainstream and when Woodstock was rebooted to commemorate the festival's 25th anniversary. What few people seem to know, however, is that 1994 was also an extremely busy year in the world of Rory Gallagher. Far from the belief that he had slowed down or even stopped working altogether following the departure of Gerry McAvoy and Brendan O'Neill in 1991, Gallagher was still touring extensively and recording new material. And in 1994, despite increasingly poor health, Gallagher's pace of activities grew to pre-*Jinx* levels, with guest appearances on three sessions (see 1.5) and roughly eight months on the road.

Whether this gruelling work schedule was because Gallagher knew no different or had nothing else outside his life as a musician is not a question that this essay will attempt to answer. What it will seek to highlight, however, is just how remarkable it is that, in the year prior to his death, Gallagher was still pushing himself to deliver both emotionally and physically intense performances. In the summer of 1994 alone, the guitarist played an extensive festival circuit, taking in 14 cities within a one-month period. These shows are some of the most memorable of his career, demonstrating his ceaseless development not only as a guitarist but also as a storyteller of the blues. But like so many other events in the last decade of Gallagher's life, they have been unfairly disregarded in accounts of his career to date.

In a recent article, *Kerrang!* magazine described 1994 as a year of musical renewal,[1] and that is precisely what can be seen when watching many of Gallagher's 1994 festival appearances. Behind the scenes, he may have been hurting considerably, yet publicly, he rarely displayed that chink in his armour and still came across as the great musician he always was. This echoes comments made by Dónal Gallagher that his brother was often "in complete turmoil inside," but would "never cower down" and always insisted on performing or giving an interview.[2] In the same interview, Dónal cited the lyric "whatever you do don't show that hurt" from Gallagher's classic 1976 song 'Calling Card', describing this as the mantra by which his brother lived his life.

This essay takes a fresh look at Gallagher's 1994 festival appearances, shining a spotlight on two of his most significant performances: the Pistoia Blues Festival and the Montreux Jazz Festival. It seeks to reset the balance by moving the narrative beyond one simply centred around Gallagher's physical appearance and declining health, and instead directing attention to the quality of each performance and its significance as part of his body of live work. SDR3 radio presenter Stefan Siller notes that it was "quite risky"[3] to book Gallagher at this time, given his worsening health. Yet, as this chapter will show, Gallagher was still a man determined to give everything he had and do all he could to send his fans away with smiles on their faces.

Part 1: Pistoia Blues Festival

A rumour surfaced a long time ago that 'Blues Boy' — a deep cut by Thin Lizzy — was written about Rory Gallagher. The blues boy who could silence people with the sound of his guitar. While it has since come to light that frontman Phil Lynott, in fact, had BB King in mind when he wrote the lyrics, I still like to think that it is true because a blues boy is exactly how I have always seen Gallagher. I stress *boy* because, even as he grew older, Gallagher forever maintained a childlike excitement and curiosity for music, no more apparent than in the look of joy that overtook his face whenever he performed. And when I think of that youthful sense of wonder and infectious love of music that Gallagher had, my mind constantly drifts to his 1994 performance at the Pistoia Blues Festival.

The concert is full of snapshots that capture Gallagher in time as a sprightly child, not a man of 46 years old — and a gravely ill man of 46 years old at that. From his big, blue eyes full of emotion as he delivers the lyrics to 'I Wonder Who' to his cheeky schoolboy smile over his shoulder to bassist David Levy when things are really cooking during 'Tattoo'd Lady'. Or his silly dancing in 'Messin' with the Kid' and his little bounces after the guitar solo in 'La Bamba'. Right down to the way he tosses his harmonica across the stage to one of the road crew through to his sloppy attempts at Italian and Spanish — both acts followed by warm laughter.

It is funny then that so many people are all too keen to stress how much Gallagher appears to have aged in later years. Illness aside, it is almost as if he is expected to be some kind of Dorian Gray or Peter Pan who remained eternally young. Gallagher's age should not be marked by physical signs like the number of lines on his face, grey hairs on his head or pounds on the scales. Rather, it should be marked by his internal passion and enthusiasm to perform that shone like a beacon from his very soul. And by that token, it can be said that Gallagher had drunk from the Fountain of Youth. "[Rory was] an eternal teenager with fingers of fire," Breton musician Dan Ar Braz fondly states.[4]

Music is a powerful thing that has the ability to bring about complex physiological changes to the body. Indeed, when Gallagher slipped into a coma following his liver transplant in March 1995, it was the sound of Mark Feltham's harmonica-playing that had a "dramatic effect" on his body heat, colour and complexion, according to Dónal, and produced a temporary improvement in his condition.[5]

Although on a far lesser scale, at Pistoia 1994, Gallagher's transformation from the beginning to the end of the concert is truly palpable. His body language, posture and facial expression all physically alter as soon as his beloved Stratocaster is in his hands. He walks with a spring in his stride, a grin on his face. Offstage, he may have been "troubled" and "carried the weight of the world on his shoulders,"[6] but in those hours onstage, the weight was handed firmly back over to the mythical Titan Atlas. Save for the psoriasis on his arms and occasional breathlessness, Gallagher gives few hints to his illness here, of his inner anguish. A miraculous metamorphosis takes place thanks to the mysterious power of music.

Giancarlo Trombetti, a music journalist who was at Pistoia 1994, perhaps said it best. No matter what Gallagher looked like or his age in literal terms, he had the perpetual "passion and impetus of a 16-year-old."[7] He was a true *bambino* of the blues.

An Italian Affair

So, when did the *bambino* of the blues first come to the attention of Italy?

Although Gallagher's first visit to *il Bel Paese* was in 1972, his Italian fanbase had slowly developed throughout the late 1960s as Taste were regularly featured in the country's music press. This meant that, by the time Gallagher turned solo in 1971, there was huge momentum around him. As if to make up for lost time, Gallagher toured Italy twice in 1972—February and July—playing a host of small venues across major cities, including Brescia, Milan, Florence, Rome, Verona, Viareggio and Rimini. His concerts were warmly received by critics who marvelled at how such "great energy and virtuosity" could come from such a "small man."[8]

Fan memories of Gallagher's 1972 tour compiled in Fabio Rossi's *Rory Gallagher: Il Bluesman Bianco Con La Camicia a Quadri* are also highly positive. Giuseppe Ospici describes seeing Gallagher as being at the "concert of a friend" because of his honesty, passion and humility, while Dante Colavecchi believes his soul has been "shaken forever" by Gallagher's cry of "Well, did you ever…" at the start of 'Bullfrog Blues'.[9] Gallagher's Florence gig on 18 February was particularly memorable because of some unintentional acrobatics. Recalling the gig in a 1992 *Hot Press* interview, Gallagher stated that there was a hollow pit by the stage that he did not see and which he fell straight into as he was running. He immediately grabbed onto a metal bar and started "swinging from it like Tarzan,"[10] leading his Stratocaster to give off feedback. The Florentine crowd thought it was part of the act and went wild. His legend was cast that night.

Due to endless other touring commitments, it was ten years until Gallagher returned to Italy again, playing at Milan Rolling Stone and Bologna Music Show in 1982. Once more, press reviews were highly favourable, praising Gallagher's ability to produce "otherworldly sounds" from his Stratocaster and deliver a version of 'Nothing But the Devil' so powerful that it "would send a shiver down the spine of a dead man."[11] However, it was his next visit in 1984 to the Pistoia

Blues Festival, where he would really make his mark.

The Pistoia Blues Festival was established in July 1980 by Raffaele Barki and the Associazione Isola del Tonale (of which Barki was president at the time), with the support of both Pistoia City Council and the Tuscany Tourist Office. The inaugural Festival set the standard high with performances by Muddy Waters, Fats Domino, BB King, Alexis Korner and Dizzy Gillespie, which quickly established Pistoia as *the* place to be for blues lovers in Europe.

Gallagher was invited to the Festival's 1984 edition, along with Jimmy Page, Georgie Fame and Ginger Baker, to take part in an Alexis Korner tribute night. The 'Father of British Blues' had passed away in January and Pistoia's organisers wanted to arrange a special event in his honour. Gallagher had become good friends with Korner, the two of them once delighting German fans by plugging into a streetlight and playing skiffle and blues on the pavement together, so he willingly accepted the invitation. Pistoia 1984 was also significant because it was the first time that harmonicist Mark Feltham played with Gallagher. Feltham had been asked to come along by Dónal Gallagher "purely as a sideman,"[12] yet he went on to stay with Gallagher until 1995, playing a pivotal role in the band's later sound. From bootleg recordings of the Festival, Feltham's influence is immediately clear, his expertise on the harp enriching old classics like 'I Wonder Who' and 'Off the Handle'. Fan Mario Valentini remembers Pistoia 1984 fondly, particularly his encounter with Gallagher backstage who he found to be a "simple man, kind and friendly to everyone." During their conversation, Valentini asked Gallagher what he thought of Johnny Winter to which Gallagher replied that, "unlike him," Winter was "a true guitar hero." It was this humility that left a lasting impression on Valentini, even more so than Gallagher's music.[13]

"Mamma mia!"
There was some doubt over the future of the Pistoia Blues Festival when the 1984 edition was cut short due to financial problems. Luckily, the Festival was saved after being taken over by new management (Associazione Blues In and Giovanni Tafuro) and came back in 1985 with BB King as headliner. Throughout the rest of the 1980s, the Pistoia Blues Festival went from strength to strength, reaching a high point in 1988 with a guest list that included John Lee Hooker, Johnny Winter, Bo Diddley, Otis Rush and Louisiana Red. This was also the first year that the event was broadcasted on the Italian television channel *Videomusic*—a tradition maintained until the mid-1990s.

In 1994, the organisers decided to pull out all the stops to make the Pistoia Blues Festival the biggest and best edition to date. As it had been ten years since Gallagher first performed at the Festival, he was invited back to close the second evening. Joining him on the bill were John Mayall (celebrating 30 years in the music business) and Paul Rodgers with Neil Shon and Jason Bonham. While all performances usually took place in the city's main square—Piazza del Duomo—the 1994 edition spilled out into the town's Casermette district, with young artists and emerging bands taking to the streets and local bars.

Gallagher's return to Italy was much awaited by both music journalists and fans alike. An article from *La Repubblica* described him as "one of the great guitarists of English [sic] blues rock,"[14] making it unsurprising that he had been chosen as headliner. Umberto Berlenghini, a long-term fan of both Gallagher and Paul Rodgers, bought tickets as soon as he found out that his two idols were playing Pistoia. The big day could not come around quick enough for him, but when it did, he was so overcome with emotion that everything passed in a blur and he remembers very little of the actual performances. However, he does recall that Gallagher's audience was "adoring" and that Gallagher looked like he was "having fun" on stage.[15]

Gallagher lived up to the hype surrounding his return to Italy, delivering an impassioned two-hour set before a crowd of several thousand spectators that newspapers described as "superb."[16] "The audience practically fell silent as soon as he started playing," said *L'Unità* newspaper, "Everyone was enraptured by his way of delivering music and by his sincerity, something hard to find in the music business." For fan Franco Serena, seeing Gallagher at Pistoia 1994 was "the fulfilment of a dream" he had carried for twenty years. From his response, it is clear just how special the evening was for him:

> I had been to many concerts up until then, but I had never seen so many people come away with a smile on their faces and overjoyed by such an intense, hot and enthusiastic performance by an artist literally feeding off the audience and playing as if this were his last ever chance. Rory was physically on the stage, but he and his guitar emanated so much feeling, warmth, charisma that everyone present felt his heart beating as if he was playing individually for every one of us. The phrase that I heard repeated over and over by the crowd was 'Mamma mia!' An unforgettable memory that will be forever engrained in my brain and still today gives me shivers. I would have so liked to have met Rory and shook his hand, but it's like I did because I consider Rory to be one of my friends. He's been part of my family for a long time.[17]

Martino Palmisano also still remembers the emotions of the concert as if it were yesterday. According to Palmisano, watching Gallagher perform was "sweat, tears and goosebumps at full throttle," followed by "more tears" during the "devastating" encore. However, he believes that it is "useless to try and describe the feelings" because for those who were not there, it is impossible to understand just how incredible Gallagher was.[18] Luca Guiotto, a presenter for local Italian radio covering the Festival, also speaks positively of the concert. Despite being more of a heavy metal fan at the time, Guiotto appreciated "the energy and power that [Gallagher] unleashed on the public." He particularly recalls 'Out on the Western Plain' ("I was enchanted by the fluidity of his movements on the fretboard... I was beginning to fall in love") and with 'La Bamba' ("[he made] the square jump and dance at the feet of a genuine person"). Guiotto notes that Gallagher's health problems were evident in his appearance and lack of mobility on stage, yet the crowd "realised this [and] welcomed him with a renewed warmth."[19]

Given the absence of Pistoia 1994 in any previously published works on Gallagher, despite their claims to be a "testament to [Gallagher's] musical life" (Vignoles) and offer "the insightful biography that [Gallagher] deserves" (Connaughton),[20] these fan accounts are gold dust in helping to fill in the glaring gaps in the story of Gallagher's later years.

For those not present at Pistoia, it is still possible to get a sense of Gallagher's enduring power from the available video and audio bootlegs. The start of the concert reveals a subdued—even slightly tired—Gallagher, yet this changes by the time he reaches the guitar solo in the opener 'Continental Op'. From that point on, Gallagher transforms and is on fire for the rest of the concert, squeezing every last note out of his Stratocaster and preaching the blues as if his life depends on it. Gallagher himself said similar in a 1986 interview with French magazine *Hard Rock*: "Sometimes half an hour before the show, I feel like I'm 90 years old. I feel unable to even walk, but once on stage, I forget everything and I feel nothing."[21]

One of the high points of the evening comes early with a 12-minute rendition of 'I Wonder Who'. Here, Gallagher takes the listener on a rollercoaster of emotions, smiling as he places his hand on his hip and acts out the scene of his "little girl" walking on down the street. The song then takes a more sombre turn with his improvised, quasi-autobiographical lyrics about getting nervous and crying himself to sleep. The mood is lifted once again on the next line, however, with the humorous: "I think about divorcing you, honey, but even in Mexico the price ain't so cheap." Gallagher shows his mastery of the blues genre here, letting the song breathe as he hands the floor over to Frank Mead (who was filling in for Mark Feltham that evening) and John Cooke for harmonica and keyboard solos, respectively. He then follows this up with his own harmonica solo. As Gallagher rolls up his sleeves, we catch a glimpse of the painful psoriasis on his arms, serving as a fleeting visual reminder of his vulnerability, strangely juxtaposed with the sheer strength of his performance. The rest of the song is filled with a beautiful assortment of borrowed lyrics and weeping notes. There is everything from Bob Dylan's 'Just Like a Woman' to Buddy Guy's 'The First Time I Met the Blues', complemented by a stunning piece of closing slide guitar.

The concert proceeds with so many other memorable moments, from an intense solo in 'Tattoo'd Lady', which demonstrates the song's progression over its 21-year history, to an emotional version of 'Out on the Western Plain', which illuminates Gallagher's prowess on the acoustic guitar. Here, Gallagher rather poignantly sings "I've found you, Jesse" after almost 20 years of singing "Look out, Jesse."[22] The double encores of 'Messin' with the Kid' and 'La Bamba' are also true crowd-pleasers. Gallagher is in his element here as he teases the audience and laughs in his struggle with the Spanish lyrics. The interplay between Frank Mead on saxophone and Gallagher on rhythm guitar is so instinctive, each delicately balancing the other. The whole band look like they are having so much fun, making it the perfect feel-good end to a formidable concert.

Italian blues expert, Ernesto De Pascale, provided a short account of Gallagher's Pistoia 1994 performance on the June 2002 edition of his radio show *Il Popolo del Blues*. Echoing many of the testimonies above, De Pascale said that Gallagher gave a "rousing show" and that his music was just as good as when he last saw him play in 1972, even if he looked "tired and bloated."[23] A similar opinion was given by Silvano Martini, a long-term Gallagher fan who now works as a security guard at the Pistoia Blues Festival. On his music blog *Last Music Rebel*, Martini writes that Gallagher was "clearly fatigued" and "heavier" in 1994 than when he saw him in 1972 in Florence, but he "didn't spare himself on stage" and was "S-P-E-C-T-A-C-U-L-A-R."[24] He also notes that, despite the temperature being around 30°C, Gallagher dressed in a thick long-sleeved denim shirt and black leather jacket, perhaps in a bid to hide his body.

Behind the Curtain

When Gallagher left the stage at Pistoia and headed to his dressing room, the weight of the world seemed to pass back from Atlas to his shoulders once again. He was not happy with his performance and felt that he could have done better. Being the perfectionist that he was, Gallagher rarely came off stage satisfied, but these feelings of disappointment at himself seemed to worsen in his later years. Even if he would have preferred to be alone, Gallagher never refused to meet fans and Pistoia was no exception, where he obligingly welcomed them backstage.

Silvano Martini and Ernesto De Pascale were two of the fans who managed to meet Gallagher after the concert. Martini notes that when they entered the dressing room, they could see that Gallagher was "clearly upset." Nonetheless, he thanked the two men politely when they complimented him on his performance. They then presented Gallagher with a gift: a photo that they had taken of him when he performed at the Space Electronic Club in Florence in 1972. According to Martini, Gallagher inspected the photo for a while, thanked them and then smiled sadly. "The smile betrayed his embarrassment at seeing himself young and in perfect physical shape," Martini mused.[25] De Pascale gave an almost identical account of meeting Gallagher in his 2002 *Il Popolo del Blues* programme, explaining how Gallagher tried to "hide his physical pain, his sadness too" as he looked at the photo.[26] Although these memories are somewhat bittersweet, they demonstrate Gallagher's kindness and loyalty to his fans, even when he was not feeling his best.

Music journalist Giancarlo Trombetti also met Gallagher backstage at Pistoia, describing their meeting as a "long goodbye"[27] because he had spent part of the afternoon with Gallagher and his brother Dónal helping to arrange the television shoot and then returned throughout the evening to speak on and off to Gallagher about the blues. Trombetti had first seen Gallagher at his 1972 show in Viareggio, but it was eight years later at the Reading Festival when he met him for the first time. Trombetti approached Gallagher's trailer with several other journalists and, although the guitarist had just come off stage "half destroyed" and "dripping in sweat," he agreed to an interview. According to Trombetti, Gallagher went "above and beyond any request" by not only answering all questions, but expanding on topics as well. He remembers a particular moment when a German journalist spilt beer on his tape recorder and swore. To Trombetti's amazement, Gallagher waited patiently for the man to fix the recorder before continuing to speak— something that he describes as a "surprising gesture of courtesy."

Trombetti met Gallagher briefly once again in the mid-1980s, although he does not recall the encounter. He does, however, vividly remember their last meeting at Pistoia. Trombetti admits that he felt a "little shocked" when he first saw Gallagher, describing the Irishman's extra weight and swollen face as typical of someone with "serious health problems" who required "large doses of medication" to help. Just as before, Gallagher was very attentive and precise when answering Trombetti's questions. However, sometimes "his gaze became absent." Trombetti told Gallagher about their meeting at Reading Festival in 1980 and was surprised that not only did Gallagher recall it, but he even remembered the German who had spilt beer on his recorder. "I don't speak German very well," Gallagher told Trombetti, "But since I've often played in Germany, I remembered at least some of the bad words and, goodness, that man was saying really bad words!"

Trombetti had brought some records with him for Gallagher to sign. However, a strange premonition came over him that Gallagher "would pass away soon" and he decided not to ask him, worried of being like a "vulture." Reflecting on his encounters with Gallagher today, he describes him as a kind, respectful, sensitive and shy gentleman who "lived for the stage" and spent the other hours of his day thinking about music. Music journalist Stefano Tavernese, who was also backstage to secure an interview with Gallagher the next day at his hotel for *Chitarre* magazine, speaks with equally warm words about the occasion. He was astounded at how "on fire" Gallagher was on stage, considering his "questionable physical condition" and noted how, in their interview, Gallagher really came alive when he spoke about music.[28]

At the end of his set at Pistoia, Gallagher blew a kiss to the audience and called out *"ciao ciao bambinos."* This was goodbye, but it could have equally been hello, given the polysemy of the word in Italian. It was optimism and hopefulness rolled into one. Not so much "farewell" as "we'll meet again." But sadly, that was not to be, and Gallagher's second time at Pistoia would also be his last. However, he is still warmly loved in Italy and, since 2016, an annual tribute festival has been established in Bergamo to honour this kind-hearted, multi-talented *bambino* of the blues.

Part 2: Montreux Jazz Festival

> *"I was over the moon, thinking it would do Rory a lot of good. I was wrong. After that, he fell into a deep depression and wouldn't leave his room for four days."*[29]

These words from Dónal Gallagher describe the immediate events surrounding his brother's sensational performance at the Montreux Jazz Festival in 1994, which took place just ten days after the Pistoia Blues Festival. Gallagher had been a regular visitor to Montreux since the days of Taste in 1970 (see 2.2) and was invited back by organiser Claude Nobs for the sixth time in 1994, where he would feature at the top of the bill alongside Bob Dylan—one of his ultimate heroes.

Prior to Gallagher's set, Dylan called into the dressing room to talk to him. Watching them exchange stories was a moment that bassist David Levy told us that he felt "honoured" to witness and of which he still has "very clear" memories.[30] The two musicians' "great respect" for one another shone through as they spoke. Towards the end of their conversation, Dylan suggested that he and Gallagher should record a song together. Ever since first hearing *Live! in Europe*, Dylan had been impressed by Gallagher's music and had even planned at one point to record his own version of 'I Could've Had Religion'. Dónal was delighted at the prospect of collaboration, describing the opportunity as "manna from heaven"[31] as it could potentially raise Gallagher's profile again and help him out of the rut in which he found himself.

However, that evening after Gallagher left the stage in the Auditorium Stravinski, he suffered a depressive episode and locked himself in his hotel room, refusing to let anybody inside. According to Dónal, Claude Nobs was "going crazy"[32] because Gallagher's room was one of the best in the hotel and it was supposed to be taken over the following night by Quincy Jones. But try as they might, Gallagher would not emerge until four days later.

Just a week or so after Montreux when Gallagher was back in London in his room at the Conrad Hotel, he was still in a fragile condition. One evening, he received a phone call from his good friend Rudi Gerlach who found Gallagher in a "very terrible state." According to Gerlach, Gallagher answered the phone confusedly and told him, "Rudi, you've just saved my life." He explained that he was about to jump out of his hotel window when the phone rang and interrupted him. Gerlach describes how "heavy" his friend's words weighed on him, especially as he lived so far away in Cologne and was unable to just "take the next cab" and call in to check on Gallagher.[33] In other calls to Gerlach, Gallagher would talk further about his "precarious" health, explaining that he felt like "a corpse," was "suffering a bit of damage," feeling "angst" and everything was getting "too much" for him. However, at the same time, he also expressed his guilt and obligation as an "Irish Catholic" to keep going for the sake of his fans.[34]

While Gallagher had always suffered from stagefright, this worsened throughout his career and, by the 1990s, his crisis of confidence led him to doubt that anybody would still want to see him perform. As the Montreux Jazz Festival approached, Gallagher was particularly nervous, uncertain of how the crowd would react to him nine years on from his last appearance there in 1985. During this time, folk musician Martin Carthy was a great source of comfort. Gallagher had always been an admirer of Carthy's music and took the opportunity whenever he could to see him play live. Speaking on *The Rory Gallagher Story* radio documentary in 2005, Carthy recounted how Gallagher had even managed to get himself thrown out of one of his concerts at the Troubadour once for "cheering too loudly."[35] Leading up to Gallagher's Montreux 1994 performance, Carthy (who was on tour at the time) would buy a phone card wherever he was and call Gallagher from the train station, spending hours trying to ease his worries and reassure him that everything would go okay. As he recounted in the *Ghost Blues* (2010) documentary:

> He was really jumpy about [Montreux]. I phoned him up and sure enough he was as jumpy as hell. 'I'm not sure if I can do this'. Of course you can. You've done it before. Just lay the table. Go back and lay the table and decide what you are going to go and sing and do that, and people who turn up will actually want to see you. They're not there to shoot you down. They're there because they love you. You are Rory Gallagher. They know your albums, they know what you can do and they'll be really excited that you are coming to Switzerland, so you have to tell yourself, 'What's the problem?'

A Thin Beam of Magic Light

These stories paint a rather bleak picture of life for Gallagher in July 1994. A life full of self-doubt, anxiety and depression. However, to see Gallagher at Montreux, it is hard to believe that it could be the same person. Whatever crisis he was going through offstage, a "thin beam of magic light"—as he sang in 1978's 'Shadow Play'—always shone through onstage. And that light gleams particularly bright in the portion of the set with American banjo virtuoso Béla Fleck.

Gallagher is beaming throughout their ten-minute impromptu jam session, even throwing his head back in uncontrollable laughter at one point. He is clearly enjoying every minute of performing with Fleck, the two playing off one another in a cordial musical duel that goes from 'Amazing Grace' into 'Walkin' Blues' and 'Blue Moon of Kentucky'. The latter was a song choice that surprised Dónal as he had never heard his brother perform it before that night. Clearly caught in the moment, Gallagher slipped in the bluegrass classic and Fleck expertly responds.

It is rather unbelievable that Gallagher and Fleck had never even met before. Gallagher had been, in fact, expecting Bob Dylan to walk out, but when he did not appear, Fleck was quite literally "grabbed by the scruff of the neck and pushed out onto stage"[36] by the promoter. Despite not knowing Gallagher's music "in the slightest," Fleck said that he became "an instant fan"[37] as soon as the guitarist started playing. Gallagher's acoustic guitar and Fleck's banjo meld perfectly together, with Gallagher constantly alternating between lead and rhythm, happy to let Fleck share his moment in the spotlight. Every now and then, he cries out an unrestrained "YEAH!" truly immersed in the magic of their performance, and even breaks into a playful Irish jig during Mark Feltham's harmonica solo.

It is a fine example of music as Gallagher's "salvation,"[38] as Johnny Marr of the Smiths has often said. In musician Mícheál Ó Súilleabháin's view, Gallagher's music always appeared to offer "a necessary healing that he constantly pursued."[39] And it is comforting to know not only that the guitarist had this light in his life to restore him, even at his darkest times, but that he so selflessly shared and reflected that light back on his fans, allowing them to bask in its warmth and splendour.

Speaking to Dónal in June 2023 about 'Amazing Grace', he noted how "the musically plaintiff song of repentance slides into the 'gospel blues' cannon" of which his brother was always so fond. Dónal also believes that the song was influenced by the "acute difficult health times" that Gallagher was going through at this stage of his life. The spiritual hymn, thus, took on a broader meaning for him as a "life-line link to healing." While for the original composer John Newton, 'Amazing Grace' was about the greed of slavery, for Gallagher, it was about healing from the physical and mental health issues that plagued him, and he saw it as a "soothing 'blues prayer' for peace of mind."[40]

Recovering the Pearl of the Swiss Riviera

Montreux is often described as the "pearl of the Swiss Riviera" for its glorious sunshine and picturesque views across Lake Geneva, but its nickname could equally come from Gallagher's many performances in the town, which were always the highlight of its annual jazz festival. Gallagher himself can be viewed as the rare pearl that offered priceless joy to the spectators who gathered to see him play. However, to date, accounts of this rare pearl's appearances at Montreux have not been fair, overwhelmingly centred on the 1970s and only mentioning his 1994 performance in the context of his poor psychological state.[41]

Gallagher's Montreux 1994 concert is one of the few concerts from the final decade of his life to have had an official release. In a 2012 interview for the *Shadowplays* website, Daniel Gallagher stated that he chose to include the full 1994 show on the *Rory Gallagher: Live at Montreux* (2006) DVD boxset because he felt that Gallagher's later performances had not been documented. According to Daniel, his uncle was not "as vibrant looking as *Irish Tour*," but his "playing and spirit were really captivating."[42] Unfortunately, several press reviews critiqued the decision to include the full 1994 show, Michael Heatley of *Record Collector* describing it as "understandably less impressive" than the rest of the collection, given that it took place just one year before Gallagher died.[43]

The idea that Gallagher's 1994 performance has less value than his other appearances at the Montreux Jazz Festival has also not been helped by the fact that the *Live at Montreux* CD (released in 2006) does not contain a single song from 1994. Instead, it features two from 1975, three from 1977, five from 1979 and two from 1985, which has further fed into the young/healthy/good versus old/unhealthy/bad dichotomy. In the aforementioned *Record Collector* review, Heatley praised Daniel Gallagher for "sensibly" choosing nothing from the 1994 concert for the CD release.[44]

While the liner notes by Chris Welch for the original DVD and accompanying CD release were generally positive, the updated notes by Pierre Perrone for the 2013 rerelease leave a lot to be desired as far as Gallagher's 1994 appearance is concerned. Perrone gives positive accounts of Gallagher's 1975, 1977, 1979 and 1985 Montreux performances, but then cruelly describes 1994 as "bringing home how much the years of alcohol and prescription medication abuse had taken their toll on Gallagher." Perrone goes on to say that *"thankfully* [our emphasis], the bonus acoustic tracks from 1975, 1977 and 1985 restore the blue-collar musician to his glory years when few white bluesmen could touch him." These remarks form an opinion about Gallagher's music largely based on the way he looks, brushing aside the 1994 performance as if it is less important than those that came before simply because the guitarist was older, heavier and in poor health. Moreover, claiming that the 1970s were Gallagher's "glory years" discredits the superior level of musicianship he had reached by this later stage of his career and continues to perpetuate the 'fall' narrative about his life.

It is comments such as Heatley's and Perrone's that seem to miss the point when viewing Gallagher's later outputs. If whether Gallagher remains an impressive musician or not is going to be defined simply by comparing the way he looked in the 1970s with the 1990s or the way he used to leap all over the stage versus his later more sedate movements, then it is to fight a losing battle. Gallagher in 1994 may not be the same performer that he once was, but that has nothing to do with illness or age and all to do with evolution as a musician. His career was one of continual musical development, a quest for perfection and personal fulfilment, not one that ground to a halt after *Jinx* and saw no further progression. This is something that Mark Feltham was keen to address in our interview: "[Rory] was always good. In fact, I think he just got better. Certainly from '84 when I joined [...] He was just starting his career when he died really."[45]

Writing with the knowledge that Gallagher would pass away less than one year later, it is all too easy to tag Montreux 1994 as his *last* appearance and, therefore, not as good as earlier appearances at the Festival, but this is a weak argument. Had Gallagher lived, he would no doubt have gone on to headline many more Montreux Jazz Festivals throughout his career and 1994 would just be considered as one more great performance in a long line of great Gallagher performances. But instead, it gets sadly pushed to the margins of Gallagher's story and cast in a negative light. The overwhelming focus on his appearance—because most reviews and comments about this concert tend to be related to his *appearance* rather than his *music*—overshadows and detracts from some of the strongest 90 minutes in his career.

One of the rare music journalists who seems to understand this is Shawn Perry of *Vintage Rock*. When reviewing the *Live at Montreux* boxset, Perry singles out the 1994 concert as a particular highlight and says that, along with the *Irish Tour '74* documentary film, it best captures what it is like to see Gallagher live. Perry also gives a special mention to both the *Irish Tour '74* and *Fresh Evidence* albums to "fully assess" Gallagher's talent as a musician.[46] Too often, *Irish Tour '74* is held up as 'peak' Gallagher and is the benchmark to which everything else is compared, but Gallagher's live performances can only be fully appreciated by viewing them on a continuum rather than as essentialist demarcations by age, weight, health or other meaningless characteristics. A continuum allows for subtle differences and developments in Gallagher's musicianship across his career, recognising that he carried many of the things forward from *Irish Tour '74*, yet constantly improved upon them through his years of experience. Mark Feltham concurs, acknowledging that *Irish Tour '74* is an iconic album and that there will always be fans who see the classic four-piece with Rod De'Ath and Lou Martin as their favourite era, but Gallagher was doing "just as magical things" in the early 1990s and that he was "at the peak of his abilities" when he passed away. It is only right then that *Irish Tour '74* and Montreux 1994 should be both equally appreciated and introduced to new fans as, together, they provide a well-rounded view of the consummate musician that Gallagher always was.

Man on Fire
Wistful wizardry is perhaps the best way to describe Gallagher at Montreux 1994. Here, we see a man who is noticeably less tired than at Pistoia ten days earlier, yet seemingly more melancholic, both factors resulting in a highly emotional performance that encapsulates his talent as a sincere, exhilarating and multi-faceted musician. For bassist David Levy, Montreux is his favourite performance with Gallagher, recalling the guitarist as "on fire" and putting on a "really good show."

These thoughts were echoed by fan Marlène Rivet who was in the Auditorium Stravinski that evening in 1994. Rivet was an established member of the Swiss Rory Gallagher fan club and had seen Gallagher in concert around 20 times, meeting him on many occasions throughout the 1970s and 1980s (Gallagher even sent her a congratulatory card when she got married in 1986 to a French member of the fan club!). According to Rivet, despite the guitarist's health problems, his "pleasure and willingness to still give everything he had to his audience" at the Montreux concert was apparent from the moment that he walked out on stage.[47]

Alongside Rivet at the concert were many other long-term fans who had followed Gallagher since the late 1960s and travelled from Switzerland, Holland, Germany, France and Belgium to be at the Festival. Together, they all rooted for Gallagher, staying right until the end of his performance and enthusiastically cheering him on, even when some spectators left early. For Rivet, Gallagher's "humility, kindness and simplicity" meant that he was always well received at Montreux and were key reasons why festival organiser Claude Nobs felt such affection for him.

Writing in the liner notes for the *Rory Gallagher: Live at Montreux* CD (2006), Chris Welch notes that the Gallagher of 1994 was "fuller faced" and had a "more sombre dress-sense," but fundamentally, "*the guitar remained the same*" [our emphasis]. With a cry of "Let's go to work!" Gallagher hits the stage, driving his band into a fiery rendition of 'Continental Op', followed by 'Moonchild'.

'Moonchild' was a song that Gallagher had also performed at earlier Montreux appearances in 1979 and 1985, but this 1994 version is particularly striking, with the guitarist drawing on his tried-and-tested repertoire of unique techniques, such as string-pulling and bending behind the nut for tremolo effect. Here, his high energy is conveyed not by running around the stage like he did in earlier performances of the song, but simply by fuelling every note and every word with great passion and intensity. It is a refreshing contrast to the 'shredding' style of guitar playing that was popular at that time and shows the subtle vitality of a wise bluesmaster who knows that slow and steady wins the race.

Gallagher always had an astonishing ability to captivate the audience by constantly shifting the pace of his performances and playing around with tempo, often within the same song. By 1994, he had fully perfected this art. This is attested by the Montreux version of 'Tattoo'd Lady', where the slow Hispano-Celtic opening abruptly cuts into the song's familiar up-tempo chords or 'Ghost Blues' later in the set, where Gallagher skilfully lowers the volume to practically zero at the end of his own solo, before Newman's rumbling drums start up, setting the whole band in motion once again for a climactic finish. 'Off the Handle' also showcases this finesse with Gallagher's raunchy blues and rough vocals giving way to an almost spoken delivery of the lines, "Well, my cat won't scratch or show its claws. It just prowls around the house all day," accompanied by actions and screeching sound effects courtesy of his trusty Stratocaster. 'The Loop', on the other hand, offers an opportunity for Gallagher to display his aptitude as a bandleader, subtly directing each member with just a head nod or hand gesture, until they come together with "all the power that [they] could command."[48]

Welch believes that the "true emotional core" of Gallagher can be found in his acoustic performances, which is certainly evidenced by the Montreux version of 'She Moved Thro' the Fair/Out on the Western Plain' with its exquisite fretwork, fingerpicking and lyrical delivery. However, the emotion of Gallagher's slow blues is equally noteworthy, offering him a rare opportunity to bare his soul. There are perhaps no finer examples of this than 'I Wonder Who' and 'I Could've Had Religion'. Gallagher played both songs throughout his career, yet they subtly evolved over time in response to his own life experiences. In a 1991 interview with *BURNN!* magazine, Gallagher claimed that a sense of "melancholy" or "tragedy" was needed to play the blues well.[49] It is this sense of melancholy that makes his delivery of the two songs at Montreux 1994 particularly authentic and powerful. From his lyrical improvisations to the weeping of his guitar, the sense of catharsis that Gallagher finds in playing the songs is evident, enabling him to articulate his inner turmoil in ways that he struggled to do in everyday life. His choice of lyrics in 'I Could've Had Religion' is particularly perturbing when viewed retrospectively, Gallagher stating how he "was sick" but "got cured" and asking for a "nurse" to "take away [his] pain" as he "can't take it" anymore and is "gonna have to pray." Although it can admittedly be difficult to watch Gallagher—usually such a reserved man—weaving his pain into his music, the result is stunning.

Montreux comes to a thundering end with two encores: the evergreen 'Messin' with the Kid' and a cover of Muddy Waters' 'I'm Ready', where Gallagher and his band are joined by both Béla Fleck and Claude Nobs. This version of 'I'm Ready' is superior (and far less chaotic) to the version performed at the 1982 *Rockpalast* jam session, which saw the stage flooded with a dozen or so musicians, including Eric Burden and David Lindley. The harmonica exchanges between Feltham and Nobs are particularly enchanting, as is the opportunity to hear Gallagher and Fleck trade licks again.

As Gallagher takes his curtain call, he looks truly overwhelmed by the crowd's standing ovation. In the *Ghost Blues* (2010) documentary, Martin Carthy recalls speaking to Gallagher later about the concert and him being "slightly perplexed" that the Swiss audience had responded so warmly and still wanted to see him perform. "We'll see you again... hopefully... sometime soon," Gallagher says hesitantly to the crowd. Although he sadly never did return to Montreux, he did play in Switzerland for a final time one month later at the Thun Open Air Festival.

When Gallagher died in June 1995, Claude Nobs declared that "rock and blues in Montreux would never be the same."[50]

He was right.

Almost thirty years later, the absence of Gallagher is still firmly felt at the festival.

Part 3: "Whatever you do, don't show that hurt..."

After a short period of rest, Gallagher's festival commitments resumed in August, with appearances in Germany, France, Switzerland and Belgium. Like Pistoia and Montreux, there was a marked contrast between Gallagher's dynamism onstage and his low spirits offstage, although there were times when the lines began to blur between the two.

On a high point was the Langenau Nau-Rock Open Air Festival in Germany, where press reports described Gallagher as "the star of the evening [who] fascinates just as much as he did twenty years ago."[51] According to *Schwäbische Zeitung*, Gallagher acquired many new young fans in the audience, leaving no doubt that there is still a place for him on the current music scene and that "the time is ripe" for a resurgence in his career.[52] Similarly positive reviews came from the *Festival de la Foire aux Vins d'Alsace* where, despite "a few wrinkles," Gallagher delivered a "breathtaking" performance full of "energy, mastery and feeling."[53] The guitarist was also still capable of drawing in large crowds, his performance at the *Festival Interceltique de Lorient* (see 4.6) attended by 4,500 people—a record-breaking figure at that time for the Kervaric Sports Palace.[54]

By contrast, Gallagher's show at the SDR3 Festival in Stuttgart two weeks later was weighed down with lethargy and musical malaise. There are moments of mental distraction, almost as if he is caught up in the rush of the live experience. He can also be seen frequently clenching and unclenching his hands between songs—a sign of the pain and numbness that he is reported to have experienced in his extremities towards the end of his life. Gallagher's acoustic set, which comprises a medley of Leadbelly's 'Out on the Western Plain' and the Irish traditional 'Dan O'Hara', is the strongest part of the concert. Here, he seems to find the 'feel' of the music quicker and easier than in the electric portion of the set, the transitions effortless in order to create a melancholic nostalgia. According to SDR3 moderator Stefan Siller, Gallagher had been due to participate in a two-hour live interview prior to his performance, but this was cancelled.

A glimpse into Gallagher's vulnerabilities is offered by Patrick Kerihuel, who volunteered at the *Festival Interceltique de Lorient* between 1973 and 2020. Speaking to the Breton newspaper *Le Télégramme* in 2010, Kerihuel shared how Dónal "demanded that there should be no one between the stage and backstage" when his brother performed. Furthermore, rather revealingly, he explained how Gallagher "had to be carried to the stage [...] played for the two hours flat out [then] had to be carried when he came off."[55] Stefan Siller shared a similar story with us when talking about Gallagher's SDR3 Festival appearance, adding how the guitarist injected so much passion into his performance that he played until his fingers were "literally sore [and] bleeding." Mark Feltham also notes how Gallagher played so hard in his later concerts that his fingers and the guitar's scratchplate "would be covered in blood."[56]

Gallagher's bleeding hand at Stuttgart is also the result of punching the microphone stand during the first song due to his dissatisfaction with the volume. While biographer Julian Vignoles takes Gallagher's action as a sign that he was "clearly struggling,"[57] there are, in fact, multiple documented occasions throughout the guitarist's career when he frustratedly "lashed out" at a microphone stand.[58] According to journalist Brian Harrigan who witnessed such action at Gallagher's 1977 Hammersmith Odeon concert, this turned the guitarist into a "new man" and brought a higher level of energy to his performance that sustained throughout the set.[59] Framing Gallagher's action as "completely out of character"[60] at Stuttgart, therefore, overstates its significance and casts a cloud over the whole performance.

For those who met Gallagher during this time, they admit that his fragility was apparent, although he remained his courteous and affable self. Fan Joël Winkin, who was at the 1994 Geel House Rock Festival, recalls a rather restrained Gallagher performance, but notes that there were some particular highlights, including an emotional rendition of 'Mean Disposition'. Winkin spoke to Dónal after the concert and remembers him being quite "disillusioned" and expressing concern about his brother's wellbeing. Gallagher had returned to his dressing room and was not feeling well enough to meet fans. After some coaxing from Dónal, he finally emerged but, in Winkin's view, looked ill and sounded "really despondent and hopeless." However, then a "miracle" occurred. Belgian fan Ronny De Craemer passed Gallagher a Big Bill Broonzy record, which the guitarist inspected admiringly. When Gallagher tried to give it back, De Craemer told him that it was a present. According to Winkin, Gallagher was deeply overwhelmed and his mood instantly lifted:

> His face completely changed, illuminated by a joyful smile like a child in the presence of Father Christmas. 'It's for me? It's a gift?' As if he couldn't believe it: that his fans still loved him! He was literally transfigured for the rest of the meeting.

Then, in the next moment, Frankie Miller—who had also been playing at the festival—appeared in the dressing room. He and Gallagher started improvising a skit together, impersonating two prisoners meeting again after a successful jailbreak (in reference to the 1981 film *A Sense of Freedom*, for which they composed the soundtrack). Miller's cheerful presence put Gallagher "back into a good mood" and, for the rest of the evening, he spoke warmly to fans.

Nathalie Simon, a young photographer who was working at the *Festival Interceltique de Lorient* at the time, also witnessed Gallagher's complexities firsthand. Due to insecurities over his appearance, the guitarist had insisted that there would be no cameras at the show. However, this did not stop an array of photographers and journalists from gathering in the hallway, waiting for him to leave his dressing room. As Gallagher later headed towards the stage, he spotted Simon. Sensing that she was starting out on her career path, he told Dónal that she was the only one who could photograph him; all the other photographers were "furious" as they were "pushed back to the hall." Although Simon had just "twenty seconds" to react, her photographs offer a poignant window into Gallagher's soul. They candidly capture the portrait of a man who has lost his smile, is overwhelmingly exhausted and haunted with sadness—such a contrast to the man he became when he hit the stage. Despite his evident ill health, Gallagher took the time to exchange "some kind words of support" with Simon, "encourage" her and listen attentively. Speaking to us in April 2022, she describes the moment as "the most incredible highlight" of her career and has kept Gallagher's advice "preciously" in her memory ever since.[61]

Last Man Standing

1994 was one of Gallagher's busiest summers in years, with festival appearances from 2 July right through to 21 August across Europe. As demonstrated throughout this chapter, on the whole, Gallagher's sets were well received by both fans and critics, despite concerns over his physical appearance and general wellbeing. Watching Gallagher's 1994 performances is to see a man clearly still in love with what he does, but that is not to say that it always came easy for him at this stage in his career. While Gallagher may have lived by the mantra "whatever you do, don't show that hurt," it seemed to become increasingly difficult for him to do so when in the public eye.

What significantly helped and lifted at these moments of weakness was the support of Gallagher's band. Bassist David Levy and drummer Richard Newman provided a solid and consistent foundation, while harmonicist Mark Feltham was always one step ahead, looking out for his close friend and quickly reacting with his instrument to fill in any wobbles. Notwithstanding his challenges at times, Gallagher continued to showcase intuitive leadership skills throughout these concerts, directing solos or signalling the end with a wave of his hand, to which the band immediately responded—a sign of their well-rehearsed and coherent union. Gallagher's lyrical improvisation and soloing were also particularly well developed at this time, often tinged with wistfulness given his personal circumstances, yet with light added to the shade of his blues by the trusty Feltham on harmonica or keyboardist John Cooke. His slow blues and acoustic numbers also stand out as key examples of how he was able to channel his deep unhappiness on a personal level into emotional renditions that personify the genre.

Speaking to the European public service channel ARTÉ in July 1994, a weary Gallagher confessed, "I'm not happy as a person, but I'm happy as a musician." The guitarist lived, breathed and embodied music, perhaps to his detriment, but that is what—rightly or wrongly—made him so good at what he did right until the very end. In 1994, he may not have had the same levels of stamina and energy as 1974, he may not have been able to flick that 'on' switch as easily as he could before, but his musicianship and craft were arguably stronger than ever. And most importantly, he never lost his passion, emotion and *feel*. In an interview for the *Berner Agenda* conducted shortly before Montreux 1994, Gallagher was asked why he decided to play the blues and not another genre of music. His answer was simple: "The blues decided for me."[62] For Gallagher, blues was a "way of life," a chance to express his "angst" and "look the devil and [himself] in the eye." It was those characteristics that enabled him to push through the pain and channel his inner torment in a beautifully haunting way.

He stands alone in that regard.

LAO and RM

Footnotes

1 Stevie Chick, 'How 1994 Changed Rock Music Forever', *Kerrang!* (2 July 2021), https://www.kerrang.com/how-1994-changed-rock-music-forever
2 See: https://rory-gallagher.forumactif.org/t160-calling-card-calling-card
3 Interview with Stefan Siller, 1 August 2022. All subsequent quotes from Siller come from the same interview.
4 Alexandre Fillon, 'Dan Ar Braz, l'héritage du Celte', *Le Figaro* (9 March 2007), https://www.lefigaro.fr/lefigaromagazine/2007/03/09/01006-20070309ARTMAG90388-l_heritage_du_celte.php
5 Dan Muise, *Gallagher, Marriott, Derringer & Trower* (Milwaukee: Hal Leonard Corporation, 2002), 76.
6 Richard Fitzpatrick, 'From Che Guevara to Thin Lizzy: Jim FitzPatrick's 10 greatest hits', *Irish Examiner* (6 May 2021), https://www.irishexaminer.com/lifestyle/artsandculture/arid-40282277.html
7 Giancarlo Trombetti, 'Un brutto giorno per il blues' (4 August 2020), *Rock Around the Blog*, https://www.rockaroundtheblog.it/ricordo-di-rory-gallagher/
8 Review by Bruno Casini (18 February 1972), reproduced in Fabio Rossi, *Rory Gallagher: Rory Gallagher - Il bluesman bianco con la camicia a quadri* (Genoa: Officina di Hank, 2021), 107.
9 Ibid., 107-112.
10 Liam Fay, 'Tangled Up in Blues', *Hot Press* (July 1992), http://www.roryon.com/Tangled.html.
11 Review no longer available online, but copied in comments section of the Bologna 1982 bootleg on YouTube: https://www.youtube.com/watch?v=BEG5BT5CLFQ
12 Mark Feltham interview with Shiv Cariappa (13 September 1998), published originally in fanzine *Stagestruck*, http://www.roryon.com/mark20.html
13 Rossi, *Rory Gallagher*, 113.

Part 3 - A Year of Musical Renewal

14 Ernesto Assante, 'Sua Altezza la música del diavolo', *La Repubblica* (21 June 1994), https://ricerca.repubblica.it/repubblica/archivio/repubblica/1994/06/21/sua-altezza-la-musica-del-diavolo.html
15 Interview with Umberto Berlenghini, 26 April 2022.
16 Wolfango Tedeschi, 'Il guru del funk incendia Pistoia', *L'Unità* (5 July 1994), n.p.
17 Rossi, *Rory Gallagher*, 113-115.
18 Ibid.
19 Interview with Luca Guiotto, 22 August 2023.
20 See blurbs of Marcus Connaughton, *Rory Gallagher: His Life and Times* (London: Collins, 2012) or Julian Vignoles, *Rory Gallagher: The Man Behind the Guitar* (London: Collins, 2018).
21 Jean-Pierre Sabouret, 'Rory Gallagher', *Hard Rock* (July 1986), https://rewritingrory.co.uk/2022/06/05/hard-rock-july-1986-1-article/
22 My thanks to Jody Buckley-Coogan for drawing my attention to this.
23 Ernesto Di Pascale, 'Seventies Recollection – Rory Gallagher', *Il Popolo del Blues* (16 June 2002), http://www.roryon.com/ernesto234.html
24 Silvano Martini, 'RORY GALLAGHER-Viareggio 1972-Pistoia 1994', *Last Music Rebel* (17 April 2010), https://lastmusicrebel.blogspot.com/2010/04/rory-gallagher-viareggio-1972-pistoia.html
25 Martini, 'RORY GALLAGHER...'
26 Di Pascale, 'Seventies Recollection...'
27 Trombetti, 'Un brutto giorno per il blues'.
28 Stefano Tavernese, 'Rory Gallagher and the Irish Blues', *Chitarre* (August 1994), n.p.
29 'ITW de Donal Gallagher – Une affaire de famille', *Paris Move* (May 2011), https://www.paris-move.com/portrait/itw-de-donal-gallagher-une-affaire-de-famille/
30 Interview with David Levy, 22 February 2024. All subsequent quotes from Levy come from the same interview.
31 'Rory Gallagher', *Record Collector* (11 May 2018), https://recordcollectormag.com/articles/rory-gallagher
32 'ITW de Donal Gallagher...'
33 Muise, *Gallagher, Marriott, Derringer & Trower*, 69.
34 Ibid., 80.
35 'The Rory Gallagher Story (Audio Broadcast)', https://www.youtube.com/watch?v=ovFQu3vF5n0
36 Nicki French Davis, 'Banjo Great Rekindles his Passion for Trad', *Irish Examiner* (23 January 2012), https://www.irishexaminer.com/opinion/commentanalysis/arid-20181057.html
37 Tom Macintosh, 'Rory Gallagher - His Marvellous Acoustic Styles', *Guitars Exchange*, https://guitarsexchange.com/en/unplugged/690/rory-gallagher-his-marvelous-acoustic-styles/
38 'The Rory Gallagher Story...'
39 'Rory Gallagher: Tributes from famous friends', *Hot Press* (December 1995), https://www.hotpress.com/music/rory-gallagher-tributes-from-famous-friends-14356545
40 Email exchange with Dónal Gallagher, 22 June 2023.
41 See, for example, Vignoles, *Rory Gallagher* and the *Ghost Blues* (2010) documentary.
42 'Riding the Crest of the Rory Wave: An Interview with Daniel Gallagher', *Shadowplays* (18 February 2012), http://shadowplays.com/blog/?page_id=2234
43 Michael Heatley, 'Live at Montreux 1975-94 - Rory Gallagher' (22 May 2013), *Record Collector*, https://recordcollectormag.com/reviews/dvd/live-at-montreux-1975-94
44 Ibid.
45 Interview with Mark Feltham, 19 October 2023. All subsequent quotes from Feltham come from the same interview.
46 Shawn Perry, 'Rory Gallagher - Live at Montreux', *Vintage Rock* (2013), https://vintagerock.com/rory-gallagher-live-at-montreux/
47 Interview with Marlène Rivet, 24 October 2023.
48 Chris Welch in the liner notes to *Rory Gallagher: Live at Montreux* DVD (2006).
49 Masanori Ito, '"Whether I'm asleep or awake, I am always thinking of the blues"', *BURRN!* (May 1991), https://rewritingrory.co.uk/2022/06/27/burrn-may-1991/
50 Cited in the liner notes to *Rory Gallagher: Live at Montreux* DVD (2006).
51 Pierre LaQua, 'Brillante Bluesballaden verzaubern', *Neu Ulmer Zeitung* (8 August 1994), n.p.
52 'Ganz der ungezähmte Blues', *Schwäbische Zeitung*, 8 August 1994, n.p.
53 Newspaper clipping uploaded to https://www.flickr.com/photos/philippe_haumesser/3080139008
54 Françoise Rossi, 'Rory Gallagher: bâti sur du rock', *Ouest-France* (12 August 1994), 14.
55 'Patrick Kerihuel: Le dernier concert de Rory Gallagher', *Le Télégramme* (10 June 2010), https://www.letelegramme.fr/morbihan/lorient-56100/patrick-kerihuel-le-dernier-concert-de-rory-gallagher-967049.php
56 Muise, *Gallagher, Marriott, Derringer & Trower*, 81.
57 Vignoles, *Rory Gallagher*, 193.
58 Brian Harrigan, 'Rory's Rocking Rave-Up', *Melody Maker* (29 January 1977), https://www.roryon.com/raveup218.html
59 Ibid.
60 Vignoles, *Rory Gallagher*, 193.
61 Interview with Nathalie Simon, 14 June 2022.
62 Damian Bugmann, 'Blues ist eine Lebenshaltung', (1 July 1994), *Berner Agenda*, https://rewritingrory.co.uk/2022/07/01/berner-agenda-july-1994/

3.3 Just Remember the Good Things: The Final Tour (1995)

In January 1975, Gallagher stayed at the Rotterdam Hilton in the Netherlands over a period of three days for an extended jam with the Rolling Stones, often thought to be an audition to replace guitarist Mick Taylor. This "perhaps over-celebrated[1] episode, as termed by Julian Vignoles, has been associated with the 'high' in Gallagher's historical narrative, with critics theorising over time how the Irishman "could have single-handedly revived [the Rolling Stones'] creative spark" in the mid-1970s.[2]

In contrast, Gallagher's appearance at the Nighttown club in Rotterdam exactly two decades later has epitomised his 'fall'—quite literally, "he even collapsed onstage [in Rotterdam]"—as the "demon drink" supposedly "got the better" of his life.[3] The guitarist's 'collapse' has unfortunately dampened what would become his final concert and, in recent years, has been framed as Gallagher "literally [playing] until he dropped," as written on the Estate-approved official website. Among the fan community and journalists, Gallagher's reputation as a performer in his later years has been sullied by the conflicting (and often unclear) reports surrounding the evening in Rotterdam.[4]

When planning out this book, we often debated on the inclusion of this chapter and, if included, what would the purpose be? Occasionally, our opinion veered towards discarding the idea—if, indeed, there even *was* an idea to share. Nevertheless, we could not claim to write a book about the final decade of Gallagher's life without including *the* final year—no matter how brief. We do not write this chapter to put Gallagher's fragile wellbeing on a pedestal, dissect the contents and critique. We do not present our research as a disrespectful gesture towards a man clearly plummeting deeper into the murky gulf of depression. We simply present the *stories* and, as best possible, the *facts* of Rory Gallagher on his short Dutch tour in 1995. As we gathered research for this chapter, we came across multiple versions of Gallagher's 'collapse' in Rotterdam, ultimately challenging our perceptions of how the concert (and the tour overall) unfolded. As such, we hope the reader can be guided by our balanced approach to question the many speculations associated with Gallagher's final tour.

Picking up from 3.2, we begin with a general overview of Gallagher's touring schedule across Europe from October-December 1994, which eventually led to his concert dates in the Netherlands the following year. From there, the chapter winds through the tour using first-hand accounts from fans and newspaper reviews, as well as Gallagher's final interview. Through our lengthy and detailed interview with chauffeur Toine van Berlo, we track Gallagher's day-to-day movements from Rotterdam on 10 January to his return to London three days later. In our concluding statements, we evaluate what possible outcomes laid ahead in Gallagher's future had he lived on, supported by our conversations with band members Mark Feltham and David Levy.

"Force and fury":
Gallagher's 1994 European Tour Continued

Gallagher focused on France for his 1994 autumn European tour, with various dates interspersed throughout October. On 16 October, he played the Olympia concert hall in Paris for the final time—coincidentally, the same venue he debuted as a solo act with Gerry McAvoy and Wilgar Campbell in March 1971. While audience footage of 'Bullfrog Blues' and 'Tattoo'd Lady' has surfaced on YouTube in previous years, we recently obtained the entire concert from a fellow Gallagher fan. With the fan's permission, we uploaded the footage to *Rewriting Rory*'s YouTube channel on the 29th anniversary of the concert, receiving a positive response from our regular blog readers. Joël Winkin, for example, expressed gratitude for the rare find, appreciating the "superb rendition" of 'A Million Miles Away' and the "memorable" 'Off the Handle', as well as tracks from Gallagher's later years, such as 'Mean Disposition', which Winkin deemed "the high [point] for [him]."[5] Hopefully, with continued efforts on our YouTube channel, we can increase awareness of Gallagher's numerous performances in his later career for future fans to access.

The day after the Olympia concert, Gallagher participated in a live broadcast for Europe 1's Top Live Radio Show. Gallagher's short acoustic set featured the tender 'Out on the Western Plain', Walkin' Blues' and 'Ghost Blues'. Later on, he joined the Gypsy jazz group Au Petit Bonheur for 'J'veux du soleil'. The lyrics celebrate the innocence of childhood, the disillusionment of adult life and desire to return to a simpler time, enhanced by Gallagher's Django Reinhardtesque delivery. Notably, Au Petit Bonheur singer Jamil Leroussi can be heard calling out in French, "Maman oui c'est bien moi je suis avec Rory!" ("Mum, yes it's me, I'm with Rory!"). Thirty years on, Leroussi deemed his quick jam with Gallagher as "a moment of absolute kindness, disarming simplicity and supremely dizzying talent," recognising the "great lesson in modesty" such an opportunity taught him.[6]

On 25 October 1994, Gallagher arrived in Lille for his concert at the Aéronef. In attendance was Gallagher's friend and journalist Jean-Noël Coghe, who provides a detailed account of the evening (and next day) in his book. Coghe detected a "desperate [and] undeniable sense of force and fury" in Gallagher's Lille performance, comparing his guitar playing to a "machine gun [shooting] bursts of tortured intensity."[7] He also noted Mark Feltham's heedful observation of Gallagher during the show, "as if covering him," Coghe interprets, "[and] carrying him through a battlefield." Critics at Gallagher's *Festival Interceltique de Lorient* show two months prior mirrored Coghe's analysis, as indicated by the *Le Télégramme de Lorient* review, which compared the Irishman's guitar playing to an "artificial hell," where his "attacks are precise and powerful."[8] Once offstage, Gallagher greeted Coghe by "hugging [him] tight for what seemed like an eternity," a gesture "he had never done before."[9]

After the concert, Gallagher joined Coghe and friends at a restaurant, where he drank "very little" and "hardly touched" his dinner. In spite of this, Gallagher was "in a talkative mood," revealing his productive afternoon browsing stores during his wander around Lille's streets. "He had bought some miniature guitars for his collection, as well as lots of other little knick-knacks that he'd found amusing." Gallagher's high spirits extended into the following evening, accompanied this time by Feltham and Levy. In between "a couple of mouthfuls of steak" and "a single beer," Gallagher raised various topics of conversation, such as his admiration for French actor Lino Ventura. The table received a bottle of champagne when the restaurant's landlady recognised its well-known visitor, which Gallagher "discreetly avoided drinking [...] preferring to pour it into a flowerpot next to the table when the landlady had gone."

Notwithstanding one Belgium show on 29 November, Gallagher resumed regular gigging on 1 December with a series of dates in France and Germany. He reunited with Irish band Energy Orchard on 3 December for his concert at Saar-Mosel Halle in Konz. Keyboardist Kevin Breslin revealed how "great"[10] it was to see Gallagher again after their collaboration on 'Remember My Name' earlier in the year (see 1.5). In particular, Breslin recalled Gallagher's animated state backstage: "When we pulled up to the venue, Rory came in and he was full of beans. I mean *really* full of beans. He was just on top of everything." By Breslin's account, the crowd at the Saar-Mosel Halle were also greeted with the guitarist's genial mood:

> [When] Rory [went onstage], he just opened up with this song, and I was just shocked. He was playing these notes that I didn't think existed. I was like, 'Where did that come from?' I turned to the [stage manager], and he said, 'I don't know what it is, but he hasn't been playing like that until you guys arrived'.
>
> There was a guy on crutches at the front of the stage, and [Rory] reached out and asked him for one of his crutches, and he played a solo using his crutch. It was incredible. Not one note was bent slightly wrong; it was just perfect. And then he gave the crutch back to the guy, and there was just this glow coming from him.[11]

Energy Orchard joined Gallagher for a handful of dates in December, which were "just as brilliant," in Breslin's opinion. Gallagher would quite often hang out with the band after the gig and, at one point, discussion centred on forming a "supergroup" together. "He was talking about 'Rory Gallagher and Energy

Orchard', and we would all [get together] and go out and tour. But unfortunately, that didn't happen." Years later, Breslin prefers to focus on the positive, realising the "great honour" of working with such a "phenomenal performer." "[Rory's] energy level onstage [will] always stick with me," said Breslin, elaborating on the "flawless" connection between Gallagher and his fans. "It was like he melted into the audience, and they melted into him. It was a great thing to watch, especially from the stage."

On 11 December, Gallagher performed at the rock club Le Plan in Ris-Orangis. The club attracted a diverse range of sounds, from reggae and soul to blues and electronic, and was created as an affordable space for both amateur and professional musicians. Aware of Gallagher's "legendary friendliness and authenticity,"[12] Le Plan's owners extended an invitation for him to appear at the venue's ten-year anniversary. Trouble emerged, however, when Gallagher eventually accepted the offer, with management fearing they would be unable to pay him. Coghe recounts that payment was of "no importance" to Gallagher and he carried through with an "extraordinary" concert. Gallagher later compared the Le Plan gig to his first trip to France, playing the Piblokto Club in Dourges in 1967. "He felt the same passion [and] the same love," from the "packed [and] [intimate] audience," wrote Coghe. Moreover, Gallagher's appearance at Le Plan reunited him with French guitarist and songwriter Louis Bertignac, who he first met in 1981. Bertignac was invited by a mutual acquaintance to Gallagher's show at the Palais des Sports, joining him for a jam during the encore. Bertignac describes the moment as "wonderful,"[13] particularly when Gallagher handed over his white Telecaster to play. "Such a nice guy!" he recalled. Years later at Le Plan, Gallagher spotted Bertignac in the crowd during his set. "After a while, [Rory] asked me to come onstage and put in my hands the same white Telecaster!"

Five months after Gallagher's passing, the owners of Le Plan convinced local council to have the street renamed to Rue Rory Gallagher, which is "the first time a street in France has been named after a rock star—Irish or otherwise."[14] Speaking at the ceremony, Gallagher's mother Monica said that this was a "wonderful moment" that helped her "a little bit" through the grief that she was feeling at the "tremendous loss" of her son.[15] She also expressed her great "pride" in Gallagher, as well as her gratitude to the people of France for this "honour bestowed" on him. Gallagher concluded 1994 by returning to the studio for a fruitful session with violinist Roberto Manes and percussionist Peter Lockett (see 1.5).

Geleen (5 January 1995)
In 1988, Gallagher disclosed on *The Late Late Show* how he was "less together" when not touring: "I get more worn out when I'm off the road from nervous tension."[16] Aside from a genuine enjoyment of playing music, Gallagher's 'nervous tension' at home gradually transformed into the main force keeping him working. "It was a dilemma," Dónal explained, "[Rory] needed rest, but was only happy when he was on tour."[17] In conversation with Robert Haagsma, Dónal

identifies the absence of a personal life to return home to after months touring as "the big tragedy" in his brother's life. Over time, Gallagher's deteriorating health became closely monitored by Dónal, particularly at this late period. The short Dutch tour in January 1995 was scheduled from the year before, with Dónal optimistic that this arrangement would prevent his brother from "getting lazy"[18] and "isolated"[19] over the New Year:

> Normally, we'd break for Christmas and take a break and think about touring the following year [usually in May or June] [...] [But] the Dutch tour was relatively easy. There were only six shows, and five of the nights were spent at the one hotel, so there wasn't a lot of travelling to do.[20]

Although "[Rory's] health wasn't perfect" at this stage, Dónal hoped regular gigging would act as "therapy", providing the chance to "sweat out the toxins from his body [and] acquire an appetite." Prior to leaving for the Netherlands, Dónal determined Gallagher to be "trimmed down [enough] and thinking straight at least"[21] to sustain the short tour, which is a fair assessment since he joined Eamonn McCormack in the studio on 1 January to record 'Falsely Accused' (see 1.5).

Unfortunately, the momentary rest over Christmas deepened Gallagher's depression (as simultaneously his liver was failing), with Dónal realising at the first performance in Geleen on 5 January that "[Rory] was much too sick to give a coherent show."[22] In addition, Gallagher had "picked up a flu"[23] due to his weakened immune system, escalating tensions backstage when Dónal suggested the remaining concerts be cancelled. "It was the only time in thirty years that we had a big fight," stated Dónal to Haagsma. Unable to convince his brother, Dónal "drew back and went home [to London]."[24] Feltham echoed Dónal's opinion in our interview, stating that Gallagher's illness had "started to affect his playing" during the 1995 concerts, particularly "his chording and pick work."[25] As a result, Feltham considers the final tour an inaccurate "representation" of Gallagher's talent, knowing in retrospect that "we shouldn't have done those last couple of shows" as the band was playing with "a different [and severely ill] Rory."

Despite failing health, however, Gallagher's ability to reach out and connect with his audience remained to a moderate extent, as attested by fan Nicole D. Gunung. Gunung's introduction to Gallagher was a family affair. "[My Dad] was listening to blues at home when I was still young, and that definitely shaped my taste for music."[26] Her dad was a technician at the 1993 Tegelen Bluesrock Festival, where the Rory Gallagher Band was on the bill. Gunung fondly remembers the gig as her dad was presented with Gallagher's recently removed strings off his Takamine acoustic from a roadie. Two years later, Gunung found herself at the front of the stage at what would be Gallagher's final appearance in Geleen at the De Hanenhof, accompanied by, of course, her dad:

> At the beginning of the concert, [my dad] dragged me to the front of the stage, [with] everyone making room for us. I am not that tall, and he wanted me to be able to see Rory up close. And it worked– Rory saw me! Halfway through the concert, [Rory] pulled me up onstage. He hung his guitar around my neck, stood behind me, and while he was moving my hands we played together. I was so in awe that I cannot even remember what song we played.

Gunung then recalls Gallagher leaving the stage, guitar *still* in her hands. "I obviously cannot play!" she admitted to us, "[and] I felt quite intimidated by the huge crowd." But shortly after, Gallagher returned, having removed his leather coat and rolled up his sleeves. "I could see his arms were covered in some sort of rash [and] it looked painful." As a mark of gratitude, Gallagher slid off the purple scarf from his neck and draped it around Gunung's, which she describes as "a once in a lifetime experience." In the present day, the gifts are enshrined: "I have [the Takamine strings] wrapped around a bottle of Mississippi Mud, [along] with the scarf Rory gave me."

Enschede (6 January 1995)
"I saw Rory five times," said fan Paul ten Thije, "[and when] Rory came onstage [in Enschede in 1995], we were a bit shocked at how he looked [...] His face was very bloated and he just didn't look healthy."[27] Although the quality of guitar playing was still good, Thije detected less intensity in the performance, perhaps a result of Gallagher's stagnant position onstage. "I remember Rory as someone who used the whole stage, but he just sat down for the entire concert, which didn't really suit him." Thije's recollections fly off his tongue and dissolve into a bittersweet atmosphere, "now knowing that we would never see Rory live again."

Similar remarks were made to us by fan Hank Mennes. "Rory did not look good, very bloated and sweating profusely, but as usual he gave everything for his audience, and despite his poor condition, the performance—especially the guitar work—was unparalleled."[28] A bootleg of this concert exists on YouTube, with Gallagher showcasing moments of his usual musical prowess, such as the evocative 'A Million Miles Away'.

Following his concert in Enschede, Gallagher participated in what would be his final interview for the station Radio Hengelo. The interview was broadcast on 11 January as part of the 'Aerial in the Area' segment and replayed on 21 June in tribute to Gallagher.[29] Overall, Gallagher was "[feeling] good" about returning to the Netherlands. "We're hitting not the usual big cities, but quite a span of places, and [I think] that's very important." The conversation sweeps across the usual line of questioning in a Gallagher interview, from his defiant stance on singles to his opinion on his musical peers, especially those he would like to work with, such as Bob Dylan. When asked about the gap between *Jinx* and *Defender*, Gallagher expresses general frustration—perhaps a hint of fatigue, even—towards the demands of the music industry. "I'm not a machine, you know? It takes time to write things and it takes time to feel the moment is right to record [...] what's the point in being a bread-factory?" Justifiably so, Gallagher's words give the impression of being slightly irked. "I did have six albums in three years, for instance," he reminds the interviewer.

Gallagher's concluding comments regard the making of a great performance: "[...] a million notes on the guitar is one thing, [but] it's to perform and to absorb the feelings of the people in the crowd." Gallagher relates this to his field of the blues, and specifically how musicians of the past balanced passion and technique with a theatrical element, which the British blues movement in the 1960s lacked. "The blues is not all academic," he states. "[...] People used to dance at Muddy Waters concerts [...] [and] Howlin' Wolf used to crawl up curtains to get a reaction."

Amsterdam (7 January 1995)

In an obituary from *Het Parool*, Gallagher was reported to have been "so drunk that he could barely stand on his feet"[30] at his show in Amsterdam's Paradiso club. Allegations of Gallagher's 'drunkenness' are now read as ancient conjectures from an uninformed press, and today we are enlightened to the fact that Gallagher's behaviour was the primary result of mixing medication. Jan-Willem Sligting, promoter for the Paradiso, provides a dismal account of Gallagher's concert on 7 January for *De Volkskrant*. "The first half hour was sad, but after that it sounded a little better."[31] After 45 minutes, more than half the audience had disappeared. "Maybe they should have gotten their money back," says Sligting, "but that should have happened sooner." On the other hand, those who persevered "asked for an encore."

Fan Jan Van Bodegraven, who was also in the audience, shows great sympathy for Gallagher, recalling the audience booing and asking himself, "How can you boo a musician that you have come to see who is noticeably ill and unhappy?"[32] Sligting admits that discontinuing the show had crossed his mind. Promoter Willem Venema even brought in a doctor to check Gallagher who advised that he return to London immediately. Quashing rumours about drunkenness, Venema told *De Volkskrant*, "It is not true that the man rolled out on stage intoxicated. His medication just wasn't right."

As stated in *Het Parool*, Energy Orchard had planned to support Gallagher's show at the Paradiso on 7 January 1995, as well as Leeuwarden the subsequent evening. In addition, the band was scheduled to appear alongside Gallagher for his concert in Tilburg[33] on 12 January. However, for unknown reasons, the Martin Hutchinson Band replaced Energy Orchard as a support act for Gallagher. Born in Kildare, Ireland, Hutchinson has been described as "a restless drifter" captivating audiences with his merging "of folk, ballads and blues,"[34] making him a well-suited opener. Despite Gallagher's evident health problems at the Paradiso show, Mark Feltham shared a poignant memory to *Guitarist* magazine about Gallagher crossing the street in Amsterdam to give money to a busker. "[Gallagher] would do that often," said Feltham, "He was always a man for the underdog."[35]

Leeuwarden (8 January 1995)

The diminished crowd attendance continued the next night for Gallagher's show at De Harmonie in Leeuwarden. "The organising foundation De Ooievaar declared the FIB room sold out with about 750 visitors, although according to Ivan Pel of De Harmonie another 100 people could join."[36] Contrastingly, Gallagher attracted close to 1,000 people on his previous trip to Leeuwarden in 1993. "[Gallagher] dragged himself through the set with difficulty," published J.H. from the *Leeuwarder Courant*, "and the weak sides of his musical personality came to the fore." Sympathetically, the article explains Gallagher's behaviour as a consequence of a bad flu, with the performance consisting of highs and lows overall. While the electric set was "one-dimensional and boring," the acoustic intermission provided "the only breathing space." Although "he can still play the guitar, and the audience would know that too," the reviewer believes Gallagher has lost his direction with the blues. "Our Irishman had less vision and more scruples and got stuck in a blues idiom that nowadays leans more and more towards the muscular blues of a Walter Trout." Read retrospectively, it is hard not to feel a sense of anger at the review, given how gravely ill Gallagher was and his desire to still fulfil the expectations of his audience.

Gallagher's Farewell to the Stage:
Rotterdam (10 January 1995)

"I spent three days with him," said Toine van Berlo, "I remember him as being a very kind man, but he was a really, really lonely man too."[37]

And in that moment, staring out towards the Wadden Sea, enveloped in the salty fragrance swirling around him, Rory Gallagher was perhaps at his loneliest.

Persistent gusts of wind obscure his vision, as tendrils of his black hair fling across his face. The only other person is frozen and carved out of bronze… glancing over, and Gallagher views the statue of Dutch politician and civil engineer, Cornelius Lely. Lely strongly advocated the Zuiderzee Works, a project dedicated to enclosing the Zuiderzee bay and preventing further flooding. In 1927, construction began on the Afsluitdijk, a 32km dike linking North Holland and Friesland, which successfully barricaded the Zuiderzee, and was eventually renamed to the Ijsselmeer Lake.

The statue of Lely was not the sole accompaniment with Gallagher… there was also, of course, his driver…

On Monday 9 January 1995, Toine van Berlo received a call from the Dutch promotion company Mojo about a musician who had stepped out in the middle of the Afsluitdijk on his drive from Amsterdam the night before. Berlo was informed, "He got into a fight with his current driver [Hein Fokker], who was a good friend of mine, and he got upset and said, 'Stop the car', and got out on the dyke! [There are] no buildings, nothing. [But] he got out. And that was Rory."[38] Mojo required one task from Berlo, and the task was simple: drive Gallagher from Amsterdam to Rotterdam for his show on 10 January. "One day, one job.

'Okay, I'll do it'."

Founded in 1968 by Berry Visser, Mojo worked with both Dutch and international groups touring around Europe. While studying at university, Berlo was employed at Mojo, beginning as a scaffolder for Pink Floyd's set at the Pink Pop Festival in 1988. "[It] was the biggest stage I ever worked on. It was 22 metres high and it was climbing with no ropes, no helmets, no safety gear [...] [As a scaffolder] you got about 100 *guilder* a day, and for a student, that was excellent." Over the years, Berlo carried out various jobs for bands, from lighting and PA to limo driving (transporting artists such as Art Garfunkel, Joe Cocker and Rage Against the Machine), and even worked as a tour manager for support acts.

By the time Berlo crossed paths with Rory Gallagher in 1995, his employment with Mojo had been terminated for quite a while. He had since dropped out of university, instead completing IT work for the Roman Catholic archives and administrations. Fokker, Gallagher's (now-ex) driver, recommended Berlo based on his encounters with mental health problems, including depression, within his family and friendship circles. "I wasn't afraid of that. I have experience of that in my [background]. So, I think that led to the decision that I was suitable." In addition, Mojo did not technically employ Berlo, which he soon discovered was the reason Gallagher had stopped the car on the Afsluitdijk that cold Saturday night.

"It was all Mojo's fault [...] that was one of the first things [Rory] asked when I met him: 'Are you from Mojo?' I said, 'No. I'm freelance'. [But] they instructed me [on this]. I knew I had to say I was freelance." On Monday, Berlo caught the train from Nijmegen to Amsterdam and picked up the latest Mercedes 3SSL, meeting Gallagher at the Hyatt Hotel:

> I didn't know what Rory looked like, [but] had a faint idea of who he was. Later on, I realised I was mistaking him with Gary Moore. I thought, 'Guitarist. Black hair'. So, in my mind, I saw Gary Moore, [but] then it was Rory. I had heard of him, [but] had no records of and no CDs of him. [In the Hyatt lobby] I looked around [and] saw a man sitting in the corner, leather jacket, black hair. I thought, 'It must be him'. I stepped over to him [and] said, 'Mr. Gallagher, I presume?' He said, 'Yes?' I said, 'I'm Toine. I'm your limo driver. I've come to take you to Rotterdam'. He said, 'Oh, nice.' He didn't say much [else].

Berlo noted that Gallagher was looking at him rather than talking, perhaps taking in his "white, albino Rockabilly" aesthetic at the time. "I was dressed in jeans, [a] bomber jacket and my hair was bleached white in those days." Gallagher carried with him one suitcase, a briefcase and an old guitar case. Initially, the two cases were to be placed in the trunk. "The guitar [stays] with me. It has to ride in the car," said Gallagher. However, Berlo was able to secure the guitar case in the backseat using the seatbelts. "We have to be sure that's safe," he reassured

Gallagher. During the drive to Rotterdam, Berlo offered to play music, choosing a recent CD of Dutch guitar band Fatal Flowers:

> We engaged in conversation, and he wasn't very happy. He had a chip on his shoulder. But after talking a bit, he became a bit more relaxed [and] mellow [...] one thing was evident and it was [that] he felt mistreated. More than once, he said, 'People don't respect me anymore'. It really bothered him. He didn't demand that they respect him as a rock star [or] as a well-known artist, but just [to show] common decency and respect. That's what he wanted and that wasn't anymore in the day-to-day context that he encountered in Amsterdam, in Holland, everywhere.

Gallagher asked if he could stop at the Hilton Hotel before heading to the Nighttown centre. Berlo left the Mercedes with the valet service, assisting Gallagher with his luggage to the hotel front desk. "He said to the clerk, 'I want to rent the suite at the top', the most expensive room in the Hilton." After settling payment, Gallagher requested a doctor visit him as soon as possible in his room. In the meantime, Berlo stayed in the lobby:

> After about ten minutes, a very young female doctor arrived. I think she was about 30 [and] just out of university. [She] went up in the elevator and came back after 15 minutes pale as a sheet and eyes like death. 'Bye!' and off she went. I don't know what happened upstairs [when she examined Gallagher], but she got a fright of her life one way or another.

Following this medical interlude, Gallagher returned to the lobby and Berlo drove him to the concert venue. Meanwhile, "tremendous tension" was building backstage at the Nighttown due to Gallagher's absence and, according to online user 'Dennis', the band took to the stage and "[played] to keep the fans calm."[39] When the guitarist eventually arrived, fans were "angry" at the delay and, in a very uncharacteristic reaction, Gallagher "got mad" to the point that he "stopped playing his second song." Shortly after, "Mark Feltham and some roadies" escorted Gallagher offstage, causing many in the audience to leave as well. In this version of events, the remaining band members (along with Feltham) briefly resumed playing until the performance was officially called off. Gallagher's alleged onstage collapse is excluded from this narrative and, while Dennis states that fans were (supposedly) "updated" with news of Gallagher's condition, the reason or explanation is absent from his account. Another fan, Bram Pescador, shed some additional light on the "strange" Rotterdam evening:

> It turned out to be a very chaotic night. What I can remember is that [Rory] and his band had different agendas when it came to the songs. It was hard to recognise any of the songs they were playing and at some point, it led to an argument with the audience. They were disappointed and left the concert [...] I actually stayed until

the concert ended prematurely. The few people left were really baffled and confused. I actually felt sorry for [Rory]. I couldn't believe that someone of his status sank so deep.[40]

Pescador remembers Gallagher "[walking] off the stage soon after the arguments he had with the audience," verifying that many "were not pleased with his performance" and, therefore, "already gone" by the time the show ended. For the backstage perspective, we return to Berlo's account:

> The show started. I went downstairs. I [was talking] with [promoter] Willem Venema [when] suddenly news came that the show wasn't going very well. I went up to the [wings] of the stage [...] [when] the band came off and went to the dressing rooms, they were crying. Real tears. They were really upset. Rory stayed out and was challenging people to come and fight with him onstage. The crowd of people didn't know exactly what was going on, but something was really off. The band wouldn't go out on the stage again. They'd had enough. They just wanted to go back home to England.

We then posed the possibility that Gallagher had collapsed backstage rather than onstage, and somehow the two events had muddled overtime. "On the stage, maybe he swerved or was uncertain in his movements," said Berlo, "[But] Rory did not collapse *backstage*, and I was there all the time." Both Mark Feltham and David Levy later confirmed to us that Gallagher, in fact, did *not* collapse—at any point—during his Rotterdam concert. As Levy simply told us, "We started the show and then Rory couldn't continue."[41]

Moving on, we encountered another fictional claim that Gallagher was admitted to Amsterdam's Academic Medical Centre (AMC) following his 'collapse' (and in some cases, he was transferred from the AMC to a London hospital for his liver transplant).[42] Berlo, however, firmly denies this, stating that the only medical treatment Gallagher received was from doctors he consulted in his hotel suites in Amsterdam. As stated previously, the band was scheduled to appear in Utrecht on 11 January and Tilburg the day after, with the tour—at least in Gallagher's mind—to continue, even after the (quite disastrous) Rotterdam performance. Once offstage, Berlo remembers that Gallagher was a mixture of "upset [and] furious," even planning to contact Gerry McAvoy and Charlie Watts [of the Rolling Stones] to join him in Utrecht. "[Watts] was, in Rory's mind, hopping on the bus, coming over, and playing with him. In fact, that was absolutely unrealistic, but that was his mind setting," said Berlo.

Gallagher's paranoia worsened as the hours progressed. After the concert, Berlo drove Gallagher, accompanied with his sound engineer, back to Amsterdam. "Where to—the Hyatt?" "No. They don't respect me anywhere anymore," he said. The American Hotel was decided instead, and the trio headed straight for the hotel bar, drinking wine and *pastis* until close at 1AM. Apparently, this annoyed the guitarist, who wanted to stay up and have a few more drinks. When Gallagher awoke the next afternoon on Wednesday 11 January, he wanted to move on to another hotel because he was convinced "they didn't respect him" due to refusing service after the hotel bar closed.

Next stop: the Grand Hotel.[43] However, the trip did not last very long due to the lavish interior. "[With] the way I looked and Rory in his leather jacket, [when] we walked into the lobby, Rory looked around and said, 'Let's go!'" Although the Barbizon Palace was newer, yet still expensive, Gallagher was satisfied. He checked in as Alain Delon and "sprinted to his room," worried about being recognised by journalists. As he did at the Hilton, Gallagher wished for a doctor to check in on him. Berlo had a chance to talk with the doctor after at the hotel bar:

> I don't know what was wrong with Rory or how his physical condition was, but the doctor was shocked also. I asked the doctor, 'Is everything okay with him? Is something wrong with him?' He said, 'There's a lot of things wrong, but I can't say anything. I'm a doctor […] I just gave him some vitamin shots, but the problem is everywhere he goes, he wants to see a doctor. Every doctor writes him a prescription, he mixes up all those prescriptions, throws down the pills with some wine or something. He doesn't eat. And it can't go on like this. He has to go back to London to get treatment. That's it. Try to get him back to London'.

Due to the cost, Berlo was unable to stay at the Barbizon Palace, and instead roomed at the Hotel Prins Hendrik. Berlo walked the streets of Amsterdam's city centre, recalling Gallagher's kind words from a day ago: "Toine, you're doing a great job. Before I go back, I want to buy you a gift." Berlo appreciated the gesture, selecting a present for Gallagher as well. "I bought him a money clip because [he had a lot of credit cards and notes of money] in his shirt." Berlo requested the message, 'Rory, just remember the good things', be engraved on the clip.

On Wednesday night, Gallagher invited Berlo to have dinner with him and the sound engineer at the Barbizon Palace restaurant. Gallagher ordered fish and spoke about working with Bob Dylan on a studio album. At 5AM the following day, Berlo received a phone call from Gallagher's sound engineer, saying that Gallagher wanted to return to London as soon as possible and, therefore, needed transport to the airport for the morning flight. At Schiphol, Berlo asked Gallagher if he could sign his CD copy of *Tattoo*. "It says, 'To Toine, the best Dutchman. Thanks, Rory Gallagher'."

> And then Rory [said], 'I wanted to buy you a gift, but I didn't dare go out of the hotel. Sorry'. I said, 'It's okay. I bought you one'. So, I gave him [the money clip]. He took it out, he unwrapped it, he looked at it, and he started crying. Big tears falling from under his sunglasses. That was very emotional for me too. I didn't expect that to happen.

Wanting to reciprocate, Gallagher then took off his watch and gave it to Berlo. "It is sort of a granite watch with a red copper backing. It's really thin with a large bulb shaped cover glass on the top and then marble greenish speckles. Brand New Age." Berlo observed how the red copper back was very oxidised, most likely a result of Gallagher's acidic sweat.

Unfortunately, Berlo would not hear of Rory Gallagher again until five months later.

Driving home to Nijmegen after working at the Pink Pop festival in Landgraaf, Berlo switched on the radio to learn of Gallagher's untimely passing. Although Berlo was aware that Gallagher had been admitted to hospital for a liver transplant, the news came as a shock, especially since the two had become friendly during their three days together. "[Rory] liked me, because on the way to Schiphol, he asked, 'Will you come and work for me? Come with me on the plane to London'." In 1996, the organisers of the Tegelen Bluesrock Festival dedicated the night in honour of Gallagher. Willem Venema suggested Berlo attend. "I was brought up onstage like, 'This is the last Dutchman who shook [Rory's] hand'." Berlo's time with Gallagher is "not something that I easily forgot," and those three days are cherished memories forevermore:

> Rory was super nice and super gentle and a super courteous person [...] but I had the feeling he was alone. He was a very lonely man. And [I'm unsure] if that was because of his paranoia getting the better of him, his drinking, his wellbeing, but he struck me as a lonely guy. He kept his distance.

Gallagher in London (February-June 1995)
Following his return to London from Holland, Gallagher's health "got worse really quickly,"[44] as his lingering flu quickly turned into pneumonia. Dónal recounts to Dan Muise that, around the same time, he also picked up "a horrendous flu" and, thus, "laid low for about three weeks"[45] until he recovered. By this stage, Gallagher had "isolated himself" into his apartment in Chelsea Harbour. Although Dónal attempted contact with his brother on several occasions, Gallagher persistently "blocked him out [and] [refused] to see him."[46] Dónal even resorted to sending food parcels to the apartment to ensure Gallagher was eating regularly. In an interview with Dutch magazine *Aardschok*, Dónal mentions the few instances he saw Gallagher at this time, highlighting the guitarist's "lonely and depressed" state of mind. "He acted like a man who wanted nothing else other than to die. It was a mess and you could not talk to him [...] There was nothing I could have done."[47] Although Dónal tried to "settle the fight" with his brother, "coherent communication was hardly possible" as Gallagher's health rapidly deteriorated.

In the Rory Gallagher tribute edition of 1995's *Hot Press*, Gary Moore recalled his telephone conversation with Gallagher prior to his hospitalisation. During the call, Gallagher informed Moore about his recent difficulty with the Mojo promoter in Holland, which had "[really affected] his confidence." Gallagher revealed he had not left his apartment "since the New Year"—or at least early January—sounding, in Moore's view, "pleased to hear from anyone." He explains further: "I think [Rory] thought nobody cared about him." Although Gallagher "didn't sound too well" and was clearly "beaten down," he nevertheless maintained his "selfless" nature, shifting focus onto the "problems" in Moore's life as opposed to his own.[48]

At some point between February-March, Dónal visited (the now "saffron"[49]) Gallagher and, after much "coercion,"[50] was able to convince his brother to seek treatment at Cromwell Hospital. Following Gallagher's admission, it would take several weeks before doctors advised a liver transplant, moving to King's College Hospital for the procedure. Though touring had ceased as Gallagher recuperated, his bandmates continued to care for his wellbeing. "I think I can speak for everybody when I say our main concern was that [Rory] was well and better," said Levy. "There was no talk about, you know, Plan A or Plan B. I was quite happy having been privileged to know the man and work with the man."[51] Gallagher's previous agent, Paul Charles, also expressed both concern and hope for the guitarist's wellbeing: "Sure, he was Rory Gallagher, wasn't he? He walked on water. I knew he was ill, but we all felt he was going to be okay [...] [he] was going to recover and get back where he belonged: on the boards again [...] that was our wish, that was our dream."[52]

The progress of Gallagher's recovery was documented in an article from the *Evening Herald* in June, claiming "accidental overdoses of prescription medications over a number of years"[53] had led to the surgery. During the same month, Dave Fanning bumped into Dónal at the London Fleadh:

> I was talking to him and asked, 'How's Rory?' [Dónal] said, 'Ah, not too good'. That was the first time I heard that Rory was actually sick, and possibly in the face that Dónal was making, there seemed like the word 'terminal' was coming through. But I didn't know what he was talking about. I had no idea about this.[54]

According to *L'Humanité*, Gallagher was scheduled to be entertaining fans in Bourges, France in June 1995. Instead, news travelled that he was undergoing a liver transplant. "Many of us are waiting for [him]," wrote *L'Humanité*.[55] "I had prepared two press releases – one to say that Rory had an operation and was recovering; the other that Rory had died as a result of complications," journalist Harry Doherty wrote in his 2002 memoirs, "I hoped never to have to use the second, but the phone call came..."[56] On 14 June, he received news that Gallagher had passed away at just 47 years old, struck with an MRSA infection during his recuperation.

Dermot Bolger, chair of Musicbase (a company that offered support to young musicians), shared a poignant memory with us from Gallagher's final weeks in hospital: "[He] regularly phoned our receptionist from his hospital bed, just for a voice to talk to, and very often in the late afternoon, so that long after her working day was over, she was still chatting to this man in a hospital bed whom she had never known."[57] Although Bolger had never met Gallagher, he was a "constant presence" in his youth. Wanting to do something to commemorate him, he set up a book of condolences in the Musicbase office in Temple Bar. On the first page, he wrote the poem 'In Memory of Rory Gallagher', which he had penned on the day that the guitarist died:

There came a time on those summer nights
When a free house had been found,
And a cheap stereo rigged with strobe lights
                That froze each moment in your mind.

You just knew when the crowd had waned
And the wasters had long gone
That soon the wised-up boys who remained
                Would put Rory Gallagher on.

Picking Up the 'Fall':
Rethinking the 1995 Tour and Gallagher's Final Projects

While, in the past, Gallagher's 1995 tour has attracted much controversy and confusion in the fan community, we have tried to dilute the muddied waters by presenting various angles of the story in this chapter. With the uncertainty (partially) dissolved, the image revealed to us is Gallagher's solid commitment to his music, even at the point of critically poor health. Sligting claimed that "there was no stopping Gallagher" from walking onto the Paradiso stage in Amsterdam; "he had to perform."[58] And even Berlo attested to Gallagher's endurance on the tour: "Rory wanted to play. He wanted to do the next gig in Utrecht." Unfortunately, Gallagher's farewell to the stage does not encapsulate his irrefutable talent and showmanship. As put by Dónal, "It's painful that such a dedicated artist had to say goodbye to the stage in this way."[59]

Throughout persistent health battles, however, Gallagher's inner circle—such as his band—provided a musical foundation, particularly when there was an obvious effect on his performance. "[Rory] would have his good days and bad days," Levy agreed, "and part of being a bandmate is to actually back him up if he was having an off day." Levy then quickly asserted, "[But] when he was on, he was unbelievable. He would make the hairs on the back of my arms stand up straight."

As revealed in Enschede during his final interview, Gallagher was looking beyond the 1995 tour, expressing many career goals and ambitions. "I hope, in the future, to write for the cinema," he stated, showing an interest in composing for others. "The songs I write are the songs I would love to hear from someone else, if you understand me."[60] A double album, with an electric and acoustic side each, was a project Gallagher spoke of quite frequently. "I have the material all ready. But there was a time [when] I could record and tour, [and] at the moment [...] the older I get the more intense my performances become, really!"

While Gallagher displayed an enthusiasm for getting back in the studio, he wanted to do so according to his own terms. "After the Dutch tour I'm taking a little break in Ireland and then [starting] the albums. I have them written, [and] I'm really looking forward to doing them." Gallagher desired a production "without too many gimmicks," and alluded to guest appearances, "I've asked a number of people that are of the same mind as myself."

As written by Jean-Noël Coghe, Gallagher envisioned recording with his new band in the summer of 1995, with Dónal encouraging his brother to establish his own studio. An uncertain Gallagher passed on the suggestion, "preferring to go where the urge and the inspiration took him."[61] Plans were (almost) set in motion to purchase the Stones mobile recording truck from Bill Wyman; however, Gallagher (again) did not warm to the idea of being tied down. This sentiment carried over to his living situation, with the proposal of Gallagher buying a flat in Lille. "It would be good for Rory," Coghe wrote, "a place where he could work in peace and quiet," while still able to attend business in London through the newly opened Channel Tunnel.[62]

In an obituary for the *Irish Independent*, concert promoter Jim Aiken stated his plans to help Gallagher get back out on the road, particularly in Ireland, as "there would have been a market for him"[63] leading into the 21st century. Even Gallagher's bandmates expressed optimism regarding the many options for his musical pathway, as outlined by Feltham:

> I think [*Defender* and *Fresh Evidence*] were great albums as well. I think a lot of [people] loved those last two albums. He was doing great business in Germany. He was at the height of his career really. We could have gone around the world, finished the world tour in London and then gone off around the world again. It could have gone on and on and on.

From this, we can reassess if indeed *Mojo*'s Colin Harper was correct in his assertion that Gallagher's career was nearing "full circle"[64] by the time of his death. With this chapter, we reinforce the point that Gallagher's aspirations soared as opposed to fell—that he, in fact, did not play 'until he dropped', but remained standing until the very end. As we neared the end of our conversation with Feltham, he shared a bittersweet anecdote regarding the final period of the guitarist's life, hinting that—somewhere in the cosmos—there was more to come from Rory Gallagher:

> It's funny because I have a postcard here from Rory. I keep it and it's framed. And it's half written. And I think that it was when he was back in Ireland. A black and white photo, it is. Got it here framed. And he wrote, 'Dear Mark, I hope you're okay. I'm back at the fort'. He called it the fort [laughs]. 'I'm back at the fort', and

Part 3 - *Just Remember the Good Things*

then, 'I hope you're…' and it just ends. And he put stamps on. And he posted it to me. And it's kind of an unfinished letter. And it was very apt.

RM

Footnotes

1 Julian Vignoles, *Rory Gallagher: The Man Behind the Guitar* (London: Collins, 2018), 127.
2 Ibid., 128.
3 Frédéric Lecomte, 'Rory Gallagher 1948-1995', *Guitare et Claviers* (July 1995), https://rewritingrory.co.uk/2022/06/04/guitare-et-claviers-july-1995/.
4 In much the same way as the 1992 Town & Country Club show (see Introduction and 3.1).
5 Email exchange with Joël Winkin, 1 November 2023.
6 Interview with Jamil Leroussi, 13 May 2024.
7 Jean-Noël Coghe, *Rory Gallagher: A Biography* (Cork: Mercier Press, 2001), 162. All subsequent quotes from Coghe are from the same passage (162-166).
8 '"Toro" Gallagher met Kervaric en transe... celtique', *Le Télégramme de Lorient* (10 August 1994), 1.
9 Ted McKenna recounts a similar situation to Dan Muise when Gallagher greeted him at the 1992 Scottish Fleadh. As we argue in other chapters (such as 1.2), this could also be another example of Gallagher's medication influencing his moods and emotional state.
10 Interview with Kevin Breslin, 10 April 2022. All subsequent quotes from Breslin come from the same interview.
11 When we spoke with Breslin in April 2022, he initially confused the December 1994 dates with the original arrangement of supporting Gallagher on his 1995 Dutch tour. As a result, he (unintentionally) challenged our bleak impressions of Gallagher's final tour and, therefore, partly inspired this chapter.
12 Coghe, *Rory Gallagher*, 166.
13 Quoted from the Rory Gallagher Facebook page (12 December 2020), https://www.facebook.com/RoryGallagher/posts/pfbid0Pkr3yDcAQBYqj9LBHjx582p8XN1FyPkNG8Awu8afvJDQoe5iN9BYRESUofifmHEwl.
14 'Paris Honours Rory Gallagher', *RTÉ* (4 November 1995), https://www.rte.ie/archives/2020/1028/1174445-rue-rory-gallagher/.
15 Audio recording included on the CD in the 2000 deluxe edition of Coghe's book (Paris: Le Castor Astral).
16 'Rory Gallagher – The Late Late Show – 12th February 1988', https://www.youtube.com/watch?v=lKJ3ploCKv0&t=695s.
17 Robert Haagsma, 'Rory Gallagher: An Irishman not to be forgotten!', *Aardschok* (July 2000), http://www.roryon.com/Aardschock.html.
18 *Ghost Blues: The Story of Rory Gallagher* (2010).
19 Dan Muise, *Gallagher, Marriott, Derringer & Trower* (Milwaukee: Hal Leonard Corporation, 2002), 71.
20 Ibid.
21 Ibid.
22 Haagsma, 'Rory Gallagher'.
23 *Ghost Blues*.
24 According to Toine van Berlo, concert promoter Willem Venema acted as a stand-in manager for the guitarist. Dónal agreed to this arrangement, with Dónal advising the team to pay particular attention to his brother's eating habits.
25 Interview with Mark Feltham, 20 October 2023. All subsequent quotes from Feltham come from this interview, unless stated otherwise.
26 Interview with Nicole D. Gunung, 16 October 2023.
27 Interview with Paul ten Thije, 30 October 2023.
28 Interview with Henk Mannes, 19 February 2024.
29 'Famous Last Words', *Radio Hengelo*, https://www.roryon.com/famous221.html
30 'Rockgitarist Rory Gallagher overleden', *Het Parool* (15 June 1995), 21.
31 'Rory Gallagher: 'klein menselijk drama', *De Volkskrant* (13 January 1995), 2.
32 Interview with Jan Van Bodegraven, 21 January 2024.

33 This date (as well as one in Utrecht) was cancelled by the De Ooievaar promotion organisation, and Gallagher promptly flew home to London.
34 Martin Hutchinson Official Website, https://www.martinhutchinson.com/.
35 Cited in Julian Vignoles, *Rory Gallagher*, 254.
36 J.H. 'Rory Gallagher: nog net niet in Las Vegas', *Leeuwarder Courant* (9 January 1995), 13
37 Interview with Toine van Berlo, 23 December 2023. All subsequent quotes from Berlo come from this interview, unless stated otherwise.
38 From the Afsluitdijk, Berlo is unsure how Gallagher made it back to Amsterdam without a driver (22 March 2024).
39 'Rory Gallagher Biography', *HotShot Digital*, https://www.hotshotdigital.com/WellAlwaysRemember/RorysBio.html.
40 Interview with Bram Pescador, 23 May 2024.
41 Interview with David Levy, 22 May 2024.

42 See: Harry Knipschild, 'Herinneringen aan Rory Gallagher (1948-1995)' (29 July 2022), https://www.harryknipschild.nl/harryknipschild.nl/?view=article&id=857:467-herinneringen-aan-rory-gallagher-1948-1995&catid=79:artikelen-popmuziek; Herman Veenhof, 'Neef Daniel Gallagher vond honderden tapes van Rory Gallagher in de BBC-archieven, nu is er een 3cd met veel moois', *Nederlands Dagblad*, (14 June 2019), https://www.nd.nl/cultuur/muziek/525995/neef-daniel-gallagher-vond-honderden-tapes-van-rory-gallagher-in-de-bbc-archieven-nu-is-er-een-3cd-met-veel-moois
43 In his 2002 article, 'When the Good Guys Die: Remembering Rory Gallagher' (*Rock's Backpages*), Harry Doherty mentions Gallagher "book[ing] into three different hotels in the same evening in Amsterdam, but does not elaborate further.
44 Haagsma, 'Rory Gallagher'.
45 Muise, *Gallagher, Marriott, Derringer & Trower*, 72.
46 Ibid.
47 Haagsma, 'Rory Gallagher'.
48 'Gary Moore remembers Rory Gallagher', *Hot Press* (1995 Rory Gallagher Tribute Issue), https://www.hotpress.com/music/gary-moore-remembers-rory-gallagher-14356584
49 *Ghost Blues*.
50 Muise, *Gallagher, Marriott, Derringer & Trower*, 72.
51 Interview with David Levy, 22 February 2024.
52 Interview with Paul Charles, 24 October 2023.
53 'Liver Op for Rock Legend', *Evening Herald* (19 April 1995), 4.
54 Interview with Dave Fanning, 24 April 2022.
55 'Rory Gallagher n'est plus', *L'Humanité* (16 June 1995), https://www.humanite.fr/rory-gallagher-nest-plus-106733.
56 Doherty, 'When the Good Guys Die'.
57 Interview with Dermot Bolger, 17 January 2024.
58 'Rory Gallagher…', 2.
59 Haagsma, 'Rory Gallagher'.
60 'Famous Last Words'.
61 Coghe, *Rory Gallagher*, 148.
62 Ibid., 164-165.
63 Tony O'Brien, 'Hometown Resting Place for Rory', *Irish Independent* (16 June 1995), 9.
64 Colin Harper, 'Rory Gallagher (1948-1995)', *Mojo* (August 1995), https://www.roryon.com/colin.html.

Part 4:
Ireland

4.1 He Came, He Saw and He Certainly Conquered: Cork Opera House 1987

With his new album *Defender* (1987) receiving much critical attention, Gallagher was back out on the road, beginning with shows around Germany and Great Britain from late July through to October. News of Gallagher's 'comeback' grew as reviewers raved about the "vigorous" and "lively" Irishman, continuing to be "full of ideas as he was twenty years ago."[1] *Kerrang!* editor Derek Oliver noted the "capacity crowd" at Gallagher's show at the Hammersmith Odeon on 16 October, commending him on "being as relevant in 1987 as he was treading the Marquee's boards in 1967."[2] Gallagher's performance left such an impression that Oliver even hinted at a possible career revival: "Is Rory Gallagher in danger of becoming, er, fashionable again?" Commentary such as Oliver's, coupled with Gallagher's absence from Ireland in the mid-1980s, intensified anticipation from fans for his return in November for a filmed appearance at the Cork Opera House.

And so, while it seemed that Gallagher was finally being rewarded for tireless hours in the studio during the last five years, when returning to Ireland, he discovered that he was neither fashionable nor square, but instead "rounding out."[3]

John Andrews, for instance, reminded readers in the *Nationalist and Leinster Times* of the "seriously over-weight"[4] Gallagher during his previous trip to Dublin for the Self Aid Festival in May 1986, adding that the show was "average" due to Gallagher's "out-of-tune guitar" and "a large sprinkling of bum notes." Ann Marie Hawthorne of the *Irish Press* made similar remarks: "There is more to Rory Gallagher than there used to be," and the 'more' is not a new album, but rather "a bigger size of Wrangler jean."[5] Gallagher defends himself, "I'm going to get the weight off by walking a lot, rehearsing a lot and starving a lot," reassuring fans that he will soon be "fighting fit" again. Next, Hawthorne dissects his age, deciphering how late into his thirties Gallagher is. "Just late," he answers. When the conversation turns to the length of his hair, Gallagher seems withdrawn. "'Sort of long', he said helpfully." Gallagher's "cagey" demeanour provokes Hawthorne to claim that "interviewing Cork people [is] a real challenge" as they lack a "loquacious" persona. Even an article for the *Meath Chronicle* comments on Gallagher's weight, noting a "new slimline appearance" as he has been busy "fighting the dreaded flab" in preparation for the European leg of his *Defender* tour.⁶ Aside from being "back in his hometown and playing for his home crowd,"⁷ such examples of distasteful coverage from Ireland's media may have affected the already "extremely emotional" and "nervous" Gallagher backstage at the Opera House.

Thirty-four years on, Barry Barnes, lead guitarist and vocalist for the Rory Gallagher tribute band Sinnerboy, nervously awaited the likelihood of his next gig. Unlike Gallagher, Barnes' trepidation arose from the external rather than the internal. In 2021, the world was bound by the restrictions of the COVID-19 pandemic, with daily interaction temporarily paused due to curfews, travel restrictions and the cancellation of many outdoor events. The music industry suffered to a large extent, with creative outlets such as rehearsal halls and studios to pubs and auditoriums forced to close (in some unfortunate cases, permanently) as a result of the economic crisis from the pandemic. Barry Barnes was all too familiar with this reality. However, the air momentarily cleared during this bleak period when promoter Tom Keating contacted Barnes about Sinnerboy recreating Gallagher's 1987 Cork Opera House performance.

Although Barnes missed out on the original Cork show, he was honoured to commemorate such an important milestone in Gallagher's touring history. Barnes was first impressed with Taste's *On the Boards*, attending the trio's gig at the Free Trade Hall in Manchester in early 1970. He recalls initial "disappointment"⁸ when noticing Gallagher's minimal set-up of a small Vox amplifier, as opposed to the wall of Marshall amps preferred by bands such as the Jimi Hendrix Experience and Cream. "Anyway, Rory ran on, plugged his Stratocaster into the Vox, turned it up and *woah*. The rest is history, and I've been a mega fan since then."

Barnes tried to see Gallagher whenever he played in Manchester, including his visit in 1987, just a month before his Cork Opera House date. Since forming in 2000, Sinnerboy have participated in many landmark shows commemorating Gallagher, including the first London tribute at the Irish Arts Centre in Hammersmith in 2003. Sinnerboy have trekked from England to Spain, from Greece to Ireland, celebrating Gallagher's music with his fans, supporting Dónal's claim that the band is "proof that my brother's music lives on."⁹

Therefore, Sinnerboy were an obvious choice to pay homage to Gallagher's "triumphant return"¹⁰ to Cork in 1987. According to Barnes, the tribute show aimed to capture the "spirit" of the original by "[recreating] the atmosphere [and] the memories."¹¹ While the idea sounded "amazing" on paper—or rather, phone screen—the difficulty lay in how to enact this idea in a stagnant world. Barnes confessed to his apprehension, "I was waiting any day now for Tom [Keating] to ring me and say, 'No, we're not on, Barry. We can't do it'." Thankfully, Barnes did not receive such a call, and a show was scheduled for 18 September 2021. "There was a small window where we came out of lockdown and then we went back into it about a week later. But we were so lucky that we got this little clear window," said Barnes. "We [were] due to fly out on the Friday and the gig was on the Saturday, so on the Monday I got a phone call from Jonny Brutal [Sinnerboy's drummer]. 'Barry, I've got COVID'. Oh no. Everything was conspiring against us to do this." Barnes quickly contacted Sean Reynolds, a drummer from Ballyshannon, who was more than happy to replace Brutal for the show.

Sinnerboy's tribute concert in 2021 is merely one example of how Gallagher's connection to the city of Cork has been honoured in the present day. In this chapter, we explore the impact of Gallagher's show at the Cork Opera House in 1987 using fan accounts (many of whom were young teenagers witnessing their first concert experience), as well as press articles and interviews with band members, such as Mark Feltham. In addition, we investigate the current commemorations for Gallagher in Cork, such as a proposed festival to influencing contemporary composers like Anselm McDonnell. Overall, this chapter establishes the theme for 'Part Four: Ireland', which explores Gallagher's position in the history of Irish music and culture, whether in Dublin (see 4.2 and 4.4) or Derry (4.3), as well as assess the ways he connected with his Gaelic roots on an international level (4.6).

"Rory Rory, Hallelujah!":
Kickstarting the *Defender* tour, from Great Britain to Cork
As record stores stocked the recent *Defender*, Gallagher started his promotional tour with appearances at two German festivals in July: Deggendorf's Blue Danube Festival on the 12th and Out in the Green in Babenhausen six days later. Gallagher's show in Babenhausen attracted a mixed reaction from photographer Micha Thieme, as described to us in a 2022 Q&A. Although "brilliant" in 1987, Thieme sensed an element lacking when compared to seeing Gallagher previously at the Stadthalle in Offenbach. "I had the feeling that performing onstage wasn't as easy for Rory as it looked like in 1982," Thieme explained.[12] Nevertheless, Gallagher had certainly found 'the feeling' by early August for the Seepark Open Air Festival at Arbon, Switzerland. Beyond the concert itself, Gallagher's new album had begun to generate a positive response from his fans, as indicated by a review from *Deuce Quarterly*: "[At Arbon], there were storms of enthusiasm for 'Continental Op', even though the LP *Defender* had only been released a few days earlier."[13] On 21 August, Gallagher entertained fans at the Trochtelfingen Open Air Festival in Germany for close to three and a half hours, joined briefly onstage by guitarist Tony McPhee from the Groundhogs. As the show finished, "the band as well as the audience was totally knackered–but just as satisfied."[14]

During soundcheck at Glasgow's Pavilion on 4 October, Gallagher spoke with Tom Russell about treating his Edinburgh audience the night before to "a long set" with "the best blend we could [of new stuff in between the old stuff]."[15] Russell asked Gallagher if he was feeling "more nervous" tonight, as Radio Clyde was to record his performance at the Pavilion. "You're more cautious of buzzes and mistakes and broken strings and so on," he revealed, keeping primarily optimistic about the "extra tension." "If tonight works, it'll be great because we do a few numbers that aren't on [*Defender*]—tracks for the next album, so to speak—and that'll be nice to get them on tape and see how they happen."

Reviewer Peter Grant hailed Gallagher's return to the Royal Court in Liverpool on 9 October as "the best indoor gig of the year," complimenting the guitarist's ability to "bring out the best in [his] audience."[16] Speaking with the *Liverpool Echo*, Gallagher expressed delight to finally "be back on the road again,"[17] remembering Liverpudlians as "a great bunch of people [with] a real warmth."[18] Gallagher's agent at the time, Paul Charles, recalled to us "the buzz of excitement" in the air at the guitarist's City Hall gig in Sheffield on 14 October.[19] "Rory and the band were in fine form that night, but then again if my memory serves me correctly, they were in fine form every night [on the *Defender* tour]."

A raving review by Frank Edmonds echoed Derek Oliver's remarks at the beginning of this chapter regarding Gallagher's appearance at the Hammersmith Odeon in mid-October. Edmonds admits to his initial worry when watching the "chubby-faced, portly middle-aged"[20] Gallagher walk onto the stage, wondering if he was "a spent force [after] such a lengthy absence." Edmonds was ultimately proved wrong. "From the moment [Gallagher] powered into the first chords of the night, one thing was abundantly clear: you can't keep a good guitarist down." Around the same time, Gallagher was featured in the "first comprehensive account"[21] of Ireland's rock music history with the release of *Irish Rock: Roots, Personalities, Directions* by Mark J. Prendergast in November 1987. Such positive press reinforced to fans (both old and new) about "the man who put Ireland on the rock map" years before "Saint Bob [Geldof] and Bono," preparing Irish audiences for Gallagher's return to the stage in Cork.[22]

Taking a short break following his Birmingham concert on 18 October, Gallagher recommenced his *Defender* tour by flying to Cork to take part in a concert series devised by RTÉ'S Television Variety Department. In addition to Gallagher, the other acts included Paul Brady, Johnny Logan and Freddie White. RTÉ recorded each musician separately across 4-7 November to be eventually broadcast at Christmas for public viewing, with Gallagher the first to be televised. According to the *Evening Herald*, Gallagher's Opera House concert had "been sold out for ages,"[23] indicating the high demand still cultivated by the guitarist at this time in his career. The Opera House was a suitable venue for Gallagher due to its "intimate 'club' feel [and] acoustic values," while at the same time providing a "broad theatrical stage" for the band's "'tour de force' set to be technically and perfectly captured for posterity."[24]

During his interviews with Gerry McAvoy and Dónal, Dan Muise directs the questioning to his "personal observation" of the "sadness in Rory's eyes" at the show. McAvoy's primary explanation was that Gallagher could not accept that "there were things he could deliver ten years previous that he couldn't deliver that particular night. And he felt that." "Rory always wanted to think that he could still do what he was doing when he was twenty-one," he added.[25]

Mark Feltham offers an alternative perspective, assessing Gallagher's "procrastination" to be the faction of his life that began to "deteriorate" around late 1987. Feltham observed "a very, very nervous [Gallagher]" offstage, "but once [he was at the show and playing], everything was brilliant right up until the end." Feltham firmly attested that, apart from the 1995 tour, he "never saw any problems [with Gallagher's performing] at all" and, therefore, disputes any negative press surrounding the Opera House gig.

Moreover, McAvoy mentions the auditorium lights being on for the television cameras interfering with the "ambience" of the performance—a topic that Gallagher had discussed in his Tom Russell interview in Glasgow a month before. "A live TV thing is very [difficult] sometimes because they have to use bright lights," Gallagher explained. The challenge lay in balancing his attention between "trying to please the audience out front" while also "directing [his] act to the camera."[26] All in all, Gallagher described the process as "harrowing." Dónal fleshes out the circumstances surrounding his brother's "extremely emotional" [27] return to his hometown, recalling the few hours prior to walking onstage in Muise's book:

> We sat with a photographer friend of ours, John Minihan, from *The London Evening Standard*, who had photographed Rory a lot and was a good pal of Rory's. And he was finding it hard to understand why Rory was so glum. There he was with a sold-out Opera House. A seven-camera shoot. All the ordeal, the trucks, everything that goes with it. Yet Rory was despondent and keeping low key.

Dónal provides two explanations for the 'sadness' Muise had previously noted. On the one hand, Gallagher's "remorseful" attitude could have been "a side effect of the medication he was taking," while, on the other, Dónal suggests that his brother had begun to "feel the pressure" of the music business. He explains further: "Do an album. Go and promote it, which would take a year to go around the world and cover every territory. And then you were expected to deliver yet another album. It was an abnormal pressure road."

Carolyn Fisher of *Sunday World* framed Gallagher as "a workaholic and a recluse," unable to resist the typical comments about his wardrobe: "I bet you he'll be wearing the same shirt too [at the Opera House]!"[28] Interestingly, an article published in *The Kerryman* a month prior to Gallagher's Cork show critiqued the 1980s trend of music on television, particularly with the launch of MTV in 1981. The article argued, "TV can use music to fill [air time]," citing a recent example of the Pogues' Shane McGowan drinking and smoking throughout a performance on the late night programme *Session* as a "bad mix of music and TV."[29] With critics disapproving of filmed concerts for primetime viewing, pressure was possibly increased onto the RTÉ team (or even Gallagher himself) regarding audience reaction to the broadcasts.

In addition, Dónal attributed Gallagher's innate "blues heart"[30] to his melancholic demeanour at Cork, which mirrored Feltham's assessment. "I always saw a sadness there," he attested, "That was part of him […] [but] I don't think that it reflected on anything technically [at Cork or at any other performance]."[31]

Contradicting McAvoy's words, Feltham stated several times throughout our conversation that, apart from the few shows in 1995, Gallagher maintained a high quality of musicianship during their 11 years working together. "[At Cork] he was as fearsome and as fiery as ever," Feltham said, "He was always good. In fact, I think he got better." As the *Evening Echo* reported, Gallagher "always kept something special in reserve for his appearances in Cork," guaranteeing a memorable night for his fans.[32]

"The master's return"

For almost three hours,[33] Gallagher entranced fans at the Opera House with a mixture of old and new material, showcasing his strengths as a bandleader and performer, demonstrated immediately in the strong opener 'Continental Op'. As the crowd enthusiastically greets Gallagher, he hints to the next song as the "old one you might like to hear again," drifting into the hypnotic introduction of 'Tattoo'd Lady', which ignites applause. As argued by Greg Barbrick on *Blogcritics*, Gallagher is "at the top of his form"[34] at the Opera House, highlighted in his effortless musical seduction, from cooling the audience in 'I Ain't No Saint' to firing up the blood in 'Don't Start Me Talkin''. Gallagher produces an exhilarating cover of 'When My Baby She Left Me', as well as easing into mild-tempo jams, such as on the electric version of 'Loanshark Blues'. He also showcases his great ability to improvise and extend the potential of his guitar, as depicted in the momentary deviation to Dave Brubeck's 'Take Five' during 'Off the Handle'. In conjunction with the release of *Live in Cork* (2009), Barbrick rightfully concludes that the video "should be viewed by all fans of great blues playing."

To further enhance the mood of each song, Gallagher is cascaded in deep hues of turquoise and purple lightning, with occasional bursts of yellow and orange to enliven the atmosphere. Producer of the show Avril MacRory shared an amusing anecdote involving Gallagher's preference for a black stage and set. To prevent him from camouflaging into the background, MacRory advised Gallagher to wear blue jeans, to which he (initially) agreed. However, when he arrived for the concert in head-to-toe black clothing, MacRory admitted she "nearly slaughtered him" and, as a result, the RTÉ team had to "adjust" the lighting so that Gallagher could still be seen on film.[35] "But that was Rory," she later reflected, "He would be charming and nice and then do exactly what he had intended all along."

According to fan Paul O'Sullivan, the auditorium was "packed for the master's return," an instant and "rousing applause" erupting in the Opera House as the band reached the stage.[36] O'Sullivan contributed a lengthy review for the members of fanzine *Deuce Quarterly*, reporting the "many standing ovations" Gallagher received throughout the evening, such as during the lively 'Messin' with the Kid'. As written by O'Sullivan:

> The mixture of the new and the not-so-new in the set seemed just right. New material like 'Road to Hell' and 'Don't Start Me Talkin'' (new?) fitted in well amongst the older classics like 'Tattoo'd

> Lady' and 'A Million Miles Away'. The passage of time seems to have lent even more magic to these latter two tracks and to the way they are reproduced on stage by the band [...] Throughout the performance, Rory's Strat produced those familiar hard-edged sounds that we know only *it* can produce–particularly effective on 'Off the Handle' and 'Brute Force and Ignorance', which were played with true venom and power. [...] All in all, this for me was a concert to savour. RORY IS BACK!

As stated in the introduction, many Irish teenagers attended Gallagher's appearance at the Opera House, challenging claims from the *Southern Star* that a majority of Gallagher's audience at this time was comprised of "males in their mid thirties reliving the good old days."[37] For some of Gallagher's newest fans, such as 17-year-old Mark Gillis, the Opera House gig became a milestone in their youth. Aside from growing up in Cork, where "it's hard not to know of Rory,"[38] it was Gillis's father who encouraged his appreciation of Gallagher's music. "I love [Gallagher's] honesty and integrity that comes through in his music, from the beautiful ballads to straight out rockers." Gillis recalled the "exciting" time watching Gallagher in his hometown while accompanied by his father to then reliving the experience when viewing the show on television a month later:

> It was my first gig and I was blown away by the sound, so loud [...] It was then with great anticipation that we awaited the [Christmas] broadcast [of the show]. I taped the concert on a blank VHS video, which I still have, and made a cover for it out of magazine articles. I can actually be seen in the film.

Gillis would go on to see Gallagher at Cork City Hall in 1988 (4.2), Lark by the Lee in 1992 and the acoustic gig in honour of Gallagher's Uncle Jimmy at the Regional Technical College in 1993 (4.5). Gillis's father passed away in 1990 and, in a strange twist of fate, is buried not far from Gallagher in St Oliver's Cemetery. Whenever Gillis goes to visit his father, he stops to say hello to Gallagher as well.

Another young Gallagher fan to attend the Opera House show was Gary Cotter. "I was fourteen, [and] I'd never seen anything like it. Fantastic. I had never heard a guitar player that loud before. He just blew me away," Cotter shared with us in July 2023.[39] Cotter was particularly spellbound by Gallagher's "rapport with the crowd," as well as watching "his [guitar] technique and seeing [in] reality what I'd only seen him do on video." Although not a strictly blues-rock fan—citing The Stranglers as his favourite group at the time—when a neighbour loaned him Gallagher's 1975 LP *Against the Grain*, Cotter was suddenly buying "anything I could get my hands on to listen to him." A guitar player from a young age, Cotter learned song craftsmanship from listening to Gallagher's records. "It was the fact that his solos didn't need to be note perfect. They had to have feel, emotion, and that's what I loved about them." Following the Opera House concert, Cotter managed to meet Gallagher backstage, an experience he recalls as "absolutely incredible":

He still had sweat on his hair–he was literally just off the stage–and my Dad brought me around the back and I got a photo taken with him from an actual professional photographer. It's a big, black and white photograph of the two of us. And he had a kind of promotional picture of himself, [and] he signed that for me on the front of it and on the back as well. My Dad told him that I play guitar as well and [Gallagher] put a little message to me about keeping up playing the guitar on the back of it. He was such a nice man. That was the only time I met him.

24-year-old fan Stephen Murphy, another attendee reporting to *Deuce Quarterly*, confirmed that Gallagher performed four acoustic tunes. However, only two were featured in the broadcast: Leadbelly's 'Out on the Western Plain' and John Lee Hooker's 'Want'ad Blues'. In addition, Murphy mentioned, "On two occasions [...] an extremely happy fan" joined Gallagher onstage, with the band appearing "delighted to be back home after such a long time." The broadcast includes one moment when an audience member—later identified as Denis Cronin—jumps onstage and whispers into Gallagher's ear during 'Out on the Western Plain'. This has since become an iconic moment in the fan community, with Barry Barnes intending to recreate the interaction at his 2021 Sinnerboy tribute gig. Unfortunately, Cronin was ill at the time and, therefore, unable to attend the show. Instead, promoter Tom Keating enacted the moment "for fun."

During an autograph signing after the concert, Gallagher told Stephen Murphy that he was "looking forward to a few Christmas gigs" in Ireland. In fact, praise of Gallagher's Opera House appearance lingered in the Irish press into the New Year (partly due to the RTÉ broadcast at Christmas), generating a warm welcome for the start of his Irish tour in February 1988 (see 4.2). As highlighted by Dan Collins, "Gallagher ripped out the best of his repertoire [for almost three hours]" at the Opera House, predicting a similar "ecstatic audience" to return for his concert at Cork's City Hall on 28 February.[40] During his 1988 tour, Gallagher exhibited a generally favourable outlook on his Opera House concert in an interview with Dave Fanning. Gallagher enjoyed the "general mood of the place," particularly the lighting and sound, and while "the cameras did constrict us a wee bit[41] [...] as televised things go, I think it was a success."

Overall, Gallagher's performance was considered by the Irish press as "the most exciting" of the four RTÉ Christmas broadcasts and that, without question, the guitarist had "conquered" the "serene surroundings" of the Opera House.[42] Peter Cross of the *Cork Examiner* made similar observations, stating that, while "the last traces of paint are almost gone from [his] '61 Fender Stratocaster, rock supremo Rory Gallagher has lost none of [his] lustre."[43] Cross then declares: "never has such a performer on the hallowed boards of the Cork theatre received so many standing ovations." Avril MacRory noted how it was "amazing" to be at the Opera House and see the "pride and emotion in the crowd," including "people in tears."[44] In recent years, however, Gallagher's appearance at the Opera House has attracted some negative press, such as Carol Clerk's review for the 1999 video release of *Messin' with the Kid: Live at the Opera House*.

As opposed to the "much-loved" *Irish Tour '74*, Clerk comes across as slightly disheartened for "a concert filmed in the late stages of Rory's career [...] in his hometown in 1990 [sic]" and, as such, it was "the last thing" she expected to be released from the Estate's archives.[45] Clerk, however, could not overlook the fact that 1987 Gallagher had sustained the "passion and magic" in his guitar playing, regardless of how "subdued" or "measured" he appeared.

Critics recently echo Clerk's sentiments, for example, Ed Power's review for the *Irish Examiner* in 2021. Power emphasises Gallagher's "tired eyes" and his loss of "previous leanness and intensity," even comparing the guitarist to a "warhorse who'd spent [too] long at the front line."[46] Nevertheless, further on in the article, Power does acknowledge Gallagher's extraordinary display of skill and showmanship: "Gallagher blazed through his blues blitzkrieg. It was as if an earthquake had struck Emmet Place." Therefore, despite the occasional criticism (largely shaped around Gallagher's appearance), his return to the Cork stage in 1987 is, on the whole, regarded as "one of the greatest gigs ever to grace any Irish venue"[47] in both a past and contemporary context.

From Visual Bible to Recreation:
Paying Tribute to the 1987 Cork Opera House Show

Compared to many of the other Gallagher concerts mentioned in this book, the Cork Opera House broadcast has received considerable coverage in biographies, such as Vignoles and Muise, as well as appeared on Estate-approved VHS and DVD releases, therefore maintaining access for future generations. Initially released under *Messin' with the Kid* on VHS in April 1990, the press soon referred to the video as a testament to "why Rory is still one of the most respected guitar-pickers in the business,"[48] with both he and his band "in peak form."[49]

K.Y Lee of the *South China Sunday Morning Post* observed Gallagher's "spellbinding" fretwork, claiming "the Irish guitarist can still play a mean lick or two."[50] Similarly, Monty Smith of *Q* magazine praised the high level of musicianship exhibited by the Irishman. "[Gallagher's] voice, light but strongly melodic, is superior to, say, [Eric] Clapton's, while his extraordinarily fluid fretwork is powerfully dramatic without resorting to flashy tricks."[51] Furthermore, Smith outlined how Gallagher treated all his guitars with "the ease and comfort of old and respected friends" and that he had "an impressive set of songs old and new."

Over a decade later, Shawn Perry of *Vintage Rock* shared similar insights following the DVD release in 2009. By Perry's account, *Live in Cork* demonstrated Gallagher's exquisite ability to give even his "memorable riffs," such as 'Tattoo'd Lady', that "needed juice of sustainability," as well as captivate the audience with his recent material from *Defender*.[52] Perry highlights Gallagher's acoustic interval as epitomising his "mastery [as a bluesman]," and considered tracks such as 'Want'ad Blues' and 'The Loop' to be the DVD's "defining moments" because it "[showcases] an innate talent no longer here and sorely missed."

Zach Demter, another contemporary critic, also singled out Gallagher's acoustic technique, particularly on 'Out on the Western Plain', as "a perfect example of his talent."[53] In addition, *Live in Cork* was regarded as a "vastly superior documentation" due to the "crisp [and] clear" sound quality, with Christel Loar of *Popmatters* complimenting the RTÉ stage crew on the brightly coloured lighting, which allows "viewers to completely geek out on exactly what and how Gallagher is playing."[54]

The DVD also contained the special feature 'A Rough Guide to Rory's Cork', which tracked significant landmarks in Gallagher's hometown with his life. According to Ronan Leonard of *Echo Live*, both the VHS and DVD versions of the Cork show have become "a visual bible for Gallagher fans," continuing to be a high spot in the canon "as an iconic snapshot of Gallagher [as] the revered bluesman."[55] In recent years, the Gallagher official page have uploaded remastered versions of 'Continental Op', 'Tattoo'd Lady' and 'Out on the Western Plain' from the Cork broadcast to their YouTube site, possibly hinting at a future rerelease of the DVD in HD quality. If not, then these videos at least serve to introduce Gallagher's latter-day performances to the new 'tech-generation'.

Sinnerboy's Barry Barnes seemed to agree with Ronan Leonard's 'visual bible' description, attributing the DVD's popularity as a partial influence in organising their 2021 tribute show:

> It's a big video for the Rory fans in Cork. Well, it's a big video for *all* Rory fans. It's a fantastic video. I think it's the best filmed gig we've got, and Rory that night was really, really on it. It was later in his career, in the eighties, as we know, and he wasn't as fiery, like running about as he was when he was young, but his guitar playing... every solo was a symphony. It was fantastic, [and he had] really matured as a player. It was a big thing for Cork, [and] that's why we recreated that.

Growing up in Ballyshannon, drummer Sean Reynolds easily became a Gallagher fan, discovering "a whole new world of music"[56] when dropping the needle on *Live! in Europe* (1972) for the first time. "The album became my door to a dimension of blues and rock that to this day I am still discovering," wrote Reynolds, recalling 'Bullfrog Blues' in particular as "[his] calling to play drums." Reynolds enjoyed Gallagher's music to the point of joining the tribute band Moonchild for a decade, playing at various festivals, such as the Rory Gallagher International Tribute Festival in Ballyshannon, where he first met Sinnerboy's Barry Barnes. When Barnes phoned him four days prior to the 2021 Cork Opera House gig, Reynolds immediately recognised the importance of such an opportunity. As he later disclosed: "This was way too good of an offer to refuse—and for three reasons. Firstly, I get to play in the same venue Rory famously played. Secondly, I get to play with [Sinnerboy]. Thirdly, I get to play a gig filled with Rory Gallagher songs."

While, on the surface, it all seemed too good to be true, once reality settled in, then the nerves truly kicked in for Reynolds. During the next two days of rehearsals, Reynolds received an "overdose" of Gallagher material. "My mind was in overdrive wanting to prove to [Sinnerboy] and to Rory that I could do it." On the night of the concert, as Reynolds looked out across the "enormous" stage of the Opera House, everything suddenly became "a little bit daunting." Nevertheless, as the show got underway, his mood soon shifted. "The gig was unbelievable in the sense that [the band] played with such joy and passion. We seemed to gel together quite well, which is what I was worried about all week." Reynolds enjoyed the experience of playing songs like 'Continental Op', 'Don't Start Me Talkin'' and 'Off the Handle' for the first time, feeling "so proud" to honour Gallagher (as well as his former drummers) with his performance.

Tom O'Flaherty, a Gallagher fan since 1973, attended both 1987 and 2021 concerts. "I missed numerous opportunities to see [Gallagher] […] [and so] when the Opera House gig was announced [in 1987], I got tickets immediately."[57] O'Flaherty fondly remembers the show as it was his first time seeing Gallagher live. "He looked older and a little heavier, but when he started playing, he was amazing [and] the crowd loved it." Over the years, O'Flaherty has attended many commemorative celebrations for Gallagher, such as the Ballyshannon Festival and Cork Rocks for Rory. He highly regards Sinnerboy amongst the other tribute groups, particularly "his favourite tribute guitarist" Barry Barnes because "he's so passionate about it." O'Flaherty considered Sinnerboy's performance a "fantastic tribute" to the original, even expressing support for the idea that the 2021 concert should appear on DVD someday.

Sinnerboy's commemorative concert aimed to revive interest and appreciation for Gallagher in his hometown, especially during a period when "there was nothing happening in Cork for Rory [in terms of tribute events]."[58] In Barnes' opinion, the Cork tribute was not one of Sinnerboy's best performances due to the COVID-19 restrictions limiting rehearsal time as well as the addition of a new drummer. Nevertheless, he did highlight the powerful connection formed between the band and the crowd as a result of playing Gallagher's music, particularly after an extended period of social isolation. As stated by Barnes, "[…] if you were to analyse the gig, the audience were so excited and so happy that [they] managed to get over and listen to some Rory music. It was really well attended, 1,000 [to] 1,200 people, something like that. Everybody had a ball, we had a fantastic time." As such, Sinnerboy's tribute to Gallagher strengthened the legacy of his 1987 Opera House appearance, as well as emphasising the healing relationship between music and people, specifically in the context of COVID-19.

Tributes and Triumphs:
Sustaining Gallagher's Memory in Cork

Since 1995, Gallagher has been honoured in his hometown through various tribute shows and events, such as Ger Kenneally's Cork Rocks for Rory festival (hereafter Cork Rocks) from 2005 to 2019. Musician Dave McHugh remembers Kenneally as "a very kind-hearted man,"[59] who curated a "more intimate" tribute attended mainly by Corkonians, as opposed to the annual Rory Gallagher International Tribute Festival in Ballyshannon founded by Barry O'Neill. Although popular throughout the years, Cork Rocks was nevertheless affected by the Estate-endorsed festival in Ballyshannon, and since Kenneally's passing in 2017, tributes for Gallagher in Cork have gradually "petered out," according to McHugh. Many factors, such as fewer large venues and street events, contributed to the lowkey atmosphere of Cork Rocks, instead hosting gigs at spots such as the Rory Gallagher Music Library. In addition, tensions slightly arose due to the fact that Gallagher was born in Ballyshannon yet grew up in Cork, creating confusion over which location was most suitable to honour Ireland's first 'rockstar'. This "rivalry" reached a point where Kenneally would invite bands to Cork Rocks that O'Neill had rejected for Ballyshannon (and vice versa), often "working against each other as opposed to working forward" in establishing multiple sites for fans to remember their musical hero. In spite of this, McHugh argues that Kenneally's efforts helped "sustain the memory of Rory in Cork," thus strengthening Gallagher's legacy in his hometown.

Kenneally's death seemed to mark a decline in tribute gatherings for Gallagher in Cork, perhaps worsened by the subsequent COVID-19 pandemic restrictions. McHugh raised another issue regarding the timing of festivals, since both Cork Rocks and the Ballyshannon festival occurred within the early June period to coincide with the anniversary of Gallagher's passing on the 14th, therefore creating difficulty for fans to attend both.

In late 2021, news circulated regarding a new Rory Gallagher festival in Cork. Following Councillor Shane O'Callaghan's successful application to Cork City Council, the annual weekend festival will possibly be held in Rory Gallagher Place in years to come. As stated by O'Callaghan, not only will this event advance Cork's tourism, but also—and more importantly—it will increase awareness of Gallagher's "enormous contribution to Cork and to music."[60] Although no new information has come to light since the initial announcement in 2021, Gallagher's legacy has been commemorated for a new wave of fans to enjoy within the past year.

In February 2024, Irish composer Anselm McDonnell was announced as the winner of the Seán Ó Riada competition for his piece 'Gallagher'. McDonnell discovered Gallagher's music when he expressed interest in the guitar at 11 years old. His father bought him a five-CD Rory Gallagher boxset and, from there, "*Top Priority* was rarely out of the hi-fi."[61] McDonnell credits Gallagher as "a major inspiration" for his guitar playing in addition to "studying rock and blues," leading him to a "predilection towards Fender guitars" in adult life. Gallagher's presence in McDonnell's early musical education has subtly crept into his classical works. Key features, such as Gallagher's "melodic writing" and "raw emotion and immediacy," have been areas that McDonnell strives to "emulate" in his music making. This is epitomised in 'Gallagher' (2024), which integrates various "iconic riffs of phrases [of Rory's] into its choral textures," such as the chorus line of 'Follow Me', utilised for the countermelody to the main soprano melody. As demonstrated in 1.2-1.5, Gallagher experimented with many musical ideas and sounds during his 'Cubist' period; McDonnell agrees, referring to the "harmonica [imitation]" on Gallagher's guitar in some *Fresh Evidence* tracks. McDonnell takes inspiration from such methods in his composing, "pushing instruments to extremes of expression."

On 3 May 2024, 'Gallagher' premiered at the Cork International Choral Festival, with McDonnell "very honoured" due to the attendance of Dónal and his family. 'Gallagher' derived primarily from McDonnell and poet Tim MacGabhann's "mutual love of Rory's music" and, thus, for the composition to "find a home at the festival [in Cork]" was a "moving and appropriate" gesture. The McDonnell-MacGabhann collaboration shows a different angle to Gallagher as a creative influence, emphasising his impact on both blues artists, as well as "the musical landscape of Ireland." Moreover, tributes continue in his hometown, with Gallagher remembered at the Cork Jazz Festival by band Deuce performing at Fred Zeppelins on 26 October 2024.

The Ulster Hall in Belfast "became the shrine every Christmas to Rory,"[62] eventually memorialised with a plaque in 2007 to "[show] respect to one of the great Irish performers of his—or any—generation."[63] In a similar way, perhaps the Opera House in Cork is gradually transforming into another place of commemoration for the guitarist in Ireland, with even Band of Friends (along with special guest, the Pat McManus Band) performing at the venue on 16 September 2023.

Many fans regard the Opera House as an essential location to visit when travelling to Cork, signifying the meanings created between specific spaces in Ireland with being a Gallagher fan.[64] As indicated in the reflections by fan Monique Frie from her trip to Cork: "Finally standing there in front of the Cork Opera House was so special. Here, Rory played a very good concert with many of my favourite songs."[65] Frie strongly felt Gallagher's "presence with every breath of wind that [passed her]" while walking the streets of Cork. As such, future tribute events and dedications are to be encouraged in order to further cement Gallagher's legacy in his hometown.

RM

Footnotes

1 Review from *Bünder Zeitung* (October 1987), published in *Deuce Quarterly*, no. 43 (January 1988), 25.
2 Derek Oliver, 'Rory Gallagher – Hammersmith Odeon, London', *Kerrang!* (14 November 1987), https://www.roryon.com/hammer351.html
3 Ann Marie Hawthorne, 'Rounding on Rory', *Irish Press* (3 September 1987), 9.
4 John Andrews, part of the 'Your Scene' column, *Nationalist and Leinster Times* (18 December 1987), n.p.
5 Hawthorne, 'Rounding on Rory'.
6 'Rhythm 'N' News', *Meath Chronicle* (12 September 1987), 20.
7 Dan Muise, *Gallagher, Marriott, Derringer & Trower* (Milwaukee: Hal Leonard Corporation, 2002), 64.
8 Interview with Barry Barnes, 11 September 2023. All subsequent quotes from Barnes come from this interview unless stated otherwise.
9 Bill Browne, 'Sinnerboy set to follow the 'Blueprint' laid by Rory Gallagher at the Cork Opera House', *Irish Independent* (13 September 2021), https://www.independent.ie/regionals/cork/news/sinnerboy-set-to-follow-the-blueprint-laid-by-rory-gallagher-at-the-cork-opera-house/40845178.html
10 Julian Vignoles, *Rory Gallagher: The Man Behind the Guitar* (London: Collins, 2018), 185.
11 Ed Power, 'Cork Opera House 1987: How Rory Gallagher showed he could still rock', *Irish Examiner* (26 October 2021), https://www.irishexaminer.com/lifestyle/artsandculture/arid-40729227.html
12 Interview with Micha Thieme, 3 August 2022.
13 Markus Gygax, 'Arbon 8.8.87 Seepark-Open-Air-Festival', *Deuce Quarterly*, no. 43 (January 1988), 12.
14 Edith Viertelhausen, 'Trochtelfingen 21.8.97 8. Open-Air-Festival', *Deuce Quarterly*, no. 43 (January 1988), 12.
15 'Radio Clyde Interview' (4 October 1987), http://www.roryon.com/clyde349.html.
16 Peter Grant, 'Rory's return brings out the best', *Liverpool Echo* (10 October 1987), 3.
17 Peter Grant, 'Rory set to roar back', *Liverpool Echo* (10 September 1987), 28.
18 Peter Grant, 'Rory roars back into town', *Liverpool Echo* (9 October 1987), 7.
19 Interview with Paul Charles, 24 October 2023.
20 Frank Edmonds, 'Rory Rory, Hallelujah!', *Bury Free Press* (23 October 1987), 76.
21 'Book Review: 'Irish Rock: Roots. Personalities. Directions'. *Bookseller* (9 October 1987), 47.
22 'Choice Cuts', *Sandwell Evening Mail* (15 September 1987), 15.
23 Philip Nolan, 'That other Cork festival', *Evening Herald* (4 November 1987), 21.
24 Dónal Gallagher in the *Live in Cork* (2006) DVD liner notes.
25 Muise, *Gallagher, Marriott, Derringer & Trower*, 64.
26 'Radio Clyde Interview'.
27 Muise, *Gallagher, Marriott, Derringer & Trower*, 63.
28 Carolyn Fisher, 'Glory for Rory', *Sunday World* (8 November 1987), 9.
29 'Music and Television', *The Kerryman* (16 October 1987), 22.
30 Muise, *Gallagher, Marriott, Derringer & Trower*, 63.
31 Interview with Mark Feltham, 20 October 2023.
32 Tony O'Mahony, 'Looking In: Treat for Gallagher fans', *Evening Echo* (30 December 1987), 6.
33 Although Gallagher delivered an almost three-hour performance, only 90 minutes were used for the RTÉ broadcast in December. As such, our review of the show is based on the songs included in the recording.
34 Greg Barbrick, 'Music DVD Review: Rory Gallagher – *Live in Cork*', *Blogcritics* (21 March 2009), https://blogcritics.org/music-dvd-review-rory-gallagher-live/
35 'Rory Gallagher: Tributes from famous friends', *Hot Press* (December 1995), https://www.hotpress.com/music/rory-gallagher-tributes-from-famous-friends-14356545
36 Paul O'Sullivan, 'Cork Opera House – Nov. 4th 1987', *Deuce Quarterly*, no. 43 (January 1988), 7.
37 'Concerts', *Southern Star* (31 October 1987), 10.
38 Interview with Mark Gillis, 17-18 May 2022.
39 Interview with Gary Cotter, 22 July 2023.
40 Dan Collins, 'Rory Gallagher returns', *Weekend* (6 February 1988), n.p.
41 According to fan Stephen Murphy, Gallagher even stated to him backstage after the show that "he was dissatisfied with a cameraman standing in front of him a lot of the time."
42 'Rory rocks back for City Hall concert', *Evening Echo* (7 January 1988), n.p.
43 Peter Cross, 'Rory rolls back', *Cork Examiner* (5 November 1987), n.p.
44 Vignoles, *Rory Gallagher*, 185.
45 Carol Clerk, 'Videos', *Uncut* (1 August 1999), 111.
46 Power, 'Cork Opera House 1987'.
47 Browne, 'Sinnerboy set…'
48 'A video feast of music and comedy', *Formby Times* (5 April 1990), 27.
49 K.Y Lee, 'Storm still rages inside Rory's guitar', *South China Sunday Morning Post* (7 October 1990), 90.
50 Ibid.
51 Monty Smith, 'Messin' With the Kid: Rory Gallagher in Cork', *Q* (April 1990), https://www.roryon.com/messin357.html
52 Shawn Perry, 'Rory Gallagher I Live in Cork – DVD Review', *Vintage Rock*, https://vintagerock.com/rory-gallagher-live-in-cork-dvd-review/
53 Zach Demter, 'Rory Gallagher: Live in Cork DVD Review', *Pop Geeks* (11 March 2009), https://popgeeks.com/rory-gallagher-live-in-cork-dvd-review/?amp
54 Christel Loar, 'Rory Gallagher Live in Cork', *Popmatters* (31 March 2009), https://www.popmatters.com/71973-rory-gallagher-live-in-cork-2496040581.html

Part 4 - *He Came, He Saw and He Certainly Conquered*

55 Ronan Leonard, 'Sinnerboy recreating Rory Gallagher's iconic 1987 Cork Opera House show, in Cork Opera House!', *Echo Live* (28 October 2021), https://www.echolive.ie/entertainment/whatson/arid-40731657.html
56 Interview with Sean Reynolds, 23 May 2024.
57 Interview with Tom O'Flaherty, 4 April 2024.
58 Interview with Barry Barnes, 11 September 2023.
59 Interview with Dave McHugh, 30 May 2024.
60 Carl Kinsella, 'Cork given go-ahead to launch Rory Gallagher Music Festival', *Yay Cork* (27 October 2021), https://www.yaycork.ie/cork-given-go-ahead-to-launch-rory-gallagher-music-festival/
61 Interview with Anselm McDonnell, 14 May 2024.
62 *Rory Gallagher: Calling Card* (RTÉ and BBC NI, 2024).
63 'Belfast pays tribute to Rory Gallagher', *Hot Press* (3 January 2007), https://www.hotpress.com/music/belfast-pays-tribute-to-rory-gallagher-2902233
64 For further commentary on meanings created between fan and space (*semiotic musicscapes*), see: Lauren Alex O'Hagan, 'Walkin' Blues: Exploring the Semiotic Musicscape of Rory Gallagher's Cork' (2024), *Ethnomusicology Forum*, https://doi.org/10.1080/17411912.2024.2331432.
65 Interview with Monique Frie, 8 June 2024.

4.2 Just a Man with a Mission (and a Guitar): The 1988 Irish Tour

1988, as declared by some sources, was "the year Ireland was doomed."[1] As written by John Gibney, "The Republic of Ireland in the 1980s was a state gripped by a recession, burdened by a huge national debt, and ravaged yet again by emigration on a huge scale."[2] Furthermore, Irish citizens in 1988 were still grappling with a "deep and widespread revulsion" over the "appalling" tragedy on 8 November 1987 when a Provisional Irish Republican Army (IRA) bomb exploded at a Remembrance Day service in Enniskillen, County Fermanagh. Greater misfortunes lurked around the corner, with "one of the most strikingly memorable and shocking periods of the northern conflict" to occur, following the deaths of three IRA members in Gibraltar on 6 March 1988.[3]

John Meagher balances the "doom" of 1988 in his contemporary article for the *Irish Independent*, reminding readers that "there was plenty to lift spirits."[4] He mentions Ireland's "legendary victory" over England at the Euro 88 football tournament, as well as the "wide range of initiatives" spurred by Dublin's millennium. Although "small things," Meagher raises the importance of such distractions as "they counted for much in the pre-boomtown Ireland." In this chapter, we build upon Meagher's argument by highlighting the return of Rory Gallagher in February 1988 as yet another example of lifting Ireland's spirits during a period of political, financial and psychological turmoil.

As mentioned in 4.1, Gallagher had hinted in his conversation with fan Stephen Murphy at the Cork Opera House in November 1987 about his plans to (hopefully) return to Ireland for a few Christmas concerts. Although he would not return until three months later, "great interest" had nevertheless sparked concerning his 1988 Irish tour, particularly following "his sell-out Opera House show," as well as the continued success of *Defender* (1987), "which [had] brought him a host of new converts in Ireland."[5] While, for some fans, the phrase 'Irish Tour' will inevitably bring to mind the year 1974—an extremely significant tour on many social and cultural levels—we take the opportunity in this essay to explore Gallagher's later Irish tour, which is, unfortunately, lesser known. We argue that, just as in 1974, Gallagher's return to his home country in 1988 brought momentary escapism and enjoyment for his fans, with concerts receiving similar praise in the press to those 14 years earlier. In addition, we detail the few events succeeding Gallagher's Irish tour, such as his performance in Dublin celebrating Nelson Mandela's

70th birthday in July. As a final note, we examine Gallagher's pioneering role in shaping Ireland's music scene (both in 1988 and beyond), with the aim of moving him beyond the status of simply a "last crusader of the blues."[6]

Gallagher in the International and Irish Media, 1987-1988

Shortly after his Cork Opera House performance on 4 November 1987, Gallagher travelled to mainland Europe, where he toured mainly around Germany for the next five weeks. He used the opportunity to make a number of television appearances to promote the recently released *Defender* album. On 9 November, he appeared on *WWF Club* in the WDR Studios performing 'Loanshark Blues' in front of a small audience, as well as participating in a brief interview with presenter Jürgen Triebel. Four days later (after brief concert detours to the Netherlands and Belgium), he stopped by Studio 3 in Mainz to perform 'Don't Start Me Talkin'' on the ZDF show *Tele-Illustrierte*. This was followed on 18 November by a collaboration with accomplished German musician Götz Alsmann for the programme *Roxy*. Together, they performed a medley of Muddy Waters' 'I Can't Be Satisfied' and the Edith Piaf signature tune 'La Vie En Rose'. As Alsmann shared with us in May 2022:

> While preparing a new episode of my WDR-show *Roxy* [...] I had an evening's appointment with the head of WDR Youth Television, Peter Rüchel [...] We met in a hotel bar and, preparing a concert recording for WDR, Rory was there, too, celebrating and drinking with us. Rory and I had never met before. When Peter learned that we were shooting our program the next day in the outskirts of town at a fast food stand and also learning that I had my banjo with me, he suggested Rory and myself to 'do something together'. And sure enough, the next morning Rory and Peter showed up at the site, we fooled around a little bit, chose the song and off we went. As far as I remember, we did it in two takes. To add a little 'La Vie En Rose' at the end of the song was Rory's idea.[7]

Alsmann recalled that the 'restaurant' was "just about the dirtiest food stall" he had ever encountered, "an extremely dirty and seedy place" where he "wouldn't even have bought a coke." Apparently, Gallagher was equally "appalled by the surroundings" and had hoped to order some breakfast, but "wouldn't touch anything" once he had checked out the place. According to Alsmann, the whole recording took just 30 minutes, including rehearsal and soundcheck. Gallagher left immediately after to make a series of other WDR appointments. When asked of his lasting memories of the Irishman from the day of the recording, Alsmann described him as somebody "very friendly and even shy." Although Alsmann does not follow rock music himself, he has fond memories of the performance and says he feels "honoured" to have met Gallagher and played with him on this occasion.

The day after his spontaneous performance with Götz Alsmann, Gallagher travelled to Düsseldorf, where he played a concert at the Philipshalle. During afternoon rehearsals, he was joined by the crew from infotainment magazine *Aktuelle Stunde*, who filmed a backstage interview and a short performance of 'I Can't Be Satisfied' with Mark Feltham. In the interview, Gallagher challenges the presenter's claim that he has played the same music for 22 years and voices his negative opinion of "flimsy" music videos, which tend to be full of cliches like "the swimming pool, the Rolls Royce, the parties."[8]

Meanwhile, back in Ireland, viewers were treated to a special RTÉ Christmas broadcast of Gallagher's November Opera House concert (see 4.1). This was his first appearance on Irish television since 1986's Self Aid. The guitarist had been scheduled to make a return to Irish screens earlier in the year (June) with an appearance on RTÉ's *The Session*—a new music show that brought Irish and American musicians together to perform, but unfortunately had to pull out when he injured his back by tripping over a cable in the studio. As a result, he was replaced on the show by Bobby Whitlock.

In late January 1988, Gallagher returned to Ireland to enjoy some downtime before beginning his Irish tour the next month. There was much excitement in the air about his visit and the *Sunday Independent*, in conjunction with HMV, had even been running a competition to give away free copies of *Defender* and five pairs of tickets to one of his concerts at the Dublin Olympia. To mark his return, a number of television and radio appearances, as well as magazine and newspaper interviews, were scheduled. However, having finally given himself a moment to slow down and take some rest, Gallagher came down with a nasty bout of flu. In true Gallagher style, he still pushed ahead with the pre-arranged media appointments, the first being on *Evening Extra* on 6 February (broadcast on 24 February).

In this short television appearance, "the great blues journeyman" is interviewed by Shay Healy.[9] Gallagher enthuses about his 1932 National Resonator, before becoming noticeably ill at ease when the conversation takes a more personal turn towards his "permanent exile" from Ireland and his feelings of homesickness. Then, joined by Mark Feltham, Gallagher—sweating profusely from his fever—performs a rather sedate version of 'Walkin' Blues', his husky voice adding a nice vibrato to the vocals.

Six days later, Gallagher—still unwell but noticeably recuperating—appeared live on *The Late Late Show* with Gay Byrne, performing 'Out on the Western Plain' and then joining the presenter for an interview.[10] Byrne remarks that Gallagher is "a busy little lad" for the next fortnight, reading out the tour dates of Ireland, including four nights at the Olympia. The interview covers various topics, including Gallagher's childhood and his introduction to the guitar, as well as his early gravitation towards African American country blues and rock & roll via the radio.

As a point of contrast, Byrne rolls a clip of Gallagher's 'Messin with the Kid' from the 1987 Opera House concert for the studio audience (and those at home) to view how the guitarist "behaves when he's really surrounded by all his adoring fans." As the segment draws to a close, Gallagher discusses his cautious approach regarding the business aspect of the music industry, concluding, "In general, I just like to play, and play every night." On a final (and bittersweet) note, Byrne asks if in 20 years' time, when Gallagher has turned 62 [sic], will he still be playing music? "Chuck Berry just turned 62," replied Gallagher, "and if I can be anything like he is at that age, I'll be more than happy."

Gallagher expressed similar remarks to Bill Graham of *Hot Press* who sat down with him on the afternoon of his first show at the Dublin Olympia. "My dream would be to be fit and healthy at 65 and still playing," he says, before rather poignantly adding, "But that's asking too much of the man upstairs, it really is." The guitarist also elaborates on his struggle to "get over the workaholic thing," commenting that he would be "much healthier" if he could only learn how to "switch off." He notes, however, that the blues is a "true creed" that he needs "on a spiritual level" and in which he can always find comfort.[11]

Speaking to Molly McSnailly Burke of the *Sunday Press*, Gallagher also expresses a certain restlessness, but explains how these emotions can be channelled positively into his music:

> I've felt every emotion you can name and sometimes I feel neglected, but if you had a settled life, it would be harder to build up a climax in the music [...] When you just live from hotel to suitcase to gig, the music is bound to become nastier. In a particular way, I don't feel bad in a lonesome room – that's where I do a lot of writing.[12]

On 16 February—the eve of his first of four concerts at Dublin's Olympia Theatre—Gallagher participated in a lengthy interview with Dave Fanning for 2FM. While Fanning later remarked to us that he often "felt guilty" speaking with Gallagher, believing his every question to be "an intrusion" on the shy guitarist,[13] this 1988 interview nevertheless displays Gallagher in a very relaxed and talkative mood. Fanning allocates much of the conversation to this 'post-*Defender*' Rory Gallagher (see 1.2), enquiring how the guitarist has settled into the musical changes of the 1980s, including the up-and-coming generation of rock fans. Gallagher has observed the "real mixture" arriving at his concerts: "we've got everything from fans from the beginning right through to young teenagers, in all forms, from suits to leather jackets and back again."[14]

Despite his recent turmoil with the record industry, Gallagher appears undeterred from his long-term musical ambitions, expressing the desire to "aim high" and "elevate [himself] into that realm where [Muddy Waters and Chuck Berry] are at," rather than be remembered as simply a "good ol', reliable" blues guitarist—a discussion we return to at the conclusion of this chapter. Halfway through the interview, Gallagher performs a cover of John Lee Hooker's 'Want'ad Blues', sustaining the listener's attention through shifting rhythms and emotions, from the passionate sweeps of his slide playing to the utilisation of his boot-tapping as a percussive technique.

Four Nights in Dublin:
Gallagher at the Olympia (17-20 February 1988)

Gallagher played in Dublin on numerous occasions throughout his career, but 1988 marked the first time that he would play at the city's Olympia Theatre on Dame St. Boasting a capacity of roughly 1,600 people, the venue offered an intimate and energetic environment for his four-night run. Fans "eagerly awaited" Gallagher's return to the Dublin stage on 17 February, emerging "from every neck of the musical woods" to honour "one of Ireland's original troopers."[15] While the "occasional long haired renegade" could be spotted in the audience, Paul Russell of the *Evening Herald* noted the general absence of check shirts, replaced instead by a swarm of "Ozzy and Anthrax tee shirts," alluding to the presence of a younger, heavy metal-based crowd.

Whether for "nostalgic reasons" or "pure admiration," fans of all "age, rank and profession" gathered in the Olympia to watch Gallagher—a musician who, according to Russell, "has lost none of [his] power" and brought "simplicity and craftsmanship back to the Irish stage." Throughout his set, there were "gasps and cheers" from the crowd, with the whole audience getting to their feet for a standing ovation at the end of the show. Russell notes that Gallagher was genuinely "taken aback" by [the] enthusiasm [from his fans]."

"It's been a long time, thanks for waiting for me," the guitarist had politely greeted the crowd on his first night at the Olympia. Clearly, for many, it had been worth the wait. For the next three nights, Gallagher continued to captivate audiences, emphasising his "larger than life"[16] onstage persona every evening, as stated by long-time fan Des White. White attended three out of the four concerts at the Olympia, fervently recalling the "fantastic" atmosphere within those "two hours and thirty minutes—even three hours." "[Gallagher] completely occupied the stage. I can't think of anyone else that I have seen who achieved this presence of place," he added, "Literally the entire building filled with sound as it seemed to vibrate through your body."

On all four nights, Gallagher made the bold decision to start his shows with the instrumental number 'The Loop'—a track unknown to fans and one which would appear later on *Fresh Evidence* (1990). Spectacular covers of T Bone Walker's 'Stormy Monday' and Hambone Willie Newbern's 'Rollin' and Tumblin' followed shortly after, setting the tone for an extremely bluesy evening ahead in stark contrast to the more rock-oriented set delivered on his last Irish tour in 1983-1984 (as seen in the *Rory at Midnight* concert recorded at Belfast's Ulster Hall for BBC Northern Ireland). Gallagher, in fact, carried very few songs over from the 1970s, with a clear preference for material from *Jinx* and *Defender*, as well as more obscure blues covers, such as Big Bill Broonzy's 'Keep Your Hands Off Her'. "There's no point in me trying to be three different people just to keep everyone happy. I stick with what I believe in," Gallagher would later tell Paul Russell of *Evening Herald*.[17]

Fan Paul O'Sullivan saw Gallagher on his second night at the Olympia.[18] He describes the show as a "tour de force by any standards," noting how Gallagher was "hoarse" by the end yet still giving it all he had. It was the faster numbers that seemed to go down particularly well with the Dublin crowd who were on their feet, "clapping, roaring and generally making complete idiots of themselves." "Nadine came off the speakers like rock 'n' roll hadn't really happened until now!" recalls O'Sullivan, Gallagher having rejuvenated the song with his "hell for leather guitar work, the driving rhythm section and the energetic vocal delivery." Overall, it was a "totally committed performance" from the Irishman, with the cheers and applause from the crowd "[speaking] volumes for the vibrancy and honesty" of his music.

Prior to 1988, American fan Amy Maloney had heard of Gallagher from an Isle of Wight Festival bootleg, with "Taste being a highlight on the album."[19] Growing up, she continued to come across Gallagher's name, as well as "see his photos in many rock magazines." On her way to Wales in February 1988, Maloney stopped by Dublin to connect with a group of Led Zeppelin penpals, who suggested seeing Gallagher at the Olympia during his four-night stint. Unfortunately, the concerts were "sold out." Nevertheless, Maloney and her friends managed to locate a "broken window" that led to a lower level of the venue and soon "found ourselves on the floor in front of the band." She recalls the music "being very loud" and was initially "a little bummed at the distortion." However, as soon as Gallagher began to play slide, she was instantly "so impressed" at the "searing and crystal clear" sounds. Leaving the Olympia, Maloney began to question how, on the one hand, she could appreciate Stevie Ray Vaughan, Led Zeppelin and Little Feat, and yet, on the other, lack the same knowledge regarding Gallagher and his music. Reflecting in the present-day, she feels "fortunate to have seen [Gallagher] play live," even if it was her only experience.

Another person with fond memories of Gallagher's Olympia concerts is Carmel Murphy who worked for *Hot Press* at the time. Backstage at one of the shows, Gallagher noticed that she was wearing a navy-blue neckerchief—rather similar to the one he too was wearing on that evening. He signalled to exchange them, telling Murphy that his was a "good luck one" from Mexico. Sometime later, she met Gallagher again and asked him if he wanted it back, knowing what a superstitious person he was. "Not at all," he replied. Sharing a fear of flying with Gallagher, Murphy went on to bring the neckerchief with her whenever she was on a plane, using it to help ease her anxiety.[20]

Writing about Gallagher's final night at the Olympia for the *Deuce Quarterly* fanzine, one anonymous fan described it as "one of the best Rory has ever played in Ireland."[21] The fan had the chance to talk with Gallagher and his brother Dónal before the concert in the bar at Blooms Hotel where they were both staying. Gallagher was "relaxed" and talked freely about the guitarists he had jammed with over the years, but as it approached showtime, he suddenly became "very tense" and quiet. The fan notes that there were many famous faces in the crowd that evening at the Olympia, including The Edge and Adam Clayton from U2, Ted Hawkins, Chris Rea and Paul Brady. But the real highlight came later into the early hours of the morning when Gallagher—never passing up an opportunity to play music—made a surprise appearance with the Olympia's house band, Hank Halfhead and the Rambling Turkeys.

As recounted to us by musician Niall Toner (aka Hank Halfhead), Dublin's pubs in the 1980s were still "based on old rules"[22] and, therefore, forced to close after 11PM. The Olympia Theatre, however, had "found a loophole" and continued to serve alcohol until 2AM for patrons. As a result, the venue began a regular series of live gigs across Friday and Saturday nights following regular theatre shows, featuring many up-and-coming bands, which often followed the main act. Irish country rock band Hank Halfhead and the Rambling Turkeys were in the middle of an eight-week run at the Olympia when Gallagher began his four-night stint as the main draw. Toner shared a pleasant memory of Gallagher visiting the Rambling Turkeys at a soundcheck following his final gig. He "appeared to be enjoying what we were doing," recalls Toner. After Gallagher graciously "introduced himself" to the band, he stated that "he'd love to play a few songs with us later that night!" Around 1AM, Gallagher returned to the Olympia "with a crate of beer and his trusty Strat" and "much to the excitement (and delirium) of the crowd," he joined the Rambling Turkeys onstage for the old Taj Mahal song 'Six Days on the Road' and several country rock songs, followed by two instrumentals.

Paul Russell reviewed the show in the *Evening Herald*:

> [...] for fifteen minutes of the set the surprise guitar player for the cousins of country was none other than Rory Gallagher supported by Nine Below Zero harmonica man Mark Feltham. And what a storm that crowd blew up, to say nothing of the reaction of the audience. What a set! A little bit country, a little bit rock n roll. The packed house was up and hoppin' for the whole thing. Gallagher has come back on the scene with the vitality that modern music lacks so much. And the applause he won left him speechless.[23]

Russell also notes that it could have been an all-star event as Van Morrison was spotted in the wings, but he never came out to join them.

"Return of the Prodigal":
Belfast, Limerick, Galway and Cork (22-28 February 1988)

Following the four hugely successful nights in Dublin, Gallagher took one day off, before travelling up north to Belfast to play at the Ulster Hall on 22 February. This was a venue that the guitarist knew well, having performed there almost every Christmas throughout the 1970s to a grateful crowd deprived of live music, so it felt like being back on home territory. In fact, in the weeks leading up to the concert, neon posters appeared all over the city with the slogan "Welcome home, Rory." And on the evening itself, Gallagher was given a true hero's welcome with a standing ovation not just when he came out on stage, but after almost every song. In contrast to Dublin, it was Gallagher's acoustic set that seemed to go down particularly well with the Belfast audience. Bootleg recordings reveal that 'Out on the Western Plain' attracted so many claps and cheers of "Rory! Rory!" that Gallagher even had to stop playing until the noise died down before starting the song again.

Fan Declan McKinney still remembers what a great evening he had at the Ulster Hall—the "first and only time" he would ever see his musical hero. McKinney was first introduced to rock music through Thin Lizzy's 1976 release *Jailbreak*, becoming "well aware" of Gallagher's "legendary reputation when [he] picked up the *Stage Struck* tape" four years after.[24] Gallagher's "primal roar" as he introduces 'Shin Kicker' still elicits "goosebumps" for McKinney, who considers the 1980 live album to be "very special" in the guitarist's catalogue. It was a "dream come true" to finally see Gallagher live in 1988, especially at such an "iconic venue" that played an "integral" role in his "legend":

> The energy and pure physicality he brought to his performance was incredible. He was relentless and [...] mesmerising to watch, literally wringing that Strat's neck. He'd ping off harmonics, then reach over and bend them behind-the-nut; real showmanship, and it was hard to take your eyes off him. I'm pretty sure I elbowed my friends hard when I first saw him grab the headstock and brutally bend the whole neck. No wonder he didn't need a whammy bar!

Such colourful memories accompanied McKinney on his "chilly walk home, clad in a sweat-soaked Rory t-shirt." Reflecting on Gallagher's legacy today, McKinney emphasised the guitarist's impact for those growing up in Northern Ireland who are "particularly proud of him and appreciative that he played here right throughout the Troubles." McKinney also identified the "rare honesty and integrity" in Gallagher's music, as well as the fact that there was "nothing fake" about him, which comforted many fans, including McKinney, living in the "quite conservative" Ireland of the 1980s.

Another fan, Pete McCarter, shares similar insights regarding the Belfast show: "The atmosphere that night was really lively—more than I'd felt at any other gig before—and you really got the feeling you were in for something memorable."[25] Gallagher was "full of energy" as he made his way onto the Ulster Hall stage and, as McCarter observed, he "clearly loved the maniac reception he received," describing the guitarist as playfully "blessing people as if he was the Pope!" The evening carried all sorts of memorable moments for McCarter, from Gallagher's Stratocaster slipping off his shoulder mid-song and the roadie swiftly reattaching it without the guitarist missing a note, to a female fan invading the stage to hug Gallagher and him jokingly trying to hold onto her when security dragged her away.

He also remembers a poignant moment when "a projection of a starry night background was displayed on the Ulster Hall's organ backdrop as [Gallagher] sang 'A Million Miles Away'." Due to the fact that McCarter, at the time, "only knew a handful of Rory songs," the entire concert was "quite the [learning] experience" for him. As the show drew to a close, he stayed behind and was able to obtain one of Gallagher's guitar picks. "[Rory] had left three taped to the front of his speaker cabinet. I couldn't believe my luck when the roadie grabbed them and handed me one, throwing the other two into a small handful of eager fans." McCarter has "guarded" the pick "like gold dust" and it remains in his possession, along with the original 1988 ticket, tour t-shirt and sweatshirt. He concludes that Gallagher was "a very special kind of talent who could fill a room with his music" and doubts that "we will ever see his like again."

Press reviews echoed McKinney and McCarter's words, emphasising Gallagher's endurance and noting that the concert was just as good as his concerts 20 years before when he started out at the Maritime with Taste. Brian Hunter of the *Belfast Telegraph* singled out new numbers 'I Ain't No Saint' and 'Loanshark Blues' as particularly strong and commented on Gallagher's ability to generate "a sound wall of power-driven licks" and make his guitar not "so much gently weep as sob buckets." Hunter also noted how Gallagher "seems recharged" and that his "guitar still shines brighter than most in the firmament."[26] In other words, this was not a simple case of nostalgia for the audience; it was to witness a progressive artist still at the top of his game and offering something new and exciting with his music.

The next date on Gallagher's tour—the Savoy Theatre in Limerick (24 February)—did not go ahead, despite being widely advertised in advance. Just a few weeks before the concert, the Savoy's promoter and co-manager Brendan Murray was tragically killed in a car crash on his way home to Lisnagry. His partner Tony O'Mara had no plans to keep the Savoy running without him and, in March 1988, the venue closed its doors for good.[27] While there was a short-lived campaign to save the Savoy, with Gallagher himself sending a good luck telegram, it was to no avail. As Mike Maguire notes in his brief history of the Savoy, it is a shame that Gallagher's concert did not go ahead because it would have offered a "neat bookend" to the venue's history: Gallagher's concert with Taste in October 1970 was the "first real rock concert" at the Savoy.[28] The Savoy was also where Rod De'Ath made his debut in the Rory Gallagher band, featuring in the 1972 RTÉ *Music Makers* documentary.[29]

Gallagher's next concert at Leisureland in Galway on 26 February was met with similar positive reactions to his Dublin and Belfast appearances. The *Tuam Herald* expressed great anticipation for the "artist who has become an institution both on the Irish and International stage," convincing fans that Gallagher's "overdue visit is worth catching."[30] The article referenced Gallagher's latest visit to *The Late Late Show*, where he appeared "to be as fresh, relaxed and buoyant as ever."

Following the concert, arranged by the University of Galway's Student Union, the same newspaper described Gallagher's performance as "gut punching stuff," the guitarist still able to "create a sense of excitement that many electro-pop bands could never produce."[31] "It was obvious Gallagher has never lost it," they concluded in direct defiance of claims that the bluesman could no longer perform like he once did. After the concert, Mark Feltham and Gerry McAvoy were spotted at De Lacy's club enjoying the local Blues Band. Feltham said that he was particularly impressed with the harmonica player Paul Jones.

The final stop of Gallagher's Irish tour was his home city of Cork, where he played a sellout gig at City Hall (28 February). Religious hyperbole was abound in the local press, with the guitarist's homecoming described as the "return of the prodigal" and the *Evening Echo* reporting on a "plea" from four emigrants planning on return to the "holy ground" to see Gallagher yet unable to obtain tickets.[32] Fan Mark Gillis remembers that the gig was all seated, yet as soon as Gallagher appeared on stage, he ran to the front and shook the guitarist's hand, before security escorted him back to his seat. They proceeded to stop any attempts of the audience standing up. However, by the time the third song, 'Moonchild', had started, "the whole hall rushed the stage, and security gave up." In Gillis's view, there is "nothing close" to Gallagher's concerts, his "honesty and integrity" always shining through in his music.[33]

Paul Hunt, who was introduced to Gallagher's music at age 13 through the *Top Priority* (1979) album, was also at City Hall on 28 February. Hunt was unwell for most of 1982 and credits Gallagher's January 1983 concert in Cork as "instrumental in [his] recovery," returning to school just a week after seeing the show and "never looking back."[34] "Because of this," Hunt concludes, "Rory has always been close to my heart." Hunt lived less than a mile away from Gallagher's mother, Monica, and can recall bumping into the guitarist "from time to time." He added that Gallagher "always had time for a quick hello."

Hunt attended the Cork Opera House recording in November 1987, managing to see Gallagher backstage, where he autographed his *Defender* cassette. Hunt also had his photograph taken with Gallagher by a professional from the *Cork Examiner*. At Gallagher's 1988 Cork show, Hunt found himself backstage again, where the guitarist was already chatting with a group of fans outside his dressing room, "discussing working with [Deep Purple's] Roger Glover [on *Calling Card*]." Hunt asked Gallagher to sign his poster, which he "gladly did." Then, "what really threw" Hunt was when Gallagher "excused himself to everyone" and disappeared back into the dressing room with Hunt's poster. "Within minutes he emerged again and handed me the poster, telling me that Gerry, Brendan, and Mark had all signed it. I have been a massive fan since, with both of my sons Rory fans, too."

Stag/Hot Press Awards (1 March 1988)

After a few days of rest in Cork, Gallagher was back in Dublin on 1 March for the Stag/Hot Press Awards. First established in 1978 (with huge input from Dónal Gallagher), the Awards celebrated and recognised musical talent in Ireland, as well as acknowledged the achievements of Irish artists on the international music scene. The first ceremony, captured on film in the German television programme *ELF ½*, saw an embarrassed Gallagher pick up an award for headlining the Macroom 'Mountain Dew' Festival, as well as receive a silver disc from Dan Young of Chrysalis Records for sales of *Against the Grain* within the UK. At the 1980 Awards, Gallagher was ranked number four for Best Male Singer and number three for Best Group, and won Best Album for *Stage Struck*, seeing off fierce competition from U2's *Boy* and the Undertones' *Hypnotised*. Two years later in 1982, Gallagher was honoured with the Best Musician Award.

The 1988 Stag/Hot Press Awards took place at the Waterfront Nightclub in Dublin. This time, Gallagher won Best Album for *Defender*—a mighty achievement that challenged any hearsay about the quality of his new music and yet which is rarely talked about in modern-day accounts of his life. The award also undoubtedly meant a lot to the guitarist, given how much he had put into the recording over the past five years. Other awards that evening were picked up by Something Happens (Best New Band), Sinéad O'Connor (Best Emerging Artist), U2 (World Domination), Paul Cleary (Songwriting), Paul McGuinness (Services to Industry) and the Stars of Heaven and Microdisney (Best Breakthrough Albums). Van Morrison, Christy Moore and Mary Coughlan were also all honoured with awards for their services to music.

Newspaper reports of the awards rather sarcastically described Gallagher, Morrison, Moore and Coughlan as a reflection of "the old guard holding their ground (or maintaining their stranglehold)," but also expressed optimism at the "new faces" who were recognised for their talents.[35] Indeed, photos from the event show Gallagher, Moore and Coughlan sticking together and seeming to have a good time in each other's company. Coughlan later told the *Irish Examiner* that she made Gallagher laugh by telling him an anecdote about going to one of his concerts in the 1970s:

> I remember wanting to see Rory in Galway years ago, and I wasn't allowed to go by my father who thought I was too young. But I had arranged to meet a fella at the gig, so I wasn't about to be stopped. I got out the bedroom window and went to the gig. Afterwards, who was outside the gig in a car, but my father and I was caught red faced and red handed. I was never so mortified in all my life.[36]

Highlights from the Awards were shown later in the evening on *Borderline*, together with a pre-recorded interview that Gallagher did with presenters Rónán Johnston and Maria Doyle. Gallagher also took part in a small promotional piece for *Borderline* live from the Awards, joking how he had to cancel a session in the studio to be here and that he "could go to hell for that."[37] Johnston begins the interview with Gallagher's latest win at the Stag/Hot Press Awards, referring to him as "the total and utter king of rhythm and blues."[38] Gallagher reveals the lessons he has learnt from his "more or less" 25 years on the road and that, as time goes on, touring becomes "more challenging." He explains: "The longer you do it, the more you find you don't really understand the whole thing, the more you need to challenge yourself." Therefore, what ultimately drives Gallagher is the need "to keep pushing [himself] further and further," as opposed to producing "one or two good albums" or delivering one "good concert." Towards the end, Gallagher comments on the "healthy" blues scene of the late 1980s, particularly with the success of Robert Cray and Stevie Ray Vaughan.

Rónán Johnston, a musician at the time, admitted that he felt slightly "intimidated" to be interviewing Gallagher, yet was "struck" by how "incredibly shy" the guitarist was.[39] "I chatted to him before and after the show, and it was much like the interview itself—really quick and stilted." Gallagher had brought a guitar with him to the *Borderline* set, playing offstage both before and after his interview. "The minute [Gallagher] [strapped on his guitar], he was relaxed again," observed Johnston, "The guitar did the talking for him." Now a licensed psychotherapist, Johnston—has since re-examined his interaction with Gallagher, concluding that this "sensitive gentle guy with immense talent" had a "haunted look" and, "even as a thirty-eight-year-old man, was already in the grip of the demons that got him in the end."

While Gallagher may have cancelled a session in the studio to appear at the Awards, he never really took an evening off, and as soon as he learnt that Hank Halfhead and the Rambling Turkeys were the house band hired for the Awards, it was "inevitable," according to Niall Toner, that he would get up to play with them again. Toner remembers that they played 'Honky Tonk Woman', 'Close up the Honkytonks', 'Lost Highway', 'My Baby She Worships Me' and 'Hey Good Lookin'' among other country and blues rock numbers. Toner surmised his "fondest memories" of Gallagher to be "his friendliness and warmth," in addition to his "ability to put others at complete ease in his company." "[Gallagher] was the kind of man anyone would be happy to call a friend," he concludes.

The day after the Awards, Gallagher and his brother Dónal headed home once again to Cork where the guitarist was planning to spend his 40th birthday with the family. However, on the drive back, they stopped off in Cashel for a quiet pint at one of the town's only two pubs. Being recognised by a local, Gallagher was approached and told that the owner of the town's other pub—the Moor Lane Tavern—was a huge fan and asked if it would be possible for him to stop in and say hello. Gallagher kindly obliged, much to owner Liam M. Malone's surprise. He describes the moment as "unbelievable," having been a Gallagher fan for so many years, and recalls the guitarist as a "really humble man."[40] Gallagher agreed to a photo, which Malone hung on the wall of his pub until it closed in 2013. It speaks volumes to the Irishman's character that, after a sellout Irish tour, a prestigious awards ceremony and countless jams along the way, he always remained grounded and was happy to blend into the background and remain inconspicuous when offstage.

Part 4 - *Just a Man with a Mission*

Nelson Mandela 70th Birthday Event (17 July 1988)

Following his birthday, Gallagher remained in Ireland, taking time out to recuperate after his successful Irish tour. It was here where he received the crushing news that his uncle Jimmy had passed away suddenly and unexpectedly. According to Jimmy's son, Jim Roche, Gallagher and his mother Monica went to sit with the Roche family that night and they emotionally reflected on how many great evenings had been spent in the very room in which they were sat.[41] Gallagher had always been very close to Jimmy (see 4.5) and, according to Dónal, he took the death "very much to heart."[42]

Plans had been arranged for Gallagher to take part in a concert to mark Dublin's millennium. However, presumably grieving over his uncle's death, he decided to withdraw from the project and did not return to the international stage until September that year. Nevertheless, between March and July, Gallagher did participate in two public events in Ireland, beginning with his donation of a guitar to a charity auction at the Imperial Hotel on 16 June to raise funds for the Cork Film Festival and Rehabilitation Institute. Along with Gallagher, "some of the top people in politics, entertainment and the arts,"[43] such as Sir Richard Attenborough and Samuel Beckett, contributed to the cause.

The second event occurred on 17 July 1988 when Gallagher took part in a special music event at the Olympia Theatre in Dublin to mark Nelson Mandela's 70th birthday. The event was inspired by the tremendous success of the Mandela birthday event organised by producer Tony Hollingsworth and held at Wembley Stadium in London the month before, which was widely praised for raising worldwide consciousness of Mandela's imprisonment by the South African apartheid government. The 12-hour concert had brought together a range of global stars, from Dire Straits, George Michael and Whitney Houston to the Bee Gees, Sting and Stevie Wonder, raising $5 million and watched by over 600 million people in 67 countries.[44] The Irish press expressed disappointment, nonetheless, that no Irish act had been included in the concert.

This oversight was swiftly rectified with the organisation of Dublin's own 'Freedom at Seventy' concert—a four-hour musical extravaganza featuring Rory Gallagher, Christy Moore and Sinead O'Connor at the top of the bill, with support from Louis Stewart, Terry Woods, Ella Mental, Frank Harte, Ndor Khuze and Liam O'Flynn. According to the *Irish Independent*, the concert was "a highly charged celebration of Mandela and a determined denunciation of racism [...] a night of stomping feet, clenched fists and a thousand voices calling in song" for his release.[45] It was the perfect culmination to an important day that had begun with Dublin City Council awarding Mandela with the Freedom of the City.

Despite one caustic comment about Gallagher in the press ("oh no, it's Rory Gallagher. Who the hell let that fella on?"[46]), journalists and fans alike were impressed with his performance. Gallagher launched with a "tougher-than-the-rest set of black-inspired R 'n' B,"[47] producing a mixture of original and traditional blues numbers, such as 'The Loop', 'I Wonder Who', 'Continental Op', 'Don't Start Me Talkin'' and 'Nadine'. Fan Paul O'Sullivan recounted Gallagher's "full-fledged blues" for readers of *Deuce Quarterly*, describing the guitarist's "onstage energy" as "infectious" for the entire evening.[48] O'Sullivan writes in thorough detail of Gallagher "duck walking across the stage [with] one guitar string broken," captivating audience with his "magic sounds," as the "band behind him [fired] on all cylinders." Gallagher guided the band (and crowd) through the gospel tune 'Let's Go Home', accompanied onstage by the South African A.N.C choir. While some critics (e.g. Chris Donovan of *Hot Press*) referred to the rendition of 'Let's Go Home' as "shambolic," it was undoubtedly a "moving" scene for an "inspiring and uplifting occasion."[49] Gallagher closed his show with a cover of Bob Dylan's "beautiful hymn-like ballad" 'I Shall Be Released'.

Beyond the "Last Crusader of the Blues":
Rethinking Gallagher's Outlaw Music

In February 1988, Rory Gallagher returned to Ireland for his first Irish tour in four years. Speaking to *Tuam Herald* about his long absence from the country, the guitarist admitted that he had "found it hard to come home" because he was not too happy with the Irish music scene and the way that politics and music were becoming mixed.[50] While he was not "afraid" that the Irish people would forget him ("they are a great loyal audience"), he was worried that they might start taking him for granted and expressed hope that they would see his validity alongside new bands like U2 ("they are going up a different road than I am"). In his appearance on *The Late Late Show*, Gallagher reflected on the "sad" reality that many Irish popular groups "overlook" the blues, yet remained quietly hopeful that people were beginning to "reappraise these great original blues players" because "that's the source."[51]

Despite his fears, Gallagher's 1988 Irish tour was deemed an overwhelming success, with critics describing his musicianship as "refreshing" and praising his "warm, good humoured, visceral and unashamedly non-intellectual" approach to the blues.[52] Michael Ross of the *Sunday Tribune* claimed that, despite "pushing 40," Gallagher was playing "as sharply and energetically as most musicians half his age."[53] Although the guitarist's changed appearance continued to attract media critique ("He has got a little more plump [and] a little less varnish on his battered Fender guitar," says Ross), the overall consensus was that "he still has fire in his belly" and has retained his musical "flexibility" and "respect for his audience"—both signs "essential for career longevity."[54]

In most press articles leading up to and around the tour, Gallagher was portrayed as a 'survivor'—someone who has stuck to the blues with religious devotion and never strayed from his traditional beliefs about music. While, to a certain extent, this is accurate, as we have argued throughout this book, Gallagher was always pushing the boundaries of the blues, whether with his lyrical themes, Celtic motifs or cross-genre experimentation. Although he wanted spectators to enjoy his blues and even learn something from them, he never wanted them to feel like they were "part of some blues society."[55] Furthermore, he wished to be recognised as "some sort of original performer,"[56] not just a blues interpreter. We reflect on these points further in 4.6 and the book's Conclusion, which address Gallagher's influence on young musicians, both then and now.

But there was far more to Gallagher than simply being a "last crusader of the blues." We forget that he was also a "founding father of Irish rock music,"[57] "a comet in a land of glow-worms" who "exploded out of the melancholy world [of showbands] to form Taste"[58] in 1966 and had an undeniable influence on those who came after him (see 4.6). Paul Russell remarked in his 1988 article for the *Evening Herald* on how "the past" can be "so easily forgotten" and that, on occasion, "it is hard to imagine there was Irish rock before U2."[59]

Gallagher's return to Ireland in 1988, however, must be remembered for "[bringing] it all back again" and that for those few hours—whether at Dublin's Olympia or Cork City Hall—the "innocent days of rock and roll" thrived once more.[60] In his obituary for Gallagher written seven years later, Declan Lynch reminds readers of the guitarist's importance to the (Irish) rock world: "rock stars are now general all over Ireland, but Rory was the first. There was nothing remotely like him. He was not so much the Columbus of Irish rock as its Brendan The Navigator."[61] Gallagher's impact beyond the blues genre is something that broadcaster Dave Fanning is also keen to address, emphasising that it is a disservice to Gallagher's tremendous talent to pigeonhole him into just one box.

> He wrote brilliant rock songs and he's never given enough praise for that. He was a blues guy. He was based on the blues, but he was a brilliant rock guitarist and he was a brilliant rock writer [...] I just hope [people] see he was a great songwriter as opposed to just a guy who brought the blues into some more decades from the old blues guys from years ago, which is great that he did that, but I just thought he was more than what a lot of people think he was.[62]

Indeed, Gallagher was more than what a lot of people think he was, his music "transcending all trends"[63] and even crossing beyond blues and rock into jazz, folk and Irish trad at times. In doing so, he attracted a diverse range of fans, offering something for everyone, whether they identified with his sound, attitude, style or musical philosophy. This diversity and resistance to trends kept him relevant throughout his career.

When asked by Fanning in 1988 how he would like to be remembered, Gallagher himself reflected on the different aspects of his musical identity:

> I'd like people to say 'he plays the toughest rock around, but he does it with the minimalist of frills'. And I wanna play tough blues as well [...] you get to a certain point in your life where you've got to beat these European blues stigmas, which was connected to,

say, Fleetwood Mac and Blue Horizon, Chicken Shack, and all that. They did their thing, but they all stopped at a certain point, and while writing my own material and trying to play modern music, I—at the expense of being unpopular—dig deeper and deeper [...] it's just a great hobby for me.[64]

So, rather than categorising Gallagher as strictly a bluesman or a rockstar, perhaps we should instead look at him within the broader framework of an outlaw musician. This is how Molly McSnailly Burke of *Sunday Independent* frames him in her 1988 article, defining Gallagher simply as "the Cork boy with a mission and a guitar" who plays "outlaw music" with the "spirit of risk or fortitude."[65] In an industry where "integrity is a real liability," Gallagher was never "willing to sell out" or "be tomorrow's throwaway." Instead, he was a "free spirit" who felt akin to Muddy Waters and Woody Guthrie, musicians who "seem like a pirate, [men] with a mission, and a sense of destiny." "I've always believed that the best music should be dangerous," Gallagher insisted, "It's like taking it to the edge where a riot could break out [...] the best blues and rock is a collision." 'Collision' is a good term to describe his own body of work, bringing together multiple influences, sounds and genres in exciting new ways. As McSnailly Burke nicely put it, as Gallagher arrived in Ireland for his 1988 tour, he brought home with him "a pirate's legacy."

"Some people see me as the last crusader of the blues or some kind of independent because I do a certain amount of things my own way," Gallagher told Mark Stevens in a 1978 interview.[66] "I don't mind being an independent, but I don't want to be the last of anything." Maybe then we should also rethink Gallagher's musical legacy in terms of *firsts* rather than *lasts*: the *first* Irish rockstar, the headliner of Ireland's *first* rock festival, the *first* person to appear at Reading Festival the most times, star of the *first* rock film (*Irish Tour '74*) to enter Cork Film Festival, the biggest draw on the *first* ever *Rockpalast* Rock Night, the owner of the (allegedly) *first* Stratocaster in Ireland... The list goes on... Even in passing, Gallagher continues to achieve firsts, from Bank of Ireland commemorative coins and An Post stamps to street name unveilings and magazine special editions.

"[Twenty years ago] we rarely would have thought that you would ever see the day an Irishman—a Corkman—*in* Cork get such adulation,"[67] Gay Byrne told Gallagher in his 1988 *The Late Late Show* interview. Thirty-six years on with an ever-growing fanbase, Byrne's statement seems even more significant. Such is the timeless appeal of the humble, softly-spoken Irishman who thought like a folk musician, yet had the soul of a bluesman and the energy of a rockstar.

RM and LAO

Part 4 - *Just a Man with a Mission*

Footnotes

1 John Meagher, '1988: The year they said Ireland was doomed', *Irish Independent* (19 January 2008), https://www.independent.ie/irish-news/1988-the-year-they-said-ireland-was-doomed/26345635.html.
2 John Gibney, *A Short History of Ireland: 1500-2000* (New Haven: Yale University Press), 236.
3 Richard English, *Armed Struggle: The History of the IRA* (London: Pan), 256-258.
4 Meagher, '1988'.
5 Paul Russell, 'Gallagher roars back with a burning ambition', *Evening Herald* (18 February 1988), 19
6 Mark Stevens, 'Rory Gallagher: Meat 'N Potatoes Rock 'N Roll', *Triad Magazine* (February 1979), https://www.roryon.com/meat3.html
7 Interview with Götz Alsmann, 3 May 2022.
8 'Rory Gallagher - I Can't Be Satisfied - Germany 1987', https://www.youtube.com/watch?v=QTG5UnXcCPQ
9 'Walking Blues - Rory Gallagher & Mark Feltham, 1988', https://www.youtube.com/watch?v=qx0gcPksufs
10 'Rory Gallagher – The Late Late Show – 12 February 1988', https://www.youtube.com/watch?v=lKJ3ploCKv0&t=695s.
11 Bill Graham, 'On this day in 1987: Rory Gallagher released Defender', *Hot Press* (1 July 2023), https://www.hotpress.com/music/on-this-day-in-1987-rory-gallagher-released-defender-22977026
12 Molly McSnailly Burke, 'Pirate Rory revisits for his destiny', *Sunday Press* (2 February 1988), https://www.roryon.com/pirate183.html
13 Interview with Dave Fanning, 24 April 2022.
14 'Rory Gallagher - Dublin 1988 + Interview', https://www.youtube.com/watch?v=JZVjd8JaI-A
15 Paul Russell, 'Roaring Rory lets rip just like old times', *Evening Herald* (18 February 1988), 3. All subsequent quotes in this paragraph come from Russell.
16 Interview with Des White, 1-3 May 2023.
17 Russell, 'Roaring Rory lets rip just like old times'.
18 Paul O'Sullivan, 'Dublin 18.2.88, Olympia Theatre', *Deuce Quarterly*, no. 44 (1988), 4.
19 Interview with Amy Maloney, 20 May 2023.
20 Julian Vignoles, *Rory Gallagher: The Man Behind the Guitar* (London: Collins, 2018),148-149.
21 'Dublin 17-20.2.88, Olympia Theatre', *Deuce Quarterly*, no. 44 (1988), 4
22 Interview with Niall Toner, 4 October 2023. All subsequent quotes from Toner come from this interview.
23 Paul Russell, 'Trot along to see Hank', *Evening Herald* (24 February 1988), 30.
24 Interview with Declan McKinney, 4 April 2022.
25 Interview with Pete McCarter, 2 April 2022.
26 Brian Hunter, 'Gallagher's Blues', *Belfast Telegraph* (23 February 1988), 12.
27 In the years leading up to its closure, the venue had been increasingly struggling to compete with Galway's Leisureland and its shows were often not achieving full capacity, leading to mounting running costs. Another problem came in April 1987 when Declan McNelis, bassist with the jazz band Hotfoot, was tragically attacked after a concert at the Savoy and later died in hospital. The tragedy shocked the local community, with many Irish artists stating that they could never contemplate playing the Savoy again because of the association.
28 Mike Maguire's history of the Savoy Theatre was available on the Limerick City Council website, but was removed when the Council updated its website in early 2024.
29 The last concert instead was given by folk singer Mary Black on 14 March and the last ever show being the *Tops of the Town* final on 26 March.
30 'Guitar ace Gallagher for Leisureland', *Tuam Herald* (27 February 1988), n.p.
31 N.E. 'Rory Gallagher: Defender of Rock and Blues Traditions', *Tuam Herald* (12 March 1988), 9.
32 Brian O'Brien, 'Music Scene', *Evening Echo* (11 February 1988), 9.
33 Interview with Mark Gillis, 17-18 May 2022.
34 Interview with Paul Hunt, 27 February 2023.
35 George Byrne, 'Accolades and Gongs from Hot Press', *Irish Independent* (2 March 1988), 7.
36 Mary Coughlan – Western Star', *Irish Examiner* (19 March 1988), 22.
37 'Rory Gallagher does an impromptu sting for RTE', https://www.youtube.com/watch?v=YwAwzp0Abbw
38 'Rory Gallagher on Borderline – 1988', https://www.youtube.com/watch?v=drQW3EJiz2s&t=6s
39 Interview with Rónán Johnston, 25 May 2022.
40 Interview with Liam M. Malone, 17 February 2024.
41 Interview with Jim Roche, 25 March 2023.
42 Marcus Connaughton, *Rory Gallagher: His Life and Times* (Cork: Collins Press, 2012), 150.
43 'Celebrity sell out', *Sunday Press* (12 June 1988), 51.
44 'When Pop Went Political: Nelson Mandela 70th Birthday Tribute Concert', *Classic Pop* (2 August 2018), https://www.classicpopmag.com/2018/08/nelson-mandela-70th-birthday-tribute-concert/
45 Senan Molony, 'Songs of freedom for SA hero', *Irish Independent* (18 July 1988), 9.
46 'Free Nelson, free gig', *Evening Herald* (25 July 1988),12.
47 Chris Donovan, 'Mandela Day', *Hot Press*, included in Paul Sullivan, 'Dublin 17.7.88, Olympia Theatre, Nelson Mandela's 70th birthday', no. 45 (1988), *Deuce Quarterly*, 6.
48 O'Sullivan, 'Dublin 17.7.88…'
49 Ibid.
50 N.E. 'Rory Gallagher: Defender of Rock and Blues Traditions', 9.
51 'Rory Gallagher – The Late Late Show – 12 February 1988'.
52 Michael Ross, 'Rory Gallagher – Fire Bellied', *Sunday Tribune* (21 February 1988), 11.
53 Ibid.
54 Ibid.
55 Graham, 'On this day in 1987…'

56 Ibid.
57 Embassy of Ireland. 'Rory Gallagher (1948–1995), A Founding Figure of Irish Rock Music' (October 2014), https://www.dfa.ie/irish-embassy/great-britain/about-us/ambassador/ambassadors-blog-2014/october2014/rory-gallagher-founding-figure-of-irish-rock-music/
58 Declan Lynch, 'Bad day for the blues', *Sunday Tribune* (18 June 1995), https://www.roryon.com/badday.html
59 Russell, 'Roaring Rory lets rip just like old times', 19.
60 Ibid.
61 Lynch, 'Bad day for the blues'.
62 *Rory Gallagher: Calling Card* (RTÉ and BBC NI, 2024) and interview with Dave Fanning, 22 April 2022.
63 Harry Doherty, 'Caught in the Act', *Melody Maker* (6 May 1978), https://www.roryon.com/hammer170.html
64 'Rory Gallagher - Dublin 1988 + Interview'.
65 McSnailly Burke, 'Pirate Rory revisits for his destiny'.
66 Stevens, 'Rory Gallagher…'
67 'Rory Gallagher – The Late Late Show – 12th February 1988'.

4.3 In Sunshine or in Shadow: Irish Festivals and Cultural Celebrations, 1983-1989

In 1977, Rory Gallagher made history when he headlined Ireland's first major open-air festival at Macroom. Nobody was quite prepared for the crowd of 20,000 that he attracted to this sleepy, little town in County Cork. And when he returned a year later, performing to an even larger audience, his legend was well and truly sealed. Ever since, Macroom has been synonymous with Gallagher's name, so much so that a mural was unveiled in 2022 on Main Street to commemorate the momentous occasion when he first performed in the town's castle grounds.

Yet, as pioneering as it was, Macroom 'Mountain Dew' Festival was not the only Irish music festival or cultural celebration in which Gallagher was involved. Macroom might receive the most coverage because it broke new ground in Ireland and was tied to the founding of *Hot Press* magazine (which Gallagher and his brother Dónal helped fund). But the overfocus on this festival in publications about Gallagher's life downplays the fact that he continued to obtain firsts on the Irish music scene throughout the 1980s, appearing at all sorts of events—in the North, the Republic and across the sea in London—that showcased his deep pride and love for his homeland.

In some cases, his appearances were for worthy social causes, such as the Self Aid benefit concert for unemployment in Ireland (1986) or the Irish Rock Week to promote new, young Irish talent (1989), while others, like Lisdoonvarna Folk Festival (1983) or Ballyronan Rock Festival (1989), were simply for the *craic*. What they all have in common, however, is that, despite the high quality of Gallagher's performances, they are typically neglected when telling his story. As with most topics in this book, this neglect stems partially from their occurrence in the latter part of Gallagher's career rather than the 1970s. But on this occasion, there is also a deeper reason: all four events are tied up with something negative— whether national tragedy or scandal, unfavourable press coverage or economic difficulties—which has skewed public opinion towards them and often, in turn, towards Gallagher.

This essay seeks to rethink these four events, providing much-needed context in order to recover Gallagher's appearances and highlight the extenuating circumstances that have shaped their (negative) portrayal to date. In doing so, we argue that—in their own way—such events were just as noteworthy as

Macroom. Reporting at Macroom in 1977, Niall Stokes of *Hot Press* wrote that Gallagher "lifted the audience into other dimensions," delivering "rock n roll of the finest shape and hue," while his "undiluted energy" resulted in a "festival victory, a celebration."[1] Here, we make the case that Gallagher's 1980s festival appearances were equal *victories* and *celebrations* that demonstrated both his continued ability to excel in the live setting and to inspire a whole new generation of fans.

Lisdoonvarna Folk Festival (30 July 1983)
Established in 1978 by local men Paddy Doherty and Jim Shannon, the Lisdoonvarna Folk Festival was conceived as the "Irish Woodstock" or "Irish Glastonbury," seeking to bring people together in "part-scout jamboree, part-Bacchanal frenzy, part-hippy-dippy roots-embracing finger-in-the-ear jig-'n'-reel extravaganza."[2] Staged in a valley halfway between the villages of Lisdoonvarna and Doolan in County Clare, the festival quickly became the largest and most famous outdoor music event in Ireland.

While the early years of the festival centred around traditional Irish music, its growing reputation led to the appearance of a range of cross-genre international artists, from Chris De Burgh and UB40 to Jackson Browne and Wishbone Ash. In addition to several days of music, the festival also featured art and mime sideshows, aerobatic and skydiving displays and fireworks, making it a highlight of the Irish summer and a "rite of passage"[3] for many young people.

The 1983 edition of Lisdoonvarna was set to be bigger than ever, with Rory Gallagher and Van Morrison—"two of the country's great rock luminaries"[4]— confirmed as headliners. Also on the bill were blues guitarist Peter Green, folk legend Christy Moore, Celtic rockers Moving Hearts and Scottish singer-songwriter John Martyn, ensuring that festivalgoers received real value for money with their £18.50 weekend ticket. For the first time, the festival was moved from July to the August Bank Holiday "to allow more people to partake of the music and the festivities." The stage was set for an exciting event.

In his iconic song, Christy Moore paints an idyllic notion of Lisdoonvarna: mighty *craic*, loads of frolics, pints of stout, good music, open air.[5] That is exactly how the 1983 edition was advertised by its organisers in the festival programme: "a happening, a festive event, crowd participation and enjoyment as much part of the festival as the artist and background organisation." However, this imagined congenial atmosphere was a far cry from reality due to a set of tragic happenings that marked an abrupt end to the festival's six-year run and overshadowed the legacy of Gallagher's remarkable performance.

The festival got off to a flying start on the Saturday afternoon, with the sun beating down and record high temperatures when the first act—Pulling Faces—began their set. The crowd was buzzing, and these feelings only grew as the afternoon continued. By the time that Rory Gallagher took the stage just after 10PM to the sounds of 'Double Vision', the entire valley was electric. Earlier in the week,

Gallagher had performed two nights at the London Marquee Club; the concerts were in aid of the venue's 25th anniversary, but also served as warm-up shows for Lisdoonvarna. Gallagher was always especially nervous when performing before a home crowd, so he wanted to be well prepared. As attested by bootlegs, he had no reason to be concerned and was on his usual fine form.

Gallagher's setlist at Lisdoonvarna marks the gradual transformation in his live performances from this date onwards—still energetic and full of fire, yet with an added maturity and emotional depth, greater attention to detail and a more blues-based core. Of course, there were timeless favourites like 'Moonchild', 'Shadow Play', 'Shin Kicker' and 'Tattoo'd Lady' (the latter beautifully blended with The Band's 'Loving You Is Sweeter Than Ever'), but these were accompanied by equally strong newer material from *Jinx* like 'Big Guns', 'Ride on Red, Ride On' and 'The Devil Made Me Do It'.

But perhaps the most striking aspect of Gallagher's Lisdoonvarna performance was the addition of Ray Beavis and John Earle on saxophone, the brass echoing splendidly across the valley and accentuating the tones of Gallagher's guitar. Beavis and Earle added a new layer to Gallagher's songs, whether in the highly moving version of 'What in the World', the cheeky cover of Chuck Berry's 'Nadine' or the mystical sounds of 'Philby'. Also of note is their role in this early appearance of the Sonny Boy Williamson classic 'When My Baby She Left Me', which went on to become a highlight of Gallagher's late 1980s concerts.

Fan 'Fran K' was one of the many lucky people to witness Gallagher's performance at Lisdoonvarna. He had travelled down from Arklow on a bus with a group of friends and, while he recalls that the whole festival was strong, it was Gallagher who stood out for him and really "showed his class." 'Fran K' describes the whole gig as "energy and freedom," his particular highlight being 'Shadow Play', where bright shining lights beamed from one side of the stagefront and Gallagher's shadow was silhouetted on the other side. 'Fran K' also remembers the way that Gallagher effortlessly tuned his guitar as he played a solo, not dropping a single note. For 'Fran K', Gallagher was an inspiration for a whole generation of Irish people because he showed them that there was something more to life than "getting a full-time job and maybe buying a house"; like him, they too could dream big and strive for more.[6]

Despite the strength of Gallagher's performance and the immediate warm response from fans such as 'Fran K', it was during his set that the first signs of trouble at Lisdoonvarna flared up. The concert area was protected by a 10-foot fence of corrugated metal backed up with wooden props. However, with insufficient security to monitor the area, roughly 1,000 people breached the fence and obtained free entry into the festival site. For now, these people were well behaved, simply happy to witness their hero Gallagher in the flesh, yet things turned sour the next day.

Around 6PM, as John Martyn started his performance, more and more people tried to obtain entry to Lisdoonvarna by scaling the fence. With security increasingly struggling to cope, a group of Hells Angels took it upon themselves to offer reinforcement. Nobody is entirely sure who or what started the next chain of events, but, suddenly, there was a swarm of stones, bottles and cans and a fight broke out between the gatecrashers and the Hells Angels, leading the protective barrier to collapse.

According to a report by Margaret Collins of the *Galway Advertiser,* the gatecrashers "defied the best efforts of the security men"[7] who fled in dismay. Then, oddly cheered on by some of the crowd, the Hells Angels turned into "animals" and "caused havoc," wielding bottles and drawing knives. The gatecrashers, in turn, began to burn the Hells Angels' motorbikes and tents. Witnessing the violence from the safety of a hilltop, Collins described the scenes as "barbaric." Although Sunday's headliner Van Morrison still came on stage at 10PM and delivered a crowd-pleasing set, it was too late. The music did not really matter anymore. It had now taken second place to "violence and vandalism."

Then things got even worse.

Throughout the evening, rumours started amassing about a group of young festivalgoers who had got into trouble after going for a swim in Doolin to cool off from the summer heat. Apparently, they had been reported as missing. When the festival came to a close in the early hours of Monday with a set by Moving Hearts, all that people could talk about was the earlier displays of violence and the fate of the young swimmers. The music had been well and truly forgotten.

As the festival clean-up operation began the next day, the true extent of what had happened became clear in the local newspapers. Eight people — all between the ages of 17 and 25 — had lost their lives in the treacherous waters of Doolin. Ignoring warning signs on the beach, they had gone swimming and strong undercurrents had pulled them under at a dangerous sandbar. Newspaper coverage of Lisdoonvarna, thus, became dominated by this appalling tragedy, as well as the violence that had broken out at the festival.

While the drownings could be seen as a terrible accident, what happened inside the festival grounds was less easy to fathom and threatened to jeopardise the future of Lisdoonvarna. As Gene Kerrigan of *Magill* wrote:

> The employment of Hells Angels, the kicking down of fences, the use of dogs and bottles, are all peripheral to the joy of the music and the adventure of the weekend in the beautiful and scarred countryside. But they determine the future of events like this. Those things, and developments elsewhere.[8]

Similar thoughts were aired in the recent RTÉ documentary *How Ireland Rocked the '70s.* According to Doherty and Shannon, the disaster "took the good out" of Lisdoonvarna and unveiled a "wave of sorrow and depression" amongst both spectators and organisers. It was inevitable that things could never be the same again, and they made the difficult decision to cancel the festival, bringing an end to six successful years of entertainment.

With 1983's Lisdoonvarna finishing so badly and being the last ever edition, it is no wonder that so little is mentioned today about this festival. Its name may be immortalised in Christy Moore's song, but the event itself is largely forgotten under a cloud of misfortune. Gallagher—just like the other artists who took part in the 1983 edition—had nothing to do with the mindless violence that erupted. In fact, he was already well on his way to the US where he would kick off a tour in Palo Alto on 1 August when the worst of the violence took place. Yet, his performance—along with the other musicians' performances—is sadly soiled and often overshadowed by the infamous events. It is important to look past the reckless actions of a small few and remember the *good* of Lisdoonvarna and the positive aspects of its legacy. As Christy Moore reminds us:

> Something happened at Lisdoonvarna that still reverberates in Ireland today... different genres brought together... taking place on the side of a hill in a valley open to Atlantic winds and rains... a great atmosphere in the air of love and friendship and music and drink...[9]

In short, we should not forget what happened at Lisdoonvarna and, of course, we should learn from it, but we must also remember the bands and the bonhomie, the fun and the friendships, the love and the laughter. On that Saturday evening in 1983, Gallagher brought happiness to the crowds who flocked to see him. For those two hours, he held them in the palm of his hand, transporting them to a new world where anything was possible. That is the real magic of Lisdoonvarna and, by the same token, the real magic of Rory Gallagher.

Self Aid (17 May 1986)

In 1986, Ireland was at a critical level for unemployment. Within just five years, the number of people without a job in the country had doubled; 17.3% were now out of work and 500 people were emigrating each week, most of whom were under 25.[10] Seeing the success of Live Aid the year before, Tony Boland and Niall Mathews—two experienced RTÉ producers and programme makers—decided to approach RTÉ in December 1985 about copying the format to help combat Ireland's growing unemployment problem.[11] Their aim was to put on a 14-hour live music event that served several purposes: to celebrate Irish enterprise and Irish rock music, while helping create jobs and boost national morale (particularly amongst young people). In short, they wanted to "retain all the good things about Live Aid," especially the viewers' sense of involvement, and direct this against unemployment under the strapline "Make It Work."[12] They decided to call the event Self Aid.

Once Self Aid was given the green light by RTÉ, Boland and Mathews began to receive immediate interest from musicians, as well as state training and employment agencies. Bob Geldof was one of the first artists to sign up and, according to Boland, his support acted as a catalyst for many others to follow suit. As someone with a strong track record of involvement in charitable causes,[13] Rory Gallagher was also keen early on to participate. However, as he told Dave Fanning for the *Self Aid: Behind the Screens* documentary, he sat down with Boland and Mathews to run through "the general format and the idea and the spirit behind the thing" before saying yes.[14] As soon as Gallagher learnt more about the aims of Self Aid, he felt that it was "above board" and "worth doing" and agreed to sign up.

By the beginning of 1986, the entire Self Aid line-up was confirmed, reading like a who's who of Irish musicians. There was Gallagher, U2, Boomtown Rats and Christy Moore, but also Van Morrison, Paul Brady, The Chieftains and Clannad, as well as honorary Irishmen Chris De Burgh and Elvis Costello, to name but a few. All musicians agreed to give their time for free, with profits going to the Self Aid Trust for job creation. The concert would take place at the RDS stadium in Dublin and be broadcast live on RTÉ and Radio 2.

Boland and Mathews borrowed a revolving stage from Live Aid, as well as the concert structure. With each act given just 15 minutes to perform, the stage was divided into three sections and each performer's equipment was numbered and lodged in a tunnel behind, ready to be rolled on for assembly by a 25-man road crew. Throughout its 14 hours, there would be a telethon with two separate pledge systems for the public: one for jobs pledged by employers and one for money donated into a jobs creation fund to finance various employment projects. On the day, there would also be a number of local events arranged around Ireland, with various businesses donating a percentage of their day's takings to Self Aid. Like Live Aid, Self Aid also had its own song—'Let's Make It Work'—written especially for the event by Paul Doran and Christy Moore.

Just one month before the concert, 30,000 tickets went on sale, the publicity handled by legendary concert promoter Jim Aiken. Tickets cost £15 for the general public and £25 for the press and artists' guests. There were also £10 discounted tickets for the unemployed at one end of the spectrum and £100 VIP tickets in the Anglesea Stand at the other. After initial slow sales ("jobs [are] a more practical thing than the emotional sight of a starving child,"[15] Geldof justified), all 30,000 tickets sold out. Leading up to the event, Self Aid received much positive international attention: it was featured in the ITV investigative current affairs programme *World in Action*, while Geldof and Boland promoted it on British breakfast television and BBC Radio 4, respectively. MTV and *Rolling Stone* also flew over crews from the US in preparation.

Back home in Ireland, however, opinions on Self Aid were far more negative. For many, a rock concert was seen as side-tracking people from the main problems facing the country, while also taking responsibility away from politicians and creating the illusion that unemployment could be dealt with by charity. Others felt that Self Aid "blames the unemployed for being unemployed" and "does damage" by "reinforcing"[16] negative attitudes around unemployment. There were also troubling reports that employers were deliberately holding back planned jobs in order to obtain good publicity during the show, and that the monitoring committee to oversee the money was not trustworthy.

At a time when RTÉ were shedding 300 jobs, their support was also seen as hypocritical, while Paul Cleary of new wave band The Blades considered it to be "patronising" and "self-indulgent"[17] for musicians to preach about unemployment. As a means of protest, a series of alternative concerts were arranged at the Underground Bar and McGonagle's Club in Dublin, but half of participants pulled out at the last minute for fear of RTÉ "blacking"[18] (i.e., a blanket ban on their music across all RTÉ channels). "Suspend your cynicism!"[19] was the parting message of Boland and Mathews to the nation before the big day.

For Gallagher, expectation around his appearance at Self Aid had built long before 17 May, with the Irish press noting that it would be his first performance in Ireland in several years. The programme for the event produced by *Hot Press* emphasised how it was fitting that Self Aid would "mark his return" to Ireland, given that he had "pioneered the Irish open-air festival" with his appearance at Macroom in 1977.[20]

Gallagher was due on stage at 10PM and had taken time out of a very busy schedule to be in Dublin for the event. He had been performing in Lille just the night before, flew in for his 15-minute set at Self Aid and then would be flying straight back out again to Bremen, where he would give a concert at the Bruchhausen-Vilsen Open-Air Festival the following evening.[21] Speaking to Dave Fanning in 1988, Gallagher recalled Self Aid as "very, very odd," noting how he was "off the stage before [he] had cooled down."[22] He remembered running out before the crowd, seeing the three traffic-light system ("if you weren't off by the red light... you were kicked off"), his guitar lying on stage with "the wind blowing around it" and being "twenty feet away from the band," all of which was "not good for [his] calm." "We got through it," Gallagher self-deprecatingly concluded, "As long as a bit of it was good."

And good it certainly was!

Indeed, what makes this performance so special is the way that Gallagher expertly turns things around after a somewhat shaky start. He looks nervous when he opens with 'Follow Me', experiencing both pitching and tuning issues throughout the first verse. Biographer Julian Vignoles unfairly claims that this was a sign that "cracks were now showing"[23] in Gallagher's concerts, yet he fails to mention the remarkable magic that occurs next. In the chorus, Gallagher takes a momentary step back from the microphone, inhales deeply and shakes his head. When he moves forward again, it is like a switch has been flicked on. He transforms and is now in a completely different zone, brimming with confidence and his familiar neon intensity—not a "crack" in sight.

For the rest of the set, he is at the height of his abilities, moving from 'Follow Me' into an emotional rendition of the slow blues 'I Wonder Who'—a bold move at a stadium concert before a general audience, yet deftly pulled off. 'I Wonder Who' then transitions into 'Messin' with the Kid', Gallagher all smiles now as Feltham impresses with his harmonica skills and the crowd sing along to the chorus. The set finishes all too soon with a rousing interpretation of 'Shadow Play', complete with duckwalking, dancing and an exciting series of breaks in the chorus.

For many, Gallagher's performance was one of the high points in an incredibly strong night of music that showcased the very best of Irish talent. Despite initial fears of disruption due to an anti-Self Aid protest outside the gates of the RDS Stadium, the concert "ran as smoothly as a well-oiled engine running on full throttle"[24] and "the music was a triumph."[25] According to *The Blackpool Sentinel* blog, the "quality and breadth" of the final two hours of Self Aid is unlikely to "ever again be replicated on any national stage,"[26] with Gallagher followed by Christy Moore, Elvis Costello, Chris De Burgh, Van Morrison and, finally, U2. The event also saw the last ever performance of The Boomtown Rats and a reformed Thin Lizzy with Gary Moore on lead vocals paying special tribute to frontman Phil Lynott who had passed away just four months earlier.

Self Aid was watched by almost 2.4 million people across Ireland (the equivalent of over 90% of all homes in the country). On the day, over £500,000 was raised and 750 jobs were created. Although there was much scepticism before the event, most initial press reviews were positive, describing Self Aid as a "fitting acknowledgement that Irish rock music has come of age, and can take its rightful place in the world."[27]

According to the *Irish Independent*, it was a "landmark"[28] that such an impressive bill of artists was all Irish, while for the *Sunday Independent*, it was "the greatest celebration of popular music the country has ever seen."[29] However, there was some criticism of the fact that there were no television screens in the stadium, nor pledge updates from the studio, meaning that spectators lost a sense of what Self Aid was about. There was also disappointment in Cork when a giant RTÉ transmitter disk erected on top of the Opera House blew down in strong winds, cracking the roof and temporarily disrupting transmission of the concert.

Following Self Aid, the Self Aid Trust continued to raise money through a live double album *Live for Ireland*, which featured 'Follow Me' from Gallagher's set (mixed by Gallagher himself). Funds were also raised through an exhibition at the Bank of Ireland in Dundalk, which featured photographs taken by Colm Henry at the event. Seven months later, the *Sunday Independent* reported that there was now £800,000 in the job creation fund, with 88 small firms approved for funding and 815 people with new jobs.[30]

However, as time went on, it began to seem that the sceptics had been right and Self Aid did not have a lasting impact in terms of helping Ireland's unemployment problem. According to later press reports, no jobs actually arose from Self Aid other than already existing vacancies. Furthermore, almost one in three of the jobs pledged on the day never came into fruition or did not come with the terms of reference outlined by the National Manpower Service. By the start of 1987, the general public view was that, despite the best intentions of Boland and Mathews, they were naïve in their aims and Self Aid did little more than temporarily raise the nation's spirits.

Self Aid may be remembered with mixed feelings today, but many of the people involved in the concert did not regret their decision to participate. In an interview with *Hot Press* in 2019, Eddie McCarron—the commercial manager of RDS—described Self Aid as an "epic thing" with "such an incredible amount of goodwill"[31] from the musicians, while Boland and Mathews felt that it had ultimately been "a celebration of positive thinking."[32] Speaking to *La Nueva España* in July 1986, Gallagher said that he was happy to have taken part in Self Aid because "Ireland has the highest rate of unemployment in Europe" and he was eager to raise awareness of issues in his own country.[33]

So, perhaps the success and legacy of Self Aid should not be measured in money raised or jobs created, but rather in the power of music to provide comfort and hope to a nation going through a difficult time—something that Gallagher strived for throughout his career. Without ever needing to be overtly political, Gallagher said all he needed to say on political matters through his guitar. His participation in Self Aid, thus, stands as a key example of his kind heart, his ardent support for the underdog and his undying love for his country. More than 35 years on, Ireland's economy is highly developed and unemployment levels are far lower at just 4.4%. Today, one of the most pressing issues facing the country is affordable housing, leading journalist Mick Lynch to ask whether it is time that we have a 'House Aid' benefit concert.[34] If this ever came to pass, filling the gap that Gallagher left on stage would be a mammoth task.

Irish Rock Week (10 April 1989)
For over four decades, Vince Power was a major figure on the British music scene. Originally hailing from County Waterford, Power moved to London as a teenager and worked in various manual labour jobs, before establishing a chain of lucrative second-hand furniture shops which enabled him to pursue his first love: country and western music. Keen to bring the sounds of Nashville to London, Power set up the Mean Fiddler club in 1982 in Harlesden. Built on the site of an old boxing gym, the venue swiftly became *the* place for country stars to perform.

Shortly after opening, Power recognised that the Mean Fiddler could also provide a home-from-home for the increasing number of Irish expats in London and decided to introduce Irish Music Nights, which showcased up-and-coming Irish bands like the Pogues. Spurred on by the success of the Nights, Power went one step further in 1989, launching an Irish Rock Week—a whole seven nights in April featuring the "cream"[35] of Ireland's new talent and sponsored by Ryanair and BMI. Despite its focus on the *new*, Power was adamant that he wanted Gallagher to kick off the Week, given his legendary status as the first man to put Ireland on the world map for music. And Gallagher, as a proud Irishman, willingly said yes.

In the weeks leading up to its launch, the event was talked about frequently in both the London and Irish press. In a bid to attract English spectators, organiser Tim Hegarty stressed to journalists that the week should not be seen as a "cultural festival" of Ireland, but rather just a celebration of great rock and pop music.[36] The *Evening Herald*, nonetheless, took the opportunity to capitalise upon the Irish aspect of the Week, describing it as a place for the "liggers of the world" to "unite" over "seven drunken nights."[37] They continued this emphasis in a later article, reporting on the "new breed of London Irish" who are unable to "resist the lure of music from home."[38]

Not all press coverage was positive, however. George Byrne of the *Irish Independent*, for example, praised the decision to include Aslan, Something Happens!, The Fleadh Cowboys and Cypress, Mine! as headliners, but followed this statement up with the sarcastic "and, er, lots of other people"[39] to signify their lack of importance. Not one to mince his words, Byrne also described Thursday night's entertainment (The Stunning, The Swinging Swine and The Sawdoctors) as one that he "certainly wouldn't wish on [his] worst enemy," cheekily adding that "life really is too short."

Despite their differing opinions about the aims of Irish Rock Week and the talent involved, the majority of newspaper articles were united in one surprising factor: they did not seem to recall who Rory Gallagher was. It had only been four months since Gallagher had last performed in England, ending his one-month tour with a concert at the Borderline Club in London that was positively reviewed by the British press. He donated all proceeds from the concert to fellow blues musician Jo Ann Kelly who was in ill health at the time.[40] Gallagher had also attracted local media attention when he opened the PA section of Carlsbro Music Shop in Leeds (despite being unwell with a cold). Yet, by the time of Irish Rock Week, the guitarist had clearly been forgotten.

While Gallagher may have been away from the stage for early 1989, he had remained busy, carrying out session work for the Fureys, Davy Spillane and Phil Coulter—three important names in the area of traditional Irish music (see 1.4). It is surprising then that recollections of him were no different in the Irish press. In his article for the *Irish Independent,* the aforementioned George Byrne described Gallagher as a "promising guitarist who'll doubtless be doing his utmost to impress the 18 year old A&R men in black 501s and rollneck jumpers."[41] Equally, the *Evening Herald* reported that Irish Rock Week is "designed to showcase emerging Irish talent like Rory Gallagher."[42] The *Sunday Independent* at least recognised who Gallagher was, but were eager to point out that he was "somewhat long in the tooth"[43] to be chosen for a week promoting new Irish talent.

Interestingly, this was not the first time that Gallagher had taken part in an event to celebrate Irish culture and promote new Irish talent. In 1980, he had closed London's six-week Sense of Ireland festival (also featuring a young, unsigned U2) with a barnstorming performance on St Patrick's Day at the Lyceum, yet in this case, the press was enthusiastic and made no comments about him not fitting the category of new talent. By 1989, however, Gallagher was 41 and his 'old age' was now a regular feature of press articles, often used as a cheap shortcut to imply that playing the blues was something unfashionable. It is no wonder then that the few journalists who remembered Gallagher not only questioned his right to play at Irish Rock Week, but also subsequently gave him an unfavourable review, based not on the quality of his actual performance but on the assumption that his music was old hat.

One of the most negative in this respect came from Eamonn Carr of the *Evening Herald* who claimed that Gallagher "flopped" and that the support act (the Foremen) "completely wiped [him] out."[44] According to Carr, "connoisseurs" dismissed Gallagher's performance as "abysmal" and it was only attended by "leftovers from the sixties with long hair and those who wished they still have any." Carr's report paints a damning picture of the evening for Gallagher. A picture of him unrecognisable to Irish audiences familiar with his jaw dropping performances of the 1970s. A picture of him as obsolete and out of touch with young people. A picture of him that feeds into the 'fall' narrative and suggests that he was no longer the performer that he once was by this stage in his career. However, by accumulating other perspectives, we expose the dubiousness of this review, especially as another review by Eugene Maloney can be found in the very same copy of the newspaper and describes an entirely different concert to the one supposedly observed by Carr.

Maloney outlines the excitement and anticipation of fans around seeing Gallagher again, with queues lining up down the street and the "house full" sign going up long before he hit the stage. He describes the chants of "RORY RORY" filling the air—chants that come mainly from fans who were not even born when Gallagher was "treading the boards with Taste"—and praises his "searing powerhouse version" of 'Messin' with the Kid' that sent the crowd "wild with delight."[45] Reading Maloney's review, we get a completely different sense of Gallagher's performance: one that was engaging and powerful, that brought together young and old fans, that left them crying out for more.

These views are echoed by others who were in the audience that night. For fan Byrne Norry, the gig was "great" and it was "such a thrill" to be so close to Gallagher.[46] Likewise, fan Aidan Russell described it as the "best, most ecstatic, exciting gig ever." Elaborating further to us in June 2022, Russell's emotion is still apparent:

> Rory's gigs were the best ever gigs I have seen. Such powerful, special and unique performances. So honest and sincere […] How one man could give so much on stage was mind-blowing. He was so energetic. […] It was truly a unique and memorable gig, a great performance from Rory. The pinnacle of the night was when my Irish hero, dear Rory, played the song of my American hero, Bob Dylan, 'I Shall Be Released'. A special night, which I and my fellow Irish music lovers were proud and privileged to be part of in the Mean Fiddler with Rory and his band.[47]

Organiser Robert Stevenson also saw the evening as "very special" and viewed the entire Week as good for the audience, the bands and the Irish music industry as a whole.[48] Gallagher himself was so impressed with Dublin band the Foremen that he appeared on stage wearing a Foremen lapel badge and, according to the *Evening Herald*, was still wearing it when he headed for home.[49]

One week after his performance, Gallagher was interviewed by Dave Fanning for his RTÉ radio show. Fanning tells Gallagher that he heard from spectators that it was a "brilliant show" and, in a rare display of self-confidence, Gallagher agrees and says that the band was "on form" and "really cooking" and he was "really coasting with them."[50] Given that Gallagher was always his own worst critic and the first to acknowledge when he performed badly, his account of the evening can be taken as reliable.

Overall, Irish Rock Week stands as another opportunity that Gallagher proudly embraced out of love for his country and a desire to entertain his compatriots. Subjected to unfriendly media reports that ranged from mocking his 'old age' at one end of the spectrum to failing to recall who he was at the other, Gallagher set out to prove critics wrong and show that if anybody deserved to headline a week that celebrated Irish talent, it was him. Added to the tension was the fact that Gallagher had been off the road for four months prior to Irish Rock Week, so the evening marked both his 'big return' and his first gig of 1989. However, Gallagher had no need to worry about being rusty. As usual, he rose to the occasion and pleased both fans and critics (Eamonn Carr aside) with his performance, imbuing his fellow countrymen and women with pride. As fan Aidan Russell recalls, "we were all very proud of [Rory]. Special sincere and honest music from a sensitive, caring soul and gentleman."

Ballyronan Rock Festival (29 July 1989)
The tranquil shores of Lough Neagh experienced a shakeup in July 1989 when the Ballyronan Rock Festival returned for a second year, this time with Rory Gallagher as headliner. Known informally as 'Rock the Lough', this short-lived festival was established in 1988 by local company Island Concert Promotions who wanted to host a large-scale music event in Northern Ireland, which had historically been deprived of concerts since the outbreak of The Troubles in the late 1960s.

The first year saw British hard rock band Magnum as headliners, with Irish jazz singer Mary Coughlan second on the bill (replacing Bonnie Tyler who had pulled out due to illness). While an unlikely pairing on paper, the two acts complemented each other well and the festival was a resounding success. Spurred on by the triumph, Island decided that 1989's headliner would be a homegrown talent and who better—or more significant to Northern Ireland—than Rory Gallagher?

With its 600 inhabitants, the village of Ballyronan was hardly where you would expect a rock festival to take place, let alone a rock festival featuring somebody of such high calibre and international status as Gallagher. Yet, Gallagher was never one to give too much attention to geographical location or size of an audience. If people wanted music, then he would quite happily take the music to them, far ahead of any thoughts about financial gain or even personal safety. The fact that this festival was in Northern Ireland—and County Derry of all places—may have just twisted his arm on this occasion, however. Not only did County Derry have huge personal significance to Gallagher (see 1.4), but he had expressed a desire to perform there since at least 1975.[51]

Although Ballyronan Rock Festival was a fledgling in the world of outdoor summer concerts, the organisers pulled out all the stops to obtain a "red hot line-up" to support Gallagher.[52] Sharing the bill was hard rock band Mama's Boys from County Fermanagh, as well as Dare (featuring ex-Thin Lizzy keyboardist Darren Wharton), Elixir, This Obsession, The Mockers and Krakatoa, who could all be seen for the bargain ticket price of just £11.50. For many, the festival was considered a "brave undertaking,"[53] given the precarious situation in Northern Ireland at the time, as well as its unique choice of location. But then again, previous Irish successes like Macroom had equally been deemed a huge gamble when they first started out.

Pat McManus, lead guitarist and fiddle player for Mama's Boys, did not think twice when presented with the opportunity to perform at Rock the Lough. He and his fellow band members saw the festival as a "good warm-up gig"[54] to get into shape for their forthcoming European tour. Furthermore, they were particularly excited about the prospect of being on the same bill as Gallagher. Speaking to *Derry Now* in 2020 about Rock the Lough, McManus stated:

> We always jumped at the chance to share the stage with Rory. He was one of my heroes growing up, and still is. He was marvellous. From that point of view, it was great. We'd shared the stage a couple of times with Rory in Germany and various places like that, but this was the first time on home soil, which we were delighted about.[55]

The local press was also equally excited about the return of Gallagher to Northern Ireland—his first visit to the region since February 1988, when he performed at the Ulster Hall in Belfast, and his first performance on the island of Ireland since the Nelson Mandela 'Freedom at 70' tribute concert in July 1988 (see 4.2). In stark contrast to the lukewarm press response leading up to Gallagher's appearance at Irish Rock Week in London, the Northern Irish press lauded the decision to select the "legendary" Gallagher as headliner for Rock the Lough, describing him as the "Irish King of blues and rock and roll."[56] Likewise, they saw his age as insignificant, stressing that he had "lost nothing with the passing of time," was "one of Ireland's most enduring musicians" and that the years had "done nothing to diminish his legendary status in the eyes of countless fans."[57] They also noted Gallagher's continued relevance and popularity amongst young people, arguing that he was now "firmly established among the album collections of many a second generation fan."

Another key feature of these Northern Irish press articles is the praise that they steeped on Gallagher for his "uncompromising" attitude towards music, emphasising that many of the critiques around him only exist because people have "difficulty reconciling the man's offstage modesty with the intensity of his performances."[58] To support this point, Paddy Fitzsymons of *Sunday Life* cites a short interview with Gallagher where he describes his only real ambition as playing "for as long as many of [his] own heroes."[59]

In their articles, the Northern Irish press showcase a clear understanding of Gallagher and a deep sensitivity and respect for his authenticity and values. This love and loyalty towards Gallagher is grounded in the fact that he never turned his back on the people of Northern Ireland and always included them in his tours. Consequently, the press stands by him faithfully, rightly imbuing him with the title of "legend" and acknowledging his remarkable talent, regardless of his age, health problems or current music trends.

On the day of Rock the Lough—29 July—thousands of fans from across the island of Ireland eagerly converged on the shores of Lough Neagh, excited about the rare opportunity to attend a festival in the North. It was not without the overhanging threat of violence, however. A bomb scare and a Chinook helicopter flying overhead meant that many festivalgoers were forced to wait on incoming buses for several hours until the all-clear was given. Despite the bomb turning out to be a hoax, the news had filtered backstage. Yet, all bands had a "steely determination"[60] to perform. After all, 11 bombs had once gone off around Belfast when Gallagher performed at the Ulster Hall, some even shaking the venue, but he still played on. So, this was not going to faze him. As Pat McManus told *Derry Post*: "We were determined, come hell or high water, we were going to get on that stage and play and the rest of the artists that day felt the same."[61]

The concert went ahead as planned, with Gallagher hitting the stage early evening. "Good to see ya!" he humbly addressed the audience, before launching into a typically energetic 'Continental Op'. His 90-minute set was raw, hard-hitting and full of all sorts of surprises, including a rare opportunity to hear 'Kickback City'—the opening track of 1987's *Defender*—and a surprising return of 'Cradle Rock', not performed regularly since the days of *Irish Tour '74*. 'Cradle Rock' seems to be a spur of the moment choice, video footage showing bassist Gerry McAvoy quickly telling drummer Brendan O'Neill what song it is when Gallagher starts up the opening riff. Despite Gallagher unable to remember some of the lyrics, the performance sends the crowd into a frenzy, particularly during the two slide solos—a testimony to how much Gallagher had developed and matured as a guitarist since the *Irish Tour '74* version. "We haven't done that one for a million years," he says with a laugh as the song comes to a close.

Gerry McNally was in attendance that evening and had only recently become a Gallagher fan. He describes Gallagher as a "ball of energy," noting that he was "awestruck" by his "amazing" playing and had "never seen or heard anything" like him before or since. Darren Seaton was only 17 when he attended Rock the Lough and more a fan of Bon Jovi than Gallagher, yet he was well aware of Gallagher's "legendary status" and was in awe at the "epicness" of what he witnessed. It is only since Gallagher's death that Seaton has fully appreciated how lucky he was to see him, especially in such an unusual setting as Ballyronan.[62]

While it was Gallagher's music that stunned both the crowds and fellow musicians at Lough Neagh, his kindness and generosity had an even bigger resonance on some. Following his performance, Gallagher met a group of fans who had travelled all the way from Tipperary for the festival and did not have anywhere to stay. Touched by their efforts to see him and hearing that they were planning to sleep in their car, Gallagher insisted on giving up his hotel room for them.

Despite attendees praising the "wonderful afternoon's music" and "beautiful venue,"[63] a lack of marketing and issues with accessibility undermined the success of Rock the Lough and the 1989 edition would sadly be its last. Ultimately, the crowd of 4,000 people was not enough for the festival to be lucrative and the overly ambitious bill of musicians and costs to stage the event were not offset by ticket sales. This rather blunt end to a promising Northern Irish festival has, unfortunately, marred its memory and rendered it somewhat forgotten. However, it deserves to be remembered for its significant place in Gallagher history alone as both a *first* and a *last*: the *first* time that he headlined a festival of this scale in the North and the *last* time that he ever played in Northern Ireland. Full video footage online attests to the continued quality of Gallagher's live performances at this stage in his career, ensuring that—although he never played again in the North—he certainly left his mark and secured his status as a local treasure.

Bolts from the Blue(s): A Reappraisal
Between 1983 and 1989, Rory Gallagher participated in four important musical events, all of which had a celebration of Ireland and the island's rich cultural heritage at their core. Whether in the North or the Republic—or even across the sea in London—Gallagher enthusiastically took up the opportunity to participate, keen to showcase his love for his homeland by performing for his fellow compatriots. All four events were important in their own way, yet all were characterised by bolts from the blue that have negatively shaped their legacy in the public imagination. And somehow, these same feelings are often unfairly transferred over to Gallagher himself, almost guilty by association.

Speaking of Gallagher's performance at the 1980 Sense of Ireland festival, journalist John Stephenson stated that there was no better representative of the country than the "angel of the guitar"[64]—Rory Gallagher. The same can be said for the four events under study here, which are all clear manifestations of the guitarist's pride in his homeland. At a time when it was difficult to be Irish—especially when living in England—Gallagher never shied away from his identity. At a time when to be Irish was often seen as to be second-best or inferior, Gallagher always proved otherwise. Over and over again, he showed that, if Ireland could produce a musician of his stature, then the country was surely capable of anything.

If we look beyond surface level, we see then that there is much to commemorate about Gallagher's four 1980s festival appearances. We should celebrate the fact that he was the last person to headline Lisdoonvarna and Ballyronan, not view his appearance on the bills as a 'kiss of death'. We should commend his decision to want to help the unemployed and be part of a once-in-a-lifetime concert that raised over £500,000, not dwell on the fact that Self Aid did little to relieve Ireland's unemployment problem. And we should applaud his willingness to support new Irish talent by opening Irish Rock Week, not to mention his bravery to do so in the face of many hostile press reviews. Ultimately, we should reappraise these four events, seeing them not as *millstones*, but as *milestones* in Gallagher's career.

"You wouldn't want to lose your roots in Ireland," Gallagher told presenter Alan Bangs in 1982, "I suppose everyone secretly hangs onto their roots, even though they travel here and there."[65] It was this deep connection with his roots that led Gallagher to embrace opportunities to support Irish events and promote Ireland across the British Isles.[66] In 1994, he would have the opportunity to extend this connection internationally by taking part in the *Interceltique Festival de Lorient* in Britanny (see 4.6). Gallagher had also expressed a desire to play the Folk Festival in his birth town of Ballyshannon, once telling his brother Dónal, "God, if they only asked me, I'd love to play that. I'd play that for free"[67] — testimony of his attitude to music making, always putting personal beliefs before profit. Despite never getting to fulfil this ambition, today, that very birth town is home to the Rory Gallagher International Tribute Festival, which Dónal believes Gallagher would be "so pleased to bits" about, albeit also deeply "embarrassed."[68]

Gallagher was a true ambassador and role model for his country, a beacon of light for the people of Northern Ireland and someone who brought constant joy in sunshine and in shadow. As his agent, Paul Charles, put it, he was a "true gentleman and one of the genuine great men of modern Ireland."[69]

LAO

Footnotes

1 Niall Stokes, 'Ridin' Down a Country Mile', *Hot Press* (9 June 1977), http://www.roryon.com/macroom376.html
2 'Rainy Days and Festivals', *Irish Independent* (7 October 2004), http://www.independent.ie/unsorted/features/rainy-days-amp-festivals-162560.html
3 *How Ireland Rocked the '70s* (RTÉ, 2021).
4 As stated in the 6th Lisdoonvarna Folk Festival official programme.
5 In a later interview with Eamonn McCann for RTÉ's *Exhibit A*, Moore admitted that he wrote 'Lisdoonvarna' the Wednesday before the festival after hearing that he would be performing after Gallagher. Worried of how he would go down with the guitarist's fans, he decided to write a song that would "get through" to them and encourage them to chant.
6 Interview with 'Fran K', 11 February 2023.
7 Margaret Collins, 'Oh Lisdoon…', *Galway Advertiser* (4 August 1983), 15.
8 Gene Kerrigan, 'Lisdoonvarna', *Magill* (31 July 1983), https://magill.ie/archive/lisdoonvarna
9 *How Ireland Rocked the '70s*.
10 David Orr, 'Rock and Dole', *Irish Independent* (16 May 1986), 10; Tony O'Brien, Alan O'Keefe and Mairtin Mac Cormaic, 'Self Aid Brings Jobs Rock n' Rolling in', *Sunday Independent* (16 May 1986), 1.
11 Boland had, in fact, led RTÉ's coverage of Live Aid in 1985.
12 Orr, 'Rock and Dole'.
13 Following the Miami Showband Massacre in 1975, Gallagher was one of the first people to donate to the Fund set up to support the band's families and also played several concerts to raise further funds for the cause.

Part 4 - *In Sunshine or in Shadow*

14 'Rory Gallagher Self Aid 1986 Part II', https://www.youtube.com/watch?v=dRzuyNSNRnY
15 Tony O'Brien, 'If It Makes One Job, It's O.K.' - Bob', *Sunday Independent* (18 May 1986), 3.
16 Tony O'Brien, 'It's Self Aid for the Bosses' - Alternative Group', *Irish Independent* (14 May 1986), 6.
17 Emily O'Reilly, 'Ireland's Self Aid Will Be Great Gig', *Sunday Tribune* (11 May 1986), 5.
18 Brian Trench, 'Fear of RTE Ban Hits Protest', *Sunday Tribune* (18 May 1986), 4.
19 O'Reilly, 'Ireland's Self Aid Will Be Great Gig'.
20 As stated in the Self Aid official programme.
21 According to Gerry McAvoy, Gallagher was meant to headline the festival, but on seeing that James Brown was second on the bill, he "refused" the headlining slot and offered it to the funk legend instead.
22 'Rory Gallagher - Dublin 1988 + Interview', https://www.youtube.com/watch?v=JZVjd8JaI-A
23 Julian Vignoles, *Rory Gallagher: The Man Behind the Guitar* (London: Collins, 2018), 62.
24 O'Brien, 'If It Makes One Job, It's O.K.'. - Bob'.
25 Tony O'Brien, 'Belting Out a Song of Hope', *Irish Independent* (19 May 1986), 11.
26 'Self-Analysis', *The Blackpool Sentinel* (27 June 2020), https://theblackpoolsentinel.com/2020/06/27/self-analysis/.
27 O'Brien, 'Belting Out a Song of Hope'.
28 Ibid.
29 O'Brien, O'Keefe and Mac Cormaic, 'Self Aid Brings Jobs Rock n' Rolling in'.
30 Colin Kerr, 'Making It Work - Self Aid Goes On', *Sunday Independent* (28 December 1986), 2.
31 'On This Day in 1986: Self Aid Took Place at the RDS in Dublin', *Hot Press* (17 May 2022), https://www.hotpress.com/music/on-this-day-in-1986-self-aid-took-place-at-the-rds-in-dublin-featuring-u2-christy-moore-the-pogues-more-22906663
32 Una Mullally, 'Self Aid: When Irish Rockers Banded Together Against Unemployment', *Irish Times* (25 April 2020), https://www.irishtimes.com/culture/heritage/self-aid-when-irish-rockers-banded-together-against-unemployment-1.4230636
33 'Rory Gallagher: Soy antes un trabajador que un músico', *La Nueva España* (13 July 1986), 49.
34 Mick Lynch, 'Self Aid: 20 Years On', *CLUAS*, https://www.cluas.com/music/features/self-aid-20-years-on.htm
35 Chris Stephen, 'Irish Rock Tougher than the Blarney', *Pinner Observer* (6 April 1989), 23.
36 Ibid.
37 Fiona Looney, 'Rockin' Fiddler', *Evening Herald* (5 April 1989), 27.
38 Eugene Maloney, 'Rocked by the Irish Invasion', *Evening Herald* (12 April 1989), 3.
39 George Byrne, 'Bags Full of Jollity', *Irish Independent* (5 April 1989), 10.
40 Kelly was later diagnosed with a brain tumour and sadly passed away one year later.
41 Byrne, 'Bags Full of Jollity'.
42 Looney, 'Rockin' Fiddler'.
43 'London Rockfest', *Sunday Independent* (2 April 1989), 18.
44 Eamonn Carr, 'Foremen in Charge as Poor Rory Flops', *Evening Herald* (12 April 1989), 26.
45 Maloney, 'Rocked by the Irish Invasion'.
46 Interview with Byrne Norry, 25 April 2022.
47 Interview with Aidan Russell, 25 June 2022. All subsequent quotes from Russell come from this interview.
48 Maloney, 'Rocked by the Irish Invasion'.
49 Eugene Maloney, 'Now', *Evening Herald* (15 April 1989), 9.
50 'Interview with Rory' (12 April 1989), http://www.roryon.com/casey169.html
51 'Previously unpublished 1975 interview with 2JJ', https://rewritingrory.co.uk/2022/12/30/previously-unpublished-1975-interview-for-2jj/
52 Mary Carson, 'Rory to Rock Around the Lough', *Sunday Life* (9 July 1989), 11.
53 Liam Tunney, 'Rory Gallagher's 1989 Ballyronan Gig Recalled', *Derry Now* (6 August 2020), https://www.derrynow.com/news/features/563752/rory-gallaghers-1989-ballyronan-gig-recalled.html
54 Ibid.
55 Ibid.
56 Carson, 'Rory to Rock Around the Lough'.
57 Ibid; Paddy Fitzsymons, 'The Music Man!' *Sunday Life* (23 July 1989), 17.
58 Ibid.
59 Ibid.
60 Tunney, 'Rory Gallagher's 1989 Ballyronan Gig Recalled'.
61 Ibid.
62 Both testimonies from the aforementioned Tunney article.
63 Ibid.
64 John Stephenson, 'AGAINST THE GRAIN: Rory Gallagher at the A Sense of Ireland Festival 1980', *Hot Press* (11 June 2015), https://www.hotpress.com/music/against-the-grain-rory-gallagher-at-the-a-sense-of-ireland-festival-1980-14356578
65 'Rory Gallagher Rockpalast 1982 (video interview)', https://www.youtube.com/watch?v=-0mcx5hECd8&t=73s
66 In April 1989, the guitarist had agreed to appear at RTÉ's People in Need Telethon, aimed at raising £1 million for charity, but was sadly prevented by ill health.
67 'Remembering Rory Gallagher 2024', https://www.youtube.com/watch?v=xE8LArN63VA
68 Ibid.
69 Interview with Paul Charles, 24 October 2023.

4.4 Like a Phoenix from the Ashes: The Temple Bar Blues Festival 1992

"It's been three years now since he played in Ireland, played in Dublin, so when he comes out, I want you to give him a real welcome home, Ireland's own blues legend, Rory Gallagher..."

With these introductory words by Ronnie Drew of The Dubliners, Rory Gallagher hit the stage at the inaugural Temple Bar Blues Festival in Dublin on 15 August 1992, giving a free concert before 20,000 spectators on the steps of the Bank of Ireland on College Green. Three days prior, he had kicked off the festival with an intimate masterclass with five budding young guitarists at the Guinness Hopstore in the city's St James's Gate district (see 4.6).

Leading up to Gallagher's appearance at the Festival, there was much expectation. He had not performed on the island of Ireland since 1989 and now he was back without long-term band members Gerry McAvoy and Brendan O'Neill. Would he still be liked? Would his new band make a good impression? Was he still capable of headlining a major festival? He was also back with a heavier build as a result of his worsening health problems. What would people say about the way he looked? Would they comment on his weight gain? Would they still want to see him? Gallagher was never a confident man, but he was increasingly riddled with insecurity at this time and whether he would be able to live up to the high standards that people had of him (let alone his own, given that he always demanded so much from himself). "They just expect too much of me," he would tell new drummer Richard Newman.[1]

Gallagher's nerves were not eased by pre-festival press articles, which were keen to write him off before he had even set foot in Dublin. While the guitarist was likely hurt by such remarks, to some extent, they appear to have spurred him on, knowing that he had something to prove. Just as he had come back from the devastating break-up of Taste with an impressive solo debut in 1971, which stopped critics in their tracks, a similar situation occurred here. From the opening bars of 'Continental Op', it was immediately apparent that this was going to be a night like no other. Gallagher came with the strength of a hurricane, leaving no doubt that he was back and stronger than ever before. Like a true phoenix, he had risen from the ashes, proving the age-old proverb that you should never judge a book by its cover.

Mr Blues Comes to Dublin

The Temple Bar area of Dublin underwent significant development from the mid-1980s onwards, with then-Taoiseach Charles Haughey expressing desire for the space to appeal to the younger generation "to relax and enjoy themselves."[2] As part of a Streets Improvement Scheme, sponsored by Dublin Corporation and the European Regional Development Fund, many parts of Temple Bar were pedestrianised. As reported in a 1991 RTÉ news broadcast, this pedestrianisation made way for "lots of art space, activities, small businesses [and] low to moderate priced restaurants" in the area. To promote this new cultural quarter of Dublin, the city decided to launch a blues festival in 1992, alongside other cultural initiatives like open-air film screenings, concerts and street theatre.

Running for three days and organised by Guinness and Temple Bar Properties, the Temple Bar Blues Festival—as it came to be known—promised a 'Guinness 12 Bar Blues Trail' (which offered free live music at 12 pubs in the area) and a series of midnight blues concerts by different artists at the Olympia. It would end on 15 August with an open-air concert by Gallagher, widely publicised as the highlight. According to the *Evening Herald*, the Festival had the potential to "equal the Cork Jazz festival in content and popularity."[3]

Although organisers framed Gallagher as the Festival's 'highlight', the Irish press was not so enthusiastic. Articles prior to the concert questioned Gallagher's ability to 'pull off' a headlining performance and triggered a rumour mill around the reasons behind his bloated appearance. A particularly scathing piece in the *Sunday Tribune* entitled 'Return of a Flawed Prodigal' seemed to set Gallagher up to fail.[4] In the article, journalist Tony Clayton-Lea frames the 1970s as Gallagher's "most inspiring period," differentiating this by informing readers that he now "has problems":

> Dreams of conquering the world with his guitar technique and genuine style have been lost in the mists of time [...] Due to a glandular disorder, he appears far too overweight for his size. Even a small degree of light hurts his eyes, so sunglasses are a constant accessory. He has an obsession about straightening pictures and can't stand to be in a room unless they're angle perfect [...] He no longer wears his fashion trademarks – the standard check shirt and denim jacket – blaming a psychological problem.

The article also briefly discusses the recent compilation *Edged in Blue* (1992), describing this selection of material as how "clear and sharp Gallagher's vision— in every sense of the word—*once was* [our emphasis]." Ironically, six out of the 11 tracks on *Edged in Blue* were chosen from *Jinx* (1982), *Defender* (1987) and *Fresh Evidence* (1990). Therefore, the majority of this "stunning collection" of Gallagher "at his blues best" was not from the supposed "prime" stage in his career. The failure to recognise this from Clayton-Lea's perspective is either from poor familiarity with the material or just journalistic carelessness. Clayton-Lea concludes by questioning whether Gallagher is capable of obtaining a "happy and satisfactory ending" at the Temple Bar Blues Festival.

Similar issues can be found in a piece for *Hot Press* by Liam Fay. Gallagher himself was particularly upset by this interview, which claimed that he was "an obsessive painting straightener" with a "ragbag of neuroses"[5] and requested an interview with Joe Jackson of *Irish Times* to offset the damage. While the Jackson interview does set the record straight somewhat about Gallagher's health problems, it still overemphasises his superstitions and includes rather disturbing themes of premature death, excess in rock and fear of illness and dying,[6] which are latched onto by biographer Julian Vignoles in such a way that frames the Gallagher of Temple Bar as a tragic victim rather than a glorious victor. This portrayal is not helped by the fact that Vignoles then segues into an account of the infamous Town and Country Club performance a few months later (see 3.1).[7]

Nervous with Evidence of Fragility?
Elaborating further on the Temple Bar Blues Festival, Vignoles writes that Gallagher was "apprehensive about how he would go down with the audience."[8] To support this, he recounts the story of musicians Brian Palm and Mary Stokes meeting Gallagher in the bar of Blooms Hotel before the gig and noting that Gallagher was "nervous" and showed "evidence of fragility."[9] While we know that Gallagher was plagued with self-doubt at this time and his stagefright was getting progressively worse, Vignoles appears to frame this as something *new*, something that was *suddenly* having a detrimental effect on the Irishman's later performances. The reality was, however, that anxiety leading up to a concert was something from which Gallagher had suffered throughout his career.

Clips of Gallagher backstage in the *Irish Tour '74* documentary film provide a sense of the tension he felt before performing, while Dónal Gallagher has often described "walking on eggshells"[10] around his brother before a concert as he was so nervous. Even Gallagher himself frequently talked about the topic in interviews, including in the 1978 *Elf 1/2* documentary ("I'm always nervous before a concert, particularly in Ireland"),[11] at *Rockpalast* 1982 with Alan Bangs ("I'm a bit nervous as usual")[12] and with Def Leppard's Vivian Campbell in 1991 ("I've always gotten nervous about everything"),[13] to name but a few examples. So, understood in this broader context, we see how Vignoles—and others—have a tendency to dramatise Gallagher's stagefright in this period, which encourages misconceptions around his ability to perform like he did in the 1970s. Yes, Gallagher was undoubtedly more nervous than before and perhaps more fragile too—and who could blame him with the damning press reports?—but like a true professional, he knew how to channel his nerves into giving a high-energy, adrenaline-fuelled performance. As he joked in the aforementioned interview with Alan Bangs, "As Sarah Bernhardt said, 'You need the nerves to give you the extra injection of adrenaline'," and that is exactly what he did at the Temple Bar Blues Festival.

In a 2020 interview with *Hot Press*, Mary Stokes reflected further on her encounter with Gallagher in Blooms. She notes how she was helping Brian Palm hang up paintings of his favourite blues artists for an exhibition and that she saw Gallagher sitting at the bar. She introduced herself to which he replied, "I know. Who else would be hanging up paintings of Sonny Boy Williamson?" They then started talking about the blues and swapping stories about other musicians. Seeing that Gallagher was clearly nervous, Stokes spent a long time reassuring him that "it would be great, that he was loved by Dublin, by Ireland, that people were excited that he was back."[14] Brian Palm corroborates this story, explaining to us that—to his amazement—Stokes tried to boost Gallagher's confidence and ensure him that everyone was going to love seeing him perform. However, Palm also adds that the three of them "had a good laugh together" and Gallagher even bought them both a pint.[15]

In this narrative, we see similarities with the way that folk musician Martin Carthy would reassure Gallagher two years later before the Montreux Jazz Festival (see 3.2). It paints a far different picture from the hackneyed image of Gallagher as a lonesome figure drowning his sorrows in a bar and, rather, Gallagher as someone who could confide in others if he felt at sufficient ease with them and even relied on their words of encouragement to comfort him.

Fan Eamon Maguire also came across Gallagher in Blooms that day. In a sheer stroke of fortune, he had entered the hotel for a drink and, when searching for the bathroom, took a wrong turn and ended up in the foyer. As he turned back around, he bumped straight into Gallagher. Maguire describes himself as being "tongue tied," having "twenty years of questions" yet unable to ask one. He remembers being concerned at Gallagher's appearance, "heavier" than he had ever seen him with "watering eyes" and constantly squeezing his hands together. Nonetheless, he was taken by his usual graciousness; Gallagher talked to him for a short while and signed two autographs, which are now Maguire's "prize possession." Maguire recalled the rumours circulating in the press before the Festival that Gallagher was "washed up," which "broke [his] heart." He prayed that he would soon be proven wrong.[16]

To read only what has been published so far then is to build up an unfair and inaccurate image of Gallagher at the Temple Bar Blues Festival. It is to see the event as one of little significance in his career, as the Dublin swansong of a 'neurotic' man, as somebody long past his best. To listen to the bootleg of the open-air concert, however, tells a very different story. It captures the intensity and emotion of Gallagher's performance, his powerful vocals, his expert musicianship. This is a Gallagher with the fire of *Irish Tour '74* and Macroom 'Mountain Dew' Festival combined, yet honed by the experience of the mature bluesman into which he had developed. Wanting to get the *real* story of the Temple Bar Blues Festival, we turned to those who were there and witnessed Gallagher's concert first-hand.

Views from the Ground
"It was the first and only time I saw Rory play live, but it's a gig I'll never forget," says Paddy T. Meakin.[17] Despite being a long-term Gallagher fan, Meakin was

unaware that Gallagher was playing the Temple Bar Blues Festival or that there was a festival on at all in Dublin in August 1992. That Saturday, he had travelled into the city centre with his friend to go record shopping. On their way to Tommy Teigh's Sound Cellar in College Green, they noticed a stage being set up as they rounded the corner from the O'Connell St direction. Being curious, they decided to go and investigate what was happening. As Meakin recounted to us in July 2022:

> We could see drums, amps and lighting equipment being set out on the stage. One of the roadies was quite close to the railing just off the street. As we approached him, I shouted over to him asking, 'What's happening? Is there live music on here?' He yelled back over the railing, 'Yeah!' 'Who's on?' I asked. 'Rory Gallagher', the roadie replied. I looked at my friend and said, 'Rory's playing!' I then quickly asked the roadie, 'You're not having me on, are you?' 'No, buddy', he replied and added, 'He's playing later'. 'Jesus!' I said to my friend, 'We have got to see that!' He replied eagerly that we have to get the DART [Dublin commuter train] and get home. 'It's Rory! and I'll walk home if I have to!' I said. I then added, 'I'm not missing the chance to see Rory play!' My friend then quickly agreed.

Several hours later, Meakin and his friend made their way to the concert amid throngs of people of all nationalities that had gathered. The large street and footpath areas around the stage were full, leading some to "take up positions on the Trinity College gates." A couple of "eager spectators" had even turned a lamp post into a "good lookout tower." Meakin recalls the sense of anticipation in the air as cans cracked around him, the audience chattered and "mounting excitement" grew as Gallagher's performance approached. He still clearly remembers the moment when Ronnie Drew suddenly appeared on stage giving a warm welcome to Gallagher, to which the crowd erupted into thunderous applause.

In the next breath, there was Gallagher running onto the stage in his black leather jacket and trusty Stratocaster in hand. Meakin can still hear the guitarist's cry of "YEAH!" which was closely followed by his "ever humbling thank you." The audience were then "overleveraged" with the opening number 'Continental Op'. As the bootleg attests, Gallagher is a force of nature from the very first note. He sounds revitalised by his new band, releasing all the nervous tension from the days building up to this big concert. Despite his fears that nobody would want to see him, the crowd is immediately on his side and pushing his performance to new heights with their cheers and claps.

While there were so many musical highlights for Meakin across Gallagher's two-hour set, he has particularly fond memories of 'Tattoo'd Lady', where he was left in "pure amazement and disbelief" at Gallagher's playing. 'Tattoo'd Lady' is a song that Gallagher seemed to feel with every part of him. While it was written about his childhood memories of the fairground, as Dónal stated in a 2023 interview with *Lust for Life*,[18] it also had a secondary meaning for his brother. As a travelling musician, Gallagher emphasised with the peripatetic life of the fairground workers and recognised himself in their status as outsiders who did not quite fit into mainstream society. In the fairground, he saw a non-judgemental space where he belonged.

The Temple Bar bootleg provides evidence of the importance of 'Tattoo'd Lady' to Gallagher, as well as his incredible delivery of its message. He introduces the song with his usual self-effacing charm: "This song isn't rhythm and blues, but I wouldn't mind having a bash at it for old times' sake. I love playing it [hugs his Stratocaster to his chest]. You may like it…" He then starts up the iconic opening, adding a little Hispano-Celtic flavour to the riff, before a cry of "look out, baby!" Gallagher pulls out all the stops here, using his repertoire of guitar techniques, from string-pulling and bending behind the nut to random pinch harmonics and volume swells. The song ends triumphantly, Gallagher holding his guitar like a machine gun and firing at the crowd.

'Off the Handle' was another high point for Meakin, which followed straight after 'Tattoo'd Lady' to "cool it down a little" (as Gallagher says). It is clear to understand why from the bootleg, which reveals a strong groove laid down by David Levy that perfectly supports Gallagher's rhythm playing. The song reaches a crescendo with an astonishing piece of jazz guitar by Gallagher interspersed with beautiful melody on the harmonica by Mark Feltham.

Meakin also praised Gallagher's acoustic set, stating how he was intrigued at Gallagher's ability to stand there on his own and "keep the audience in the palm of his hand." The acoustic set at Temple Bar begins with a moving instrumental of the Irish folk song 'She Moved Thro' the Fair', which leads into the timeless 'Out on the Western Plain'. Gallagher feeds off the crowd's enthusiasm here, his fingers moving faster and faster on the fretboard in the solo, almost of their own accord. Video footage shows him smiling during the call and response part with the audience, clearly overwhelmed at the positive reception on his homecoming to Ireland. After a huge cheer from the spectators, he starts up 'Walkin' Blues' with an emotive piece of slide. Again, as he moves into the familiar rhythm part of the song, the crowd claps along. Feltham's accompaniment is impeccable here, adding his own flavour to the blues classic and demonstrating why he and Gallagher were so often described as musical kindred spirits.

The jewel in the crown of the acoustic set, however, is Gallagher's duet with Ronnie Drew on 'Barley and Grape Rag', which he dedicates to "the people from Belfast and Cork City and Derry City and for various parts of the globe." Gallagher and Drew were good friends and the camaraderie between them is particularly apparent in this performance. The two banter back and forth with one another, Gallagher asking Drew, "What do you think?" to which he responds, "My baby's done me wrong…" in his iconic gritty voice, and later "Good God, Ronnie, you look like you could do with it too" which Ronnie, in turn, answers, "One for you too, Rory!" Then, their two voices meld together on the chorus in a wonderful blend of gravel and soul. Having the opportunity to witness two of the finest Irish talents together on stage was a truly iconic moment for many of the people present, including Meakin.

All in all, Meakin considers it a "high privilege" for him to have seen Gallagher, who was so "full of energy" and "really packed a punch" at the Temple Bar Blues Festival. He marvelled at the contrast between how shy Gallagher was offstage and his "dynamic energy" on stage, where the guitarist "really came to life," "let it all go" and was "so comfortable with his audience."

Mick Shanahan is another fan who still remembers Gallagher's performance at Temple Bar Blues Festival with great affection, being not only the last time that he saw the guitarist live, but also the first time that his son (just a baby in a pram) attended a concert.[19] Shanahan had been a Gallagher fan since hearing *Live in Europe*, which "changed everything" for him, and he first saw Gallagher live in 1978 when he hitchhiked from Waterford to Macroom for the 'Mountain Dew' Festival. On the day of the Temple Bar Blues Festival, Shanahan and his family drove from Waterford to Dublin and headed to College Green "just in time for the master to arrive on stage." He describes Gallagher's performance that evening as "wonderful" with "so many favourites," including the "epic closer" 'Bullfrog Blues'.

'Bullfrog Blues' was indeed epic, extended into a blistering 12-minute version with the energy of *Rockpalast* '77 or '79 renditions, yet taken up a notch with Gallagher's maturity and experience. Every member of the band makes a strong contribution here—bass, drums, harmonica and keyboards all adding to Gallagher's magnificent slide-playing—while Gallagher's addition of "Dublin" to the lyrics sends the crowd into a frenzy. The feeling is so good that Gallagher bursts into a spontaneous medley, starting with a few licks of Eddie Cochran's 'Summertime Blues' before weaving into Larry Williams' 'Dizzy Miss Lizzy' and then finally an up-tempo version of 'All Around Man'. He then smoothly moves back into 'Bullfrog Blues', bringing his set to an end and delivering the musical equivalent of a knock out punch to any critics who had doubted him beforehand.

Johnny McMonagle was also at the Temple Bar Blues Festival in 1992 and remembers the "great atmosphere" on College Green and how good it felt to finally see one of his "musical idols."[20] McMonagle hailed from Donegal, but moved to Cork in the late 1980s to go to college. It was at college that he made friends with one of Gallagher's cousins who asked him if he was a Gallagher fan when she noticed his long hair, check shirt and denim jacket. The cousin mentioned McMonagle to Gallagher, telling him, "There is a guy in my class from Donegal who looks like you and dresses like you." Gallagher (jokingly) replied, "At least I still have one fan!" McMonagle received some limited-edition records, a *Top Priority* badge and *Defender* tour t-shirt in return. Reflecting on Gallagher and the Temple Bar concert, McMonagle uses four words to describe him: "passion, virtuosity, honesty, integrity."

When speaking to other fans about the Temple Bar Blues Festival, the topic of Gallagher's health understandably came up. However, in contrast to unfavourable press reports before the concert, all were keen to stress that this did not affect Gallagher's performance in any way. Kieran Devitt, for example, told us that it was "apparent that Rory was struggling with his health," but that he still gave an excellent performance and there was a huge crowd who "all wanted to be there to see a proper legend." For Devitt, "every song reached a whole new level of excellence" when performed live.[21] This is certainly clear from the intense and spirited version of fan favourite 'Shadow Play', which carries tinges of the iconic Montreux '79 version of the song in Gallagher's high energy and the way that he constantly brings the pace up and down, playing to the crowd and receiving a rapturous response that fuels him on further.

Eugene Curran's thoughts on the Temple Bar Blues Festival also echo Devitt's own. He could see from Gallagher's appearance that he was unwell and "retaining a lot of fluid," but "he had lost none of his energy." Curran was "amazed" at "how smoothly" the concert went from start to finish, as well as the "massive buzz" from the crowd who "really got going" right from the first notes that Gallagher played.[22] Equally, Barney Toal described Gallagher's performance as "brilliant," even though he was "not in the greatest of health."[23]

That energy and brilliance mentioned by both Curran and Toal is particularly captured in Gallagher's blazing rendition of 'Messin' with the Kid'. Here, he makes a nod to the 15th anniversary of Elvis Presley's passing (on 16 August), improvising some lyrics halfway through: "There's a man in New Orleans who plays the guitar | He's up there in heaven living on a star | oh, Mr Presley we know where you are!" He then follows this up with his own dazzling sample of Presley's 'You're So Square (Baby I Don't Care)', before transitioning back into 'Messin' with the Kid' again.

Another topic that arose often when speaking to fans was Gallagher's new band with David Levy and Richard Newman. Considering it was only their second performance together (after a warm-up concert in Rhyl), many were surprised at how tight they already sounded and how well they gelled. They felt that Levy and Newman made a brilliant rhythm section, providing solid support for Gallagher and Feltham and adding a fresh, youthful and invigorating sound. For Kieran Devitt, the addition of Levy and Newman signalled the "possibility of a new era" and a chance to "reinspire Rory."[24] The cover of Sonny Boy Williamson's 'Don't Start Me Talkin'' at Temple Bar certainly showcases the new Rory Gallagher Band at its very best, with all members looking like they are having a blast on stage. There is a real sense of optimism about this performance, from the smiles exchanged between members and Feltham's lip-synching side of stage to Levy's nods to Newman and Gallagher's 'musical faceoff' with Feltham. It is easy to share Devitt's sadness over the short-lived final band because "perhaps Rory didn't realise just how delicate his health was."[25]

A Slice of Humble Pie

While the fans were well and truly satisfied with Gallagher's performance at the Temple Bar Blues Festival, would it be enough to win over the tough critics that had been so searing of Gallagher beforehand? In short, the answer is a resounding yes.

Many of the very same journalists who had previously criticised Gallagher were now forced to eat a big slice of humble pie after watching him play. It was clear that something magical had occurred in Dublin. Contrary to what many had been predicting—and even hoping, in some cases—Gallagher more than lived up to his role as headliner and proved that he was still a major force to be reckoned with and that few compared to him on the live scene.

Eugene Moloney's report for the *Irish Independent*, headlined 'Thousands Thrill to Rory's Blues', noted how Gallagher's outdoor concert "stopped the traffic in the centre of Dublin" and "blew Guns N' Roses away." He describes the wide range of people in the crowd, dispelling the myth that Gallagher had lost audiences and was failing to connect with young people: "blues buffs, heavy metal heads, fans from the old days—some with their grown-up kids—mingled with tourists and the just plain curious." Reflecting Paddy T. Meakin's own account, Moloney describes fans "spilling out from the railings of the Bank of Ireland to the gates of Trinity College," with some even "climbing on top of the traffic lights to get a better view of the show." He emphasises how watching Gallagher's hands "move up and down" and "respond to the emotions he was feeling inside" was "more electric, more fascinating than any amount of high-tech special effects."[26] Now—unlike before the concert—Gallagher was being recognised for the accomplished musician that he was, rather than simply a man with "problems."[27]

Eugene Moloney wrote another review for the *Evening Herald*, entitled 'Rory Still So Sharp'. Despite the unnecessary remark that Gallagher was a "somewhat portly man of his 40s," the report is highly favourable, noting how the guitarist "squeezed out note after note of raw, passionate blues" and showed that "he is still resisting any attempts to dull the edges of his music."[28]

Once again, these comments stand in marked contrast to some of the prior claims in the press that Gallagher's music was becoming boring and showing no progression. Moloney goes on to write how it was "intoxicating to watch a man perform a music that still trod that thin line between being liberating and heartfelt and being downright wicked." These words perfectly encapsulate Gallagher's ability to push the limits with his performances and be an outlaw for doing so. Always sticking to his guns and staying true to his own musical vision made him far more of a rebel and a bad boy of the blues than other musicians who lived a cliched sex, drugs and rock & roll lifestyle.

Another glowing review of the concert came from Tony Murphy of *Bray People* who described Gallagher's performance as "tremendous."[29] Equally, writing in the *Irish Times* upon Gallagher's death in 1995, John Waters stated that Gallagher was "if possible, even better than I remembered at Temple Bar." "He captivated the huge crowd—half curious bystanders, half now-greying lumberjack-shirted hordes—like the angel he was," Waters continued.[30] These reports, again, show how not only was Gallagher attracting all sorts of people to his concerts, but that, as always, he was able to create a deep, meaningful connection with them.

Away from critics, those close to Gallagher were also rightfully proud of his performance. Mary Stokes, who had provided Gallagher with some encouraging words before the gig, told *Hot Press*: "As I stood beside the stage that evening, I saw Rory Gallagher take the stage like a man possessed—and the audience roared back in affirmation."[31] Equally, Brian Palm remembers watching Gallagher "absolutely ripping it up, with the crowd going wild in a sea of bodies crammed right up to the stage." For Palm, it was "a brilliant atmosphere and a triumphant return from exile" that put him "in a great mood" for his own show. Although he and Stokes never saw Gallagher again after that day, they cherish the lasting image of him "shredding it in his element on stage [...] before a massive, happy crowd."[32]

For Dónal Gallagher, the show was "one of the best" that he ever saw his brother play and included one of his favourite versions of 'Tattoo'd Lady'.[33] And Ronnie Drew also thoroughly enjoyed the concert, describing it as "a great thrill" and "one of the big times" of his life to introduce Gallagher and later perform 'Barley and Grape Rag' with him. When interviewed in 2001, Drew stated that his tape of the show is "probably one of [his] most treasured possessions."[34] Speaking to us in April 2022, bassist David Levy described the concert as "something else" and said that it made him realise "how much Gallagher was loved and what a huge and talented artist he was."[35] Along with Montreux Jazz Festival 1994, Temple Bar Blues Festival is Levy's standout concert when he reflects on his time in the Rory Gallagher Band. Drummer Richard Newman echoed Levy's words when we spoke a month later, noting that Gallagher really "blew the roof off" that night in Dublin and that seeing the thousands of people who had turned out to see him was remarkable.[36]

And what did Gallagher himself think of his performance? Well, according to Dónal, he was "quietly satisfied rather than particularly happy."[37]

Moving Mountains

In a piece for the *Evening Herald* to mark the fourth anniversary of the Temple Bar Blues Festival in 1995, journalist Aileen O'Reilly lamented the recent passing of Rory Gallagher and noted that his presence would be "felt even more strongly" this year as the Festival was dedicated to his memory. She reflected back on that evening in August 1992 when:

> Blues brothers—and sisters—merged in the fading light of College Green, fans from Ringsend to Ringaskiddy, half of them lost in the ecstatic throes of air guitar, the other half just lost in music as Gallagher plied them with riffs in a myriad of blues hues.[38]

This powerful description of Gallagher's concert was certainly not what journalists had expected beforehand. Their unkind views knocked Gallagher's already low self-esteem and, being the sensitive man that he was, wounded him personally. Requesting an interview with Joe Jackson of *Irish Times* to counter these rumours, Gallagher explained that he had never had any interest in the excesses of rock 'n' roll and expressed his frustration at his achievements being "glossed over" as if he "didn't open the doors for anyone." He also criticised the Irish rock scene for becoming too "conservative" and quietly acknowledged that he had "advanced the blues," taking the songs beyond the level of 'Little Red Rooster'.[39] Following his performance, journalists had to concede that all this was true.

Of all the post-concert reviews, the article by Michael Ross of *Sunday Tribune* stands out for its sensitivity and understanding of Gallagher's complex character. Ross does not conform to typical judgements based on Gallagher's weight gain and instead describes the "mutterings" of alcohol dependency by journalists as a "cruel suggestion" for a man like Gallagher—a man so full of "dignity," yet so "evidently in distress." Moreover, Ross does not see Gallagher as an artist of the past, but rather as an artist "trying to progress blues beyond Muddy Waters and Robert Johnson," which makes him still "one of the leading modern interpreters of the blues." While Ross outlines the many challenges that Gallagher has faced, both professionally and personally, he does so in a compassionate manner. Moreover, rather than use these challenges to create the image of a haunted man, he flips the narrative to argue that Gallagher has an underlying optimism and tenacity that helps him through any crisis that he faces.[40]

Today, people who walk the streets of Temple Bar in Dublin may come across Rory Gallagher Corner—a tucked-away square that features a statue of his beloved Fender Stratocaster, unveiled in 2006. But how many people who stand there know of Gallagher's performance at the inaugural Temple Bar Blues Festival? How many people are aware of the crowds—young and old—who flocked in their thousands to see him play that summer evening? And how many people realise what a tremendous professional and personal achievement it was for him? The Temple Bar Blues Festival put Dublin on the world map for blues music and it was Gallagher at the spearhead. More must be done to remember this accomplishment and celebrate Gallagher's triumph as the magnificent phoenix who defied all odds, rose from the ashes and soared high on 15 August 1992.

LAO

Footnotes

1 Nick Dent-Robinson. 'Richard Newman - Interview', *Pennyblack Music* (23 February 2013), https://pennyblackmusic.co.uk/Home/Details?Id=20894
2 'Temple Bar Dublin's Left Bank 1991', *RTÉ*, https://www.rte.ie/archives/2016/1206/836872-temple-bar-cultural-quarter/
3 Catherine Murphy, 'Guinness Sings the Blues', *Evening Herald* (25 June 1992), 10.
4 All quotes here and in the next paragraph come from Tim Clayton-Lea, 'Return of a Flawed Prodigal', *Sunday Tribune* (9 August 1992), 27.
5 Liam Fay, 'Tangled Up in Blues', *Hot Press* (July 1992), http://www.roryon.com/Tangled.html
6 Joe Jackson, 'Black Cat Blues', *Irish Times* (14 August 1992), 6.
7 Julian Vignoles, *Rory Gallagher: The Man Behind the Guitar* (London: Collins, 2018), 188-189.
8 Ibid., 190.
9 Ibid.
10 Treacy Hogan, 'The Legend's Going Strong', *Irish Independent* (26 June 2004), 62.
11 'Rory Gallagher - ELF 1/2 - 1978 Documentary', https://www.youtube.com/watch?v=BGlCX91VEj4&t=9s
12 'Rory Gallagher Rockpalast 1982 (video interview)', https://www.youtube.com/watch?v=-0mcx5hECd8
13 Vivian Campbell, 'The Wearing of the Blues', *Guitar for the Practicing Musician* (August 1991), http://www.roryon.com/guitar91.html
14 Mary Stokes, 'Mary Stokes on Rory Gallagher: "He Freed the Audience from the Brown and Grey Drabness of 1970s Ireland"', *Hot Press* (24 July 2020), https://www.hotpress.com/music/mary-stokes-on-rory-gallagher-he-freed-the-audience-from-the-brown-and-grey-drabness-of-1970s-ireland-22823453
15 Interview with Brian Palm, 24 April 2023.
16 Interview with Eamon Maguire, 13 February 2023.
17 Interview with Paddy T. Meakin, 10 July 2022.
18 Caya Forman, 'Terug naar Rory´s roots in roerige tijden', *Lust for Life* (October 2023), https://rewritingrory.co.uk/2023/10/29/back-to-rorys-roots-in-turbulent-times/
19 Interview with Mick Shanahan, 4 July 2022.
20 Interview with Johnny McMonagle, 22 March 2022.
21 Interview with Kieran Devitt, 5 June 2022.
22 Interview with Eugene Curran, 7 April 2022.
23 Interview with Barney Toal, 16 July 2022.
24 Interview with Kieran Devitt, 5 June 2022.
25 Ibid.
26 All quotes in this paragraph from Eugene Moloney, 'Thousands Thrill to Rory's Blues', *Irish Independent* (17 August 1992), 12.
27
28 Eugene Moloney, 'Rory Still So Sharp', *Evening Herald* (17 August 1992), 12.
29 Tony Murphy, 'Tony Murphy's Musical Miscellany', *Bray People* (21 August 1992), 26.
30 John Waters, 'Nobody Did It Better', *Irish Times* (17 June 1995), http://www.roryon.com/nobody.html
31 Stokes, 'Mary Stokes on Rory Gallagher'.
32 Interview with Brian Palm, 24 April 2023.
33 Ross, 'While My Guitar Gently Weeps'.
34 'Dino McGartland's 2001 interview of Ronnie Drew', *Stagestruck* (20 April 2001), http://www.roryon.com/ronnie388.html
35 Interview with David Levy, 29 April 2022.
36 Interview with Richard Newman, 20 May 2022.
37 Ross, 'While My Guitar Gently Weeps'.
38 Aileen O'Reilly, 'Dublin's Got the Blues', *Evening Herald* (13 July 1995), 19.
39 Jackson, 'Black Cat Blues'.
40 Michael Ross, 'Praying at the Temple of the Blues', *Sunday Tribune* (16 August 1992), http://www.roryon.com/praying.html

4.5 Going to My Hometown: The Rebel Returns to Cork, 1992-1993

"It's always nice to head for home"
Rory Gallagher, *Irish Tour '74* documentary film

Cork always held a very special place in Rory Gallagher's heart. Although he left his adopted home city in the late 1960s to pursue his musical dreams—first in Belfast and then in London—Cork was never far from Gallagher's mind, and he relished the rare moments of downtime when he could return to visit his mother Monica and catch up with old friends. Cork was also the place where Gallagher did his best songwriting, finding that the city's calmness helped him think better and gave him fresh ideas. The guitarist favoured the "uncomplicated way of living"[1] typical of the south of Ireland and regularly acknowledged that his Cork upbringing had given him a strong foundation, which made it easy to remain level-headed and realistic when it came to success.

Speaking about Cork in a 1975 interview with Hermann Haring of *Sounds*, Gallagher stated that he would not trade the city for any other place in the world. Furthermore, he did not wish to be put into a "golden cage" by his fellow Corkonians and just wanted to be seen as "someone from their own town."[2] When back home, Gallagher saw no reason not to continue doing what he had always done—visiting Crowley's Music Centre, frequenting the local pubs, attending mass, walking his dog and going fishing in the River Lee. He relished the opportunity to continue "rambling around the streets" of the city's Victorian Quarter and, later, Douglas (where his mother subsequently moved), living an "ordinary walk down the street without being recognised sort of life," as he asserted in the now iconic *Irish Tour '74* documentary film.

When Gallagher's fear of flying worsened in the 1980s, he went through long periods of time without being able to make the short one-hour flight back home to Ireland. As a result, he became increasingly homesick for Cork, telling Liam Fay of *Hot Press* that he would "love to go back and live there" if he could get his "old mind sorted out."[3] Gradually, Gallagher learnt how to manage his phobia enough to resume travel and, after a four-year break from performing in Cork, he returned to the city in August 1992 as a surprise headliner at the Lark by the Lee.

Adhering to the old saying that you wait ages for a bus and then two come along at once, Gallagher then played again the next day at the Everyman Palace Theatre on MacCurtain St. Two days after, he was given an award for his contributions to music at a civic reception with the Lord Mayor. Just over a year later, Gallagher was back in Cork again, this time headlining the Inaugural Cork Arts Festival with a unique acoustic set in honour of his uncle Jimmy who had been Principal of Cork Regional Technical College. This was Gallagher's last-ever performance in both Cork and on the island of Ireland.

Here, we provide a detailed account of each of these important events, arguing that they stand as representations of Gallagher's deep love for his adopted home city and respect for his fans, as well as his strong sense of benevolence and compassion for others. While 4.1 concluded with an assessment of Gallagher's lasting legacy in Cork from a musical tribute perspective, here, we conclude with a focus on his commemorative legacy in the form of plaques, statues and exhibitions. We argue, that with his unwavering commitment to the blues, his own unique identity and unwillingness to play to anyone's rules but his own, Gallagher well and truly put the *rebel* into the Rebel County, making him the embodiment of Corkonian values.[4]

Lark by the Lee (30 August 1992)
After his triumphant performance at the Temple Bar Blues Festival in Dublin on 15 August 1992 (see 4.4), you would be forgiven for thinking that Rory Gallagher deserved a well-earnt break. Yet wanting to keep the momentum going with his new band, he travelled out to Germany for the Open Flair Festival in Eschwege. Only then was the guitarist satisfied to fly back to Cork with his brother Dónal to spend a few days of rest with their mother. However, even this was mixing business with pleasure as Gallagher had been chosen to headline the city's annual Lark by the Lee festival on 30 August.

The Lark by the Lee was "a backbone of musical life in Cork"[5] throughout the late 1980s and early 1990s. Funded by a collaboration between RTÉ 2FM and Cork 89FM Radio, the Lark provided a free annual open-air concert in the city's Lee Fields on a Sunday afternoon. It was based on a similar initiative—the Lark in the Park—which was held yearly in Blackrock Park in Dublin and hosted by RTÉ 2FM and *In Dublin* magazine. Similar roadshows were also arranged at the time in St Anne's Park in Rahiny and Salthill Park in Galway.

The inaugural Lark by the Lee took place in 1985 and was an instant success thanks to a surprise appearance by U2, who were then in the middle of touring *The Unforgettable Fire*. According to broadcaster Dave Fanning, "the place went insane" when he announced U2, with many people who were leaving all charging back across the Lee Fields at once, some even fainting with excitement.[6] Three years later, in 1988, 2FM and 89FM came up with the idea of extending the Lark by putting unsigned bands on stage at the city's iconic Sir Henry's nightclub to help showcase new rock talent. This marked the beginning of what became known as Cork Rock, the Lark now making up just one part of this thrilling musical weekend. While the open-air concert was a family-friendly event that catered to a broad cross-section of Corkonians, the Sir Henry's gigs were aimed at rock enthusiasts, talent scouts and A&R people. By the end of the 1980s, the musical weekend was attracting over 15,000 spectators.

In the years prior to the 1992 Lark, 2FM's Aidan Stanley had formed a close friendship with Dónal Gallagher. Speaking to us in December 2023, Stanley explained that he, therefore, "set [himself] the target" of getting "Cork's favourite musical son"—Gallagher—to headline the festival.[7] To Stanley's delight, Gallagher agreed. The 1992 Lark, thus, promised to be the biggest one yet, with Something Happens, The Stunning, Belsonic Sound, Rubyhorse and Colour Tide all joining Gallagher on the bill. According to both the *Evening Echo* and *Cork Examiner*, this bold display of "Ireland's finest musical talents" would guarantee a "full house," while also being a "bonanza" for business and trade in the city.[8]

At first, Gallagher was billed only in the press as "a special guest," but the cat was out of the bag long before the name of the special guest was finally revealed, and Cork began to fill with excitement at the guitarist's much-anticipated homecoming. Unlike negative views prior to the Temple Bar Blues Festival, Cork journalists all assured that Gallagher would provide one of the highlights of the weekend. Ralph Riegel of the *Evening Examiner* boldly announced that the "King of Rock is about to retake his throne" and that the newer bands would have to "take an undoubted backseat to the adopted Corkman." He also pointed out that Gallagher was "enjoying an enormous revival," but made it clear that "his profile has never dropped" on mainland Europe.[9] Dermott Hayes of the *Irish Press*, on the other hand, directly challenged recent reports that Gallagher was "a bloated and neurotic hypochondriac," emphasising that this was an unfair portrayal of the "always affable" man that he knew.[10]

After two months of preparation, Sir Henry's was also gearing up for three unforgettable nights of music that dovetailed perfectly with the Lark. This year was extra special because, instead of Cork Rock ending on Sunday evening with the Lark After Dark in Sir Henry's, Aidan Stanley had arranged an extra concert at the Everyman Palace Theatre on Monday evening. And the performer would be none other than Rory Gallagher. In the summer leading up to the festival, Stanley had come up with the idea of Gallagher doing an extra concert while back in Cork to raise money for the Irish Red Cross Yugoslav Refugee Appeal. Gallagher was only too happy to oblige, having "very strong feelings about getting a charity contribution going" for those affected by the conflict, as Stanley told us.

The Lark sounded outstanding on paper, but its fate was in doubt when torrential rain on the day before the concert left the Lee Fields waterlogged. There were particular concerns that the electricity needed to power the event could become a danger to the public if it came into contact with surface water. Lorries carrying equipment also became bogged down in heavy mud, resulting in a forklift rescue in order to set up the stage and PA system. On Sunday morning, experts were called in to assess the site. Luckily, it had dried out enough for them to deem it safe and, at 1PM, Rubyhorse took to the stage to kick off the Lark. By the time that Gallagher launched into his late afternoon set, the atmosphere was buzzing, the bad weather now well and truly forgotten.

"It's brilliant to be back! Four years away is too long!" Gallagher greeted the audience after his opening number of 'Continental Op'. This was met by a series of cheers and claps, the warm reception clearly touching the guitarist. Although delivering a much shorter set than usual (the Gardaí requested that the Lark wrapped up by 6:30PM), Gallagher went down a storm with critics. Articles heaped praise on the "local hero and Ireland's greatest ever bluesman"[11] and welcomed his mixture of old and new material, which appealed to the wide range of age groups in the audience. Dave O'Connell of the *Evening Examiner* even went so far as to claim the Lark as "Gallagher's day." "The legendary blues guitarist didn't disappoint [...] Home was the hero and he looked like he was enjoying himself," he concluded.[12] Even one month later, the *Irish Examiner* was still talking about Gallagher's performance, where crowds were "spellbound by [his] sheer brilliance."[13] Journalist Dan Collins described Gallagher as "part of a rare class of virtuoso performers whose musical genius and consequent popularity transcends physical borders" and lauded his lifelong devotion to both preserving and improving upon the blues.

The other bands who shared the bill with Gallagher at the Lark were also mesmerised by the Corkman's performance. For many of these young musicians, Gallagher was an icon and to perform alongside him was a dream come true. Tom Dunne, lead singer with Something Happens, fondly recalls standing side of stage to watch Gallagher play, describing it as "one of the greatest 'Take me now, Lord' moments of his life."[14] Joe Philpott of Rubyhorse was also side of stage during Gallagher's performance and recalled the experience with awe to us in February 2024:

> The vibrant charge and power of Rory Gallagher's timeless music reverberated through The Lark by the Lee in Cork [...] I witnessed a performance that transcended mere entertainment; it was a musical pilgrimage, a sound that shook the foundation of the packed field and rattled the cage of my heart. As Rory Gallagher took the stage, what emerged from the Marshall twinned with an AC 30 created a sound that remains etched in my memory, a sound unlike anything heard before or since. His music, a fusion of passion and skill, left an indelible mark on everyone present.[15]

The Vox AC30 amp that Gallagher used at the Lark was, in fact, borrowed from Steve Wall of The Stunning, who still owns it and considers it a sacred item. Gallagher's Vox AC30 was giving him trouble and, seeing Wall's new Rose Morris model on stage, he sent one of his backline technicians to the dressing room to ask if he could borrow it. "I think I actually got down on my knees and said, 'I would be so honoured to have Rory play through my amp!'" Wall told us in March 2023. For Wall, Gallagher played a "great set," but like many who met the guitarist, he was even more impressed by Gallagher's kindness than his musicianship. Somewhat naively, Wall approached Gallagher the moment that he came off stage, told him that the Vox AC30 was his and asked what he thought of it. Despite being exhausted and sweaty, Gallagher stopped, thanked Wall and told him that it sounded "really good," asked if it was a Rose Morris model and said that he might purchase one for himself. Wall was "blown away" at the fact that Gallagher took the time to speak to him when he had just finished performing—something that many other musicians would not do.[16]

While critics and fellow musicians were impressed with Gallagher's set, opinions were slightly more mixed amongst fans. Those seeing Gallagher for the first time were enamoured, while more seasoned fans felt that he was not up to par. Rob Harrington was just 16 at the time. Although he acknowledges that Gallagher was "out of step" with the current music interests of most young people, Harrington saw him as a "legend" and had been introduced to his music by his father—a fan since the days of Taste. Speaking of the Lark, Harrington states:

> The music was awesome in the truest sense of that word and there was a deep appreciation in the crowd, both for his genius and the local boy done good. That Strat was a tired looking yoke, but he made the thing talk. The whole experience was... fucking cool. We left that show completely openmouthed and walking a foot taller. At thirty years' distance it is hard to remember any more beyond my impressions, but it was definitely a door opened for me in terms of exploring the blues and guitar rock.[17]

For Ben Cuddihy, on the other hand, Gallagher "was in great form, mood wise, but the playing was very loose, a bit sloppy initially." In comparison to his performance at the Temple Bar Blues Festival several weeks before, Cuddihy saw the Lark as "very poor" and "some fans who'd not seen Rory since his mid 70's peak were disappointed."[18] Other older fans, who prefer to stay anonymous, equally felt that Gallagher was "not his meticulous self" and "wasn't at his best that day." They also mentioned how Gallagher slipped and fell backwards against the drum platform at one point during his performance. This was due to a wet puddle on the stage from the torrential rain, but fuelled unfounded rumours that he was drunk.

Such comments—while valid—need to be taken from a broader perspective. Often, when thinking of Gallagher's later-day performances, comparisons are made with the 1970s, the former typically coming up short. Such comparisons are unhelpful because Gallagher was two entirely different—yet equally skilled—performers in these periods. As he himself reflected in a 1992 interview with the *Irish Press*: "when you were younger, you just wanted to go out and rock the hell out of it and play a few blues numbers."[19] Now, he liked to maintain the rock 'n' roll intensity, but give increasing presence to folk and the blues, constantly developing his playing in new ways.

We must also remember that Gallagher was performing back home for the first time in four years. Whenever he played Cork, he felt an added pressure to put on a good performance so as not to let his 'people' down, and this pressure was heightened in 1992 by his long absence. Coupled with this was the stress of playing a short set to fit with the Lark's time constraints. Gallagher never liked to be under time pressure when performing and found that this affected his calm considerably. In such situations, he would often begin nervous before gradually relaxing into the set (see Self Aid in 4.3, for example). Another factor to consider is that the Lark was a family affair, consisting of a party in the park complete with balloons and face painting for children. Both the audience and setting were, therefore, not typical for Gallagher, posing an additional challenge, especially for the type of music that he played, which compounded his anxiety.

What is clear from the Lark is that the majority of people in attendance were not disappointed by Gallagher. Families who had come for a free day out with their children simply enjoyed the live music for what it was: a chance to sing, dance and have a good time. Young generations, on the other hand, revelled in the chance to see a man who was an integral part of Cork's musical history and about whom they had heard so much from their parents. Having not seen Gallagher in the 1970s, these young people came with no preconceptions and judged him at face value. Many of these people went on to champion Gallagher's music and are still fans today. For them, the Lark marked the start of this love affair in much the same way as *Irish Tour '74* or Macroom 'Mountain Dew' Festival did for their elders. Gallagher's performance may not have been entirely convincing for long-term fans, but he hit all the right spots for most, proving his continued relevance in the modern age and making him the standout act of the Lark.

Everyman Palace Theatre (31 August 1992)
With his confidence boosted by the hero's welcome he had received at the Lark by the Lee, Gallagher was feeling more upbeat about his performance the next day at the Everyman Palace Theatre. He would be back on familiar territory now in a small 650-seat venue, playing before an audience of adoring fans and facing no time restrictions with his set.

Designed by Richard Henry Brunton, the Everyman was a beautiful Victorian theatre that Gallagher knew well. Located at 15 MacCurtain Street, it was just a few doors down from where he had grown up above his grandmother's Modern Bar. With the arrival of the 'talkies' in 1930, the Everyman had been converted into a cinema and, as young children, Gallagher and his brother Dónal—both movie buffs—had been regular visitors. When the cinema closed down in 1988, the Everyman Theatre Company took on the challenge of saving the listed building and turning it back into a theatre. As a strong supporter of the venue, Gallagher played an active role in funding its restoration and was delighted when it was saved and reopened in 1990.

In an interview with the *Evening Echo* several days before his Everyman performance, Gallagher explained how he had particularly fond memories of his 1985 tour of Yugoslavia (see 2.1) and felt that, "in his heart," he wanted to do something to help.[20] Therefore, he would be donating all proceeds from the concert directly to the Irish Red Cross Yugoslav Refugee Appeal. "It's for the innocent people affected by this conflict; the children," he elaborated to the *Cork Examiner* on the day of the concert, "I follow politics, but I can't fathom this war. This is to help those children who are caught in the middle."[21] The tickets were priced at the attractive sum of £10 and local blues band Floating Opera were chosen as support. As maintained by the *Evening Echo*, the "measly" amount of money for the "world-class standards" associated with Gallagher, in addition to the "nature of the appeal," would ensure a sell-out gig.[22]

In his interview with us, Aidan Stanley revealed that he had originally wanted Gallagher to play an acoustic gig at the Everyman. When he approached Dónal with the idea, he was encouraged to ask Gallagher directly at the Temple Bar Blues Festival in Dublin. So, following Gallagher's performance, Dónal escorted Stanley backstage to his brother's dressing room. It was Stanley's first one-on-one meeting with Gallagher and he remembers feeling nervous as he entered. After some initial awkwardness, Stanley got straight to the point and asked Gallagher if he would consider performing acoustically at the Everyman. Gallagher mulled over his response before politely declining. Although Stanley was disappointed, he accepted the guitarist's decision, musing that it was "good enough" for him that Gallagher had agreed to perform twice for free.

Stanley still fondly recalls Gallagher today as a kind and shy man, and is particularly "touched" by his second one-on-one encounter with him at the Everyman. The day prior at the Lark, Stanley had passed Gallagher's caravan and noticed a "downcast look on his face." When he nodded at Gallagher, the guitarist "barely saluted" him. The following evening when Stanley met Gallagher's car at the backstage door of the Everyman, Gallagher immediately smiled and apologised, stating that he had been feeling "a bit down" yesterday and was "okay" now. Stanley was stunned that Gallagher had said sorry for having a "momentary dark cloud over his face."

As predicted, the low-ticket price meant that the Everyman was packed to the rafters on Monday evening and Gallagher—always eager to please—ensured that everybody got more than their value for money, playing for over three hours. Indeed, the Everyman gig has acquired somewhat of a cult status amongst fans today who marvel at the extraordinary contrast between the first and second parts of the show. Fan Cormac Sheehan—just 17 at the time—recalls that Gallagher initially seemed to be "going through the motions," playing skilfully yet "there but not there." After an hour, he went offstage, and that is when the magic happened. Chants of "Nice one, Rory. Nice one, son. Nice on, Rory. Let's have another one," started up and Gallagher came back out. According to Sheehan:

> The man that left the stage was not the same man that came back on. He came on, like a man possessed, all the talent, all the energy of *Irish Tour* or *Live in Europe* erupted on stage. The bouncer turned his back for a second and that was all the time the crowd needed. It was like a dam breaking, and we left our seats and all rushed forward. Song after song he played, and even did the Chuck

Berry walk across the stage. It was unbelievable. The set before was a distant memory. I remember turning and looking up at the balcony and seeing faces I knew from around Cork, screaming Rory's name. I had my arm around a friend, and I think I became overwhelmed with emotion and tears were in my eyes. I found out that day that I was going to be a Rory fan for the rest of my life. It was I think the best gig I was ever at. He seemed to play forever, and we all stayed to the very end, not wanting it to end [...] He gave so much that night, he must have been very unwell underneath it all, but he knew that we loved him, and I think through the haze that night he loved us.[23]

Also in attendance that night was Gallagher's cousin Jim Roche.[24] Roche was 8 or 9 years old when Gallagher released his first solo album and can remember seeing copies in the basement kitchen of the *Modern Bar*, where the family used to gather. Roche often spent time at the bar because Gallagher's mother Monica was his "favourite aunt"—a woman who "made [everyone] feel special" and "paid attention to children at a time when it wasn't really done." As a teenager, Roche regularly attended Gallagher's gigs at City Hall and cherished the moments when Gallagher would pay a visit to the family house, where Roche and his siblings "hung on [Gallagher's] every word" and would "carefully remember" any bands or artists that he mentioned to check out later.

At the time of the Everyman concert, Roche ran the Acadian Bar in Douglas Street. The influence that Gallagher had on his musical taste was reflected in the bar and many local Gallagher fans were customers. For Roche, the Everyman concert was "brilliant" and being back in MacCurtain Street "meant a lot" to him and the family. Following the concert, Gallagher signed his ticket "To Jim and all at the Acadian Bar"—a memento that he still holds dear. Although Roche has been to many concerts throughout his life, he still maintains that the "unity of performer and audience Rory created was never matched."

Given the high praise steeped on the Everyman concert, it is rather astounding that so little has been written about it to date. On the scant occasions that it is mentioned, the concert seems misremembered in an attempt to give it retrospective poetic meaning based on Gallagher's untimely death. A piece in *The Echo* by theatre producer and playwright Pat Talbot, for example, describes it as "a dark, intense midnight gig which pre-figured the further darkness that would soon envelop [Gallagher]"[25]—an unrecognisable retelling of a concert full of such positive memories for the other spectators.

What is perhaps even more astounding, however, is that the date of the concert is frequently cited incorrectly by both official and unofficial sources. The interactive map bonus feature on the *Rory Gallagher: Live at Cork Opera House* DVD release (2006) marks the gig as occurring in 1993, while even a recent piece in the *Cork Examiner* to celebrate the Everyman's 120th birthday records the concert as taking place in November 1993. The same article also wrongly claims that the concert was to mark the reopening of the theatre and that it was the last time that Gallagher performed in Cork.[26] These oversights are disappointing when the concert was one of such personal significance in Gallagher's later career. Speaking later to friends about the concert, Gallagher described the Everyman as a "superb venue" and said that he was really "taken" with the facilities and the reception he had received.[27]

Hearing news of Gallagher's Everyman concert, the Red Cross were delighted and requested that a delegation and six Yugoslav refugees come to Cork for a photo opportunity and to receive the cheque at RTÉ. Not wanting to receive any publicity, Gallagher requested that the presentation be organised for some weeks later when he had returned to London. That way, he was able to send Dónal in his place to present the funds, along with Aidan Stanley. Speaking to us in February 2022 about the event, Dónal shared a humorous anecdote:

> I enquired as to what 'day out' plans they had for the six refugees. The train ride was more or less it! So, I called my friends at Ballymaloe Hotel - they would provide a lunch, Micheál Martin invited them to the mayor's chambers at City Hall and another pal arranged a tour of the Midleton Distillery. At the day's end, the only English speaking person of the six said they wanted me to take them to a favourite bar of mine, so, they could thank me with a pint. Their Red Cross minders reluctantly agreed to their request, as I promised to have them back at the station for the 5:30PM train to Dublin. On route to the pub, I showed them some of the City's sites and pointed to them, however, when I looked around, they had all vanished on me!! Luckily, I found them in a department store, telling them that if they jumped their handlers, it would be a worst curfew, etc. I took them back to the station a very relieved man![28]

Civic Reception at City Hall (2 September 1992)
On 2 September 1992, Rory Gallagher walked up the steps of the imposing Georgian-style building on Albert Quay, accompanied by his brother Dónal, mother Monica and aunt Kathleen. He was at City Hall, a place that he had been countless times before. City Hall was a regular stop on his annual Irish tours throughout the late 1960s and 1970s. But today was different. Today, he was here as a guest of honour, invited for a civic reception with Lord Mayor of Cork Micheál Martin (now Ireland's Minister for Foreign Affairs and Minister for Defence and former Taoiseach). Gallagher's first visit to City Hall was back in 1961 when he entered the T.V. Talent Competition and won first prize, even getting his photo on the front page of the *Evening Echo*. How far he had come in those three decades since. How much he had done for the city of Cork and the island of Ireland. And now — on what would become his final visit to City Hall — it was time that he got an official expression of gratitude.

A press photograph taken at the civic reception shows Monica signing the visitors' book on behalf of the Gallagher family. She is dressed in a houndstooth skirt suit and smiles proudly at the camera. Standing behind her is Dónal, wearing a black suit and tie, while sat on her left is the Lord Mayor in his livery collar. Alongside the Lord Mayor is Gallagher in a black sweater, black shirt and white neckerchief, his trademark black leather jacket on top. He looks sheepish, with his hunched shoulders, right elbow on the table and chin resting on his thumb — almost bashful to be the centre of attention.

The civic reception had been arranged as a surprise for Gallagher by Aidan Stanley, who saw it as a way for the guitarist's hometown to give something back to him. As he elaborated to us in December 2023, "Very often in a player's career, they might be international figures, but their homebase might have a particular way of expressing how strongly they feel about him, how much they love him. *That* was the avenue." Stanley had also decided months before that it would be fitting to honour Gallagher with an award for his musical accomplishments and that this award could be presented at the civic reception. He, therefore, approached Tipperary Crystal who donated a piece and inscribed it to Gallagher.

On arrival at City Hall, Gallagher and his family were met by Micheál and Mary Martin, and led to the Lord Mayor's chambers, where a small gathering was assembled. These included Stanley, Tadgh Kidney (an old friend), Vincent O'Shea (the artistic director of the Everyman Palace Theatre), Colm Ross (director of Murphy's Brewery, the official sponsor of Cork Rock), Joe Philpott (guitarist in Rubyhorse) and several local reporters and photographers. Once gathered, Martin delivered a short speech in which he described Gallagher as "a world figure in his field" with a "unique" talent.[29] Martin also stated that the city could be "justifiably proud" of Gallagher because he is "one of Cork's greatest sons and has become part of the city's folklore."[30] He then presented Gallagher with the inscribed Tipperary Crystal. Gallagher also made a short speech in response, thanking the city for honouring him and expressing his delight at being back home in Cork. He also thanked Dónal, affectionately referring to him as his "twin."[31]

In Stanley's view, the presentation particularly "touched" Rory's mother Monica who "finally got to sit in the inner sanctum of City Hall" and experience a "lovely private moment" with her sons. According to Dónal, Gallagher was rather embarrassed and surprised about receiving the award, but was also extremely proud. Jim Roche (son of Gallagher's Aunt Kathleen) concurs, noting that Gallagher was "very happy" to get recognised in City Hall and "honoured" to accept the Lord Mayor's invitation. Such recognition came at an important time in Gallagher's life when his self-esteem was low. It, thus, served as a welcome tonic, especially coming off the back of receiving the Arbiter/Fender Hall of Fame award just two weeks before (see 4.6). While the 'Cork Rock Award' had been intended as inaugural, this was the only time that it was given. Reflecting today, Stanley believes that this turn of events was fitting because there was "nobody in the same league" as Gallagher at that time.

The official presentation was followed by light refreshments. Joe Philpott feels privileged to have had the opportunity "to spend an hour with the greatest guitar player in the world in a relaxed non-showbiz setting." He recalls Gallagher being "humble and shy," while Dónal was much more outgoing and enthusiastically spoke to him about Rubyhorse and offered helpful career advice. Vincent Kelly of the *Cork Examiner* interviewed Gallagher at the reception, noting that he was very "eager" to address the rumours that he had been "plagued by health problems" in recent years and assure that he was "in great form."[32] Kelly acknowledges that the "two superb shows" that Gallagher delivered at the weekend certainly indicate that "his physical, mental and creative capacities, after more than a quarter of a century on the road, are still at a peak."

Gallagher was also keen to talk about his future plans, telling Kelly that he wanted to tour more regularly on a national basis, finish his long-overdue acoustic album and collaborate with Bob Dylan. He also hoped to spend far more time in Cork and soak up its "peace and quiet."[33] Speaking of his musicianship, Gallagher candidly acknowledged that it is only now that he feels in "control" of his music. However, he takes "nothing for granted" and is always learning; just recently, he started to develop his use of a thumb pick and finger picks when playing guitar. Gallagher also stated how he continues to play and sing every day, whether on the road or not, because he finds it both therapeutic and relaxing. "If I'm away from a guitar for a few days, I really miss it," he admitted. Overall, the interview is optimistic and shows that Gallagher had so much more that he wanted to accomplish as a musician. Kelly concludes that music has always come first with Gallagher, which is what makes him so "special" and why he is likely to be "at the top" for a long time to come.

Cork Arts Festival (17 November 1993)
Despite Gallagher's plans to spend more time in Cork and tour Ireland with greater frequency, a prolonged period of ill health, followed by summer festival commitments, meant that it was over a year until he returned to his home country. His return—which would turn out to be his Irish swansong—saw him performing a unique acoustic set in the atrium of Cork Regional Technical College (RTC) as part of the inaugural Cork Arts Festival.

Described as "the most comprehensive multi-dimensional cultural event ever in Cork,"[34] the Cork Arts Festival was organised under the auspices of the RTC and was designed to mark its recent amalgamation with Crawford College of Art and Design and Crawford School of Music. Running from 15 to 20 November, the Festival sought to emphasise the college as "a resource and creative force"[35] by celebrating music, art and poetry, with a series of concerts, recitals, exhibitions, theatrical performances and film screenings. The events would be open to the general public and run across the three College venues in order to acknowledge the "changed emphasis" of college life and show the people of Cork that it was now about "a great deal more than engineering and science."[36] If successful, the Festival hoped to become an established annual event, marking a "new cultural venture" in Cork.[37]

For the organisers, it was essential that an event to celebrate the arts in Cork would have Rory Gallagher on the bill—especially an event held at RTC. Gallagher was one of Cork's most famous sons, of course, but he also had a strong personal connection to the College: his uncle Jimmy was principal there from 1968 to 1988.

Jimmy, or James Roche was the brother of Monica Gallagher and an "inspirational figure"[38] for Gallagher to whom he was "very, very close."[39] Jimmy had spent part of his early adult life in Canada, before returning to Cork in the 1950s where he obtained undergraduate and postgraduate degrees in Experimental Physics. Jimmy was a huge music lover and, during his time across the pond, he was exposed to many artists that he had never heard before in Ireland. He avidly spent his wages on the latest country, blues and folk records, which he later shared with the young Gallagher.

According to Dónal, "the feel of American music became more real because of and thanks to Jimmy."[40] While Gallagher had been trying to develop a sense of what America was like through the songs of Lonnie Donegan or the cowboys Roy Rogers and Gene Autry, Jimmy provided him with first-hand accounts, further developing his love of travelling musicians and the Wild West. Jimmy was also a very fine singer, as well as the first person that Gallagher ever saw in a leather jacket—a piece of clothing that fascinated him.

Jimmy spent some time as a Research Assistant at Birmingham University, then in positions with the Department of Posts and Telegraphs and Waterford Glass, before beginning his career in education as a Class 3 teacher at the Crawford Municipal Technical Institute in Cork. After various teaching roles around Ireland, he returned to Cork in 1968, securing the position of principal back at Crawford. Jimmy was a pioneering principal who modernised Crawford through an expansion of the arts and the introduction of new learning technologies. Keen to improve his own knowledge of ICT, Jimmy would regularly travel to London in the late 1960s to take computer courses at IBM. Dónal has fond memories of picking his uncle up in the Taste van and bringing him to their bedsit, where he would crash on the floor. Gallagher had such "huge *grá*"[41] for Jimmy that the Taste debut album featured a cover of Hank Snow's 'I'm Moving On' (Jimmy's favourite song) as a subtle tribute.

Jim Roche (Jimmy's son) recalls how "immensely proud" Jimmy was of Gallagher's achievements. Roche describes the release of a new Gallagher album as a "big event" and remembers Jimmy reading out a positive review of *Against the Grain* to the whole family in 1975. Jimmy also regularly attended Gallagher's annual City Hall concerts, which earnt him some "bewildered looks" from students wondering what their principal was doing there. Whenever Gallagher was back in Cork, he was a regular visitor to Jimmy's house, where the two men and Dónal would stay up late exchanging tales and joking with one another. Sadly, in March 1988, Jimmy passed away suddenly at just 58 years old. He was at a social function with his wife Kathleen when he collapsed, suffering a fatal heart attack.

Given the great affinity between Gallagher and Jimmy, it is unsurprising that he agreed to perform at the Cork Arts Festival. According to Dónal, Gallagher was eager to honour his uncle musically, but the idea also appealed to his superstitious side: he saw performing in Jimmy's former workplace as having a "Ghost Blues" element.[42] For Jim Roche, it was "very moving" for the family as RTC had played such a "huge part" in their lives.

Despite Gallagher's willingness to perform, Dónal notes that his brother was "very nervous" and "wasn't particularly well at the time," yet he "rose to the occasion."[43] Gallagher worried that the atrium of RTC would not lend itself to a full rock band, but more importantly, he felt that a rock band would be distasteful and too raucous for Jimmy. While he had been reluctant to play acoustically when approached by Aidan Stanley the year prior, this time, Gallagher felt that an acoustic set would be the most appropriate way to pay tribute to Jimmy, given his musical tastes. However, once he had settled on this, he became anxious about performing on his own without a band. Although Gallagher always incorporated an acoustic element into his set and had performed short acoustic concerts before, this would be his first full-length acoustic concert. He feared that people would not be interested or, worse still, that he would not be able to do his uncle justice. Therefore, he decided to bring in Mark Feltham and Lou Martin for moral support.

The official press release for the Cork Arts Festival took place in the CERT Catering Course restaurant on 5 October. Here, the full schedule for the five-day event was announced. There would be a range of traditional, classical, jazz and blues performances, an art exhibition featuring the work of students, lecturers, local collectives and famous Irish artists, and a series of lectures by Tomas O'Canainn, PJ Curtis and Ciarán Mac Mathúna. But what most caught the attention of the press was the surprise announcement of Gallagher's acoustic concert.

In the following days, local newspapers were filled with excitement about Gallagher's return to Cork. David O'Connell described him as the "undoubted musical highlight" of the Festival,[44] while Pat Brosnan assured that there was "nobody more qualified to deliver a rock encyclical" than Gallagher, given that he was "the man who unquestionably drove the entire Irish rock movement."[45] Later articles referenced Gallagher's "storming set" at the Lark by the Lee and how it was "still ringing in the ears" of all those who attended.[46]

Tickets for Gallagher's concert were in high demand and sold out quickly, the *Evening Echo* noting that fans were travelling from as far as Dublin and Donegal for the occasion. The article also mentioned a special touch by RTC: 'As the Crow Flies' was used as the music on hold when people phoned for tickets. On the day of the concert, Dónal spoke to the *Evening Echo*, telling them that "Cork is always very special for Rory" and that the concert would be "a little bit of an experiment in styles."[47] When asked about Gallagher, he informed them that he had arrived back home the night before, just in time to watch the Northern Ireland-Republic of Ireland football match on television.

On the evening of the concert as the atrium filled with fans, Lou Martin was sent out to warm them up with some piano playing, while Gallagher psyched himself up backstage. PJ Curtis—who had previously worked with Gallagher on Davy Spillane's *Out of the Air* album (see 1.4)—was chosen to introduce Gallagher to the stage. He brought along his ticket stub from a Gallagher gig that he had attended in Bournemouth on St Patrick's Day in 1972 and displayed it to the audience, much to their amusement. Curtis met Gallagher and his mother Monica backstage beforehand. In our interview in March 2023, he admitted that he was "shocked" at Gallagher's condition: "his face puffed and swollen, greatly overweight and generally lacking that vital youthful life-force he so possessed both on and off stage." However, Gallagher was his usual polite and courteous self and turned in a "great performance" for his hometown audience, despite his evident ill health. This was the last time that the two men ever met.[48]

Fan Ben Cuddihy also remembers the concert as a "fantastic evening," with Gallagher on top form. The crowd was full of young students who had never seen Gallagher before and, subsequently, went on to become lifelong fans. Despite drafting a setlist on this occasion (something that Gallagher rarely did), he worked from it very loosely, changing the order and adding in new songs as he saw fit. Jim Roche recalls that Gallagher opened with 'Ghost Blues'—a bittersweet choice that felt "sad and funny" and which Jimmy would have enjoyed very much. For Cuddihy, the rare inclusion of 'I'm Not Awake Yet' was a particular highlight. Like many others, Cuddihy expected Gallagher to tour more acoustic shows and was "confident" that he would see him perform in this format for years to come. Very sadly, this was not to be.

The reviews that followed Gallagher's concert were glowing and paint a vibrant picture of the evening. Dan Collins of the *Evening Echo* joked how "there are few places on earth where the accolade 'good man—kid' will be shouted at a performer," but that this was "just one of the many tributes" paid to Gallagher by the appreciative audience at RTC. Elaborating further, Collins writes that Gallagher played for two hours, working his way through a wide range of blues material in a performance that was "nothing short of perfection." Feltham and Martin were the "perfect accompaniment," offering a "feat of harmonica and blues piano rarely witnessed this side of the southern American states." Collins reserved particular praise for 'Walkin' Blues' and its touching 'Amazing Grace' opening, as well as the closer 'Goin' to My Hometown'—performed for the first time in well over a decade. Gallagher left the stage to the usual "Nice one, Rory..." and, according to Collins, had "the glow of somebody who knew he had struck all the right chords."[49]

Equally, Brian Hennessy of *Southern Star* noted how Gallagher did not "put a foot wrong" and performed "with the passion and feeling of old." He praised the guitarist for being a "true musician" with the "same passion and enthusiasm" for music that he has always had and for the evident "great buzz" that he still gets playing live. He also singled out 'As the Crow Flies', 'I Wonder Who' and 'Out on the Western Plain' as his favourite moments. The fact that journalists, along with family and fans, all chose different songs as their highlight attests to the consistently high level of Gallagher's two-hour set. Hennessy ends by saying how it might be hard to assess Gallagher's popularity in the 1990s, but that he is still without doubt the "king of rhythm and blues."[50]

There were only some rare criticisms. Con Downing of *Southern Star* felt that Gallagher was not the same without "the power and raw" energy of the electric guitar and that Lou Martin's warm-up "dragged a bit," while the sound engineer did such a poor job that none of the instruments "came close to what they should sound like."[51] Fan Dónal de Róiste wrote into the *Examiner* two weeks later, grumbling about the price of the concert (a meagre £10!), that there was standing room only and that Gallagher had gone on stage late and "never connected" with the audience.[52]

Dónal hoped that the concert would mark a new direction for his brother. He saw Gallagher under increasing stress and anxiety, juggling several roles and struggling to cope with the everyday administration of running a band and funding his own musicians. Back at Jury's Hotel that night, the two had a drink in the bar and Gallagher, in his own modest way, expressed satisfaction with how the concert had gone. He disclosed that he wanted to focus more on folk and do more acoustic performances.

Also at Jury's Hotel was Lou Martin. Martin recalls that Gallagher was "very nervous" before the concert, but "in good spirits" after[53] and they sat up until 5AM talking. Martin was smoking and, at one point, Gallagher picked up his packet of cigarettes and said, 'You know, there have been times when I really thought I would enjoy one, but it's bad for you'[54]—a heartrending statement considering the damage that Gallagher's medication was unknowingly doing to his body. Martin hung out with Gallagher again the next day, noting that Gallagher seemed "genuinely happy" to spend time with him and said that they should do it more often. Regrettably, this was the last time that Martin ever saw Gallagher.

That afternoon, an interview was scheduled with journalist Marcus Connaughton to discuss the concert. Reflecting on the show, Gallagher stated:

> One's hometown show is a joy, yet it's very tense. You don't want to let anybody down, your family, or the audience, or yourself. So we brought Mark Feltham, the great harmonica player, along to help out on some songs and Lou Martin, my old buddy from the old days, to play some piano and to open the show. I was a little apprehensive but once we got there and checked it out, the audience was beautiful and warm. It was serious but there was an element of fun as well, which doesn't hurt. It wasn't exactly a Segovia recital but it's great for me cos I can write and play but until I get on stage, the X factor comes into being, because an audience, you can really draw from them and get inspiration and fire and all kinds of

qualities that you think you have lost or can't find [...] We had a great night and I'm relieved and happy and still getting rid of the perspiration but I'm fine otherwise.[55]

Gallagher expressed his enjoyment at playing old songs like 'I'm Not Awake Yet' and 'Bankers Blues' and singled out 'She Moved Thro' the Fair' and 'I'm Ready' as specific highlights for him. Connaughton then praised Gallagher for the effortless way that he moved from one acoustic instrument to another, telling him that it was great to see him playing the mandolin again. In his typically self-deprecating manner, Gallagher played down his mandolin skills, stating that he was not "a great single string player" and had simply found his "own way of doing it."[56] He told Connaughton that he was hoping to include more mandolin songs on his planned acoustic album and that he had recently picked up the bouzouki and was planning to use it on several tracks, along with a 12-string, acoustic piano and double bass.

As we now know, Gallagher never did record his acoustic album and his concert for Uncle Jimmy ended up being his very last on Irish soil. In 2018, plans were put forward to unveil a plaque in Gallagher's honour in what is now called the Rory Gallagher Theatre at RTC (today, Munster Technological University). The unveiling was to be carried out by Dónal and followed by an acoustic performance by Jacques Stotzem. Unfortunately, the event was cancelled due to adverse weather and is set to be rescheduled in the near future.

Following the RTC concert, Gallagher told Dónal that he only hoped that he had done his uncle proud. According to Jim Roche, there is no doubt about that. He believes that his father would have enjoyed the concert immensely and been extremely proud of Gallagher.

Local Boy Makes Good
After a four-year break, Rory Gallagher returned to his adopted home city of Cork in 1992 for an unforgettable few days that saw him perform at the Lark by the Lee Festival, play a benefit concert for the Irish Red Cross, win an award for his musical achievements and receive a civic reception with the Lord Mayor—all remarkable feats that have been overlooked in previous works on Gallagher. One year later, he returned again, this time to the Cork Arts Festival where he delivered an astounding acoustic set in honour of his uncle Jimmy, truly leaving his mark on the city.

"I'll definitely be buried there," Gallagher had said back in 1972 when speaking about Cork to *New Spotlight*.[57] And this was sadly the case when he returned to Cork for the last time in June 1995. On the day of Gallagher's funeral, the Church of the Descent of the Holy Spirit was overflowing with family, friends, fans, colleagues and music industry figures, while the city streets were lined with wellwishers out to bid the guitarist a final farewell. The day was full of symbolic meaning, from the pouring rain representing the city's tears to the stray dog who wandered into the church and rested beside Gallagher's coffin—a sign of protection and loyalty.

Following Gallagher's untimely passing, the city was quick to memorialise his life. In 1996, a commemorative plaque was placed on MacCurtain Street outside Crowley's Music Centre, while one year later in 1997, a bronze memorial sculpture was unveiled in the newly named Rory Gallagher Place (previously Paul Street Plaza). 2004 saw the city's music library renamed the Rory Gallagher Music Library, 2009 marked the opening of the Rory Gallagher Music Studios and 2015 witnessed the inauguration of the Rory Gallagher Theatre at RTC. Numerous lectures, tribute concerts, walking tours and bars were also set up across the city.

Today, Gallagher continues to be commemorated around County Cork. In 2023, to mark his 75th birthday, photo exhibitions were arranged at Gallagher's Pub on MacCurtain Street, Cobh Library and Macroom Library. The Cobh Readers and Writers Festival also dedicated their 2023 event to Gallagher, with a talk by Dónal on *Kickback City*, a special viewing of the *Irish Tour '74* documentary, a Gallagher-themed poetry competition and the unveiling of another plaque at 19 West Beach (where the brothers spent many summers as children with their relatives, the O'Mahony family).

Speaking of Gallagher's significance to Cork, Joe Philpott of Rubyhorse says:

> Rory, to us, was more than a guitarist; he was ingrained in Cork's DNA. His accent, a testament to Cork's distinctive identity, spoke of a connection never claimed by Donegal. And Donegal could never boast Crowley's Music Store—the essence of pure Cork [...] Cork embraced Rory as its own, and he reciprocated with a genuine connection that resonates to this day.

It is fitting then that the 2025 Cork Person of the Year Awards will include a new *in memoriam* category, with Gallagher rightly chosen as the first winner in recognition of his role as "Ireland's first international star."[58]

Despite his success, Gallagher remained down-to-earth, "a humble, gentle and unassuming man who always kept in touch with his roots," as Canon Cashman said at his funeral.[59] It is these qualities that made Gallagher so loved by old fans and why he continues to attract so many new fans today. Walking around Cork, it is still easy to come across people who knew him. Their eyes light up when they speak about him and fondly recall his grace and dignity—words not typically used to describe a rockstar. From MacCurtain Street and City Hall through the Lee Fields to the Bishopstown Campus, it is clear that the whole of Cork city still beats strongly with Gallagher's heart.

LAO

Footnotes

1 Hermann Haring, 'Rory Gallagher: Our Fellow Worker from Cork', *Sounds* (June 1975), https://www.roryon.com/fellow184.html
2 Ibid.
3 Liam Fay, 'Tangled Up in Blues', *Hot Press* (July 1992), http://www.roryon.com/Tangled.html
4 For more on this topic, see: Lauren Alex O'Hagan, "It's always nice to head for home": Music-Making, Sense of Place, and Corkonian Identity in the Rory Gallagher Irish Tour '74 Documentary', vol. 17 (2022), *Journal for the Society of Musicology in Ireland*, 47-77.
5 'Glory Days! Remembering the finest gigs Cork's ever staged', *The Echo* (26 August 2021), https://www.echolive.ie/entertainment/whatson/arid-40366958.html
6 Interview with Dave Fanning, 24 April 2022.
7 Interview with Aidan Stanley, 7 December 2023. All subsequent quotes from Stanley come from the same interview.
8 'Leeside Rock is Ready to Roll', *Evening Echo* (28 August 1992), 2; 'Charity Concert', *Cork Examiner* (29 August 1992), 4.
9 Ralph Riegel, 'Gallagher Tops the Bill at 'The Lark'', *Cork Examiner* (29 August 1992), 3.
10 Dermott Hayes, 'Rory Is Still Rocking All Over the World', *Irish Press* (12 August 1992), 19.
11 Dave O'Connell, 'Rory Banishes Leeside Blues!', *Cork Examiner* (31 August 1992), 1.
12 Dave O'Connell, 'Sun to the Rescue', *Cork Examiner* (31 August 1992), 24.
13 Dan Collins, 'Classic Stuff from Rory', *Irish Examiner* (19 September 1992), 18.
14 Tom Dunne, 'Tom Dunne: Cork — The City Where I Sported, Played and Enjoyed So Many Gigs', *Irish Examiner* (22 September 2022), https://www.irishexaminer.com/lifestyle/artsandculture/arid-40967162.html
15 Interview with Joe Philpott, 26 February 2024. All subsequent quotes from Philpott come from the same interview.
16 Interview with Steve Wall, 27 March 2023.
17 Interview with Rob Harrington, 31 August 2022.
18 Interview with Ben Cuddihy, 28 March 2023. All subsequent quotes from Cuddihy come from the same interview.
19 Hayes, 'Rory Is Still Rocking All Over the World', 19.
20 Ibid.
21 O'Connell, 'Rory Banishes Leeside Blues!'
22 'Cork Rocks It!', *Evening Echo* (28 August 1992), 38-39.
23 Interview with Cormac Sheehan, 24 May 2023.
24 Interview with Jim Roche, 25 March 2023. All subsequent quotes from Roche come from the same interview.
25 Pat Talbot, 'A Taste of What Made Rory Great', *The Echo* (22 November 2017), https://www.echolive.ie/corklives/arid-40175652.html
26 John Daly, 'Palace of Theatrical Delights - The Everyman Celebrates 120 Years', *Irish Examiner* (31 March 2017), https://www.irishexaminer.com/lifestyle/arid-20446540.html
27 Vincent Kelly, 'Rory Proud of His Native City', *Irish Examiner* (10 October 1992), 16.
28 Email exchange with Dónal Gallagher, 26 February 2022.
29 Kelly, 'Rory Proud of His Native City'.
30 Vincent Kelly, 'City Honours Gallagher', *Cork Examiner* (3 September 1992), 26.
31 Ibid.
32 Kelly, 'Rory Proud of His Native City'.
33 Vincent Kelly, 'Gallagher Happy Just to Be Singing the Blues', *Cork Examiner* (8 September 1992), 4.
34 Paul Dromey, 'Arts Festival '93', *Evening Echo* (15 November 1993), 8.
35 Frank O'Donovan, 'Arts Festival for Cork Regional Tech', *Southern Star* (16 October 1993), 9.
36 David O'Connell, 'Gallagher Heads Star Line-Up', *Evening Echo* (6 October 1993), 9.
37 'Arts Fest '93', *Cork Examiner* (17 November 1993), 13.
38 Marc O'Sullivan, 'My Brother's Keeper – Guarding the Legacy of the Legendary Rory Gallagher', *Irish Examiner* (4 June 2011), https://www.irishexaminer.com/lifestyle/arid-20156734.html
39 Marcus Connaughton, *Rory Gallagher: His Life and Times* (Cork: Collins Press, 2012), 150.
40 Ibid.
41 Ibid.
42 Ibid.
43 Mark McAvoy, *Cork Rocks: From Rory Gallagher to the Sultans of Ping* (Cork: South Bank Press, 2009), 158.
44 O'Connell, 'Gallagher Heads Star Line-Up', 9.
45 Pat Brosnan, 'College Cuisine', *Evening Echo* (8 October 1993), 6.
46 David O'Connell, 'Local Hero', *Evening Echo* (18 November 1993), 18.
47 Ibid.
48 Interview with PJ Curtis, 12 March 2023.
49 Dan Collins, 'Nice One Rory', *Evening Echo* (19 November 1993), 13.
50 Brian Hennessy, 'Old Faithful', *Southern Star* (27 November 1993), 10.
51 Con Downing, 'Rory Gallagher – Unplugged!', *Southern Star* (27 November 1993), 10.
52 Dónal de Róiste, 'Gallagher's Cork Gig', *Irish Examiner* (13 November 1993), 7.
53 Gerry McAvoy and Pete Chrisp, *Riding Shotgun: 35 Years on the Road with Rory Gallagher and "Nine Below Zero"* (Chicago: SPG Triumph, 2005), 210.
54 Ibid.
55 Connaughton, *Rory Gallagher*, 152.
56 Ibid, 153.
57 Shay Healy, 'I'm Not Afraid of Failure Here', *New Spotlight* (21 September 1972), http://www.roryon.com/spotlight419.html
58 Donal O'Keeffe, 'Rory Gallagher to be honoured at annual Cork Person of the Year ceremony', *Cork Echo* (2 September 2024), https://www.echolive.ie/corknews/arid-41467894
59 Tony O'Brien and Dick Cross, 'Cork's Final Tribute to Rock Star Son', *Irish Independent* (20 June 1995), 7.

4.6 Carrying the Celtic Blues Torch: Television Interviews and Recordings, 1992-1994

For the final section of Part Four, we examine various aspects of Gallagher's musicianship within the framework of three important events in his career from the early 1990s. We begin with Gallagher's involvement with Welsh television for the 30-minute programme *Stratocasters* in January 1992, pinpointing his position in the history of the Stratocaster, as well as its emblematic attachment to his 'image'. We devote the middle section to Gallagher's appearance at the Guinness Hopstore in August of the same year for a guitar Masterclass, investigating his matured outlook on (electric and acoustic) playing as he finds himself in the role of instructor, passing on knowledge for the next generation of blues enthusiasts. Lastly, we look at Gallagher's inclusion in *Rock 'n the North*, a television docuseries exploring Northern Ireland's music history, taped and broadcast in 1994. We conclude with a focus on Gallagher's connection to his Celtic roots overseas, specifically in reference to Brittany and his friendship with Breton musician Dan Ar Braz. Through our analysis, we aim to further awareness of (often) overlooked musical moments in Gallagher's later life, while also highlighting his role as a pioneer of Celtic blues and his (self-imposed) 'responsibility' to carry that torch, "bringing it through and keeping it on track,"[1] both within his native Ireland and abroad.

***Stratocasters* Television Documentary (1 January 1992)**
In July 1990, filmmaker Michael Bayley Hughes approached rock journalist Bob Hewitt at the Bodelwyddan Blues Festival about a forthcoming project on the Fender Stratocaster for the Welsh TV station S4C. "I had already interviewed several of the top rock [players] for [*Guitarist*] magazine, so it was not too difficult to get back in touch," said Hewitt in early January 1992.[2] Realistically, the short documentary would not be completed until the autumn of 1991, and was set to be broadcast on New Year's Day 1992. With the passing of Leo Fender in March 1991, public interest of the Stratocaster had renewed, leading to documentaries such as Mark Over's *Curves, Contours and Body Horns* (see 3.1), released the year after Bayley and Hewitt's feature. In a 1991 conversation with Shiv Cariappa, Gallagher casually raised the topic of both "Welsh [and] Irish" television companies expressing interest in "a documentary on [him] in the future."[3]

As discussed in 2.4, Gallagher underwent a lengthy period of medical treatment for various ailments following the release of *Fresh Evidence* in May 1990. We, therefore, estimate that his interview with Hughes and Hewitt occurred somewhere between late 1990 and early 1991. As confirmed by Hewitt, Gallagher was filmed at the small Fender showroom inside the Nomis Complex in London's Earl's Court. Hewitt also revealed that Gallagher was the "first name" to be considered during the initial stages of production:

> Rory's inclusion [in *Stratocasters*] was important because he was the people's choice. He had a rapport with his audience and fans like no other, and that is witnessed today via social media, [with] his following as strong as ever.[4]

Alongside Gallagher, guitarists such as Robert Cray, Hank Marvin and David Gilmour shared insights on the Stratocaster's distinctive sound, as well as detailing the instrument's history. Additional footage from Gallagher's interview was later used in the Bayley-Hewitt documentary *Stratmasters*—conceived in 1994, but not officially released until 2007 due to "complications getting permission to take a UK film unit to work in the USA."[5] In our April 2024 phone call, Hughes admitted that, prior to making *Stratocasters*, he "didn't know a great deal about [Gallagher]," though found him to be a "very humble person," as well as "natural and friendly" during the interview process.[6] Hughes attended Gallagher's 1992 warm-up gig in Rhyl, Wales (see Interlude), recalling his "striking performance" as he led his new band. "I saw Eric Clapton perform in an arena stadium the same week and you couldn't compare the two things [...] you couldn't imagine a better performance."

Returning to *Stratocasters*, Gallagher spoke with evident affection about acquiring his 1961 sunburst Fender Stratocaster when he was 15 at Crowley's Music Centre, as well as connecting with the guitar's image at an early age. "The Stratocaster looked sort of futuristic when it came out on [Buddy Holly's] *The Chirping Crickets* album [...] and the sound off a Strat, which was so chirpy and zingy, appealed to me." While Gallagher talked often in interviews about the personal significance of the Stratocaster to him (see 3.1), in *Stratocasters*, he highlights the key attributes of what makes the Stratocaster as an instrument so special:

> It's just the versatility. You've got three pickups, but you have the in-between positions, which are used by a lot by people. The tone control is really near your hand. The volume control... the guitar stays alive as it goes down, whereas in some guitars, if you take it below eight, the guitar starts becoming very dead and unresponsive. Plus, the scale of the guitar, you know? Your hand feels right on the E chord. It's just, obviously, a perfect design, for some people [...] It's the sound of a Strat really, when all is said and done, that's the main feature.

Part 4 - *Carrying the Celtic Blues Torch*

When not talking with his voice, Gallagher does so with his guitar. This takes the form of bluesy riffs between pauses, almost like a musical punctuation point to his answers that feel entirely instinctual to his vocabulary. On other occasions, Gallagher showcases longer pieces, producing an array of styles, from rockabilly to funk, to highlight the Stratocaster's flexible tone. For *Stratmasters* (2007), Hughes and Hewitt incorporated footage of Gallagher playing 'Off the Handle' from his 1987 Cork Opera House performance, demonstrating his versatility on the Stratocaster in a live setting. Although Gallagher was initially "a little uncomfortable sitting under the studio light being filmed in a confined space," this unease gradually evaporated while chatting with Hewitt and Hughes to the point that Gallagher even "willingly demonstrated a few techniques and tricks on camera [while] most other interviewees refused."

In an interview with Jas Obrecht the year before *Stratocasters*, Gallagher modestly stated his desire to get to the point one day where his music had an identifiable "Rory Gallagher feel."[7] For Hewitt and Hughes, the guitarist undoubtedly had his own unique "feel", and they encourage him in *Stratocasters* to summarise it by explaining his technique and approach to guitar—specifically the Stratocaster—throughout his career.

> It's quite hard really to look in on yourself and say, 'I do this, I do that' [...] I don't really have little tricks that I can think of. I use a lot of damping for certain parts. Also, if I'm doing a solo, I quite often take the edge off the song, so it's not quite as bright as most Strats. I try and aim at something like a cross between a Tele sound, a P-90 pickup, and a Strat sound [...] Sometimes I do this string-pulling thing, which is something like a tremolo-arm thing [demonstrates] or if you want to be really showy, you can pull the string out [demonstrates], but you have to be in full flight for that kind of thing. So I just try and do everything I can that feels right for the song.

Gallagher always enjoyed playing rhythm guitar and often cited Keith Richards as one of his favourite rhythm guitarists. In *Stratmasters*, he mentions how the Stratocaster's versatility enables him to switch seamlessly between rhythm and lead guitar. It was this dual function that Gallagher, in fact, used to persuade his mother back in 1963. As Dónal recounted in a 2013 *Hot Press* interview: "[Rory] convinced her that if he got the guitar, not only could he play lead guitar but he could play rhythm at the same time and therefore could play in a band that required only one guitarist [and earn more money]."[8]

Gallagher ends the interview by stating that somebody else would be better at explaining his style because he does not really "have a textbook style." In 2022, guitarist Davy Knowles did just that, taking part in a Fender Play LIVE! 'How to Play Guitar Like Rory Gallagher' Masterclass. Knowles breaks down a range of Gallagher guitar techniques, including pinch harmonics, volume swells, finger vibrato, bending behind the nut, string pulling to mimic tremolo, natural minor string bending, tapping, slide misdirection and tone wah-wah effect. He also gives great emphasis to the "Irish inflections" in Gallagher's playing, such as the way that he blended triplets from a traditional jig or reel with 12-bar blues licks, his frequent use of a major third with a flat seven and his fondness for DADGAD tuning.[9]

Speaking to Vivian Campbell in 1991, Gallagher himself acknowledged that elements of Irish music crept into his playing, including triplets, minor keys, oblique suspended chords and modal chords and 'hanging' open-middle strings.[10] He also compared the bending of notes to the sound of uilleann pipes or vocal wailing and attributed slide playing with his little finger to his familiarity with the mandolin. Guitarist Jim Kirkpatrick believes it was this Irish side of Gallagher's playing that helped him "stand out against Eric Clapton or Peter Green."[11]

Celebrating Gallagher's Stratocaster in the 21st Century
Throughout his career, Gallagher often spoken about his fondness for the Stratocaster. In a 1985 *Guitarist* article, for example, he referred to the Stratocaster as his "Desert Island" guitar, which is "about the classiest" instrument to own.[12] "It's a good, tough guitar—you never have to treat it like a baby," he added. In November 1979, Gallagher received one of the 25th Anniversary Stratocasters from Fender representatives Don Johnston and Larry Newman while staying in New York. Gallagher admitted in a later interview that Fender presumed "[he] couldn't afford a nice and clean guitar," providing him with the "lovely [and] white" Anniversary guitar because "they were slightly embarrassed by the [worn] finish" of his 1961 Stratocaster.[13] Gallagher used it in the studio on occasion, such as the recording of *Jinx* (1982), but preferred to stick with his trusty 1961 Stratocaster, remarking later in *Stratmasters* that "people are no longer offended by the look of the old guitars" thanks to Stevie Ray Vaughan and Adrian Belew.

A year after *Stratocasters* was broadcast, Gallagher appeared at the 40th Anniversary Celebration of the Fender Stratocaster on 15 September (see 3.1), playing a significant part in honouring what he claimed to be "the best 'primary' guitar."[14] Rather fittingly, Fender's 50th anniversary concert in November 1996 was billed as a "Tribute to Rory Gallagher" and featured a host of stars celebrating the life of the guitarist, from Hank Marvin and Jack Bruce to Peter Green and Yngwie Malmsteen. At the end of the evening, Dónal Gallagher was presented with a Stratocaster signed by all the artists who had taken part. The guitar is now on permanent display at the Rory Gallagher Music Library in Cork.

Fender has since paid tribute "to one of the finest guitarists of his, or any, generation"[15] by producing a replica Rory Gallagher Signature Stratocaster, immortalising the Irishman's contributions towards the instrument's sound and design for future players to access. Critics and fans alike have hailed it as "the best sounding Strat [from the Fender Custom] shop,"[16] insisting that "this guitar will elicit gasps of astonishment," despite "the [obvious] ageing [exterior]."[17] Further consolidating Gallagher's association with Fender, in 2015, Fender Headquarters in Scottsdale, Arizona unveiled a Rory Gallagher conference room, while in 2018, the boardroom in Fender's Irish Headquarters was renamed after the guitarist. In recent years, fans have also had the opportunity to see Gallagher's original Stratocaster up close and personal in the *Born to Rock* exhibition at Harrods (2007), *The Guitar Show* at London's Olympia (2018) and the *Play It Loud* exhibition at the Rock & Roll Hall of Fame in Cleveland (2019). A replica is now permanently exhibited at the Irish Rock 'n' Roll Museum in Dublin.

Along with the check shirt, the Fender Stratocaster has always been associated with Gallagher's 'image'—an image that is mainly attributed to him by the press (and, to an extent, fans also). In the media, the image of Gallagher's Stratocaster shifted throughout his career in accordance with the ebbs and flows of musical fashion. By the 1980s, the guitar was swept up in criticism, attracting descriptions such as "old," "beat-up," "battered," "moth-eaten," "sandblasted," "weather-worn" and even the "world's worst looking" in leading music magazines.[18]

For fans and critics of the 21st century, however, what was once considered outdated is now "the best Stratocaster in the world," the guitar's worn finish inextricably linked to Gallagher's back-to-basics style, contrasting the current technological and AI climate. Bob Hewitt agrees, arguing that Gallagher brought "integrity" to the Stratocaster. "[He] made people realise it wasn't something to play occasionally, polish and keep under the bed in pristine condition. It was made to be played, and Rory really showed everyone he was the one to do it."

In his final radio interview in 1995 (see 3.3), Gallagher spoke of his admiration for the "theatrics" of the early blues and rock 'n' roll artists. On stage, Gallagher himself often utilised such 'theatrics', some involving his Stratocaster, such as his ten-minute version of 'Shadow Play' at the 1979 Montreux Jazz Festival. This thrilling interaction between performer and instrument is often forgotten within the iconic moments of the Stratocaster, such as Jimi Hendrix settling alight his guitar at the 1967 Monterey Pop Festival.

In April 2024, *The Guardian* celebrated 70 years of the Fender Stratocaster, highlighting well-known players of the guitar, from Nile Rodgers to Joe Bonamassa. Fans in the comments section expressed disappointment at the exclusion of Gallagher from the article, even prompting a letter to *The Guardian* referring to him as "the greatest Fender Stratocaster player you've never heard of."[19] On a positive note, such mentions of Gallagher encouraged many to seek out his music for the first time, as confirmed by this commentator: "I have now [been] introduced and heard some Rory Gallagher."[20] *The Guardian* writer Andy Welch revealed that, during his interview with Bonamassa for the Stratocaster article, the two "talked about Rory for twenty minutes." Although there was limited space to include Gallagher in the piece, Welch hinted to a possible article in the future dedicated solely to the Irish guitarist.

In his lifetime, Gallagher was regarded as one of the "Fender Stratocaster 'Hall of Fame' Members," indicating his high rank—at least, from the media's perspective—amongst his guitar contemporaries. Such commentary continues to the present day, with Gallagher positioned at number two on the 'Ten Great Strat Tones' in *Guitarist* magazine's Stratocaster Handbook edition from June 2024. *Guitarist* cites *Irish Tour '74* in particular for those who seek "a Strat player giving their all." Gallagher's pairing of the Fender Stratocaster with the Top Boost Vox AC30 ultimately cemented his "reputation as one of the most intense, visceral guitar players in blues-rock history."[21]

In July 2024, the Gallagher estate made the surprise announcement that Gallagher's beloved Stratocaster would be sold at auction, along with the rest of his instrument collection. Mounting insurance and storage costs, coupled with the inevitable "conveyor belt of life" and numerous unsuccessful attempts to secure a permanent museum home for the guitar, led Dónal Gallagher to make this difficult decision.[22] The news sent shockwaves through the fan community, who view Gallagher and his iconic Stratocaster as a single entity, given his close relationship with the guitar throughout his career. A crowdfunding campaign, spearheaded by Sheena Crowley (daughter of Michael Crowley who originally sold Gallagher the guitar in 1963), was set up to secure a permanent home for the instrument in Cork, where it would be preserved as a "national treasure" and "modern-day Book of Kells."[23]

Guinness Hopstore Masterclass (12 August 1992)
In a 1978 interview with *Guitar Player*, Stefan Grossman asked Gallagher to design a "hypothetical" lesson about "blues guitar" for music students. Gallagher answered that he would "keep it within a reasonably rigid blues framework" and that his teaching would mostly "depend on what music the student had been exposed to."[24] The next year, he had the opportunity to put this into practice when he was invited to give a guest seminar at the YMCA in Belfast in his role as Honorary President of the Northern Ireland Guitar Society. Founder Joseph Cohen remembers meeting Gallagher before the seminar to discuss the format and reassuring the "very concerned" guitarist that he would not be "quizzed" on music theory and that it would be "very laidback," with members of the Society asking him questions.[25] Following the successful seminar, Gallagher was presented with an engraved tankard.

Although Gallagher was reluctant to ever appear academic or "preach the [blues] in a too intellectual way," he "inevitably [became] his own professor" through years of hard study and dedication, as a 1987 *Hot Press* article noted.[26] It was this hard study and dedication that led the organisers of the inaugural Temple Bar Blues Festival in 1992 (see 4.4) to call upon him to deliver a guitar Masterclass to a selected audience at the Guinness Hopstore on 12 August. Five recent graduates from the Ballyfermot Rock School (Colm Quearney, Daragh Brennan, Michael Duff, Eamonn Griffin and David Gunning) were some of the lucky few to attend this underpublicised event.

Gallagher divides his Masterclass 'lessons' to showcase the numerous blues styles, such as ragtime ('Pistol Slapper Blues'), country blues ('Walkin' Blues') and the electrified Chicago blues ('I Wonder Who'). For the first track ('Walkin' Blues'), he reviews slide tunings and bottleneck varieties, demonstrating the copper brass. For 'Out on the Western Plain', Gallagher explains his preference for the 'Celtic tuning' (otherwise known as DADGAD), popularised by singer-songwriter Davey Graham on his 1961 instrumental 'Anji'. Gallagher also displays the importance of interacting with fellow musicians in a live setting on his duet of 'Barley and Grape Rag' with Ronnie Drew, to then jamming with the Ballyfermot graduates on known blues standards, such as 'Gypsy Woman'.

For present-day fans, the Masterclass was, fortunately, recorded and has circulated on the internet on various platforms (from YouTube to Soundcloud). However, unfortunately, the Estate has never treated the tracks to an official remaster and release. Consequently, fans without regular usage or access to technology, such as an older generation, may have never listened to (or indeed lack awareness of) some of the best renditions of Gallagher's material. When we contacted Colm Quearney for this chapter,[27] he informed us that additional tracks were recorded on the day, yet did not appear on the Soundcloud listing. Quearney was 19 when he met Gallagher at the class, noting that the "shy" guitarist appeared to be more nervous than him. Journalist Michael Ross concurs, revealing in his article that Gallagher worried before the Masterclass "if he would still be liked" and that "someone would remark upon his low profile of late, or upon his unhealthy appearance."[28]

Listening to the audio, Gallagher's nerves are indeed apparent at the beginning. With a shaky voice, he greets the audience, apologising for being "a wee bit nervous" and self-effacingly claiming that the young players will "come up and blow [him] off the stage." He then transforms as he starts up 'Walkin' Blues', delivering a powerful and confident vocal performance. Ross describes this very moment in his article, remarking how the audience "applauded warmly" after the song finished and Gallagher looked "grateful and relieved."[29] The guitarist would later tell Ross that he felt "the gods were with him [...] for the first time in a long time" at that moment.

Despite Gallagher's own nerves, he had a great ability to put others at ease, as Quearney recollects:

> I was dizzy walking to the stage. I had never played in front of a crowd like that before. They were so enthusiastic. I was getting to step in and share Rory's light. I could see his fans truly loved him. What a vantage point. I knew I was privileged and lucky. Going into it I knew I had an advantage. I had learned a lot of his songs and guitar licks from watching a VHS that my Dad had recorded from TV [*Messin' With the Kid* released in 1990].

He introduced me and we got straight into playing. 'Blues in A?' he said. I sneaked an eye open once or twice to see what he was doing, [and] he was just smiling his way through the song/jam and that made me think it must be going okay. He was encouraging. After the first jam we played (and the applause calmed down), Rory said to the crowd, 'Colm's playing speaks for itself really, he has a similar sound to Buddy Guy'. That really gave me a confidence that I still carry with me today.

[…] At the end of the Masterclass we spoke for a while and then he signed my cassette tape and then it was over [and] I was walking home back down James Street. Why was it me that got to play with him? It gave me inspiration to keep going. And I'm still playing the blues thirty years later.[30]

Daragh Brennan, another Ballyfermot attendee, recalls a similar experience when exchanging guitar licks with Gallagher:

It was intimidating initially as I was a young metal/rock player with no blues influences at the time and had only found out about the session a couple of days beforehand. The other guys chosen were much more suited and influenced by Rory and more mature players than I was, but once I sat down with him, I was less nervous and he helped me feel at ease by being very relaxed and chilled. He was a total gent and very easy to play with. I had to have a distortion pedal which mostly sounded terrible, and he was smiling away being very relaxed and making it a pleasure to jam with him.[31]

Brennan admitted to listening mainly to "rock and metal players" during the 1990s. It was only a few years ago that "I really started to find myself looking to move out of my comfort zone and explore the bluesier side of guitar playing." This eventually led Brennan to delve further into Gallagher's catalogue, in particular his live recordings and blues covers. Rediscovering Gallagher years after meeting and jamming with him "really brought home" to Brennan just "how amazing [Rory] was as a player, whether using slide or not, and how great his voice was."

Furthermore, Gallagher's "engagement with [the] up-and-coming guitarists [from Ballyfermot]"[32] was a highlight of the class for long-time fan Joseph Cavenagh. After attending Gallagher's concert at the National Stadium in Dublin in 1972, Cavenagh became an immediate admirer of his "talent, energy and music," realising then that he had found a musician who was "very special." Cavenagh's sister happened to be listening to RTÉ radio when they announced that only two tickets were available to Gallagher's 1992 Masterclass. She immediately called the station, winning the tickets by informing the presenters that "[Joseph] and her husband Alan followed Rory everywhere." Cavenagh fondly reflects on meeting Gallagher after the class:

> [Alan and I] were immediately brought over to him by one of his 'bodyguards' whom we had met earlier and had a quick chat with him. It was there that he signed all my albums that I had bought over the years and I still proudly have today. We then got our photo with him, which I have on my wall to this day.

Another fan who was lucky enough to grab one of the few tickets for the Masterclass was Hank Wedel. In 1974, at 11 years old, Hank Wedel arrived in Mallow, Co. Cork from New York City. By the time Gallagher visited the Guinness Hopstore in Dublin, Wedel—now a full-time musician—greatly appreciated his impact on the music scene in Ireland, even briefly chatting with him on one occasion backstage at the Cork City Hall. Wedel recounts a fascinating anecdote from the Masterclass, highlighting Gallagher's patience and simplicity when faced with flashy technique:

> There were three [sic] guitar candidates, and one of them in particular was what we would now call a shredder. That is to say, the dude played an amazing array of multiple scales, arpeggios flying up and down the frets over a basic boogie blues chord progression, which Rory was laying out for him. As I recall it, this went on for what seemed an eternity—a full 10 plus minutes, at least—and was somewhat uncomfortable listening, although Rory kept the pace up and an eye on the young student. When the student finally gave Rory **a chance to play, a magical thing happened. Rory simply turned his guitar volume up, picked, bent and held** one note for about a minute. The relief in the room, full of guitarists and musicians, was palpable. Less is more.[33]

Following Gallagher's impressive Masterclass, the Lord Mayor of Dublin, Gay Mitchell, along with Fender representative Tom Nolan came out on stage to present the guitarist with the Fender/Arbiter Hall of Fame Award. The award—a Fender headstock mounted on an inscribed wooden base—was given to the guitarist in recognition of his loyalty to Fender and longevity as a musician. Speaking to us in December 2024, 2FM's Aidan Stanley explained that Dónal was partly responsible for getting Fender to acknowledge Gallagher in this way. Sensing his brother's despondency at this time, Dónal was "very thoughtful" about what he did to try and raise Gallagher's spirits.[34]

As reported by Eilish O'Regan in the *Evening Herald*, behind James Burton of Elvis Presley's TCB band, Gallagher is the second guitarist in the world to receive this award. Nolan warmly praised Gallagher for the well-deserved achievement, as he stated in the *Cork Examiner*: "There are only a handful of people in the world at that level, and he's one of them."[35] At the Inaugural Rory Gallagher Memorial Lecture in 1995, Marcus Connaughton revealed that Gallagher was "deeply touched" by the induction because, firstly, he "valued and respected James [Burton] as a player," and secondly, he felt he had received very few accolades in his career, putting this down to the fact that he "always stay[ed] true to the blues."[36] At a time when Gallagher was struggling with self-doubt and felt that he had been forgotten by the music industry, this award served as a boost to his morale and evidence that he was still well respected by his peers.

Revisiting the Lesson:
The Importance of Gallagher's 1992 Masterclass
for His 21st Century Students

On the whole, Gallagher hesitated in straying from the fundamental purity of roots music, yet understood the need to stay relevant for the everyday listener. Above all, he valued the earthy sentiment of "the old names" like Scrapper Blackwell and Blind Boy Fuller, who produced "[natural] boogies back to front" without "[trying] to be clever."[37] While Gallagher was curious about the electric guitar from an early age (as evident in his 1992 interview with Hewitt and Hughes), the acoustic also presented intense appeal. "I was [initially] more interested in American folk songs and the acoustic guitar and the image of the American travelling musician—the drifter, you know?" said Gallagher to Shiv Cariappa in 1991. He continues: "I was keen on rock and roll, but I thought it was not the same."[38] In addition, Gallagher frequently advocated for young guitarists to purchase an acoustic, highlighting the advantage of "heavier strings" to give "a good tough start" as well as "develop fingering."[39] He also encouraged exposure to "other kinds of guitar playing," such as flamenco, which he viewed as "another kind of blues."[40] When playing acoustic, Gallagher tended to use a flatpick together with his index and middle finger, which not only allowed him to play very "fast and precise" runs, but also enabled him to combine strumming with "delicately finger-picked notes."[41]

The acoustic interval in Gallagher's concerts was a crowd (and often critic) pleaser, as evident in a 1979 review from *New Musical Express*. While, electrically, Gallagher is "numbingly predictable," *NME* claims his "two-song acoustic set [to be] exquisitely tasteful and richly sonorous."[42] *Photo-Finish* (1978), *Top Priority* (1979) and the live album *Stage Struck* (1980) are noted in the Gallagher catalogue for their absence of acoustic material. A decade on, Gallagher referred to *Stage Struck* as "not [his] favourite album," as it was "a little too harsh" and offered only the "hard-rock aspect" of his playing.

Many factors contributed to Gallagher's sudden hard rock edge in the late 1970s, including pressure from the record company, beginnings of the New Wave of British Heavy Metal and 'back-to-basics' philosophies of punk, as well as a general revolt (even malaise?) of his past. As Dónal notes to Dan Muise, "[During the scrapping of the 1977 San Francisco album] Rory took a turn against the whole time period. Just took an attitude against it."[43] In the press, Gallagher seemed agitated by the popular "anti-lead guitarist" attitude during the late 1970s. He vented to David Fricke in 1979 about the matter: "That whole critical commandment—'thou shalt not do long guitar solos'. You're not even allowed to say 'lead guitar' anymore. I still want to be modern and valid, but I haven't sold out on the past [and] on the thing I love and refuse to drop."[44] Gallagher's acoustic playing seemed to reflect this defiance, as heard, for instance, in his fervent 'Too Much Alcohol' at the Montreux Jazz Festival in 1979 or 'Out on the Western Plain' at 1980's Reading Festival, brimming with Celtic buoyancy as he warns "Jesse [James]" to 'watch out' for trouble ahead.

Gallagher's relationship with the studio brought about many trials as he emphasised the need for quality over quantity, resisting "big projects"[45] to allow the music to speak for itself. In 1.1-1.3, we discussed the modified soundscape of Gallagher's discography, from the "garage band sound"[46] of the late 1960s and early 1970s to the 1977 brassy "American album"[47] with Elliot Mazer in sunny San Francisco, before finally reaching the middle ground of "old magic [with] modern material"[48] on *Defender* (1987) and *Fresh Evidence* (1990). Around this time, Gallagher's guitar technique and style—particularly onstage—adapted to fit his updated ambitions, especially in response to the influx of hard rock and heavy metal guitarists of the 1980s. Speaking with Gay Byrne on *The Late Late Show* in 1988, Gallagher remarks upon his departure from being "European clever" with blues standards, instead focusing on creating "[his] original stamp" with the material. He concludes: "In the last five years I'm moving back towards the real origins of the music [...] simplifying [and] cutting down."[49] Three years later, Gallagher shared his observations in *Young Guitar Magazine* about the preoccupation with "guitar players being *lead* guitar players" amongst the new wave of musicians. "There's more to guitar than just lead guitar," he said, "It takes you a long time to learn to take it cool and easy and laidback in a song. If every song you do is a hundred miles an hour, there will be no time for depth or soul."[50] Gallagher's 'laidback' lesson is superbly displayed at the 1992 Guinness Hopstore, as heard in the very mild (yet hypnotic) 'Out on the Western Plain' and even more so in the electric 'I Wonder Who', given that he is unaccompanied by his band.-

In his 1975 interview with Australia's *Double JJ*, Gallagher was asked to evaluate his spot on the musical spectrum, from "Leadbelly [to the Rolling] Stones."[51] While he "appreciates [emotionally] what the blues does," Gallagher acknowledges his role "as a contemporary writer" and rejects the idea of "doing Elmore James stuff over and over again." Gallagher references the 1960s British blues boom as a point of contrast, justifying "[his] new contemporary way [and] slant" attempted on his blues interpretations. "I don't wanna be just an imitator or recreator of the old blues country stuff," he explains. Gallagher's "stamp" is displayed in his choice of tunings, such as DADGAD for 'Out on the Western Plain', blending a 'semi-Celtic' flavour to the country blues. Furthermore, Gallagher's enhancement of ragtime elements in the Piedmont blues style, as heard in his demonstration of 'Pistol Slapper Blues' at his 1992 Masterclass (where he briefly plays Fuller's slower version for comparison), exemplifies his ambition to go beyond 'imitator'.

Gallagher adjusted (or added) lyrics to blues standards quite often, signifying another 'contemporary slant' of his covers. In a 1992 conversation with Joe Jackson for *The Irish Times*, he discusses the predominant theme of "sexism [and] violence" within a large portion of blues material and contrasts this to his songwriting, citing the 1987 track 'Continental Op', which he (fairly) assesses to be "no way connected" to those "worrying questions."[52]

Gallagher's attitude to composing, therefore, pushed his songs beyond traditional blues themes and boundaries. This has been recognised by even Gallagher's newest fans, such as Rosie, a member of the Instagram community. Rosie highlighted Gallagher's "culturally relatable" song topics, admiring his "stories," such as 'Daughter of the Everglades' (*Blueprint*, 1973), which "reminds [her] of [Henry Wadsworth] Longfellow's poem Evangeline, with this very well-developed plot with a sweet [and] tragic ending."[53]

In addition, Gallagher's acknowledgement of African American artists has deeply resonated with a young audience, particularly in the recent inundation of copyright cases in classic rock.[54] "Rory was very upfront about the blues musicians who had influenced him," said Rosie, even to the point of "[putting] it in a song," referring to 1978's 'Mississippi Sheiks' (*Photo-Finish*) about the Delta blues group of the 1930s. Gallagher's rich musical knowledge is exhibited to a great degree at the Masterclass when explaining the link between Tampa Red's "trademark lick" with Robert Nighthawk, Earl Hooker and Muddy Waters on 'I Wonder Who'. Similarly, Gallagher mentions how Robert Johnson is famously "the man of the 'Walkin' Blues'," despite the song being "written by Son House." Such examples raise Gallagher's musical profile as not simply blues interpreter or 'imitator', but rather, dare we say, blues educator.

Overall, Gallagher's strengths on both the acoustic and electric come to light on his 1992 recordings at the Guinness Hopstore, capturing a solid attempt to balance "enough technique" with "enough primal [grittiness]."[55] Although Gallagher orchestrated many solo acoustic and/or electric performances throughout his career, such as the 1972 session at Cleveland's WNCR[56] or the RTÉ *Me and My Music* programme in 1977, the significance of his 1992 Masterclass should not be underestimated, particularly as a documentation of his growth as an artist. With 'less is more' anecdotes from attendees such as Hank Wedel, we learn the value of keeping composed and sympathetic in a collaborative atmosphere, as well as gain insight into Gallagher's humble nature.

Aside from the guitar playing, Gallagher receiving the Fender/Arbiter Hall of Fame Award magnifies the importance of the Masterclass as a latter-day achievement, contrasting earlier (and often mentioned) accolades of his career, such as topping the 1972 *Melody Maker* 'Best Guitarist' poll. Finally, Gallagher's credibility as a musical mentor and creative influence is enhanced when listening to the Masterclass recordings, and not only for the Ballyfermot students or few fans, but also those accessing the tracks in the present day (and beyond). As we explore later in this chapter, Gallagher's musical guidance also extended to his peers, such as Breton songwriter Dan Ar Braz.

Rock 'n the North Television Documentary (9 August 1994)

Throughout his career, Gallagher spoke of Belfast with great affection, often referring to the city as "[his] second home," which he "adopted" during the Taste period (1966-1970).[57] Audiences, in return, felt the same. Gerry McAvoy disclosed to Dan Muise that Gallagher's concerts in Northern Ireland, particularly Belfast, during the Troubles prompted an "amalgamation"[58] between both sides of the conflict. As opposed to the labels of 'Catholic' and 'Protestant', the crowd simply identified as "music fans"—more specifically *Rory Gallagher* fans—and "for three hours, everything was forgotten about." Sound and lighting technician Joe O'Herlihy states that Gallagher's music "crossed the [political] divide" and that his shows served as a platform to celebrate "an Irish guy making it on the international stage."[59]

In a contemporary setting, footage of Belfast's streets in the *Irish Tour '74* documentary film read less like a film and more like a record of Ireland's political and cultural history. In doing so, Gallagher also demonstrates the "new direction" musicians were pursuing in the 1970s, as "it was rare in those days for a band to film a documentary."[60] From a musical standpoint, Belfast cultivated a "certain mentality," particularly in the early-mid 60s blues scene, where "a kind of casual but seriously way of playing" crept into the psyche of many working musicians, including Gallagher.[61] The predominance of rhythm and blues music created "an ESP" between Belfast players, which ultimately strengthened the working relationship between Gallagher and Belfast-born McAvoy.

Gallagher maintained his connection with the Belfast music scene up until his final decade, exemplified in his final television interview with Terri Hooley for the six-part documentary *Rock 'n the North* (1994). The series was created by Adare Productions, working on behalf of Ulster Television, and traced Northern Ireland's music history. Gallagher featured in the second episode (aired on 9 August 1994), which explored the 1960s blues movement in Belfast. The first half of the programme highlights the significance of the Maritime Club in cultivating an appreciation for African American roots music in Ireland. Most notably, Van Morrison and Them debuted at the Maritime, with Morrison himself, as well as keyboardist Eric Wrixon and guitarist Billy Harrison, appearing in the episode.

The success of the British blues boom granted 60s youth a voice of expression, rebellion and individuality. By contrast, the political, cultural and musical foundation on the island of Ireland differed from Britain and America. Therefore, to become a successful Irish musician—particularly on international soil—proved a difficult task. As Gallagher notes in the programme, "Don't forget, it wasn't an open door then for Irish bands, [and] to be taken seriously as a rhythm and blues band or something like that was quite a challenge." *Rock 'n the North* emphasises the relationship—or the "intertwine," as described by former Thin Lizzy guitarist Eric Bell—between Irish traditional music and the Delta blues. Gallagher builds upon Bell's explanation through his rendition of Arthur Crudup's 'That's All Right, Mama' (1946) on his Stella 12-string acoustic, again utilising the DADGAD tuning to magnify the Celtic element. Gallagher offers less of a performance and more of a tutorial, demonstrating the link between chords like "the Celtic G" to those with an "African influence." He also adjusts the lyrics, which read more like a sorrowful poem then a song.

The latter half of the episode follows the timeline of Gallagher's late-60s trio Taste. He fondly reflects through a bittersweet nostalgia his "ultra clear" memories from that period in his life, as he concludes: "I miss those days, to be honest with you." Also featured in the documentary is John Wilson (Taste's drummer from 1968-1970), as well as songs from the band's self-titled debut album (1969), such as 'Leaving Blues' and 'Dual Carriageway Pain'. In a similar fate to the Irish group Them, poor business decisions and personal differences led to the (arguably premature) demise of Taste, alluding to Gallagher's previous comments about the "challenge" many Irish musicians faced in the industry. In what would be Gallagher's final public statement about the trio, such a loss continues to weigh deeply upon him decades on, shown in his body language and pauses between sentences. He states:

> Oh, it's like why does any band split up? There's no clever answer to that. It's just that things came to a crisis point, unfortunately. I'm still... we've... the whole thing's been reviewed now and we're all sort of in contact again. It's just communications breakdown, right? And it was a shame because it was a great band, and it shouldn't have been allowed to happen is the way I would put it.

Shortly before Gallagher's death, drummer John Wilson had sent several letters hoping to regain contact with the guitarist, but never received a reply.[62]

The episode draws to a finish by highlighting musicians who never ventured over to England, but instead found popularity in Ireland, such as David McWilliams. Nevertheless, as the 60s drew to a close, Ireland's popular music scene was to drastically shift as tensions arose with the Troubles (1968-1998) in Northern Ireland, hindering any development of a rock movement in the 1970s and beyond. "The bands might have disappeared," the narrator reflects, "but the blues and beat era was to be remembered fondly for igniting the spirit of a generation."

Unseen portions of Hooley's interview with Gallagher, such as discussing his admiration for Lonnie Donegan, Leadbelly and Woody Guthrie, were included in the 1995 documentary *Gallagher's Blues*, released on Ulster Television shortly after Gallagher's death. He recalls his introduction to Muddy Waters during his regular listening to American Forces Network and how "it just changed [his] life." In addition, Gallagher reflects on his time with the Fontana Showband (later the Impact) during his adolescence with a balanced perspective, recognising "[his] opportunity to learn chords and play with brass sections," despite it never being "[his] thing [from the start]." *Gallagher's Blues* also previews 'That's All Right, Mama', as well as Gallagher's musical plans for the future: "I'd like to keep on touring. I'd like to learn more. I'd like two great albums in the charts, not for my sake but for the people that have supported me over the years and fans—if I may use that expression." Reflective of his kind heart and gentle nature, Gallagher's overall wish is to simply "do well for other people."

The circumstances surrounding Gallagher's participation in *Rock 'n the North* are well documented in Vignoles' biography, as well as Colin Harper's essay for *Irish Folk, Trad and Blues: A Secret History* (2004). According to cameraman Brian Reddin, when he and Hooley arrived in London, they received a message from Dónal that Gallagher was withdrawing from the project. Many hours later, however, Dónal placed another call with the news that his brother had changed his mind—albeit if Hooley and Reddin would conduct the interview at Gallagher's hotel room in Chelsea Harbour as opposed to the prearranged studio location. "[Rory] was anxious about the interview," Reddin recalled to Vignoles, "Anxious about everything. He didn't want to play anything."[63] Despite this, Gallagher held his H912 Stella 12-String acoustic close throughout the interview, explaining to Reddin that it made him "feel comfortable."[64] "It was the first time I ever heard Rory feel comfortable in my life," Hooley notes, reflecting on how "nervous" the shy musician could be.

Gallagher initially hesitated to discuss "his past musical career," preferring to "talk about what he was doing [at the time]."[65] He finally relaxed when prompted with, "why do Irish people like the blues so much?" which, to Hooley's recollection, "set [Rory] off and he talked for [what] seemed like hours." To thank Gallagher for the interview, Hooley gifted him a bottle of Bushmills Black Bush whiskey in a presentation case. The gesture deeply moved the guitarist, who then invited Hooley and the crew to stay and share it with him. According to Hooley, Gallagher was so gentle and unassuming that if he had asked him that day to pick up his amp and carry it all the way to Australia, he would have done it without hesitation.[66] Hooley reminds readers in Harper's obituary for *Record*

Collector of how "very important" Gallagher's involvement was in *Rock 'n the North* and that he was "definitely a big hero of mine."[67] He reflected in a later interview that Gallagher was "one of the nicest guys you could meet, but if you walked into a room with six people in it, [he] was the last person you would ever expect to be a rock legend."[68]

Since his passing, Gallagher has been commemorated in a variety of ways in Belfast, such as the Ulster Hall plaque in 2007 (aforementioned in 4.1). In addition, the Belfast City Council announced the approval of a Rory Gallagher statue on Bedford Street outside the Ulster Hall in 2016. The project, proposed by East Belfast's Wilgar Community Forum, was warmly received by Dónal, who emphasised his brother's fondness for Belfast throughout his life: "[Rory] was looking for a place where he felt he was at one with the music, and Belfast offered that."[69] Barry McGivern—one of the leading figures behind the Rory Gallagher Statue Project Trust—regularly plays fundraising concerts with his band to support the statue campaign, demonstrating the continued efforts to honour Gallagher in Belfast to the present day.

"He carried the torch of Celtic blues":
Gallagher as a Musical Ambassador

In his later years, Gallagher continued to celebrate his Irish roots in a manner of ways, whether collaborating with young (or established) Irish musicians (see 1.4-1.5) to performing traditional Gaelic songs, such as 'Dan O'Hara' at the 1994 SDR3 Festival in Stuttgart, Germany. Furthermore, Gallagher often played on the bills for various festivals embracing Celtic music, arts and culture, such as the 1992 Scottish Fleadh (see Introduction) and the *Festival Interceltique de Lorient* in 1994.[70] As briefly highlighted in 3.2 and 3.3, Gallagher's two-hour set at Lorient was hailed by the media as a "truly magical night."[71] Even at this late stage in the Irishman's career, he was seen as continuing to carry "the torch of Celtic blues-rock very high."[72]

Prior to Gallagher's trip to Lorient in 1994, he had visited Brittany on a number of occasions, including: Brest in 1975; Quimper in 1980, 1982 and 1984 and Rennes in 1980, 1981 and 1983. Being a region with strong Celtic roots in its language, culture, customs and music, it is easy to see why Gallagher felt such an affinity with Brittany. When he performed in Lorient, he even declared that he felt "right at home,"[73] while organisers noted that Bretons have "always [had] a warm welcome" for Gallagher and that, "In the Celtic country, the Irishman is King."[74]

Gallagher's frequent appearances in Brittany during the early 80s were particularly significant for Breton musician Dan Ar Braz, who befriended and frequently collaborated with his musical hero. Braz had followed Gallagher's career since the days of Taste, first meeting him at the Montreux Jazz Festival in 1975. Braz recalls Gallagher's "immediate kindness and simplicity" and that "to be yourself" was "the lesson I shall never forget" from the Irishman.[75] When Gallagher played at the Salle Omnisports in Quimper (Braz's hometown) in 1982, Braz was delighted to join his guitar idol onstage:

> My friend Jean Théfaine wanted to have an interview with Rory and asked me to come to help for translation. So I did and took my new guitar with me to show it to Rory. So [we] went [to] the interview and, in the end, I asked Dónal if there could be an opportunity for jamming with Rory at the following concert. He said, 'We will see how it goes'. So I took my guitar just in case and left it in my car outside the concert hall. The concert was warm and great and, towards the end, Dónal came to me and said, 'You're on...'
>
> I then had to jump outside quickly to get my guitar, which was cold from being in the car for so long. I got onstage and honestly I just remember being so happy to be on Rory's side. I don't remember how I managed sound or music wise, but I did my best. My playing was probably so weak compared to the fire set up by Rory. [But] I was so happy, and so was the audience—I hope.

Two years later, Braz played onstage with Gallagher in Quimper, this time at the Stade de Penvillers. "We got to meet in Rory's dressing room [and] had a drink—two in fact!" shared Braz, "And later on, there I am once again onstage with him. That show was much easier for me—my guitar was warm enough this time!" After the gig, Gallagher joined Braz and his wife at a restaurant opposite the Gradlon Hotel. Braz recalled a heartfelt moment when Gallagher, understanding his fellow musician's "[struggle] to make it [in the industry]," informed Braz's wife that "his day will come" in the music business. During Gallagher's absence in Brittany across the late 80s, Braz continued his "daily struggle from club to club," continuing to write and practice music as often as possible. Eventually, his hard work led to the creation of the Héritage des Celtes, a 50-piece group of musicians playing and celebrating Celtic music, their self-titled debut record (1994) selling one million copies.

When Gallagher returned to Brittany for his final time in August 1994, he and Braz shared a tender reunion onstage, trading riffs with a medley of 'Don't Start Me Talkin'/Revolution/Treat Me Nice/Dust My Broom' for the encore. Leading up to the event, Braz had expressed his eagerness to "throw an amp and guitar in [his] car and get to Lorient" to see his old friend.[76] Speaking to us about the reunion, he recalled:

> This time again I phoned Dónal and he said, 'Come on, Dan, we'll see how it goes'. Fortunately, I came because it was going to me last meeting with [Rory]. Again, I'm not very happy with my playing

as the delay on my pedal board was all over the place and I didn't know how to turn it down! But the true emotion was there, and it is difficult to express it with any words.

In an email exchange in June 2022, Dónal described Braz as a "wonderful guy," noting that Gallagher was "very fond of him and his musicianship" and enjoyed their "great jam sessions" together.[77] Such was Gallagher's impact on Braz that he recorded two instrumentals in his honour: 'To Rory' in 1979 and 'Gwerz Rory' in 2001. For Dónal, 'Gwerz Rory' "remains one of [his] favourite instrumentals." An emotional piano-led song with poignant Celtic guitaring from Braz, 'Gwerz Rory' encapsulates a sombre and reflective atmosphere. "Gwerz in Breton language means 'Lament'," Braz told us—a fitting term that evokes the Gaelic Celtic tradition of keening (*caoineadh*). Here, Braz's repetition of basic motifs, almost in the form of wails, mimics these vocal laments for the dead, embodying a powerful expression of mourning that captures the sorrow of Gallagher's untimely passing. "I was so lucky to get to know Rory. [He was such] a great human being and a wonderful guitarist," Braz concludes.

RM

Footnotes

1 As stated by Dónal Gallagher in the 2000 Irish music documentary *From a Whisper to a Scream*, https://www.youtube.com/watch?v=2HpNNlEBLJg
2 Mike Davison, 'Musicians pay their respects to a legend', *The Visitor* (9 January 1992), 23.
3 Shiv Cariappa, 'Conversation with Rory Gallagher', *Christian Science Monitor* (29 July 1991), https://www.rorygallagher.com/conversation-with-rory-gallagher/
4 Interview with Bob Hewitt, 22 May 2024.
5 Interview with Bob Hewitt, 30 October 2023. All subsequent quotes from Hewitt come from this interview unless stated otherwise.
6 Interview with Michael Bayley Hughes, 24 April 2024.
7 'Rory Gallagher - The Complete 1991 "Guitar Player" Interview', https://www.youtube.com/watch?v=9gA9vGWieAs&t=2437s
8 Dónal Gallagher, 'The Day Rory Gallagher Bought His Fender Strat', *Hot Press* (15 August 2013), https://www.hotpress.com/music/the-day-rory-gallagher-bought-his-fender-strat-10091644
9 'How to Play Guitar Like Rory Gallagher: Riffs, Licks & Tones', https://www.youtube.com/watch?v=6Nai5JnybdA&t=2125s
10 Vivian Campbell, 'The Wearing of the Blues', *Guitar for the Practicing Musician* (August 1991), https://www.roryon.com/guitar91.html
11 Jim Kirkpatrick, 'Rory Kept It Simple', *Total Guitar* (May 2024), 54-55.
12 Bob Hewitt, 'Rory Gallagher', *Guitarist* (February 1985), https://www.roryon.com/guit231.htm.
13 '1979 Fender – 25th Anniversary Stratocaster', *Rory Gallagher Official Website*, https://www.rorygallagher.com/1979-25th-anniversary-stratocaster/.
14 'Rory Gallagher', *Music Maker* (June 1978), https://www.roryon.com/mm678-315.html.
15 'Fender Rory Gallagher Stratocaster review', *Guitarist* (23 November 2007), https://www.musicradar.com/reviews/guitars/fender-rory-gallagher-stratocaster-24518
16 'Fender Custom Shop Rory Gallagher Tribute Stratocaster Reviews', *Sweetwater* (23 August 2019), https://www.sweetwater.com/store/detail/StratRGTrib--fender-custom-shop-rory-gallagher-tribute-stratocaster/reviews.
17 Ibid.
18 See: Lauren Alex O'Hagan, 'Fashioning the "People's Guitarist": The Mythologization of Rory Gallagher in the International Music Press', vol. 9, no. 2 (2022), *Rock Music Studies*, 174-198.
19 Graham Mort, 'The greatest Fender Stratocaster player you've never heard of', *The Guardian* (18 April 2024), https://www.theguardian.com/music/2024/apr/18/the-greatest-fender-stratocaster-player-youve-never-heard-of
20 Andy Welch, "With a Strat you can rule the world!' Nile Rodgers, Bonnie Raitt and John Squire on the electric guitar that changed everything', *The Guardian* (10 April 2024), https://www.theguardian.com/music/2024/apr/10/fender-stratocaster-turns-70
21 'Ten Great Strat Tones', *Guitarist* (June 2024), 34.
22 Rachel Roberts, '"You can't just hang the Strat up over your fireplace"', *Guitar* (30 August 2024), https://guitar.com/news/gear-news/rory-gallagher-auction-1961-stratocaster

Part 4 - *Carrying the Celtic Blues Torch*

23 See https://www.gofundme.com/f/bring-rorys-strat-home
24 Stefan Grossman, 'Rory Gallagher: An Irish Guitarist Traces His Roots in Acoustic and Electric Blues, and Tells How He Plays Them', *Guitar Player* (March 1978), https://www.roryon.com/GP78.html
25 Interview with Joseph Cohan, shared on https://rory-gallagher.forumactif.org/t622-photos-de-joseph-cohen-belfast-annees-70
26 Bill Graham, 'Rory Gallagher: Revisiting his classic 1987 interview with Hot Press legend Bill Graham', *Hot Press* (17 July 2020), https://www.hotpress.com/music/rory-gallagher-revisiting-his-classic-1987-interview-with-hot-press-legend-bill-graham-22822714
27 The 1992 Guinness Hopstore Masterclass section was originally featured in a *Rewriting Rory* post from August 2022.
28 Michael Ross, 'Praying at the Temple of the Blues', *Sunday Tribune* (16 August 1992), http://www.roryon.com/praying.html
29 Ibid.
30 Interview with Colm Quearney, 5 August 2022. All subsequent quotes from Quearney come from this interview.
31 Interview with Daragh Brennan, 27 July 2022.
32 Interview with Joseph Cavenagh, 7 July 2022.
33 Interview with Hank Wedel, 8 February 2024.
34 Interview with Aidan Stanley, 7 December 2023.
35 Vincent Kelly, 'Gallagher happy just to be singing the Blues', *Cork Examiner* (8 September 1992), 4.
36 'Inaugural Rory Gallagher Memorial Lecture', https://www.roryon.com/marcus.html
37 Royston Eldridge, 'The Sounds Talk-In with Rory Gallagher', *Sounds* (10 April 1971), https://www.roryon.com/talkin303.html
38 Cariappa, 'Conversation with Rory Gallagher'.
39 Hewitt, 'Rory Gallagher'.
40 'Rory Gallagher interview 1991', https://www.youtube.com/watch?v=fNpaun5s1CE&t=814s
41 John Carnie, 'The Acoustic Styles, Influences and Techniques of Rory Gallagher', *Signals* (1997), http://www.johncarnie.com/articles-1.html
42 'What Rory did for fame', *New Musical Express* (6 October 1979), https://www.roryon.com/fame.html
43 Dan Muise, *Gallagher, Marriott, Derringer & Trower* (Milwaukee: Hal Leonard Corporation, 2002), 39.
44 David Fricke, 'Rory Gallagher Roars Back', *Circus* (January 1979), https://www.roryon.com/circus140.html
45 'Rory Gallagher interview Houston Texas 1985', https://www.youtube.com/watch?v=dqc3l8viC_I&t=203s
46 Dónal Gallagher, as quoted in the *Deuce* 50th Anniversary Edition (2022).
47 Julian Vignoles, *Rory Gallagher: The Man Behind the Guitar*, (London: Collins, 2018), 156.
48 Jon Lewin, 'Rory's Story', *Making Music* (October 1987), https://www.roryon.com/Rorystory.html
49 'Rory Gallagher - The Late Late Show - 12th February 1988', https://www.youtube.com/watch?v=lKJ3ploCKv0&t=1s
50 'Rory Gallagher interview 1991'.
51 Rory Gallagher Interview with Tony Maniaty, Double 2JJ studios (8 February 1975), Library of NSW archives.
52 Joe Jackson, 'Black Cat Blues', *Irish Times* (14 August 1992), 6.
53 Interview with Rosie, 13 April 2022.
54 See: Radiohead vs. The Hollies, Pharrell Williams, Robin Thicke vs Marvin Gaye's Estate (2015), Led Zeppelin vs. Spirit (2016). In addition, discussion on the interpretation of African American music by Anglo-Saxon artists has come to light again with such films as *Elvis* (2022).
55 Charley Crespo, 'Here Comes the Irish Rory Attack', *Relix* (1979), https://www.roryon.com/crespo.html.
56 This session was subsequently released under *Cleveland Calling Pt. 1* (2020).
57 'Rory Gallagher interview Houston Texas 1985'.
58 Muise, *Gallagher, Marriott, Derringer & Trower*, 31.
59 Ibid.
60 Ibid., 32.
61 'Rory Gallagher interview Houston Texas 1985'.
62 Muise, *Gallagher, Marriott, Derringer & Trower*, 31, 70.
63 Vignoles, *Rory Gallagher*, 250.
64 'Rory Gallagher Tribute evening Belfast 1997', https://www.youtube.com/watch?v=G1Dumui60nA&t=782s
65 'In Love with the Blues', *Irish News* (13 June 1998), https://www.roryon.com/news11.html.
66 'Rory Gallagher Tribute evening Belfast 1997'.
67 Colin Harper, 'Rory Gallagher', *Record Collector* (August 1995), https://www.roryon.com/harper.html
68 'In Love with the Blues'.
69 'Rory Gallagher: Belfast statue of rock legend gets approval', *BBC* (19 October 2016), https://www.bbc.co.uk/news/uk-northern-ireland-37699194
70 As a sign of Gallagher's importance as an ambassador of Irish music, the 1996 Fleadh was dedicated to him.
71 'Rory Gallagher: Guitar Hero', *Le Télégramme de Lorient* (10 July 1994), 9.
72 Ibid.
73 Ibid.
74 Françoise Rossi, 'Rory Gallagher marche au blues', *Ouest-France* (10 July 1994), n.p.
75 Interview with Dan Ar Braz, 13 June 2022. All subsequent quotes from Braz come from this interview.
76 Rossi, 'Rory Gallagher marche au blues'.
77 Email exchange with Dónal Gallagher, 14 June 2022.

Conclusion: The Rise and Rise of Rory Gallagher

In a 1973 interview with Jerry Gilbert of *Sounds*, Rory Gallagher stated how he would hate his life to one day be summarised as "The Rise and Fall of Rory Gallagher."[1] This is something that clearly bothered him as just four months later, he broached the topic again with *Music Scene,* stating that "the title 'Rise and Fall of Rory Gallagher' should not be all there is to say about my career."[2] Gallagher's words are unsettlingly prophetic, given that this is exactly how his life has been summarised to date in the majority of publications.

In fact, as these 1973 remarks show, this 'rise and fall' account of Gallagher's life was widely circulating long before his untimely death and only worsened throughout the 1980s and beyond. When Gallagher passed away in 1995, Irish journalist Joe Jackson made a poignant remark: "Rory Gallagher may be on the minds of many people this morning, following his premature death at 47 in a London hospital on Wednesday, but how many of them were thinking about him on Tuesday?"[3] As obituaries for the guitarist poured in, most were filled with the cliched 'rise and fall' narrative, focusing predominantly on Gallagher's successes in the 1970s and asserting that his best years had long been behind him.

At the worst end of the scale were pieces like those of Frédéric Lecomte (*Guitare and Claviers*), who unfairly claimed that Gallagher spent the 1980s "sinking into oblivion" and "becoming obese, bloated and a raging alcoholic"[4] [sic] and Michael Ellison (*The Guardian*), who bizarrely chose to dedicate half of his article to Gallagher's ill-fated Town & Country Club gig in 1992. However, even the more favourable obituaries still peddled the idea that "in the last 10 years, it had all turned quiet"[5] for Gallagher and that he "had shown signs of exhaustion and began to age and put on weight."[6]

Gallagher felt that he made some of his best music in the 1980s and early 1990s, but that it was often not given a chance by the fickle music industry. This is something that Shu Tomioka, a close friend to Gallagher in his final years, emphasised in an April 2022 interview with us:

> In the early 90s, Rory was underrated in the rock world. When some magazines made special articles like 'Great Blues Guitarist' or 'Great Fender Guitarists', Rory's name was often omitted. This made me so angry with it, and Rory was really hurt too.[7]

Similar sentiments were also emphasised by Gallagher in conversations with Toine van Berlo, the chauffeur on his 1995 Dutch tour, where he expressed his sadness that people "[didn't] respect [him] anymore" and he felt forgotten.[8]

Gallagher wished to "find a niche" one day, but stoically accepted that it would be "okay" if he never did.[9] Speaking to Dermott Hayes of the *Irish Press* in 1992, he noted that he was happy to "just fade away and just keep playing music and, lo and behold, every couple of years there's a renaissance of interest in what I'm doing."[10] In a cruel twist of fate, that renaissance of interest seems to be stronger than ever before, with generations of new fans today attracted to the Irishman's beguiling music.

Despite this boost in popularity, the uncomfortable 'rise and fall' narrative has stuck and continues to be recycled in most articles about Gallagher. With a rapidly growing fanbase, it is more important than ever to tell a *balanced* story of his life. In a world where people are now far more attuned to mental health challenges, where body positivity is embraced and where greater compassion is shown towards those considered 'unconventional', Gallagher's final decade in particular can be looked upon with a much needed fresh and empathetic understanding. So much has been written about his challenges offstage and so many labels have been attached to his name. It is time to reframe these discussions and focus instead on all that he continued to achieve musically from 1985 to 1995, despite these personal struggles.

It is our hope, then, that *Rory Gallagher: The Later Years* can offer an entry point for these new fans to gain an understanding of Gallagher's musical achievements *throughout* his life, not just in the 1970s, but that it can also serve as a touchstone or even a revelatory text for older fans who may be less familiar with Gallagher's work in the post-1970s period.

Remembering Rory

As we have highlighted throughout this book, Gallagher's final decade was marked by a number of important accolades, hitherto undocumented in any depth. In 1988, he won the Stag/Hot Press Award for Best Album with *Defender*, while 1992 saw him receive the dual honours of the Fender/Arbiter Hall of Fame Award and the Cork Rock Award for his musical achievements. These sat alongside such earlier distinctions as his 1972 *Melody Maker* Best Guitarist award, his 1980 award for most headlining performances at the Reading Festival and his 1982 award for selling out the Glasgow Apollo, to name but a few examples, demonstrating his continued excellence as a musician. In his final years, Gallagher remained a highly sought after musician, with requests to play all over the world and to feature as a guest artist in the studio.

Since Gallagher's death in 1995, so many more accolades have been bestowed upon him, standing in the face of the 'rise and fall' narrative that continues to be perpetuated. We take pause to summarise the most notable below:

Conclusion - *The Rise and Rise of Rory Gallagher*

November 1995	Inaugural Rory Gallagher Memorial Lecture at Cork Regional Technical College
	Unveiling of Rue Rory Gallagher in Ris-Orangis, Paris
June 1996	Establishment of Hot Press Rory Gallagher Rock Musician Award
1997	Creation of Fender Custom Shop Rory Gallagher Stratocaster
October 1997	Unveiling of Rory Gallagher Memorial Sculpture in the newly named Rory Gallagher Place (formerly St Paul's Street Square) in Cork
February 1999	Induction into Blues Hall of Fame (Memphis, Tennessee)
1999	Unveiling of Star Club plaque in Hamburg
2000	Unveiling of Rock Hospital plaque in Ballyshannon
2002	Release of Rory Gallagher An Post Stamps
June 2006	Unveiling of Rory Gallagher Corner and Fender Stratocaster Sculpture in Dublin
December 2007	Unveiling of Ulster Hall plaque in Belfast
June 2010	Unveiling of Rory Gallagher statue in Ballyshannon
2013	Winner of Tommy Vance Inspiration Award, Classic Rock Roll of Honour
2015	Unveiling of Rory Gallagher Conference Room at Fender HQ in Scottsdale, Arizona
June 2015	Unveiling of Rory Gallagher Music Studios in Camden Palace Hotel Community Arts Centre, Cork
	Shandon Bells in Cork ring to mark the 20th anniversary of Gallagher's passing
February 2016	Winner of Ireland's Greatest Love Song 'I Fall Apart', Irish Rock 'n' Roll Museum
March 2018	Unveiling of Rory Gallagher Boardroom at Fender HQ in Ireland
	Release of Central Bank of Ireland commemorative coin
2019	Winner of Planet Rock Radio's Best Blues Artist
2020	Induction into Vintage Guitar Hall of Fame
2020	Gallagher's Stratocaster on display at the Rock 'n' Roll Hall of Fame (Cleveland, Ohio)

June 2020	Special edition of Hot Press to mark the 25th anniversary of Gallagher's passing
2021	Gallagher's Telecaster on display at the 1971 Reading Festival exhibition (Reading, UK)
June 2021	Cork poet laureate William Wall writes 'Hometown Blues' about Rory
August 2021	Winner of Ireland's Greatest Music Artist Award, Newstalk Radio
March 2022	Launch of Hot Press Rory Gallagher performance series
2022	Unveiling of three Gallagher murals in Ballyshannon, Cloyne and Macroom
March 2023	Gallagher photography exhibition at Gallagher's Pub, Cork
	Replicas of two of Gallagher's guitars exhibited in the Irish Rock 'n' Roll Museum
April 2023	Gallagher photography exhibition extended to Cobh Library
April 2023	Cobh International Readers and Writers Festival dedicated to Rory
	Unveiling of plaque at 19 West Beach, Cobh
May 2023	Gallagher photography exhibition extended to Irish Rock 'n' Roll Museum
June 2023	Gallagher photography exhibition extended to Macroom Library
May 2024	Anselm McDonnell's composition 'Gallagher' wins the Seán Ó Riada composition competition (February 2024) and is premiered three months later at the Cork International Choral Festival
June 2024	Rory Gallagher: Calling Card documentary premieres on RTÉ and on BBC NI and BBC iPlayer as The Rory Gallagher Story
August 2024	Gallagher mural unveiled on electricity box in MacCurtain Street, Cork

The list shows a huge acceleration in accolades over the past five years, acting as testimony to Gallagher's unceasing popularity, as well as recognition of his important role as Ireland's first international rockstar, paving the way for the many Irish musicians who followed. Gallagher continues to make the front pages of music magazines across Europe and North America, while his music has featured in a range of recent television shows and films, from *Irma Vep* through *Woman in the Wall* to *Dead Shot*. The future looks even brighter, with plans to unveil a statue of Gallagher outside the Ulster Hall in Belfast and a plaque in his memory at Munster Technological University in Cork. Gallagher will also be awarded at the 2025 Cork Person of the Year Awards in a newly created *in memoriam* category.

"If I didn't, who would?" The Work of the Gallagher Estate

It is very clear that none of the above would have come about without the tireless work of the Gallagher Estate, led by Gallagher's loyal brother Dónal and, more recently, by his nephews Daniel and Eoin. Throughout Gallagher's career, Dónal was always at his side, serving as his manager, best friend, confidant and so much more. As Carol Clerk of *Classic Rock* noted, Dónal:

> Assumed all the responsibilities of the road manager, supervised the equipment and the stage, humped the gear, mixed the live sound, and co-managed the band with Rory and his agent David Oddie [in the 1970s]. Dónal was also Rory's driver, his trouble-shooter, and an unusually well-meaning PR who saw to it that journalists and fans alike received time with Rory in the dressing room and were sorted for a safe trip home.[11]

As the years progressed, Dónal assumed increasing responsibilities for both Gallagher's professional and personal life, essentially becoming his brother's keeper. In a 1992 interview, Gallagher described Dónal as a "superb character, a gift from God" and admitted that he would not have "stuck with it" so long without his support.[12] Speaking candidly to *Young Guitar* magazine, Gallagher also acknowledged that his brother was "very clever" and very switched on businesswise, and that it was a good feeling to have a manager who had his best interests at heart.[13]

In a 2000 interview, Dónal Gallagher was asked what the best part of his brother's career was for him. His reply is telling:

> I personally feel that the best had yet to come. If all factors were taken into account and his health being the primary one, he was maturing as an artist, maybe in the genre of Muddy Waters whom he highly respected, and had held their own, despite things like age or the like. Others talk of the Isle of Wight gig, or his tenure with Taste or even when he was voted the world's top musician in the Melody Maker Poll of 1972 - they were milestones, but I feel that there was still much more that he wanted to contribute to music.[14]

While Gallagher's untimely passing in 1995 cut short his many future musical goals, Dónal has worked relentlessly to ensure that his brother's legacy is protected and his name lives on. It was down to his consistent hard work and effort that Gallagher's entire back catalogue was remixed and rereleased in Europe in 1998-

1999 when Capo Records partnered with BMG. Many of Gallagher's filmed appearances, including at *Rockpalast* and the Montreux Jazz Festival, were also released in the early 2000s on DVD. Gallagher's albums were reissued again in 2010-2011 under Eagle Rock (in the US), 2012-2013 under Sony Music (in Europe) and in 2018 under Universal (worldwide). The 2018 releases proved to be particularly successful, with 14 of Gallagher's albums positioned within the Top 22 UK Jazz and Blues chart in just one week, *Irish Tour '74* scooping the number one slot. *Hot Press* editor Niall Stokes highlighted this achievement as "an extraordinary statement about the enduring appeal of Rory's music," adding that not only do his songs indicate immense talent and hard work, but that they are still "revered by fans all over the world."[15]

The Gallagher Estate has always produced very thoughtful releases, carried out with Gallagher's own wishes in mind. Take *Wheels Within Wheels* (2003), for example, which sought to fulfil Gallagher's lifetime ambition of releasing an acoustic album, or *Kickback City* (2013), which endeavoured to bring together Gallagher's music and his love for noir, with Ian Rankin producing an accompanying novella. *Notes from San Francisco* (2011)—based on the album that Gallagher scrapped before *Photo-Finish*—offers a fascinating insight into 'what could have been' if the guitarist had stuck with Elliot Mazer as producer. Shortly before his death, Gallagher had given Dónal permission to release the original San Francisco versions of the songs if they were remixed.[16] Other well-received releases include the *BBC Sessions* (1999), *Beat Club Sessions* (2010) and *Taste - Live at the Isle of Wight* (2015)—all showcasing Gallagher's fine skills as a live performer.

Largely taking over the helm from his father, Daniel Gallagher has continued this stellar work, producing the three-disc album *Blues* (2019), which debuted on the Top 50 Official Irish Albums Chart at number four, and the live album *Check Shirt Wizard – Live in '77* (2020), which reached the top of the Billboard Blues Album Chart. Dónal later reflected on the momentous occasion in an interview: "[when] I saw that, I thought, 'Well, I can die happy now' – not that I want to – but to me, that would be the feather in his cap, and nothing less than he deserved."[17] Daniel also oversaw 50th anniversary editions of *Rory Gallagher* (2021) and *Deuce* (2022), a range of Record Store Day releases, including such hidden treasures as *Cleveland Calling* Parts 1 and 2 and *Live in San Diego '74*, and the all-encompassing *BBC Collection* (2024). But the pièce de résistance came in 2023 with *All Around Man – Live in London*, documenting Gallagher's two concerts at the Town & Country Club in December 1990 and demonstrating the continued strength of his later-day performances (see 2.4).

2024 has seen the release of a new Gallagher documentary, broadcast on RTÉ as *Rory Gallagher: Calling Card* and on BBC NI and BBC iPlayer as *The Rory Gallagher Story*. The documentary offers a more personal look into Gallagher's life and career through the perspective of Dónal, delving into his own archive and following him around various sites of significance to Gallagher on the island of

Ireland and in London. Speaking to us via email in December 2023, Dónal stated that *Rewriting Rory* "connects well to the endeavours of the 'new' documentary,"[18] which balances out Gallagher's offstage struggles with his continued musical excellence throughout his life. The documentary has received overwhelmingly positive reviews from fans and critics alike.

Just as Gallagher saw music as a "lifetime affair,"[19] so Dónal views looking after his brother as his own vocation. "I'm still not retired yet," he asserted at the end of the documentary, "There's always something new on Rory on the horizon." In a 2011 interview with *Paris Move*, Dónal was asked specifically why he has chosen to dedicate his entire life to his older brother. He replied that he always felt "there was some injustice" to Gallagher and that he "didn't get the recognition he was due." He, therefore, saw it as his responsibility to take care of him: "if I didn't, who would?"[20]

According to former RTÉ disc jockey and producer Aidan Stanley, Dónal's "thumbprint" is over everything related to Gallagher and he should be commended for always seeking to protect his brother's name and ensure that "we remember the right things" about him.[21] For Johnny Marr, guitarist with the Smiths, it is "a real blessing that [Gallagher's] manager was his brother,"[22] while producer Avril MacRory describes Dónal as a "solid and loyal support" to Gallagher, one of the "foundation stones" in his life along with his mother Monica and Tom O'Driscoll.[23] Equally, Paul Charles describes Dónal fondly as "a great ideas man" with "so much enthusiasm for Rory and his work."[24] "Dónal's priority was always what was in Rory's best interests. He was hands on, 24/7 and totally dedicated to the cause," he adds.

Fan Lori Murphy concurs:

> Everything that Dónal has done and is still doing is such a testament to his love for Rory. His loyalty, hard work, patience, affection and devotion is outstanding! He went way beyond what most brothers would have done [...] Rory may have been the performer, but Dónal did so much of the work to get him noticed. He continues to keep his memory and legacy alive and well, and has done an incredible job so far. Really remarkable.[25]

On 1 June 2024, Dónal took part in a live Q&A with Dave Fanning at the Rory Gallagher International Tribute Festival in Ballyshannon. At the end of the Q&A, Fanning and festival organiser Barry O'Neill presented Dónal with a lifetime achievement award for his services to music. "I'm sharing this with you guys," an emotional Dónal told the audience, "It'll be on my mantelpiece, but I'll think of all you Rory fans every time I look at it."

"Keeping his memory alive": The Work of Fans

Although Gallagher was often characterised as "a very lonely man"[26] during his life, the opposite could be said in the years following his death. Everything about

Gallagher, from his music captured on vinyl to duplicating the flannel he adorned, has been cherished by an exceptionally loyal (and growing) fanbase. Gallagher would, therefore, never be 'lonely' again, his career enjoying a "remarkable revival"[27] throughout the 21st century. In addition to the Estate, a substantial effort to preserve Gallagher's work and uphold his musical integrity has been achieved through the fans, both of older and newer generations. We explore the trajectory of Gallagher's memory in the eye of the fan and how this has adapted across time, from the rise of technology to the impact of the COVID-19 pandemic.

Brigitte 'Bibi' Lehmann

Lehmann met Gallagher on several occasions throughout the 1970s. Her 1973 interview with him and the band in Düsseldorf appeared in the March edition of German magazine *Popfoto* under 'The Rory Gallagher Story'. "The first time I met him, he was special. And I was intrigued because I never got eye contact [from him]," Lehmann told a reporter at the 2017 Ballyshannon Festival.[28] "He was so shy, maybe he was frightened of women, but that was really something I've never forgotten."

In 1975, Lehmann caught up with Gallagher again in Blankenberge (Belgium) when he appeared on the television programme *Golden Lion*. Later that year, Lehmann attended Gallagher's concert in Amsterdam. Their final meeting occurred when Gallagher headlined the Torhout Festival in 1979. In a 2011 interview, Lehmann fondly recalled the moment when Gallagher spotted her as he made his way offstage, interrupting her conversation with David Byrne of the Talking Heads to kiss her hand. Lehmann highly appreciated Gallagher's chivalrous nature, which was refreshing from the perspective of a woman in the very male-dominated environment that is rock 'n' roll. "[Rory and I] had this respectful relationship every time we saw each other. I think he was the only artist who ever kissed my hand."[29]

In her later years, Lehmann set up a YouTube account and tribute site on Facebook titled 'Bibi's Rory Gallagher Page'. "The purpose of my video page on Facebook is to keep his memory alive, but also to introduce him to the new generation and to discover how great he was, because it would be a shame to forget about him and to lose his music."[30] Lehmann regularly uploaded audio interviews, concert footage and press articles, maintaining the circulation of Gallagher information. On top of this, she was primarily responsible for the petition to the Irish Government in 2012 for Cork Airport to be renamed after Gallagher, as well as frequently assisting the Ballyshannon Festival over the years. Lehmann sadly passed away in December 2022. Gallagher's nephew, Eoin, honoured Lehmann in a statement on behalf of the family, expressing gratitude for her many years of sustaining Gallagher's legacy.

Barry O'Neill

Since 2002, O'Neill has been involved in many Rory Gallagher festival events, culminating in the establishment of the Rory Gallagher International Tribute Festival in Ballyshannon, of which he is the current chairperson. The annual four-day event in June honours Gallagher's music with concerts and exhibitions, connecting fans from around the globe. Over the last two decades, a wide variety of performers have appeared on the town's stages, from the Michael Schenker Group, Horslips and the Walter Trout Band to the Bernie Marsden Band, Ronnie Drew and the Eric Bell Band, as well as Band of Friends and numerous other tribute bands, including Sinnerboy, Laundromat and The Loop. Even to the present day, the festival continues to attract much interest. Following a two-year hiatus during the COVID-19 pandemic, O'Neill revealed that 2022 saw not only "the largest Rory Gallagher festival ever staged," but also "the largest Ballyshannon has ever witnessed."[31] The festival appeals to both an older and younger league of fans, either to relive experiences of the past or to hear those memories being told. As O'Neill observes, "No matter where people come from, whether from Greece or Holland or Germany, they'll tell you about the experiences they had at a concert or meeting Rory after a concert. He had time for his people, and I think that respect is still there [after his sad passing]."

Although casual listeners or critics might "box Rory off as being a rock guitarist," O'Neill considers there to be "much more to him," citing Gallagher's collaborations with Ronnie Drew and Lonnie Donegan (as released on 2003's *Wheels Within Wheels* compilation) as embodying this other side of his music-making. Gallagher's exploration into other genres, whether jazz, folk or flamenco, as well as being "organic to himself" is "why the fans to this day still connect with him." O'Neill credits this to his Irish heritage and upbringing. "From the start Rory had a natural introduction to traditional Irish music, and I think that those values always stayed with him."

John Ganjamie

In early 1998, Ganjamie travelled to Cork—or, as he soon discovered, 'Home of Ireland's first rock star'—though his relationship with Gallagher's music began months prior when he purchased a copy of *Irish Tour '74* and was "taken in by the variety of songs he did."[32] At this time, Ganjamie was welcomed by a very active and substantial Gallagher fanbase online and learnt more about Gallagher through reading a wide collection of articles. "I found a great musician, a great man and great fans," said Ganjamie, encouraging his participation in the community. Although much information about Gallagher existed on the internet, many of the sites that Ganjamie sourced were incomplete or eventually unusable, prompting the genesis of his own webpage called *RoryON!!*

"I decided to see what I could do to make a complete site and draw in the best of what I had found. I had no idea how to create a website, but it was fun learning," he told us in February 2024. The *RoryON!!* site was finalised in 1999 and provided links to Gallagher interviews, press articles and fan anecdotes, as well as a touring timeline compiled by Joachim Matz. In addition, the circulation of many forum pages and mailing lists led to Ganjamie creating his own. The Loop mailing list was set up in May 2000 and is connected to the *RoryON!!* page.[33] "It became very active for a long time [and] I still run it as it's the easiest way to set up my daily posts and for people who refuse to use Facebook."

Moreover, Ganjamie was fundamental in the launch of the official Rory Gallagher Facebook page. The page was initially created by Hugo Angel in 2008, with Ganjamie and several other fans invited to moderate in 2010. Some years later, it evolved into the official Facebook site. Today, Daniel Gallagher and long-time fan Milo Carr (who also runs the *Shadowplays* website) have joined Ganjamie as moderators for the page. Ganjamie uploads the daily timeline as part of the 'On This Day' component, while Carr manages the comments section and reviews concert anecdotes or encounters with Gallagher from fans.[34] Daniel, on the other hand, reports new information or current articles circulating about Gallagher (this includes pages on X, Instagram, TikTok, YouTube and Spotify). Daniel's input ensures the accounts' integrity and authenticity and, just like his uncle and father, he maintains a close relationship with fans, regularly responding to their messages and reposting videos of them playing Gallagher songs.

Over the course of interacting with the online community, Ganjamie has most enjoyed introducing Gallagher to an older generation who, for one reason or another, missed out on his music. Compared to online activity in 1998, he claims that "the initial excitement" surrounding Gallagher in the forums and mailing lists has somewhat quietened, with many members fading away across the decades. Although Gallagher's fanbase has remained relatively consistent since his death, Ganjamie attributes the absence of blues and rock as the dominant form of popular music to be limiting Gallagher's coverage. While partly true, as we argue in the following section, Gallagher has attracted a younger crowd on social media, in particular Instagram, igniting another wave of 'excitement' for his legacy on a new platform.

Stepping into the World of the Rory Gallagher Instagram Community: A Personal Perspective

In 2020, the Rory Gallagher Estate launched the 'RememberRory' campaign in commemoration of the 25th anniversary since Gallagher's passing. As part of the proceedings on 14 June, Eoin Gallagher was invited to perform a rendition of 'Tattoo'd Lady' on the Shandon Bells in Cork. Simultaneously, four radio stations broadcasted the album version of the track, while a tribute band delivered a live rendition in Rory Gallagher Place on Paul Street. In the evening, Gerry Murphy recited Louis de Paor's poem 'Rory'. From day to night, and in many different forms, "Rory Gallagher will ring out all over the city."

Fans were encouraged to participate in RememberRory by using the hashtag on social media outlets, loudening the 'ring' of Rory Gallagher to an international level. At that time, confined to a bedroom on the east coast of Australia, for me, the 'ring' of Rory Gallagher was instead associated with the *ding* of an Instagram notification. As a consequence of the COVID-19 restrictions, sluggish days blurred with other sluggish days as the unpredictability of the pandemic quickly manifested into a mixture of dread, loneliness and irritability. To combat these feelings, people engaged in a variety of activities, including indoor sports and gyms, writing poetry, listening to and playing music, and adopting pets for company. In my case, the main salvation was creating my Instagram profile in March 2020. In the subsequent months, my mornings were accompanied with a burst of energy from the anticipation of logging in and catching up on the many messages, comments and posts shared by the members of Rory Gallagher's online fanbase.

As a result of social distancing and mandatory lockdowns, the role of technology in our daily lives heavily increased during COVID-19. On the one hand, current literature has primarily focused on the harm of social media during the intermittent and long periods of isolation in the pandemic.[35] On the other, my findings uncover how social media interaction, in fact, positively shaped the routine of many members of the Rory Gallagher Instagram community, particularly in regard to sharing, expressing and identifying with music. On a more significant level, this section shows how the image and narrative of Rory Gallagher is represented by a young and virtual audience, while also addressing the impact of Irish popular music on an international scale. Lauren and I interviewed several members, some still active and others since deactivated, of the Gallagher Instagram community from 2021-2024.

"A sense of belonging":
Building Connections During and Post-COVID-19

During the COVID-19 pandemic, a sense of connection, while difficult to achieve, was highly important to maintain. The United States Census Bureau reported "more than 42% of people"[36] experiencing periods of depression and anxiety in December 2020. For Beatrice,[37] joining the Gallagher Instagram group during the pandemic was "a blessing." She discovered the online interaction generated "a sense of belonging" and was most beneficial on her lowest days as "it helps to stay positive and take your mind off of things." Beatrice confesses that, during COVID-19 isolation, "I didn't want anyone to know about [my love for] Rory," stating that Instagram was the only space for her to understand and share the "awakening" Gallagher's music brought for her. "It's another side to me not many know of, not even my own family."

In doing so, Beatrice noticed her relationship with Gallagher's music strengthen. "I have learned *so* much information that I didn't know about him previously, [especially] his emotional state and meaning behind songs." In comparison, Denise has enjoyed Gallagher's music since 2015 and since joining Instagram, she has "become an even bigger fan because you hear from other people about how special they think he is," as well as "sharing the joy" of not only original material, but also the many posthumous releases from the Gallagher Estate.[38] In this regard, being a Rory Gallagher fan in the 21st century goes beyond the love of his music, acting as a catalyst for social bonding and stimulating positive mental health, particularly during a period of global unease.

Moreover, with the COVID-19 pandemic keeping us indoors and, therefore, close to our listening devices, many young people had spare time to discover and learn about artists of the past. Cathleen had always preferred 1960s and 1970s music, but on a trip to Ireland in 2019 with her parents, she was finally exposed to the Rory Gallagher sound. "That's when I started listening to Rory's music, even though it would take another year [during the first COVID lockdown] until I actually started digging deeper." Our interview with Cathleen occurred in a post-pandemic world. Nevertheless, her opinion of the Gallagher Instagram community echoed observations made by Beatrice and Denise, especially concerning low moments in her mental health. "I can't say how important being in contact with those people was during the beginning of my depression. As overwhelming as it was, I knew I wasn't alone and there was someone I could talk to." Cathleen credits Gallagher's music and personality as an additional source of comfort:

> Rory and his music always reach the people that need it most, [and] that includes many people with mental health issues [...] Listening to his music when I wasn't feeling great started to feel as if a dear friend was telling me, 'It's alright, I understand'. [...] Feeling less alone, having the motivation to fight your fears [by] someone who is your hero [...] [and] telling you, while playing his Fender in the most wonderful way, that you might hit the floor, but you'll get back up at the count of nine.

To celebrate the 50th anniversary deluxe edition of Gallagher's self-titled debut album, Sanjoy Narayan wrote an article called 'Rory Gallagher, The Forgotten Guitar God'. From a social media perspective, the reality of Gallagher as 'forgotten' is far from the media's truth. "I first heard Rory's music back in 2019 when someone on Instagram posted about Taste performing at the Isle of Wight," said Taylor, "I decided to check him out on Spotify because I'm always looking for new music." Soon after, Taylor was regularly uploading photographs and videos of Gallagher:

> When I first started posting about him, I didn't see him at all [on Instagram]—just what I posted. Gradually more people followed my page, and I started seeing him more and more [...] I feel like I actually have opened people's eyes to Rory on my fan page, and I'm thankful. I want everyone to know about him and how greatly he contributed to the music industry. I feel good in knowing more people are aware of him.

Taylor highlights the importance of the Instagram fanbase on Gallagher's quick rise in popularity within the past couple of years. "[We] help keep his presence alive [because] the more we share pictures, thoughts, his music, the things we love about him, and his craft, [the more] it helps other people to discover him as well." In fact, it was the "active presence" of Gallagher's fanbase on Instagram that persuaded Katerina to join the community. From listening to 'Laundromat' on YouTube, Katerina describes the "build up" of her relationship with Gallagher's music, ultimately leading to 28 November 2020: "I remember because I put it [as a post] on Instagram. I realised, 'Yeah, I really wanna be a fan of this guy.'" Katerina has used her profile to "get [her] [creative] energy out" through making photographic edits and affectionate memes of Gallagher. Despite passing almost three decades ago, Gallagher's image continues to be reshaped, becoming relevant to 21st century popular culture, which increases his coverage to a new generation of fans.

Is Less More?
The Pros and Cons of Technology
in Rory Gallagher's Legacy

Although known for his 'back-to-basics' country blues musicianship, Gallagher has, ironically, attracted the digital generation. At the age of 15, Erik was introduced to Gallagher's music through his YouTube recommendations. "My first song was 'Moonchild', and after hearing the solo in 'Shadow Play', I became hooked." Erik suggests that Gallagher's appeal to a younger, and radically different, audience is found in the humility of his blues playing and lyrics, especially in the context of today's heavily technological environment:

> I think part of it is the fact that there is currently a revival of rock and similar music, which is driving young people to search for new music more than ever before. As a member of the latter part of Generation Z, I have seen how terrified my generation is for our future and we're all looking for a piece of hope in a very scary world. Rory is the perfect musician to deliver that hope because it shines through his music that he, too, felt hopeless at times.

Another user, Kelly, agrees. "Among the throngs of artists from the analogue age, I feel Rory's music sticks out for being so human. He was a very talented multi-instrumentalist who held nothing back from his music and that dedication resonates with people." Daniel Gallagher has made similar remarks in the press. "[Rory] kept himself looking and sounding [quite relevant] all the way through [...] and I think that rings true to people when they discover him and they see a clip of him on YouTube. He looks like a really cool guy from [the present]."[39] Daniel has described Gallagher's resurgence as "really quite eye-opening," particularly the many guitar players who upload renditions of classic Gallagher songs on Instagram. "It's really wonderful seeing people who weren't even born when Rory passed away doing great covers and playing his riffs."[40] Streaming platforms also show a steady global interest in Gallagher, from the US to Greece.[41]

In a 2020 interview for the *Irish Examiner USA*, Daniel presented the idea of a Rory Gallagher biopic. As a means of adhering to Gallagher's private nature, Daniel proposed a film centred on a defining moment in the guitarist's life. Ultimately, the biopic would serve as a starting point to discover Gallagher's music. "Rory is on the high again and I think [fans would] be interested in some stories from his career."[42] The influx of music biopics in recent years has generated a rise in listeners for the classic rock genre. Following the release of Baz Lurhmann's *Elvis* (2022), for instance, "Presley gained 1.9 million monthly listeners on Spotify, 43 million YouTube channel views, and even 63.2 thousand Instagram followers."[43]

While portraying a fictional Gallagher on the big screen could increase his younger fanbase and maintain relevancy, the estate following such trends risks overexposure, particularly to a figure so anti-establishment. Since his passing, Gallagher's public persona is out of his control, creating debate amongst fans about the best methods to celebrate him. During his lifetime, Gallagher himself was mixed, expressing disinterest at reaching the 'Best Guitarist' polls in magazines, while at the same time not wishing to be overlooked entirely. "I'm aware of the fact that I must mean something as a guitar player. I'm not naïve," he told *Circus Weekly* in 1978.[44] If Gallagher's popularity continues to rise, should we be wary of this line of exposure, and even more so, should we care?

John Ganjamie recounted a revealing anecdote about visiting Gallagher's mother, Monica, during a trip to Ireland in 2001:

> I remember saying we were disappointed that Rory's fame wasn't greater. She cautioned, 'Sometimes you have to be careful about getting what you wish for'. [...] To me, the early celebrations of Rory were wonderful, personal and heartfelt. It grew into the Ballyshannon [Festival], which is bigger [but] not better, involving people and bands with no connection to Rory. [But] isn't that what we wanted–more? See what I mean?

A popular discussion amongst Gallagher fans is the decision to induct him into the Rock 'n' Roll Hall of Fame. On the one hand, ex-band members have publicly supported the idea. Gallagher "deserves" to be in the Hall of Fame, according to Gerry McAvoy, on the basis of his "uniqueness" as well as influence on players such as Brian May and Johnny Marr.[45] Some fans, on the other hand, disapprove of such judgements since Gallagher was against music as an institution.

Most recently, the surprise announcement in July 2024 that Gallagher's extensive instrument collection, including his beloved 1961 Fender Stratocaster, would be sold at auction ignited passionate discussions among fans about the guitar's future. Some argued that this iconic instrument, revered as a secular relic, should be acquired by the Irish state and displayed in a museum in Cork, preserving its cultural significance for future generations. Others wished to see the Stratocaster in the hands of a musician like Joe Bonamassa or Slash, bringing it back to life on stage once more. Others still held a more sentimental view, suggesting that the guitar—fondly referred to by Daniel Gallagher as his uncle's "wife"[46]—should find its final resting place alongside Gallagher himself at St Oliver's Cemetery. Amidst these diverse opinions, technology has played a crucial role in driving the conversation, enabling crowdfunding efforts by Sheena Crowley of Crowley's Music Centre in Cork and the Irish Rock 'n' Roll Museum Experience in Dublin.

In terms of how Gallagher's music—or music generally—is remembered in the public sphere, Dave Fanning had this important lesson for us: our love of music should not be based on how, or even *if*, an artist is widely acclaimed, but how we relate to the music, both now and in the future:

> 'Legacy' and 'credit' [are] things I don't think Rory gave two hoots about. [And] that's the way I look at it. Was his music any good and was he any good at what he did and all the rest of it? Well, I thought he was great, [and] that's all I care about.
>
> I've moved on to other music [...] But Rory's [music] has stayed with me, and I love when that happens. [For example] John Lennon released his first solo album *John Lennon / Plastic Ono Band* [1969], and it sounds as good today as it did then, but that's not necessarily the way I judge anything. I just like the music. I happen to like Rory's music now too, and that's enough. End of story.[47]

Perhaps we can learn from Fanning's perspective and care more about the 'ring' of Rory Gallagher from the speakers in our home, and less about the 'ring' in our local cinema or museum hall.

"Timeless and honest":
Gallagher's Influence on Fellow Musicians

Gallagher never shied away from expressing admiration towards the many blues, folk and rock 'n' roll guitarists that impacted his playing. Since his passing, he has received high praise from well-known peers, such as Slash, Brian May and Johnny Marr. However, there is also a whole new generation of musicians that continue to be inspired by the Irishman and acknowledge that he has shaped both their playing and their attitude towards music. With this in mind, in this section, we track Gallagher's influence on a smaller (and more recent) scale.

Belfast-born musician Dom Martin discovered Gallagher at a very early age when his father made a cassette with *Live! in Europe* on one side and *Blueprint* on the other. Even as a young boy, Martin was struck by the "sheer energy and raw power"[48] of Gallagher's music. Growing up during the Troubles, Martin spent much of his adolescence listening to music in his bedroom, absorbing the sounds of his father's records, from Pink Floyd and Led Zeppelin to folk singer-songwriter Ralph McTell and Australian guitarist Tommy Emmanuel. Martin is well known for both his acoustic and electric guitar playing, covering a range of Gallagher tunes onstage with his trio, including 'Laundromat', 'What's Goin' On' and 'Morning Sun'. In October 2022, he was filmed at Belfast's Scott's Jazz Club to coincide with the release of the 50th anniversary edition of *Deuce*, performing tracks such as 'Used to Be' and 'Don't Know Where I'm Going'.

In our email exchange with Martin, he wrote of particular admiration for the light and shade in Gallagher's songcraft. "[Rory] had an almost musically violent way of playing at times, but it always had that feeling he was playing from the heart and soul and that he was in control of it." Martin noted the 1971 Beat Club session of 'In Your Town' as epitomising this 'violent way', which is also "an absolute masterclass for slide players." By the same token, Gallagher had "a much deeper and gentle side to his playing," referring to original compositions 'I'm Not Awake Yet' and 'I'll Admit You're Gone'. Martin also commends Gallagher for the many covers of blues standards in his repertoire. While "[Rory made] them [his] own," he also showed "adoration and respect" for the original recordings. Overall, Martin credits Gallagher for making him "fearless" in "hitting a stage and playing [my] own songs":

> Rory went his own way when it came to his music. He did his own thing […] He wasn't just playing a guitar; he lived through that guitar and you could tell the man had a real calling from it […] [Playing] was a way of life and it was much more important to him to be true to himself musically than to change for fame or fortune. He wasn't trying to impress anybody. He just loved to make music openly and freely […] so that's a massive and beautiful influence.

Gallagher's music has been celebrated in various ways since his passing, including the abundance of international tribute bands formed over the years. We spoke to guitarist Stephen Graf about the impact of Gallagher's onstage and offstage persona on his tribute trio Double Vision. "[Rory] always gave it his all and was never an arrogant star. He was a good person and his music reflects that for me."[49] Graf's interest in Gallagher can be traced to 1994 when his father played him 'Philby' on the car stereo. "I immediately loved the [electric] sitar and the chorus, which was easy to sing along to as a child."

Along with Muddy Waters and Freddie King, Gallagher's music was an important focus in Graf's musical education. "I really taught myself to play guitar with his songs. I always wanted to sound like him with the Stratocaster and an old Tweed amp or an AC30." Though primarily a tribute act, Double Vision has also experimented with original blues rock material, releasing albums such as *May Day*, *Roots* and *Top Secret*. Since 2020, Graf has been invited to perform across Europe with Band of Friends, contributing vocals and guitar. For Graf, Gallagher is a "cornerstone of rock" whose music is "timeless and honest […] never boring, full of surprises, sometimes wild, sometimes tender" with a "breathtaking" variety of styles. For this reason, he believes that Gallagher will continue to be an inspiration for many young musicians for the foreseeable future.

Furthermore, Gallagher's influence can be spotted in many young and up-and-coming musicians. The Zac Schulze Gang were established in the UK four years ago, incorporating a spectrum of classics from the rock and blues field, such as Gallagher's 'Shadow Play', 'I Fall Apart' and 'Same Old Story'. In addition, the trio has appeared at numerous Gallagher tribute festivals, from Ballyshannon to Wijk aan Zee, and even dedicated their track 'Ballyshannon Blues' to the late guitarist. Drummer and vocalist Ben Schulze discovered Gallagher's music in 2018 when a friend showed him a live version of 'Bullfrog Blues' and was immediately impressed by the bluesman's "no nonsense raw sound" and "the intensity of [his] live recordings."[50] Speaking to us about Gallagher's appeal on his own group, Schulze said, "[Rory is] no nonsense. [He had] a raw sound. We try to play with that same intensity and passion that Rory did. To keep things simple onstage [and] focus on the music and the playing."

Dea Matrona originated around the busking streets of Belfast, inspired by the records of Fleetwood Mac, Led Zeppelin and, of course, Rory Gallagher. Since February 2022, the female trio has reduced to a duo, supplementing with session drummers. Mollie McGinn and Orláith Forsythe became Gallagher fans while learning to play the electric guitar during adolescence. For this younger generation, Gallagher's legacy lies not only in his musical output, but also in his Irish identity. As Forsythe told us, "Generally British and American guitarists come to mind whenever the term 'guitar hero' is spoken about. To have a legend like Rory to look up to is inspiring to us as Irish musicians when you can sometimes feel cut off from the rest of the music world geographically."[51]

McGinn attributed Gallagher with the increase of her slide guitar usage, especially since the addition of 'Cradle Rock' to Dea Matrona's setlist. "We toured across Europe in May 2022 and every time we played 'Cradle Rock' the crowd went mad!" said McGinn. Both recognise the relevance of Gallagher in the modern musical landscape, with Forsythe reflecting on the "timeless" effect of 'Bad Penny' in a film she viewed at the cinema years ago. Lastly, McGinn touched upon Gallagher's wide reach across generations from her experience as a musician. "I think his legacy is only getting stronger each year, [and] having played at the Rory Gallagher festival in Ballyshannon you can tell that he was special and that people across the world treasure him as a hero of blues music."

Reassessing Gallagher's Legacy: The Academic Turn
In recent years, the growing field of Irish musicology has also started to turn its attention to Gallagher. While the guitarist was mentioned in seminal academic works on Irish music,[52] it was often only as a passing reference or subjected to short-sighted views that failed to appraise his contributions as a musician in both the context of Ireland and internationally. A case in point is *Rock and Popular Music in Ireland* (2012) by scholars Martin McLoone and Noel McLaughlin, which was not very complimentary of Gallagher, claiming that his music had "the tedium of a relatively unchanging format" and he was "content to work within a style he had mastered in the 1960s."[53] The book also stated that the "sophistication and technical brilliance" of Gallagher's guitar playing was "in stark contrast to the undistinguished and indistinguishable nature of many of the songs and the often obscure banality of their lyrics."[54]

Colin Harper's *Irish Folk, Trad & Blues* (2005) fared better, with a rather empathetic portrayal of Gallagher's career, as did Noel McLaughlin and Joanna Braniff's *How Belfast Got the Blues* (2020), which dedicated an entire section to Gallagher's legacy in Northern Ireland. Gallagher has also occasionally been the subject of conference papers, such as Eamonn Wall's 2005 presentation at the American Conference for Irish Studies[55] and Wesley Callihan's 2013 lecture at New Saint Andrews College in Idaho.[56]

However, it is only since 2020 that full-scale academic studies of Gallagher's music have emerged and have been led by *Rewriting Rory* in a bid to reassess Gallagher's importance as a true pioneer in his field. Publications have explored fan identities in the comments sections of the Rory Gallagher YouTube channel,[57] articulations of Gallagher's Corkonian identity in the *Irish Tour '74* documentary film,[58] the mythologisation of Gallagher in the international music press,[59] the use of Irish stereotyping in the international music press,[60] the Rory Gallagher Instagram fan community[61] and Gallagher's presence in the semiotic musicscape of Cork.[62] This work has also led to Gallagher becoming an established part of OpenLearn—the Open University's open educational resources platform. To date, Gallagher has featured in curriculum materials on the Belfast music scene,[63] the benefits of online music fandoms for mental health[64] and the influence of crime fiction on his songwriting.[65] Gallagher has also been the recent subject of a conference presentation for the British Association for Irish Studies[66] and a guest lecture at the Cowper and Newton Museum.[67]

Recognising Gallagher as a fundamental figure of study in Irish musicology reinstates his historical significance and emphasises his continued importance as both a musician and an Irishman. Furthermore, reappraising the complexities of his songs, lyrics and live performances, as well as representations of him in the music press and fan identities, offers new narratives on the evolution of Irish music throughout the 20th and 21st centuries.

Another particular boost to Gallagher's status within the field of Irish musicology is the increasing number of archives that hold items related to the musician in their collections. There is the well-established Rory Gallagher Music Library in Cork, which houses music and memorabilia of Gallagher, as well as a permanent tribute exhibition, and the Irish Rock 'n' Roll Museum in Dublin, which contains replica Gallagher guitars. More recently—and perhaps most excitingly—the Oh Yeah! Music Centre in Belfast received four scrapbooks belonging to the late music journalist Carol Clerk. Dating from 1970 to 1972 when Clerk was a music-mad teenager, they document the early years of Gallagher's solo career, each containing newspaper clippings, photographs, press releases and souvenirs, such as an old Doublemint packet from which Gallagher took a stick of chewing gum when Clerk saw him in concert in 1972. The scrapbooks capture tangible memories of a turbulent time in Belfast and the important role of music as a means of escapism and upliftment. They offer rich possibilities for researchers to explore, suggesting exciting prospects for further academic studies on Gallagher.

Final Word
In a 2023 interview with the *Irish Examiner*, Julian Vignoles summarised the "great story" that was Rory Gallagher's life:

> A kid joins a showband at 15. He's an excellent guitarist, everyone loves him, and he becomes a global star in the seventies. He takes to drink; he can't handle the idea that the career slides, and he has nothing to fall back on—not children, relationships, or golf—he becomes depressed and dies at 47. All you have to do is write it up.[68]

Conclusion - *The Rise and Rise of Rory Gallagher*

While, in theory, this does sound like a "great story", we cannot resist asking the obvious question: is there *more* to Rory Gallagher than simply a former "global star" struggling through a "career slide" as he "takes to drink"? Even *Irish Examiner* journalist Sue Leonard concludes that the narrative is "more complicated than that." Regardless, commentary such as Vignoles highlights the unwavering pattern that frames most critiques of Gallagher's 47 years of life. Throughout this book, we have endeavoured to challenge this oversimplistic and distorted view by filling the many gaps of knowledge associated with his final decade and providing a fresh angle to the "great story" of Rory Gallagher. Previous career narratives have often fallen into an all-too-easy trap of depicting Gallagher's life as a 'rise and fall' or comparing him to Dashiell Hammett, one of his favourite novelists. Colin Harper even went so far as to claim that Gallagher was "all but dictating his own epitaph"[69] when he mentioned Hammett's problems with health, drink and relationships with women in a 1992 *Hot Press* interview. We repeatedly show that such a narrow view of Gallagher has perpetuated an unjust mythology around his life that takes away from his many musical achievements.

In a 1992 article for the *Irish Times*, Gallagher expressed his opposition to the rock 'n' roll cliché of an early death, stating that "there's nothing glamorous about dying young, even if the journey makes you the greatest musician in the world."[70] Despite passing at quite a young age, Gallagher often considered his music as a life-long ambition, desiring to "reach 65" to properly learn "the old magic" of past African-American blues artists.[71] As he remarked to Gay Byrne in 1988, "I've got 25 more years to try and learn [to play T-Bone Walker riffs with [my] own original stamp]."[72] Although unable to reach the subsequent 25 years, for his remaining seven, Gallagher tried to seize every opportunity to engrain his 'stamp' on the blues, whether in a concert setting or on vinyl.

So, let us return to the question posed by Françoise Rossi in the book's Introduction: "what became of Rory Gallagher?" With all the research we have compiled, perhaps the question should be: what—or rather *who*—did Rory Gallagher become? The 'great story' we discover ourselves writing is of a musician still enthused by what he does, constantly innovating and pursuing various identities as he navigates an unpredictable music industry. From mentor to collaborator, from folk to jazz fusion, Rory Gallagher has not *one*—nor even two—but *many* phases of his artistry. Despite his numerous personal and professional challenges, there was never any 'fall'; right until the very end, Gallagher was recording, performing and writing new songs, and had great ambitions for the future. And now almost 30 years since his untimely death, a flourishing young fanbase indicates that he remains relevant and essential.

Indeed, Rory Gallagher continues to rise.

LAO and RM

Rory Gallagher - *The Later Years*

Footnotes

1 Jerry Gilbert, 'Rory – The Sounds Talk In', *Sounds* (4 August 1973), https://www.roryon.com/talkin280.html
2 Pierre F. Haesler, 'Rory Gallagher – I stand for the blues!!', *Music Scene* (6 December 1973), https://www.roryon.com/stand212.html
3 Joe Jackson, 'Lest We Forget', *Irish Times* (16 June 1995), 16.
4 Frédéric Lecomte, 'Rory Gallagher 1948-1995', *Guitare et Claviers* (July 1995), https://rewritingrory.co.uk/2022/06/04/guitare-et-claviers-july-1995/
5 Uli Twelker, 'Rory Gallagher – "They don't make them like you anymore"', *Good Times* (June 1995), https://rewritingrory.co.uk/2022/06/13/goodtimes-june-1995/
6 Chris Welch, 'Obituary: Rory Gallagher', *The Independent* (15 June 1995), https://www.independent.co.uk/news/people/obituary-rory-gallagher-1586663.html
7 Interview with Shu Tomioka, 24 April 2022.
8 Interview with Toine van Berlo, 23 December 2023.
9 Stephen Roche, 'Rory Gallagher: King of the Blooze', *Seconds*, no. 15 (1991), https://www.roryon.com/blooze412.html
10 Dermott Hayes, 'Rory Is Still Rocking All Over The World', *Irish Press* (12 August 1992), 19.
11 Carol Clerk, 'Rory Gallagher: Goodfella', *Classic Rock* (1 June 2005), https://www.loudersound.com/features/rory-gallagher-goodfella
12 Liam Fay, 'Tangled Up in Blues', *Hot Press* (July 1992), http://www.roryon.com/Tangled.html
13 'Rory Gallagher interview 1991', https://www.youtube.com/watch?v=fNpaun5s1CE
14 Michael McHugh, 'Rory Gallagher - World renowned blues and rock guitarist, singer and songwriter', *Donegal Democrat* (June 2000), https://www.roryon.com/Donegal.html
15 Niall Stokes, 'Rory Gallagher Has Record 14 Albums In UK J and B Top 20', *Hot Press* (25 March 2018), https://www.hotpress.com/music/rory-gallagher-has-record-14-albums-in-uk-j-and-b-top-20-21860731
16 In a 1992 interview with Uli Twelker, Gallagher also said: "Maybe eighty percent of the San Francisco album could come out in some form—remixed."
17 'Donal Gallagher', *Eon Music* (June 2020), https://www.eonmusic.co.uk/donal-gallagher-rory-gallagher-eonmusic-interview-june-2020.html
18 Email exchange with Dónal Gallagher, 17 December 2023.
19 Colm McGinty, '"Music is not a job, more of a hobby," says Rory', *Evening Herald* (1983), https://www.roryon.com/job156.html
20 'ITW de Donal Gallagher – Une affaire de famille', *Paris Move* (May 2011), https://www.paris-move.com/portrait/itw-de-donal-gallagher-une-affaire-de-famille/
21 Interview with Aidan Stanley, 7 December 2024.
22 *Rory Gallagher: Calling Card* (RTÉ and BBC NI, 2024).
23 'Rory Gallagher: Tributes from famous friends', *Hot Press* (11 June 2015), https://www.hotpress.com/music/rory-gallagher-tributes-from-famous-friends-14356545
24 Paul Charles, *Adventures in Wonderland* (Hot Press: Dublin, 2023), 116.
25 Interview with Lori Murphy, 26 June 2023.
26 Interview with Toine van Berlo, 11 December 2023.
27 Lee Zimmerman, 'Rory's Remarkable Revival: A New Best-Of Gives A Great Guitarist the Fuller Focus He Deserves', *American Songwriter* (8 October 2020), https://americansongwriter.com/the-best-of-rory-gallagher-album-review/.
28 'SheRocks Interview with Rock Journalist & Photographer Brigitte 'Bibi' Lehmann', https://www.facebook.com/DonegalTV/videos/sherocks-interview-with-rock-journalist-photographer-brigitte-bibi-lehmann-2017/691854439157822/
29 'Bibi talks about Rory Gallagher and other rock legends', https://www.youtube.com/watch?v=NmJcZyI6KbA.
30 'SheRocks Interview…'
31 'Barry O Neill Interview on Rory Gallagher Tribute Festival Ballyshannon', https://www.youtube.com/watch?v=WM3DRX_pPaM. All subsequent quotes from O'Neill come from this interview.
32 Interview with John Ganjamie, 20 February 2024. All subsequent quotes from Ganjamie come from this interview.
33 Prior to setting up The Loop, there was an active mailing list called The Bullfrog, though, according to Ganjamie, it "deteriorated into a mess [with] rude people posting ignorant things."
34 The forum on the official Rory Gallagher website was moderated by another fan, Jay Jay Joyce, who sadly passed away in August 2024.
35 Scholarship has highlighted a number of areas, including: the increasing loneliness of being on social media during the COVID-19 lockdown, the relationship between social media and panic buying, and the spread of health misinformation online.
36 Jaffar Abbas, Dake Wang, Zhaohui Su and Arash Ziapour. 'The Role of Social Media in the Advent of COVID-19 Pandemic: Crisis Management, Mental Health Challenges and Implications', vol. 14 (2021), *Risk Management and Healthcare Policy*, https://pubmed.ncbi.nlm.nih.gov/34012304/
37 Some of the following names are pseudonyms, as per the interviewees' request.
38 Across the COVID-19 pandemic, there were five releases: *Check Shirt Wizard - Live In '77* (2020), *The Best of Rory Gallagher* (2020), *Cleveland Calling Pt. 1* (2020), *Cleveland Calling Pt. 2* (2021) and the 50th anniversary edition boxset of Gallagher's 1971 solo debut *Rory Gallagher*.
39 Brad Balfour, 'Rocker Daniel Gallagher Does His Best to Keep Alive Uncle Rory Gallagher's Blues Music Legacy', *Irish Examiner USA* (4 November 2020), https://irishexaminerusa.com/wp/?p=17673#:~:text=Because%20there%20wasn't%20a,him%20on%20YouTube%20or%20something.
40 'Barry O Neill interviewing Rory Gallagher's nephews Ballyshannon 2022', https://www.youtube.com/watch?v=L-KZiQP47Z0
41 Ed Power, 'Rory Gallagher: New live album created from 1990 concert in London', *The Examiner* (11 July 2023), https://www.irishexaminer.com/lifestyle/artsandculture/arid-41180998.html.
42 Balfour, 'Rocker Daniel Gallagher…'

43 Sarah Kloboves, 'The Elvis Presley Shake-Up: How Music Biopic Movies Are Revolutionizing Music Catalog', *How Music Charts* (18 July 2022), https://hmc.chartmetric.com/music-biopic-movies/
44 David Fricke, 'Rory Gallagher', *Circus Weekly* (2 January 1979), https://www.roryon.com/circus.html
45 Steve Newton, 'Rory Gallagher's longtime bassist thinks Rory's 'uniqueness' makes him worthy of Rock Hall induction', *Ear of Newt*, (9 December 2018), https://earofnewt.com/2018/12/09/rory-gallaghers-longtime-bassist-thinks-rorys-uniqueness-makes-him-worthy-of-rock-hall-induction/
46 Phil Weller, '"'I don't think he would have swapped it for anything in the world'"', *Guitar Player* (9 July 2024), https://www.guitarplayer.com/news/rory-gallagher-strat-auction
47 Interview with Dave Fanning, 24 April 2022.
48 Interview with Dom Martin, 5 February 2024. All subsequent quotes from Martin come from this interview.
49 Interview with Stephan Graf, 2 February 2024. All subsequent quotes from Graf come from this interview.
50 Interview with Ben Schulze, 21 February 2024. All subsequent quotes from Schulze come from this interview.
51 Interview with Dea Matrona, 21 October 2023. All subsequent quotes from Dea Matrona come from this interview.
52 For example, Gerry Smyth, *Noisy Island: A Short History of Irish Rock* (Cork: Cork University Press, 2005); John O'Flynn, *The Irishness of Irish Music* (London: Routledge, 2009); Martin McLoone and Noel McLaughlin, *Rock and Popular Music in Ireland: Before and After U2* (Dublin: Irish Academic Press, 2012); Mark Fitzgerald and John O'Flynn, *Music and Identity in Ireland and Beyond* (London: Routledge, 2014); Áine Mangaoang, John O'Flynn and Lonán Ó Briain, *Made in Ireland: Studies in Popular Music* (London: Routledge, 2020).
53 McLoone and McLaughlin, *Rock and Popular Music in Ireland*, 91-92.
54 Ibid.
55 'What in the World: Reading Rory Gallagher's Blues' (5 October 2008), https://shadowplays.com/blog/?p=2792
56 'Rory Gallagher and the Continental Op' (5 May 2013), https://shadowplays.com/blog/?p=170
57 Lauren Alex O'Hagan, '"Rory played the greens, not the blues": Expressions of Irishness on the Rory Gallagher YouTube Channel', vol. 29, no. 3 (2021), *Irish Studies Review*, 348-369.
58 Lauren Alex O'Hagan, '"It's always nice to head for home": Music-Making, Sense of Place, and Corkonian Identity in the Rory Gallagher Irish Tour '74 Documentary', vol. 17 (2022), *Journal for the Society of Musicology in Ireland*, 47-77.
59 Lauren Alex O'Hagan, 'Fashioning the "People's Guitarist": The Mythologization of Rory Gallagher in the International Music Press', vol. 9, no. 2 (2022), *Rock Music Studies*, 174-198.
60 Lauren Alex O'Hagan, '"Rory Gallagher's Leprechaun Boogie": Irish Stereotyping in the International Music Press', vol. 4, no. 2 (2023), *Review of Irish Studies in Europe*, 38-72.
61 Lauren Alex O'Hagan, 'Music for Mental Health: An Autoethnography of the Rory Gallagher Instagram Fan Community', vol. 52, no. 5 (2023), *Journal of Contemporary Ethnography*, https://journals.sagepub.com/doi/10.1177/08912416231162077
62 Lauren Alex O'Hagan, 'Walkin' Blues: Exploring the Semiotic Musicscape of Rory Gallagher's Cork' (2024), *Ethnomusicology Forum*, https://doi.org/10.1080/17411912.2024.2331432
63 Lauren Alex O'Hagan, 'Music as a Source of Unity: When Rory Gallagher Came to Belfast', *OpenLearn* (18 May 2023), https://www.open.edu/openlearn/history-the-arts/music/music-source-unity-when-rory-gallagher-came-belfast
64 Lauren Alex O'Hagan, 'Supporting Mental Health Through Online Music Fandoms', *OpenLearn* (15 December 2023), https://www.open.edu/openlearn/openlearn-ireland/ireland---health-social-issues/supporting-mental-health-through-online-music-fandoms
65 Lauren Alex O'Hagan, 'Hardboiled Blues: Rory Gallagher's Blues Lyrics Revisited', *OpenLearn* (28 May 2024), https://www.open.edu/openlearn/openlearn-ireland/ireland---places-culture-heritage/hardboiled-blues-rory-gallaghers-blues-lyrics-revisited
66 Lauren Alex O'Hagan, '"Rory played the greens, not the blues": Expressions of Irishness on the Rory Gallagher YouTube Channel', *British Association for Irish Studies 2021 Conference*, https://www.youtube.com/watch?v=3An1GJUHWms&t=3s
67 Lauren Alex O'Hagan, 'Amazing Grace in the Life and Work of Rory Gallagher', *Cowper and Newton Museum* (August 2023), https://www.youtube.com/watch?v=aqdMcwdsnr8
68 Sue Leonard, 'Book Interview: Julian Vignoles looks at dementia in fourth book Tides Go Out', *Irish Examiner* (1 July 2023), https://www.irishexaminer.com/lifestyle/artsandculture/arid-41173783.html
69 Colin Harper, 'Ballad of a Thin Man', *Mojo* (October 1998), https://www.roryon.com/mojo.html
70 Joe Jackson, 'Black Cat Blues', *Irish Times* (14 August 1992), 6.
71 Jon Lewin, 'Rory's Story', *Making Music* (October 1987), https://www.roryon.com/Rorystory.html
72 'Rory Gallagher - The Late Late Show - 12 February 1988', https://www.youtube.com/watch?v=lKJ3ploCKv0

Acknowledgements

First and foremost, we want to thank both Dónal and Daniel Gallagher for their permission to pursue this book project. Since the launch of *Rewriting Rory* in November 2021, the Gallagher Estate has always been very supportive of our work, for which we are most grateful. Throughout the process of writing this book, Dónal and Daniel were very helpful at answering many of our questions and sharing their insights into this period in Rory's career. We also want to give a special mention to Rory's cousin, Jim Roche, for his support, encouragement and guidance from the very beginning of this project.

We also wish to say a big thank you to Mark Feltham, David Levy and Richard Newman, who all kindly agreed to be interviewed for our book and provided precious memories and anecdotes of working with Rory. Our heartfelt thanks also to Rory's dear friends Bob Hewitt, Shu Tomioka and Roberto Manes for their memories, not to mention their kindness and support for the project from day one. And to Dave Fanning for taking time out of his busy schedule to have a long conversation with us.

Special thanks also to Vincent Wolting for his expert knowledge of Rory's guitars and rigs, and for putting us in touch with so many other valuable contacts within the Rory community. And Wim Wizenberg for his graciousness in sharing his large Rory collection with us. For specialist advice on Hungary and Yugoslavia, we also thank Ádám Ignácz, Anna Zsubori, Catherine Baker, Éva Mihalovics and Tijana Rupčić.

We extend our gratitude to the archives that we used and visited when researching this book: Biblioteca Nacional de España (Madrid), British Newspaper Archive, Cork City and County Archives Service, Cork City Library, Croatian State Archives (Zagreb), Everyman Theatre (Cork), Irish News Archives, National and University Library (Zagreb), National and University Library of Bosnia and Herzegovina (Sarajevo), National and University Library of Ljublana, National Archives of Hungary (Budapest), National Széchényi Library (Budapest), Newspapers.Com and State Library of New South Wales (Sydney)

In alphabetical order, we also wish to thank the following people—musicians, photographers, producers, friends and fans—who all spoke to us (either via Zoom, telephone, email or social media) in preparation for this book. Your wonderful memories and knowledge have been essential in helping us 'rewrite' the story of Rory's final decade: Götz Alsmann, Amelie Scheidt, Bertrand Alary, Bob Andrews, Dan Ar Braz, Gwyn Ashton, Beatrice, Philipp J. Bösel, Bob Daisley, Barry Barnes, Michael Bayley Hughes, Ray Beavis, Umberto Berlenghini, Dermot Bolger, Derry Bray, Daragh Brennan, Kevin Breslin, John Carnie, Cathleen, Joseph Cavenagh, Paul Charles, Gary Cotter, Ben Cuddihy, Eugene Curran, P.J. Curtis, Kieran Devitt, Paul Dufficy, Denise Ebner, Matthew Fisher, Orláith Forsythe, Joby Fox, Monique Frie, John Ganjamie, Robert Gannon, Mark Gillis, Stephan Graf, Chris Grotz, Simon Grundy, Luca Guiotto, Nicole D. Gunung, Wolfgang Gürster, Bob Hall, Ani Harr, Rob Harrington, Paul Hunt, Žikica Ivković, Rónán Johnston, Ferenc Kálmándy, Fran K, Jeff Lang, Jamil Leroussi, Juan Lloret, Katerina Ludwig, Eamon Maguire, Liam M. Malone, Amy Maloney, Dave Mangin, Henk Mannes, Toni Mantis, Megumi Manzaki, Dom Martin, Juan Martín, Marc 'Jake Lee' Martin, Paul Patrick Martin, Marc 'Jake Lee' Martin, José Martos Arellano, Pete McCarter, Declan McKinney, Anselm McDonnell, Dave McHugh, Mollie McGinn, Johnny McMonagle, Paddy T. Meakin, Csaba Mester, Mark Morrison, Kelly Munro, Lori Murphy, Marianne Murphy, Byrne Norry, Fiachna Ó Braonáin, Mike O'Connor, Tom O'Flaherty, Takayuki Oi, Carlos Olabarria, Robert Orr, Brian Palm, Harry Pater, Bram Pescador, Carolyn Phillips, Coleen Phillips, Joe Philpott, Erik Plaku, Colm Quearney, Sean Reynolds, Vince Rampino, Taylor Ray, Marlène Rivet, Rosie, Jesús Ruipérez, Aidan Russell, Jean-Pierre Sabouret, Ben Schulze, Mick Shanahan, Stefan Siller, Nathalie Simon, Cormac Sheehan, John Spreckley, Aidan Stanley, Saiichi Sugiyama, K.G. Takeda, Kouki 'Dannie' Taniguchi, Micha Thieme, Paul ten Thije, Andrew Thompson, Barney Toal, Niall Toner, Lothar Trampert, Toine van Berlo, Jan Van Bodegraven, Zoran Veselinović, Christian Wagner, Steve Wall, Hank Wedel,

Des White, Joël Winkin, Pete Wood and Milan Živančević. Our sincere apologies to anyone who we may have accidentally overlooked.

For use of photographs, we thank: Umberto Berlinghini, Philipp J. Bösel, Joseph Carlucci, John Carnie, Luca Guiotto, Nicole D. Gunung, Wolfgang Gürster, Colm Henry, Bob Hewitt, Ferenc Kálmándy, Gerard Koot, David Levy, Liam M. Malone, Henk Mannes, Pete McCarter, Herman Nijhof, Byrne Norry, Tony O'Connell, Robert Orr, Harry Pater, Michael Pellegrini, Marlène Rivet, Jim Roche, Nathalie Simon, Micha Thieme, Shu Tomioka, Lothar Trampert, Toine van Berlo, Jan Van Bodegraven, Ann Wilson, Vincent Wolting and Wim Wezenberg.

On a personal level, Lauren wishes to thank her partner Diego and parents Tina and Kevin for their constant belief and motivation in completing this book, and Sonny and Tubby for always putting a smile on her face. Thanks also to her supportive work colleagues, particularly Göran, Jörgen, Jane, Caroline, Victoria and Michael, and good friends Natalie, Axel, Kelly, Mandy, Amelie and Ani for their encouragement. And, of course, Rayne—her co-author and "partner in crime."

On a personal level, Rayne would like to thank her family Kelly, Ben and Caesar for their unwavering guidance, love and patience through the lowpoints (as well as highpoints) while completing this project. In addition, a sincere thank you to her grandmother Marie and uncle Paul for their ceaseless support and faith in her abilities. Thanks also to Erika for her constant friendship, as well as Hayley Costello and the Carnes Hill Dan Murphy's ('Cubs') Team for their kindess and understanding. Lastly, to the confidante she admires on many levels—her co-author, Lauren.

We would also like to thank everybody who has supported *Rewriting Rory* over the past three years. Your kind words and feedback really mean so much and inspired us to take on this momentous book writing task.

And, last but most definitely not least, we thank Rory. Thanks seems such a small word for someone who has blessed our lives in such a huge and immeasurable way, but, as actions speak louder than words, we hope our book—a true labour of love—goes some way to conveying what you mean to us.

www.ingramcontent.com/pod-product-compliance
Lightning Source LLC
Chambersburg PA
CBHW071941220426
43662CB00009B/943